Géza Jeszenszky

Hungary and Its Neighbors, 1988–1994

Géza Jeszenszky

Hungary and Its Neighbors, 1988–1994

Attempts to Heal the Wound of 1920

Helena History Press

English edition © 2025 Géza Jeszenszky

Originally published as
Kísérlet a trianoni trauma orvoslására © 2016 by Osiris

All rights reserved

Published in the United States by:

Helena History Press LLC

A division of KKL Publications LLC, Reno, NV USA

www.helenahistorypress.com

Publishing scholarship about and from Central and East Europe

ISBN: 978-1-943596-49-2 (paperback)
ISBN: 978-1-943596-50-8 (Ebook)

Copy Editor: Jill Hannum, József Litkei

Graphic Designer: Zsolt Gembela

Printed by: Könyvpont Nyomda: Budapest

To the memory of József Antall (1932–1993)
... teacher, scholar, statesman

"Attention, tense interest, striving for understanding, empathy, respect and love for this special breed of people, the Hungarian beyond the border—this was his characteristic feature in his relations with Hungarians beyond the border."

Béla Markó, former President of RMDSZ
(Democratic Alliance of the Hungarians of Romania)
on József Antall

Contents

Figures, Maps, and Tables x
Acronyms xiii
Preface xv

Introduction 1

Chapter 1
Hungary and Its Neighbors before 1988 7
    The roots of an antagonism 7
    "Possession is nine tenths of the law" 11
    The alarming situation of the Hungarian minorities:
    The engine of the regime change 18
    Dramatis personae: The players 19
    The winds of change start blowing 26
    The illusions of the regime changers 35
    The Romanian drama in December 1989 45

Chapter 2
The Government's Foreign Policy Program 59
    Haunting dilemmas 59
    Internal political conditions 61
    Foreign policy in the government program 65
    "Prime minister of fifteen million" 70
    Illusions and reality in neighborhood policy 72
    The personnel 76
    Conference of the Heads of Missions, July 25–26, 1990 83

Chapter 3
The First Steps: The International Reception 87
    Touring the neighborhood: Novi Sad–Belgrade–Zagreb 94
    Opposing trends in Czech and Slovak relations 99
    The toughest neighbor: Romania 107
    On international forums for minority rights 114

Diplomatic conflict with Romania 119
　　　Is Europe helping? 127
　　　Poland, the old friend 132

Chapter 4
An Attempt at Cooperation: Visegrád and Further Efforts
for the Protection of National Minorities 135
　　　Visegrád or the new Central Europe 135
　　　Visegrád in action 143
　　　The Central European Initiative 153
　　　Renewed efforts to enforce minority rights 156
　　　The anti-Hungarian atmosphere in Romania and its causes 160
　　　Disappointment in Geneva 163
　　　Results and failures 168

Chapter 5
Accusations and Reality: The New Eastern Policy 177
　　　The neighboring superpower and its break-up 177
　　　Relations with Ukraine 186
　　　The new Russia 193

Chapter 6
The Break-up of Yugoslavia 203
　　　The "Kalashnikov case" 205
　　　Serbian nationalism in communist guise 208
　　　At the crossroads: Confederation or separation 211
　　　Active Hungarian policy in the period of the moratorium 214
　　　War along the southern border—towards
　　　accepting disintegration 221
　　　A turn in international reactions? 225
　　　Reassuring international action 227
　　　The successful endgame 237

Chapter 7
Successes and Disappointments in 1992 245
　　　Croatia and Slovenia 247
　　　Serbia 251
　　　Bosnia and Herzegovina 256

    Macedonia 257
    Austria 258
    More disputes with Romania 260
    Ukraine 270
    Central European solidarity and minority rights 271

Chapter 8
Czechs and Slovaks: The "Velvet Divorce" 281
    Slovak-Hungarian conflict over the Danube barrage project 283
    Hungarian aspects of the "velvet divorce" 289
    The Hungarian offer 292
    The Slovak response 296
    An attempt to enlist foreign mediation 299

Chapter 9
The Hungarian-Ukrainian Treaty and "Nation Policy" 307
    Has Hungary given up Subcarpathia? 308
    Between signature and ratification 311
    The hot debate over ratification 316
    The afterlife of the treaty 326
    Policy towards the neighbors caught in the crossfire 329

Chapter 10
Slovakia and Romania Join the Council of Europe 339
    A new state unfriendly towards its minorities 339
    Democracy in Slovakia—a cursory examination 343
    The mechanism of abandoning principles 346
    A premature decision 355
    A new tone in Romania? 359
    Romania on the threshold of the Council of Europe 362
    My official visit to Romania 366
    Membership—with conditions 380
    The Summit of the Council of Europe 382
    Semi-Private visit to Háromszék 386

Chapter 11
Instead of Stabilization, Conflicts Are Put in the Freezer 391
    The death of the hero of the transition 391

A cancelled visit 396
Two trips to Serbia 398
Election campaign linked to neighborhood policy 404
The Balladur Plan—the last attempt to mitigate minority
problems 412
My 1500 days—the balance and the lessons learned 423

Chapter 12
The Outstretched Hand and the Embracing Arm 439
Changes under the Horn Government 440
The Hungarian-Slovak treaty 446
The Hungarian-Romanian treaty 448
From the law on benefits to simplified naturalization 451
"Requiem for a former province" 459
In the 2010s and 2020s 464
The situation today and the perspectives 470

Bibliography 479
Appendix 497
Index 505

Figures, Maps, and Tables

Figure 1. At the summer camp of the young Hungarians of Slovakia, July 1989 26
Figure 2. The first mass demonstration allowed in communist Hungary since 1956: against the oppression of Hungarians in Transylvania, Budapest, June 27, 1988 30
Figure 3. Press conference held by S.O.S. Transylvania in Geneva protesting village erasing in Romania, February 10, 1989 33
Figure 4. Dedication of the memorial to the Iron Curtain on the border with Austria, with FM Alois Mock and our wives, August 24, 1991, Nickelsdorf/Miklóshalma 91
Figure 5. With Croatia's former FM Zdravko Mršić 97
Figure 6. Arriving in Prague, August 27, 1990 100
Figure 7. With Czechoslovak FM Jiří Dienstbier, Prague, August 27, 1990 103
Figure 8. Hungary's PM József Antall welcomes Poland's President Lech Wałęsa, Budapest, February 15, 1991 139
Figure 9. Presidents Havel and Wałęsa and PM Antall signing the Visegrád Cooperation, Visegrád, February 15, 1991 140
Figure 10. The founders of the Visegrád Cooperation: myself, Poland's FM Krzystof Skubiszewski, PM Jan Krzysztof Bielecki of Poland, President Lech Wałęsa, Hungary's President Árpád Göncz, Czechoslovakia's President Václav Havel, PM Antall, FM Dienstbier of Czechoslovakia, Budapest, February 15, 1991 141
Figure 11. The Visegrád foreign ministers at the Cracow summit, October 5, 1991 149
Figure12. Submitting Hungary's application for membership in the European Union: Athens, April 1, 1994 152
Figure 13. Climbing the highest peak of Czechoslovakia (now Slovakia), Gerlachovský štít (2655 m), with PM Ján Čarnogurský, FM Demeš in the background. August 16, 1991 165
Figure 14. Signing Hungary's accession to the European Convention on Human Rights, with Secretary General of the Council of Europe, Catherine Lalumière, Strasbourg, November 5, 1992 169
Figure 15. Dissolving the military part of the Warsaw Pact, together with Minister of Defense Lajos Für, February 25, 1991 180

Figures, Maps, and Tables

Figure 16. With Ukrainian FM Anatoliy Zlenko in Kyiv, July 9, 1991 190
Figure 17. Welcome by Hungarians from Visk, Subcarpathia,
  Ukraine at the Uzsok Pass, August 10, 1991 191
Figure 18. Speaking at the First World War Memorial at Uzsok Pass,
  August 10, 1991 192
Figure 19. At the Turul Monument at Tiszaújlak (Vylok),
  celebrating the Rákóczi uprising, 1703–11 193
Figure 20. Wreath-laying at the memorial to the mass deportation
  of Hungarians of Subcarpathia in 1944/45. Makkosjánosi (Yanoshi),
  August 11, 1991 194
Figure 21. With Russia's FM Kozyrev in Budapest, August 22, 1991 195
Figure 22. Signing the last international treaty of the Soviet Union with
  President Mikhail Gorbachev, Moscow, December 6, 1991 198
Figure 23. President Boris Yeltsin and PM József Antall,
  Budapest, November 10, 1992 200
Figure 24. Received by President George H. W. Bush in the White House
  to discuss the South Slav war, September 1991 219
Figure 25. Austria: the best friend, FM Alois Mock, Vienna, April 14, 1992 259
Figure 26. Ministerial meeting of the North Atlantic Cooperation
  Council: with Slovak FM Milan Kňažko, December 18, 1992 294
Figure 27. In Transylvania: visiting András Sütő, the renowned author
  at Marosvásárhely/Târgu Mureș, September 17, 1993 376
Figure 28. Visiting the house of my first visit to Transylvania in 1969 (Parajd/
  Praid), with the leaders of RMDSZ, Béla Markó and László Borbély 377
Figure 29. In Transylvania: dedicating the bust of Mózes Turóczy,
  who cast the copper guns in the War of Independence, 1849,
  Kézdivásárhely/Târgu Secuiesc, November 6, 1993 387
Figure 30. Visiting war-torn Sarajevo, March 17, 1994 402
Figure 31. Meeting Bosnia's FM Irjan Ljubijankić in Sarajevo,
  March 17, 1994 403
Figure 32. Discussing NATO membership with Secretary of State
  Christopher, Budapest, October 21, 1993 417
Figure 33. Addressing the Paris Conference of the Pact on Stability in Europe,
  May 26, 1994 421
Figure 34. Speaking in Transylvania at the cemetery of fallen Hungarian
  soldiers in the Úz valley in the Carpathians, in today's Romania,
  August 26, 1996 457
Figure 35. Celebrating March 15, 1848, in Bratislava/Pozsony, 2008 462

xi

Figures, Maps, and Tables

Figure 36. Speaking at the birthplace of the poet Kölcsey,
Sződemeter, August 8, 2010...463
Figure 37. At the peak of the Hargita Mountains
   in Transylvania, February 2020..464
Figure 38. Talk at Subotica/Szabadka in Serbia, 2006..465
Figure 39. Decorated with the Commander's Cross
   of the Order of Merit by President Duda of Poland,
   Budapest, March 20, 2016...476

Figure A1. Change in the number of Romanians, Hungarians and Germans
   on the present territory of Transylvania (historical Transylvania,
   Maramureș, Crișana, Rumanian Banat), 1910–1992....................................501

Map A1. Ethnic map of the Carpathian Basin...497
Map A2. Ethnic map of the present territory of Transylvania in 1910..................500
Map A3. Ethnic map of the present territory of Transylvania in 1992..................500
Map A4. Ethnic map of the settlements of the present
   territory of Slovakia in 1941 and 1991..502
Map A5. Ethnic map of Slovakia, 1991..502
Map A6. Ethnic map of Sub(Trans)-Carpathia, Ukraine, 1999...............................503
Map A7. Ethnic map of the present territory of Vojvodina,
   Yugoslavia, in 1910...504
Map A8. Ethnic map of the present territory of Vojvodina, Serbia, in 2002.........504

Table A1. Ethnic structure of the population of the Kingdom
   of Hungary (1495–1910) and the Carpathian Basin (1930–2001)..............498
Table A2. Ethnic structure of the population of the countries and
   regions of the Carpathian Basin...499

Acronyms

CEI: Central European Initiative

COE: Council of Europe

CSCE: Conference on Security and Cooperation in Europe

EC: European Community (until 1993)

EU: European Union (since 1994)

HCNM: High Commissioner on National Minorities

HHRF: Hungarian Human Rights Foundation (New York)

HTMH: Határon Túli Magyarok Hivatala (Office for Hungarians Beyond the Border)

HTMT: Határontúli Magyarok Titkársága (Secretariate for Hungarians Beyond the Border)

HuMFA: Hungary's Ministry of Foreign Affairs

KMKF: Kárpát-medencei Magyar Képviselők Fóruma (Forum of the Hungarian Representatives of the Carpathian Basin)

KMKSZ: Kárpátaljai Magyarok Kulturális Szövetsége

MTI: Magyar Távirati Iroda (Hungary's official news agency since 1880)

MP: Member of Parliament

PACE: Parliamentary Assembly of the Council of Europe

PSE: Pact on Stability in Europe

Preface

The year 1989 was indeed an *annus mirabilis,* a year of miracles, when the dominoes of the Soviet Empire fell in rapid succession. The accompanying applause in the West still rings in my ears, it is a beautiful memory. However, soon doubts were also voiced: will the former "captive nations" really change into liberal democracies? Will history really come to an end, as Francis Fukuyama optimistically predicted?[1] Will "the new Europe" not become a powder-keg led by nationalist demagogues, resuming their old quarrels about territory? The break-up of Yugoslavia in brutal wars seemed to justify such fears, but the rest of Central Europe opted for peace, prosperity and European integration. The close cooperation of Czechoslovakia, Hungary and Poland in the "Visegrád" association offered a promising model.

Nevertheless, there was a potential time bomb: compared to the linguistically relatively homogeneous Western European countries, which had stable borders, in Central and Eastern Europe, as a result of the border changes following the two world wars, most of the states contained large national minorities. Their overall number is estimated at 30 million. One of the potentially most serious post-1989 time bombs involved the condition of the more than 2 million people who were Hungarian by language and identity but had been separated from the main body of the Hungarian nation by the borders drawn in the 1920 peace treaty signed in the Greater Trianon Palace near Paris.

The very existence of these Hungarian minorities living in the states around Hungary raised both hopes and fears. In general, they were ill-treated by the states the treaty had assigned them to. Between the two world wars, Hungary, in accordance with the principle of national self-determination, strove for the peaceful revision of its borders. After the Second World War, voluntary and involuntary population movements, industrialization and urbanization, and the oppressive policies of the communist dictatorships changed the ethnic composition of the territories lost by Hungary. The numbers and even more so the proportions of the Hungarian minorities were reduced, but the core problem remained: whether those minorities were bound to be assimilated and disappear, or whether, in a democratic environment, they could survive and keep their language and traditions. After the regime changes, the question became: How would the democratically elected governments

---

[1] Francis Fukuyama, *The End of History and the Last Man* (New York: Macmillan, 1992).

of the new Europe get on with each other, how would they treat their national minorities that have a kin-state (or mother state) beyond the borders?

Three of my four grandparents, with Hungarian identity, were born in pre-First-World-War Hungary, but their birth-place was soon outside the present borders of what was left of the historical country. That fact may have contributed to my becoming a historian of twentieth century Central Europe, one well versed also in the problem of the national minorities. My academic career took me to the United States in the mid-1980s as a Fulbright scholar. Returning home, I became closely involved in the transition of my country from communism to democracy, and József Antall, elected prime minister on May 23, 1990, asked me to serve in his government as minister for foreign affairs. Since leaving that office, I have felt obliged to give an account of the foreign policy goals and achievements of the first freely-elected government of Hungary. However, a comprehensive account of four years of foreign policy in an entirely new international setup, based on my notes, speeches, statements, interviews, and memories, and using the documents in my possession, would have resulted in far too extensive a book. Therefore, I decided to focus on the most difficult and controversial aspects of Hungary's foreign relations: its attitude toward and relationship with its neighbors. Alongside many substantial achievements in that quarter, the eventual outcome also brought many disappointments for me and my compatriots.

Therefore, the subject of the present book is not the history of Hungary's foreign policy in the years of the regime change, but only the history of a distinct part of it: Hungary's relations with the neighbors and the efforts to guarantee the survival and well-being of the Hungarian national minorities. I examine how, following the collapse of communism, the Hungarian government tried to overcome the memory of past conflicts between Hungary and its neighbors, to replace animosity with friendly relations, and, at the same time, to help the Hungarian national minorities secure the right to participate in the decisions affecting them and preserve their language and culture. To secure fair treatment for the Hungarian minorities, gaining international protection of national minorities offered the best tool. It was a major aim of the Antall government to improve the instruments, the recommendations and laws adopted in various international institutions in the service of protecting the national minorities in Europe.

Whereas there are many publications in English on the great changes of 1989/90 and also on the various attitudes to the problem of the national minorities, very little scholarship is available on the course of Hungary's foreign policy in the last four decades, and there is practically none on how the political transformation affected the Hungarian minorities living in the seven states around Hungary. The subject of this book is likely of primary interest to Hungarians living both inside and outside of Hungary, but by presenting the events for the first time in English, it will hopefully also catch the attention of scholars, politicians and general readers among Hungary's neighbors. Political scientists interested in inter-ethnic relations, and historians of Central Europe will find little-known but interesting details in the present volume. Finally, since most countries of the world are multinational, having a large number of ethnic and national minorities, this case-study of the Hungarians also offers object lessons for political leaders and analysts.

This book is a combination of memoir and historical analysis based mainly on documents I preserved and my personal memories; it is a real-time account of an attempt to "heal the wound" inflicted by the Treaty of Trianon. My position was unique due to my special relationship with Prime Minister Antall, to whom this book is dedicated. Since his death, I have considered it one of my primary duties to keep the direction of Hungary's foreign policy on the path he laid, and to protest whenever I see the principles, aims and practices of the regime change being abandoned or altered.

The first Hungarian edition of this book was especially well received in Transylvania, where I presented it in several towns and even villages. It has long been out of print. When Katalin Kádár Lynn of Helena History Press came up with the idea of an English version (not a strict translation), I jumped at the possibility. The interest and generous support of Hungarian-Americans made both a second Hungarian edition and an English-language version possible. I would therefore like to express my special gratitude to the following people: Károly Balogh, Géza Kádár, Katalin Kádár Lynn, the late Szabolcs Kálmán, Judith Némethy, Klára Papp, Zsolt Szekeres, Endre Szentkirályi, and Katalin Vörös, with special thanks to Csaba Zoltáni and to a friend, a freedom-fighter in 1956, who wishes to remain anonymous. Their contribution helped my Hungarian publisher, János Gyurgyák of Osiris Publishing House, to bring out the second Hungarian edition, to which I had added a new chapter, a summary of publications and government actions, and an account of my personal involvement in advancing the case of the Hungarian minorities from 1994 to the present.

Discussing the subject of this book with my former collaborators, with participants in and witnesses of those memorable, full of hope days, was of great help in writing this book. I owe special gratitude to Ambassador János Herman, who was my spokesman and adviser then, also to the chiefs of my cabinet, Emőke Sillár, followed by Ferenc Oberfrank. I found the observations and suggestions of my reviewers and critics Csaba Gy. Kiss, Ignác Romsics, Géza Entz and Béla Király well placed. Special thanks are due to the English edition's copy editors, Jill Hannum and József Litkei. They did much more than careful reading and bringing the text to high stylistic standards; Jill became such an expert on the subject of Hungarian history and the minorities that her recommendations clarified my sentences for the English-speaking reader. My wife, Edit, who was an active participant in so many important meetings and discussions, contributed greatly to all my achievements with her involvement and ideas during the years of action, and with her patience and encouragement during the writing processes—words cannot express my gratitude.

I take full responsibility for any misinterpretations, shortcomings and errors.

Géza Jeszenszky
November 2025

Introduction

The end of the Cold War and the bipolar world that characterized it marked the beginning of a new era in world history. The balance of power was transformed, the unchallenged supremacy of the United States seemed to justify President George H. W. Bush's optimism that now freedom and justice would prevail in the world, the rule of law would supplant the rule of the jungle and the strong would respect the rights of the weak.[1] New countries emerged on the ruins of artificially created federations, and an independent Hungarian foreign policy became possible.[2]

Hungary's role in the collapse of the communist dominions made it a key player in the international transformation, contributing to post-Soviet history, and therefore deserving of special attention.[3] As then, so today, I am of the opinion

---

[1] George Herbert Walker Bush, "Toward a New World Order," address to a joint session of Congress and the nation, September 11, 1990. http://www.sweetliberty.org/issues/war/bushsr.htm.

[2] My first summaries: Géza Jeszenszky, "A magyar külpolitika fő irányai a század utolsó évtizedében" [Key fields in Hungarian foreign policy in the last decade of the century], in *Magyarország helye a XX. századi Európában* [The place of Hungary in twentieth century Europe], ed. Pál Pritz et al. (Budapest: Magyar Történelmi Társulat, 2002), 169–84; and Jeszenszky, "Hungary's Foreign Policy Dilemmas after Regaining Sovereignty," *Society and Economy* 29, no. 1 (2007): 43–64. Critical examinations: Pál Dunay and Wolfgang Zellner, *Ungarns Außenpolitik 1990–1997: Zwischen Westintegration, Nachbarschafts- und Minderheitenpolitik* (Baden-Baden: Nomos Verlagsgesellschaft, 1998); Margit Bessenyey Williams, "European Integration and Minority Rights: The Case of Hungary and Its Neighbors," in *Norms and Nannies: The Impact of International Organizations on the Central and East European States*, ed. Ronald H. Linden (Oxford: Rowman & Littlefield Publishers, 2002), 227–59; Pál Dunay, "Az átmenet magyar külpolitikája" [The foreign policy of the transition in Hungary], *Mozgó Világ* 30, no. 2 (2004): 51–65; and Márton Benedek, "Conditionality and Kinship: Hungarian Neighbourhood Policy towards Romania and Slovakia, 1990–2004" (D. Phil. Thesis, Oxford University, 2009). Among Nándor Bárdi's thorough studies, his *Tény és való: A budapesti kormányzatok magyarságpolitikája és a határon túli magyarok társadalomtörténete; Problémakatalógus* [Fact and reality: The "nation policy" of the Budapest governments and the social history of the Hungarians beyond the border] (Pozsony: Kalligram, 2004) is particularly noteworthy. Inaccuracies and hasty judgments weaken Zsolt Kéri Nagy's study, "The role of Hungarian nation policy in the context of regional stability," *Magyar Kisebbség* 9, no. 3 (2004): 223–56. My successor presents and analyzes the first period of the foreign policy of free Hungary in a broad context in János Martonyi, *Európa, nemzet, jogállam* [Europe, nation, Rechtstaat] (Budapest: Magyar Szemle–Európai Utas, 1998).

[3] Several contemporary accounts stand out among the significant body of literature on 1989/90: Timothy Garton Ash, *The Magic Lantern: The Revolution of 1989 Witnessed in Warsaw, Budapest, Berlin, and Prague*

that 1988–1991 was one of the brightest periods in world history, and was also Hungary's "finest hour." During those turbulent times, I often referred to the words of Lajos Kossuth, the leader of Hungary's War of Independence in 1848/49, who saw Hungary as becoming the "master of its own future," and said that foreign policy would play a key role in it. Hungary's historical role did not end with the end of the Cold War in 1990. Due to its geographic location and history, Hungary was—and has remained—particularly interested in developing norms and methods for resolving an ongoing international problem: the internal tensions of multi-ethnic countries, which usually have external repercussions as well.

After 1989, Hungary strove to ensure that, in addition to bilateral agreements, universally valid norms would come into force to secure the future of the millions of Hungarian minorities living in the neighboring countries. Hungary initiated the dissolution of the Warsaw Pact and Comecon, the economic version of Soviet domination, and also the establishment of the "Visegrád Group," a strong cooperation between the core Central European countries. As a neighbor to the bloody crisis zone in the Balkans, Hungary played an active role in the efforts to stop the bloodshed and find a just and lasting settlement. The "exploded Yugoslav ethnic mosaic"[4] confirmed the Hungarian thesis that problems arising from the multi-ethnicity of countries and the violation of minority rights could lead to serious crises. The security of Hungary and of Central Europe as a whole was assured by NATO membership, but first, the old members of the alliance had to be convinced of the usefulness of accepting former Warsaw Pact countries as members.[5] I took a most active part in that convincing.[6]

(London: Random House, 1990); Andrew Nagorski, *The Birth of Freedom* (New York: Simon & Schuster, 1993); Robert L. Hutchings, *American Diplomacy and the End of the Cold War* (Washington D.C.: Woodrow Wilson Center Press, 1997); Lee Edwards, ed. *The Collapse of Communism* (Stanford: Hoover Institution Press, 1999). András Oplatka, *Egy döntés története* [History of a decision] (Budapest: Helikon, 2008) provides an authentic and unbiased account of the key events that led to the first breach in the Iron Curtain, the opening of the border between Hungary and Austria. I summarized Hungary's role in an international context in: Géza Jeszenszky, "The Collapse of the Soviet Empire and Communism," in *The Berkshire Encyclopedia of World History* (Great Barrington, MA: Berkshire Publishing Group, 2016). http://www.grotius.hu/publ/displ.asp?id=UWRNDR. Cf. Géza Jeszenszky, "Magyarország és a kommunista dominók eldőlése" [Hungary and the fall of the communist dominoes], *Hitel* 22, no. 10 (2009): 70–79.

[4] Károly Kocsis, *Egy felrobbant etnikai mozaik esete* [The case of an exploded ethnic mosaic] (Budapest: Teleki László Alapítvány, 1993).

[5] For an authentic account of NATO's enlargement by one of its advocates, see Ronald D. Asmus, *Opening NATO's Door* (New York: Columbia University Press, 2002). M.E. Sarotte, *Not One Inch: America, Russia and the Making of Post-Cold War Stalemate* (New Haven, CT: Yale University Press, 2021) weighs the pros and cons of NATO moving East.

[6] Géza Jeszenszky, "NATO Enlargement: Anchor in a Safe Harbor," in *Open Door: NATO and Euro-Atlantic Security after the Cold War*, ed. Daniel Hamilton and Kristina Spohr (Washington, D.C.: Foreign Policy

Introduction

My aim in this book is to present the intentions and actions of József Antall's post-1989 government in an authentic manner, not for the sake of self-justification but only for the record. I feel it is also my duty to respond to distorted interpretations and unfounded accusations. Supporters of the radical right accuse the Antall government of not being "tough" enough with our neighbors, meaning that we did not reclaim from our neighbors any of the territories lost in 1920 and still inhabited mainly by Hungarians. To any clear-thinking person who is aware of the balance of power, of the ethnic composition of the population, and the unambiguous position of foreign powers, this accusation of weakness is ridiculous. Revision of existing borders in order to reclaim territory was neither possible nor was it our intent. This book will document the many ways in which we tried to improve the fate of the millions of Hungarians separated from the main body of the nation by the borders imposed by the 1920 and 1947 peace treaties. Revision was not among them. Rather, we focused on negotiating with our neighbors and striving for good relations with them. In the eyes of the contemporary left-wing opposition, however, the Antall government was thinking in terms of the "fifteen million Hungarians," also embracing those living outside the country's borders, and was unnecessarily paying too much attention to them. This "spiritual irredentism," the critics claimed, exacerbated relations with the neighbors. Another accusation focused on the government's alleged unfriendliness toward the Soviet Union and its legal successor, Russia, ostensibly for "ideological reasons," which destroyed economic relations between the two.[7] I hope that my book will prove most of that criticism to have been unfounded. Unfortunately, however, many people abroad gave credence to the leftist critics, and some of our neighbors themselves spread their views. Since the 2010 elections, in consequence of the criticism leveled at Viktor Orbán's

---

Institute and Henry A. Kissinger Center for Global Affairs, Paul H. Nitze School of Advanced International Studies, Johns Hopkins University, 2019), 117–50.

[7] László Lengyel, "Külpolitika vagy nemzetpolitika" [Foreign policy or "nation policy"], in *Kormány a mérlegen, 1990–1994* [Government—the balance sheet], ed. Csaba Gombár, Elemér Hankiss, László Lengyel, and Tibor Várnai (Budapest: Korridor Politikai Kutatások Központja, 1994), 346–68; Dunay and Zellner, *Ungarns Außenpolitik 1990–1997*; Dunay, "Az átmenet magyar külpolitikája"; my response: Géza Jeszenszky, "Tanulmányok a szuverén Magyarország külpolitikájáról" [Studies on the foreign policy of Hungary after the restoration of sovereignty], *Külügyi Szemle* 4, nos. 1–2 (2005): 274–90; and Jeszenszky, "Válasz egy doktrinernek" [Reply to a doctrinarian], *Külügyi Szemle* 4, nos. 3–4 (2005): 290–93. A complete misinterpretation of the Antall government's foreign policy and a series of false assertions can be found in Béla Galló's superficial presentation: "Nemzeti mozgástér, magyar külpolitika" [National room for maneuver, Hungarian foreign policy], in *Húsz éve szabadon Közép-Európában: Demokrácia, politika, jog* [Twenty years of freedom in Central Europe: Democracy, politics, law], ed. János Simon (Budapest: Konrad Adenauer Alapítvány, 2011), 311–13. The Hungarian Socialist Party gradually revised its position on dual citizenship and eventually voted for the law enabling Hungarians living beyond our borders to obtain Hungarian citizenship.

government, the image of Hungary as a "nationalist" country that is destabilizing its neighborhood and is even speculating about border changes has been projected back onto the Antall government as well.

The first edition of the present book, published in Hungarian in 2016, did not offer any reassuring solutions for healing the trauma caused by Trianon, and since then there have been no signs of recovery. However, we must not give up the fight; it is worth making further efforts to alleviate that sad legacy.

Admittedly, the change of regime did bring some improvement to the Hungarian minorities' situation. Today, our neighbors enjoy civil liberties, Hungarians have their own press, political parties, and are represented in parliaments, local governments, and occasionally even in national governments. All this was lacking during the communist era, and between the two world wars they lived in a politically oppressed situation. The Antall government was able to make it understood at the international level that there is a big difference between indigenous and immigrant minorities and that the two require different treatment. Building on the Helsinki process, which brought human rights (including the rights of national minorities) to the forefront, the international community, governments and organizations accepted that the protection of national minorities is a duty and must be ensured by legal means. The Hungarian government under Antall turned the problem from a bilateral issue into an international one, bringing Hungarian parties and representatives abroad into the arena of international diplomacy. It achieved that after the break-up of the neighboring, artificially created, and in principle federal states. We had serious disagreements with four of our seven neighbors, but with the other three we avoided any conflicts and established exemplary, friendly relations. In sum: we prevented the rebirth of the Little Entente that had isolated and shackled Hungary between the two world wars. Its revival was not far from the thinking of the nationalists of Slovakia, Romania and Serbia.

Under Antall, Hungary supported the struggle of Hungarian parties in neighboring countries to improve the situation of their communities. We refuted the claim that Hungarian policies protecting minorities had a destabilizing effect, arguing that it was precisely intolerance toward national minorities that led to internal and international tensions and conflicts. Unfortunately, our neighbors did not follow, or did so only to a limited extent, European examples such as the genuine autonomy granted to South Tyrol, which is part of Italy, and we failed to ensure that in any of those neighbors the Hungarians who had been forced to become citizens of other countries against their will were granted territorial or personal autonomy or co-national status by law. However, subsequent Hungarian governments were also unable to achieve this. Nevertheless, in those settlements and districts where

Hungarians constitute a majority or a significant minority, they are able to assert their special interests through democratic local elections.

In addition to valuable books and studies that were published on the occasion of the 100th anniversary of the Treaty of Trianon, a number of misleading articles and messages spread on the Internet. Rather than encouraging self-examination and a search for root causes, these have tended to scapegoat countries and politicians. This dissemination of unrealistic desires and illusions has only made the pain of Trianon more acute. Recent talk of the supposed possibility of border changes has not only mislead gullible people but has also caused serious damage to our neighborly relations; and it is the Hungarian communities outside our borders that suffer the consequences.

The victims of Trianon are the Hungarians living on both sides of the border. The real grievances cause serious internal tensions among our neighbors and complicate relations between countries. Only European integration can alleviate the pain of the Trianon trauma and, over time, make it disappear. I strive to raise awareness of this and promote it both within Hungary and abroad.

Chapter 1

Hungary and Its Neighbors before 1988

The roots of an antagonism

A good ethnic map of early twentieth-century Central and Southeast Europe looks like a colorful mosaic. A mosaic, as we know, is composed of small pieces of variously colored material. That part of Europe was not a melting pot of peoples; many smaller national/ethnic groups lived there, side by side, overlapping each other, often mixed in the towns, but in separate quarters. The twenty-odd ethnic groups in that region were submerged within four empires: the Russian, German, Habsburg (after 1867 Austro-Hungarian), and Ottoman. The Kingdom of Hungary (Regnum Hungariae) was established around 1000 A.D., composed of seven nomadic tribes that settled in the Carpathian Basin, mixing with its sparse, mainly Slavic population. Most likely they spoke a Finno-Ugric language and absorbed some Turkic groups, like the Cumans.[1] German-speaking settlers in the northeast in the twelfth century and the southeast in the eighteenth, following the final expulsion of the occupying Turks in 1740, were granted privileges, and they preserved their language and customs until the mid-twentieth century. From the thirteenth century, Romanian shepherds from the Balkan Peninsula gradually moved to the mountains of Transylvania,[2] and, following the Ottoman conquest (sixteenth–seventeenth centuries) immigrated in larger numbers. Serbs, escaping from Ottoman rule, settled in the southern part of the Great Hungarian plain. As

---

[1] The term "Hungarian" refers to the people who speak a Finno-Ugrian language ("Magyar"), who arrived from the Euro-Asian steppe region. "Hungary" denotes the territory surrounded by the Carpathian Mountain range, the state established in the eleventh century by King (Saint) Stephen. After the First World War, Hungary was reduced to one third of its former territory, to the central region inhabited almost exclusively by the Hungarian ("Magyar") speaking population. See Stephen Borsody, ed., *The Hungarians: A Divided Nation* (New Haven, CT: Yale University Center on International and Area Studies, 1988).

[2] Transylvania was an integral part of the historic Kingdom of Hungary (Regnum Hungariae), comprising its eastern region with varying degrees of autonomy. See Béla Köpeczi, ed., *History of Transylvania*, 3 vols. (Boulder, CO, Highland Lakes, NJ, New York: Social Science Monographs, Atlantic Research and Publications, Distributed by Columbia University Press, 2001). On its ethnic variety, see Csaba K. Zoltani, ed., *Transylvania Today: Diversity at Risk* (Budapest: Osiris, 2013).

a result, by 1900, the Hungarians were reduced to forming only around 50 percent of the population.[3]

Neither the medieval Hungarian kingdom nor any states in Europe were monolingual countries composed of only one ethnicity. Rather, a leader, a king, or a dynasty united and kept together in a political organization peoples of different origins and languages. The multilingual character of the countries of Europe became a source of tensions and conflicts only in the nineteenth century, with the so-called "national awakening," the formation of modern nations based on language, culture and common history. Before that, all the inhabitants of the Kingdom of Hungary, irrespective of the language they spoke, were considered *Hungarus*, Magyars and non-Magyars alike. Following the French Revolution and the Napoleonic Wars, loyalty based on language and culture replaced loyalty based on social status (nobility versus peasantry) or on the territory under a given ruler and its dynasty. *Natio* gave way to nation. In the short term, this resulted in demands for linguistic and administrative rights being made by the various national groups, but, in the long run, state borders and even the survival of the empires composed of different nations came to be questioned.[4]

In 1526, after the Battle of Mohács was lost to the Ottoman Turks, the Hungarian crown passed to the Habsburgs, who also ruled over the German, Czech, and later some Polish lands; but legally Hungary remained separate and was never part of the Holy Roman Empire.[5] Up until 1918, the break-up of the Habsburg Monarchy, the relationship between the Hungarians and the other peoples living in the historical kingdom was primarily a domestic issue. In contemporary usage, it was referred to as "racial problems," and later as "the nationality problem."[6] What made friendly coexistence among ethnic groups having a strong national identity so difficult was the existing settlement pattern of the various nationalities. Homogeneous blocs mingled with areas having a mixed population, where the various nationalities lived side-by-side in separate villages or had separate quarters in towns. Some ethnic

---

[3] R. W. Seton-Watson [Scotus Viator], *Racial Problems in Hungary* (London: Methuen, 1908), Geographical and statistical note [based on the census of 1900], 3–14. Croatia-Slavonia joined Hungary in a personal union in the thirteenth century; it remained a separate unit of the kingdom, enjoying considerable autonomy.

[4] On modern nationalism, see Hugh Seton-Watson, *Nations and States: An Enquiry into the Origins of Nations and the Politics of Nationalism* (London: Methuen, 1977), on the Hungarian case, 137–69 and 493.

[5] C.A. Macartney, *The Habsburg Empire, 1790–1918* (London: Weidenfeld & Nicolson, 1968). The latest and rightly acclaimed works are Martyn Rady, *The Habsburgs: The Rise and Fall of a World Power* (London: Allen Lane, 2020); and Rady, *The Habsburgs: To Rule the World* (New York: Basic Books, 2020). The most up-to-date history of Hungary in English is Bryan Cartledge, *The Will to Survive: A History of Hungary* (London: Timewell Press, 2006 [2nd ed. London: Hurst & Company, 2011]). Less thorough, but perhaps more easily available is Peter F. Sugar, ed., *A History of Hungary* (Bloomington: Indiana University Press, 1990).

[6] The basic and most widely used, though biased, work on that is Seton-Watson, *Racial Problems in Hungary*.

groups, like the German Saxons in Transylvania, had their own legal system, and all groups had their own churches.[7] During the 1848/49 revolution and war for independence, some of the non-Hungarians, instigated by the Court in Vienna, already demanded and fought for territorial autonomy. Following the settlement of relations between the Habsburg dynasty and the Hungarian body politic in 1867 (the "Ausgleich"), the co-existence of the various national groups came to be regulated by a liberal law (Nationalities Act of 1868), which guaranteed linguistic rights to the various national groups but declared all citizens to be members of "the unitary Hungarian nation."

The Nationalities Act failed, however, to recognize "group rights" or grant any political, let alone territorial, autonomy to the non-Hungarians.[8] But since in many regions the population was ethnically mixed, especially in the towns, it would have been rather difficult to create autonomous units within the country. However, the execution of the originally quite generous law increasingly left much to be desired, as was expressed by the representatives of the nationalities and also by the more enlightened members of the Hungarian body politic, such as Oszkár Jászi.[9] Nevertheless, the charges of oppression and "ruthless Magyarization" so often leveled against Hungary's conduct by its national minorities and later historians are unwarranted, given the liberal character of the state. Between 1870 and 1910, a small percentage of Germans and Slovaks (mostly those living in the towns or working in the factories) and most of the Jews assimilated and came to call and regard themselves (even more so their offspring) Hungarian. This was not a forced process, and the Romanian, Slovak and Serb peasant masses were not affected at all by the Hungarians' desire to increase their percentage and influence in the overall population. It is often overlooked that the Romanian and Serb churches and that of the German-speaking Lutheran Saxons in Transylvania enjoyed full autonomy. Liberal capitalism even helped the growth of the middle class among the non-Hungarians.[10] So it can be safely said that before 1914 national antagonism did not affect the majority of the people—yet.

---

[7] Béla Köpeczi, ed., *History of Transylvania*, vol. 1 (Boulder, CO, Highland Lakes, NJ, New York: Social Science Monographs; Atlantic Research and Publications, 2001–2002).

[8] Cartledge, *The Will to Survive*, 264–74. The role this issue played in the eventual collapse of the Hungarian state in 1918 was best described by one of the protagonists, see Oscar Jászi, *The Dissolution of the Habsburg Monarchy* (Chicago: University of Chicago Press, 1929, republished in 2008).

[9] Oszkár Jászi (1875–1957): Hungarian social scientist, historian, and politician. Minister for National Minorities (October 1918–January 1919). From 1925 he lived in exile in the United States, a professor at Oberlin College, Ohio.

[10] Péter Hanák, "Polgárosodás és asszimiláció Magyarországon a XIX. században" [The middle class and assimilation in nineteenth century Hungary], *Történelmi Szemle*, nos. 3–4 (1974): 513–36.

At the beginning of the twentieth century, most peoples who lived within the framework of the Habsburg, Russian and Ottoman (Turkish) Empires were already dreaming about establishing independent states and unification with their kin abroad, but without the support of one of the great powers any change of the borders—let alone the dissolution of an empire—was illusory. The assassination of the heir to the Austro-Hungarian throne (who happened to have pro-Slav and anti-Hungarian sentiments) by a Bosnian Serb terrorist led to a world war only because of the conflicting interests of the great powers and the system of their alliances. Originally, the break-up of the Austro-Hungarian Monarchy was not among the war aims of the Entente powers.[11] The stalemate that ensued on the war's fronts increased the value of the neutral states; both alliances competed to win them over in the hope of tipping the balance, so each offered territories of the enemy's side as a reward for joining their side. Recognition of this historic opportunity guided the respected representative of the Imperial Parliament in Vienna, the Czech professor Tomáš G. Masaryk, and also several Croatian politicians to emigrate to Britain or France. There, with the help of sympathetic politicians and journalists, they started a campaign to convince the Entente of the need to dissolve the Austro-Hungarian Monarchy and replace it with nation states. They had to contend with those who thought that the balance of power, the need for a great power in Central Europe, would be best served by transforming the domains of the Habsburgs into a democratic federation.[12] But by endorsing the strivings of the "oppressed peoples" for independence, the Entente was able to justify the war on moral grounds, too. However, it was not until the spring of 1918 that both Britain and the United States decided to accept the dissolution idea, concluding that with Germany having facilitated a social revolution in Russia, a good response to that would be to weaken and then disrupt the Monarchy by initiating "national revolutions" in that multinational empire.[13] Starting in April 1918, about 150,000 leaflets were dropped every day on the enemy on the Italian front. These propagated the Czech and South Slav program for independence, illustrating it with maps of proposed new states, and calling for the Slavic and Romanian soldiers to desert.[14] The perspective of

---

[11] Arthur May, *The Passing of the Hapsburg Monarchy, 1914–1918*, vol. 2 (Philadelphia, PA: University of Pennsylvania Press, 1966), chap. 6, "Entente Opinion and the Danube Monarchy"; Hugh Seton-Watson and Christopher Seton-Watson, *The Making of a New Europe: R.W. Seton-Watson and the Last Years of Austria-Hungary* (London: Methuen, 1981), 102; Géza Jeszenszky, *Lost Prestige: Hungary's Changing Image in Britain 1894–1918* (Reno, NV: Helena History Press, 2020), 329–32.

[12] Jeszenszky, *Lost Prestige*, 338–43.

[13] For the process leading there: Jeszenszky, *Lost Prestige*, Chapter 7.

[14] Mark Cornwall, *The Undermining of Austria-Hungary: The Battle for Hearts and Minds* (Basingstoke: Macmillan, 2001).

achieving independence with generous borders greatly contributed to the collapse of the Austro-Hungarian Monarchy. On October 28, the Czechs proclaimed their independence in Prague. They were followed by the Croats in Zagreb on October 29, and the Slovaks on the 30th in Turčiansky Svätý Martin (Turócszentmárton).

"Possession is nine tenths of the law"

The ceasefire signed in Padova on November 3, 1918, entitled the Entente to occupy any area of the Monarchy. In line with that, the Serbian and Romanian armies, led by French generals, took over the southeastern regions of Hungary by the end of the year. Czechoslovak Foreign Minister Eduard Beneš, who stayed in Paris, managed to get authorization for the newly formed Czech army (led by French and Italian officers) to occupy the territories that Czechoslovakia claimed. In Hungary, Count Mihály Károlyi's[15] new, radical, pro-Entente government, formed on October 31, placed all hopes in the fairness of the peacemakers and in President Woodrow Wilson's noble principles, and therefore saw neither reason nor a chance for armed resistance. The Hungarian public at that time could not even imagine that towns such as Pozsony, Kassa, and Kolozsvár, all having played a prominent role in Hungarian history, would become Bratislava, Košice and Cluj, or that the purely Hungarian Szeklerland (Székelyföld) would be placed under foreign sovereignty—in contradiction to the principle of self-determination proclaimed by the victorious powers.

This *fait accompli* settled the fate of historic Hungary. The debate is still going on as to whether there was any opportunity to fight for at least the areas inhabited mainly by Hungarians. We now know that the French and the English did not want to sacrifice a single soldier to satisfy the territorial greed of Hungary's neighbors, nor were the Hungarian soldiers, tired of the war, eager to join the small, newly organized Hungarian army. Many of the vanquished Germans and Hungarians were captivated by the idea of a new world order based on social justice and flirted with Bolshevism, while the Romanians, Serbs and Czechs were driven by the possibility of realizing their national dreams. Their success was an antidote to the attraction of the Leninist utopia.

Contrary to their declaration on self-determination, the great powers that made the decisions over Central Europe were driven by selfish, short-term interests,

---

[15] Count Mihály Károlyi de Nagykároly (1875–1955): Hungarian politician, president of the Republic in 1918–1919. The scion of one of the wealthiest Hungarian landowning families, he gradually espoused radical political views and was opposed to the German alliance in the First World War. In exile after the proclamation of the Hungarian Soviet Republic in March 1919 and its collapse 133 days later, he flirted with Bolshevism.

instead of adhering to the principle of nationality, equity and stability. The Peace Conference (originally planned to be only a preliminary one among the victors to agree upon what to propose for the defeated countries), met on January 18, 1919, in Paris. The new borders of Hungary were drawn up by the junior diplomats who made up the territorial committees. The pattern was typical: the American experts proposed frontiers as close to the ethnic lines as possible (where it was possible to draw such a line), the British were wavering between a sense of fairness and the drive to punish the vanquished and reward the smaller new allies, while the French gave all possible support to the often extravagant claims of the "successor states" of Hungary. The main argument was based on military and economic strategy, particularly the existence of railway lines in the most disputed areas. Eventually, that is what decided the fate of more than three million Hungarians, who were separated from the compact bloc of Hungarians, despite their protests against the denial of the principle of self-determination. Nevertheless, it must be pointed out that the most outrageous claims, like the creation of a "corridor" in Western Hungary between Czechoslovakia and Yugoslavia, the incorporation of the Börzsöny, Mátra and Bükk mountains into Czechoslovakia, or the cession of the towns of Baja and Pécs to Yugoslavia, were turned down by the Great Powers, despite the many false figures presented to the Conference by the Czech, Romanian and Serb leaders. By the time Hungary had a government recognized by the victors and the head of the Hungarian delegation, Count Albert Apponyi,[16] presented the Hungarian objections on January 16, 1920, Hungary's neighbors had already consolidated their hold over the debated areas, expelling from them hundreds of thousands of Hungarians. The Hungarian proposal to the peace conference to hold plebiscites on the territories to be detached was of no avail. The only person who paid attention to the Hungarian arguments was David Lloyd George, the British Liberal prime minister. He spoke out against detaching so many Hungarians from their country and proposed revision of the planned borders. Francesco Nitti,[17] the new Italian prime minister, supported him, but in the end, the "expert" advisors and the foreign ministers foiled the only serious attempt to mitigate the terms to be imposed upon Hungary. It was claimed that the special treaties drawn up for the protection of the national minorities would resolve any problems that might arise from having three million Hungarians detached from Hungary.[18]

---

[16] Albert Apponyi de Nagyappony (1847–1933): the scion of an old Hungarian aristocratic family. Minister of Cults and Education in 1906–10, Apponyi was Hungary's chief delegate at the League of Nations.

[17] Francesco Saverio Nitti (1868–1953): Italian economist and politician, prime minister (1919–20).

[18] From the vast literature on the peace conference dealing with Hungary the classic one is Francis Deak, *Hungary at the Paris Peace Conference: The Diplomatic History of the Treaty of Trianon* (New York:

From pre-war Hungary's territory of 283,000 km² (without Croatia), the size and nationality composition of the territories detached in the Peace Treaty signed at the Grand Trianon palace in Versailles (based on the 1910 census data).

Romania received 103,093 km² with 5,257,476 inhabitants, including

1,704,851 Hungarian	31.6 percent
2,828,522 Romanian	53.8 percent
559,824 German	9.8 percent

Czechoslovakia received 63,000 km² with 3,576,000 inhabitants, including

1,084,000 Hungarian	30.3 percent
1,702,000 Slovak	47.6 percent
436,000 Ruthenian	12.2 percent
266,000 German	7.4 percent

Yugoslavia received 21,000 km² with 1,514,999 inhabitants, including

458,252 Hungarian	30.2 percent
382,149 Serb	25.2 percent
303,583 German	20.0 percent
91,571 Croat	6.1 percent
76,780 Romanian	5.1 percent
46,000 Slovak	3.0 percent

Columbia University Press, 1942); Béla K. Király, Peter Pastor, and Ivan Sanders, eds., *Essays on World War I: Total War and Peacemaking, A Case Study of Trianon* (New York and Boulder, CO: Atlantic Research, 1982); and Béla K. Király and László Veszprémy, eds., *Trianon and East Central Europe: Antecedents and Repercussions* (Boulder, CO, Highland Lakes, NJ: Atlantic Research, 1995) are collections of insightful studies. A succinct monograph is Ignác Romsics, *The Dismantling of Historic Hungary: the Peace Treaty of Trianon*, 1920, trans. Mario D. Fenyo (Boulder, CO: Columbia University Press, 2002); my review: "The Genesis of a Lasting Quarrel in Central Europe," *The Hungarian Quarterly* 44 (Winter 2003): 113–18. Recently, in connection with the hundredth anniversary of the Trianon peace, a large number of detailed and objective monographs and document collections appeared in Hungary under the direction of Balázs Ablonczy. A report on the conference *Trianon 100 Years After*, LSE IDEAS and Babes-Bolyai University held in Cluj/Kolozsvár in 2020, edited by Megan Palmer and Mădălina Mocan, was published at the London School of Economics. A good guide in English to the literature is in Bryan Cartledge, *Trianon egy angol szemével* [The Treaty of Trianon as seen by an Englishman] (Budapest: Officina Kiadó, 2009). One of the foremost Hungarian experts, Miklós Zeidler, collected a large number of sources, essays and studies, with an excellent bibliography: *Trianon* (Budapest: Osiris, 2003); while János Gyurgyák edited an impressive three volume collection, *Trianon 100* (Budapest: Osiris, 2020).

Austria received 4,000 km² with 292,000 inhabitants, including

    26,000 Hungarian   8.8 percent
    266,000 Austrian   91.2 percent

....

Hungary (post-war) 92,963 km² with 7,615,117 inhabitants, including

    6,612,000 Hungarian   88.4 percent
    521,000 German   7.0 percent
    166,000 Slovak   2.2 percent

If historic Hungary was a multinational country and not a unitary Hungarian state, the same can be said of the successors:

The national composition of the new states of Central Europe (based on the 1920 census):

Czechoslovakia: 14.7 million.
50 percent Czech, 15.7 percent Slovak, 22.5 percent German,
5.5 percent Hungarian (Jews excl.), 3.5 percent Rusyn

Romania: 16 million.
72 percent Romanian, 9.1 percent Hungarian, 4.5 percent German,
4.2 percent Ukrainian

Yugoslavia: 12 million.
47.7 percent Serb, 23.3 percent Croat, 8.5 percent Slovenian,
5.5 percent Albanian, 3.9 percent Hungarian, 3.4 percent Macedonian

Hungary: 8 million.
89.5 percent Hungarian, 6.9 percent German

These numbers make it clear why Hungarians will always consider the 1920 peace treaty seriously unfair. These "successor states" defined themselves as nation-states, despite the substantial number of citizens who belong to a national minority. The Hungarian minorities did not receive the rights guaranteed in the minority protection treaties, which were part of the peace treaties. Their fate was expulsion, expropriation, and discrimination. In addition, the governments of the successor states hoped to gradually reduce their numbers. Discriminatory land reforms expropriated the Hungarian large landowners and the Hungarian Catholic, Calvinist and Lutheran churches, without compensation. Ownership passed to members of the majority nation, often to people coming to Hungarian-inhabited areas as settlers and colonists. In the schools, false myths were spread, like speaking of "a thousand years of oppression" by the barbarous Hungarians. The debates and conflicts that had previously been confined almost exclusively to a relatively narrow, well-educated circle, now penetrated the deeper layers of society. Hungary could think only of a single solution: a change of the borders—preferably peacefully.

The anti-minority policies distorted the thinking of the majority peoples, too. Genuine democracy could not take root and operate between the two world wars as political freedoms were denied to the minorities, except in Czechoslovakia. To the contemporary slogan in Hungary of "No, no never!" (shall we accept the imposed borders), the answer was "Not a furrow!" (shall we give back). István Bibó, a prominent Hungarian scholar and politician observed: "If for some reasons a territorial dispute becomes a dominant cause in the life of a nation, it can block the road to democratic progress for any not yet democratic community, and may lead to a relapse of the democratic spirit even in a democratic community."[19]

The Trianon peace treaty has indeed proved to be the apple of Eris for Central Europe, the root of animosities between the Hungarians and their neighbors. If the borders established in 1920 had conformed to the ethnic-national principle, legitimizing the decisions made by referendum (as proposed by the Hungarian Peace Delegation), eventually the Hungarians would have reconciled themselves to the loss of some of their historical provinces, and today the relationship between the Hungarians and their neighbors would be much easier. There are no national tensions and territorial conflicts in Hungarian-Austrian, Hungarian-Croatian, and Hungarian-Slovenian relations today, because in 1920 an ethnically fair, acceptable boundary was drawn and only a small number of national minorities were created. Compared to this, the Slovaks still remember that in 1938 the Hungarian-inhabited areas were returned to Hungary, and they fear its repetition. If the Hungarian-Slovak border had been drawn a little to the north, on the then-existing ethnic

---

[19] István Bibó (1911–1979): Hungarian legal scholar and political theorist. Minister of state in the 1956 revolutionary government, for which he was sentenced to life imprisonment, amnestied in 1963. The quote is from István Bibó, *A kelet-európai kisállamok nyomorúsága* [The misery of Eastern Europe's small states] (Budapest: 1946 and London: 1960), 143. Cf. István Bibó, *Democracy, Revolution, Self-Determination: Selected Writings*, ed. Károly Nagy (Boulder, CO: Atlantic Research and Publications, 1991); and István Bibó, "The Miseries of East European Small States," in *The Art of Peacemaking*, ed. Iván Zoltán Dénes (New Haven, CT: Yale University Press, 2015), 130–80.

dividing line, there would be no serious tensions between the two nations today. However, the loss of purely or mostly Hungarian-populated areas is still a painful wound, especially for those affected by the change. Its healing is prevented by the anti-minority sentiments often perceptible even today. In the face of intolerance and discrimination, a sovereign Hungarian state can never be indifferent. Only a fair minority policy that does not try to change the ethnic proportions could calm Hungarian society. There are analogous Western European examples for the fair handling of national minorities, for example, the case of South Tyrol, but also the example of the Åland Islands and Schleswig.

Almost all objective historians and analysts considered Trianon to be a harmful and bad peace. A few quotations can serve to show the connection between the Trianon peace treaty and the ensuing conflicts between Hungary and its neighbors: "There is not one of the peoples or provinces that constituted the Empire of the Habsburgs to whom gaining their independence has not brought the tortures which ancient poets and theologians had reserved for the dammed."[20] "Legitimate rights to national independence in the Danube region could have been safely satisfied without placing one-third of the Hungarians under the foreign domination of triumphant neighbors. Justice as well as common sense dictated reconciliation. The peace dictated by the Danubian victors to the vanquished Hungarian perpetuated national conflicts. Trianon did the opposite of true peacemaking. Instead of encouraging regional union and cooperation, peacemaking in the Danube region after the First World War placed the issue of nation-state boundaries at the top of Danubian politics, thus fanning the flames of rivalry and territorial imperialism."[21] "In each of the new states there prevailed a narrow official nationalism …This state of generalized and mutual hostility provided opportunities for any great power intent on disturbing the peace." This latter was written by the sons of R. W. Seton-Watson (Scotus Viator), one of the creators of the new Central Europe.[22] In his writings in the 1930s, the British historian C. A. Macartney drew a particularly realistic picture of inter-war Central Europe.[23] In 1938–1941 Hungary was lured into the

---

[20] Sir Winston Churchill, *The Gathering Storm* (London: Cassell & Co, 1948), 14. Cf. István Deák, "The Social and Psychological Consequences of the Disintegration of Austria-Hungary in 1918," *Österreichische Osthefte* 22 (1980): 22–32.

[21] Stephen Borsody, "Hungary's Road to Trianon: Peacemaking and Propaganda," in Király, Pastor, and Sanders, *Essays on World War I*, 35.

[22] Seton-Watson and Seton-Watson, *The Making of a New Europe*, 435.

[23] C. A. Macartney, *Hungary*, with a foreword by H.A.L. Fisher (London: Ernest Benn Ltd. 1934); Macartney, *Hungary and Her Successors: The Treaty of Trianon and its Consequences 1919–1937* (Oxford: Oxford University Press, 1937 [1965]). Cf. Macartney, *The Danubian Basin: Oxford Pamphlets on World Affairs*, no. 10, Oxford, 1939.

camp of Nazi Germany by the offer of territorial gains: the return of predominantly Hungarian areas from Czechoslovakia, Romania and Yugoslavia.

During the Second World War and immediately afterwards, almost all the peoples in Europe learned the horrors of total war and their consequences. Mass murders, cruel civil wars, concentration camps and gas chambers, the transfer of millions, and open or concealed "ethnic cleansing" all comprised the fate of tens of millions.[24] In Central Europe mutual grievances only increased. Communism, nominally anti-nationalist, internationalist, could not, in fact did not want to help. It only wrapped national oppression in a red mantel. For decades majorities and minorities were victims of state terror, the confiscation of property, the forcing of peasants into collective farms; all suffering the consequences of harmful economic policies. At the same time, the national minorities suffered under double oppression; they could not rely on their own press, political parties or the church. A new peace treaty with Hungary, signed in 1947 again in Paris,[25] repeated the territorial clauses of 1920. In addition, the protection of minority communities was abandoned and replaced by the general protection of codified human rights, which were totally disregarded in the communist-dominated countries. The principle of the *status quo* and (supposed) stability has been overwriting the concern for the fair treatment of the minorities.

The ethnic map of the Carpathian Basin (identical with the historic Kingdom of Hungary) has changed considerably due to the Second World War and the subsequent population transfers and expulsions, to communist industrialization and deliberate colonization (transferring a large number of non-Hungarians to territories traditionally inhabited mainly by Hungarians and thus changing the ethnic composition of the area), and finally to free emigration following the regime changes. In the course of a hundred years the number of Hungarians detached from Hungary fell from 3.4 million in 1920 to a little over 2 million, and their proportion in the transferred territories fell from 35 percent to 10–20 percent.[26]

---

[24] See Timothy Snyder, *Bloodlands: Europe Between Hitler and Stalin* (New York: Basic Books, 2010).

[25] The authoritative account of "the second Trianon" is the generally acclaimed monograph: Mihály Fülöp, *The Unfinished Peace: The Council of Foreign Ministers and the Hungarian Peace Treaty of 1947* (Boulder, CO: Social Science Monographs; Wayne, NJ: Center for Hungarian Studies and Publications, 2011; Second, revised and enlarged edition: Budapest: Ludovica University Press, 2025).

[26] The proportion of the Hungarians has fallen drastically from 30 to 11 percent of the population in Slovakia; from 32 to 17 percent in Romanian Transylvania; from 28 to 16 percent in the Vojvodina (Serbia); and from 31 to 12 percent in Subcarpathia (Transcarpathian Ukraine). The ethnic composition of the cities has changed even more dramatically, as graphically demonstrated by the case of the capital of Transylvania, Kolozsvár. In 1910, 82 percent of the city's population was Hungarian and 14 percent Romanian. Today it is called Cluj-Napoca, where—largely due to the methods of the deposed dictator Ceaușescu and the notorious mayor Funar—Hungarians comprise only 15 percent of the population. See map A1 in the Appendix.

Post-1990 democratic Hungary respects the boundaries prescribed for it in 1947 but continues to feel responsibility for the Hungarian minorities beyond its borders. All successive, democratically elected Hungarian governments will endeavor to live up to this responsibility.

The alarming situation of the Hungarian minorities: The engine of the regime change

Despite the reputation of János Kádár's[27] communist regime in Hungary as "the jolliest barrack in the Soviet camp," opposition to it emerged from the 1970s.[28] The Western media noticed that independent-minded intellectuals started to point out many of the shortcomings of that system in clandestine publications, "samizdats," often openly revealing the authorship. There was, however, a much larger section of the population equally or even more critical of the system, mainly "intellectuals": writers, artists and social scientists who, for existential reasons, represented a more cautious, less outspoken opposition. Their criticism was hidden "between the lines" but grew loud in private conversations. I call that group the silent opposition. Due to the background and the subjects of the publications of those intellectuals they were quite often considered by some as "too patriotic," nationalist or populist.[29] I hope that the following pages will modify, or even refute such a representation.

It has long been a common view in Hungary that the Czechoslovak-Hungarian project for the construction of a barrage system on the Danube, between Gabčíkovo/Bős and Nagymaros, was opposed by an increasing number of people throughout the 1980s for fear of serious environmental damage. Protests against "the damned dam" certainly had a galvanizing effect on the population, and it contributed to the growth and consolidation of an organized opposition to the Hungarian regime. It hasn't been noted, however, how strong was the concern for the fate of the

---

[27] János Kádár (1912–1989): Hungarian communist politician. Interior Minister from 1948 to 1950, imprisoned in a show trial, released by reformist Prime Minister Imre Nagy in 1954. Following the Soviet suppression of the uprising in 1956, he was imposed on his country as the general secretary of the Hungarian Socialist Workers' Party, a position he held for thirty-two years until 1988.

[28] A collection of essays on the regime change, partly by the participants, is Béla K. Király and András Bozóki, eds., *Lawful revolution in Hungary, 1989–94* (Boulder, CO: Atlantic Research, 1995). There is a detailed monograph on Hungary's peaceful revolution: Ignác Romsics, *From Dictatorship to Democracy: The Birth of the Third Hungarian Republic 1988–2001* (Boulder, CO: Columbia University Press, 2007).

[29] On the "populists," see the works of Gyula Borbándi, a prominent member of the anti-communist Hungarian emigration. His seminal work: *Der ungarische Populismus* (Munich, 1976). A more thorough account by the same author: *A magyar népi mozgalom: A harmadik reformnemzedék* [The Hungarian People's Movement: The third reformer generation] (New York: Püski, 1983; Budapest: 1989).

Hungarian minorities in Romania and Czechoslovakia. That apprehension and related actions taken are the *leitmotiv* of the present volume.

Dramatis personae: The players

The majority of the members of the political parties elected to Parliament in 1990 were born between 1930 and 1950. As a result, their thinking about the world, foreign policy and neighboring countries was largely shaped by the recent past—that is, by the Trianon peace and the fate of the Hungarians annexed by the neighboring countries; the (temporary) successes of the territorial changes between 1938 and 1941; the German and later Soviet occupation of the country; the deportation and murder of a significant part of Hungarian Jewry; the pillage, mass rape and other atrocities by the Red Army; the strangulation of Hungarian democracy by Moscow and a handful of Hungarian communists, despite that it began promisingly in 1945; the political crimes and disastrous economic policies of the Rákosi era;[30] the 1956 revolution and its armed suppression by the Soviet superpower; the brutal reprisals under the name of János Kádár; the crushing (with Hungarian complicity) of the "Prague Spring" of 1968; the historical friendship towards the Polish people and the example of the Solidarity movement of 1980–81; the official disinterest in the situation of Hungarian minorities beyond the borders and the actions taken against those who spoke out for them; and, finally, by the growing anti-Hungarian policy of the Ceaușescu regime[31] in Romania. These were collective experiences, but they had a concrete, personal impact on everyone. Those who took an active part in the defeat of the communist regime, who joined the new or revived old political parties, who formed the National Assembly and the new political elite after the free elections of 1990, were all intensively concerned not only with the subject of democracy and the political system but also with the complicated relationship between Hungarians and their neighboring nations, which was fraught with many bad memories.

---

[30] Mátyás Rákosi (1892–1971): Hungarian communist politician. Returning from exile in the Soviet Union he became the *de facto* leader of Hungary from 1947 to 1956. Modeled upon Stalin's personality cult, his terrorizing the population and a disastrous economic policy made his rule highly unpopular, ending in revolt in 1956. Following the suppression of the democratic revolution he was not allowed to live in Hungary and died in exile in the Soviet Union.

[31] Nicolae Ceaușescu (1918–1989): Romanian communist politician. De facto dictator from 1965 until his death by execution in December 1989. On his oppression of the Hungarians, see Elemér Illyés, *National Minorities in Romania: Change in Transylvania* (Boulder, CO: East European Monographs, 1983).

József Antall[32] is the real hero of the present volume. He was the key figure in the peaceful transition from dictatorship to democracy in Hungary, and in 1990 won the first free elections to be prime minister until his untimely death. He was, however, more than that. Antall was also an educator for his whole nation on Hungarian history, on parliamentary democracy, on foreign policy, and also on the problems of the Hungarians beyond the borders. His father came from the small nobility engaged in farming and viticulture in the heart of the Transdanubian region, in the region of Somló Hill, noted for its excellent wines. Antall Sr. was a civil servant in the Ministry of Home Affairs. From 1939 to March 1944, he was responsible for war refugees, and, with the tacit approval of Prime Minister Pál Teleki[33] and his successors, helped about a hundred thousand Poles to settle in Hungary or to escape to Western Europe and continue the fight against Nazi Germany. Following the March 1944 German occupation of Hungary he was arrested by the Nazi Gestapo. After the war, Yad Vashem recognized him as Righteous Among the Nations. In 1946 Antall Sr. became Minister for Reconstruction in the coalition government led by the centrist Smallholders' Party. His democratic convictions and social sensitivity had a decisive influence on his son's thinking and political sympathies. Antall Jr. became a convinced Anglophile democrat and a fearless opponent of the communist regime. He studied history, literature, law, art and became an archivist and later a schoolteacher (an extremely popular one with the students), and he took an active part in the revolution of 1956. Following its suppression, he was arrested several times, but no charges could be proven against him, and he got away with being banned from the teaching profession. After spending several years as an assistant in a lending library, in the mid-1960s he joined the then-modest Semmelweis Memorial House, which, in just a few years, he made into an internationally renowned institution focused on the history of medicine, eventually becoming its director. It was also a place where his many friends could gather to discuss informally the political situation at home and abroad.

József Antall was one of the founding members of the MDF (Hungarian Democratic Forum) in 1988 and was elected president of that party on October 22, 1989. Foreign policy had been of deep interest to him since his youth. He was also very familiar with the history and internal conditions of Hungary's neighbors. His aim, based on the lessons of history, was to join Hungary to the West, integrating

---

[32] József Antall (1932–1993): archivist, historian, politician, statesman. Prime minister from May 1990 until his death on December 12, 1993, caused by non-Hodgkin's lymphoma.
[33] Count Pál Teleki (1879–1941): geographer, university professor, politician, from a distinguished Transylvanian family. Prime minister in 1920–1921 and 1939–1941. He detested Nazism and tried to keep Hungary out of the Second World War, and when that looked impossible he committed suicide.

it into NATO and the European Union while simultaneously establishing cordial relations with his country's neighbors. However, at the same time, he considered safeguarding the rights of the Hungarian minority communities to be an indispensable element of good relations. He hoped that the need for cooperation in Central Europe would be stronger than the mentality of the inter-war Little Entente,[34] the alliance against Hungary.[35]

Thanks to Antall's confidence in me, I became Hungary's minister for foreign affairs. Born in November 1941, I grew up in the fearful atmosphere of the Rákosi era. I listened to Western radio broadcasts with my father. Later, witnessing and remembering the beautiful days of the 1956 revolution, I came to firmly reject the dictatorship and to be a strong believer in multi-party democracy. That is why, unlike many of my contemporaries, I refused even to consider membership in the MSZMP, the communist party,[36] even though many Western acquaintances used to say, "the system can be changed only from within."

The history of Central Europe and Hungary's relations with its neighbors preoccupied me from my early youth, partly because of my family background: three of my grandparents were born outside the present borders of Hungary while having a strong Hungarian identity. My very surname leads to questions, is it Polish? Slovak? On our walks in the Buda hills, my father would tell me the story of the 1278 Battle of Marchfeld fought against the King of Bohemia, in which the ancestor of the Jeszenszky family fell and his sons received as compensation from King Ladislaus IV a piece of forest in the heart of today's Slovakia. My forebears, staunch Lutherans since the Reformation, have spread from the ancestral home Nagyjeszen (now Jaseno) in Turóc county to all parts of the historic kingdom. Those Jeszenszkys who remained in Turóc became Slovaks and still make up the majority of the inhabitants of the village. My great-great grandfather, Péter Jeszenszky, was a Lutheran pastor who, in the second half of the eighteenth century, moved to the Southlands, then recently liberated from the occupying Turks. He was the founder of the village of Glozsán, near today's Novi Sad in Serbia, and he built its church. His grandson was the Lutheran pastor at Nagyszentmiklós (today Sânnicolau Mare in Romania). In that multi-ethnic small town, which was also the birthplace of the famous composer Béla Bartók, Hungarians, Germans, Serbs and Romanians lived together, generally in peace. My maternal grandmother was born in Transylvania, her father

---

[34] "Little Entente" was the informal name of the alliance of Czechoslovakia, Romania and Yugoslavia between 1921 and 1938, mainly directed at Hungary.
[35] On Antall's foreign policy, see my essay in Géza Jeszenszky, ed. *József Antall, Prime Minister of Hungary: Selected Speeches and Interviews (1989–1993)* (Budapest: József Antall Foundation, 2008), 15–48.
[36] MSZMP: Hungarian Socialist Workers' Party, the name of the ruling communist party after 1956.

was born in Eszék (today Osiek in Croatia) and became the director of the forestry service at Teke/Tekendorf (today Teaca in Romania). He was of Czech origin (he changed his name from Kofranek to the more Hungarian-sounding Kovács) and married a daughter of the well-known Transylvanian Saxon Lutheran Gräser family. My grandmother married János Miskolczy-Simon, a strong Calvinist from Miskolc, a historian and archivist. As the chief archivist of Nógrád County, he fell in battle near Lemberg (Lwów, today Lviv in Ukraine) on September 1, 1914, aged 34, leaving two small children. My paternal great-grandfather was János Puchly, a colonel in the 1848/49 Hungarian Home Defense army. When Hungary was crushed by the Russian intervention, as a former officer of the imperial army he was sentenced to 16 years' imprisonment. (Ten years later he was pardoned.) So, I grew up with the knowledge that my ancestors played an active role in the history of Hungary. I was also aware of the fact that the population of the old Kingdom of Hungary was multinational, consisting of Hungarian, Saxon, Swabian, Slavic and Romanian speakers, with a strong Jewish immigrant population, and that before the spread of nationalism (and partly afterwards) they jointly defended and enriched the homeland.

After graduating from the prestigious Toldy Grammar School in Buda in 1959, with honors, I spent two years as a manual laborer, having been banned from higher education as a political punishment for my class having shown its dedication to the memory of 1956. From 1961 I was able to study history and English at Eötvös Loránd University, and in 1966 I obtained a teacher's diploma with distinction. Unlike most of my fellow students, my interest was not restricted to Hungarian history but also encompassed international relations. I wrote my thesis on the colonization of East Africa and my Ph.D. dissertation in 1970 was titled "The Colonial Question in the First World War and at the Paris Peace Conference." I was most interested, however, in how Hungary became involved in the First World War, with disastrous consequences that explained why my country ended up on the wrong side in the Second World War, leading to the imposition of Soviet domination, which affected my life so much.

I was twenty-three years old when a gap opened in the previously closed borders, and I could travel with a friend via Prague to Poland. While hitchhiking around that country I fell in life-long love with the extremely friendly Poles. By then I had learned a great deal about the outside world from reading books and not least from foreign radio broadcasts. Thanks to knowing the English language, which I had learned from childhood, I also had a thorough knowledge of the democratic political system in the West. I became convinced of the common destiny of the peoples living in and around the Carpathian Basin and also deduced from the mixture of my genes the need for mutual understanding and national tolerance in Central Europe.

I saw that the independence of the peoples of this region was always threatened and often destroyed by the expansion and influence of the surrounding great powers. I concluded that the way of defense is cooperation and a coordinated policy.

In the 1960s and '70s, I travelled by rail and auto, also by hitchhiking, in all the neighboring countries except the Soviet Union, and also spent memorable days in England, Scotland and Switzerland. As a certified ski instructor, I took my students and groups of tourists to the mountains of the Carpathian Basin. Between 1968 and 1976, I was a librarian at the National Széchényi Library, in the company of eminent but politically sidetracked scholars. One of them, Gábor G. Kemény, invited me to work on the final volumes of his major publication of documents on the issue of Hungary's minorities.[37] It was at the library that I started to study Hungary's foreign image. Between 1973 and 1976, on a scholarship from the Hungarian Academy of Sciences, at the Institute of History, I was under the guidance of the brilliant historian Péter Hanák. My research focused on how, in the wake of the 1848–49 War of Independence, the enthusiastic sympathy felt for the Hungarians throughout Western Europe turned into antipathy and severe criticism, even before the outbreak of the First World War. Once Hungary became the enemy of Britain and France, it was easy to arrive at the cruel judgment of Trianon.[38]

In 1976, without giving in to attempts to recruit me to spy on my friends or join the MSZMP,[39] I achieved my original goal of teaching at a university. On the recommendation of Professor Gyula Juhász (1930–1993), a renowned diplomatic historian, I became an adjunct professor in the Department of International Relations at the Karl Marx University of Economics, i.e., today's Corvinus University of Budapest. For thirty-five years, with interruptions due to my service as ambassador to the United States of America and later to Norway and Iceland, I taught history, from 1981 as an associate professor, after 2008 as a *Privatdozent*. Specifically, I taught both in Hungarian and in English the history of international relations, Hungarian foreign policy, Central and South-Eastern Europe, and the problems of national minorities. In 1984, I was awarded a Fulbright Grant, and for two and a half years I taught the history of Central and Eastern Europe at the University

---

[37] Gábor G. Kemény, ed., *Iratok a nemzetiségi kérdés történetéhez Magyarországon a dualizmus korában* [Papers on the history of the nationality problem in Hungary in the age of the Dual Monarchy], 8 vols. (Budapest: Tankönyvkiadó, 1956–2019).

[38] The result was Géza Jeszenszky, *Az elveszett presztízs: Magyarország megítélésének megváltozása Nagy-Britanniában (1894–1918)* [Lost prestige: The changing image of Hungary in Great Britain, 1894–1918] (Budapest: Magvető, 1986; 2nd ed., Budapest: Magyar Szemle Kiadó, 1994; 3rd enl. ed., Budapest: Fekete Sas Kiadó, 2020). For the English edition, see Jeszenszky, *Lost Prestige*.

[39] See my essay, "László Péter: Hungarian Patriot, British Scholar and a Threat to Hungary's Communist Regime." Forthcoming.

of California, Santa Barbara, and also at UCLA. As a result of my stay in the U.S. and trips to Western Europe (still before the change of the regime) I came to know many Hungarians who had fled from communism and built successful careers in the West, but preserved their mother-tongue and Hungarian identity. A list of them all would be long and, inevitably, some would be left out, therefore here I mention only the most prominent ones, who were well-known at least in their local community and showed a strong interest in the political developments in their native country. In alphabetic order they are: Gyula Borbándi, István Borsody, Lóránt Czigány, Ernő Deák, István Deák,[40] László Deme, László Hámos,[41] Béla K. Király,[42] György Kopits, Ferenc Koszorús,[43] John Lukacs,[44] Károly Nagy, László Péter,[45] István Siklós, Peter F. Sugar,[46] Mátyás Sárközi, László Cs. Szabó, István Szépfalusi, Szabolcs and Zsolt Szekeres, Sándor Taraszovics, and Gyula Várallyay. In addition, my family and I made lasting friendships with several leaders of the Hungarian Scouts Association in Exteris (Külföldi Magyar Cserkészszövetség).

Together with my friends I kept thinking about how to survive and be of use to the country enduring a detested dictatorship. We had an informal (practically underground) debating society; we were aware of the serious limitations on action but tried to enlighten our students and the general public about the past and present, without any distortion or unprincipled compromise. Publishing was done within the framework of the "three T's": writings were *támogatott*, *tűrt*, *tiltott* (supported, tolerated and banned). As the pressure of the dictatorship eased, the number of outspoken like-minded people increased. The formation of an open opposition in the

---

[40] István Deák (1926–2023): Hungarian-born American historian at Columbia University, New York.
[41] László Hámos (1951–2019): Hungarian-American political activist, fighter for the rights of national minorities as co-founder in 1976 of the Committee for Human Rights in Rumania, since 1984 the Hungarian Human Rights Foundation.
[42] Béla K. Király (1912–2009): Hungarian army officer before, during, and after the Second World War. He was sentenced to death under the communist regime, but his execution was postponed. He commanded the National Guard in the 1956 Hungarian Revolution, then fled to the United States, and became an academic historian. He returned to Hungary after the collapse of the Soviet Bloc and was elected a member of the Hungarian Parliament.
[43] Ferenc Koszorús (1947–2024): Hungarian-American lawyer, an advocate for the collective rights of the millions of Hungarians living in the Carpathian Basin, detached from Hungary. President of the American Hungarian Federation in the 2000s.
[44] John Lukacs (1924–2019): Hungarian-born American historian, who wrote a best-selling tribute to Winston Churchill, and produced a substantial body of writings on the politics and culture of Europe and the United States, including *Budapest, 1900*.
[45] László Péter (1929–2008): Hungarian-born British historian, professor of Hungarian History at University College, London, School of Slavonic and East European Studies, a specialist on the history of political ideas and the constitutional history of Hungary.
[46] Peter F. Sugar (1919–1999): Hungarian-born American historian, an expert in the history of East Central Europe.

late 1980s revealed, and the free elections of 1990 proved, that what was thought to be a small, silent opposition in the country had grown into a majority.[47]

The Hungarian minorities were a permanent subject in conversations with my friends; almost all of them had ties beyond the borders. One of my closest friends was Gyula Kodolányi,[48] my fellow student at the English Department of Hungary's most prestigious Eötvös Loránd University, a specialist in American studies, and also a poet. He came from Transylvania on his mother's side and was instrumental in setting up interviews on the harassment of the Transylvanian Hungarians[49] between Gyula Illyés, the renowned poet (his father-in-law), and foreign journalists. I also had personal ties and friends among Hungarians in the neighboring countries. Among them, Miklós Duray, who after 1990 turned out to be one of the leading Hungarian politicians in Slovakia.[50] Following the suppression of the Prague Spring of 1968 he devoted himself to the cause of his Hungarian compatriots. In the 1970s he organized an underground group for defending Hungarian schools which were about to be compelled to use Slovak as the language of instruction. Duray compiled several reports of the *Committee for the Protection of the Rights of the Hungarians in Czechoslovakia* which were published in France in the series *Magyar Füzetek* (Hungarian pamphlets) by Péter Kende, a political exile. Eventually some of his associates, frightened by the security people, revealed Duray's activities, and in 1982 he was arrested and imprisoned for fifteen months. (Eventually he was released, thanks to international protests.) After that I had many clandestine meetings with him on skiing and mountaineering trips. I wonder how much of those were known to the Czechoslovak (or also the Hungarian) authorities.

---

[47] In an essay I showed how the memory of 1956 survived under the surface to influence the great political changes in 1989. Jeszenszky, "1956 és a rendszerváltozás" [1956 and the regime change], *Kommentár* 5 (2009): 103–15.

[48] Gyula Kodolányi (1942–): Hungarian essayist and Kossuth Prize-winning writer of poetry. Fulbright scholar at the University of California, Santa Barbara in 1984–1985. State secretary and senior foreign policy adviser to Prime Minister Antall, 1990–94. Editor-in-chief of the re-founded high-quality journal *Magyar Szemle* (1992–2019) and *Hungarian Review* (2010–19). His memoir, Gyula Kodolányi, *Antall Józseffel a világszínpadon* [With József Antall on the world stage] (Budapest: Batthyány Lajos Alapítvány, 2023), is an important source.

[49] There is a vast literature on the problem of Transylvania and the issue of its national minorities. A very thorough bibliography is Elemer Bako and William Sólyom-Fekete, *Hungarians in Rumania and Transylvania: A Bibliographical List of Publications in Hungarian and West European Languages Compiled from the Holdings of the Library of Congress* (Washington D.C.: U.S. Govt. Print. Office, 1969). For an excellent introduction to the problem, see John F. Cadzow, Andrew Ludanyi, and Louis J. Elteto, eds., *Transylvania: The Roots of Ethnic Conflict* (Kent, OH: Kent State University Press, 1983). A recent collection of essays with bibliographies: Zoltani, *Transylvania Today*, including Géza Jeszenszky, "Transylvania: Its Past and Present," 23–47.

[50] Miklós Duray (1945–2022): Hungarian-born geologist in Slovakia, after 1990 MP, leader of the Co-existence Party. For his activities prior to 1990, which led to his trial and imprisonment, see Miklós Duray, *Kutyaszorító* [Dog collar] (New York: Püski, 1983); and Duray, *Kutyaszorító II* [Dog collar II] (New York: Püski, 1989).

Figure 1. At the summer camp of the young Hungarians of Slovakia, July 1989

In 1988, not even hoping for an imminent end to communism, I was invited to a traditional summer camp for young Hungarians in Slovakia, near Komárom/Komarno. There I spoke about the borders in Western Europe that were disappearing, with border controls abolished and unimpeded traffic within the European Community. Once Hungary and its neighbors would be able to join European integration, the significance of the borders in Central Europe would be reduced, I said, overcoming the baneful legacy of Trianon. In Transylvania, too, I came to know many Hungarians: historians, other scholars, writers and churchmen. I helped them by supplying them with books, and when austerity measures made everyday life very difficult, with food and medicine. Many of them played some political role after 1989.

The winds of change start blowing

In a lecture I gave in April 1985 at Indiana University in Bloomington, at the invitation of the Hungarian chair, Professor György Ránki, I described Hungarian foreign policy in the twentieth century as an impassable road because of the lack of options and choices. My conclusion was that we must prepare for the time when Hungary would once again have the opportunity to pursue an independent and active foreign policy, to consider alternatives freely. At the time, I saw this as a challenge for the next generation. Two years later, real political activity, which had been in abeyance for a long time, was being taken up by people who had until then only pondered the factors that had repeatedly wrecked the ship of the Hungarian state.

In the mid-1980s the Western media discovered that there was a Central Europe encapsulated within the Soviet Bloc, and it was re-emerging.[51] The memory of the anti-communist risings (1956, 1968, and the many in Poland) was a bond uniting the core countries of "the sick heart of Europe"[52] and directing them towards internal and external changes. The follow-up conferences of the Helsinki process put the issue of human rights, and their concomitant right of national minorities, in the limelight. The isolated opposition movements developed solidarity with each other, and there was an encouraging consensus on the need to speak out for the protection of minority rights. When Duray signed Charter 77[53] and was arrested, there was protest against his imprisonment in Hungary, too. So, at the time of the regime change, it was a realistic hope that the countries emerging from communism would follow the example of the West, and that the old policy of oppressing minorities would be replaced by tolerance and sincere reconciliation. Was this naivety? Perhaps, but the alternative was confrontation and conflict.

On the problem of national minorities, I thought that the era of assimilation or conflict was over, to be replaced by multiple loyalties, additional rights, autonomy. Essays and books by respected authors had a galvanizing effect on Hungarian society, and it became known that in the United States a Committee for Human Rights in Rumania (later known as the Hungarian Human Rights Foundation) had been formed by three American Hungarians: László Hámos, Ferenc Koszorús and Bulcsú Veress.[54] In Romania a clandestine Hungarian publication *Ellenpontok* (Counterpoints) lived to see ten issues before being discovered by the dreaded *Securitate* (Security Agency). In Czechoslovakia several reports of the underground

---

[51] Milan Kundera, "The Tragedy of Central Europe," trans. Edmund White, *New York Review of Books*, April 26, 1984; Timothy Garton Ash, "Does Central Europe Exist?," *New York Review of Books*, October 9, 1986.
[52] Hugh Seton-Watson, *The "Sick Heart" of Modern Europe* (Seattle & London: University of Washington Press, 1975).
[53] Charter 77 was an informal civic initiative in Czechoslovakia, named after the document issued in January 1977. It called for implementing and honoring the human rights provisions of the 1975 Conference on Security and Cooperation in Europe and other documents, including the Czechoslovak Constitution and the 1966 United Nations covenant on political, civil, economic, and cultural rights. The 242 signatories (including Václav Havel) represented various political viewpoints and religions.
[54] Bulcsú Veress (1941–2012): Hungarian-American jurist and political adviser. As a high-school student in Budapest he was sentenced to eight months in prison in 1958 for underground political activities. Emigrated to the U.S., where he was admitted to the Graduate School of Columbia University and received a degree in political science/international relations in 1976. He was legislative assistant to Senator Christopher Dodd in the 1980s. An expert scholar on minority rights issues and a political analyst of Communist societies.

Committee for the Protection of the Rights of the Hungarians in Czechoslovakia, set up by Miklós Duray, were drawn up in the late 1970s. Hungarians leaning toward various versions of the opposition could easily agree to standing up for the Hungarian minorities[55]

A kind of unwritten but nevertheless perceptible general change of mood and the growing demands from society explains why in 1985 the authorities established the Institute for the Study of Hungarian Nationality (*Magyarságkutató Intézet*) as part of the National Széchényi Library, "for the purpose of comprehensive research into the social and cultural conditions of Hungarians living outside our borders and for the study of the nationality question in general."[56]

The increasingly oppressive character of the regime in Romania and the deteriorating situation of the Hungarian minorities, especially the plan to erase their villages, alarmed an element of the Hungarian political leadership. Feeling at least the tacit approval of Moscow, it started to criticize Romania's policies openly. The critics must have felt some remorse for their silence on the subject for decades. Yet, as Nándor Bárdi, the prominent expert of this issue, noted

> at this point the associates of Mátyás Szűrös,[57] who became the head of the Foreign Affairs Department of the Central Committee of the Hungarian Socialist Workers' Party after his return from Moscow in 1983, were already working on a more visible representation of Hungarian interests in foreign policy.
>
> At the Helsinki follow-up conferences (1985 in Ohrid and 1987 in Madrid) Hungary and Yugoslavia spoke out for extending the rights of the national minorities. Hungary took the same definite position at the follow-up conference in Vienna (1986–87), too. The basic question was to what extent is the minority issue merely a country's domestic affair, and the extent to which international standards apply to it. Szűrös, in radio statements, kept talking about Hungarian foreign policy interests, and about the wave of refugees from Romania. The final point of this communication process was the statement of January 1988: Hungarians living beyond the borders form part of the Hungarian nation. [...] In February 1988, members of

---

[55] Duray, *Kutyaszorító II*, gives a detailed account of the human rights activist's efforts and the reactions. For our close connections, see Duray, *Kutyaszorító II*, 143.

[56] Oto Psenak, "A Magyarságkutató Csoport (Intézet) története 1985-1991," https://www.watson.sk/index.php?option=com_content&id=4326.

[57] Mátyás Szűrös (1933–): Hungarian communist, later socialist politician. He served as provisional president of the Republic in 1989–90.

his staff, Csaba Tabajdi[58] and Imre Szokai,[59] explained in detail in a memorable newspaper article that issues related to Hungarians abroad are essential parts of neighborhood relations.[60]

Tabajdi and Szokai's article "asked for no less than the redefinition of a modern, European sovereign national program, essential for the future of the country, the need to recognize and appreciate national values, and to raise all-national goals to the level of a national policy."[61]

In September 1987 a group of the "silent opposition" calling itself the Hungarian Democratic Forum (*Magyar Demokrata Fórum*, MDF) met at Lakitelek, a small settlement in east-central Hungary, to evaluate Hungary's situation. Their ensuing Declaration addressed mainly internal political issues but mentioned also that "the Hungarian ethnic group is suffering from having been cut into pieces."[62] Subsequent meetings of MDF were attended by a large number of people; eventually, many of them joined other political parties. Recommendations adopted at the March 21, 1989, Forum on the Transylvanian Hungarians at the Jurta Theater in Budapest's City Park adopted some basic principles of the foreign and minority policy of the regime change. Based on the plight of the Hungarians in Romania, this forum proposed that a new Hungarian Constitution should include solidarity and commitment for Hungarians living anywhere in the world. The Parliament—with broad social participation—should draw up the necessary practical measures "to protect the nationalities and ethnicities living in our country, and the Hungarian minorities and diasporas living beyond our borders.[...] Hungarian foreign policy should be based on new principles, including striving for the expansion of human and cultural relations with Hungarians across the border. [...] Hungary should continue to initiate the recognition of the collective rights of national and ethnic minorities in international forums. [...] It is necessary to create a body under the prime minister, which set force the tasks related to Hungarians beyond the borders at the government level."[63]

---

[58] Csaba Tabajdi (1952–): Hungarian politician, former member of the European Parliament for the Hungarian Socialist Party (2004–2014).
[59] Imre Szokai (1951–): Hungarian economist. Deputy State Secretary at the Foreign Ministry, 1990–1991; Director of the State Privatization Agency (1994–1996).
[60] Bárdi, *Tény és való*, 19, referred to the article Szokai Imre and Tabajdi Csaba, "Mai politikánk és a nemzetiségi kérdés" [Our present policies and the nationality problem], *Magyar Nemzet*, February 13, 1988.
[61] Ferenc Mák, "Az új nemzeti politika és a Határon Túli Magyarok Hivatala (1989–1999)" [The new national policy and the Office for Hungarians Beyond the Border], *Magyar Kisebbség* 6, no. 3 (2000): 240.
[62] *Magyar Nemzet*, November 14, 1987, 7.
[63] The text of this document is among my papers.

Figure 2. The first mass demonstration allowed in communist Hungary since 1956: against the oppression of Hungarians in Transylvania, Budapest, June 27, 1988. Future PM Antall in the left corner (with tie and white jacket), myself somewhere in the crowd

On September 3 the Democratic Forum (MDF) became a formal political party. I was among its 200-odd founders.

For information abroad, a detailed report on Romania's president Ceaușescu's increasingly oppressive policies towards the Hungarian minority was prepared under the auspices of the MDF and edited by one of the Forum's founders, Rudolf Joó.[64] The report was sent to the delegations of the Helsinki follow-up meeting in Vienna, the member states of the UN Security Council, the most important international church organizations, the two houses of the American Congress, Amnesty International and many internationally renowned experts. The destruction of villages in Transylvania stirred up Hungarian society, including the part of the Communist party leadership that was more sensitive to national issues, and so by the summer of 1988 such "national unity" was created in this matter that the authorities allowed an unofficially organized demonstration for the first time in decades. The émigré organization "Romania Libera" also participated in the one hundred thousand-strong demonstration held on June 27 against the destruction of villages in Romania. The first demonstration permitted in Hungary since 1956, it underlined that the

---

[64] Rudolf Joó (1946–2002): political scientist, deputy state secretary (1993–94 and 1998–2000), ambassador to the United Nations in Geneva (2000–2002). He edited: *Jelentés a romániai magyar kisebbség helyzetéről* (Budapest: 1988); and *Report on the Situation of the Hungarian Minority in Rumania* (Budapest: 1988). A revised new edition came out later: *The Hungarian Minority's Situation in Ceausescu's Romania*, ed. Rudolf Joó, rev. ed. Andrew Ludanyi (Boulder, CO: Social Science Monographs, 1994).

Hungarians wanted to see democracy and minority rights in Romania in cooperation with the Romanians. Thus in 1988, in line with the framework of the "third basket" of the Helsinki Final Act, the diplomatic struggle for the enforcement of human rights was coupled with the demands for minority rights.

In response to the protest march in Budapest, Ceauşescu had the Hungarian Consulate General in Cluj/Kolozsvár closed. Relations between the two countries deteriorated, and Hungary, breaking with its previous shameful practice, stopped deporting back to Romania the increasing number of refugees from that country. Romania's international image also deteriorated spectacularly, while Hungary's, in appreciation of its internal reformist tendencies, became very positive. That prompted the Romanian president to invite the new prime minister and party secretary General Károly Grósz[65] to a meeting. Grósz immediately accepted, against professional advice. The "summit" in Arad (part of Hungary before 1920) on August 28 was a complete failure on the Hungarian side: instead of a firm refusal and a presentation of the actual Hungarian grievances, Grósz accepted the Romanian president's explanations and accusations and swallowed the closure of the Consulate General in Cluj/Kolozsvár. At the international press conference, he even accepted that there were no programs to erase villages in Romania, only "reorganizations."[66]

The response in Hungary was practically unanimous in its condemnation of the prime minister. On September 1 a delegation from the emerging opposition (the MDF and the Bajcsy-Zsilinszky Society) called upon Minister of State Imre Pozsgay,[67] and Mátyás Szűrös, now chairman of the Foreign Affairs Committee of the National Assembly. A member of the delegation, József Antall, handed over a five-page memo in which he pointed out the traditional skill of Romanian diplomacy ("The creation of Greater Romania was achieved without a single victorious war"), that in major national affairs Romanians are always united, and the failures of Hungarian negotiations ("the policy of concessions, gestures, tact has not led to any result in the past decades"), and he proposed how to proceed.[68]

---

[65] Károly Grósz (1930–1996): Communist politician, general secretary of the Hungarian Socialist Workers' Party from 1988 to 1989, chairman of the Council of Ministers of the People's Republic of Hungary, 1987–88.

[66] Pál Szűts, *Bukaresti napló* [Bucharest diary] (Budapest: Osiris, 1998), 142–57. (Szűts was Hungary's ambassador to Romania then.) See also: http://adatbank.transindex.ro/html/alcim_pdf1835.pdf.

[67] Imre Pozsgay (1933–2016): Hungarian communist politician. Minister of culture (1976–1980), minister of education (1980–1982) and minister of state (1988–1990). He played a key role in Hungary's transition to democracy after 1988. Member of Parliament from 1983 to 1994.

[68] Antall's type-written copy from September 1, 1988. Among my papers.

At that time, on the initiative of art historian Géza Entz[69] and the children of prominent members of the former Peasant Party (Katalin Bodor and Ádám Farkas), an exhibition of the treasures of Transylvania was under preparation, with my participation, to be displayed at the Council of Europe in Strasbourg. The exhibit was opened in Budapest by Mátyás Szűrös, the new speaker of Parliament. This act was in itself a minor sensation. At the end of 1988, a nationwide letter-writing campaign was launched to call upon the UN Human Rights Committee to put the situation of ethnic and national minorities in Romania on its agenda. The campaign was begun on the initiative of the S.O.S. Transylvania movement, founded by Éva Csekme Zabolai, who worked for the International Labor Organization in Geneva, and Pál Benczédi, a refugee from 1956 living in Geneva. As part of this effort, the organization mentioned convened an international press conference in Geneva on February 10, 1989, at which Rudolf Joó and I reported on the village reorganization plan and other anti-minority actions in Romania. In my capacity as the MDF's spokesman for foreign affairs, I sent a letter to several European leaders on November 15, 1988, describing the deplorable conditions in Romania. Prominent among the replies I received was a letter from Swedish Foreign Minister Sten Andersson. In it he included his answer for an interpellation by opposition MP Margaretha af Ugglas (three years later, as foreign minister, my dear colleague), protesting the destruction of villages in Romania and its serious impact on Hungarian and other minorities. The minister himself described the situation as worrying and outlined the means the Swedish government was using in trying to dissuade Romania from implementing the plan. On behalf of the British prime minister, Helen Pugh from the Foreign Office assured me that the British government shared our concerns. She informed my party that Foreign Secretary Howe had raised the issue both in a letter on September 12 and also verbally during the visit of his Romanian counterpart to London in November, and that all the foreign ministers of the European Community had made a joint protest on September 7. An encouraging sign was the statement of U.S. Secretary of State George Schultz at the Helsinki follow-up conference in Vienna, where he condemned Romania for its behavior towards its minorities. Points 18 and 19 of the final document of the meeting, which ended on January 19, 1989, reaffirmed the importance of the rights of "persons belonging to minorities" and of the preservation of their identity.

József Antall's note of March 30, 1989, "The Chance for Change in Romania," and his letter of April 2 to the new speaker of the House, Mátyás Szűrös, show

---

[69] Géza Entz (1949–): Hungarian art historian and politician, state secretary and president of the Office of Hungarians Beyond the Borders (1990–94), president of the National Monument Protection Office, 1998–2000.

Figure 3. Press conference held by S.O.S. Transylvania in Geneva protesting village erasing in Romania, February 10, 1989. Rudolf Joó is in the left corner, our wives between.

not only insight but foresight. Six veteran (communist) Romanian politicians (including Silviu Brucan, well known in the West, as well as Gheorge Apostol and Corneliu Mănescu, the former foreign minister), seeing that Romania's image abroad had plummeted, criticized Ceaușescu's policies in an open letter. Antall saw in that a revelation of the "Romanian national savior reflex." The elite of the secret service, the army, the diplomatic corps and a group of the party leadership "will first remove the [Ceaușescu] 'family.' [...] This can be expected within a year." But Antall warned against excessive optimism. The phraseology will change, it will be welcomed by foreign countries, the value of Romania will go up, "the 'prodigal son' will be enthusiastically welcomed back without real concessions [on the minority question] …" Antall's warning continued: "Hungary's prestige and position vis-à-vis the former Little Entente countries has never been better than it is today, or still today," but "we must be aware that these countries are in a better position than we are, both in terms of connections and weight. The slightest Czech opening will put them above us, as will the changes in Romania." In the words of the future prime minister, "We have to be in a race against time," and by this he meant radical internal changes as soon as possible, the preparation of a "comprehensive national political strategy" and the constant supply of information to the outside world.

"All of this, of course, without giving any chance for accusations of nationalism, revisionism, irredentism, etc..."[70]

By this time, Pál Köteles, a writer who had been forced to flee Transylvania, had already founded the Transylvanian Alliance, originally to bring together those who had left Transylvania or had been compelled to leave it. The membership of this "independent, democratic social organization" ranged from professionals such as the renowned international lawyer Géza Herczegh to those who dreamed of territorial change. Köteles asked me to head the Alliance's foreign affairs committee. Unfortunately, irresponsible radicalism, the result of the new, free atmosphere, soon raised its head in the organization. I tried to warn of the dangers of this before its first general meeting to elect the leadership. I noted that Ceaușescu's regime had been exposed, and said, "the world is reeling from the condemnation of the violations of human rights in Romania, [...] the heir to the British throne [Prince Charles] has criticized the policy of barbaric madness that is about to destroy the grave of his great-grandmother. The special rapporteur of the UN is planning to go to Hungary to get direct information of the situation in Romania, if Romania does not allow him in." I also praised the role of Hungarian organizations abroad in raising international awareness:

> Alongside the strength of our arguments based on indisputable facts, our best weapon was our moderation and sobriety, the total absence of hatred and incitement, and solidarity with the Romanian population. [...] It is interesting that abroad, almost all our friends—Hungarian and non-Hungarian—warn us relentlessly against irresponsibility, unfulfillable demands, words that can be turned against us, but at home, empty hectorizing, demagoguery, personal attacks easily become popular and gain credibility. This is only partly explained, but in no way excused, by the long period of enforced silence, the lack of free, instructive debate, the despair over the tragedy in Romania.[71]

In my program for the foreign affairs committee of the Alliance, I stated: "Since the citizens of Romania in general, but especially the national minorities, including the Hungarian, are not in a position to represent their interests publicly and in an organized manner, this task must be taken over by international public opinion, in accordance with the intentions and interests of the parties concerned, and

---

[70] Note by József Antall on March 30, 1989, and his letter to Mátyás Szűrös on April 2. Typewritten copy among my papers.

[71] My own statement for the general meeting of the Transylvanian Alliance, May 26, 1989.

especially by Hungarian society, which is best acquainted with their situation and problems, and has family, historical and friendly ties with them." Among the tasks of the committee I listed the maintenance of contacts with the foreign missions in Budapest and with visiting foreign journalists, the preparation and distribution abroad of petitions and memoranda, participation in scholarly and political forums, the establishment of a guest escort service, and close contact with Hungarians living in the West and their organizations. I reminded the members of the Association that instead of wishful thinking we must take note of the present ethnic composition of Transylvania, that "our policy must be in harmony with the interests of the Romanian community," that any proposed solution "can only be supported within the existing international legal framework," and that "we must seek a solution until the last possible moment that does not involve abandoning the ancestral settlement area of the Transylvanian Hungarians." I then set as a goal for the Alliance "the restoration of cultural institutions and rights to 1947 level, [...] the enactment and guarantee of the specific minority rights of all national minorities living in Romania, by adopting the principle of autonomy," and the assertion of rights at both individual and collective levels, through local autonomy for the various groups (villages, workplaces, towns, counties), following the Swiss cantonal model. Finally, I stated that these goals "are a prerequisite for the democratic transformation of Romania" and that it is necessary to be prepared "for a post-Ceaușescu era."[72] Pál Köteles fully agreed with this document. Unfortunately, the June General Assembly was divided and scandalized by the advocates of wishful and irresponsible radicalism (led by the lawyer László Nagy), and I felt I had no alternative but to leave the fledgling organization, together with Köteles, its founder. Those who remained at the meeting naively imagined that their wish would magically create an "independent, sovereign and neutral Transylvania."[73] No wonder the Transylvanian Alliance became an insignificant organization, unnoticed abroad.

The illusions of the regime changers

By this time, the MDF had become the leading force of the opposition, with a membership of 24,000 and more than 400 local organizations. From the outset, foreign journalists showed a keen interest in the "Eastern European" opposition. On the eve of regime change, the by-then legalized political parties came to be cultivated by

---

[72] "The Prerequisites for the Successful Operation of the Transylvanian Alliance—from a Foreign Political Aspect." My own memorandum, among my papers.
[73] Letter of the Transylvanian Alliance to President George H. W. Bush, July 11, 1989. Copy among my papers.

foreign governments, which had been cautious until then. "At that time, in 1988–89, it became customary [for the government] to take visiting foreign politicians on so-called 'opposition safaris,' during which they had the opportunity to meet various representatives of the opposition movements of the time at embassy receptions, garden parties and hotel lobbies, as if they were natives from the colonies," recalled József Antall.[74] At the MDF's temporary headquarters, a building company's barracks, and also at the party spokesman's, i.e., my own, apartment, foreign visitors arrived one after the other. On the occasion of the reburial of Imre Nagy and his fellow martyrs of 1956, on June 16, 1989, the MDF, in talks with Romanian émigrés who had arrived for the event, laid down the foundations for the settlement of Hungarian-Romanian relations in a Declaration.

> Today, on 16 June 1989, when Hungary mourns the victims of the reprisals following the 1956 Hungarian Revolution, [...] a meeting was held between the Hungarian Democratic Forum and members of the Romanian emigration of democratic convictions living in the West. The participants of the meeting agreed to publish the following Declaration. [...] We expect the improvement of Hungarian-Romanian relations to be based on a democratic transformation affecting the whole of Europe. [...] Transylvania, which was and remains a land of mutually complementary cultures, should become a model of cultural and religious pluralism. It is in the interest of our peoples that the diversity of cultures, religions and traditions, which has always been a unique characteristic of Transylvania, should be preserved. The right of each nation to autonomous political representation and cultural autonomy must be guaranteed. This requires, among other things, the re-introduction of Hungarian-language instruction at all levels, including the restoration of the Hungarian University of Cluj/Kolozsvár.[75]

Among the signatories were several future members of the Hungarian government of 1990–94 (Géza Entz, Lajos Für,[76] Géza Jeszenszky, Gyula Kodolányi), other widely

---

[74] Péter Sárközy, "A Közép-Európai Kezdeményezés és Magyarország: Beszélgetés Antall József miniszterelnökkel" [The Central European Initiative and Hungary: A conversation with József Antall], *Európai Utas* 4, no. 2 (1993): 3.

[75] The text of the Declaration was published in the Hungarian daily *Magyar Hírlap* (June 20, 1989), in Géza Jeszenszky, *Post-Communist Europe and Its National/Ethnic Problems* (Budapest: Kairosz, 2009), 346–47.

[76] Lajos Für (1930–2013): Hungarian politician and historian, one of the founders of the Hungarian Democratic Forum (MDF), and its president (1994–96). Minister of defense (1990–94).

respected Hungarians (e.g. Mária Illyés,[77] Sándor Csoóri,[78] Gusztáv Molnár[79]), and prominent Romanians living in exile (Mihnea Berindei, Ariadna Combes, Mihai Korné, Ion Vianu and Dinu Zamfirescu.) In the following days, the signatories were joined by future MPs and well-known intellectuals: Attila Ara-Kovács, József Annus, Kálmán Benda, Pál Bodor, Endre Bojtár, Lajos Csőgör, Árpád Göncz,[80] András Gyekiczki, János Gyurgyák,[81] László Hámos,[82] Gábor Hunya, Mihály Ilia, Ferenc Kulin, György Litván, András B. Vágvölgyi, and Miklós Vásárhelyi on the Hungarian side, and Paul Goma, Marie-France Ionesco, Eugene Ionesco, Virgil Ierunca, Monica Lovinescu, and even King Michael I of Romania. It was also signed by Mihai Korné, the director of the Romanian exile newspaper *Lupta* (Fight), who added: "Transylvania must become a model of pluralism, because we cannot measure by two political standards: one for the Romanians in Bessarabia [today's Republic of Moldova] and another for the Hungarians in Romania." Education in the Hungarian mother tongue and the restoration of the Hungarian university are necessary "so that the Hungarian tradition can be preserved in Transylvania alongside the Romanian one."[83] At the same time, Ion Rațiu, the president of the World Federation of Free Romanians in the UK, who later became vice-president of the Christian Democratic National Peasant Party, distanced himself from the statement, saying:

> Cultural autonomy and the restoration of the Hungarian university in Cluj is unacceptable from the point of view of Romania's traditional Transylvanian policy. The overwhelming majority of the Romanian political and cultural elite still considers any kind of "autonomy" as separatism. It is therefore understandable that the Romanian press after 1990 was, at best, silent about this event, and at worst, labels the Hungarian signatories of the Budapest Declaration as irredentists and the Romanian signatories as traitors.[84]

---

[77] Mária Illyés (1944–): Hungarian art historian and teacher, curator of the Gyula Illyés Foundation, being the poet's daughter.
[78] Sándor Csoóri (1930–2016): Hungarian poet, essayist, and politician, a founder of MDF.
[79] Gusztáv Molnár (1948–): Hungarian political scientist and philosopher born in Oradea/Nagyvárad.
[80] Árpád Göncz (1922–2015): Hungarian writer and politician, sentenced to life imprisonment for participation in the Hungarian Revolution in 1956. President of Hungary (1990–2000).
[81] János Gyurgyák (1956–): Hungarian historian, prominent in the regime change. Founder and director of the publishing house Osiris.
[82] László Hámos (1951–2019): Hungarian-American jurist, fighter for the rights of national minorities as co-founder in 1976 of the Committee for Human Rights in Rumania, since 1984 the Hungarian Human Rights Foundation. Was prominent in several Hungarian organizations in the U.S.A.
[83] *Lupta* (Geneva), July 22, 1989.
[84] Ferenc Takács, "România Erdély-politikája 1989 után" [Romania's Policy on Transylvania], *Magyar Kisebbség*, nos. 3–4 (1998): 312–30.

The significance of the Declaration lay in the very fact that it was created, and also in the specific Romanian promises it contained. I still believe today that if a genuine democratic revolution had taken place in Romania at the end of 1989, if the new Romanian leadership, the National Salvation Front, had acted on the basis of that document, the relations between the two neighboring countries, and that between the Romanian majority and the Hungarian Minority in Transylvania would be different, setting an example for the whole of Central Europe.

Even then, there were people in Hungary who were dissatisfied with the MDF's stance, because it had "renounced" territorial revision and thus "sold" Transylvania. All the signatories of the 1989 Declaration considered the peace treaty imposed on Hungary in 1920 to be unjust and wrong and regretted the unfair borders in Central Europe set after the two world wars, which disregarded the principle of self-determination. But they were aware that in 1989 no country, no major foreign politician or expert would have supported a change in Hungary's borders. Those who called for a border change demonstrated their political dilettantism, but also their ignorance of the ethnic relations that have changed to the detriment of the Hungarians in recent decades. Given the large numbers of Romanians, Slovaks and Serbs who had settled in towns which had a clear Hungarian majority before 1945, even a referendum would not have brought any results favorable for Hungary. As a member of the MDF Executive Committee and as the organization's foreign policy spokesman, I tried to enlighten the radical dreamers, both orally and in writing, by setting forth a positive strategy for the protection of minorities:

a./ The enforcement of the general freedoms guaranteed by international conventions and also in Romanian law.
b./ Restoration of the cultural institutions and rights of the Transylvanian Hungarians in accordance with the principles laid down in the 1919 Treaties for the Protection of Minorities and the promises made by the Romanian governments in 1944–47, before the borders were settled.
c./ To enact into law and guarantee the specific minority rights of all national minorities living in Romania by adopting the principle of autonomy. This should be enforced both at the individual level (the right of the citizens to choose and preserve their language and culture) and at the collective level, through local autonomy for the various groups (villages, workplaces, towns, counties), following the Swiss cantonal model. [In the case of the hoped-for political turnaround in Romania] the test of internal transformation is to address the minority question, to implement the requirements described

above. A precondition for international support for a new Romanian government must be the elimination and remedying of current violations and the development and implementation of new norms of coexistence. International public opinion should be won for the changes that are imperative in the post-Ceaușescu era."[85]

My memo also warned that the broad international support for Hungarian minorities could be jeopardized by raising the issue of the border, "because Western attitude above all seeks peace and tranquility." I admit that my thinking at the time harbored a major illusion, which was, however, quite common among Hungarians at the time: that the countries embarking on the path of European integration "can only be accepted if they pursue an enlightened, tolerant minority policy in line with contemporary Western practice."[86] It is now clear that this was a blind hope.

In the summer of 1989, the negotiations of the National Roundtable created the framework for peaceful regime change. On October 20–22, immediately before the anniversary of the outbreak of the 1956 revolution, the MDF held its second congress. In his program speech before being elected as president, Antall outlined the foreign policy background to the changes in Hungary, speaking of the need to "develop a new type of East-Central European policy." Reiterating the importance of the historic friendship with Poland, he added the need "to seek renewed friendship with other neighboring nations!" He also expressed his belief that friendship should be established with the Russian people and with the other peoples of the Soviet Union on the basis of independence and on an equal footing. Many Hungarians had suffered together with them in the Gulag concentration camps.[87] In a special declaration, the Congress appealed to the UN member states to act against the continuing violation of human rights and persecution of minorities in Romania.[88]

The founders of the MDF have long been known for their commitment to the cause of Hungarians living beyond the borders. Writings by Sándor Csoóri, Rudolf Joó, Lajos Für testify to that, and the whole of the Forum's early membership was characterized by a keen interest in this issue. They knew history, many of them had relatives or friends in the areas that used to belong to Hungary.

---

[85] "The Road for Hungarian-Romanian Reconciliation." My memorandum presented for the MDF at the end of June 1989. Among my papers.
[86] "The Road for Hungarian-Romanian Reconciliation."
[87] Jeszenszky, *József Antall, Prime Minister of Hungary*, 91–92.
[88] MDF Bulletin 2, October 21, 1989, 6. Among my papers.

However, their interest and commitment were generally free from unrealistic desires or irresponsible statements. A good example is a speech given on March 15, 1989, by Ferenc Gyurácz, one of the founders of the MDF in Szombathely: "We must respect the internationally guaranteed borders [of our country]. The unity and common destiny of the Hungarian nation across national borders should be expressed as much as possible in school education, culture, state policy and our everyday life."[89] Two years later, at a commemoration of the Trianon treaty, he stressed the importance of "working for the friendship of the peoples of Central Europe [...] because only through this friendship can Central Europe, buried 71 years ago, be revived."[90]

In the first months of its existence, the MDF established contacts with the Austrian People's Party, with Solidarity in Poland, and with the Czech and Romanian opposition.[91] The program adopted by its first national convention bears witness to its common sense:

> Our aim is to develop a minority policy in line with European standards, which is equally applicable to Hungarian minorities beyond the borders and non-Hungarian minorities within our borders. Our interests lie in the permeability of the borders. We consider it natural for people to have a double allegiance, both loyalty and to the state one resides in, while preserving loyalty to one's ethnicity, and to his or her nationality. The system of local and community autonomy is of paramount importance in guaranteeing the future of the minorities. The creation of the conditions for the exercise of these rights is the task of the state, and the minorities are entitled to that. [...] Hungary bears responsibility for the fate of Hungarians living beyond its borders. Regular attention to Hungarian minorities must become part of a comprehensive national strategy.[92]

I contributed to this document with a draft, which also contained the ideas that guided my later work as foreign minister. I always bore in mind the international precedents going back to before 1914, including the fact that before the First World

---

[89] Ferenc Gyurácz, *Egy "populista" följegyzései: Politikai esszék, tanulmányok, cikkek, 1981–1993* [Notes by a "populist": Political essays, studies, articles] (Szombathely: Életünk könyvek, 1993), 88.
[90] Gyurácz, *Egy "populista" följegyzései*, 95.
[91] Rudolf Joó, "Az MDF nemzetközi kapcsolatairól" [On the international contacts of MDF]. Summer, 1989. Manuscript among my papers.
[92] *A Magyar Demokrata Fórum programja* [Program of the Hungarian Democratic Forum], October 1989, 143–63.

War, Romania could provide financial support to the two Romanian denominations and their schools in Hungary without any hindrance or obstacle. The solution "we seek," the program asserts, "is good relations with neighboring countries and maximum rights for our own minorities."

> Our goal is to eliminate all open and concealed discrimination, [and to secure] special minority rights, the possibility for autonomous development, self-administration in the place of residence, in local administration, in the churches and in culture. Educational institutions in their own language, from kindergarten to university. Use of own language in public: inscriptions, administration, in the judiciary. In short: a free minority in a free state. [...] This program should be acceptable to all democrats in the neighboring countries. For as long as the Hungarian minorities do not have a voice and democracy does not prevail, we will be constantly making our grievances known to world public opinion, seeking the support of friendly governments, "bombarding" international institutions, while constantly seeking contact with the democratic forces of neighboring peoples. That is why we cultivate their emigrants, why we support the refugees who come here from them.[93]

I presented this program in English at an international conference organized by Professor János Radványi[94] at the University of Mississippi in September 1989,[95] a conference to which I was invited along with Miklós Vásárhelyi[96] and Gábor Fodor.[97]

Similar principles were set out in the program adopted at the Second Congress of the Federation of Young Democrats (Fidesz) on October 15, 1989:

> In addition to fundamental human rights, collective minority rights must be guaranteed. [...] We consider the Hungarian minorities outside our

---

[93] *A Magyar Demokrata Fórum programja*, Executive summary, 4–5.
[94] János Radványi (1922–2016): Hungarian diplomat, ambassador to the United States between 1962 and 1967, when he applied for political asylum. Having earned a degree in history at Stanford University he joined the history department at Mississippi State University, where in 1982 he founded and directed the Center for International Security and Strategic Studies.
[95] "Hungary's Foreign Political Options," September 1989. Among my papers.
[96] Miklós Vásárhelyi (1917–2001): Hungarian journalist and politician. Press secretary in the government of Imre Nagy during the Hungarian Revolution of 1956, for which he was sentenced to five years in prison. Was closely involved with the Soros Foundation in Hungary, was a founding member of the Alliance of Free Democrats and was its MP in 1990–94.
[97] Gábor Fodor (1962–): Hungarian jurist and politician, MP from 1990 to 2019. Minister of Education (1994–96), Minister of Environment and Water Resources (2008–2009).

borders to be an integral part of the Hungarian nation, for whose survival and fate the Hungarian state is responsible. It has a similar responsibility for the national minorities in Hungary. We fully recognize the principle of national and ethnic self-determination. At the same time, we must help to ensure that minorities are not forced to change their place of historical residence. [...] Our organization sees it as its task to establish intensive contacts with those groups of the Hungarian nationalities which hope for a solution to the nationality question through the democratization of the country in which they live. At the same time, it seeks to build relations with the democratic opposition in these countries and with their members and groups forced into exile. [...] Our fate is shared with that of our neighbors. Attention to Europe cannot make us forget that we must resolve our disputes with them. In order to establish closer relations with them education must take on the task of teaching the cultures, histories and languages of the neighboring countries and of the national minorities. [...] we propose the creation of a ministry for national minorities, abolishing the current deputy-minister level administration. Similarly, we consider it essential to establish an Institute for Nationalities capable of providing a scientific basis for political decisions.[98]

The last "reformed communist" government of the party-state system, with a responsible patriot, Miklós Németh at its head,[99] was already competing with the opposition to take the necessary steps in foreign policy. One of these was the establishment on November 11, 1989, of the Quadrangolare, the Italian-Austrian-Yugoslav-Hungarian intergovernmental cooperation. We in the opposition saw that as an important political step on the road which would enable the Central European states, above all the later Visegrád Three, to break free from the Warsaw Pact and the Comecon, and to move towards European integration. A social event was organized by the opposition parties on the initiative of the Debrecen branch of MDF for August 19, 1989. It was to take place on the Austrian-Hungarian border, symbolizing the need to reduce the signs of the division of Europe. This "Pan-European Picnic" was utilized by close to a thousand East German citizens to escape

---

[98] The program adopted at the II. Congress of Fidesz is published in Csaba Lőrincz, Zsolt Németh, Viktor Orbán, and Zoltán Rockenbauer, *Nemzetpolitika '88–'98: Tanulmányok, publicisztikák, beszédek, interjúk* [Nation-policy '88–'98: Articles, speeches, interviews] (Budapest: Pro Minoritate Alapítvány, 1998), 280–84.

[99] Miklós Németh (1948–): Hungarian economist and "reform communist" politician. As prime minister (1988–1990) he was one of the founders of the Hungarian Socialist Party (October 1989), a left of center successor of Hungary's Communist Party. He deserves credit for facilitating the regime change.

through a temporary hole in the Iron Curtain. That prompted tens of thousands of their compatriots to come to Hungary, hoping they, too, could leave from there for the West. Pressed by that crowd, also by the political opposition and by the Federal Republic of Germany, the Hungarian government announced on September 10, 1990, that the citizens of the "German Democratic Republic" would be permitted to cross the erstwhile Iron Curtain border and leave for the West.[100] Now, with tens of thousands of East Germans escaping from their communist prison, it was pointless to keep the Berlin Wall closed. When a new, reformist leadership in East Berlin decided to open it, the people tore the Wall into pieces on November 9, 1989. That monstrosity, the symbol of the division of Europe, was gone, and a new democratic coalition was formed in Berlin, preparing the way for the reunification of Germany.

Spurred on by this, the "Velvet Revolution" took place in Prague and Bratislava in the last days of November. "Every week, a party state collapses," I said in Radio Free Europe's newly opened Budapest studio. On December 15–16, at the invitation of the Hungarian Democratic Forum, representatives of democratic movements from Central and Eastern Europe met in Budapest for an "Interforum." The joint declaration advocated self-determination, representative democracy, further close cooperation and the rights of minorities, in a highly idealistic spirit:

> Now, in our hands we have a great opportunity to put an end to the conflicts that traditionally turned the peoples of this region against each other. Free nations ought to develop free contacts with each other; borders should not obstruct the movement of people, information and ideas. Our new democracies should be determined not to let old conflicts spring up, so that attention could be focused on creating a better future. This sentiment was universally expressed at the meeting of Polish, East German, Czech, Slovak, Bulgarian and Hungarian democrats on December 15–16, 1989 in Budapest, convened by the Hungarian Democratic Forum. We propose that all the democratic organizations in Central and Eastern Europe publicly commit themselves to the preservation of our unity and the realization of our democratic, pluralistic ideals. One of the cardinal prerequisites of democracy is toleration for those whose political views, religion or language differ—for the various minorities. The practical realization of that principle is recognition of these groups' organization and autonomy in order to facilitate their free development. It is our hope that in the future social integration in the new

---

[100] Andreas Oplatka, *Der erste Riss in der Mauer: September 1989—Ungarn öffnet die Grenze* (Zürich: Zsolnay-Verlag, 2009). For the wider background, see my essay: "One Thousand Years at the Crossroads of History: History and the Politics of Transition," *Macalester International* 2 (Fall 1995): 97–113.

democracies will go side-by-side with respect for regional, national and ethnic distinctions, and that representative democracy will be based upon local self-government. We hope that in the not too distant future all the nations and countries of Europe will endorse these ideals, including the concept of European unity, and thus will create the foundations for a real European home. In past centuries, the peoples of East-Central Europe could never stand together on the same side. Today, history offers us a unique opportunity for such a unity.[101]

This rather naïve appeal reflected the atmosphere of the blissful moment of Christmas 1989. At least that was how most of the democrats in Hungary felt then.

The hope was genuine in late 1989 for the settlement of Hungary's neighborly relations and the rights of the Hungarian minorities—in the event of the hoped-for regime changes all over Central Europe. There was the Hungarian-Romanian Declaration of June 16, Czech-Hungarian solidarity shown by the activists of the Free Democrats, Fidesz and the trade unions who participated in a protest demonstration in Prague on August 20, Romanians opposed to the Romanian regime who found refuge in Hungary, and the statements of the Czech dissident Václav Havel (whose grandfather, Hugo Vavrečka, was Czechoslovakia's envoy to Hungary in the 1920s),[102] as well as King Michael I of Romania appearing on Hungarian television. The West seemed receptive and supportive of those goals. Together with József Antall, I participated in the formation of the Hungarian branch of the European Movement, founded in 1947, and of the League of Human Rights in Paris. That is how I came into contact with the Young European Federalists (JEF). In their periodical I explained the need to settle the situation of national minorities and argued that the best way to achieve that was European integration, in the long run a federal Europe.[103]

Since the foundation of MDF I was the party's foreign affairs spokesman. On September 15, 1989, at the request of the MDF presidency, I took over the leadership of the party's Foreign Affairs Committee from Rudolf Joó, who had resigned from that post due to an invitation to be a guest professor in Lyon, France.

---

[101] The Christmas Manifesto of the Hungarian Democratic Forum: "An appeal to the new democratic organizations in Central and Eastern Europe," December 16, 1989. Among my papers.

[102] Václav Havel (1936–2011): Czech playwright opposed to Communism. President of Czechoslovakia (1989–1992), of the Czech Republic (1993–2002).

[103] "Eastern Europe and the European Federal Idea," *The New Federalist*, nos. 5–6 (1988): 10–11; "Federation as a Solution for National Minorities," *The New Federalist*, no. 2 (1989): 6.

I put together a team consisting of Enikő Bollobás,[104] Ákos Engelmayer,[105] Csaba Gy. Kiss,[106] Gyula Kodolányi, László Ódor,[107] László Szarka,[108] János Szávai,[109] Bálint Varga and Tünde Vajda, with occasional contributions from others. At the first two national conventions of the MDF, the committee informed a significant number of diplomats and foreign journalists via English-language bulletins prepared by Enikő Bollobás, Tünde Vajda and my wife, Edit Jeszenszky.

The Romanian drama in December 1989

The hoped for and yet unexpected turn of events in Romania, starting with defiant acts by the Calvinist minister in Timișoara/Temesvár, László Tőkés,[110] led to the collapse of Ceaușescu's dictatorship.[111] The dramatic events triggered an emotional shock and action in Hungary not seen since 1956. Hungarians spent the last days of Advent and Christmas day in front of television screens, watching the drama unfold in Romania. The Romanian flag, with its communist coat of arms torn-out, was a reminder of the similar act in Hungary in 1956.

When the news of the uprising in Timișoara/Temesvár[112] spread to the Romanian capital and led to two days of street fighting, causing hundreds of deaths, the Democratic Forum, now led by Antall, saw the need to enlist foreign support

---

[104] Enikő Bollobás (1952–): Hungarian literary scholar, member of the Hungarian Academy of Sciences, and professor at the School of English and American Studies of the Faculty of Humanities at Eötvös Loránd University, Budapest.
[105] Ákos Engelmayer (1938–): Hungarian author, expert on Polish studies, ambassador to Poland, 1990–94.
[106] Csaba Gy. Kiss (1945–2025): Hungarian literary historian, founding member and vice-chairman of MDF, specialist on Central Europe, professor at several universities in Central Europe.
[107] László Ódor (1945–): Hungarian linguist, cultural historian and diplomat. Ambassador to the Confederation Helvetica (1990–94).
[108] László Szarka (1953–): Hungarian historian born in Czechoslovakia, director of the Research Institute of Ethnic and National Minorities at the Hungarian Academy of Sciences (2001–)
[109] János Szávai (1940–): literary historian and diplomat. Ambassador to France (1990–94), professor at the Université de Paris IV (Sorbonne) (1994–2005).
[110] László Tőkés (1952–): ethnic Hungarian pastor and politician from Romania. Bishop of a Calvinist diocese in Romania (1990–2000). Honorary president of the Democratic Alliance of Hungarians in Romania (1990–2003). Member of the European Parliament (MEP) (2007–2019), its vice-president (2010–2012). A controversial hero.
[111] On the road to 1989, see Trond Gilberg, *Nationalism and Communism in Romania: The Rise and Fall of Ceausescu's Personal Dictatorship* (Boulder, CO: Westview Press, 1990); for an early analysis, see Juliana Pilon, *The Bloody Flag: Post-Communist Nationalism in Eastern Europe; Spotlight on Romania* (New Brunswick, NJ: Transaction Publishers. 1992 [Routledge, 2021]); for a larger context, see Vladimir Tismăneanu and Sorin Antohi, eds., *Between Past and Future: The Revolutions of 1989 and Their Aftermath* (New York: Central European University Press, 2000).
[112] For a detailed account of the events in Temesvár, see Árpád Szőczi, *Timişoara—The Real Story Behind the Romanian Revolution* (Bloomington, IN: iUniverse, 2013).

for the revolution in Romania. In the journal *História*, György Szabad,[113] then a member of the Forum's executive board, gave an account of the actions of his party in those tense days.[114] On December 19, 1989, the executive board of the party expressed the Hungarian people's solidarity with

> all those in Romania whose human, political and ethnic rights have been violently suppressed. [...] Our message to Romania is that Romanians, Hungarians, Germans and other nationalities, Catholics, Protestants and Jews, and people of all other religions, should show solidarity with each other. History has taught us that oppressive and divisive forces could prevail only over those who are filled with hatred, and that only love and solidarity can make those who live together invincible.[115]

That same day József Antall forwarded this statement to Foreign Minister Gyula Horn,[116] together with his letters addressed to the secretary general of the United Nations and the president of the European Parliament. The following day, December 20, the MDF executive board drew up a statement saying that "Hungary cannot stand idly by" given the bloody developments in Romania, and therefore "the Hungarian Democratic Forum calls on the Government of the Republic of Hungary to initiate the convening of an extraordinary session of the UN Security Council to examine the events in Romania, which threaten peace."[117] This was all the more justified as there was a danger that the Romanian dictator might try to stabilize his position by a military attack on Hungary, citing provocations from the Hungarian side.[118]

On December 21, at a rally convened by Ceaușescu, the crowd turned against the dictator, forcing him and his wife to flee by helicopter. The army leadership changed its stance and joined the rising. On December 22, the National Salvation

---

[113] György Szabad (1924–2015): renowned Hungarian historian and politician. Founding member of MDF, speaker of the National Assembly (1990–1994).
[114] György Szabad, "Román forradalom és Magyarország, 1989" [The Romanian revolution and Hungary]. *História* 22, no. 8. (2000): 26–27.
[115] Szabad, "Román forradalom," 26.
[116] Gyula Horn (1932–2013): Hungarian communist, later socialist politician. Foreign minister (1989–1990), prime minister (1994–1998).
[117] Szabad, "Román forradalom," 26–27.
[118] This is supported by the then Hungarian minister of defense, Ferenc Kárpáti, and the operational reports of the state security services. See Ferenc Kárpáti, "A román forradalom és Magyarország 1989" [The revolution in Romania and Hungary's reactions, 1989]. *História* 22, no. 4 (2000): 26–29; and Zoltán Haszán, "Megoldani Erdély ügyét ügyes-okosan" [To solve Transylvania—cleverly], *Index.hu*, December 22, 2009, http://index.hu/belfold/1989/. The risk of Romanian military action subsided after December 20.

Front, chaired by Ion Iliescu,[119] took over the country, essentially with the support of the military. Aid in the form of food, medicine and clothing, donated by the people of Hungary, started to flow into Romania. However, the well-armed secret police, the notorious Securitate, seemed to stand by Ceaușescu. Armed struggle and civil war spread throughout the country, with rumors (rumors?—there is still no conclusive proof) that Arab and other mercenaries were involved. The situation appeared critical, and in Hungary there was fear that the revolution might be crushed. On December 22, the MDF sent a telegram to Bucharest hailing the success of the Romanian revolution, but at 1 p.m. the next day, the driver of an MDF aid convoy was shot dead near Arad, and in response, Antall and I appealed to Prime Minister Németh "to take steps for convening the UN Security Council immediately. In our neighboring country, where foreign mercenaries are trying to suffocate the struggle for freedom of the people of Romania with blood, [...] it is fully justified to ask for UN intervention, sending peacekeeping troops and anti-terrorist commandos."[120]

The MDF was not alone in making such a proposal. The Alliance of Free Democrats (SZDSZ, the party formed by the earlier "dissidents," the main rival of MDF) addressed an open letter to Prime Minister Németh:

> The Romanian masses fighting against the dictatorship and the Romanian army need immediate military assistance. This is also necessary for the security of Central Europe, especially in the light of reports that the forces of the dictatorship are using foreign mercenaries against the unarmed masses. At the same time, it is also clear that Hungary, for known historical and political reasons, cannot take on the responsibility of providing military assistance alone. We call on you to immediately initiate the urgent convening of the Security Council and the immediate initiation of an international military intervention with the deployment of UN-led forces. Clearly, this can only be aimed at assisting the National Salvation Front and the Romanian army, and it must be withdrawn immediately after its mission is accomplished. Irrespective whether Hungary participates in the operation or not, Hungary must once again formally declare its respect for Romania's territorial integrity. What Hungary can do immediately, as a sign of its friendly intentions and in fulfilment of its democratic duty, is to assist the Romanian army units

---

[119] Ion Iliescu (1930–2025): communist politician, a protégé of Nicolae Ceaușescu until 1971, when he fell out of favor. In December 1989 he headed the National Salvation Front, was elected president in 1990. In 1996 he was defeated by Emil Cobstantinecu, but was re-elected president in 2000 to 2004. He openly called Romania's Hungarians a danger to the "unitary Romanian State."

[120] Fax letter by J. Antall and G. Jeszenszky to PM Németh, on December 23, 1989. Copy among my papers.

with ammunition. The Romanian army has publicly requested assistance in this very regard.[121]

The Hungarian government was clearly on the side of the rebels, and on December 23 it recognized the National Salvation Front. It was ready to support the revolutionary leadership, reportedly being threatened by Securitate units, with arms and ammunition.[122] However, in the memoirs of the then foreign minister Horn, and again in April 1994 (as part of the election campaign), Horn claimed that the MDF had—irresponsibly and in an amateurish way—proposed sending armed Hungarian guerrillas to Romania.[123] I immediately refuted that in the press. In 2000, former minister of defense Ferenc Kárpáti[124] repeated the allegation. According to him, on the evening of December 23, a delegation of the MDF called upon the Hungarian military leadership with the "hair-raising" idea that they "should facilitate the arming and sending of volunteers to Romania."[125] In 2003, MDF co-founder Lajos Für recalled in his memoirs that "at the outbreak of the Romanian Revolution," he and Zoltán Bíró[126] "were discussing [...] that—in the bloody upheaval—it may be necessary to help the Hungarians of Transylvania not only verbally and diplomatically." According to Für, Antall "considers the idea itself to be madness. No matter how Romania's internal relations develop, we must not intervene even indirectly on the military level." In Für's account the Hungarian military leadership rejected the idea of any Hungarian interference in "another country's civil strife, possible civil war." According to Für "we asked, a little timidly, but nevertheless: if they [the new Romanian leaders] asked for weapons or ammunition from us, would they [the Hungarian government] provide, say, to the anti-Ceauşescu forces? No way, they replied again firmly." György Szabad, a member of the delegation, agreed with this, "and praised the prudent and wise conduct of the military leadership."[127]

I do not know why the minister of defense of the Antall government tried to portray Antall and Szabad in an unfavorable light in his memoirs. György Szabad, in his article cited above, gave a different account of the meeting: "As I recall, I

---

[121] The open letter is among my papers.
[122] Gyula Horn, *Cölöpök* [Piles] (Budapest: Zenit Könyvek, 1991), 272.
[123] In his memoirs the former foreign minister gave a detailed, but at some points inaccurate account of how the government reacted to the events in Romania.
[124] Ferenc Kárpáti (1926–2013): Army officer in the communist period, minister of defense (1985–1990).
[125] Kárpáti, "A román forradalom," 29. In his memoirs, published in 2011, he held on to the allegation, see Ferenc Kárpáti, *Puskalövés nélkül...* [Without a shot...] (Budapest: Duna International, 2011).
[126] Zoltán Bíró (1941–): Hungarian literary historian and politician. Served as the first, interim president of the Hungarian Democratic Forum.
[127] Lajos Für, *A Varsói Szerződés végnapjai—magyar szemmel* [The final days of the Warsaw Pact—from a Hungarian perspective] (Budapest: Kairosz Könyvkiadó, 2003), 19–22.

spoke first and foremost about the uneasy public mood, quoting liberally from the sober and justified as well as the naive and impetuous statements made at meetings and outside them." Kárpáti described the "tone" of the remarks of the MDF delegation in his recollections as "shocking" and "offensive." "Today, I still consider it important that I confronted the Minister with the real public mood. Our delegation did not put forward any 'astonishing proposals.'"[128] I have a document that refutes both Kárpáti's and Für's version.

In the temporary headquarters of the MDF, on Ó utca, the news from Romania really did cause much excitement, and the premises were flooded with donations of clothes and food. I, as head of the foreign affairs committee and a regular guest at the meetings of the presidency, did not hear a single word about sending Hungarian volunteers or irregulars to Romania. Surely Lajos Für and other members of the leadership discussed the situation that was changing hourly and the dangers that threatened the Hungarian population, but nobody authorized anyone to send guerillas. However, Für was certainly wrong that Antall categorically rejected any military intervention. On the contrary, on the morning of December 24, worried about the news from Romania, I went to the party headquarters. Antall arrived almost simultaneously. "When the trumpet is sounded, the old warhorses will move," he said in greeting. In light of the latest news, we decided immediately to approach the Hungarian government with a proposal, which we sent on the letterhead of the Hungarian Democratic Forum.[129]

> A few hours before Christmas, the situation in Romania remains grave, the defeat of the dictatorship's beneficiaries and their foreign mercenaries seems certain, but terrorist actions still kill thousands of people and could endanger public safety and aid operations for weeks. The United Nations Security Council, due to a likely veto by the People's Republic of China, is unable to live up to expectations and its inherent responsibility, therefore new frameworks must be sought to stop the bloodshed in Romania and to provide aid. The improved relations between the United States and the Soviet Union and the changes in Europe offer a real opportunity to do so. We therefore propose that the Warsaw Pact and NATO should take joint help to stop the genocide and acts of terrorism and to help the cause of democracy and peace to prevail in Romania. In line with our previous statements, we call on the Hungarian Government to contact the National Salvation Front of Romania,

---

[128] Szabad, "Román forradalom," 27.
[129] Letter by J. Antall and G. Jeszenszky addressed to Prime Minister Miklós Németh, Foreign Minister Gyula Horn, and Defense Minister Ferenc Kárpáti, December 24, 1989. Copy is among my papers.

which Hungary has already recognized, and to offer the good offices of the Republic of Hungary to organize the deployment of international anti-terrorist forces under Romanian Supreme Command. If Romania agrees, specially trained anti-terrorist units could be invited from among the member states of the Warsaw Pact and NATO. Their task would be to clear the whole of Romania of the remnants of the Securitate units and their affiliated gangs, which pose a threat to lives. If necessary, Hungary will offer its territory and direct cooperation to receive the troops.

There is no room for procrastination, because every hour of delay could mean the loss of hundreds of lives.
Budapest, 24 December 1989, 12 noon.
On behalf of the Presidium of the Hungarian Democratic Forum:

Géza Jeszenszky, Head of the Foreign Affairs Committee
József Antall, President

I phoned the foreign ministry. Gyula Horn was in and was ready to receive us immediately. He considered the situation to be less serious than we thought, he was right, but he had much more information at his disposal. He refused to forward our proposal and announced this on television the same day. Obviously, if the situation in Romania deteriorated, it was a more realistic and better proposal to send NATO and Warsaw Pact troops there than a regular or volunteer Hungarian armed force. Greater international attention and presence could only have benefited Romania's majority and minority populations, and perhaps the anti-Hungarian atrocities that took place the following March in Târgu Mures/Marosvásárhely would not have taken place.

The sympathy and helpfulness of Hungarian society was not limited to the Hungarians of Transylvania, it also extended to the Romanian people, who had also suffered much. At the end of 1989, all well-meaning Hungarians and Romanians were filled with hope that serious improvement between the two peoples would come about. All of Hungarian society was deeply moved; political parties competed with each other to send convoys to deliver donations to the destitute population of Romania.[130] On December 24, an ecumenical service was held at midnight in

---

[130] My wife recorded 550 registered vehicles (150 of which were trucks and microbuses) alone (excluding the organizations in the rural towns) which delivered aid to Romania from the MDF headquarters from 3 pm on December 22, 1989, to 2 pm on December 26, 1989. Sixty percent of the consignments were

Heroes' Square in Budapest in front of a huge crowd. Inspired, I wrote a draft statement for my party:

> The people of Hungary continue to follow the events in Romania with shock, sympathy and deep understanding. The unprecedented action of Hungarian society to help the people of Romania is a testimony to this. Food, medicine, blood, clothing, money and toys are flooding into the collection points, and great efforts are being made to get them to Romania. Hundreds of people are consciously putting their lives at risk to help the people of a country with which relations have been more strained than friendly for centuries. Ceauşescu was constantly warning his unfortunate oppressed compatriots that Hungary was their mortal enemy, that the territorial integrity of Romania was seriously threatened by events in Hungary, by the words spoken and written there. Even among the Romanian people who had risen up against the dictator, there was a fear that Hungary might take advantage of the civil war conditions to use military force for its own ends. Instead, we are witnessing the transformation of a centuries-old—and not unjustified—public mood. What is the reason, the explanation for that? We feel that this is also our revolution, because the Romanians and the national minorities in Romania have taken up the flame that started with us, because the people's uprising was given impetus by the courageous stand of László Tőkés and the solidarity of the Romanians, Hungarians, Germans and Serbs in Timisoara, because among the heroes and the dead of Romania there are a large number of members of the Hungarian minority... the democracy that is being born in Romania offers the best chance for reconciliation and true friendship between the Hungarian and Romanian nations. The membership of the Hungarian Democratic Forum is playing a prominent role in the relief effort. It is far from us to exploit a human tragedy for party political purposes, but it is no coincidence that the driver Sándor Tóth, shot while helping the Romanian Revolution, was a Hungarian citizen, and a member of the MDF, since our members started sending aid to Romania in the very first hours of the drama. ... we can say that with our moderate voice and our substantive proposals we contributed to influencing both society and the government. We therefore feel entitled, while continuing to be at the forefront of this assistance, to take political initiatives now to engage both with

---

food, 30 percent clothing and 10 percent medicine. In addition, 2.2 million Hungarian forints in cash was collected. The memory of this generosity ought not be forgotten.

the new revolutionary bodies in Romania and with the reborn Hungarian organizations. Our aim is to take advantage of this historic opportunity and to contribute to the lasting settlement of the situation of national minorities in Romania, especially, of course, the Hungarian minority, by putting interstate relations between Romania and Hungary on a new footing. It is our hope that the Hungarian and Romanian nations, freed from dictatorship, can embark together on the path of national rebirth and accession to Europe, also due to the similar geopolitical situation.[131]

The shameful lie that Hungarians are the enemies of the Romanians and would take the first opportunity to attack them in order to get back some territory was indeed exposed. Iliescu and his fellow politicians bear a huge responsibility for the fact that a sincere desire for reconciliation and friendship was so quickly swept away by a false agenda of hate mongering and enemy-building. The moment was missed.

In January 1990, Antall himself travelled to Transylvania with an aid convoy. In 2007, Béla Markó, then president of the Democratic Alliance of Hungarians in Romania (RMDSZ), recalled:

> I first met József Antall on January 7, 1990, in Kolozsvár, in one of the offices of the Hungarian Theater. ... There we met people from Hungary, including perhaps some of my old friends, but today I remember only one person vividly, the yet unknown József Antall. He listened to what we said, and he preferred to listen, but there was something of extraordinary interest in this listening. He did not seem to be the most important person there at the time, and today, I repeat, he is actually the only person I remember of all those present. This is probably also due to his later role, that is why that moment has been preserved in my memory, but also because this was in fact his characteristic feature in his relations with Hungarians beyond the border all along. The attention, the tense interest, the striving for understanding and empathy. In our subsequent contacts, in those few one-to-one conversations, I also felt the same: respect and love for this special breed of people, the Hungarian beyond the border.[132]

I have kept sharing those sentiments.

---

[131] The draft, dated December 31, 1989, is among my papers.
[132] Béla Markó, "Az antalli nemzetpolitika" [Antall's "nation policy"], *Magyar Hírlap*, September 24, 2007.

As the situation in Romania started to consolidate following the execution of the dictator and his equally wicked wife, Foreign Minister Horn flew to Bucharest on December 29. There he made detailed proposals for a radical improvement in Hungarian-Romanian relations and in the situation of Hungarians in Transylvania. These included, among other things, the abolition of discriminatory regulations, the opening of the Hungarian Consulate General in Cluj/Kolozsvár, and the restoration of an education system in the Hungarian language. These were accepted by Front President Iliescu, Prime Minister Petre Roman and Foreign Minister Celak, and the agreement was put in writing in a protocol.[133] At its first press conference in Bucharest on January 5, 1990, the Provisional Executive Committee of the Hungarian Democratic Alliance of Romania, formed at the end of December 1989, announced that the party stood on the principle of the right of self-determination for the Hungarian community in Romania, but it would pursue that right while respecting the territorial integrity and sovereignty of Romania.[134] On the same day, the National Salvation Front issued a statement condemning the policy of the previous dictatorial regime towards the national minorities and declaring its commitment to realizing and guaranteeing individual and collective minority rights. The country's new constitution would recognize and guarantee the individual as well as the collective rights and freedoms of the national minorities, a law should be drafted on the nationalities, and a Ministry of National Minorities should be established.[135]

Such a program has never been adopted. In letters to his Romanian counterpart on January 23 and February 2, Horn urged the implementation of the December 29 agreement, in particular the opening of consulates-general, and he protested against the political and physical attacks and the spread of unfounded slander against Hungarians in Transylvania. No substantive response was received, and when Horn's letters were published at the end of March, the only answer was a letter from Bucharest containing false accusations about the conduct of the Hungarian minority.[136] Then came the bloody clash that broke out in Târgu

---

[133] Horn, *Cölöpök*, 274–76.

[134] *Romániai Magyar Szó* (Bucharest), January 7, 1990. Cf. https://udvardy.adatbank.ro/, January 7, 1990. Takács, "Románia Erdély-politikája," 3–4.

[135] The statement was drawn up by Géza Domokos (1928–2007), the first president of RMDSZ, the new party of the Hungarians. Károly Király (1930–2021), then a vice-president of the Salvation Front, agreed with it, and the other leaders of the Front accepted the statement. See his interview: *Népszabadság*, January 10, 1990.

[136] Horn, *Cölöpök*, 274–78. The two letters were published in *Magyar Külpolitikai Évkönyv, 1990* [Hungarian Foreign Policy Yearbook, 1990] (Budapest: Magyar Külügyminisztérium, 1990), 110–11 and 116–18.

Mureș/Marosvásárhely[137] on March 20, 1990, caused by an incited and drunken Romanian mob that attacked the local Hungarians (then still a majority of the town's inhabitants) who were peacefully demonstrating for their language and educational rights. That was more than a cold shower for Hungarian hopes, it was a real shock. Antall summarized the events in a letter drafted by Gyula Kodolányi to the world leaders Antall had recently met. The list gives an indication of the contacts the future head of Hungary's regime-change government had already established: President George H. W. Bush, Chancellor Kohl, Prime Minister Thatcher, presidents Mitterrand and Giscard d'Estaing, mayor of Paris and later president Chirac, Spanish Prime Minister Felipe Gonzalez, Japanese Prime Minister Toshiki Kaifu, Deputy Secretary of State Eagleburger, Italian Foreign Minister De Michelis.

> It seems that our willingness to establish understanding and cooperation, which has been demonstrated with so many signs since the Hungarian moderation and the [Romanian] revolution, has not yet borne fruit. [...] The responsibility of the Romanian government in this matter is enormous. Firstly, for not fulfilling its promises to the minorities in the days of the revolution [...] the Hungarian government and people were the first and more than their strength to help the National Salvation Council from the very beginning. Secondly, during the current atrocities, it has behaved hesitantly and cowardly, it did not prevent the obvious organization of the pogrom, its armed forces stood idly by and watched the bloodshed, and now it is trying to shift the responsibility to others with transparent pretexts and falsehoods.[138]

The letter rightly pointed to the danger of aggressive nationalism: "The entire achievements of the glorious year of 1989 in Eastern and Central Europe are now at stake. [...] Romania must not be balkanized; on the contrary, we must work to strengthen the Romanian voice for democracy, so that this country can soon shed

---

[137] Târgu Mures was the center of the Hungarian Autonomous Province between 1948 and 1959. During this period, Hungarians made up 74 percent of the population of the town. Due to the measures of the Ceaușescu regime, the proportion of Hungarians steadily decreased: in 1966 the proportion of Hungarians was 70 percent, in 1977 63 percent, and in 1989 the proportion of Romanians and Hungarians was almost equal. The explanation is the massive influx of Romanian workers and other employees, mainly from Moldova. Gabriel Andreescu, *Ruletă români și maghiari 1990–2000* (Bucharest: Editura Polirom, 2001), 28, quoted in Árpád-Attila Nyitrai, *"A román-magyar kapcsolatok és a román-magyar alapszerződés megkötése (1990–1996)"* [Romanian-Hungarian relations and the conclusion of the Romanian-Hungarian basic treaty] (PhD diss., Babes-Bolyai University, 2008).

[138] Gyula Kodolányi's draft, May 23, 1990. Among my papers.

the quarter-century-old psychological stigma of fascist dictatorship and join the community of European democracies." At the time, Western democracies were more serious about their principles.

The behavior of the Romanian authorities showed that the previous policy on the Hungarian question would essentially continue. According to Transylvanian historian Ferenc Takács:

> There was no significant change in Romania's Transylvanian policy after 1989. The strategy remained the same, but the tactics had to be changed because the world had changed, and Romania, if it did not want to become completely isolated or, worse, join one of the regions outside the Euro-Atlantic bloc, had to adapt, at least formally, to the West of today. In other words, it had to renounce the use of brute and open force. […] The Romanian press and the political elite (almost without exception) once again scared the Romanian people with Hungarian revisionism, and classified any legitimate claim of the Hungarians in Transylvania as separatism.[139]

Takács explained that mainly by the fact that Romania is characterized by the Byzantine mentality of the Old Kingdom (Kingdom of Romania 1878–1918), an anti-minority nationalism that gradually infected the majority of Transylvanian Romanians, but he thought there was a possibility for change.

At the beginning of 1990, several of Hungary's neighbors made encouraging declarations towards their minorities, but from the summer of 1990 onwards the struggle between the European ("liberal") perception of tolerance towards national minorities, including Hungarians, and the impatient, centralizing, homogenizing nationalist perception that spreads false myths was perceptible. I still believe that the moment of grace at the end of 1989 could have led to sincere reconciliation among the peoples of Central Europe, but unfortunately the anti-Hungarian nationalists, now painted as democrats, gradually eroded the atmosphere of that Christmas. That the illusions of the time were not entirely unfounded, that sincere and lasting reconciliation and close cooperation with Hungary's neighbors would have been possible, is demonstrated by a statement in the *New York Times* of January 16, 1990, and beginning: "We, men and women of Romanian and Hungarian origin living in the West." Referring to the great turn of events in Romania, the role of László Tőkés and the Hungarians and Romanians of Timișoara, who stood together, and to the consignments of aid from Hungary, it expressed the signatories' conviction that

---

[139] Takács, "Románia Erdély-politikája," 317–18.

Romania and Hungary could shape a better future in unity, ensuring all liberties for the minorities and different religious denominations. From the impressive list of signatories, I highlight only the most interesting names. On the Hungarian side, Dezső Benedek (professor at the University of Georgia), Imre Bertalan, President of the Hungarian Reformed Federation of America, Ferenc Fejtő, the Hungarian-born French author, László Hámos of the HHRF, the noted philosopher Ágnes Heller, Endre Harsányi, an American Calvinist Bishop, Pál Jónás (president of the Petőfi Circle in 1956), General Béla K. Király, the commander of the Hungarian National Guard in 1956, Pál Kövi (owner of the famous Four Seasons Restaurant in New York), businessman John Lauer and his wife Edith, Attila Miklósházy (bishop of the Catholic Hungarians in the West), Ágoston Molnár (president of the Hungarian-American Foundation), Péter Nádosy (a director at Morgan Stanley), Károly Nagy (professor of political science at Rutgers University), Péter Róna (a president at Schroder & Co Bank AG), the well-known financier George Soros, Iván Szelényi (professor at UCLA), Béla Teleki (president of the American Transylvanian Association), Pál Teleki (geologist, grandson of Prime Minister Pál Teleki), Rudolf Tőkés (professor at the University of Connecticut), Nobel Prize-winning physicist Jenő Wigner; and, among the Romanians, Mihai Botez (professor at Stanford University), Matei Călinescu and Ciprian Foias (professors at Indiana University), writers Juliana Geran-Pilon, Paul Goma, Virgil Ierunca, Eugene Ionesco and his wife, as well as Professor Maria Manoilu-Manea (President of the Romanian-American Academy), Virgil Nemoianu (Catholic University of Washington), Nobel Prize-winning Professor George Palade (Yale), Vladimir Tismaneanu (professor at the University of Pennsylvania), and Dorin Tudoran (writer).[140] So it was not stubborn naivety to demand the same rights which were common in the happier parts of Europe; in fact that demand has remained the basic condition for the much desired and necessary reconciliation, friendship and alliance among the peoples of Central Europe.

Similar thoughts and hopes were expressed in early 1990 by the National Minorities Office, established in the previous year under the direction of Imre Pozsgay, and by the National and Ethnic Minorities Secretariate of the Council of Ministers, established in October 1989 under the direction of Csaba Tabajdi with the rank of deputy minister. The latter's task was to implement the recommendations of the former.[141] Welcoming the changes in Romania, Tabajdi looked forward

---

[140] *New York Times*, January 16, 1990. A copy is among my papers.

[141] For the changes in Hungary's policy towards the national minorities at home and abroad, see Róbert Győri Szabó, *Kisebbség-politikai rendszerváltás Magyarországon: a Nemzeti és Etnikai Kisebbségi Kollégium és Titkárság történetének tükrében (1989–1990)* [Regime change in Hungary in minority policy: The history

to new perspectives and a shared future in relations between the two countries and the two nations, based on common interests. While respecting the territorial integrity of Romania, he called for visible action in its minority policy "to establish institutions to fully guarantee the individual and collective rights of national and ethnic minorities living in the country, and to develop constitutional and legal regulations that meet the standards and expectations of the late twentieth century." Among these, he mentioned autonomy, "and the restoration of the entire network of Hungarian education in the mother tongue in Romania, from kindergarten to university."[142]

At the end of January 1990, Antall and I were invited by a U.S. government agency to introduce the MDF, the party which our hosts expected to be the leading factor in the future government. The issue of neighborly relations and minorities was also discussed at many of the meetings, at one of which First Deputy Secretary of State Eagleburger said that any U.S. support for Romania was conditional on democracy and minority rights there.[143] In February and March, on two other American speaking tours, I was able to speak in more detail about the nationality problems in our region and could refute the claim of the Russian *Literatura Rossiya* that "as communism retreats, Hungary has become a center of nationalism and revanchism." I gave expression to my hope that European integration will make border disputes obsolete and that improving the economic situation will prove more important for all countries than national rivalries.

At the time, Western democracies were more serious about their principles, which is why Romania was admitted to the Council of Europe and then to NATO only three years after Hungary's admission.

On May 18, 1990 (after the spring elections, won by my party, the MDF, but before the government was formed on May 23), as a candidate for the post of foreign minister, I gave an interview to the head of the BBC's Hungarian desk, István Siklós. We had become friends in 1975, when I was doing archival research in London. In the interview I expressed the hope that our neighbors would adopt the practices followed by Western European countries towards their own minorities after the Second World War. These were policies which their Hungarian minorities, their newly formed parties, could now openly demand political and cultural

---

of the College and Secretariat on Ethnic Minorities] (Budapest: Osiris, 1998); and Mák, "Az új nemzeti politika."

[142] The proposal, without date, is among my papers.

[143] My account of the visit is in Géza Jeszenszky, "József Antall and the World," in *József Antall: Prime Minister of Hungary; Selected Speeches and Interviews* (1989–1993), ed. Géza Jeszenszky (Budapest: József Antall Foundation, 2008).

autonomy, Hungarian schools, and universities. "If the neighboring states accept the multi-ethnic character of their countries and draw the logical conclusions, there will be no obstacle to the new democracies having very close relations with each other. After all, we have common goals: European integration, prosperity and internal democracy."[144]

---

[144] Hungarian broadcast monitor, May 20, 1990. Among my papers.

Chapter 2

The Government's Foreign Policy Program

The first free elections since 1945 were held in two rounds in March and April 1990, resulting in the victory of Antall's center-right Hungarian Democratic Forum (MDF). With 43 percent of the seats in Parliament, coalition partners were needed. The choice was obvious: the traditional party of the farmers and the middle class, the Independent Smallholders' Party, and the Christian Democratic People's Party. The prime minister as well as the ministers of foreign affairs and defense were professional historians; most members of the government and of the governing party were also well versed in Hungarian history. The "new" politicians wanted to learn from the historical misfortunes that had befallen the country, and even more so from the mistakes and blunders committed by their predecessors.[1]

Persons close to the last Communist governments often maintained that Hungary had already distanced itself from Moscow in the 1980s and pursued a foreign policy that served the national interest. Without denying the presence of such intentions in the minds of the foreign policy leadership of the time, in critical situations, such as the imposition of martial law in Poland in 1981 or the boycott of the 1984 Olympic Games in Los Angeles, there was no independent Hungarian foreign policy; it was aligned with that of Moscow. In the spring of 1989, even the two "bravest" foreign politicians of the MSZMP could imagine only "Finlandization" in the medium term, and identify neutrality as a long-term goal.[2]

Haunting dilemmas

In order to be able to take advantage of the opportunities offered by the new era in world history, Hungary had to avoid the trap of making ill-advised judgments and

---

[1] For the blunders committed during the Second World War, see Géza Jeszenszky, "Hungary in the Second World War: Tragic Blunders or Destiny," in *July 1944: Deportation of the Jews of Budapest Foiled*, ed. Géza Jeszenszky (Reno, NV: Helena History Press, 2017 [2018]), 65–101.

[2] Csaba Tabajdi, *Az önazonosság labirintusa* [The labyrinth of self-identity] (Budapest: CP Stúdió Bt., 1998), 36–48.

had to find solutions to the persistent, seemingly insoluble dilemmas of Hungarian foreign policy. What did these dilemmas look like in the early 1990s?[3]

Of the great powers that had threatened the independence of the Hungarian nation in past centuries, by the early 1990s only one remained dangerous, and its army continued to occupy the country. In a swan song of foreign policy steps that signaled an important part of the regime change, the Németh government signed an agreement with the Soviet Union on March 10, 1990, on the withdrawal of Soviet troops which had been "temporarily stationed" in Hungary. However, their departure was subject to financial conditions: the occupiers made demands of an absurd magnitude, citing the assets (buildings, airfields, military installations) left behind. Hungary was still a member of the Warsaw Pact (the coalition of the unwilling), and of Comecon,[4] which kept the economy in a state of dependence. In order to end the unfavorable associations and to balance foreign trade, the consent and goodwill of the Soviet leadership was indispensable. The reorientation of Hungarian foreign policy also required the goodwill and support of the Western democracies. Nor was it possible to know whether the turnaround would have a lasting impact on the Western perception of Hungary, i.e., whether the significance of 1956 and the Hungarian role in the historical 1989 turnaround would prove to be stronger than the negative memory of two world wars and the anti-Hungarian prejudices that existed in many quarters. In other words: Would the West finally reciprocate the thousand years of affection shown towards it by the Hungarians and translate into action the appreciation expressed so abundantly in words at the time? There was also the question of whether there was a solution to the shortage of raw materials and markets, as had afflicted Hungary after the First World War, without the country once again finding itself forced into a German or Russian sphere of interests. And a most important dilemma was whether it would be possible to achieve sincere and lasting reconciliation and close cooperation with those neighbors who, since 1919, had been troubled by the specter of the "Hungarian *revanche*" and who, as a countermeasure, had pursued a policy of systematic repression and forcible assimilation of the Hungarian minorities attached to them.

Hungary's neighborhood relations were characterized—in László Szarka's apt phrase—as "missed reconciliations" (elmaradt kiegyezések), sometimes the fault of

---

[3] On the continuous dilemmas, see Géza Jeszenszky, "Hungary's Foreign Policy Dilemmas," *Hungarian Quarterly* 34 (Summer 1993): 3–13.

[4] Comecon (Council for Mutual Economic Assistance): organization established in January 1949 to facilitate and coordinate the economic development of the eastern European countries belonging to the Soviet bloc. It was not a genuine, mutually advantageous integration, like the Common Market, but linked each member country to the Soviet economy through bilateral agreements.

one side, sometimes of the other. After 1848, 1868, 1918 and 1945, in 1990 history once again offered a chance for a fair settlement of relations between Hungarians and their neighbors, which many Hungarian patriots with foresight had advocated but failed to achieve, despite their fair proposals. At that most dramatic moment in the fall of communist dominoes in Europe, Christmas 1989, the authors and supporters of the MDF's Christmas Manifesto sincerely believed that, as a lesson taught by shared suffering, this could now be achieved.

To many observers today, our hopes at Christmas 1989 may seem to have been illusory. But then, at that turning point of world history, under the spell of the Romanian miracle, we had before us these examples in Western Europe: Franco-German reconciliation, which proved lasting; Scandinavia, which had once been under Danish and then Swedish rule; Finland's generous attitude towards its Swedish minority; and Iceland managing to break away peacefully from Denmark during the Second World War. Today the peoples of Scandinavia are bound together by strong friendship. We knew, of course, that in the "happy North," common ancestry and, even more, the absence of oppressive minority policies, made it much easier to establish genuine friendships. Unfortunately, however, just as the Trianon decision was the "apple of Eris," the policy towards Hungarian minorities proved to be the Achilles' heel of reconciliation.

Internal political conditions

Not even in the feverish and exciting months on the threshold of regime change, in the "halcyon days" of the MDF, did I expect to be offered the post of foreign minister. As a scholar, I was not used to the limelight, and never came to like publicity, especially having to give very short answers to questions on intricate issues. As a historian, knowing the history of Hungarian foreign policy and pondering the causes of its failures, I was also aware of the difficulties of the task. I took up the post partly because few people in the MDF had international experience and contacts, and the English language, which had become the primary language of international contacts, was either not spoken or not well enough by other MDF politicians who were available.[5] I knew that the prime minister needed someone in foreign policy who knew and fully shared his goals and ideas, and I enjoyed Antall's full confidence. This was not a post to be assigned to a former pupil or the husband of a beloved niece but one for a teacher of modern history and international relations who was

---

[5] Many of the "founding fathers" of the Forum would have liked to have had one of them, Rudolf Joó, in that position (Für, *A Varsói Szerződés végnapjai*, 35–37), but to general surprise in fall 1989 he accepted an invitation to teach at the University of Lyon, thus excluding that option.

acquainted with the English-speaking countries. In addition, and not least, it called for someone who had travelled extensively in the Carpathian Basin, was committed to the cause of Hungarians living beyond the borders, and had long-standing friendships with several among the emerging politicians.

The fact that Hungary's prestige and international image had never been as positive as at the end of 1989 gave me the confidence to take on the task, also at that time I experienced only sympathy and goodwill for Hungary, and this was reflected in the support I found then for minority rights. Although political debates were intensifying at home before the elections, there were almost no differences on foreign policy issues—in terms of programs. The program of the SZDSZ, the leading opposition party, included both cultural autonomy (compulsory bilingualism or multilingualism in local administration and in the use of public signs wherever the proportion of minorities exceeded 10 percent) and territorial autonomy for areas inhabited mainly by a national minority.[6] From the late 1970s, this party and its sympathizers took a strong stand in favor of the Hungarian minorities living under double oppression (as citizens and as minorities), and they had ties with their outspoken representatives. They were also in contact with the Polish and Czech opposition movements.[7]

The foreign policy experts of the "reform communists" (after 1990 in the MSZP, the Socialist Party), especially Csaba Tabajdi and Imre Szokai, were also known for their commitment to the cause of Hungarian minorities. In the spring of 1990, Tabajdi (and many others) did not rule out the changing of European borders by referendum.[8] (With the break-up of Yugoslavia, quite a few Western politicians and observers considered that desirable. Even today that is an option for settling the debate between Kosovo and Serbia.) At an April 19–20, 1990, meeting of European experts organized by Tabajdi, while still deputy minister, he expressed confidence that international organizations, especially the CSCE (Conference on Security and Cooperation in Europe), would adopt a binding convention on the protection of national minorities and that the autonomy of national minorities could be achieved. He also wanted to guarantee the rights of Hungarian and other minorities through bilateral agreements with "hard" commitments.[9]

---

[6] *A rendszerváltás programja* [The program of the regime change] (Budapest: Szabad Demokraták Szövetsége, 1989), 56–57.
[7] Their journal, *Beszélő*, had an appendix to the issue of April 14, 1990, that was intended to prove their long-standing commitment to the cause of the Hungarian national minorities.
[8] Tabajdi, *Az önazonosság labirintusa*, 279–80.
[9] Tabajdi, *Az önazonosság labirintusa*, 283–92.

Also, from the very beginning, the Young Democrats (Fidesz) were strong promoters of the rights of the Hungarian minorities. János Áder[10] and Zsolt Németh,[11] both among the party's founders, drew up its program on the protection of minorities (October 1989). It proved to be very close to the ideas of the MDF.

One of the first steps taken by the new National Assembly was the adoption on May 15 of a resolution ("On the situation of Hungarian national minorities in neighboring countries"), tabled by Miklós Gáspár Tamás, a Transylvanian-born SZDSZ MP well-known for his opposition activities first in Romania, then in Hungary.[12] It is noteworthy that even at this hopeful time, the Hungarian Parliament was already concerned about "the lack of tolerance towards national minorities and the rejection of their legitimate claims seriously endangering the democratization processes of the whole region and the building of good neighbor relations on new foundations." As a remedy, Tamás proposed bilateral negotiations with the governments of neighboring countries with a view to drawing up treaties guaranteeing the rights of national minorities.

> It is of fundamental importance to protect and develop the identity of national minorities, to legally guarantee the individual and collective rights of national minorities living in this region, to legally guarantee their participation in public life and in deciding over their own affairs, their self-organization and self-government, including their cultural autonomy, and to meet the needs of the nationalities in the use of their mother tongue, in education, cultural life, religious practice and communication. [...] The National Assembly of the Republic of Hungary expresses its conviction that the realization of the above-mentioned objectives will contribute to the regional and universal realization of human rights and fundamental freedoms, to the establishment of good relations between the Republic of Hungary and all its neighbors, to the democratic development of the Central and Eastern European region based on peaceful cooperation, and to the strengthening of European security and stability.[13]

---

[10] János Áder (1959–): Hungarian jurist and politician. Served as president of Hungary from 2012 to 2022.

[11] Zsolt Németh (1963–): Hungarian politician, MP since 1990. State secretary for foreign affairs (1998–2002, 2010–2014), head of the Parliamentary Committee for Foreign Affairs (2014–).

[12] Gáspár Miklós Tamás (1948–2023): Hungarian Marxist-turned radical liberal philosopher and political writer. MP for the Alliance of Free Democrats, 1989–1994.

[13] Resolution no. 40/1990 (May 24) of the National Assembly on the Situation of the Hungarian National Minorities Living in the Neighboring Countries. *Magyar Külpolitikai Évkönyv, 1990*, 166–67; also in János Sáringer, ed., *Iratok az Antall-kormány külpolitikájához és diplomáciájához*, vol. 1, *(1990. május–december 1990)* [Papers relating to the foreign policy and diplomacy of the Antall government: May to December

In the final vote on the resolution, its author essentially expressed the same objectives that the government subsequently worked for: "... we must not give up one iota of the rights that Hungarian public opinion expects to be granted to Hungarians beyond our borders [...] We would like to make a real, serious historical offer to our neighbors, preferably looking ahead to the long term, and we will hold out our hand—we hope—even if they do not accept it for the time being."[14] The resolution was adopted by Parliament with no votes against and three abstentions.

Already after the elections, but before the change of government and thus before my taking over the direction of the ministry, the old management (the Political Analysis and Information Department) prepared a foreign policy strategy, which included a proposal that was later sharply criticized by the opposition:

> The main goal of our minority policy is to enforce human rights, the collective rights of minorities, by establishing international conventions, a control mechanism, bilateral agreements and aid programs. [...] *In neighborhood policy, we should make the cultivation of relations conditional on respect for minority rights. We must make it clear to the countries with Hungarian minorities that their accession to Europe is only possible if their minorities are treated in a European way, and Budapest's judgment could be decisive in this respect.*[15]

Accordingly, what the opposition later called (erroneously) the "Antall Doctrine" was formulated by the "old guard" of the Ministry, before the formation of the new government. Was this an expression of good-faith naivety born of the European mood at the time, or a "time bomb" that could be detonated later, at the right moment?[16]

There was also agreement among the parliamentary parties on the root of the problem—the Trianon Peace Treaty, which had been imposed on Hungary seventy

---

1990] (Budapest: VERITAS Történetkutató Intézet és Levéltár - Magyar Napló, 2015), 507–8 (Doc. 114). The five volumes of the diplomatic documents of the Antall government's foreign policy, edited by János Sáringer, were published between 2015 and 2022, with introductions by the editor.

[14] Minutes of the Hungarian Parliament, May 15, 1990, http://www.parlament.hu/naplo34/004/004tart.html.

[15] My italics. Paper prepared by the Political Analysis and Information Department. Among my papers.

[16] The Ministry of Foreign Affairs was a politically very sensitive institution under the Communists. Political loyalty was doubly mandatory for people whose job involved regular contact with the capitalist world; a Communist diplomatic mission in a Western capital had a ghetto atmosphere. The wind of change reached that ministry quite early; many diplomats were indeed happy to see the end of Communism, and they were eager to serve at last the national interests of their own country.

years earlier. On May 31, the six parties in the National Assembly adopted a joint declaration stating that the peace treaty,

> while seeking to redress grievances, tragically affected the Hungarian nation as a whole [...] It also pitted the peoples of Central Europe against each other and imposed the burden of hostility on the nations living there instead of free cooperation. [...] Recalling Hungary's commitment signed in the Helsinki Final Act, the prohibition of forcible changes of borders is reaffirmed. At the same time, Hungary expects full guarantee of individual and collective minority rights for Hungarians beyond its borders. The signatory parties commit themselves to a world in which state borders lose their restrictive significance and free relations between peoples and nations, minorities and mother nations, countries and their citizens is achieved.[17]

It seemed that the new government would be able to count on the loyalty and even the support of the opposition in its efforts to ensure the broad implementation of minority rights in relations with the neighbors. In principle. However, I soon had to realize that in multi-party politics, old positions, relationships and even friendships count for little. Even more so that the opposition and the press were only looking for where to attack the government's policies. At the public hearing of the ministerial candidates in Parliament, I stated that, while we wanted to put aside the burdens of the past with all our neighbors and strive for the best possible relations, this would be more difficult with our Slovak, Romanian and Serbian neighbors, where there was a significant number of Hungarians.[18] I was severely criticized in the press for making this distinction. My assumption that our relations would not be the same with all our neighbors was realistic. I sincerely regret that my premonition was confirmed.

Foreign policy in the government program

As shown, the MDF, which won the elections, had a well-thought-out program for foreign policy; its two coalition partners embraced it without any debate.[19] The

---

[17] The Declaration, dated May 31, 1990, and released the next day, is published in *Magyar Külpolitikai Évkönyv, 1990*, 190. Sadly, it never received the publicity it deserved.

[18] Imre Szilágyi, "Magyarország és a délszláv térség 1990 után" [Hungary and the South Slav territory after 1990], *Külügyi Szemle*, 3, nos. 1–2. (2004): 4–5.

[19] On the Antall government's foreign policy, see Jeszenszky, "Hungary's Foreign Policy Dilemmas"; and Jeszenszky, "József Antall and the World. Cf. Margit Bessenyey Williams, *Foreign Policy and Transitions to Democracy: the Case of Hungary* (Bloomington, IN: Indiana University, 1997).

foreign policy part of the government program presented by József Antall on May 22 was prepared by me, together with Gyula Kodolányi (who participated in the preparation of the whole presentation), with the assistance of Ferenc Somogyi from the Ministry of Foreign Affairs.[20] The text was personally finalized by the prime minister designate. It outlined the main foreign-policy objectives of a democratic Hungary: the restoration of sovereignty and the re-orientation of its foreign policy towards Atlantic cooperation.[21] It required the development of a relationship of trust with the Western democracies and participation in European integration, but the precondition was ending Soviet military occupation and withdrawal from the Warsaw Pact, preferably by way of its negotiated termination. At the same time, Hungary offered the hand of friendship to all neighbors, the Soviet Union included. A concomitant element was standing up for minority rights, above all taking steps to ensure the survival of Hungarian communities outside the borders. The inseparability of these three tasks is obvious: freed from Soviet rule, Hungary's security and economic interests dictated that, in addition to its traditions, it should move closer to Western integration and join them as soon as possible. However, Hungary could not do this alone, without its neighbors, and by joining forces with them the speeding up of the process appeared likely.

At the same time, the guarantee of the rights of national minorities was an indispensable element and precondition of the "Danube idea," of sincere solidarity among the peoples of Central Europe. It was hoped that on the basis of common suffering under the dictatorships, and the common acceptance of the Western values, a new solidarity would emerge and the former communist countries would follow the example of post-Second-World-War Western Europe by putting aside all quarrels, old and newer, and would concentrate on political, economic, environmental and cultural recovery and reconstruction. All six parties elected to Parliament professed agreement on those basic tenets of foreign policy. It was expected that the Western governments and their countries' public opinion would share and support all those aims. In the prime minister's words:

---

[20] Ferenc Somogyi (1945–2021): Hungarian diplomat, administrative state secretary of the Ministry of Foreign Affairs (1990–91), Minister of Foreign Affairs (2004–2006), ambassador to the United States (2007–2009).

[21] After 1990, and even more so after 1994, it was often said that Hungary had already distanced itself from Moscow in the 1980s and pursued a foreign policy governed by the national interest. Without denying the presence of such intentions in the minds of the foreign policy leadership of the time, in critical situations, such as the imposition of martial law in Poland in 1981 or the boycott of the 1984 Olympic Games in Los Angeles, there was no independent Hungarian foreign policy, Hungary was organically aligned with Moscow. Even the most courageous conception, written by Csaba Tabajdi and Imre Szokai, spoke only about "Finlandization" as a future possibility. See *Magyar Nemzet*, March 18, 1989, republished in Tabajdi, *Az önazonosság labirintusa*, 36–48.

A new chapter needs to be opened in the history of Hungary, a chapter of understanding and tolerance between our much-troubled nation and the neighboring peoples, which are burdened by similar legacies. [...] The changes in Central and Eastern Europe have provided us with a great opportunity to eliminate, or at least moderate the animosities that traditionally turned the peoples of this region against each other. Nations achieving independence should develop free contacts with each other. State borders should not obstruct the free movement of persons, information and ideas. We are confident that in the future none of our neighbors will feel the need to use the Hungarians as the image of the enemy, so that they could keep their unity. European cooperation goes hand-in-hand with intensive regional cooperation; we shall seek to achieve that with all our neighbors. As Europe moves towards a federation, regionalism is the best guarantee for the preservation of national characteristics and the assertion of national interests, free of intolerant nationalism.

The principal objective of our minority policy is the enforcement of human rights and specifically minority rights, equally in Hungary and abroad. In view of the fact that one third of all Hungarians live outside of Hungary, it is a special responsibility of the State of Hungary to support the preservation of the Hungarian nation as a cultural and ethnic community everywhere. For that reason, we support the maintenance of the right of self-determination of Hungarian communities beyond our borders, in accordance with prevailing international treaties and according to their spirit, as well as in full agreement with the declared promises of the governments of the neighboring countries. The time has come for national minorities to truly form the most important bridge of friendship among countries, but this can happen only if the rights and dignity of those communities are restored. In this honest endeavor of ours we count on the support of the governments and public opinion of democratic countries as well as the political assistance of European and international organizations.[22]

The above foreign policy tasks of the reborn Hungary were a logical consequence of history. It was understandable and justified to move beyond our grave grievances with the Soviet Union, not only in view of the presence of Soviet troops on Hungarian soil, and with the Warsaw Pact still in force, but also in the interests

---

[22] For the full text of the speech, see Jeszenszky, *József Antall, Prime Minister of Hungary*, 111–37.

of good relations with the nuclear superpower and important economic partner that remained our neighbor. It was more difficult to move beyond the past with the other neighbors. What were the ingredients of this difficult legacy? The gory conflicts of 1848/49; the serious grievances felt by the non-Hungarian minorities after 1867, and especially in the twenty years before the outbreak of the First World War; the grave injustices of the Trianon Peace Treaty and the repressive policies implemented towards the Hungarians who were annexed to the neighboring countries; the scars and reprisals caused by the border changes between 1938 and 1941; the atrocities and expulsions after the Second World War; and finally, the double oppression of minorities in the communist era.

The Hungarian public at the time understood that raising the border issue would be pointless and even harmful, but it expected a radical improvement in the condition of the Hungarian minorities. The new international situation and Hungary's greatly increased prestige seemed to provide a favorable background for this. If this was an illusion, it was an illusion that both the government of the time and its opponents believed to be a reality. The words of István Szent-Iványi (the foreign policy expert of the SZDSZ, the leading force of the opposition)[23] in his response to the foreign policy program, testify to this:

> I don't think anyone doubts that the new Government intends to do its best on the minority issue. But reading the guidelines of the government's program, we are not really sure that they know how to give their best on the issue. Today, in the midst of great changes, there are great and new opportunities for the Government in the new European architecture, in the Helsinki II Treaty. There is an opportunity and a willingness on the part of the leading Western countries to set up a system of requirements codifying and establishing fundamental minority rights, and in our contribution to that. That will a precondition for all countries, including Hungary of course, to join Europe. I think this is an important national interest and it has not been mentioned in the speech.[24]

---

[23] István Szent-Iványi (1958–): Hungarian liberal politician. Member of the National Assembly (1990–2004), chairman of its Committee on Foreign Affairs (1997–2002) and the Committee on European Integration (2002–2004). State secretary of foreign affairs (1994–1997). Member of the European Parliament (2004–2009), Ambassador to Slovenia (2010–15).

[24] Speech by István Szent-Iványi, Minutes of the Hungarian Parliament, May 23, 1990. http://www.parlament.hu/naplo34/006/0060002.htm.

What some later called the "Antall Doctrine" was never enunciated or announced in speech or in writing. According to it, Hungary makes its relations with its neighbors dependent on their policy towards the Hungarian minority that lives there, and in all decisions on neighborhood policy the legal representatives of the Hungarian minority concerned would be consulted. Such an attitude would make Hungary the self-appointed protective power of the Hungarians beyond its borders.[25] In my opinion, although it would be a mistake to follow the above theses as rigid dogma in foreign policy, they can be interpreted as guidelines, and should be followed by all successive Hungarian governments. At the same time, it shows bad faith to believe that the Antall government harbored secret dreams of revising the borders and switched to a policy of minority rights based on European institutions only when it realized that the Western democracies were strongly opposed to any change in the European borders.[26]

In the spring and summer of 1990, in the euphoric mood of the regime change and in the atmosphere of optimism that filled the whole world at the time, Antall and his government felt that they had to act swiftly if they wanted to create a truly radically better Europe in which the Hungarian nation could—in the words of a later prime minister, Viktor Orbán—unite without changing borders and ensure the survival of the whole Hungarian community. Prime Minister Antall expressed this to Prime Minister Margaret Thatcher, in his toast during her visit to Budapest in September. He used Shakespeare's words:

> *There is a tide in the affairs of men,*
> *Which taken at the flood, leads on to fortune;*
> *Omitted, all the voyage of their life*
> *Is bound in shallows and in miseries.*
> *On such a full sea are we now afloat,*
> *And we must take the current when it serves,*
> *Or lose our ventures.*[27]

---

[25] Bárdi, *Tény és való*, 143.
[26] For that totally unfounded charge, see János Kis, "Nation-Building and Beyond," in *Can Liberal Pluralism Be Exported?*, ed. Will Kymlicka and Magda Opalski (Oxford: The University Press, 2002), 220–42.
[27] William Shakespeare, *Julius Caesar*. Act 4. Scene 3, Line 249.

"Prime minister of fifteen million"

Prime Minister Antall found a lasting place in the hearts of Hungarians living beyond the borders when he characterized himself as prime minister for fifteen million Hungarians. His statement, made on June 2, 1990, at the 3rd National Convention of the MDF, has only too often been misunderstood or deliberately misinterpreted, even in Hungary. His actual words were: "In a legal sense, in accordance with the Constitution, I want to act as the head of the government of all the citizens of this ten million strong country, but in spirit and sentiment, the prime minister of fifteen million Hungarians."[28] A few observers feared this statement was meant to prepare the ground for territorial claims against the neighboring states, while most Hungarians, especially those who lived outside the borders of Hungary, either in the neighboring states or in Western countries, welcomed that reversion of communist policies with enthusiasm. It was simply a memorable paraphrase of Section 3, Article 6 of the Constitution, which stated: "*The Republic of Hungary bears a sense of responsibility for the fate of Hungarians living outside its borders and shall promote and foster their relations with Hungary.*"[29] Did that go beyond the principle which was introduced into the Hungarian Constitution as a result of the 1989 round-table negotiations (in no small measure at Antall's urging)? No, this phrase only promised to reinforce and put into practice this principle. The idea was also included in the above-quoted government program. Today many remember the leader of the transformation most warmly for having espoused the cause of the Hungarian minorities.

To read into the prime minister's words the program of Hungarian irredentism and territorial claims against neighboring states required both a good deal of bad faith and an incomplete, inaccurate quotation. In Central Europe, the concept of nation is traditionally linked not to the state but to language, culture and history, so Antall added to an obvious fact (the Hungarian nation far outnumbers the citizens of Hungary) only that millions of people compelled to live outside Hungary's borders yet still claim to be Hungarian will always be present in his thinking and policies. That was indeed necessary, because during the decades of communism, official Hungarian policy ignored them, and even excluded them from much of the school curriculum. The disputed sentence sent a message to the Hungarian communities stranded outside the borders that the period of communism, when the

---

[28] József Debreczeni, *A miniszterelnök: Antall József és a rendszerváltozás* [József Antall and the regime change] (Budapest: Osiris, 1998), 137.
[29] The Constitution of the Republic of Hungary, 1989, https://en.wikisource.org/wiki/Constitution_of_the_Republic_of_Hungary_(1989).

Hungarian homeland had seemingly written them off, when it had offered them neither moral nor practical help, and when it fraternized, drank and hunted behind their backs, in comradely agreement with the leaders who oppressed them, was over. The Hungarians of Romania, as well as Czechoslovakia, Yugoslavia and the Soviet Union, immediately heard this sentence and drew strength from it, while many in the neighboring capitals took note and began to sound the alarm to their own public and the world's governments by arousing a vision of revived Hungarian territorial claims. This was facilitated by the press, both within and outside Hungary, in many cases deliberately omitting the words "in spirit and sentiment" from the critical sentence. Shortly after his speech, Antall made clear the meaning of his sentence in a statement to Hungarian Radio:

> The fact that the Hungarian government has a moral and spiritual obligation to take responsibility for all members of the fifteen million Hungarian community means nothing more than that we must stand up for their human and minority rights, we must find ways to support their cultural aspirations, their education and everything that goes with it. By the way we are not the only country that feels a responsibility for its sons and daughters living outside its borders.[30]

Indeed, the same can be said of all Western European countries having people who are linked to them by descent and/or history. In the case of former colonial powers that is taken for granted. The State of Israel is also a good example. Since the early 1990s, such care has become common in the eastern half of Europe, most countries offer dual citizenship for their kinsmen who live in other countries.

An unfortunate and damaging practice began after the prime minister's statement: instead of taking united action on a fundamental national issue, some Hungarian politicians, and, more often journalists, created the impression that a radical, extremist, nationalist foreign policy line was pursuing a path of confrontation, or even conflict, with its neighbors, and that there was also a conciliatory line. The suggestion was that the Antall government represented the former and its opponents the latter. But by quoting the words of the Hungarian prime minister authentically, and referring to the size of the Hungarian minorities, the overwhelming majority of our international partners signaled that they understood the prime minister's message. After all, the minorities "have become citizens of foreign

---

[30] For Antall's statement on Hungarian Radio, see *Magyar Külpolitikai Évkönyv, 1990*, 191–92.

countries as a result of a historical decision, but wish to remain in the spiritual, intellectual, cultural and linguistic community of the Hungarian nation."[31]

The Hungarian government's pro-minority stance was based on the principle that the rights of all national minorities have to be observed and safeguarded. The place where it was possible to change the previous practice immediately was in the treatment of national minorities at home. In September 1990, on the initiative of the prime minister, the Office for National and Ethnic Minorities was established, headed by János Wolfart (1951–2014), a member of the German minority. The drafting of a Law on Minorities, based on the collective rights of the national minorities of Hungary, began.

Illusions and reality in neighborhood policy

In the "year of miracles," in the months of the regime change, among a number of Hungarians' long-buried hopes revived that the approximation of the borders of the Hungarian state and the Hungarian nation, i.e., border adjustments in Hungary's favor, might be possible. Maps of the historic Kingdom of Hungary appeared in shops and subways, and a little later, stickers on cars depicting the contours of "Greater Hungary." Although no one could realistically hope for the Kingdom's restoration, the returning of some border areas, which were still predominantly inhabited by Hungarians, was imaginable in principle. The better informed referred to the Helsinki Final Act of 1975, which indeed stated that the borders of the signatory states "may be changed by peaceful agreement." But such a development, before the secession of Kosovo (still not recognized by Serbia, Slovakia and Romania), only took place when the two Germanies were united and a border disappeared. With the break-up of the Soviet Union, Yugoslavia and Czechoslovakia, the internal, administrative borders between the constituent republics became international borders, without changing them. Naturally, none of Hungary's neighbors showed any willingness to cede even a single village. The Antall government was fully aware of all that, while confident that in a politically and economically integrated Europe, a fair policy that respected the individual as well as the communal rights of national minorities would prevail. The position was exactly what István Bibó, the widely respected advocate of friendship between the peoples of the Danube Basin and a hero of 1956, had formulated eloquently in 1946:

---

[31] *Magyar Külpolitikai Évkönyv, 1990*, 191–92.

Hungary will faithfully respect and carry out the peace treaty, once it is signed. It would be insincere to pretend that she has become an enthusiastic adherent of the grave dispositions of the treaty. But Hungary will not create an ideology or organize political campaigns for changing the borders, and will not pursue a policy which speculates in international crises or catastrophes, so that her territorial grievances could be remedied. Hungary will comply with the conditions created by the peace treaty without any reservations, except one: she cannot give up her political interest in the fate of the Hungarian minorities [living in the states surrounding Hungary].[32]

Or what an earlier scholar turned politician, and then exile, Oszkár Jászi, dreamed of: democracy, national reconciliation, minority rights in the Danube Basin, a united Europe and an international legal order based on respect for common values. Accordingly, Hungary reconciled itself to the territorial losses but expected the adoption of laws and measures to ensure the rights and long-term survival of the Hungarians who had been transferred to the neighboring states. The same was the demand and program of the Hungarian parties formed in Hungary's neighbors in 1989–90.

This was not some kind of sloppy, cautious program. We thought that, while codifying minority rights in international forums, we would negotiate and ensure their practical implementation with our neighbors at a bilateral level. As we accept the existing borders, our neighbors should accept that their citizens of Hungarian nationality are part of the cultural community of Hungarians, that the motherland cares about them and that this does not constitute interference in their internal affairs. Although Hungary grants extensive rights and cultural autonomy to the national minorities living on its territory, it does so not on the basis of reciprocity but on the basis of its own principles. The size and the history of the mutual minorities do not even allow for a comparison to be drawn between Hungary and its neighbors. Whilst discrimination against minorities is unacceptable, all national minorities are entitled to positive discrimination, because only this can ensure genuine equality. Hungary was well aware that integration in Europe allows the free and unhindered movement of persons, goods and ideas. It followed that cross-border traffic and cooperation between Hungary and its neighbors must grow; roads, railway lines and border crossings closed after 1920 must be restored. The positive examples and solutions that had already been implemented in Western Europe,

---

[32] István Bibó, "A magyar békeszerződés" [The Hungarian peace treaty], *Válasz* (1946). In English, see Bibó, "The Peace and Hungarian Democracy," in T*he Art of Peacemaking*, ed. Iván Zoltán Dénes (New Haven, CT: Yale University Press, 2015), 181–98.

should be adopted in the countries liberated from communist dictatorship. The anti-minority mentality must change, and the foundations for this must be laid in education and school textbooks.

My first trip abroad, on May 26, 1990, in my capacity as minister took me to Vienna.[33] On the side, I visited the Central Association of Hungarian Organizations in Austria. Its driving force was Ernő Deák, editor-in-chief of the bimonthly *Bécsi Napló*, with whom I had had a personal friendship for many years. At our meeting I pointed out that as a result of the regime change, the Hungarian minorities had ceased to live in fear and in forced silence: now they were formulating their own demands, and the whole world could see that their situation needed to be improved. "In the new Europe accepted principles and forms of behavior will set the framework for political and social life. That is why I am cautiously optimistic about the future of the Hungarian minorities," I told the Hungarians in Vienna.[34] I expressed similar hopes at my first international press conference on May 30 in Budapest. "Today it is no longer Hungary that has to speak for the silenced Hungarian minorities, but they themselves can speak for themselves in an authentic way." Their program is "extremely sober and moderate, with principles and goals in line with European standards in all aspects. It is not our responsibility to fulfil them, it is the responsibility of the governments of the [neighboring] states. [...] We would like to see only those principles elaborated—and the Hungarian government itself can play an active part in this—which are suitable for solving the problems of multilingual and multinational states at the European level, and even on a global scale."[35]

The Minority College established in 1989 by Imre Pozsgay and Csaba Tabajdi, was changed into the Secretariat of Hungarians Beyond the Borders, under the prime minister's office (from 1992 it was placed under the supervision of the Ministry of Foreign Affairs with the name Office of Hungarians Beyond the Border). Its head was Géza Entz.[36] The Illyés Foundation supported the social and cultural organizations and the educational institutions of the Hungarians in the neighboring countries, making maximum use of its meagre financial resources (only fifteen million forints a year, plus donations). The hope expressed in the government program was that the new leaders in the neighboring countries would be prepared to follow the best Western European examples and meet the needs of their minorities. That

---

[33] On the official side of the visit, see the next chapter.
[34] "Az új Magyarország külpolitikájáról" [On the foreign policy of the New Hungary], *Bécsi Napló* (July–August 1990): 1.
[35] *Magyar Külpolitikai Évkönyv, 1990,* 176.
[36] For Entz, see chapter 1, note 69 in this volume.

proved to be an illusion. It was also an illusion that Western Europe and North America would firmly support these demands, if necessary, by exerting pressure.

Quite a few people at home and abroad believed, or at least claimed, that the mere mention of Trianon or the Hungarian communities in neighboring countries was irredentism, an attempt to modify the borders. The words and actions of the government refuted this accusation. On August 20, 1992, at the congress of the reorganized World Federation of Hungarians, Antall said that the injustices of the peace treaty still hurt and needed to be remedied:

> Who can doubt that the Trianon peace treaty after the First World War caused pain to this people and this country? [...] It hurts because it meant cultural separation. Every family feels pain because it has been separated from its brothers and sisters or separated from its homeland. It is difficult for a country to digest the fact that one in three Hungarians found himself or herself beyond the borders of Hungary. [...] We have renounced the policy of changing borders by force. In the Helsinki Final Act and with the signing of the Charter of Paris, we accepted this principle, together with all the peoples of Europe. But this principle goes hand-in-hand with human rights and the protection of the rights of national minorities. Let no one say that the minority question is an internal matter.[37]

Was it hidden irredentism to speak like this? Was it justified to be concerned about thinking in terms of fifteen million Hungarians? A journalist, Sándor Révész, accused Antall of being "an irredentist in spirit."[38] Talking about pain caused by Trianon, or calling for minority rights was not a political act; it simply expressed a duty to defend the interests of Hungarians living beyond the borders—or so the prime minister, his government and many of his supporters thought. Just as the authors and politicians also held in high esteem outside Hungary—from Oszkár Jászi to István Bibó to the Hungarian emigration to the West after 1947—thought and acted in the same vein. Antall's conception reflected a common Hungarian attitude.

Although Antall and his policies are nowadays viewed much more positively by any unbiased person or political force than they were during his rule, a perception lingers that Hungary's concern for its kin is irredentism and consequently a threat to peace. This is often repeated in the international press, also by politicians in the

---

[37] *Magyar Külpolitikai Évkönyv, 1992* [Hungarian Foreign Policy Yearbook, 1992] (Budapest: Magyar Külügyminisztérium, 1992), 281–81. Cf. Debreczeni, *A miniszterelnök*, 225.
[38] Sándor Révész, *Antall József távolról* [József Antall from a distance] (Budapest: Sík, 1995), 104–6.

neighboring countries. More recently the radical right in Hungary have begun to talk about the border issue, thus enabling the nationalists among our neighbors to cry wolf. The price is being paid by Hungarians living beyond the border. Irresponsible talk should be rejected by all responsible people in Hungary.

Informed observers knew (or later discovered) that Antall and his government sought to redress the legitimate grievances of the largest national minority in Europe[39] through solutions in line with international law and European practice. The Hungarian government, in accordance with the declared principles of the international community, saw the full guarantee of minority rights as the remedy for all ethnic conflicts. At that time, we believed in the importance of international recommendations and had great faith in the standards and legal mechanisms of the Council of Europe. It only took a few months to wake up.

The personnel

A good staff is essential to achieve policy goals. Foreign policy is conducted by a specialized apparatus of diplomats, but the goals and direction are set by the political leadership. In the communist era, Hungarian foreign policy, or rather just diplomacy, was directed by the Party Central Office, with the minister being supervised by the head of the Foreign Policy Department of the MSZMP Central Committee, while ultimate control rested in Moscow. The great successes of Hungarian foreign policy in 1989 would not have taken place without Soviet leader Gorbachev's[40] approval. With the change of regime, with Prime Minister Antall, Hungarian foreign policy came into very capable hands; his knowledge, intuition and active involvement brought real and lasting results. It is often said, as praise or accusation, that the Antall government's foreign policy was personally guided by the prime minister, that the ministers, advisers and the specialized apparatus merely carried out the prime minister's—often improvised—ideas. The truth is that József Antall worked with incredible assiduousness, and, in addition to his domestic responsibilities, he paid very close attention to foreign policy. However, as far as actual policy and tasks were concerned, we, his collaborators, did not need any direct guidance or instructions, as we had learned much from him and shared his ideas. He did not

---

[39] Technically the largest national minority in Europe are the Russians of Ukraine. But it is more exact to call them only Russian speakers, since most of them do not have a strong Russian identity, as shown also in the loyalty many show towards Ukraine in the war against Russian aggression taking place at the time of this writing.

[40] Mikhail Sergeyevich Gorbachev (1931–2022): Soviet politician, the eighth and final leader of the Soviet Union from 1985 to the country's dissolution in 1991.

interfere in day-to-day operational matters. Like all his ministers, I ran my portfolio in a sovereign manner, enjoyed the full confidence of the head of government, and did not need daily consultations. There was a conscious, though unwritten division of labor between us: at the most important international events and with our most important partners, the prime minister naturally represented the country, while I paid more attention to "the new Europe," the neighborhood and to minority rights. I accompanied him on his foreign trips only when the importance of the matter or the nature of the event required it as a matter of protocol. On those occasions I could discuss current affairs and longer-term tasks with him and his colleagues more thoroughly. At home, for urgent cases, there was an internal phone line; usually it was he who called me, knowing that I would use his time only for the most urgent cases. These conversations, mostly late at night, were mainly of an informative and analytical nature, decisions were not taken then. Later on, due to his illness, it became increasingly up to me to appear abroad. It was his wish that I carry on his foreign policy after his death, which is why in 1994 I chose to be a member of Parliament, and I have ever since tried to preserve his principles and represent his aims in all areas.

Antall needed a trusted direct collaborator with international experience. Gyula Kodolányi,[41] a writer and poet with an excellent knowledge of Anglo-American politics as well as European culture, and a prominent member of the intellectual opposition to communism, proved to be an ideal assistant as chief foreign policy adviser. He prepared briefs for negotiations and meetings, often relieving the head of government from having to deal with less important matters. He also received politicians, public figures and foreign businessmen on Antall's behalf. Sometimes he acted as a special envoy of the prime minister.

For my political deputy ("state secretary"), I chose—from among several possible candidates—Tamás Katona,[42] a member of the MDF parliamentary party who was well known as an editor of historical publications. Since I was not an MP, he was my main contact with Parliament, often replacing me on the government bench. He was a highly educated man, a colorful personality and an anti-communist with a background similar to Antall's. Born in the same year as the prime minister, he had the reputation of having strong patriotic sentiments. I regret that, when domestic political issues led to sharp attacks on me, his loyalty wavered. Building on his

---

[41] For Kodolányi, see chapter 1, note 48 in this volume.
[42] Tamás Katona (1932–2013): Hungarian historian turned politician, state secretary for foreign affairs (1990–1992), mayor of District 1 of Budapest (1994–98), ambassador to Poland (2000–2002).

popularity with the media, he hoped to replace me as minister.[43] András Kelemen, a psychiatrist by training,[44] replaced him. I received Kelemen with confidence and friendship, but he proved to be a disappointing schemer. He was massively involved in a 1992 rebellion in the MDF against Antall and hoped to be foreign minister.[45] For the post of administrative state secretary I chose Ferenc Somogyi, a professional diplomat, who was a fair partner in my taking over the ministry in Spring 1990, and who knew both the office and the apparatus extremely well. After a year and a half, however, he resigned because of political differences regarding my personnel policy. His replacement, János Martonyi,[46] was a great asset: his erudition, expertise, language skills, work ethic and willingness to compromise were already widely recognized. His later work as foreign minister earned him and his country worldwide respect.

In my work it was essential to rely on a well-qualified and loyal group of civil servants. Between the two world wars, Hungarian diplomacy was served by a highly educated, cultured, patriotic team, fluent in many languages.[47] Following the communist takeover in 1948, all the old diplomats were dismissed and replaced with a batch of dedicated communists, most of whom lacked the basic skills necessary for diplomatic work. Only slowly, from the 1960s, did the Hungarian diplomatic service start to acquire the necessary qualifications and expertise. Even having a distant relative living in the West disqualified an applicant from serving in the Foreign Ministry. Until the change of regime, that applied even to typists and secretaries. The secret services (including foreign ones, presumably mainly Soviet) penetrated the whole foreign ministry; everyone was afraid of everyone. To serve in Western countries was a privilege, but it required conforming to very strict loyalty

---

[43] There is a telling interview with him in the December 16, 1993, issue of *Magyar Narancs*. Tamás, this highly popular personality, never argued with me directly, personally, never expressed a different opinion, never criticized my work to me openly. He only did so indirectly, to the media. Unfortunately, he can no longer reflect on my words.

[44] András Kelemen (1940–): Hungarian psychiatrist turned politician in MDF, later in Fidesz, MP (1990–2010).

[45] In August 1992, István Csurka (1934–2012), a Hungarian playwright turned radical politician, published a pamphlet challenging the prime minister's moderate, pro-Western line.

[46] János Martonyi (1944–): Hungarian lawyer, university professor and politician, Minister for Foreign Affairs (1998–2002, 2010–14). He had a crucial role in Hungary's entrance into the European Union.

[47] Pál Pritz, *Iratok a magyar külügyi szolgálat történetéhez 1918–1945* [Papers relating to the history of Hungary's foreign service] (Budapest: Akadémiai Kiadó. 1994); Pritz, *Magyar diplomácia a két háború között (Tanulmányok)* [Hungary's diplomacy between the two wars. Studies] (Budapest: Magyar Történelmi Társulat, 1995). The memoirs of the politicians of the period that were published in Hungary after 1990 (György Barcza, István Kertész, Aladár Szegedy-Maszák, Domokos Szent-Iványi, Elemér Újpétery, etc.) also attest to this.

(reliability) criteria. Nevertheless, there were "defections," the most famous being the case of János Radványi, the head of the mission in Washington, in 1968.[48]

The cautious internal liberalization in Hungary was tolerated at the price of loyalty to Moscow in foreign policy, like participating in the invasion of Czechoslovakia in 1968, or following the order not to attend the 1984 Olympic Games in Los Angeles. It was only around 1988 that I sensed a very visible change in the policy and behavior of the Foreign Ministry. It appeared to be a proponent of political reform and took the initiative in spectacular moves such as restoring diplomatic relations with Israel and recognizing South Korea as well as South Africa. Outreach to the new parties also began; I, as the head of the MDF foreign affairs committee, received invitation to events, and also discreet curtesy calls. After the elections, in the run-up to the handover, I gained a good impression of the professional work going on in the ministry and of the people I came into contact with. Therefore, I did not feel the need for a "spring-cleaning," only to get rid of the hard-liner communists and to bring in new people with good qualities. I offered a clean slate to the inherited foreign affairs apparatus, while the compromised intelligence agents, the alcoholics, the untalented, and the philistines were to go. (The old foreign ministry had plenty of them.)

Pursuing a Western orientation, I wanted diplomats who knew the countries and their culture inside out and who had always been staunch supporters of democracy. That is why it was a necessary step, and one that was welcomed by all our Western partners, to make a major overhaul of the Foreign Ministry apparatus after I took office. I was careful not to send diplomats to NATO countries who had been compromised under the old system by working against them. I recruited mainly people who were experts in a particular language, culture or country, most of whom had previously been academics. Hungary's new ambassadors to London, Paris, Rome, Vienna, Berne, Warsaw, Prague, Helsinki, Stockholm, Tokyo, Montevideo, Brazil, and Canberra were all such. Similar people filled a few lower ranking posts in Washington, Bonn, Bucharest, and Paris. The "newcomers" came under a lot of undeserved attacks by the anti-government Hungarian press, and some of the old guard considered them dilettanti, but their education, work ethic and not least their manners won them respect, and in the eyes of the world outside Hungary they also personally signaled and authenticated the change of regime. They also had the advantage of being well acquainted with the situation of the Hungarian minority in the neighboring countries and paid particular attention to this in their daily work.

---

[48] For Radványi, see chapter 1, note 94 in this volume.

I received much criticism for my personnel policy from two sides. On the one hand that the Antall government failed to carry out the promised "spring-cleaning," and the removal of the "cadres" of the communist regime from political and economic life and from the civil service. On the other hand, between 1990 and 1994, the opposition, and the press close to it, constantly accused the government, and in particular the head of the Foreign Ministry, of filling the service with MDF buffs. After 1990, application to work in the ministry was open. I introduced an entrance examination, and even for the administrative staff, such as secretaries, cooks or drivers, I required at least a basic knowledge of the language of the country they served in. By 1994, I estimate that a good third of the total staff had entered the service after 1990. I think that was an optimal proportion. The majority of the new recruits were not MDF members, and I even asked the leadership of the SzDSz and Fidesz to recommend new people for the diplomatic apparatus. Only the leading opposition party took up the offer—to a modest extent. Agreeing with Antall, my aim was to create a politically neutral foreign service, dedicated to serving the national interest.

We also had a hitherto untapped resource: the Hungarians living in the West. They had fled, primarily for political reasons, to escape the dictatorship, and now they were happy to put their talents, experience and contacts at the disposal of the motherland, which had become free. Only a few such were considered for ambassadorial posts because their advanced age, or insufficient understanding of Hungary due to their long period of absence could prove problematic. That was unfortunately the case with Peter Zwack,[49] who was appointed to Washington but proved unsuitable and had to be recalled after a few months. But since after the Jews, Poles and Armenians, the Hungarian diaspora was the most widespread in the world, we had thousands of voluntary representatives. From among them I was pleased to enroll in the diplomatic service Pál Tar,[50] János Perényi,[51] István Siklós,[52] and Lóránt Czigány.[53] Former Hungarian diplomat Ödön Gáspár[54] set up a "foreign

---

[49] Peter Zwack (1927–2012): Hungarian businessman and politician, owner of the internationally known liqueur company Zwack, which produces Unicum. Ambassador to the United States (1990–91).

[50] Pál Tar (1931–): Hungarian born French businessman (escaped from Hungary in 1957), Hungary's ambassador to the United States (1991–94), and to the Holy See (1999–2002).

[51] János Perényi (1949–): Hungarian diplomat, ambassador to the Council of Europe (1992–96), to Austria (2014–18).

[52] István Siklós (1931–1991): Hungarian poet and orientalist; head of the Hungarian section of the BBC (1980–89).

[53] Lóránt Czigány (1935–2008): Hungarian literary historian, founder of the Szepsi Csombor Circle of Hungarians in exile in the U.K.

[54] Ödön Gáspár (1915–2001): Hungarian diplomat, escaped after the communist takeover and lived in Uruguay.

affairs advisory service" for me, based on prominent Hungarians living in the West. Its members were, among others, János (John) Lukacs, Andor Sziklay, Gábor Szent-Iványi, Ede Chászár, Béla Lipták, József Takács (all from the United States), Antal Czettler and Szabolcs Vajay (Switzerland), Kristóf Kállay (Italy), Domokos Gyallay-Pap (Canada), and Vilmos Harrach and Gedeon Fáy (Germany). It also had members who lived in Hungary, such as Imre Del Medico, Tibor Forrai and Béla Végh. They provided many useful ideas and suggestions through correspondence and two conferences.[55] In September 1990, I set up a parallel foreign policy advisory board in Hungary composed of experts in foreign and economic policy (professors Tibor Palánkai and László Csaba, law professor László Valki), eminent historians (István Diószegi, Péter Hanák), an expert on Central Europe Gy. Csaba Kiss, another on national minorities, István Zalatnay, and also Miklós Vásárhelyi MP from the Free Democrats. I also restored the Honorary Consular Service (abolished under the communist regime) from among successful Hungarians living abroad and foreigners who knew and liked Hungary. I came to appreciate the selflessness, energy and generosity of its recruited members, who represented Hungary's interests, defended the interests of its citizens, and fostered economic relations in places far from professional diplomatic representation or where there were significant Hungarian colonies. Sándor Tar (Miami), Ilona Szablya (Seattle), István Gergácz (New Orleans), Jenő Megyesy (Denver), and János Fenjves (Caracas) all became my personal friends. Hungarians in the West have always been extremely sensitive to the situation of the Hungarians minorities of the Carpathian Basin; I could count on their activities in this matter in particular. If the regime change had come sooner, many more would have been involved in helping their homeland.[56]

In order to provide a theoretical foundation and practical support for our foreign policy, I decided to supplement and strengthen the existing Institute of Foreign Affairs and the Institute of Hungarian Studies at the Széchényi Library with a Central European section, following the example of prestigious foreign academic institutions. This was the Dunatáj (Danube region) Institute directed by Gusztáv Molnár,[57] who had escaped to Hungary from political persecution in Romania in 1988. The Dunatáj team was attached to the new Institute on Central Europe under the direction of Csaba Gy. Kiss. These scholarly institutes came under

---

[55] The documents of that body fill two bulky folders, a testimony of the patriotism and high quality of those people, by 2023 all sadly deceased.
[56] I recognized the contribution of the Hungarian emigration to the cause of Hungary in several speeches and addresses, as well as in the daily *Új Magyarország*, August 18, 1991, 5.
[57] Gusztáv Molnár (1948–): Hungarian political scientist, senior researcher at the László Teleki Institute (1991–2003), since 2006 professor at the Partium Christian University in Oradea/Nagyvárad.

the management of a foundation named after László Teleki,[58] established in 1991 by the government, with a board of trustees covering a broad political spectrum. (It was headed by Domokos Kosáry, president of the Hungarian Academy of Sciences, and included Sándor Csoóri, the popular poet.) I chose Teleki's name because he had had the courage to express his opinion that the only way to preserve the historic country was to cooperate with its neighbors. As director of the foundation, my former student László Diószegi,[59] did an excellent job.

For the work within the ministry, I found excellent colleagues, some from the old guard, some from the academic world, and also a few of my former students. The post of Head of Cabinet is the most trusted position; the always exhausting work can multiply the minister's effectiveness. I owe a lot to the people who filled it, including my former student Kristóf Forrai,[60] who was replaced by my former fellow-student at the English Department of Eötvös Loránd University, Emőke Sillár,[61] who successfully tamed the old guard with her personality and manners. As the elections approached, amidst the escalating political conflicts, her post was taken over by Ferenc Oberfrank,[62] whose youthful vigor was matched by his ingenuity and indefatigability. The deputy who served them both, the versatile and precise Kati Szalai, worked throughout the cycle. My former university student Julia Kircsi[63] was my personal secretary, and her intelligence, work ethic, appearance and manners won her acclaim from a wide range of our contacts. I am grateful to all of them for their dedicated work. The other "new" diplomats, mainly having degrees in the humanities, brought a new style and work ethic to the Ministry. Their results refuted the charge of dilettantism voiced by the press and some colleagues. The same could be said of the "new" ambassadors and first officers, whose names are to be found in the Hungarian edition of this book.[64] They possessed not only an outstanding knowledge of the language and culture of the country in question but also, they were

---

[58] László Teleki (1811–1861): Hungarian politician, the envoy of the War of Independence (1848/49) to France, returned from exile to fight for the complete restoration of the Laws of 1848.

[59] László Diószegi (1957–): Hungarian historian, expert in folk dance. Director of the László Teleki Foundation (1991–2006) and, since 2007, of its successor foundation, engaged in restoring old churches and castles in the entire Carpathian Basin.

[60] Kristóf Forrai (1956–): Hungarian diplomat, Ambassador to the Czech Republic (2000–2004), to Finland (2010–14), to Estonia (2019–22). Director of the Visegrád Fund (2006–19).

[61] Emőke Sillár (née Szíjj) (1941–): teacher of English and Russian, and diplomat. Ambassador to the Philippines (1993–94), Consul-General in Cape Town (1997–2000).

[62] Ferenc Oberfrank (1960–): D. Med, researcher at the Institute of Experimental Medicine, Hungarian Academy of Sciences.

[63] Júlia Kircsi (1967–): foreign policy expert, private secretary to the minister, 1990–94.

[64] Géza Jeszenszky, *Kísérlet a trianoni trauma orvoslására: Magyarország szomszédsági politikája a rendszerváltozás éveiben* [An attempt to heal the Trianon trauma: Hungary's neighborhood policy in the years of regime change], 2nd ed. (Budapest: Osiris, 2023), 75–77.

dedicated to the cause of the Hungarian minorities and paid much attention to the expatriate Hungarian communities at their stations, helping them in many ways.

The majority of the old guard earned my trust and proved themselves in high positions. Among the many I should mention, first and foremost is my press officer, János Herman, who carried out his difficult task with great professionalism, composure and an exemplary work ethic. Having gained the confidence of József Antall, too, he became the government's foreign policy spokesman as a deputy state secretary. Later he had a most distinguished career.[65] Almost all the diplomats dealing with the neighboring countries were "old hands" (as there were hardly any candidates for such posts from outside the ministry). Most of them did an excellent job, and the newcomer Béla Borsi-Kálmán[66] was outstanding.[67]

Conference of the Heads of Missions, July 25–26, 1990

Shortly after taking office, I convened the senior diplomats and made it clear that: "Our ambition is to create a unified Hungarian foreign service apparatus, which is not divided by who studied where, who was in which party, or when they entered the foreign service."[68] The regular summer conference was a good opportunity to discuss the details of the government's foreign policy program, and how to put it into practice. Prime Minister Antall cooled rumors of the government's perceived weakness and imminent fall, declaring that his was not a transitionary government. He stressed that foreign policy is "a national task that transcends parties," the direction of which—having regained sovereignty—"will be determined by a government responsible to the National Assembly, without external instructions or influences." In outlining our attitudes and aspirations towards the various great powers, Antall made a special point of the Soviet relationship. In the wake of the end of subordination, we must "put this on a completely new basis," supporting Gorbachev's line. Diplomats trained in the Soviet Union or who had spent extended periods of time there, would not be viewed with suspicion, since they were the ones who had the best knowledge of "the negative phenomena, the internal working system of a one-party dictatorship," but we would not tolerate any conduct that serves foreign

---

[65] János Herman (1952–): Hungarian diplomat, Ambassador to Greece and Cyprus (1994–98), permanent state secretary of the Ministry for Foreign Affairs of Hungary (1998–2001), ambassador to NATO (2001–2005), deputy political director at the European Commission (2007–2009), ambassador of the EU to Norway (2009–13), and to Georgia (2014–18).
[66] Béla Borsi-Kálmán (1948–): Hungarian historian, translator, diplomat in Bucharest (1990–95) and in Paris (1999–2003, 2011–15), doctor of the Hungarian Academy of Sciences.
[67] For others, see Jeszenszky, *Kísérlet a trianoni trauma orvoslására*, 78.
[68] Records of the conference of ambassadors, 1990, 91. Among my papers.

interests. Antall reiterated that the Central European countries were of the utmost importance to Hungary and stressed that he considered Poland a priority partner. Finally, he expressed his expectation that Hungarian diplomacy should be united, with no distinction between old and new diplomats and said that all evaluations and appointments would be based on competence and quality.[69]

Having reviewed the major changes and the international context, in my presentation (which I had previously distributed in writing to the participants), I spoke about the need for consensus in foreign policy and how I intended to achieve that. I stated that our goal was to become a regional center, and said that this would require domestic political stability, economic and legal conditions attractive to foreign capital, and serious investments in infrastructure. For this statement, the Antall government later came under much domestic political attack. On the issue of the Hungarians living beyond the borders, I said that the drafting of a European Minority Charter was important. Taking our neighbors in turn, I warned them that for Austria, Hungary is no longer the single partner from the eastern bloc, that processes in the Soviet Union could be dangerous for us, and that Czechoslovakia insists on finishing and operating the power plant on the Danube, while anti-Hungarian sentiment is growing in Slovakia. In the case of Romania, I spoke of the stalling of democratization, and I did not rule out a further deterioration in our relations because of growing intolerance towards Hungarians there. With Yugoslavia, I saw an opportunity to expand our relations primarily at the level of the republics, as the country seems to be moving towards a looser confederative system. I explained that the national interest guiding our foreign policy was not the same as national selfishness, and that we were trying to pursue our national interests in harmony with the interests of the whole of Europe. Conflicts over the minorities could also be resolved and mitigated within a European framework, and we could build our security, too, on that.[70]

In response to questions, I confirmed that the Hungarian government leaves it up to the Hungarian communities beyond the borders and their elected representatives to decide what they consider necessary to secure their future, and that the issue of borders can be resolved by their diminishing significance and eventual disappearance. I pointed out that our neighbors, primarily Romania, knew fully well that Hungary did not threaten their territorial integrity and security, but they were trying to postpone the fulfilment of the legitimate demands of the Hungarian minorities by using the bogeyman of Hungarian irredentism and potential armed

---

[69] Records of the conference of ambassadors, 1990, 16–18, 23–24.
[70] Records of the conference of ambassadors, 1990, 59–64, 72–81.

conflicts, thus disinforming foreign countries. Finally, I contrasted the false, misleading propaganda with credible information and the presentation of our cultural values abroad.[71]

The change of regime brought radical changes in the internal life of the Ministry of Foreign Affairs, both in organization and spirit. The ideological distinction between "capitalist" and "socialist" countries was abolished. The Hungarian communities of the Carpathian Basin were treated with a radically new perspective, and the Hungarian diaspora in the West, which had been regarded as enemies and suspicious emigrants during the communist era, was welcome to contribute significantly to the political and economic goals of the new Hungary on the basis of their emotional and national commitment. The turnaround brought about a major change in the tasks and activities of foreign missions.

---

[71] Records of the conference of ambassadors, 1990, 89–95.

Chapter 3

The First Steps
The International Reception

On the whole, the new Hungary enjoyed considerably sympathy abroad. Forgetting that, in recent years, it had been a recurring theme that the outside world, specifically the Western powers, always let Hungary down, allowed its struggles for freedom to fail, and in some cases even helping the oppressors. In particular, the West was to blame for the Trianon verdict, the mutilation of the historic kingdom, and that drove the country first into Hitler's arms, only to be handed over to Stalin. The conclusion to be drawn is that the Hungarians are the stepchildren of the West, their relation to the *Occidens* is one of unrequited love. The peace treaties of 1920 and 1947 are cited as proof, but the trump date is 1956, the alleged betrayal of the Uprising. Mária Schmidt, director general of the Budapest House of Terror museum documenting the terror of the right and the left, exercises strong ideological influence on the Orbán government, and she has repeatedly denounced the failure of the Western democracies to provide political and military help to the freedom fighters. Several journalists follow her entirely erroneous line. It is justified to criticize the democracies for their behavior in the autumn of 1956, but only the Soviet Union can be condemned for the brutal repression of Hungary. Recently, political leaders tended to reinforce the notion that Hungary had been regularly let down, even betrayed.[1]

It is a completely unfounded notion that the Hungarians have always been left standing alone; and, for some irrational reason, the whole world tends to be

---

[1] Prime Minister Orbán said at Zalaegerszeg, October 23, 2022: "If the West had not betrayed us, for the second time after 1945, we could have succeeded." "Orbán Viktor: a Nyugat másodszor árult el bennünket 1956-ban," *Euronews*, October 12, 2022, https://hu.euronews.com/2022/10/23/orban-viktor-a-nyugat-masodszor-arult-el-bennunket-1956-ban. In the same vein László Kövér, speaker of the National Assembly said: "The political elite of the West has always failed us, looted us if possible, and tried to subjugate and humiliate us quite a few times, and if it was in its interest, pushed us into the clutches of the despised 'barbarian' east." "Kövér László: Magyarország a normalitás utolsó menedéke," *Mandiner.hu*, October 14, 2022, https://mandiner.hu/belfold/2022/10/belfold-kover-laszlo-lampas-interju-magyarorszag-normalitas-europa-veszedelem-ukrajna-haboru. The pro-government media immediately echoed that. E.g., László Petrin, "A Janus-arcú Nyugat" [The Janus-faced West], *Magyar Hírlap*, October 24, 2022, https://www.magyarhirlap.hu/velemeny/20221023-a-janus-arcu-nyugat.

hostile to Hungary, while its neighbors are liked and supported. Self-pitying beliefs are extremely harmful; in fact, the image, the perception of the Hungarians has often fluctuated between the extremes of strong sympathy and antipathy,[2] and usually the perception is that they themselves are to blame for that. The decisions that affected Hungary were most often the result of the role the country played in international politics, irrespective of whether it was the result of free choice or was imposed upon the country. Few foreign observers note that in the Second World War Hungary was the "unwilling" rather than the "last satellite" of Nazi Germany.[3] Notwithstanding that, Hungary's international image, as a result of is role in that war, was for a long time extremely poor, but the 1956 revolution reversed that. Similar sympathy emerged in 1989 following the peaceful regime change in Hungary and the chain reaction of its international repercussions. In 1990 and the following years, I personally experienced the sincere sympathy of Western democracies towards Hungary. Of particular importance was Germany's enthusiasm expressed as a reward for Hungary having allowed the East Germans to flee west, thanks to the Pan-European Picnic of August 19, 1989, and opening the border to Austria that September. The aftermath, the fall of the Berlin Wall was the consequence.

I think Hungary really did deserve gratitude for its role in the reunification of Germany. At the same time, I already observed in early 1990 (from the world press as well as from political analyses and personal conversations) that when the West's enthusiasm surrounding the collapse of the European communist system subsided, fears also emerged: instead of Fukuyama's vision of "the end of history,"[4] in the countries freed from communist rule their frozen history would melt, and serious ethnic and national tensions might resurface, including, perhaps, the national conflicts and territorial disputes of the years between the two world wars. The other fear was that a unified Germany might upset the balance of power in Europe, given its size and economic power, and it might even endeavor to recreate its former economic and political sphere of interest in the neighborhoods to

---

[2] Jeszenszky, *Lost Prestige*, esp. chapters 1 and 5.

[3] Based primarily on John Flournoy Montgomery, *Hungary: The Unwilling Satellite* (New York: Devin-Adair Co., 1947); Tibor Frank, ed., *Discussing Hitler: Advisers of U.S. Diplomacy in Central Europe, 1934–1941* (Budapest and New York: Central European University Press, 2003) is the best proof of that. Documentary evidence is in György Ránki, ed. *Hitler 68 tárgyalása keleteurópai államférfiakkal 1939–1944* [Hitler's sixty-eight negotiations with East European statesmen, 1939–1944] (Budapest: Magvető, 1983). Out of many memoirs, that of the contemporary player, Prime Minister Miklós Kállay (1954) is most relevant to the issue.

[4] Francis Fukuyama, "The End of History?" *The National Interest*, 16 (Summer 1989), had a strong impact in Hungary, too. The changes in the former Soviet bloc book seemed to justify the book titled *The End of History and the Last Man* (1992).

its east. Hungary, by its very history, has attracted considerable attention in the context of both these fears. The electoral victory of centrist/center-right political forces in 1990 and the—unfounded but by some strongly propagated—bugbear of Hungarian nationalism somewhat undermined the very favorable perception of the country.[5] Nevertheless, Antall and his government rightly felt that their actions and policies would be able to allay concerns and draw on the broad sympathy for Hungary still existing in world public opinion.

The independence and sovereignty of the states that had been subordinated to the Soviet Union was formally restored only after the dissolution of the Warsaw Pact and the departure of the Soviet occupation forces, but in practice the states were already free in their foreign policy from 1990. This meant a radical change in Hungary's neighborhood relations. Instead of the expected policy of rivalry, mutual grievances and territorial disputes that characterized the post-First World War era, the Hungarian government deliberately embarked on a path of good neighborliness and cooperation. With the addition that this must include fair treatment for the Hungarian (and other) national minorities. Our hopes in the latter respect had been confirmed by the prevailing international atmosphere, and in particular by the Conference on Security and Cooperation in Europe (CSCE) born in Helsinki in 1975.

My first trip as minister took me to Vienna in May 1990, where, in addition to meeting the local Hungarians I took part in the *Quadrangolare* meeting of the deputy prime ministers. In 1988 it was almost a sensation when Italy, a NATO member state, Hungary, a Warsaw Pact member, neutral Austria and "non-aligned" Yugoslavia agreed on a broad regional cooperation, in which, in addition to the governments, parliaments and provinces and counties would participate independently. It was meant to re-establish traditional practical cooperation among the participating countries, to be a framework for exploring possibilities for economic, infrastructural and cultural projects. After the regime change, Czechoslovakia joined the group informally. For me, however, Austrian-Hungarian relations mattered more.

In the last two decades of the communist era, it was customary to talk about the exemplary relationship between Austria and Hungary, two neighboring countries with different socio-political systems. Now with this relationship being between two countries with the same political and economic system, it was bound to be even better. In the first half of the 1990s, this proved to be the case, and Austria was a strong supporter in our neighborly relations, a stable friend. The Austrian

---

[5] For me, the most alarming manifestation of this was the title of the editorial in the prestigious Swedish newspaper *Dagens Nyheter* on the victory of the MDF: "Hungary on the downhill slope."

vice-chancellor and foreign minister, Alois Mock, a respected leader of the Austrian People's Party,[6] received me most warmly. His great international experience and authority were matched by his sincere friendship and helpfulness towards Hungary. He strongly supported our European integration. Later, at our meeting in Budapest on April 5, 1991, he said that once we were members of the European Community, we would have a very close ally in Austria, a country "privileged by history." We shared a similar world view and political outlook, our parties were both members of the European Democratic Union (EDU) and the interests of our two countries converged—especially a little later, in the handling of the unfolding crisis in Yugoslavia. From the outset, there was a mutual personal sympathy between us, and I was most pleased to note his support for the rights of the national minorities. Our personal friendship continued after his term of office. It is a great pity, and I am deeply saddened that, having successfully brought Austria into the European Community, his worsening Parkinson's disease prevented this highly educated, multilingual, ethical statesman from playing a further significant role in his own country and in world politics. Antall's personal relationship with Mock was also excellent.

Mock and I agreed, among other things, to intensify preparations for the joint Vienna-Budapest world exhibition planned for 1995, to open new border crossings, to support German language education in Hungary and to jointly promote the codification of minority rights. The *Diplomatische Akademie Wien* (where I had lectured on a few occasions) offered scholarships to young Hungarian diplomats. The agreement on the opening of new border crossings was signed during Mock's official visit to Budapest on April 5–6, 1991. On August 24, 1991, at the initiative of the Austrian government, a memorial column was erected at the Nickelsdorf border crossing "to remind people of a devilish idea of a split Europe, that divided countries and peoples, the Iron Curtain."[7] I think I rightly felt then that never before in our history had we had such cordial and good relations with Austria. In addition, right from their first meeting in Sopron (June 18, 1990), the Hungarian prime minister also found a fair and good partner in the person of the Socialist chancellor Frank Vranitzky (1937–).

The outcome of the 1975 Helsinki Final Act was the Conference on Security and Cooperation in Europe composed of thirty-four European and North American countries. On June 5 and 6, 1990, they gathered in Copenhagen at foreign ministerial level for a meeting on the "human dimension." It was the first major

---

[6] Alois Mock (1934–2017): Austrian politician. As foreign minister, he was instrumental in taking Austria into the European Union.
[7] For my speech at the inauguration ceremony, see *Magyar Külpolitikai Évkönyv, 1991* [Hungarian Foreign Policy Yearbook, 1991] (Budapest: Magyar Külügyminisztérium, 1991), 271.

Chapter 3 – The First Steps

Figure 4. Dedication of the memorial to the Iron Curtain on the border with Austria, with FM Alois Mock and our wives, August 24, 1991, Nickelsdorf/Miklóshalma

international meeting since the historic changes ending the Cold War. It was appropriate that the issue of national minorities should be brought to the fore as human rights were being extended eastwards, given the high proportion of those minorities in the countries of the "new Europe." Although this issue could be seen as a potential source of tension, it was in fact more a test of the democratic system that was replacing dictatorship, both within the states and in relations between states. About a third of my own speech was devoted to the problem of minorities. As I summarized our position: "Our aim is to develop an international political and legal regulatory framework that includes practical ways of preserving the identity of national minorities, asserting their individual and collective rights, and establishing effective mechanisms for monitoring the implementation of enforcement."[8]

To my great delight, virtually all the speeches of the participating foreign ministers included the issue of minorities as something that should be settled in the spirit of democracy. The recommendations adopted in Copenhagen (based on a joint proposal by four Central European countries, Austria, Czechoslovakia [!], Yugoslavia, and Hungary, plus Italy) are the most far-reaching in an international

---

[8] *Magyar Külpolitikai Évkönyv, 1990*, 194–98. The English (original) text is among my papers.

document in this field to date. The most important points are: national minorities are entitled to special measures to ensure genuine equality; efforts for their assimilation are prohibited; they may establish their own educational and cultural institutions from public funds; they may exercise their rights individually *and in community with other members of their group.* (My italics.) Of particular importance is Article 35, which allows minorities to establish local or autonomous administrative institutions to promote their ethnic, cultural, linguistic and religious identity. These recommendations were of great significance for our neighborly relations. At that time, I had great hopes for their implementation, since it was agreed that a Conference of Experts, to be convened in Geneva in the middle of the following year, would be responsible for the practical implementation of the Copenhagen recommendations and their transformation into a binding convention.[9]

I met a number of prominent politicians during the usual bilateral meetings held at the conference. Everyone was curious about Hungary, a country at the forefront of change and the first post-communist country to hold free elections. U.S. secretary of state James Baker and French foreign minister Roland Dumas (1922–2024) impressed me for their warmth and expressed readiness to help the economic transition. The host, Danish foreign minister Uffe Ellemann-Jensen (1941–2022) (later president of the Liberal International), welcomed me as a personal friend. His Romanian colleague, Sergiu Celac, who was found too liberal for the Romanian leadership and was shortly replaced, expressed his admiration for Hungary's policies in effusive terms and asked for the text of the five-power proposal we submitted on the rights of national minorities. The only time I felt any tension was when talking with Soviet foreign minister Eduard Shevardnadze:[10] I was facing one of the leading figures of the great power that had kept us under its rule for forty-five years. Is it really ready to let us go now? I was sincere in saying that as a free country we could be a most reliable partner for our Soviet neighbor. My dilemma was: What should we do to make our freedom lasting? Should we hasten to sever the remaining legal ties to the Soviet Union (especially the Warsaw Pact), or rather to proceed with caution, so as not to offend the great power's reflexes? I was confident that in two days' time, when Antall was due to visit Moscow, he would find the optimal way forward.

The euphoric period of regime change ended with the free elections, but the spirit of 1989 lingered on in Central Europe for some time. In the later phase of

---

[9] "Document of the Copenhagen Meeting of the Conference on the Human Dimension of the CSCE," Copenhagen, June 29, 1990, https://www.osce.org/files/f/documents/9/c/14304.pdf.

[10] Eduard Shevardnadze (1928–2014): Georgian-born Soviet politician and diplomat, foreign minister of the Soviet Union (1985–1990). President of Georgia (1995–2003).

the communist countries, nationalism was replacing Leninist internationalism; now undisguised nationalism flared up in our neighbors. However, the memory of Central European solidarity and cooperation against the communist system offered hope in the short term, as did European integration in the longer term. Most promising was a joint proposal for the CSCE meeting on the protection of minorities drafted by the Quadrangolare, joined by Czechoslovakia. The organization's summit in Venice on August 1 formally accepted Czechoslovakia as a member, and thus the *Quadrangolare* became the *Pentagonale*. Attractive infrastructure plans were drawn up (led by Italy and its energetic, unconventional foreign minister Gianni De Michelis[11]), and meetings at various levels and on various topics undoubtedly deepened the multilateral network.

We Hungarians were not the only ones who considered it particularly important that our neighbors break with the policies pursued against their Hungarian citizens since Trianon. In August 1990, one of the best known American foreign policy think tanks, the Aspen Institute, organized a conference in Prague on the changes in Central and Eastern Europe. The main points of a proposal to be discussed reflected the concerns that accompanied the general happiness about the great transformation.[12] According to the conference report, the new Eastern Europe faced two paths: either a Western-style civil society would emerge, or the old ethnic-national divisions would resurface. There appeared to be a significant difference between Central Europe (Czechoslovakia, Poland, Hungary and the GDR) and Eastern Europe (Romania, Bulgaria, the Soviet Union, Yugoslavia and Albania). For the former group to succeed, regional cooperation, and overcoming nationalism and fear of foreign intervention were the most important steps. The only serious problem between Hungary and its neighbors was the potential tension over the treatment of the Hungarian minorities, warned Charles Gati,[13] a Hungarian-born American university professor, whom I had first met six months earlier at his American university. Madeleine Albright, then a professor at Georgetown University and later U.S. secretary of state, spoke about how important it was for America to support the eastern half of Europe politically and economically: it

---

[11] Gianni De Michelis (1940–2019): Italian politician of the Italian Socialist Party (PSI), served as minister in many Italian governments in the 1980s and early 1990s.

[12] The report of the U.S. Institute of Peace of May 1990 is among my papers.

[13] Charles Gati (1934–): Hungarian-born American political scientist. Held a number of prestigious academic positions at various U.S. universities, and was member of the U.S. State Department's policy planning staff from 1989 to 1994. Author of a large number of books, mainly on Eastern Europe and the Soviet Union. His *Failed Illusions: Moscow, Washington, Budapest, and the 1956 Hungarian Revolt* (Stanford, CA: Stanford University Press and Woodrow Wilson Center Press, 2006), also translated into Hungarian, is an outstanding analysis of the events in Hungary in 1956. Charles (or Karcsi in Hungarian) is also a personal friend.

should not be abandoned, as had happened with Hungary in 1956; helping those countries also strengthened the security of the United States. The U.S. should support regional cooperation, she continued, so that those countries could "leapfrog the dangerous era of nationalism" and thus avoid border conflicts—which were not unthinkable between Romania and Hungary. The Aspen Institute's background report criticized Romania for its disregard of human rights and Western norms, saw in Yugoslavia the threat of disintegration, and in Hungary it feared the impatience of its population and the strong German influence, but found it reassuring that "Antall is a first-rate politician."[14]

Thus, in the summer of 1990 experts in North America and Western Europe were aware of the problem of national minorities, especially the Hungarian minorities, and supported the codification and enforcement of minority rights in principle, while dissatisfaction with Romania's attitude in this respect was quite common. It was also clear that all governments rejected the idea of changing the borders, so the mere raising of the issue would have spoiled the strong trust and sympathy that had developed towards Hungary and would have jeopardized the struggle for the rights of Hungarian communities beyond Hungary's borders. All this led me to be moderately optimistic about the feasibility of our goals.

Touring the neighborhood: Novi Sad–Belgrade–Zagreb

After Vienna and Copenhagen, it was a priority for me to establish contacts with our neighbors, in line with the government program. Yugoslavia was at the top of the list.[15] On the basis of an earlier agreement, the opening of the Hungarian Consulate General in Zagreb was scheduled for the end of June. In addition to the eight hundred years of Hungarian-Croatian state union, there was already intensive Hungarian tourist traffic towards the Adriatic, and, more importantly, tens of thousands of Hungarians lived near the Hungarian border in southern Baranja. Being aware of Serbian susceptibilities, I decided to visit Belgrade before Zagreb, stopping en route at Novi Sad/Újvidék, which was then the center of the Hungarians living in Vojvodina (Vajdaság in Hungarian), the north-eastern province of Yugoslavia.

Since the 1970s, Belgrade has played an active role in the international regulation of national minority rights. This was understandable, since Yugoslavia was a federal union of six nations (Serbs, Croats, Slovenes, Macedonians, Montenegrins

---

[14] I have the summary of the talks in English and in Hungarian translation among my papers.
[15] For my detailed account of the first, most critical phase of Hungary's South Slav policy, see "Hungary and the Break-Up of Yugoslavia," Part 1, *Hungarian Review* 2, no. 2 (2011): 42–52; Part 2, *Hungarian Review* 2, no. 3 (2011): 65–78.

and Bosnians) and two "nationalities" (Albanians and Hungarians). Each of the member republics had a significant number of national minorities. Former head of state Josip Tito[16] and his circle knew that ethnic divisions could blow up the country, that's why they had pursued a policy of concessions. On the international scene, Tito was one of the founders of the group of "non-aligned" countries, and he enjoyed considerable prestige. Yugoslavia continued to support the guaranteeing of national minority rights after Tito's death in 1980.

The idea of uniting the Southern Slav peoples was first mooted in the early nineteenth century, first under Croatian leadership, but following Serbia's victories in the Balkan wars of 1912–13, and especially during the First World War, Serbia took the lead in that movement.[17] On October 31, 1918, as the Austro-Hungarian Monarchy collapsed, the Zagreb National Assembly severed the union with Hungary and embraced Yugoslavism. Standing on the basis of the principle of self-determination, Hungary's revolutionary Mihály Károlyi government accepted that. The Hungarian public acquiesced, and after the Trianon treaty, Hungarian revisionist aspirations did not extend to Croatia, except for claiming the so-called Baranja triangle, which then still had a Hungarian majority. The majority of the Catholic Croats and Slovenes quickly became disillusioned with the centralized common state ruled by the Orthodox Serbs. Following the bloody conflicts between the inhabitants of Yugoslavia during the Second World War, Tito recognized the partial autonomy of each of the southern Slavic nations and introduced a form of federalism within the dictatorship, even recognizing in principle the right to secede from the federation. After his death in 1980, the economic disputes between the member republics intensified, but in the summer of 1990, in the nations' capitals, including Budapest, no one expected the country to fall apart. Following the collapse of European communism in 1989 and the introduction or restoration of democracy, Yugoslavia also held multi-party elections. In Croatia and Slovenia, in the spring of 1990, parties with a fundamentally conservative-nationalist orientation won. They rejected communism and endorsed a program of greater autonomy but did not claim independence. Serbia had held elections the previous December, which were won by the Serbian Socialist Party, led by Slobodan Milošević.[18] His combination of communism with nationalism succeeded against the purely nationalist parties.

---

[16] Josip Broz Tito (1892–1980): Yugoslav leader of the anti-Nazi partisans, after the war the Communist head (dictator) of Yugoslavia.

[17] Ivo Banac, *The National Question in Yugoslavia: Origins, History, Politics* (Ithaca, NY: Cornell University Press, 1984). See also Viktor Meier, *Yugoslavia: A History of Its Demise,* transl. Sabrina Ramet (London and New York: Routledge, 1999).

[18] Slobodan Milošević (1941–2006): Serbian-Yugoslav communist politician, president of Serbia from 1989 to 1997, and president of the Federal Republic of Yugoslavia from 1997 until his overthrow in 2000.

I set out on June 21, 1990. Imre Szokai, Hungary's deputy state secretary for Central and Eastern Europe, accompanied me with a small team, and we all traveled by car. Stopping at Novi Sad/Újvidék I called upon the provincial government of Vojvodina and visited the Institute of Hungarian Studies, where I met András Ágoston, the president of the newly formed Hungarian party.[19] However, in the presence of our Serbian escorts, we had no opportunity to have a meaningful discussion. In Belgrade, I had a brief meeting with the federal prime minister, Ante Marković,[20] a Croat from Herzegovina who told me of his promising economic plans. Unexpectedly, I was also received by the country's strongman, Slobodan Milošević. I told him about my hope that our region would follow the example of Western Europe, where, following the Second World War, economic integration put an end to centuries of conflict between nations. I mentioned that my direct ancestors had lived in that multi-ethnic region that used to be the southern part of historic Hungary, and I felt strong sympathy for its progress. The post-First World War borders had broken up the area and cut roads and railways, and economic life had experienced a set-back. Now the times were suitable for the broken economic links to be restored. The Serbian president agreed, saying that he did not fear for Serbia's integrity as a result of growing relations between Hungary and the Hungarian minority in Serbia. We agreed to make the Serbian-Hungarian border "the most open border" in our region and to improve road and rail connections. Milošević expressed his conviction that discrimination against national minorities was unacceptable and said he was ready to listen to any complaints. However, he warned that if the Serbian opposition gains power, the situation of minorities could change for the worse. Later events proved him right.

My official host was Foreign Minister Budimir Lončar,[21] also a Croat and an experienced diplomat. He appeared to be committed to Yugoslav unity with Serbia as its dominant factor. I wondered whether this was his conviction or just an expression of opportunism. Lončar was rather unhappy that the end of the Cold War had reduced Yugoslavia's international influence, but he still considered the bloc of non-aligned states to be relevant. I was therefore surprised when, meeting him in Zagreb in May 2012, I discovered that he had become an adviser to then Croatian president Ivo Josipović.

Sentenced for war crimes, he died in a U.N. detention unit.

[19] András Ágoston (1944–): Hungarian politician in Serbia, founder of the Democratic Community of Vojvodina Hungarians (VMDK).

[20] Ante Marković (1924–2011): Yugoslav (Croatian) politician, the last prime minister of Yugoslavia from 1989 to 1991.

[21] Budimir Lončar (1924–2024): Croat-born Yugoslav communist diplomat, foreign minister of the Socialist Federal Republic of Yugoslavia, 1987–1991.

Chapter 3 – The First Steps

Figure 5. With Croatia's former FM Zdravko Mršić

From Yugoslavia, we flew to Zagreb from a military airfield on a government plane; my hosts obviously hoped to impress me with the strength of the Yugoslav air force. In Zagreb the atmosphere was distinctly different. The Croats were obviously proud that their independent national identity was now recognized, and they showed high hopes for the future. They all spoke of their desire for a close and good relationship with Hungary. I was welcomed by President Franjo Tuđman,[22] who had set as his goal the "restoration" of Croatian sovereignty within a confederative Yugoslavia. Prime Minister Stjepan Mesić (1934–) confirmed that and underlined the similarities in political philosophy between the Croatian Democratic Community and the MDF. Without any trappings of formality, I was introduced to several members of the government. Foreign Minister Zdravko Mršić,[23] a mathematician, had just returned from his exile in Britain. He took me to Zagreb's main square, once again named after Josip Jelačić,[24] whose statue was removed in 1947 and was now

---

[22] Franjo Tuđman (1922–1999): Croat politician, who led the country to independence from Yugoslavia in 1991 and was president until his death. Having joined Tito's partisans in 1941, in 1960 became one of the youngest generals of the Yugoslav army, but in 1972 was imprisoned as a Croatian nationalist. In 1989 founded the Croatian Democratic Union (HDZ), which won Croatia's first free parliamentary elections in 1990.

[23] Zdravko Mršić (1936–): Croatian politician, the first minister of foreign affairs, 1990–91.

[24] Josip Jelačić (1801–1859): Croat-born general in the Imperial Austrian Army. As Ban (Viceroy) of Croatia (1848–1859) in September 1848 he led an army composed of Croats to overthrow the legal Hungarian

being restored to its former place. He reassured me, however, that the sword of their national hero would no longer point towards Hungary but towards the neutral sea. The opening of the Hungarian Consulate General was attended by a large number of representatives of Croatian public life, as well as prominent cultural and political persons from Slovenia and from the Hungarian minority. The main topic of the official talks was the establishment of intensive transport and economic relations. It was agreed that a Hungarian-Croatian expert working group would be responsible for putting this plan into concrete terms.[25]

In 1990 few, if any, outside Yugoslavia expected the imminent break-up of the country, but among the Croats the aim was independence.[26] We saw that it was possible and justified to maintain relations with each of the member republics separately, alongside Belgrade. The strengthening of our relations was reflected in the official June 27 visit to Budapest of Serbian foreign minister Aleksandar Prlja, and the celebration on October 12–14, 1990, of the 300th anniversary of the settling in central Hungary of Serbs fleeing Turkish rule. Szentendre, twenty kilometers from Budapest, became the center of their religious life.

Géza Entz, head of the Secretariat of Hungarians Beyond Borders, wrote a report on his trip to Croatia in October 1990 which supported my own positive experiences in Croatia. He noted the willingness of the Croatian leadership to improve the situation of Hungarians living there and to support Hungarian organizations.[27] Three weeks later, on a visit to Slovenia, President Milan Kučan[28] told Entz that "Slovenia is striving for a confederation, but also sees separation as an alternative. The latter, because of the expected economic and political disadvantages, is a last resort."[29] On December 7, 1990, Ante Marković, the federal prime minister of Yugoslavia, paid a one-day working visit to Budapest. Prime Minister Antall assured his guest that our Western orientation did not mean neglecting our neighborhood relations. He commended the Marković government's achievements in transforming the economy and asked for their experiences to be shared. We saw in the person of Marković a guarantee for the rights of the Hungarian minority. I

---

government. He was defeated at the Battle of Pákozd. In Croatia he is looked upon as a patriot and in Hungary as the tool of Habsburg absolutism.

[25] This account of my visit is based on my personal memories and notes as well as my report presented to the Government. Cf. Sáringer, ed., *Iratok az Antall-kormány*, vol. 1: 477–83 (Doc. 106, June 27, 1990).

[26] Kodolányi meeting Mršić on September 15 at a conference on East-Central Europe in Bratislava/Pozsony. Kodolányi, *Antall Józseffel a világszínpadon*, 327.

[27] Report on the visit of the delegation of the Secretariat of Hungarians Beyond the Border to Croatia, October 24, 1990. Among my papers.

[28] Milan Kučan (1941–): Slovenian politician, President of Slovenia from 1991 to 2002.

[29] Telegram from our Consulate General in Zagreb, November 13, 1990, secret. Sáringer, *Iratok az Antall-kormány*, vol. 1: 498–99 (Doc. 112, November 13, 1990).

held separate talks with Deputy Foreign Minister Maksić in which I told him that we welcomed the decision on their structural changes to increase the competences of the individual republics, and that we hoped to maintain particularly close relations with the three republics bordering us.[30]

Opposing trends in Czech and Slovak relations[31]

In 1990 the impending break-up of Czechoslovakia was even less conceivable to the world—including Hungary—than that of Yugoslavia. We, of course, understood the Slovaks' desire to demonstrate their separate national identity, but we believed that Slovakia's autonomy, evident in the country's new name (Czech and Slovak Federal Republic), would satisfy the smaller partner. I also had (and still have) a personal interest in our good relations with our northern neighbor, since, as mentioned, from the thirteenth century to the end of the eighteenth century, my ancestors lived in what is now Slovakia, in Túróc county. The best-known person of my family is Johannes Jessenius, a seventeenth century physician who was rector of Charles University in Prague. He negotiated an alliance between Transylvania's Prince Gábor Bethlen and the Protestant Estates of Bohemia during the Thirty Years' War. After the defeat of the Bohemian uprising in the Battle of the White Mountain in 1621, Jessenius was executed (by quartering). His name is on the Martyrs' Memorial Plaque in Prague's Old Town. It is also worth noting that Hungarian public opinion in 1968 felt great sympathy for the reform attempts in Czechoslovakia, "the Prague Spring," which were crushed by the invading forces of the Warsaw Pact. More recently, in 1989, Hungarian society and its media actively contributed to the regime change in Prague and Bratislava, to the "Velvet Revolution."

On July 12, 1990, interim Hungarian president Árpád Göncz paid an official working visit to Prague and Bratislava. President Václav Havel[32] and the speaker of the Slovak Parliament, Frantisek Mikloško,[33] responded favorably to his extremely

---

[30] Report to the Government on the visit of Yugoslav Prime Minister A. Marković to Hungary on December 7, 1990. Sáringer, *Iratok az Antall-kormány*, vol. 1: 500–505 (Doc. 113, December 17, 1990).

[31] Two surveys on Slovak nationalism and the Hungarian minority: Zsuzsa Csergő, "Beyond Ethnic Division: Majority-Minority Debate About the Post-communist State in Romania and Slovakia," *East European Politics and Societies* 16, no. 1 (2002): 1–29; and István Kollai and Bence Bánki, "Populism in the Making: The Case of Slovakia," in *Economic Policies of Populist Leaders: A Central and Eastern European Perspective*, ed. István Benczes (London: Routledge, 2024), 125–47.

[32] Václav Havel (1936–2011): Czech statesman, playwright, former dissident, the last president of Czechoslovakia and the first president of the Czech Republic. His grandfather, Hugo Vavrečka, was Czechoslovakia's first envoy to Hungary in 1922–26.

[33] Frantisek Mikloško (1947–): Slovak politician, speaker of the Slovak National Council from 1990 to 1992.

Figure 6. Arriving in Prague, August 27, 1990

friendly overtures, but Alexander Dubček,[34] and even more so Slovak prime minister Vladimir Mečiar,[35] responded with unfounded accusations of Hungarian irredentism and alleged oppression of the Slovaks of Hungary. More favorable impressions were reported by my state secretary, Tamás Katona, following his visit to Bratislava on July 27.[36]

I arrived in Prague on August 27 on an official visit. The omens, as we have seen, were mixed. President Havel and his supporters, mainly Czechs, symbols of the fight against communism, were true liberals who took seriously the rights of minorities, including that of the Hungarians. The president personally supported the idea of establishing in Komarno/Komárom an institute of higher education with Hungarian as the language of instruction. He maintained close ties with the Independent Hungarian Initiative party, which participated in the autonomous government in Bratislava. Czech prime minister Petr Pithart[37] was ready to bypass

---

[34] Alexander Dubček (1921–1992): Slovak politician, *de facto* leader of Czechoslovakia during the "Prague Spring" from January 1968 to April 1969. Chairman of the Czechoslovak Federal Assembly from 1989 to 1992.
[35] Vladimir Mečiar (1942–): Slovak politician, three times prime minster between 1990 and 1998.
[36] Sáringer, *Iratok az Antall-kormány*, vol. 1: 403–10 (Doc. 87, July 30, 1990).
[37] Petr Pithart (1941–): Czech politician, prime minister of the Czech Republic (1990–1992), president of the Senate from 1996 to 1998 and again from 2000 to 2004.

the Slovaks in building close ties with Hungary and offered to mediate between Hungary and the Slovaks. The Slovak National Council (parliament), on the other hand, was ready to consider a proposal by the nationalist organization Matica Slovenská to declare Slovak the state language, with the aim of severely restricting, if not banning, the Hungarian community's right to use their language in public. The Matica Slovenská became an exponent of Slovak nationalism in a cultural guise, and it adopted a bill on July 21, 1990, which would have given local Slovaks the right of veto in all local matters in the settlements having a Hungarian majority and made Slovak the sole language of instruction. In a memorandum sent to the UN and the European Parliament, it categorically rejected the idea of a Hungarian university to be established in Komarno/Komárom.

On August 23, 1990, the *Národná Obrada*, the mouthpiece of the Slovak government, sent a petition to the UN Commission on Human Rights and the European Parliament, which claimed, on the basis of a persistent false notion, that Hungary had forcibly assimilated nearly half a million Slovaks since 1946. It argued that the Czechoslovak Resettlement Commission, which had prepared the population exchange of 1947, had (unilaterally) found that 473,552 Slovaks were living in Hungary at the time, a number that had fallen to 7,000 by 1980, and therefore it demanded international action against Hungary. This accusation, which was raised by many Slovaks against Hungary on several occasions, is easy to refute. The facts are that following the devastating wars fought against the Ottoman Empire, which left most of the Hungarian Plain depopulated, a large number of Slovaks migrated to those areas in the eighteenth century. On the territory left to Hungary in the Trianon treaty, according to the official (reliable) statistics, the number of these Slovak speakers was only 140,000. By 1930, their number had fallen to 105,000. After the war, the Czechoslovak government had wanted to expel all the national minorities: 3 million Germans and over 700,000 Hungarians. Under pressure from the victorious great powers, a Czechoslovak-Hungarian agreement on an exchange of population (on a voluntary basis) was initiated. About 70,000 Hungarian citizens opted for Czechoslovakia and settled in the farms and houses of the Hungarians expelled from Czechoslovakia. Many of the Slovaks who remained in Hungary feared a forcible resettlement and declared themselves Hungarian at the census.[38] Today, Hungary supports the language and culture of its indigenous

---

[38] On the 1946–47 population exchange, see Kálmán Janics, *Czechoslovak Policy and the Hungarian Minority, 1945–1948* (New York: Social Science Monographs, 1982), chapters 6–7. Cf. István Tóth, "Szlovákok a 20. századi Magyarországon" [Slovaks in twentieth century Hungary], *Sulinet.hu*, https://www.sulinet.hu/oroksegtar/data/magyarorszagi_nemzetisegek/szlovakok/fejezetek_a_mo_i_romanok_es_szlovakok_tort/pages/006_szlovakok.htm.

Slovak national minority in many ways, and according to the 2011 census they number 35,208, twice the number found ten years earlier.[39]

The "liberal nationalist" Prime Minister Mečiar told the Bratislava daily *Új Szó* (August 20, 1990) that nationalism in Slovakia was a response to nationalism in Hungary and that the issue of Hungarians in Slovakia was the sole responsibility of the Slovak government. Ján Čarnogursky, a Christian Democrat leader with a record of opposition to communism,[40] rigidly rejected the idea of collective minority rights.

My counterpart, Foreign Minister Jiří Dienstbier,[41] was an active participant in the events of 1968 as a journalist, after which he could make a living only by shoveling coal. After my graduation in 1959, I had worked as a manual laborer for two years, also for political reasons, and that added to the sympathy we felt for each other. We agreed that relations between our countries should be strengthened in all areas and that to this end a joint committee should be set up, with a subcommittee to discuss minority issues. As an outspoken liberal, Jiří accepted that national minorities have special rights and that it is desirable to codify these rights—on the basis of the recommendations adopted by the CSCE in Copenhagen. He was sympathetic to the establishment of a Hungarian consulate in Kosice/Kassa, and we also discussed a Slovak center to be set up in Békéscsaba, where most of the Slovaks of Hungary lived. When I raised the issue of the rehabilitation of János Esterházy,[42] Jiří asked for data and evidence.[43] He announced that the archives in Czechoslovakia would be opened to Hungarian researchers and that the government were also prepared to examine the so-called Beneš Decrees, issued after the war, that deprived Hungarians of all political rights.[44] On the issue of the proposed

---

[39] Központi Statisztikai Hivatal, *2011. évi népszámlálás 3. Országos adatok* [2011 Census 3. National data] (Budapest: KSH, 2013), http://www.ksh.hu/docs/hun/xftp/idoszaki/nepsz2011/nepsz_orsz_2011.pdf, p. 21, official data from the 2011 census. In line with the decrease in the overall population, in 2022 the Slovaks of Hungary numbered 30,000. Központi Statisztikai Hivatal, "Népszámlálás 2022: Végleges adatok," https://nepszamlalas2022.ksh.hu/eredmenyek/vegleges-adatok/kiadvany/.

[40] Ján Čarnogurský (1944–): Slovak politician, prime minister (1991–1992).

[41] Jiří Dienstbier (1937–2011): Czech journalist and politician, foreign minister of Czechoslovakia, 1989–1992.

[42] János Esterházy (1901–1957): political leader of the Hungarians of Czechoslovakia in the 1930s. When the Hungarian region of Czechoslovakia was ceded back to Hungary in 1938 (the first Vienna Award) he stayed with the remaining 80,000 Hungarians left in Slovakia. During the war he protested against the deportation of the Jews from Slovakia, nevertheless after the war he was sentenced to life imprisonment.

[43] A few months later, János Esterházy was nominated for the Order of Masaryk on the initiative of Hungarians in Slovakia, but he was removed from the list after Slovak protests, recalling that he had welcomed the first Vienna Award. Report of Consul General Jenő Boros, November 6, 1991, 5057/Je. Among my papers.

[44] On the so-called Benes Decrees and their relevance, see Balázs Tárnok, "Why Is Ethnic Discrimination Still Legal in Slovakia?" *Foreign Policy*, March 12, 2022, https://foreignpolicy.com/2022/03/12/slovakia-benes-decrees-ethnic-discrimination/.

Figure 7. With Czechoslovak FM Jiří Dienstbier, Prague, August 27, 1990

dam project on the Danube, we agreed to involve international experts to study the environmental impact. I also found Dienstbier's suggestion that we should try to resume our traditional export deliveries to the insolvent Soviet Union with international financing a very palatable idea.

Czech defense minister Luboš Dobrovsky and Deputy Prime Minister Jozef Mikloško (brother of František, who chaired the Slovak National Council) approached the problem of the Hungarian minority in a very constructive spirit, the latter going so far as to suggest that Slovaks in areas with a mixed population should also be familiar with the Hungarian language. My positive impressions were tempered by finding that the Czechs would not expose themselves regarding the interests of the Hungarian minority in Slovakia because of the increasing disputes over the structure of the common state, and it was clear that those Slovaks who oppose nationalist plans to curtail the rights of the Hungarians there were in a minority. Our joint press conference was dominated by the territorial issue, with the press primarily interested in whether Hungary would respect the Trianon Peace Treaty. Apparently, many people gave credence to Slovak propaganda that Hungary's strong support for minority rights threatened the territorial integrity of Czechoslovakia. Already we had come a long way from the fact that a few weeks earlier Czechoslovakia was one of the co-authors of the Copenhagen proposals calling for the codification of minority rights. In Prague I participated in the Aspen conference mentioned earlier. My speech there was still marked by optimism that in Central and Eastern Europe the tradition of solidarity and cooperation was stronger than that of conflict; the border disputes could be eliminated by European integration; and there was a chance that looking back at the twentieth century it would be seen as an unfortunate, tragic episode.[45]

Between August 30 and September 3—preceding my official talks in London—at Cambridge, I attended a conference of former fellows of the Wilson Center in Washington, DC.[46] The conference was titled "Ethnicity and Nationalism," and I gave one of the keynote presentations with the title "The Threat of Ethnic Conflict in Post-Communist East-Central Europe." The point I made was that, after the joy surrounding the unexpected collapse of the communist regimes had passed, there was renewed concern: wouldn't the national differences that had been suppressed under communism now come to the surface, causing new conflicts, even wars? Will not the people, hitherto confined by the Iron Curtain and living in poverty, move *en masse* towards the countries of freedom and prosperity? To avert the looming dangers, I considered it essential to recognize that most of Europe's states were not nationally homogeneous. This was not a danger in itself, but it became one when the majority nation seeks to eliminate minorities—by expelling them, by forcible or covert assimilation. The Second World War, the subsequent displacement of millions of people, and the accelerated industrialization and urbanization under communism had led to a significant decline in the number and proportion of minorities in the eastern half of Europe, while in the West, the recognition and even extension of minority rights had become common. I then outlined the national tensions in Central and Eastern Europe, including the situation of Hungarian minorities, and explained that, in my opinion, the test of democracy was not only multi-party elections, but also the treatment of the different minorities. I said, however, that the restoration of political freedom had given minorities the opportunity to organize themselves and to express their demands; now their cause was no longer a domestic matter, and the attention paid to them was no longer an unacceptable interference. I found it reassuring that there were many sober, enlightened, well-intentioned politicians on both the majority and minority sides. Besides, people today were primarily concerned about their economic situation, and improving it required multilateral peaceful cooperation. The alternative to border changes was the opening of borders, European integration. The countries that had freed themselves from communism wanted to join the club of European democracies, but to do so they

---

[45] The text of my contribution is among my papers.
[46] In the summer of 1985, I was a guest scholar at the Wilson Center, doing research on the policy of the United States in 1918 on the future of the Austro-Hungarian Monarchy.

must accept the rules of the club, including the rights of minorities. If the Western countries were to give the expected help in this and in expanding prosperity, the real dangers mentioned could be averted.[47]

In the optimistic mood of 1989–90, this program did not seem unrealistic. I am still of the opinion that if the West had pursued a more decisive policy on this issue, as Antall constantly urged in his negotiations and speeches,[48] the South Slav crisis could have ended much earlier, and national-ethnic differences would have calmed instead of intensified. Of course, with a more generous and far-sighted Western policy, the whole Central European transition would have been faster and less painful.

On September 16, 1990, the Christian Democratic parties of Central Europe held a one-day meeting in Bratislava, attended by all three parties of Hungary's governing coalition. Representing the MDF, I reiterated the importance of dispelling the fear that our countries' newly regained freedom was bound to lead to confrontation. The Bratislava Declaration ensuing from the meeting took a stand for the effective protection of national and religious minorities and said that the solutions seen in South Tyrol should be emulated. I recall that Slovak deputy prime minister Ján Čarnogurský said that the South Tyrol model could also be applied in Slovakia.[49] In the evening, at the dinner given by Hungary's consul general Jenő Boros, Čarnogurský proposed a Slovak-Hungarian reconciliation declaration in which Hungary would acknowledge a long list of "crimes" in return for a paragraph of regret over the measures taken against the Hungarians after 1945.

The next day, I first called on František Mikloško, the Christian Democrat president of the parliament, whose past as a member of the opposition was coupled with friendship for the Hungarians. To my surprise, he also said that Slovaks in southern Slovakia were being "Hungarianized," which is why a law protecting the Slovak language was needed—but it will not have an adverse effect on the Hungarians. (In fact, a significant number of Slovaks who had been voluntarily resettled from Hungary after 1945 to replace Hungarians who had been expelled to Hungary spoke Hungarian better than Slovak, keeping southern Slovakia mainly Hungarian-speaking, and that interfered with the plan to completely Slovakize it.) I also met Prime Minister Mečiar. He kept saying that Hungary and the irredentist mood there were an obstacle to improving relations, and that the issue of Hungarians in Slovakia was none of Hungary's business.[50] He could not have seriously believed

---

[47] I have the outline of my presentation among my papers, for an extract see *Népszabadság*, September 4, 1990.
[48] For Antall's foreign policy, see Jeszenszky, "József Antall and the World," esp. 27–31.
[49] Having retired from political life, Čarnogurský's Christian political philosophy moved towards the Christianity of the Russian Orthodox Church, which is a strong supporter of President Putin.
[50] Quoted in *Magyar Nemzet*, September 18, 1990.

that simply by increasing economic cooperation our relations would improve. The minister for foreign relations, Milan Kňažko,[51] who was a popular actor, was more encouraging and was focusing on practical issues. Having also met the leaders of all three Hungarian parties and of most Slovak parties, I concluded that there was little chance of achieving a fair minority policy in Slovakia, such as we felt was necessary.

My conclusion was confirmed by the attitude and thinking of the Czechoslovak ambassador to Budapest, Rudolf Chmel,[52] as revealed in his memoirs (also published in Hungarian[53]) and also by the reports from our consul general in Bratislava. The Hungarian-speaking literary historian-turned ambassador believed that the Antall government's advocacy of collective rights for the Hungarians of Slovakia in international forums was confrontational and interfered in the internal affairs of Czechoslovakia. He thought that alongside the MDF, the (in Chmel's words) "reformist national communists" such as Miklós Németh, Gyula Horn and Imre Pozsgay, were also nationalists, as they, too, regarded the Trianon treaty as unjust, and even the opposition SZDSZ and Fidesz parties did not reject this view. According to the ambassador, the new Hungarian government talked about positive discrimination towards the Slovaks in Hungary, but in reality, they continued the assimilationist policies of the communist regimes, while expected cultural support from abroad for the minorities in Hungary. According to him even "such a sincere friend of the Slovaks as the liberal Hungarian president, Árpád Göncz" denied that there was a Hungarian policy aimed at assimilating the minorities. Chmel also criticized the Hungarian government's refusal to condemn the Hungarian minority policy of the past, let alone to apologize for it. On top of all this, he reported to Prague that Hungary wanted to be some kind of regional superpower, which the opposition rightly criticized. Czechoslovakia's "Hungarophile" ambassador thought that fortunately, the outside world had grown tired of Hungarian concepts on minorities and had rejected them.[54]

Our consul-general in Bratislava was Jenő Boros. His reports revealed not only Chmel's bias against the MDF government and his hopes for the SZDSZ to come to power, but also his utter rejection of Hungarian policy aimed at securing the collective rights of Hungarians beyond the borders. He totally misinterpreted that policy and believed that the Slovaks of Hungary were victims of continuous forcible

---

[51] Milan Kňažko (1945–): Slovak actor and politician, foreign minister in 1992–1993.
[52] Rudolf Chmel (1939–): Slovak writer and politician, deputy prime minister of the Radičová government responsible for minorities, 2010–2012.
[53] Rudolf Chmel, *Nagykövet voltam Magyarországon* [I was ambassador to Hungary] (Pozsony: Kalligram, 1997).
[54] For Chmel's 60-page summary report covering the first half of 1991, see Consul-General Boros's letter to Jeszenszky, April 16, 1991. Among my papers.

assimilation. Boros rightly assumed that the reports submitted by the Czechoslovak Embassy in Budapest did not provide an authentic picture of Hungarian government policy and did not serve the cause of better bilateral relations.[55] Yet, based on some of our subsequent meetings and conversations, I believe that Chmel was simply unable to appreciate the Antall government's efforts because of his political sympathies for the Opposition, rather than due to nationalist prejudices. In his later writings he held both sides responsible for the inability to break the deadlock in the efforts for Slovak-Hungarian reconciliation.[56]

If in Czechoslovakia (relying mainly on the beneficial influence of President Havel) there seemed to be some chance of a European solution to the Hungarian question, the dialogue with Romania was indeed a dialogue of the deaf.

The toughest neighbor: Romania

In our neighborly relations we understandably paid special attention to Romania, to our bilateral relations, an issue which was followed intensively by the Hungarian public.[57] After Hungary, Romania had the largest number of Hungarians, and naturally Hungary was interested in the well-being not only of the Hungarians of Transylvania but also in the whole of Romania, as the two were inseparable. This was instinctively felt by the people of Hungary when, on Christmas 1989, the outpouring of sympathy and massive assistance was not limited to the Hungarian communities of Transylvania.

The March events in Târgu Mures/Marosvásárhely, which the Hungarians in Transylvania rightly call a pogrom, was a cold shower on our hopes. This was compounded by the fact that on May 12, 1990, the Romanian government issued Resolution 521 on the organization and functioning of the education system, which was a step backwards even from the education laws valid before the December turnaround. The RMDSZ announced its protest against this, as well as against the abuses in the compilation of the electoral rolls, the ongoing anti-Hungarian propaganda

---

[55] Jenő Boros to Jeszenszky, April 30, 1992. Among my papers.
[56] In his essay on reconciliation, he spoke of "the dialogue of the deaf," Rudolf Chmel, *Jelen és történelem—Az etnokráciától a demokráciáig és vissza* [The present and history—from ethnocracy to democracy and back] (Budapest: Kalligram, 2014), 57–70. On multiculturalism and the Visegrád idea, ibid., 462–88.
[57] A balanced presentation is Csergő, "Beyond Ethnic Division." A large number of articles were published on Romanian-Hungarian relations in the early 1990s in various Hungarian periodicals (*Kisebbségkutatás, Pro Minoritate, Magyar Kisebbség, Külügyi Szemle*). On the Romanian side, Constantin Iordachi's, "The Romanian-Hungarian Reconciliation Process, 1994–2001: From Conflict to Co-operation," *PolSci: Romanian Journal of Political Science*, 1 (December 2001): 3–4, 88–134, does not show signs of a bias, but it completely ignores the intense anti-Hungarian agitation and actions widespread in Romania until 1996.

campaign of the chauvinist organization *Vatra Românească*, and the biased court proceedings in Marosvásárhely as well as other grievances.[58] The annual report of our ambassador, Pál Szűts, gave concrete evidence that "Ceaușescu may be dead, but his spirit lives on."[59] In mid-June, anti-government demonstrators were beaten up by miners called to Bucharest by President Iliescu.[60] In the mind of an objective observer such as Robert Hamerton-Kelly,[61] a renowned scholar who visited Romania several times in the early 1990s and conducted numerous interviews, there could be little doubt that in Romania the old nationalist-communist elite had, after the removal of the Ceaușescu clan (which was severely compromised in the eyes of the world), established a democratic-looking version of authoritarianism, and its strongest feature was anti-Hungarian sentiment and hype. Hamerton-Kelly's conclusion was that "the Romanian 'revolution' was a coup planned and executed by Iliescu and his party comrades, the Securitate and the Soviet leadership," sacrificing innocent civilian victims to make the takeover appear to be a genuine revolution. The nationalist policies of the executed Romanian leader did not disappear with him.[62]

Despite the ominous signs, we hoped that the interests of Romania, its European integration aspirations, and the forty-one Hungarian MPs elected to the Romanian Parliament would persuade the Romanian leaders to regulate the situation of Hungarians in Romania in the spirit of their needs and the standards that were gaining ground in Europe. It was in this hope that we hosted Romulus Neagu, state secretary at the Romanian Ministry of Foreign Affairs, in Budapest on July 24–26. His performance, which certainly reflected the thinking of President Iliescu and the government led by Petre Roman, was disappointing even when compared to our modest expectations. Neagu categorically rejected everything that the new Romanian leadership had promised the Hungarian community in its declarations

---

[58] Report compiled by Géza Entz, state secretary of the prime minister's office, August 10, 1990. Among my papers.

[59] Annual report of the Hungarian ambassador in Bucharest, Pál Szűts, June 5, 1990, published in Sáringer, *Iratok az Antall-kormány*, vol. 1: 427–42 (Doc. 92).

[60] Ion Iliescu (1930–): Romanian politician. A protégé of the dictator Nicolae Ceaușescu, fell out of favor in 1971 and played a major role in the December 1989 uprising. Twice served as president of Romania (1990–1996; 2000–2004). In 2018 Iliescu was charged with crimes against humanity, the verdict is still pending at the time of this writing.

[61] Robert Hamerton-Kelly (1938–2013): A theologian and researcher on religious violence at Stanford University, Center for International Security and Arms Control. (Future U.S. secretary of defense William J. Perry and Secretary of State Condoleezza Rice were fellows of the Institute.) In April 1990, as a guest at Stanford, I drew his attention to the diverse religious make-up of Transylvania and the discrimination against the Hungarian denomination, which he found worth studying.

[62] Robert Hamerton-Kelly and István Szőnyi, "The Nature of the Romanian Regime (1989–1991)." Typescript among my papers.

of late 1989 and early 1990: a law on individual and collective minority rights, a Ministry for Nationalities, regional autonomy, and a Hungarian education system with an independent university. Neagu blamed the deterioration of relations between the two countries on statements made by President Göncz and Prime Minister Antall, the allegedly hostile tone of the Hungarian press, and the "slanders" of the "Hungarian emigration," i.e., the Hungarians in the West. He dismissed the reopening of the Hungarian Consulate General in Cluj/Kolozsvár (and the Romanian one in Debrecen) as unnecessary, saying "it was an agreement between two dictatorships, and those same two closed them."

I rejected the equation of the two dictatorships, especially with regard to the previous twenty years, and I argued in favor of consulates, also referring to European examples, saying that on the basis of our personal and economic relations we needed even more Hungarian representations in Romania in addition to the consulate in Cluj/Kolozsvár. I put forward the Hungarian-Romanian opposition declaration of June 1989 as an excellent basis for the settlement of our relations. This was dismissed by Neagu, almost with disgust, as something with which the Romanian leadership had nothing to do. The Romanian signatories of that document, he said, did not represent the thinking of Romanian society. As for the assessment of the events in Târgu Mures/Marosvásárhely, we should wait for the parliamentary debate in Bucharest on the report. The state secretary stated that Romania did not interfere in Hungary's internal affairs, that the Hungarians in Romania were represented in Parliament, and that their situation was not Hungary's concern. There was, he said, no need for a bilateral agreement on the protection of minorities; Romania was abiding by the international rules, which were being drafted in the framework of the CSCE.

At the expert-level meeting chaired by Hungary's deputy state secretary Szokai, the Romanian side presented a "package plan." This included, among other things, the regularization of high-level political meetings, the introduction of the "Open Skies" military confidence-building flights, Hungarian support for Romania joining the Pentagonale and the Alpine-Adriatic Working Community, intensive Hungarian economic presence on the Black Sea coast, the excess capacities of the Romanian heavy and chemical industries to be utilized by Hungary, and the opening of cultural centers in the two capitals but depriving them of the former right to trade (i.e., to sell books and other cultural products), and, finally, starting the comparison of the school textbooks on history and geography. Then came an outright provocation: the two countries should jointly celebrate anniversaries in Romanian history, such as December 1, the "unification of Transylvania with Romania," and in addition a monument should be erected in Hungary to outstanding figures of

Romanian history, such as Eminescu (who proposed the Tisza River as the border between the two countries), Șincai and Maior (prominent figures of the early anti-Hungarian Romanian nationalist movement and authors of the—false—theory of Daco-Romanian continuity), and Bălcescu (one of the leaders of the 1848–49 Romanian revolutionary movement). Finally, the official Romanian name should be used in Hungary for the names of all Transylvanian localities! The Romanian side did not rule out sister-city and sister-county relations, but it considered participation in the emerging Carpathian-Tisza cooperation desirable only between countries and not between regions.

For its part, the Hungarian side criticized the fact that chauvinist and racist organizations were operating freely in Romania, and that the typical Romanian accusations of Hungarian irredentism had reappeared. We expected credible information about the March events in Târgu Mures/Marosvásárhely, and the June crackdown on university students in Bucharest. We explained that the treatment of minorities was a test of democracy and an inescapable element of our bilateral relationship. In return we presented a 31-point proposal for improving our relations. These included: a new treaty of cooperation (to replace the 1972 one); the establishment of a joint committee for minority affairs; economic cooperation; the drafting of a bilateral Nationality Charter; support for regular party contacts; a switch to convertible accounts; an increase in tourism by opening more rail and bus services and the opening of border crossings and railway wings that had been closed; improving the reception of Hungarian television in Romania; free circulation of books and press products; financial support for the intellectual dialogue started in March; mutually free archival research access; transfer of documents pertaining to the 1956 revolution and on the internment of Imre Nagy and his companions in Romania;[63] a memorial to the Hungarian victims of the Maniu Guards;[64] and, finally, the restoration of the monument for the martyrs of Arad.[65] The reception of our proposal to

---

[63] With the second Soviet intervention on November 4, 1956, Prime Minister Imre Nagy and a number of his close supporters were given asylum at the Yugoslav Legation in Budapest, but the puppet government of Kádár, installed by the Soviets, offered them safe conduct to leave for home. However, the whole group was kidnapped by the Soviet secret service and transported to Romania, to be interned there.

[64] Paramilitary Romanian terrorist group active in Transylvania in late 1944, which brutally beheaded a number of totally innocent Hungarians.

[65] An impressive monument by the noted sculptor György Zala was erected in 1890 in the town of Arad for the thirteen generals of the 1848/49 Hungarian Home Defense Army, who were executed on the order of Emperor Francis Joseph after the Hungarian Army had no alternative but surrender. Taking over Arad in 1918 the Romanian authorities removed the monument. Disassembled in 1924, it survived until it was restored and set up in 2004. Simultaneously, however, facing it "a counter monument" was erected, showing Romanian national heroes.

jointly erect a monument to Bishop Áron Márton[66] and to initiate his canonization at the Holy See was typical: they didn't know who the bishop was. Neagu refused to reinstall the statues in Arad on the grounds that the martyrs fought for the annexation of Transylvania to Hungary.[67]

At a press conference after the meeting, Deputy State Secretary Szokai said: "The issue of Hungarian-Romanian relations is inseparable from the development of the living conditions of the Hungarian community in Romania."[68] It was certainly the press coverage of the Hungarian-Romanian talks that prompted Radio Free Europe to ask me for an interview on this subject. I confirmed that there was a broad consensus in Hungary that our relations with Romania should be exemplary, preferably friendly, but that this depended solely on the other side. Romania should accept that it is a multi-national country and that its national minorities should be granted the same rights as provided by the enlightened states of Europe. I reiterated that the Romanian and Hungarian Communist dictatorships were very different. I criticized Romania for tolerating and even supporting extremist Hungarian-hating organizations, also for not accepting our proposals for improving our relations, and for giving at best a delaying response. I mentioned the issue of the Hungarian Consulate General in Cluj/Kolozsvár, the need for the free circulation of Hungarian books and other cultural products throughout Romania, the urgent need for improvement of rail connections, the desirable harmonization of history textbooks, and the elimination of distortions.[69] The interview provoked a strong reaction in Bucharest, with foreign affairs spokesman Chebeleu saying that it offended the Romanian people.

Subsequently, in the context of the upcoming fiftieth anniversary of the Second Vienna Award of August 1940, which returned the northern half of Transylvania to Hungary, Romanian newspapers published lengthy accounts of the alleged atrocities that accompanied the Hungarian takeover of Northern Transylvania in 1940.[70] According to the controlled Romanian press, Hungary was returning to the

---

[66] Áron Márton (1896–1980): Hungarian Roman Catholic bishop in Transylvania, harassed by the communist authorities. Yad Vashem honored him as a "Righteous Among the Nations" for his efforts to stop the deportation of Hungarian Jews during World War II.
[67] The minutes of these talks are among my papers.
[68] For Szokai's press conference of July 27, see *Külügyminisztériumi tájékoztató, 1990* [Bulletin of the Ministry of Foreign Affairs, 1990] (Budapest: Magyar Köztársaság Külügyminisztériuma, 1990), 134–35, and *Magyar Külpolitikai Évkönyv, 1990*, 220. Sáringer, *Iratok az Antall-kormány*, vol. 1: Doc. 93 (July 26, 1990), is mistaken, placing the meeting in Bucharest.
[69] "Hungarian Foreign Minister Doubtful about Romanian Relations," RFE broadcast on August 8, 1990. Among my papers.
[70] A few unfortunate incidents that claimed lives did take place in September 1940, but they were not intentional. See Krisztián Ungváry, "Félrevarrt szálak," in *Beszélő* 9, no. 10 (2004); and Ignác Romsics, "A má-

revanchist policy of the Horthy era[71] and, with its claim for Hungarian autonomy, to the policy of Stalinism.[72] The press campaign in Romania reached such worrying proportions that there were fears of further ethnic conflicts, therefore the Hungarian Ministry of Foreign Affairs issued a statement on August 24 stating that Hungary respected the international treaties and the existing borders. In addition, it stated:

> No one has any reason or legal basis to classify the sense of responsibility for the fate of Hungarians who have been placed in a minority situation as a result of the peace treaties as a hostile endeavor. [...] The Government of the Republic of Hungary hopes that in Romania [...] the various parties and organizations will refrain from any action which would make it more difficult for the peoples of our region to reconcile and accomplish the difficult historical tasks ahead of us.[73]

In the note handed over to Ambassador Simion Pop, Deputy State Secretary Dénes Tomaj "expressed the Hungarian government's expectation that the Romanian government will take decisive and effective steps to prevent the planned extremist actions and will guarantee the legal status, property and security of the Hungarian community in Romania ..."[74] Thanks to our actions and international attention, no major incidents took place on the anniversary.

I did not give up hope that our relations with Romania, which seemed to be icy, could improve, and I was convinced that instead of reacting with offended passivity we should redouble our efforts to improve the situation of the Hungarians in Romania. On the first anniversary of the Pan-European Picnic, on the initiative of the MDF, a "Europe Day" was held in eight different settlements on the border, in the spirit of the vision of a Europe without borders. "By our own peaceful means: by making friends, travelling, learning about each other's cultures, respecting each other's differences, we strive to enter the twenty-first century with borders

---

sodik bécsi döntés," *Népszabadság*, August 21, 2010. Cf. Holly Case, *The Transylvanian Question and the European Idea during World War II* (Stanford: Stanford University Press, 2009), 102.

[71] Miklós Horthy of Nagybánya (1868–1957): Hungarian admiral, regent of the Kingdom of Hungary (March 1, 1920, to October 15, 1944).

[72] Reference to the Autonomous Hungarian Region of the Székely (Szekler) province, set up in 1952. See Stefano Bottoni, *Sztálin a székelyeknél: A Magyar Autonóm Tartomány története, 1952–1960* [Stalin at the Székelys: The history of the autonomous Hungarian province] (Csíkszereda: Pro-Print, 2008).

[73] *Magyar Külpolitikai Évkönyv, 1990*, 234–35; Sáringer, *Iratok az Antall-kormány*, vol. 1: 449–50 (Doc. 96 Aug. 24, 1990). The Foreign Affairs Committee of the Hungarian Parliament issued a statement in the same spirit, *Magyar Külpolitikai Évkönyv, 1990*, 237.

[74] *Külügyminisztériumi tájékoztató, 1990*, 176.

that are only symbolic and open to all," read the text of my party's appeal.[75] Antall himself spoke on the Austrian border, in the company of Lothar de Maizière, the prime minister of the "German Democratic Republic," the state then entering its last weeks. Among the eight border settlements, I deliberately chose to speak at Ártánd, on the Romanian border, which a year earlier had been the most tense border in Europe. Both Hungarians and Romanians from Oradea/Nagyvárad and all over the Bihar region showed strong agreement with my saying that we must not forget Christmas 1989, "those wonderful moments of embracing each other." I saw in the eight border meetings the expression of the will to live together with our neighbors in a Europe,

> where borders do not separate relatives and friends, where borders are permeable and their importance is diminishing, where we can fight together to eradicate the material, moral and environmental damage of the Communist-Stalinist dictatorships. Romanian-Hungarian differences have always deepened under anti-democratic regimes, whereas under democratic conditions, rapprochement and multilateral cooperation can begin, and friendship can grow out of it. [...] In this Europe, there will be no place for the old secret police, neither for the new intolerant people and the hatemongers. Long live the new Europe! Long live the new, democratic Hungary and Romania! Se traiasca Romania si Ungaria libera![76]

At all eight meetings, a large number of people gathered from both sides of the border, not only Hungarians but also from among the neighboring non-Hungarian peoples, to call for the opening or reopening of border crossings and roads closed during the communist era.[77]

The Hungarians in Romania—along with the people in Hungary—wanted more. Only a few optimists still hoped for an independent Transylvania; and its annexation to Hungary was just a dream of Mr. István Zolcsák's Transylvanian World Alliance, incorporated in Argentina. The New York-based American Transylvanian Alliance, led by Béla Teleki, had rejected that mirage-chasing organization from its very start,[78] and in 1990, too, it saw the future of the Transylvanian Hungarians

---

[75] Declaration of the Hungarian Democratic Forum, August 18, 1990. Among my papers.
[76] For the full text of my speech, see *Magyar Külpolitikai Évkönyv, 1990*, 231–33.
[77] A good example was the petition of the Salgótarján branch of the MDF, Dr. József Várkonyi, August 23, 1990.
[78] "The problem is that those who initiate and intend to lead the Transylvanian World Alliance movement are all people who have not the slightest idea of the real situation in Transylvania, and without exception have not the slightest political acumen or sense." Letter of Béla Teleki to Dr. Áron Gábor, September 25,

in a realistic way, in achieving broad minority rights. In the autumn of 1990, the RMDSZ noted that the authorities in Bucharest had returned to Ceaușescu's centralizing and homogenizing ambitions. The party envisioned an alternative: if Soviet Moldova became independent and joined Romania, the resulting country would inevitably become a federation, and, hopefully, international support could be mobilized for that.[79]

On international forums for minority rights

The epoch-making historical changes of 1989 brought the promise—and soon the proclamation—of a new, better world order. Intolerance towards national minorities has been a long-standing source of internal and external tension in so many countries, it was self-evident that it should be tackled at the international level. It seemed to me that with the end of the Cold War (the political ice age), history, which had been on a fixed track, had run into a sort of marshalling yard, and it was now up to political leaders to set the switches in the right direction. Once that point is passed, it would be difficult to change direction, so it would be now, in 1990–91, that the political course of our country and its neighbors would be decided. In the early 1990s Hungary—partly because of the 1956 revolution and partly because of our role in the European changes—had such moral and political capital, and in Antall's person such a prestigious and far-sighted leader, that we hoped that in the present fluid state of the world we could have a greater say in the course of events than our territorial size and economic weight would suggest. In particular, we saw as essential a turnaround in the attitude of the countries liberated from the Communist bloc towards their national minorities, and this was a priority of our foreign policy. We saw that the situation of the national minorities in the western half of Europe (Catalans, Basques, Austro-Germans in Italy and the German and Danish minorities in Schleswig on both sides of the border, or the Swedes in Finland) had steadily improved after the Second World War; their rights had been extended and their survival seemed guaranteed. I thought that the time had come for a Europe-wide settlement of the issue in the former communist bloc, too.

By the end of 1990, it was already apparent that the majority of our neighbors, once free, were not willing to meet the demands of their Hungarian citizens hoping to acquire a status similar to that of the historical minorities in Western European democracies. However, as far as minority rights were concerned, it was still possible

---

1974. See Gabriella Hermann, "Az Amerikai Erdélyi Szövetség története, 1952–1977" [The American Transylvanian Alliance, 1952–1977], *Magyar Kisebbség*, nos. 61–62 (2011): 76.

[79] Géza Entz to Géza Jeszenszky, October 15, 1990. Among my papers.

to hope that foreign examples and the new norms being adopted at international level would bring about the desired change. A key question was the extent to which the great powers would accept the idea of collective minority rights and autonomy. When travelling to the annual meeting of the UN General Assembly, I spoke at Columbia University in New York, Princeton University at Princeton, and Rutgers University in New Brunswick. Many from New Jersey's large Hungarian community attended my talk at Rutgers titled "Will there be peace in the Danube Valley?" Talking about my latest impressions, I admitted that among Hungary's neighbors, politicians willing to grant the necessary minority rights were still in a minority, but with the mediation and pressure of the European institutions, the situation could change. "There is no alternative to peace—but let this peace be just," I said. The Hungarian meeting was also addressed by Dénes Csengey, a writer and one of the founders of MDF. "We have reconquered our homeland," he began, "so we will truly be the motherland of Hungarians all over the world." He saw the future's main dangers in indifference, searching for scapegoats and agitation by the old guard.[80]

In New York, in connection with the UN General Assembly, the foreign ministers of the CSCE countries held a special conference. In my speech to them, I stressed how important the Helsinki process, the struggle for human rights, had been in the miraculous events of 1989. The logical continuation of this, I said, was

> to deal properly with the problem of national minorities. It is unthinkable to move on from the past to the future without finding appropriate answers— general and concrete—to certain situations which raise questions arising from the coexistence of several ethnic communities in many countries. Promoting the exercise of nationality rights and the protection of national minorities, principles which are essential to the stability of the continent, require urgent action. For this reason, and in order to assess the scale of the action required, a major task will fall to the experts' meeting on national minorities to be held in 1991.[81]

Beginning my address to the General Assembly, I thanked the world organization "for the moral and political support it provided during and after the 1956 Hungarian Revolution and freedom fight." I expressed my conviction that the disappearance of the bipolar world order offered a good opportunity for the UN and its Charter to fulfil its original vocation of ensuring peace and universally shared values and

---

[80] Interest in Hungary at the time was such that these meetings were widely reported in the local press: *The Princeton Packet*, September 28, 1990; and *Sunday Star-Ledger* (Newark), September 30, 1990.
[81] Address by Géza Jeszenszky, October 2, 1990. *Magyar Külpolitikai Évkönyv, 1990*, 258.

the enjoyment of human rights, including minority rights. I added that for us, "it is extremely important to develop relations with neighboring countries, based on common interests and values, and on the recognition of a common destiny." I also welcomed "the growing recognition that the rights of national, ethnic, religious and linguistic minorities are an integral part of universally recognized human rights." In order to ensure the effective protection of these rights, I called for the urgent elaboration of a "binding code," accompanied by an appropriate guarantee system and monitoring mechanism.[82] It was a sign of the respect Hungary enjoyed at the time that my speech was greeted by many sincere words of congratulations, welcoming the new Hungary.

In a series of bilateral meetings, I had an extended conversation with Adrian Năstase, the then forty-year-old Romanian foreign minister, a jurist.[83] Unlike so many of his compatriots during the Ceaușescu era, he did not defect while holding a scholarship in Strasbourg, so I knew immediately where to put him; he used to be a loyal servant of the dictatorship. I found him a very tough negotiating partner who spoke English as well as French and claimed to be a social democrat. I suggested that we put aside the conflict in Târgu Mures/Marosvásárhely and the subsequent controversies, and "in one big leap" implement the agreements we had reached at the beginning of 1990. Instead, my colleague recommended a policy of small steps and rejected virtually all Hungarian proposals made since January.

At that time, we hoped above all that the Council of Europe, the guardian of democratic norms, would draw up a universally binding code of minority standards, and that no European state would be exempt from its scope. Catherine Lalumière, secretary general of the Council of Europe,[84] was sensitive to Hungarian problems, and understood that the lack of minority rights threatened the stability and even the integrity of states. At the same time as I delivered my address in New York, the Council of Europe's Committee of Ministers concluded that Hungary met all the conditions for a democratic state based on the rule of law and could join the organization—the first among the countries that had escaped from communism.[85] In his speech to the Parliamentary Assembly of the Council of Europe on October 2, József Antall expressed his hope that the other Central and Eastern European countries that meet the criteria for membership would also join in the near future. In

---

[82] Address by Géza Jeszenszky, October 3, 1990. *Magyar Külpolitikai Évkönyv, 1990*, 261–70.

[83] Adrian Năstase (1950–): Romanian politician, foreign minister (1990–1992), prime minister (2000–2004). Sentenced to two years in prison for corruption in July 2012.

[84] Catherine Lalumière (1935–): French politician, secretary general of the Council of Europe (1989–1994), member of the European Parliament (1994–2004).

[85] There were many who wanted Poland to join before or at the same time as Hungary, but since Poland had not yet held fully free elections, this was not possible.

response to a question at a press conference, he said that we were working to improve our relations with Romania, and that our interest was not to isolate Romania but to "induce it to take further steps towards a European legal system."[86]

In late 1990, Ion Iliescu and his government chose to increase anti-Hungarian agitation in order to damp down their growing domestic political difficulties, and they concocted a tale of a planned armed Hungarian uprising in Transylvania.[87] According to a Romanian opposition politician, "The post-communist leadership of the country is trying to feed nationalist, chauvinist sentiment in order to keep its power. [...] Iliescu will never forgive the RMDSZ that its members did not vote for him [in the presidential elections]."[88] The Romanian president's political opponents condemned these tactics, hoping that foreign pressure would bring down the post-communists, and they indicated that they would bring about a positive turn in the treatment of the Hungarian minority.[89] Năstase, on the other hand, who spoke very highly of Iliescu even to me privately, was an eager partner in the anti-Hungarian cause. On October 9 in the paper *România Liberă*, and next day in *Adevărul*, he sharply criticized my speech at the UN, making the unfounded charge that more than a quarter of it was about the minority issue. He particularly objected to the mention of collective rights and autonomy, claiming that they have a destabilizing effect and are rejected on the international fora. He described my statement that the international community has a duty to monitor the situation of minorities, to prevent conflicts, to provide protection in the event of violations and to hold the offending state accountable, as propagandist phraseology. Năstase explained that, from a legal point of view, "the international community" was non-existing (he was right), and neither could we talk about "the rights of minorities," only about the rights of persons belonging to minorities. As regards the system of norms for minorities, he referred to Romania's Copenhagen proposal, which was primarily about the mandatory loyalty of minorities and the prohibition of external interference. Finally, he said that my statement that Hungary feels a responsibility towards Hungarians living outside its borders (he did not refer to the fact that this is also stated in our Constitution) was contrary to international law, and from this he

---

[86] *Magyar Hírlap*, October 3, 1990.
[87] Coded telegram from Bucharest, Sáringer, *Iratok az Antall-kormány*, vol. 1: 455–56 (Doc. 98, November 28, 1990).
[88] Ambassador Rudas to Minister Jeszenszky, November 8, 1990. Among my papers.
[89] Conversation in Budapest between Dumitru Mazilu, former vice-president of the Romanian National Salvation Front, and Imre Szokai, deputy state secretary, September 20, 1990. Published in Sáringer, *Iratok az Antall-kormány*, vol. 1: 451–54 (Doc. 97). In his letter to me, Mazilu called both the March events in Târgu Mures and the June "raid of the miners" in Bucharest a deliberate provocation by the Iliescu regime. D. Mazilu to Minister Jeszenszky, February 15, 1991.

inferred that I was attacking the current European borders with "moderate language." He justified Romania's rejection of the restoration of the consulate in Cluj/Kolozsvár and the Bolyai University (which used to instruct in Hungarian and was closed down in 1959) by saying that while Hungary was officially sending out positive messages, it was "not speaking in a fair way about the situation of the Hungarian minority in our country."[90] My subsequent interview with *România Liberă* was my response. Having recalled the positive elements of our common history, and refuting the notion of "a Hungarian threat," I reaffirmed our commitment to the best possible bilateral relations. However, I stressed that an indispensable condition for this was to ensure the rights of the Hungarian community in Romania, in accordance with the demands of RMDSZ, the Hungarian party of Romania.[91]

As yet unaware of those Romanian objections, on October 5 I spoke at the international symposium of the German Helsinki Commission on Human Rights in Berlin. There I called on the German government to help draft and to recognize a binding international code on the rights of minorities. In this, it would be sufficient to codify the principles and models that are already in practice in Western Europe. I spoke about this in a broader context ten days later at the Adenauer Foundation in Bonn, under the title "Conflict or Cooperation in Post-Communist Europe." I recalled the significant role played by national minorities in conflicts between and within states in our century and said that the problem was still a serious one in the eastern half of Europe, as many examples show. I mentioned that in Romania, the ghost of Ceaușescu was haunting us again, and the government had withdrawn the promises it made to the Hungarian minority in January. However, the tried and tested solutions in the West and adherence to European standards would take the edge off the issue.[92] In response to questions, I denied that in Hungary there was "raging anti-Sovietism." On the question of borders, I said that Hungary had lost dozens of Königsbergs,[93] but we saw the solution in reconciliation, in considering the example of South Tyrol as a model.

On November 6, in Rome, Hungary—ahead of any other formerly Communist-dominated countries—became a member of the Council of Europe, the community of European democratic states. On the occasion of the fortieth anniversary of

---

[90] Open Telegram, BUC00306 and BUC003021, October 9 and 10, 1990. Among my papers.
[91] Transcript of my interview, October 1990. Among my papers.
[92] Talk by Géza Jeszenszky in Bonn, October 15, 1990. *Magyar Külpolitikai Évkönyv, 1990*, 275–78.
[93] The hometown of Immanuel Kant, annexed by the Soviet Union in 1945, was obviously a great loss to German culture, but in the 1920 peace treaty Hungary lost a large number of towns which had been important centers of Old Hungary's political and cultural life.

the Convention for the Protection of Human Rights, to which Hungary acceded, the Hungarian government issued a declaration that stated:

> Minorities can only enjoy equal rights and equal status with the majority if they are recognized as a community and can live, learn, work and develop their culture freely. In addition to the rights enjoyed by all, they must have specific rights, so as to be able to preserve their identity and existence as a community, thereby neutralizing the disadvantages of being a minority. The Hungarian Government considers the above principles to be applicable to the national minorities living in the territory of the Republic of Hungary, and regards them as communities who enrich the social, spiritual and cultural life of the country, and not as factors that diminish the rights of the majority. The Government of the Republic of Hungary wishes to take an active part in the elaboration of a universal charter for national minorities in order to achieve a reassuring and comprehensive settlement of the question of national minorities. The Government shall endeavor to establish good cooperation with neighboring states on the basis of the above principles also in the matter of national minorities.[94]

In my speech on the occasion of our admission, and again on November in 14 Strasbourg at the Committee of Ministers, as well as in several interviews, I stressed our hope that, by meeting the strict admission requirements, our neighbors would soon be admitted to the organization, and, until then, we would be ready to convey their concerns to this important European forum.[95]

Diplomatic conflict with Romania

On November 3, 1990, we hosted the foreign ministers of the six Warsaw Pact countries in Budapest to sign an agreement on national quotas for the Conventional Armed Forces Reduction Treaty. On that occasion, I had a separate meeting with my Romanian counterpart and listed the events and statements in Romania that were hindering the good relations we so much wanted. We agreed that, in order to reduce tensions and prevent misinterpretations, we would subsequently send each other the texts of our statements, not distorted or manipulated by the media,

---

[94] Statement by the Republic of Hungary on the occasion of the fortieth anniversary of the European Convention on Human Rights, November 2, 1990. *Magyar Külpolitikai Évkönyv, 1990*, 300–301.

[95] Address by G. Jeszenszky at the Ministerial Committee of the Council of Europe, November 14, 1990. Sáringer, *Iratok az Antall-kormány*, vol. 1: 382–84 (Doc. 84).

concerning our relations. After his return home, Năstase described our meeting on Romanian television as "very useful, very open, very frank," words which, in diplomacy, suggest serious differences of opinion.

A week later, on November 10 (but delivered only on November 14), Foreign Minister Năstase wrote me a letter not intended for the public, which objected to the terms of the government declaration issued at our admission to the Council of Europe, which used the term "the Hungarian community in Romania" and claimed "special rights," i.e., privileges. According to the minister, the Hungarians living in Transylvania and Bucharest were "scattered" and did not constitute a community of any kind, and "the modern concept of human rights does not recognize 'special rights.'" He rejected the idea that Hungary could bear responsibility for the Hungarian inhabitants of Romania, saying that that responsibility lay solely with the Romanian government. On the basis of the above "anachronistic" theses, he wrote, "we will not be able to find any basis for cooperation between our countries and we will not achieve any improvement in Romanian-Hungarian relations."[96]

Before my reply was ready, Deputy State Secretary Szokai was in Bucharest on November 15–17 for his scheduled talks with State Secretary Neagu. Our idea, as agreed in advance in the Ministry, was that the Hungarian side would repeat our proposals for the normalization of bilateral relations, and that they would be recorded in a protocol, which would include the points not accepted by the Romanian side, as well as any Romanian counter-proposals. Following that, we could negotiate at expert level on the basis of that "inventory." Neagu stated that the refusal to reopen the Hungarian Consulate General in Cluj was even more justified than before, and he denied the need for any Hungarian consular representation in Romania other than in Bucharest. He also rejected any bilateral cooperation or agreement on the minority issue, on the one hand because it was an "absolutely internal matter" and on the other because there was only room for a general European agreement. (Romania expected, not without reason, that because of the special considerations of some Western European countries, such an agreement would either never be reached or would be so vague that it would not conflict with Romanian concepts and methods.) The adoption of the protocol was ultimately frustrated by the Romanian side's refusal to mention the issue of Romanian refugees who had been taken in by Hungary during the Ceaușescu dictatorship.

Năstase, too, received Szokai, and now his tone had become more cordial. He said the "open and frank atmosphere" in his talks with me and my interview with Romanian Television were positive signs, but confirmed the validity of his letter

---

[96] Letter from Foreign Minister A. Năstase to Géza Jeszenszky, November 10, 1990. Among my papers.

sent to me a few days earlier. The Hungarian Deputy State Secretary also cited the Council of Europe Parliamentary Assembly's recommendation of October 1, denying that the concept of collective rights is universally rejected, and he referred to the numerous international documents on minority rights that form the basis of the Hungarian approach. Năstase—backtracking somewhat—said that Romania will be bound by the provisions of the Council of Europe when it becomes a member of that organization.

Szokai was not expected to be received by the Romanian head of state, but having been informed that Szokai wished to pass on President Göncz's oral message, President Iliescu did receive the Hungarian diplomat on November 16. The Hungarian idea was that the two presidents would meet on December 17 in Timișoara/Temesvár, on the first anniversary of the start of the dramatic events there, and that documents should be adopted on the development of bilateral relations. Iliescu said that it was unwarranted for the Hungarian president to resent the fact that the Romanian press, and even official statements, regularly criticized him for having translated Endre Bajcsy-Zsilinszky's work on Transylvania, published in English in Geneva in 1944.[97] The Hungarian press is also a constant critic of Romania's leaders, he continued, yet Romania does not raise the issue. According to Iliescu, the Timișoara anniversary was not a suitable date for the meeting of the two heads of state, and he ruled out discussing minorities alongside inter-state relations at a later date, as "the minority issue is not an inter-state problem, but an internal affair of every country."[98]

The consultations in Bucharest were not very encouraging, but what followed remains absurd even more than three decades later. According to a cable from the embassy of Hungary, immediately after Szokai's departure, Neagu called in Ambassador Ernő Rudas and confronted him. Neagu declared:

> [Szokai's] conduct can only be described as charlatanism and a series of despicable tricks. [...] He lied in a preposterous manner and deceived the Romanian side by claiming to have a message from Árpád Göncz, when he had no such message. [...] He would like to attribute the above to be merely the result of Mr. Szokai's personal qualities, but, unfortunately, he sees it as the embodiment of official Hungarian policy. [...] There are political forces in Hungary that want to worsen Hungarian-Romanian relations, to maintain the tension, and they are imposing conditions and making unacceptable

---

[97] The book *Transylvania: Past and Future* (Geneva: Kundig, 1944) proposed the creation of an independent Transylvania, made up of cantons.

[98] Report on the negotiations between Imre Szokai and Romulus Neagu in Bucharest, November 15–17, 1990.

proposals, starting with the head of state. Hungarian politics is constantly interfering in Romania's internal affairs, claiming that Hungarians are being persecuted here, even though Mr. Iliescu himself advised each side to mind its own business. Neagu concluded by saying that Hungarian behavior could no longer be tolerated, and if we wanted hostilities with Romania, all right, let there be a fight. [sic!][99]

On November 19, Foreign Ministry spokesman János Herman gave a detailed account to the press of the unsuccessful consultations in Bucharest. He was not silent about the Romanian side's rude behavior and summed up our intentions as follows:

> The Hungarian Ministry of Foreign Affairs has made and continues to make great efforts to explore the possibilities for the settlement of Hungarian-Romanian relations. However, it does not intend to abandon either Hungarian national interests or Hungary's other international legal obligations undertaken in the CSCE process. Therefore, we do not consider unprincipled compromises possible, nor can we be partners in creating the appearance of an agreement for the outside world.[100]

Adding fuel to the fire was an interview in Budapest with Romanian ambassador Simion Pop, published in the November 26–27 issue of *Tineterul Liber* and picked up by the official Rompres news agency. In it, he stated that the president of the Republic of Hungary had joined "the irredentist tide" and his actions were not in line with the aspirations expressed in the Hungarian Parliament. He called Prime Minister Antall arrogant and his ambitions contrary to legal norms. That was too much to let pass. On November 28 the government (in my absence, due to my official tour of Asia) discussed the state of Hungarian-Romanian relations and decided that we must make a public reply, at home and abroad.

Ferenc Somogyi, permanent state secretary at the Foreign Ministry summoned Ambassador Pop on November 29 and said:

> With these statements, Mr. Ambassador, you are in the most obvious violation of all the written and unwritten rules of diplomacy; you are lecturing the President and Prime Minister of the Republic of Hungary. I would remind you that, when handing over your credentials, you said that your

---

[99] Open telegram from Bucharest No 47/000, November 19, 1990.
[100] *Magyar Nemzet*, November 20, 1990. *Külügyminisztériumi tájékoztató, 1990*, 305–6.

pronouncements should be taken as if they were made by the President of Romania. That gives your current words even more weight. [...] The role of an ambassador is to facilitate, not to hinder, the development of relations between the two states and to accurately convey the official communications of the governments of the two countries. In full awareness of your responsibility, can you confirm that the Hungarian Government or any member of it has made statements to you in accordance with the accusations made in the interview? [...] I fear that it will be difficult for you to maintain relations with those personalities whom you called irredentist or arrogant. From the point of view of Romania and Hungarian-Romanian relations, it is worrying that a vacuum may be created around you, Mr. Ambassador, which will make it very difficult for you to carry out your duties. [...] I inform you, without a public apology, Prime Minister József Antall will not receive you.

I have the impression that, unfortunately, Mr. Ambassador, you have not yet got to know our country and my government well enough, since in your interview you state that "Hungary deliberately and stubbornly belittles its eastern neighbor, there is a flood of irredentist and chauvinist sentiment, the mass media provide tendentious and one-sided information about Romanian reality, and the large number of chauvinist and irredentist circles disturb and incite citizens with hundreds of books." [...] I confirm to you—and I ask you to convey my words precisely to your government—that the Republic of Hungary will continue to work hard to normalize Hungarian-Romanian relations, maintaining its principled position, consistently representing the country's interests and in accordance with its international obligations. As our Prime Minister has stated on several occasions in international fora, our aim is not to isolate Romania, on the contrary, we want Romania to become an integral part of the emerging European cooperation, in accordance with European obligations, customs and expectations. We hope that the Romanian government will show the necessary wisdom and similar willingness, bearing in mind the real interests of the Romanian people, to stop acting in a contrary way.[101]

Ambassador Pop, no doubt driven not only by his own bias, had overstepped the mark, and it became impossible for him to perform his task in Budapest. In the following weeks he reported in sick and was soon quietly recalled. But what explains

---

[101] Open telegram to Hungary's embassies, No 47/000. November 29, 1990. Cf. *Magyar Külpolitikai Évkönyv, 1990*, 321–24. *Külügyminisztériumi tájékoztató, 1990*, 322–24. A shortened version appeared in *Magyar Nemzet*, November 30, 1990.

this not only rigid but also belligerent and offensive attitude of the entire Romanian leadership? The internal power struggle was escalating in Romania at the time, and the deplorable living conditions there provided a good basis for this. Extreme nationalism, the artificial production of images of enemies has traditionally worked as a distraction operation, and distraction may be sufficient to explain Romania's behavior. This, however, was compounded by the influence of the national-Bolshevik ideology inculcated during the Ceaușescu era, the system of arguments and language adopted from it, and the repetition of the idea that the Hungarian minority threatened Romania's territorial integrity. The falsifications and manipulations confirmed the then common perception abroad that the political turnaround in our eastern neighbor was only superficial and verbal.[102] No substantial change in our relations and in the situation of Hungarians in Transylvania could be expected from that particular government. Personally, I only hoped that genuinely democratic forces would prevail in Romania, and that that would lead to an improvement in our relations. I was also aware, however, that the contemporary Romanian opposition would easily forget its promises once in power—unless the composition of the Romanian Parliament changed for the better and unless the strength of the Hungarian party, the RMDSZ, forced a change.

Meanwhile, on November 19–21, the CSCE Summit took place and the Charter of Paris was adopted, laying the foundations for a new world order. In his speech, József Antall, among other things, spoke about the danger of "a welfare wall" between the two parts of Europe, replacing the Iron Curtain; President Bush sent over a congratulatory note. The prime minister also touched on the tensions over minorities. He said that these tensions could be tackled through ongoing dialogue and by adhering to the commitments made in the Helsinki process and to the Council of Europe's standards.[103] In early December, the Hungarian Ministry of Foreign Affairs issued a Resolution on the increasing intolerant nationalism in Romania and other countries that had freed themselves from communism, and explained Hungary's policy of supporting Hungarian minorities living beyond its borders. Antall reaffirmed our commitment to the international documents then in force, adding that Hungary sees "the way to a satisfactory solution of minority problems in the establishment of democratic conditions, the enforcement of the

---

[102] The opposition in Romania, which was certainly more democratic than the ruling elite, has consistently described Iliescu's regime as a post-communist dictatorship. Gusztáv Molnár, "Új diktatúrák—csomagolva" [New dictatorships—packaged], in Gusztáv Molnár, *Alternatívák könyve*, vol. 3, *Összmagyar alternatíva* [Book of alternatives, vol. 3, All-Hungarian alternative] (Kolozsvár: Pro Philosophia Kiadó, 2014), 117–20. According to Vladimir Tismaneanu, a Romanian political scientist who fled to the United States, this was "the fifth dictatorship, the rule of the sycophantic despot." Molnár, *Alternatívák könyve*, 124.

[103] Speech by József Antall at the CSCE Summit, *Magyar Külpolitikai Évkönyv, 1990*, 315–20.

right to national self-determination, a policy based on it, unconditional respect for human rights and fundamental freedoms, and the full guarantee of the individual and collective rights of national, ethnic, religious, linguistic and other minorities."[104]

The same spirit was expressed in the statement of the Hungarian Ministry of Foreign Affairs issued on the occasion of the first anniversary of the Timișoara protests. It reaffirmed Hungary's commitment to human rights, including the individual and collective rights of national minorities, and stated that the Hungarian government continued to "wish for sincere reconciliation between the Romanian and Hungarian peoples, which must prevail among the widest strata of society, in spirit and will, and hopes that relations will not be disturbed in the future by any 'hostile image' on either side. [...] Hungary continues to follow the democratic process of renewal in Romania with the same sympathy that it showed during the dramatic days of Timișoara and Bucharest last December and the changes that followed."[105] A few days later, in a communication, we expressed our concern over the escalating tensions in Romanian-Hungarian relations.[106]

These statements may sound too strong, but they were warranted. On October 30, 1990, Csaba Tabajdi, a Socialist MP who did commendable work in the defense of Hungarian and other minorities during the last period of the party-state era, addressed an interpellation to me on the subject "Guaranteeing the rights of Hungarian national minorities living beyond the border." He pointed out, "We must make international public opinion aware that the disorderly state of national and ethnic minority affairs in Central and Eastern Europe, together with the growing nationalism and the socio-economic crisis in our region, is a serious problem which threatens the process of democratization, the integrity of certain countries, and may set off a chain reaction of bilateral conflicts with unforeseeable consequences." He did not agree with my statement in the October 13 issue of *Magyar Nemzet* that "now the support of European public opinion and political factors can be secured in the field of minority rights." In his opinion, the performance of the previous Németh government compared favorably to that of the current government with respect to the protection of the national minorities. In my reply, I praised Tabajdi's previous activities and referred to the encouraging results of the OSCE Copenhagen meeting, to my speeches and discussions on minority rights in New

---

[104] Statement of the Ministry of Foreign Affairs on the national-ethnic tensions in East-Central Europe, December 5, 1991. *Magyar Külpolitikai Évkönyv, 1990*, 338–39.
[105] Statement of the Ministry of Foreign Affairs of the Republic of Hungary, December 17, 1990. Among my papers.
[106] Statement of the Ministry of Foreign Affairs on Hungarian-Romanian relations, December 23, 1990, *Magyar Külpolitikai Évkönyv, 1990*, 338–39; Sáringer, *Iratok az Antall-kormány*, vol. 1: 464 (Doc. 102).

York, and to their positive and unopposed (apart from the Romanian) reception. I mentioned our initiatives to conclude bilateral treaties with neighboring countries, the draft international agreement on national minorities drawn up and proposed for adoption by our Ministry of Foreign Affairs, and finally, the recommendation to ministers on the rights of minorities (not just individuals!) just adopted in the Parliamentary Assembly of the Council of Europe, which was in line with our objectives.[107] I could have added that at a human rights symposium in the Reichstag building in Berlin at the beginning of October, the state secretary of the German Foreign Ministry had agreed on the need to codify minority rights.[108] My reply was accepted by Mr. Tabajdi and also by the National Assembly. The MP even added, in a fair way, that "unfortunately, no substantial breakthrough has been made on the minority issue in recent months. But that is no fault of this government, it is a very long, years-long, decades-long process, requiring further efforts."[109]

In my reply to Năstase's letter, I wrote that in the "Hungarian government statement of November 3, which he objected to, almost all the quotes are taken with words omitted and inaccurate translations." Despite my colleague's "ultimatum-like tone," as a committed advocate of improving bilateral relations, I pointed out that both the Council of Europe and the CSCE documents used the term "national minority" and "persons belonging to national minorities" interchangeably, i.e., they recognized that minorities constitute a community, so the concept could not be called an anachronistic thesis. Point 8/c of Council of Europe Resolution 95/1990 on Romania speaks of the "individual and collective rights of ethnic and national minorities." In his letter Năstase rejected and declared contrary to equality the assertion that minorities should have special rights. However, the Copenhagen document of the CSCE also talked about special measures to ensure full equality of rights, and the Council of Europe's Committee on Non-Member States identified it as a precondition for Romania's membership, stressing that special measures for the equal rights of minorities "should not be considered as an act of discrimination." I contrasted the 1946 De Gasperi-Gruber Italo-Austrian agreement and the 1975 Italian-Yugoslav treaty signed in Osimo with the Romanian Foreign Minister's rejection of the relationship between minorities and their mother country. I confirmed that Hungary was explicitly requesting the support of its neighbors for its own

---

[107] Minutes of the Hungarian Parliament, October 30, 1990, https://www.parlament.hu/naplo34/047/0470165.html. On October 1, 1990, the Parliamentary Assembly of the Council of Europe did adopt its Recommendation 1334 (1990) on the rights of national minorities.

[108] *Külügyminisztériumi tájékoztató, 1990*, 238–39.

[109] Minutes of the Hungarian Parliament, October 30, 1990, https://www.parlament.hu/naplo34/047/0470171.html.

minorities. As Năstase regularly spoke about international standards for minorities, I suggested that our experts work together in elaborating those standards, bringing into consideration the declaration of the December 1, 1918, Romanian plebiscite in Gyulafehérvár/Alba Iulia and the promises of the Romanian National Salvation Front on January 5, 1990.[110]

We had no reason to be optimistic about the Romanian government's expected behavior, and our concerns were compounded by the fact that a parliamentary committee had recently been set up, at the initiative of politicians from the nationalist Romanian National Unity Party, to hear the cases of Romanians "expelled" from the counties of Harghita and Covasna after the revolution. Unfortunately, the European tendency to turn a blind eye to manifestations of aggression and intolerance, believing that they would disappear as a result of conciliatory gestures, was already emerging. Seeing that Iliescu and his party, the Salvation Front, had won in the May elections in Romania, the European Community decided on September 17 to sign a Cooperation Agreement with Romania, on the basis of the positive experience of the "troika" of foreign ministry heads of department who had visited that country on July 1–2, 1990. In the European Parliament, Newton Dunn, a British (Conservative) MEP, asked whether the EC Council was satisfied with the way in which Romania was guaranteeing human rights for all the peoples of Romania and whether it was justified in including that country in the PHARE program? The answer was that the Convention was "merely a political signal to the Romanian government to continue on the path of reform and democracy."[111] The response to Dunn went on to state that assistance under PHARE would depend on whether the Council saw further progress in reforms.

Unfortunately, the world press had tended to see the Romanian-Hungarian dispute as an old-style nationalist frenzy, and to attribute Budapest's pro-minority statements to domestic political objectives. Even more regrettably, the source of this accusation was often the domestic opposition within Hungary.[112]

Is Europe helping?

The European Community of twelve members welcomed the change of regime in Central Europe, but not with overwhelming enthusiasm. If it had happened in just

---

[110] Géza Jeszenszky to Adrian Năstase, December 22, 1990.
[111] Stephen Biller of the Democratic Group informed me of this case in a letter dated December 4, 1990.
[112] In the *Los Angeles Times*, January 11, 1991, Carol J. Williams, in her article "Transylvania Ignites Fires of Nationalism," quoted Miklós Gáspár Tamás MP from the Opposition SZDSZ, who said that the Antall government was "trying to shore up its declining support by reviving dreams of retaking Transylvania."

two or three countries (Poland, Hungary, perhaps Czechoslovakia), those countries would probably have received considerable political and financial support and rapid integration within the Community. This was just as had happened with Spain and Portugal, then Greece—all emerging from dictatorship. But the bankruptcy of the whole communist bloc was already frightening to those who had become accustomed to prosperity. In addition, the costs of bringing East Germany, the former GDR, up to Western standards were proving to be beyond all expectations.

Continuing in the spirit of the CSCE Copenhagen Recommendations, the Parliamentary Assembly of the Council of Europe adopted Recommendation 1334 (1990) on October 1, 1990, which stated: "Respect for the rights of minorities and of persons belonging to them is an essential factor in the preservation of peace, justice, stability and democracy. The State in which they live must recognize them as a national minority and it is legitimate for them to require special measures to preserve their identity. The State has a duty to facilitate this and to eliminate prejudice." The recommendation finally reaffirmed the need for an additional protocol to the Convention on Human Rights or a Council of Europe convention on the protection of minorities.[113] This was the main hope and goal in Hungary.

Undoubtedly, time has vindicated Csaba Tabajdi's pessimism about European support—rather quickly. Our embassy in Bonn, following a visit of Prime Minister Petre Roman to that city, reported that the German side saw no chance of changing the Romanian government's policy towards the Hungarian minority. They advised Hungary to focus on multinational forums, the CSCE and even more so the Council of Europe. While Germany supported the drafting of a Minority Charter, it did not expect it to be able to provide a comprehensive settlement of the rights of national minorities in Europe. The conclusion of the Hungarian Embassy was that we could not expect recognition of collective rights—mainly because of French and Spanish opposition—and with Romania, we could only expect support for the enforcement of general democratic rights.[114]

On the basis of the German attitude, Ambassador István Horváth, who at the dawn of the regime change had made good use of the popularity of Hungarians and built up excellent contacts in the Federal Republic, wrote to Prime Minister Antall that Germany's main goal was "to accelerate the process of European unification," that in this respect it considered the demand for collective minority rights to be an

---

[113] http://assembly.coe.int/Main.asp?link=/Documents/AdoptedText/ta90/EREC1134.htm. This document is no longer accessible, but the 1992 UN Declaration on the Rights of persons belonging to national or ethnic, religious and linguistic minorities (http://www.un-documents.net/a47r135.htm) reflects its spirit.

[114] Encrypted cable from Bonn, December 7, 1990, published in Sáringer, *Iratok az Antall-kormány*, vol. 1: 528–30 (Doc. 122).

obstacle, and that the treaties planned with Poland and Czechoslovakia would not even mention such rights. The Hungarian policy to this end could not therefore be supported by the FRG. [!] The Ambassador also reported a disappointing situation in the Hungarian-Romanian dispute over the unresolved rights of the Hungarian minority in Romania: the Western European governments, especially the French, saw Hungary as trying to improve the situation of the Hungarian minority by isolating Romania, "and the Romanian leadership is unscrupulously reinforcing this impression." Hungary's German friends, he continued, would therefore like to see a change in Hungary's policy towards Romania that would only advocate "full respect for general freedoms and human rights" and the creation of conditions for education and culture in Hungarian. At the Conference of Experts on Minorities to be held in Geneva in 1991, Hungary should "temporarily" give up the demand for collective rights, so that when the international climate is more favorable, we could "return to our original legitimate demands."[115]

I don't suppose that Ambassador Horváth—an "old hand" in the ministry with a close relationship with the foreign minister of the last communist government, Gyula Horn—did not convey the German position authentically. The ambassador apparently saw no chance, using his good connections, to persuade the German government to be more understanding of Hungary's concerns. But did he even attempt to do so?[116] However, it reflects badly on the German and other European representatives in Bucharest that they did not advise their governments how anachronistically chauvinistic and anti-Hungarian Romania's minority policy was, and how perceptible was the widespread and constant violation of human rights. It is also worth asking how much effort was made by the leadership and parliamentary representation of the RMDSZ to make foreign diplomats more aware of the serious grievances of the Hungarian minority.

On behalf of the Secretariat of Hungarians Beyond the Border, István Zalatnay (soon vice president of that office) proposed a solution to overcome the reluctance for an all-European solution, namely that Hungary should first conclude a bilateral agreement on minority protection with those countries that were willing to go furthest in guaranteeing minority rights. This should include not only comprehensive individual rights but also collective rights, local government, an international

---

[115] Copy of a letter from Ambassador Horváth to Prime Minister Antall, dated December 18, 1990, sent to me on December 31.

[116] There is no indication in István Horváth's memoirs that he tried to use his good reputation and Hungary's popularity to convince his contacts to understand the cause of the Hungarian minorities better. See István Horváth, *Az elszalasztott lehetőség: A magyar-német kapcsolatok 1980–1991* [The missed opportunity: Hungarian-German relations, 1980–1991] (Budapest: Corvina, 2009).

court and NGOs responsible for monitoring minority protection measures and laws. The countries of Central and South-Eastern Europe would find it difficult to accept such binding rules for themselves because of their own minorities, and former colonial powers having large Muslim, Asian and African "new minorities," too, would not be eager to accept a binding convention. Zalatnay saw most hope for a far-reaching agreement with Ukraine, a country which aspired to independent statehood. In the case of Yugoslavia, he saw interest in such a treaty on the part of the individual member republics, as it would secure the future of their mutual minorities.[117]

At the end of 1990, leading officials of Hungary's Ministry of Foreign Affairs reviewed the possibilities of Hungarian policy for the promotion of minority rights. István Körmendy, head of the Department for European Cooperation, stated that "the obvious approach of relying on Western sympathy and helpfulness towards Hungary in order to obtain direct support and partners in the treatment of minorities, and of urging joint or corporate action and pressure against certain neighboring states, especially Romania, which could be rightly criticized for their treatment of minorities, does not seem to be promising." He cited Western fear of tensions, which could lead to military conflicts, as a primary explanation, and also a reluctance to take sides in bilateral disputes reminiscent of the Greek-Turkish relationship, regardless of the merits of the dispute. As long as the countries of Eastern Europe had been dictatorships, the Western democracies were sympathetic to the Hungarian stand for minority rights, but now they saw it as a factor hampering the democratic transition of Bulgaria and Romania, according to Körmendy.[118] The deputy head of Körmendy's department, Iván Bába, rightly pointed out in the meeting that, in relation to the Council of Europe, the majority of member states stuck to the concept of the nation state, while the concept of the cultural nation was often identified with territorial claims. Many Western European countries— notably Britain, France, Greece and Turkey—were interested in shelving the issue because of their own minorities. Bába, like Zalatnay, suggested that the issue of each Hungarian minority should be treated as a separate problem and that it should be resolved primarily in a bilateral framework. He called for a Hungarian law on nationalities to be passed as soon as possible, also bilateral agreements and declarations with the neighbors who were willing to do so, and for preliminary studies to be prepared and circulated for the summer conference in Geneva. He rightly

---

[117] Draft by Zalatnay, October 19, 1990.
[118] The issue of national minorities in European multilateral forums. Summary of the discussion at the Department for European Cooperation. Comment by I. Körmendy, January 2, 1991. Among my papers.

stressed that Hungarian foreign policy on minority protection should be on the offense but unemotional and should use legal language.[119]

At the time, Zsuzsanna Hargitai was a recognized expert on minority issues in the ministry. In a separate memo she pointed out that in the wake of the regime changes national pride was turning into nationalism in many countries, and therefore in the CSCE process conflict prevention was given priority in the minority issue at the expense of human rights. In the Hungarian-Romanian debates, Hungary was striving for the internationalization of the issue, and that was disapproved of. Among the thirty-four participating states, Bulgaria, France, Greece, Romania and Turkey rejected the notion of collective rights, and some did not even recognize the very existence of their minorities. The Netherlands, Canada, Germany, Great Britain, Norway, Italy, Austria, Switzerland and Sweden were proactive on the issue, but only Italy and Austria referred to the minority as a community. Yugoslavia, which used to be very active on the issue and also spoke of collective rights, had recently come to emphasize only territorial integrity. Czechoslovakia, Poland, the Soviet Union, the United States, Belgium, Spain and Portugal were, according to Hargitai, deliberately slow, aloof and reclusive in their involvement. Hungary, she said, "is the only country to claim the establishment of collective rights," and all states deny the concept as a legal term. The active role of governments, "positive discrimination," was not supported either. There was a general fear of "new nationalism" and "Balkanization." Many people were critical of the Hungarian behavior because of its advocacy of collective rights, its commitment to the interests of Hungarians beyond its borders, and because of the inclusion of minority issues in bilateral relations. Hungary's own minority policy (lack of representation in parliament, the situation of the Roma, and alleged anti-Semitism) was also coming under criticism. At the same time, the following concepts might be accepted: the idea that minorities should be involved in decisions concerning them, that special measures taken in their interests should not be considered discriminatory, and that in the administrative division as well as in the delimitation of electoral districts the national composition should be taken into account. Hargitai suggested that in the various forums the emphasis should be on implementing the norms already agreed upon, that instead of special rights, measures should be called for ensuring real equality, that collective rights should only be presented as a matter of personal practice, that the principle of inviolability of borders should not be linked to the "granting" of minority rights, and that, finally, it should be stressed that the best way to prevent conflicts was to ensure minority rights. Hargitai's analysis warned that the Geneva

---

[119] Intervention by I. Bába at the meeting, December 27, 1990. Among my papers.

conference in July should not be expected to produce new minority standards, and at best it would take stock of progress to date and address the implementation of the measures already agreed.[120]

Poland, the old friend

As a result of the border change in 1920, Poland, reborn in 1918, ceased to be our neighbor—except for the few months between March 1939 (Hungary's re-annexation of Subcarpathia) and the joint German-Soviet attack on Poland that September. In 1989, the two countries were moving in parallel towards complete regime change, and by 1990, like-minded, anti-communist democrats were at the helm in both countries. Both past and present dictated that we should continue to see each other as neighbors, as mutual sympathy and a community of values were more important than physical contact. And a genuine good neighbor was much needed by both countries. We also counted on Poland in our neighborhood relations because it bordered two (now three) of our actual neighbors. On June 8, 1990, less than two weeks after the Antall government was sworn in, Prime Minister Tadeusz Mazowiecki[121] arrived in Budapest for an official visit. He was accompanied by then deputy minister of national defense Bronisław Komorowski, who was president of the Republic of Poland in 2010–2015. The Polish prime minister met the entire Hungarian political leadership, including the opposition parties, and there was consensus on the need to increase cooperation in all areas, especially in the economy, and to back up words with deeds.

Already at that time, the desirability of a closer tripartite relationship, with Czechoslovakia added, was envisaged. The Polish prime minister made no secret of his concerns about a united Germany and accepted our offer to help build trust in Polish-German relations.[122] The follow-up was the official visit to Budapest by Polish foreign minister Krzysztof Skubiszewski[123] on December 11–12. A distinguished international lawyer, fifteen years my senior, he had everything that ideally characterizes a foreign minister: a thorough knowledge of law and history, a broad

---

[120] Zsuzsanna Hargitai's memo, January 2, 1991. Her arguments were realistic, and close to the views of the political opposition.
[121] Tadeusz Mazowiecki (1927–2013): Polish journalist, philanthropist and politician, one of the leaders of the Solidarity movement, and the first non-communist Polish prime minister since 1946 (1989–1991).
[122] Ministry of Foreign Affairs summary of the visit of the Polish Prime Minister, June 13, 1990. Among my papers. Cf. Communiqué of the official visit to Hungary by Tadeusz Mazowiecki, prime minister of the Republic of Poland, *Magyar Külpolitikai Évkönyv, 1990*, 206.
[123] Krzysztof Skubiszewski (1926–2010): Polish international lawyer and politician, minister of foreign affairs (1989–1993).

education, high-level command of several languages, intimate knowledge of the outside world, was at home in culture, and had urbane manners and a willingness for compromise. (He went so far as to express in Berlin in the autumn of 1990 his deep sympathy for the Germans who had been driven from their homeland when, in 1945, Poland was literarily moved westward.[124]) Moreover, he had everything a Hungarian could hope to expect from a Pole: he knew and understood us, he was convinced of our interdependence based on the past and present interest, and he always kept that in mind in his political activities. This distinguished statesman welcomed me into his personal friendship. I have been on good terms with many of my fellow ministers on the basis of political understanding and mutual sympathy, but Skubiszewski and I have always been in complete agreement on fundamental issues; I cannot even recall any differences of nuance. On bilateral relations this was natural, but until 1993, when he left office, we also had the same views on difficult issues such as the assessment of Soviet and then Russian policy, our relations with the United States, the need for the preservation of NATO and entry into it, the importance of good German-Polish relations, the independence of the Baltic States and Ukraine, and, once achieved, on political support for those countries. We were also in full agreement on our European policy, not least on the steps to be taken regarding the Southern Slav crisis. At our first official meeting, we declared that we must negotiate the complete dissolution of the Warsaw Pact, and we agreed to strengthen our cultural relations and to open a Hungarian consulate in Krakow.

I returned the visit of my Polish colleague on June 12–13, 1991, flying to Warsaw. I was received by President Wałęsa,[125] called on Prime Minister Bielecki, the presidents of the Sejm and the Senate, and Bronisław Geremek, chairman of the Foreign Affairs Committee.[126] We all noted that the difficulties of the transition were similar in our two countries: general disillusionment among the people and the activization of supporters of the old regime. We agreed that we could not accept that the Soviet Union would put limitations on our sovereignty in the treaties that were under preparation, and that we must pursue a common policy towards the West. Our countries became formal allies when we joined NATO in 1999 and the European Union in 2004. There was also mutual sympathy between Skubiszewski and Antall; in December 2003 he attended and spoke at the József Antall Memorial

---

[124] Minister Skubiszewski's speech at a symposium in Berlin on October 5, 1990, as reported by the Hungarian Ministry of Foreign Affairs on October 9. Among my papers.
[125] Lech Wałęsa (1943–:) Polish electrician, dissident, founder of the Solidarity movement in 1980. President of Poland (1990–1995), Nobel Peace Prize laureate.
[126] Bronisław Geremek (1932–2008): Polish social historian and politician, minister of foreign affairs (1997–2000).

Conference in Budapest. He recalled that the Hungarian prime minister, when they met for the final time, had stressed that "politicians must not only understand the secrets of their profession, but above all they must follow the dictates of decency and honor. Otherwise, things will go wrong sooner or later."[127]

---

[127] Krzysztof Skubiszewski on the international role of Antall, see *A politikus Antall József—az európai úton: Tanulmányok, esszék, emlékezések a kortársaktól* [József Antall, the politician: Studies, essays and recollections by contemporaries], ed. Géza Jeszenszky, Károly Kapronczay, and Szilárd Biernaczky (Budapest: Mundus Magyar Egyetemi Kiadó, 2006), 386–92.

Chapter 4

An Attempt at Cooperation: Visegrád and Further Efforts for the Protection of National Minorities

Visegrád or the new Central Europe

After the Second World War, Central Europe disappeared even from the vocabulary of the world. Those whose fate brought them to the wrong side of the descending Iron Curtain found themselves in Eastern Europe, in the Soviet empire. But in Poland, Czechoslovakia and Hungary, writers and thinkers ignored this, and their crushed uprisings proved that they hadn't accepted their immersion in the East. Their protests were expressed in 1983 in Milan Kundera's essay "A Kidnapped West or the Tragedy of Central Europe,"[1] which I read the following year in Budapest in samizdat. All my friends welcomed it as an expression of our own convictions. In the wake of the writings of Czesław Miłosz, Václav Havel, Jenő Szűcs and György Konrád, in 1986 British historian, author and commentator Timothy Garton Ash argued convincingly for the existence of Central Europe,[2] and this was brilliantly vindicated in 1989, in the *annus mirabilis*. The Hungarian regime changers lived up to the idea of Central Europe, and Antall, in his prime ministerial speech, also expressed his belief in it. The László Teleki Foundation and the Central Europe Institute, which also included the Danube Valley Institute, were set up to strengthen and institutionalize this idea.[3] The political embodiment of the idea of Central Europe was the inter-state cooperation named after Visegrád, the royal see of Hungary in the fourteenth century, where in 1323 the Polish, Czech and Hungarian kings held a royal summit.[4]

---

[1] Milan Kundera, "A Kidnapped West: The Tragedy of Central Europe" first appeared in 1983 in the French journal *La Debát*; it was translated and republished pretty much everywhere.

[2] Timothy Garton Ash, "Does Central Europe Exist?," *New York Review of Books*, October 9, 1986.

[3] Sadly, the government led by Ferenc Gyurcsány (1961–), prime minister in 2014–2019, abolished the Foundation, and no similar institution has been set up by the succeeding governments.

[4] The first account of the three Central European pioneering "new" democracies coming together is Rudolf L. Tőkés, "From Visegrád to Cracow: Security and Cooperation in Central Europe," *Problems of Communism* 40, nos. 5–6. (1991): 100–14. My most recent summary is Géza Jeszenszky, "Questions about the 25

It was said of Bismarck that after completing German unity, fearing for his achievements, he was haunted by "the specter of [anti-German] coalitions." With the transformation of Central Europe in 1990, the Antall government was haunted by the specter of the rebirth of the inter-war "Little Entente," the alliance of Czechoslovakia, Romania and Yugoslavia against Hungary. Some Slovak, Romanian and Serbian post-communist nationalist politicians would have liked to revive the alliance that had encircled Hungary in a ring of steel with a sixteen-fold military superiority over Hungary, coordinating the repression of their Hungarian minorities. The counter-example to the petty antagonism, however, was the solidarity among the intellectuals critical of the communist system and the links formed by the ideas and personal ties in the three countries, Poland, Czechoslovakia and Hungary, that rose against communism. Among the countries of the former communist bloc, in 1990 these three were the closest in terms of culture and mentality but also in terms of socio-economic development and dedication to democracy. Their center-right governments were determined to preserve and extend that solidarity and to act in unison for common goals. They wanted to go further than economic and cultural cooperation.

As early as April 9, 1990, President Havel invited Poland's and Hungary's heads of state and foreign ministers to Bratislava to discuss "integration into the European institutions, key issues of regional cooperation, and certain thorny issues in bilateral relations." That one-day meeting was attended by the Austrian, Italian and Yugoslav foreign ministers, too,[5] and for this reason alone it cannot be seen as the beginning of the Visegrád Cooperation, as it is often portrayed, especially by the Czech side. Nevertheless, in the second half of 1990 there were three follow-up meetings on lower levels between the Polish, Czechoslovak and Hungarian foreign ministries.[6]

On November 19, the Charter of Paris was signed, setting out the new principles and objectives for Europe after the political ice age. In an informal discussion (in my presence), József Antall proposed to the leaders of Czechoslovakia and Poland that they meet early in the following year in Visegrád, the site of the former triple reunion of the three kings, to agree on the tasks to be undertaken in the new historical situation. The Visegrád idea was the product of a common destiny and common interests, based on the realization, born of experience, of the need to act together against aggression, against ambitions from outside designed to conquer or threaten, defending the values and traditions of the peoples of this region. This was

---

Years of the Visegrad Group," in *Russia and Central Europe in the New Geopolitical Realities*, 38–47, XI International Scientific Conference, Moscow, December 1–2, 2016.

[5] *Magyar Külpolitikai Évkönyv, 1990*, 147–48.

[6] Sáringer, *Iratok az Antall-kormány*, vol. 1: 507–8, 565–79 (Docs. 130, 133, 134).

the main motivation for the dynastic marriages and personal unions between the Central European royal houses that had brought together what came to be called the "Visegrád" territories several times in the past. The defensive wars against the Ottoman Empire were joint actions, and while in their many wars of independence they fought separately, mutual solidarity and voluntary assistance were spectacularly manifested. Hungarian Prince Rákóczi's rising against the Habsburgs (1703–11), the Polish risings against Russian rule (1830–31, 1863), the Hungarian War of Independence (1848–49), Hungary's aid to Poland in 1939 and after, 1956 in Poland and Hungary, and the "Prague Spring" in 1968 all exemplify this mutual affinity and help, most notably is the Polish-Hungarian relationship.

The Second World War also brought a radical improvement in Polish-Czech relations—at least until Beneš abandoned the Poles at the end of 1943 in favor of a special agreement with Moscow. Unfortunately, there was also a bad tradition in Central Europe: seeking great-power patronage for selfish national goals—against each other. This was the case with the pan-Slavism of the Czechs and even more so of the Slovaks, the reconciliation of the Hungarians with the Habsburg dynasty in 1867 and its reinforcement by the German alliance, the Czech-Romanian-Serbian Entente against Hungary between the two world wars, and the Italian, and later German orientation on the Hungarian side.

The search for the causes of the common—one might say eternal—problems and the desire to find a remedy guided all those politicians, writers and thinkers who, in the past 200 years, have stood up for friendship and cooperation between the peoples who live between the Baltic and Adriatic, and between the Germans and the Russians. Instead of rivalry, looking for great power patrons, and fighting each other, many sought to foster concerted action to effectively counter and avert external threats. Among many famous and lesser-known figures, this Central European idea was represented—although not in their entire oeuvre and not with equal intensity—by the Czech František Palacký, the Hungarians Kossuth, Ady, Jászi, Bajcsy-Zsilinszky, Bibó and many other prominent writers and artists,[7] the Slovak Milan Hodža, and József Piłsudski and Władysław Sikorski of Poland. This heritage was given new content and purpose by the resistance to the communist dictatorship, by the many personal relationships that had developed, by the shared readings and writings, and by action that would build on them.

When the ground started to shift under the communist regimes, the authorities took great care to suppress expressions of solidarity, trying to turn the peoples of

---

[7] There is a long list of publications on this solidarity in the Hungarian language. In English I would single out Ignác Romsics and Béla K. Király, eds., *Geopolitics in the Danube Region: Hungarian Reconciliation Efforts, 1848–1998* (Budapest: CEU Press, 1999).

Central Europe against each other. This was in vain, given the answer by the Polish people who helped the Hungarians in 1956, by the Hungarian and Polish intellectuals who openly sympathized with the Prague Spring and protested its suppression. Charter '77, too, was the answer, and, spectacularly, so were the many Central and Eastern Europeans who came to Budapest in 1989 for the re-burial of the Hungarian martyrs of 1956. The answer was given by Havel and Dubček in 1989, and by Hungarian television, which promoted the changes in Prague and Bratislava by providing opportunities for them to address audiences in Czechoslovakia, and the Manifesto of the Hungarian Democratic Forum, addressed to "the new democratic organizations of Central and Eastern Europe" at that beautiful Faustian moment at Christmas 1989.

At the end of 1989 and the beginning of 1990, the democrats of Poland, Czechoslovakia and Hungary, and the governments that were formed following the free elections, were determined to preserve and extend solidarity, to work together for their common goals. One of the milestones in this process was the tacit and then growing support of Poland and Czechoslovakia for the stand Antall took in proposing the dissolution of the Warsaw Pact. It was in this spirit that President Havel spoke out for the rights of the Hungarian minority in Slovakia, it was manifest in numerous party programs, party meetings, personal contacts and publications that have since been forgotten.

The meeting of the foreign ministers on January 21, 1991, to prepare for the Visegrád summit was most promising.[8] It attracted widespread attention, especially since a few days earlier Soviet special military units had tried to stop the Lithuanians' growing independence aspirations in Vilnius with a series of deadly actions. In Europe, and much more so in Central Europe, people were filled with fear that the Soviet opponents of change might use military force to restore their shattered sphere of influence. After the Vilnius outrage, the need for unity and the early dissolution of the Warsaw Pact (Soviet soldiers were still stationed on our territories) was even more obvious. We expressed this in a joint communiqué.[9] However, there were a few dissenting voices. A commentary in the *Frankfurter Allgemeine Zeitung* ruled out a closer union between the three countries or nations on the basis of their historical differences.[10] The Russian paper *Izvestia*'s report from

---

[8] My report to the Government, see János Sáringer, ed., *Iratok az Antall-kormány külpolitikájához és diplomáciájához*, vol. 2, *(1991. január–1991. december)* [Papers relating to the foreign policy and diplomacy of the Antall government: January to December 1991] (Budapest: VERITAS Történetkutató Intézet és Levéltár - Magyar Napló, 2018), 867–71 (Doc. 184. January 30, 1991).

[9] The tripartite meeting of foreign ministers. HuMFA, Press Department S/V/16-1/1991, January 28, 1991. Among my papers.

[10] Johann G. Reissmüller, *Frankfurter Allgemeine Zeitung*, January 25, 1991.

Figure 8. Hungary's PM József Antall welcomes Poland's President Lech Wałęsa, on whose left is Hungary's ambassador to Poland Ákos Engelmayer, Budapest, February 15, 1991

Budapest suspected differences of opinion between the three countries,[11] and my state secretary, Tamás Katona, was quoted saying that anti-Czech, anti-Hungarian and anti-Semitic sentiment was growing in Slovakia. That latter was resented by the press there.[12] My Czech colleague Dienstbier, in a Slovak newspaper close to Prime Minister Vladimír Mečiar,[13] elegantly denied that relations between our two countries were bad, saying that we were discussing our differences on the Danube Barrage System and the issue of national minorities in a manner befitting good neighbors and that we could resolve these disputes on the basis of Western European principles. On the alleged competition among the three countries, he echoed my view: "We don't get somewhere faster by competing with each other, but by supporting each other, and we think that if one of us gets somewhere faster, it will essentially speed up the other countries' entry."[14]

Indeed, there was perfect agreement among the three countries on foreign policy. Gorbachev took note of this, and on February 13 the newspapers in the

---

[11] HuMFA, Press Telegram from Moscow, January 24, 1991. Among my papers.
[12] *Národná Obroda* (Bratislava), January 23, 1991. Among my papers.
[13] Vladimír Mečiar (1942–): Slovak politician known for his autocratic and pro-Russian policies. Prime Minister (1990–91, 1992–94, 1994–98). Instrumental in the split of Czechoslovakia.
[14] Interview with Jiří Dienstbier, *Národná Obroda*, January 23, 1991. Among my papers.

Figure 9. Presidents Havel and Wałęsa and PM Antall signing the Visegrád Cooperation, Visegrád, February 15, 1991

European capitals reported—on the basis of Antall's announcement in Budapest—that on February 25 in Budapest the foreign and defense ministers would sign an agreement on the dissolution of the military organization of the Warsaw Pact. It was also reported that the heads of state and government of Poland, Czechoslovakia and Hungary would meet at Visegrád on February 15.

The Declaration of Cooperation, adopted after the substantive negotiations held in Budapest on February 15, was signed at Visegrád, at the reconstructed site of the former Gothic Royal Palace on the Danube. The signatories were Presidents Havel of the Czech and Slovak Federative Republic, Wałęsa of Poland, and Prime Minister József Antall of Hungary. A solemn Declaration was also signed by the heads of state and prime ministers of the three countries, including Hungary's president Árpád Göncz and Prime Ministers Čalfa of Czechoslovakia and Bielecki of Poland. Foreign Ministers Skubiszewski of Poland and Dienstbier of Czechoslovakia were present, together with myself. Few of us are still alive from among the founders, but it is encouraging that the theme, the idea, has taken root. The winter sunshine that flooded snowy Visegrád was a good omen in my eyes, a promise of a good future. The document set out the long-held principles, political and economic aspirations of the new leadership of the three countries, that their aim was the "elimination of all existing social, economic and spiritual aspects of the

Chapter 4 – An Attempt at Cooperation

Figure 10. The founders of the Visegrád Cooperation: myself, Poland's FM Krzystof Skubiszewski, PM Jan Krzysztof Bielecki of Poland, President Lech Wałęsa, Hungary's President Árpád Göncz, Czechoslovakia's President Václav Havel, PM Antall, FM Dienstbier of Czechoslovakia, Budapest, February 15, 1991

totalitarian system," to build parliamentary democracy, the rule of law and a modern market economy, and to participate as soon and as fully as possible in European integration. A significant achievement was the emphasis "that national, ethnic, religious and linguistic minorities, in accordance with traditional European values and in harmony with internationally recognized documents on human rights, must be able to enjoy all rights in political, social, economic and cultural life, not excluding education." They committed "to develop a society of people cooperating with each other in a harmonious way, tolerant to each other, to individual families, local, regional and national communities, free of hatred, nationalism, xenophobia, and local strife." Practical steps to be taken included consultations on security, market-based economic cooperation, the development of North–South transport infrastructure, and that "they shall jointly develop multilateral cooperation to ensure optimum conditions for full realization of the rights of national minorities living on the territories of their countries."[15] This Solemn Declaration was pleased to note

---

[15] "Visegrad Declaration 1991," https://www.visegradgroup.eu/home/documents/visegrad-declarations/visegrad-declaration-110412-2. For the summary of the Hungarian Foreign Ministry on the meeting, see Sáringer, ed., *Iratok az Antall-kormány*, vol. 2: 882–89 (Doc. 188, February 16, 1991).

that "the awareness and the intention of the historic unity of our nations can now be expressed unhindered and in accordance with the genuine interests of our peoples at the highest level of political will."[16] There is a lingering assumption that Visegrád was born out of some kind of "Western pressure." That is totally unfounded. It is also pointless to argue over who initiated Visegrád, Havel or Antall. It was born out of the common awareness that our political aims warranted it.

The leaders of the three countries said in press statements that the meeting was extremely successful. As I recall the comment, it was: "We were saying the same things in different languages." The most detailed—and the most positive—comments were made by the Polish press, which stressed that Poland would be included in the Pentagonale and that there was agreement to phase out the Warsaw Pact. In the reports in the Hungarian newspapers—typical of the press at the time— the debate on the competence of Árpád Göncz, the head of state, and Antall, the prime minister, was given a great deal of emphasis, while the emphasis in the document on the rights of the national minorities was overlooked. Visegrád was a topic in the world press for days. According to some outlets, the declaration contained only generalities, but the majority of newspapers stressed that it had neither an anti-Soviet nor an anti-German edge, rather, the emphasis was on foreign policy consensus, rapid rapprochement with the West and deepening multilateral cooperation, a step towards free trade. Poland's *Rzeczpospolita* noted that what had been created was not a new bloc, federation or confederation, but rather cooperation among three states, while also open to other states, and not directed against anyone. According to the Romanian *Tribuna*, Visegrád was the trump in relations with the West. The *New York Times* called the three countries natural allies, but they were also competing with each other for Western investment. All major French newspapers reported in detail on Visegrád. *Libération* saw it as a way of distancing the three states from the Balkans, emphasizing the reconciliation among the Central Europeans. *Le Figaro* believed that the Soviet Union would continue to be able to exert influence on its former allies. In Britain, a commentary in the *Times* described the regional cooperation among the three countries as epoch-making, while the *Guardian* found only generalities in the Declaration of Cooperation. Italy's *l'Unità* welcomed the elimination of ethnic disputes and frictions, while *Corriera della Sera* highlighted the filling of a political void. Sweden's *Dagens Nyheter* published a long, factual report on the meeting on February 16, and the following day *Svenska Dagbladet* editorialized that the slowness of Soviet troop withdrawal could also explain the rapid rapprochement of the Central Europeans to the West. The latter

---

[16] *Magyar Külpolitikai Évkönyv, 1991*, 145.

paper warned that "it is in the interest of the Soviet Union's Red reactionaries to disturb progress in Eastern Europe and create instability in the formerly compliant countries: they lack no means of doing so."

At that time, several Moscow newspapers still had correspondents in Budapest, and their articles spoke positively of the Visegrád Declaration, stressing that the three countries were not about to ally themselves against the Soviet Union. Correspondent Lukyanov noted in *Izvestia* on February 9 that "the aspiration of the former socialist countries is to forget as quickly as possible all that tied them to the Soviet Union. One incentive for this effort is the instability in the Soviet Union and another is the desire to return to Europe." The Romanian reaction was interesting: in a television interview the day after the signing, Foreign Minister Năstase stressed the security aspects of the cooperation but did not mention that his prime minister had written a letter offering his country's membership in the tripartite cooperation. His government's official newspaper, *Azi*, however, criticized the three countries' "desire for isolating themselves" from the rest of the former Soviet bloc, apparently hinting at the rebuff of the offer to join Visegrád. Austrian foreign minister Alois Mock praised Visegrád because the huge political, economic, social and environmental burdens that these countries had inherited from the previous regime called for greater cooperation. The pithiest commentary appeared in the *Frankfurter Allgemeine Zeitung*: "The Central European countries are weak alone but together they are irresistible, a fact Gorbachev was the first to acknowledge."[17] Indeed, on July 1, 1991, the Warsaw Pact was dissolved with the acquiescence of the Soviet Union.

Visegrád in action

I personally have been and remain committed to the Visegrád idea and to the closest possible cooperation between its countries. My attitude was shared by Rudolf Tőkés, a political scientist who fled in 1956, became a highly respected professor in the United States, and was the author of the first and most thorough monograph on the Hungarian road to regime change.[18] His acerbic sense of humor and sharp language were thought by many to express cynicism, but I think he remained at

---

[17] This summary of the reactions in the world press is based on cables from the Hungarian diplomatic missions, in my possession. Cf. the news summaries of MTI, the Hungarian Telegraphic Agency, also among my papers.
[18] Rudolf L. Tőkés (1935–): Historian and political scientist. Fled Hungary after the 1956 revolution, earned a doctorate in political science at Columbia University in New York, and later became a professor of political science at the University of Connecticut. Author of *Hungary's Negotiated Revolution: Economic Reform, Social Change, and Political Succession, 1957–1990* (Cambridge: Cambridge University Press, 1996). Two

heart an anti-communist Hungarian patriot.[19] On the basis of our earlier meetings in the U.S., he accepted my invitation to become my unpaid personal adviser in the Foreign Ministry; we provided him only with an apartment to live while in Hungary. He was the author of many good ideas and advice in our discussions and correspondence.

On the basis of his experiences at a conference on European transformation held in Luxembourg on February 15–17, 1991, Tőkés put forward the following proposal: Within the former communist bloc, Hungary retained its leading role in the transformation, but this was not perceived by the outside world, due to a failure in our communication or for other reasons. To change this and to gain the necessary Western support for the economic transformation of the three countries, the László Teleki Foundation should organize a conference to assess the common problems of the Visegrád countries and to coordinate their needs.[20] He reported that the three Benelux states, and Luxembourg in particular, through special adviser to the prime minister Dr. Armand Clesse, were ready to work closely with the Visegrád countries.[21] (Clesse, by the way, had sharply criticized Romanian policy towards the Hungarian minority in a letter to Romania's prime minister Petre Roman.)

During March and April, Professor Tőkés visited Warsaw, Prague and Bratislava on my behalf, and held consultations with a total of twenty-eight Foreign Ministry experts and the "new" Hungarian diplomats there. He summarized his experiences and suggestions in a 21-page memorandum. According to him, the real antecedent of Visegrád was not the King's meeting of 1335, but the impact of the Helsinki Final Act in the three countries: the Charter '77, the Bibó *Festschrift* in Hungary in 1980,[22] the Polish Solidarity movement, and the joint appeal by opposition intellectuals in the three countries on the thirtieth anniversary of the Hungarian Revolution of 1956. Now, however, the dreams and hopes of the former "dissidents" had to be replaced by practical steps, ideas and actions, and agreements. Tőkés emphasized the importance of "Prime Minister Antall's exceptional political courage" at the Warsaw Pact summit in June 1990, when he announced Hungary's

---

years later it was published in a Hungarian translation. Tőkés acknowledged Antall's foreign policy merits but showed little understanding for his domestic policy: 436–39.

[19] Just one example: after the break-up of the Soviet Union, the conversion of the Soviet military industry to peaceful and useful production was a fashionable topic. I called the transfer of demobilized military officers to other fields "human conversion." Rudi liked the term and gave it the code name "from dog to bacon."

[20] Memorandum by Rudolf L. Tőkés, February 24, 1991. Among my papers.

[21] Memorandum by Rudolf L. Tőkés: "Three plus Three." Personal and Confidential. May 5, 1991. Among my papers.

[22] A collection of essays, a critical survey of the state of the country by seventy-five prominent authors, artists and scholars, honoring the highly respected political thinker, deceased in 1979. It could be circulated only as a samizdat.

proposal for a radical revision, practically the termination of the Pact, and the subsequent endorsement of the Hungarian position by the Polish and Czechoslovak government delegates. Tőkés perceived as a serious danger the hardliner tendencies that had been growing in the Soviet Union since the beginning of the year, threatening the three countries that had completely broken with communism and now found themselves in a no-man's land. He stressed that Romania in its bilateral treaty with the Soviet Union had accepted a clause limiting its sovereignty by a pledge never to join any organization considered to be hostile to the contracting parties, i.e., NATO. Hungary firmly rejected signing such a treaty. Professor Tőkés called Slovakia the "Achilles' heel" of the common security policy of Visegrád, since the representatives of the old regime and their "social-fascist ideology" remained almost intact there. He was right to see that even these three countries lacked the necessary internal stability, given their populations' disappointment in terms of their material expectations, and that only the fastest possible European integration could overcome that feeling. Even if the withdrawal of Soviet troops went smoothly, these countries would remain in a security vacuum, because the West feared for Gorbachev's position and was therefore in no hurry to include them in its own security system. As an antidote, Tőkés proposed the closest possible cooperation, a quasi-alliance, between the Visegrád countries, so that they could act together in international fora instead of competing and seeking individual advantages. The Benelux countries were ready to help them in this, not only with their own experience of cooperation, but also within the European Community, supporting early full membership. However, the specific interests of individual countries could limit the deepening of cooperation. A "Europe of the regions" and a "Europe without borders" created the post-war reconciliation and unity in Western Europe, and its adoption and realization would be one of Visegrád's most important achievements. Tőkés observed that the Poles and Czechs were more determined than the Hungarians to deepen cooperation, while Mečiar's nationalist-led Slovakia was more inclined to rely on the Soviet Union. He also noted that the chairman of the Hungarian Parliament's Foreign Affairs Committee, Gyula Horn, was almost sabotaging Visegrád (e.g., he blocked a visit to Budapest by the Polish Sejm's Foreign Affairs Committee), and his supporters in the Hungarian Foreign Ministry were not in favor of closer Central European cooperation. The Hungarian media behaved similarly. The Hungarian-American professor also perceived that all three countries tended to put their existing Western bilateral relations (Polish-French, Hungarian-German, Czech—the one-time Entente) ahead of joint team play. For the cooperation between the three countries to be meaningful, they needed to develop close regional cooperation alongside common security interests. The areas of cooperation were: regions and municipalities; trade, banking and finance; business and corporate relations; cultural, educational and scientific fields; and, finally, information and human contacts. He identified two serious problems: the Slovak aspirations for independence and the unresolved situation of the Hungarian minority in Slovakia—both of which he saw as representing the survival of the Slovak mentality of the communist era. Tőkés' specific proposal was that all three countries should set up permanent working groups to work out cooperation and appoint "plenipotentiary" delegates to implement the Visegrád decisions.[23]

The Hungarian-American scholar prepared his ideas in a highly condensed form in Hungarian, so that the Hungarian foreign service apparatus could become familiar with them. Iván Bába, the head of the multilateral diplomacy department, agreed with the main goals of the plan, but the "old guard" retained from communist times opposed the idea of security policy cooperation among the three countries as a "serious political mistake," because it would disrupt the security policy web created by the bilateral treaties between European countries.[24] Ferenc Somogyi, the administrative state secretary, expressed his disapproval of the involvement of an "external" (i.e., dilettante?) expert in the planning of Hungarian foreign policy, and strongly criticized Tőkés for talking about a kind of "Visegrád Alliance," and for imagining the acceleration of the European integration of Central Europeans with the help of smaller states, like Benelux, instead of relying on the leading powers of the European Community.[25]

In fact, the Visegrád Cooperation was not a formal alliance, and it was never meant as an alternative to Euro-Atlantic integration. The first results were immediately visible. On February 25, 1991, at a meeting of the Warsaw Treaty Political Consultative Council in Budapest, the foreign and defense ministers signed an agreement to dissolve the military organization. Foreign ministers, senior diplomats and other experts met regularly to coordinate their positions on the steps to be taken following the dissolution of the Warsaw Pact on July 1, 1991, and of the Comecon on June 28, 1991, and to prepare the Association Agreement with the European Communities to be signed at the end of the year. A common stand on minority rights also sent out a promising message in the face of the national disputes suppressed under communism and the manifestations of intolerance threatening in many countries. In the field of economic cooperation, CEFTA (Central

---

[23] Memorandum by Rudolf L. Tőkés: "The New Democracies of Central Europe: Cooperation, Competition and Coexistence (A Status Report)." Personal. May 6, 1991. Among my papers.
[24] Rudolf Tőkés' reply to Dávid Meiszter's note, 996/M.D., May 9, 1991. Among my papers.
[25] Dr. Rudolf Tőkés: "Three plus Three" [undated, May 1991], with comments by State Secretary Somogyi. Among my papers.

European Free Trade Agreement) was concluded in December 1992, but the re-establishment of regional links in the fields of transport, inter-enterprise cooperation, tourism and local government was a manifest intention that was moving forward, if not fast enough. Culture, education and youth relations were also not absent from the agenda of Visegrád meetings at various levels.[26]

The attempted coup in Moscow on August 19, 1991, (discussed in the next chapter) was also a test of Visegrád. The leaders of the three countries immediately contacted each other by telephone and arranged a high-level political meeting for the next day, August 20. The Hungarian side was represented by Antall's chief foreign policy adviser, Gyula Kodolányi. It was agreed that the V3 would write to the European Communities, NATO and U.S. president George H. W. Bush, asking for greater political and economic cooperation with the V3, and to prepare a common position on the situation in Moscow. The idea of calling an extraordinary Visegrád summit for August 21 was also discussed, but as the coup collapsed it was dropped.[27]

A month later, another political consultation took place in Warsaw. On the agenda, in addition to the preparations for the Cracow summit, were security policy (NATO, the arms reduction negotiations in Vienna, the deteriorating economic situation in the Soviet Union), the South Slav crisis, and the independence aspirations of Ukraine and Slovakia. Then came the annual session of the UN General Assembly. There the three Visegrád foreign ministers met separately with U.S. secretary of state James Baker. It was then that Baker and Dutch foreign minister Hans Van den Broek[28] used "Visegrád" as a noun to describe our group. Our two partners realized that there was no better, more expressive word to refer to our cooperation—perhaps because though the venue was in Hungary, the word itself was Slavic, meaning a high castle. Our Dutch friend explained that their Benelux trio, which works closely together within the European Community, could help the three of us by offering a lot of experience, and that with the realization of associate membership "the opportunities for cooperation will be greatly increased." He supported the so-called Dienstbier plan to continue to supply food and medicine to the insolvent Soviet Union in order to prevent a major humanitarian disaster, with the Western countries paying the price. The situation in Yugoslavia was also

---

[26] Károly Kriston's summary of June 20, 1991. Among my papers. A special Visegrád Fund was set up in 2000 to promote cultural programs.
[27] Gyula Kodolányi's summary of his talks in Warsaw, August 21, 1991. Among my papers.
[28] Hans Van den Broek (1936–2025): Dutch politician and diplomat, Minister of Foreign Affairs (1982–1993). European Commissioner (1993–1999).

discussed, in particular with a view to extending the size and the area of operation of the Monitoring Group.[29]

Both Presidents Havel and Wałęsa were personally strong supporters of the Visegrád idea, as they also expressed that in all their subsequent meetings with me. In 2005 in Gdańsk, marking the twenty-fifty anniversary of Solidarity, and in 2009 in London, commemorating *annus mirabilis*, these two heroes of our time recalled the first Visegrád summit and Antall's initiative with warm words. In a letter to the Hungarian prime minister in the autumn of 1991, the president of Czechoslovakia stated that "the prestige of our countries grows through our ability to formulate common positions and to coordinate our specific needs. [...] Joint action [...] will also provide a solid basis for the integrity and future stability of our region, at a time when it is going through a difficult period of trial and tribulation."[30]

The Krakow Summit of October 5–6, 1991, marked a second memorable moment for Visegrád: the unwritten alliance of the three Central European countries was sanctified in the Wawel Cathedral. It was also the day the Polish-Czechoslovak inter-state treaty was signed. (For legal considerations, the Hungarian-Polish treaty was signed by the parties in Warsaw the next day.) It was not the fault of the Hungarian side that the third treaty, the Hungarian-Czechoslovak one, was not signed, due to last minute Slovak objections. (Prime Minister Mečiar and the growing nationalism of Slovakia restricted the freedom of movement of members of the Czechoslovak government, and the autonomous Slovak government rejected that minority protection clauses be in the treaty.)[31] The foreign ministers' resolution adopted in Krakow stated that "events in Central and Eastern Europe and the Balkans make it necessary to raise the quality of the of the relation of their countries with NATO to a higher level."[32] We welcomed the statement by Foreign Ministers Baker and Genscher on October 2, which proposed the establishment of an institutional relationship between NATO and "the new democracies," essentially the countries of the defunct Warsaw Pact. The Krakow Declaration was a very substantial document. Most of it was about strengthening ties with the European Community, NATO, WEU and EFTA, also touching on the challenges arising from the drastic reduction in exports to the Soviet Union. The establishment of a working group on finance and on energy, the promotion of mutual trade and

---

[29] Memo by Emőke Sillár, my chief of cabinet, on the working breakfast of September 27, 1991. Among my papers.
[30] Letter from Václav Havel to József Antall, September 23, 1991. I have among my papers the Czech original and the unofficial translation.
[31] Sáringer, ed., *Iratok az Antall-kormány*, vol. 2: 667 (Doc. 144, October 3, 1991).
[32] The Statement of October 5, 1991, is among my papers.

investment, the simplification of banking relations, the strengthening of cooperation in the fields of infrastructure, the environment and culture were all desirable ways of deepening our cooperation. Our stance on the Yugoslav crisis was far ahead of the West's delaying and impotent attitude. Condemning "acts incompatible with the legal norms of warfare", our Declaration proposed "the dispatch of additional international peacekeeping forces." It also stated: "Solutions such as the right of nations to self-determination, including the right to acquire statehood [!] with full guarantees for the rights of minorities are considered desirable..."[33] What a pity that the European Community did not then pay more attention to the views of the Visegrád countries!

Figure 11. The Visegrád foreign ministers at the Cracow summit, October 5, 1991

Comparing the firm attitude of the leaders at the summit, as reflected in the documents adopted, with the cautious tone of the preparatory discussions, I can see that the bureaucratic apparatus of the three countries (like their Western counterparts) had difficulty in accepting the spirit of Visegrád, the essence of the "New Europe." But most Western leaders understood that Visegrád represented a promising and good example of a new kind of politics, of cooperation and the intention of taking joint action for the whole former communist bloc. It was the antithesis of the horrors unfolding in the Balkans. Rudolf Tőkés' observation that, while by dissolving the Warsaw Pact and Comecon, by rejecting the Soviet attempt at "Finlandization," they said no to the past; by their cooperation goals and methods, by establishing the values and institutions of liberal democracy, the V3 also displayed personal courage and showed the way for the future of their entire region.[34]

The Hungarian Parliament held a debate on foreign policy on October 15, 1991. In my ministerial statement I evaluated the Visegrád Cooperation with the following words:

---

[33] Declaration of October 6, 1991, *Magyar Külpolitikai Évkönyv, 1991*, 329–30. Cf. Sáringer, ed., *Iratok az Antall-kormány*, vol. 2: 895 (Doc. 191, October 6, 1991).
[34] Personal conversation with Professor Tőkés. Cf. Memorandum by Rudolf L. Tőkés, May 6, 1991. Among my papers.

We attach great importance to our regional cooperation with Czechoslovakia and Poland. The three countries, building on centuries of similar or identical historical experiences and cultural traditions, can develop an organic cooperation in the fields of foreign, security and economic policy that can serve as an example for the stabilization efforts in the post-bipolar Europe. The democratically elected parliaments and governments of the three countries face serious problems, but all three countries have made clear their ambition to integrate into Europe and to embrace Europe's political, economic and social values and norms, with all that they imply. The cooperation between the three countries can help each other to solve their problems, guarantee their security and integration into Europe. We want to develop this cooperation further, to make it more effective and deeper, and we are ready to involve regions of our neighboring countries in our work, in the framework of specific programs.[35]

In the spirit of Visegrád and Cracow, Antall informed Polish president Wałęsa and Czechoslovak president Havel of his visit to the North Atlantic Council and the EC on October 28, and said that his arguments had been well received in light of the proposal for differential treatment requested by the Visegrád Three. Secretary General Wörner agreed that in the event of an inter-state conflict in Europe, NATO should participate in a peace-building military operation in the framework of the CSCE.[36] (This is precisely what happened eight years later in the case of Kosovo, but unfortunately was not followed in 2014, when Russia started its military actions against Ukraine.)

The follow-up to the Krakow summit was dynamic and promising.[37] Here I will just outline the next stages of our cooperation.[38] In the North Atlantic Cooperation Council, which brought together NATO countries and the former Warsaw Pact countries and first met on December 21, 1991, the three Visegrád foreign ministers played a very active role, often in joint actions. In early 1992, in Washington, we argued for a "triangle deal" to manage the food crisis in the collapsed Soviet Union, which raised the threat of mass migration: the Central European countries would continue their food deliveries for the Soviet Union, and the EC would take care of the costs. Sadly, the idea was not taken up. Romania and Bulgaria, seeing

---

[35] Minutes of the Hungarian Parliament, October 15, 1991, http://www.parlament.hu/naplo34/136/1360004.html.
[36] Letter from Prime Minister Antall to Presidents Wałęsa and Havel, after October 28, 1991.
[37] Memorandum of the Regional Cooperation Department 384/refo, April 1992.
[38] For my later writings on Visegrád, see the bibliography in this volume.

the success of Visegrád, repeatedly asked to be included in this framework. Our response was unanimous: a friendly "no." This was not out of hostility or jealousy, but out of realism, because these two countries were much further behind us in the field of democracy and the market economy. We did not want to slow down the progress of our internal and international developments by adjusting our clocks to those lagging behind.

The next Visegrád summit took place in Prague on May 6, 1992. The Declaration issued declared full NATO membership as the long-term goal of the three countries. The Hungarian prime minister explained that the integration goals could be achieved speedily not by rivalry but by joint, coordinated action: "We will be more easily accepted together, and those who prefer separate ways will sober up in a few months." (Everyone knew that this was primarily addressed to Václav Klaus,[39] who was likely to win the Czechoslovak elections.) Antall stressed the need for a common European policy towards the successor states of the disintegrated Soviet Union, because "it would be naive to believe that centuries of political and foreign policy ambitions will be abandoned overnight."[40] The Hungarian prime minister had most friendly discussions with the two presidents. Knowing that Czechoslovakia was on the verge of disintegration, he told Havel how he hoped to see Hungary's relations with the two nations moving towards independence and how the separation would affect the Hungarian community in Slovakia. Antall also recalled that the Czech writer and statesman's uncle had in 1920 been the first diplomatic representative of Czechoslovakia in Hungary who had advocated Czech-Hungarian reconciliation. (I don't think anyone in Hungary knew that except Antall.) There was full agreement at the meeting with Polish president Wałęsa on the need to coordinate positions on the Russian troop withdrawal and other issues.[41]

The EC troika, too, attended the summit—to show their support for Visegrád and to help the re-election of President Havel and his supporters. However, Václav Klaus defeated the hero of the "Velvet Revolution." A few weeks later, the new Czechoslovak prime minister, invited to Budapest, unexpectedly attacked the principle of the Visegrád Cooperation. "It should not have even a single secretary," he said. With Klaus, the cooperation did falter, but it did not die. Many V3 embassies maintained regular meetings and joint actions. Independently of their ambitions for independence, the Slovaks also showed themselves to be supporters of Visegrád. Polish-Hungarian foreign policy consultations continued, including

---

[39] Václav Klaus (1941–): Czech economist and politician. Prime minister of Czechoslovakia (1992), of the Czech Republic (1993–1998). President of the Czech Republic (2003–2013).
[40] *Magyar Külpolitikai Évkönyv, 1992,* 190–94.
[41] My personal recollections of the two meetings.

Hungary and Its Neighbors, 1988–1994

Figure 12. Submitting Hungary's application for membership in the European Union: Athens, April 1, 1994

on the application for membership in the European Union. In order to promote Visegrád interests and values, it was appropriate to involve others in the cooperation on an *ad hoc* basis: Croatia and Slovenia in particular, but also the Balkan countries, the Baltic States and Scandinavia.

At the end of the decade, with the emergence of center-right governments, Visegrád was revived and entered a new, intensive phase. Membership in the European Union had brought new challenges. The four prime ministers issued a new Declaration on May 12, 2004, in Kroměříž (Czech Republic) stating with full satisfaction that the key objectives set in the 1991 Visegrád Declaration had been achieved and declaring their determination to continue the cooperation of the Visegrád Group countries as member states of the European Union and NATO.

Almost thirty years after the creation of the Visegrád Cooperation it had had its ups and downs, sometimes some people had declared it dead, only to see it rise with renewed vigor. It was founded by determined opponents of the communist dictatorship and committed supporters of Western democracy and the common interests of Central Europe. It will survive as long as this thinking remains dominant in these four countries. Lately, however, the association has weakened due to Prime Minister Orbán's attitude towards Russia's aggression against Ukraine, which the Fico-government follows. That should not be the end of Visegrád, as it rests on solid historical and political foundations.

The Central European Initiative

The Institute for East-West Security Studies (IEWSS) was established in New York in 1981, on the initiative of the late John Mroz, so as to bring the two world systems closer together on the basis of Western principles. It played an active role in promoting the stability and the success of the transition to a new Europe after the regime changes. During my visit to the U.S. in January 1990, I was invited to their headquarters together with Antall, and after the elections I was asked to be a member of its Board of Directors. The Institute organized an international conference to be held from June 6–9, 1991, at Bardejov (Bártfa in Hungarian), Eastern Slovakia. At it, politicians and academics discussed the current economic and political problems of Central Europe. In my talk addressing the gathering I asked: "Chto delat?" in Russian. (All those who grew up under communism knew that "What is to be done?" was the title of Lenin's 1902 pamphlet.) My view was that "the Iron Curtain should not be rebuilt a few kilometers to the east—to protect Europe's rich from its penniless. Rather, freedom and prosperity should gradually triumph throughout Europe, and eventually in countries outside Europe and America." In addition to the economic, political, cultural and educational tasks, I also referred to the interventions at the conference by Budimir Lončar of Yugoslavia and Yury Kvitsinsky, deputy foreign minister of the Soviet Union. Both spoke about the national minorities: one third of the population of Yugoslavia could be considered a national minority, as could 75 million in the Soviet Union. From that follows "the importance of maintaining ethnic and cultural diversity," I concluded. I recalled that Arnold Toynbee, the great philosopher of history and chronicler of international relations, argued as early as 1915 that the peace conference following the war would be far more important than the war itself; the main question to be settled would be how to bring about peace and mutual respect between the peoples, between ethnic communities who speak different languages and have a different culture.[42] The solution must be found now, not in the next century, I concluded.[43]

---

[42] Arnold Toynbee, *Nationality and the War* (London: Dent, 1915), 7.
[43] Based on the text of my presentation in Bardejov/Bártfa and my notes from the conference.

The conference was also attended by Romanian foreign minister Năstase. After the serious diplomatic clash at the end of the previous year, we had our first meeting (at the request of my colleague) in Madrid on February 21, 1991, at an extraordinary meeting of the Committee of Ministers of the Council of Europe. He complained that in the Political Affairs Committee of the Parliamentary Assembly of the Council of Europe the Hungarian representatives had abstained at voting on Romania's special invited status, and that I often criticized Romania in international fora. In my reply, I pointed out that my government could not instruct parliamentarians regarding what position to take abroad. Romania does not comply with several core standards of the Council, I said, but it was a gesture that the Hungarian members did not prevent Romania's aim by their vote. I objected, however, to the fact that foreign citizens visiting Romania are still banned from staying with relatives and friends, that Hungarian-language books and newspapers carried by travelers are checked at the border and some are confiscated. I wondered how the Romanian constitution, then being drafted, could declare Romania to be a unitary nation state, given that only Romanian was permitted to be used in the administration, courts and local government. The formation of parties on national or ethnic grounds was forbidden, even though many other national minorities besides Hungarians reside in Romania.

Năstase replied that these were issues still pending and that we should discuss them all during an official visit to Romania. I requested that the commemorations in Romania on March 15 (the National Day of all Hungarians) should not be obstructed and that there should be no provocations. My colleague promised me that.[44] One evening I invited Năstase for an informal, "friendly" chat without any escort or advisers. He accepted, and urged me to exclude Transylvania from our relations, to make Bucharest and the Black Sea coast the scene of our economic cooperation. I found his offer frivolous and explained why a rational person could not take seriously the "Hungarian irredentist threat." The Hungarians in Transylvania are realistic, and their political goals can be summed up in the word "survival." "The Romanians have never tried to assimilate other peoples," the minister, an international lawyer, replied. I asked, "Even if we completely ignore the Cumans, who inhabited present-day Romania a few hundred years ago and have now disappeared without a trace, where have the Phanariot Greeks, who only recently formed the elite of the two Romanian principalities, gone?" At first Năstase didn't want to understand my question, but when I recalled to him in detail the ethnic history of Romania, he finally gave in, saying, "My name also comes from Anastas." So he admitted his non-Romanian

---

[44] Zsolt Becsey's note on the Madrid meeting, February 27, 1991. HuMFA, 442/EEFO.

ancestry. I should have guessed from his complexion and his twisted wit that my tough debating partner must have Phanariot[45] blood in his veins.

The multilateral Italian-Austrian-Hungarian-Yugoslav cooperation, which, with the accession of Czechoslovakia, was expanded into the *Pentagonale* in 1990, added Poland to join its ranks in 1991, at the urging of József Antall, and thus the cooperation became the *Hexagonale*. It was not just a regular exchange of ideas between political leaders. From the outset, it comprised, in part, meetings of parliamentarians, social and cultural events, and working groups preparing programs for practical cooperation. From a Hungarian point of view, we considered that having a wider framework than Visegrád was important, and later we supported Romania's entry, among others, because we expected closer cooperation between the countries of this wider region, and increased trade between them, to bring economic prosperity, more jobs, a rise in living standards and even an improvement in the situation of national minorities. If the borders became more permeable, if transport links improved, the peripheral situation of the border areas and the dead-end nature of the small settlements there would disappear. In the case of Hungary, the borders of Trianon divided economically interdependent regions, cutting villages off from the big cities that were their natural markets, while roads and railways were closed. In the communist era, not only was there an Iron Curtain on the Austrian-Hungarian border, but there were very few border crossings to other neighbors, and crossing the heavily guarded "green border" was as forbidden as crossing the western one. From the very beginning, it was one of my priorities to change this situation, to open roads that had been closed long ago, to open new border crossings, or more precisely to reopen the ones that had been open before 1940. My hope, my long-term goal was to abolish borders in the same way as we were seeing in Western Europe with the Schengen Agreement (1985); abolish border control between its participants with the aim of a Europe without internal borders.

In 1990 the entry of Central Europe into the Schengen system seemed a long way off, so I did my best to (re)open as many border crossings with our neighbors as possible. The Ministry of Finance was reluctant to do so on the grounds of cost: a border crossing—usually outside a populated area—needed a nice big building for customs and border guards, and water and electricity had to be provided. Few believed that in a few years, with membership in the European Union, these buildings would become completely redundant. Also, the Ministry of Transport did not

---

[45] Phanariotes were prominent Greek families living in Phanar, the chief Greek quarter of Constantinople. They often held important positions in the Ottoman Empire, like Hospodar (ruling Prince) of Moldavia and Wallachia, the two Romanian provinces of the Empire.

want to spend money on repairing the roads to the border, which until 1919 used to carry heavy local traffic but which had then become dysfunctional, derelict, and overgrown with weeds, as a result of the border barriers. Most of our neighbors were not keen on making border crossing easier, partly because in most cases, it was Hungarians who lived on each side of the border, often cut off from close relatives, and this form of "national reunification" did not sit well with the majority nation's authorities. Western Europe and the United States, on the other hand, supported and encouraged, initially with modest but increasing financial support, trans-border programs and the strengthening of economic ties between neighboring states. I am proud that during my four years in office, the number of our border crossings by road doubled from about a dozen to more than a score.

Renewed efforts to enforce minority rights

Zsuzsanna Hargitai's analysis and that of the Analysis and Information Department, presented in the previous chapter, both proposed that our policy of advocating collective rights for minorities should be modified, owing to foreign rejection. That was pessimistic, but realistic. Nevertheless, I did not consider it feasible to radically revise the government program and the individual convictions of many of us, but rather sought to find a way out by bringing states sympathetic to the Hungarian approach on board and increasing their numbers by rational arguments. I hoped that the worldwide triumph and spread of democracy and the sober conduct of the Hungarians beyond the borders would be conducive to the fullest possible realization of minority rights. In Oszkár Jászis' apt expression, that was the "Archimedean point of democracy." The major opposition party, the Free Democrats (SZDSZ), put aside its radicalism of a few months earlier and fully embraced the assessment by Hargitai and her superior, Deputy State Secretary Dávid Meiszter. The debate at home between the government and the opposition was already then (and also later) between accepting a particular international position that was not favorable to us, or trying to change it.

The more optimistic view of the issue was supported at the conference "Liberalism and Collective Rights," held in Dunaszerdahely (Dunajská Streda in Slovakia) on January 12–13, 1991, organized by the Sándor Márai Foundation in Slovakia and the German Friedrich Naumann Foundation and held under the patronage of President Havel. Experts and politicians from ten countries (including Viktor Orbán, Csaba Lőrincz and Gusztáv Molnár from Hungary, and Oszkár Világi from Slovakia) almost without exception considered collective rights to be an inalienable part of human rights. In his opening speech, Viktor Orbán said that collective rights for minority communities were a logical corollary of liberal principles and values.⁴⁶ There was no objection to the fact that the most important collective right of minorities is that of self-government. Serious arguments were also made for the need for positive discrimination. However, a large majority rejected the position taken by Péter Kende (living in France), who argued in favor of the concept of nation being linked to citizenship.⁴⁷

On January 25, 1991, I discussed with the ministry officials Hargitai's and Ambassador Horváth's pessimistic assessment of foreign attitudes toward the rights of minorities. Deputy Director István Zalatnay's note from the Secretariate of Hungarians Beyond the Border correctly stated that several Western countries—because of their own minority problems—were reluctant to endorse the principle of collective rights. The West's primary interest being stability, we could not expect an all-European solution and acceptance of collective rights in the short term. In order to overcome that, he suggested that in our argument we should present the minority problem, the elimination of discrimination, as a condition for stability and try to conclude as many bilateral agreements as possible; these could in time become regional (i.e., for East-Central Europe) and a model. Rather than dreaming about changing the borders, which was impossible, we might expect an improvement in the situation of the Hungarian minorities through the strengthening of bilateral economic relations.⁴⁸

József Papp of the Analysis and Information Department pointed out that after the Second World War, Western Europe had taken a step backwards in the field of the legal protection of minorities and considered the minorities' separate identity from the majority nation, their collective rights and self-determination as a challenge to the unifying Europe, because it saw in them an attempt at secession. It was willing to support only individual rights. As the right of self-determination of national minorities was not recognized by the world, he suggested that the focus should be on the right to internal self-government, which did not threaten the *status quo*. The recognition of minority autonomy could only be expected after the "nation-state" stage of development had been surpassed. "Instead of a general recognition of community rights, we should strive for the acceptance of specific forms of community rights. The key issue is to acquire the right to self-government and autonomy in the fields of education, culture and information."⁴⁹

---

⁴⁶ Lőrincz et al, *Nemzetpolitika*, 25.
⁴⁷ Note by Iván Bába and Márta Kutasi, January 4, 1991. Among my papers.
⁴⁸ István Zalatnay on Hungarian Minority Policy, January 11, 1991. Among my papers.
⁴⁹ József Papp on the possibilities and limitations of minority policy. Position paper, January 22, 1991, 117/PETFO. Among my papers.

The Analysis Department concluded that our minority policy was not met with understanding, and that the Western countries "are today subordinating the assertion of minority rights in Eastern Europe to the preservation of European stability." The Western countries did not support the isolation of countries lagging behind in their democratic transition; on the contrary, they expected improvement of their policy to result from their eventual integration into the Western democracies, and this attitude came to prevail in the Council of Europe, too. However, the adoption of a Minority Charter remained on its agenda. Even though the CSCS no longer stood for collective rights, it still defended the identity of the minorities. The formerly strong advocate of minority protection, Germany, could only be relied on in the area of education in the mother tongue and culture. This was why, the Analysis Department concluded, minority rights violations should be criticized as human rights violations.[50]

Sándor Jolsvai, head of the department dealing with Hungarians living beyond the borders, said that we must not back down and that we should reference positive examples for Europe, such as South Tyrol and Switzerland, to show what the Hungarian minorities were striving for. The Copenhagen Recommendations or the Pope's message indicated that the idea of collective rights was slowly gaining ground in Europe, because that was the key to stability. It could also solve the internal problems of the Soviet Union.[51] My deputy, Tamás Katona, emphasized the importance of not allowing the Council of Europe to soften the conditions of entry. Some people might be irritated by the term "collective rights," so let us find another term with the same content, he suggested. Let us set an example in the treatment of national minorities in Hungary, and let us pass a law guaranteeing their collective rights as soon as possible. Let us build special relations with Ukraine, but also support the rights of Russians living in the member states of the Soviet Union.

Iván Bába, head of the Multilateral Diplomacy Department, pointed out that Western Europe was new to this problem in the East, and so we should explain that it is not a special "Hungarian issue," but a world-wide problem. It was advisable, however, that in international diplomacy it should not be Hungary but the parties of the Hungarian minorities who stand up for the cause of minority rights, while in our bilateral relations we should never take it off the agenda. István Körmendy of the European Cooperation Department, mindful of his negative experiences, suggested not to make a tactical retreat but only a correction. He considered it also

---

[50] Changing our minority policy in multilateral fora. Memorandum of the Analysis and Information Department, January 23, 1991. Among my papers.
[51] Jolsvai's contribution was based on a memorandum of the Department of the Hungarians Beyond the Border, dated January 10, 1991. Among my papers.

important to bring the Hungarian opposition parties on board with the government on this issue. Tádé Alföldy, deputy state secretary for Western European relations, suggested dropping the issue of collective rights and instead demanded stronger individual rights, leaving even that to the parties of the Hungarian minorities. He said it was inevitable that the Council of Europe would accept our neighbors without demanding that they change their minority policy. Perhaps the accelerated assimilation of the Hungarian minorities could be slowed if the Council of Europe were willing to exert pressure on its new members.

According to Géza Entz, head of the Secretariat for Hungarian Beyond the Borders, we needed to distinguish between our vision, strategy and tactics. Our goals would be promoted by a model minority policy in Hungary, as well as by bilateral and regional agreements. Imre Szokai, deputy state secretary for Central and Eastern Europe, said that it was desirable to establish principles with our neighbors, so that we could become a stabilizing factor. Dávid Meiszter, deputy state secretary for Multilateral Affairs, vindicated his earlier reservations, deplored Hungary's offensive policy and warned against confusing courage with blindness. He suggested that we should think with a Western mind and coordinate our bilateral and multilateral actions accordingly.

The conclusion I drew from the opinions expressed at that late January meeting was that we must continue to try convincing our Western partners that the minority problem, decentralization, and the focus on self-government were the key to peace and stability in Europe. We were at the time still before the outbreak of the Southern Slav crisis, which then proved our point.[52]

With increasingly cautious governments in Western Europe, there was more chance of support for our approach from some parties and MPs. Human rights were seen as an equal priority by Christian Democrats, Social Democrats and Liberals. Fidesz worked well to win support for the latter. Before the Liberal International's 1991 congress in Lucerne, Zsolt Németh and Csaba Lőrincz commented on the preparatory materials on minorities. They pointed out that "the minority individual is threatened precisely because of his membership in a group [...] In order to ensure that individual rights are not violated, the group must be protected. [...] The sovereignty of states must be limited by autonomy based on the principle of minority self-determination, but the self-determination of nations is limited by the sovereignty of states."[53]

---

[52] This summary is based on my papers and recollections.
[53] Lőrincz et al, *Nemzetpolitika*, 27.

The anti-Hungarian atmosphere in Romania and its causes

Among Hungary's relations with its neighbors the most acute issue was with Romania. Its gravity was felt by U.S. senator Joseph Lieberman, a Democratic candidate for vice president in 2000. The politician, who had Hungarian Jewish ancestry, was present as an observer at the Romanian elections in May 1990. He personally warned President Iliescu that the future of U.S.-Romanian relations depended largely on how the Hungarian minority was treated and strongly condemned the anti-Hungarian pogrom in Târgu Mures. On April 17, 1991, he raised the grievances of the Hungarian minority with Prime Minister Petre Roman and reiterated them in a speech to the U.S. Congress the same day.[54] On July 11, 1991, he and his fellow senator, Christopher Dodd, introduced a Senate Resolution condemning the growing anti-Semitism and anti-minority sentiment in Romania.[55]

The Visegrád Cooperation was difficult for Romania to digest, and Năstase invited me to make an official visit to Bucharest, with the prospect of a Transylvanian excursion. I made it conditional on the Hungarian complaints being remedied and the draft Romanian constitution being amended in a way that addressed what the Hungarians had complained about.[56] Given the vehement attacks on the Hungarian minority in the Bucharest parliament (RMDSZ was seriously considering withdrawing from the parliament), my visit to Bucharest, as urged by Năstase, was out of the question, and I announced that. In response, our diplomats in Bucharest, on the minister's personal instructions, were most emphatically banned from attending the March 15 wreath-laying ceremonies, and he even threatened to expel them![57] Undeterred, Ambassador Rudas and his staff did lay wreaths, without reprisals. As expected, discussions between the Foreign Affairs Committees of the two parliaments on April 23 and 24 in Budapest produced no results. I also met with the Romanian legislators and explained to them that, although we did not limit our relations to the minority problem, an inevitable element of the good relations we wished to maintain was the guarantee of the rights of national minorities, in accordance with the international principles in force and the Declaration of January 5, 1990, by the Romanian National Salvation Front.

Sensing a slight change in mood, I telephoned Năstase on May 6 and expressed my willingness to travel to Bucharest, to sign the Hungarian-Romanian Open Sky

---

[54] Hungarian Human Rights Statement, *Congressional Record*, April 17, 1991. Cf. J. Lieberman to Professor Rudolf Tokes, April 29, 1991, enclosed in a memo by Professor Tőkés, May 22, 1991. Among my papers.
[55] Senate Concurrent Resolution 52, July 11, 1991.
[56] Zsolt Becsey's note on the Madrid meeting, February 27, 1991. HuMFA, 442/EEFO.
[57] Encrypted cables from Bucharest, March 6 and 7, 1991. Among my papers.

Agreement, and to agree on the reopening of the consulates that had been closed two years earlier. Năstase rejected this, saying that a recent conference in Eger discussing the possible modification of the Romanian-Hungarian border had caused such a bad reaction in his country that he could not even negotiate on the consulates at the moment. (Eva Maria Barki, a Viennese lawyer popular in radical and uninformed circles for her statements proclaiming the invalidity of the Treaty of Trianon, had again helped Romanian chauvinists with her irresponsible words at the Eger conference, whatever her intentions were.)[58] When the Romanian foreign minister asked for our support for Romania's inclusion in the Pentagonale, I indicated in my reply that what was said at the meeting in Eger was far from the views of my government and that the Romanian press was full of similar extremist statements. The reopening of consulates would not be some kind of concession by Romania, they were necessary because of human and economic relations. Romania's membership in the Pentagonale required the agreement of five countries, Hungary would not block it.[59]

In preparation for a July 1991 meeting of experts, planned by the CSCE, the New York-based Hungarian Human Rights Foundation (HHRF) drew up a 14-page paper (with 58 pages of documentation) on Romania's policy towards national minorities since the CSCE's Copenhagen recommendations. According to the report, the Ceaușescu-era practices continued:

> National minorities are at best barely tolerated, but rather seen as a deviant element of society. Romanian official circles and the extremist Romanian media reject the aspirations of minorities to have internationally guaranteed national minority rights, and allege that such rights would somehow "endanger" the Romanian majority. The government [...] accuses minorities of inciting "separatism" and demanding "privileges."

The study on the draft constitution showed how many points contradicted the Copenhagen Recommendations and that the phrase "Romania as a nation-state" not only offended minorities but was also contrary to reality and showed the anti-minority features of several laws and bills. It also mentioned the failure to restore the Bolyai University and the Hungarian consulate in Cluj-Napoca and criticized Prime Minister Petre Roman's statement that "Romanian society is based

---

[58] Mrs. Barki liked to dispense irresponsible advice from Vienna; she was the president of the unregistered International Transylvanian Federation. Many of her statements provided ammunition for Romanian and Slovak nationalist circles, which kept on vehemently attacking the Hungarian minorities and Hungary's efforts to protect them.

[59] A transcript of our conversation is among my papers.

solely on a single nation, culture and language." After listing specific educational and cultural violations, the paper stated that "the victims of the anti-Hungarian pogrom in Târgu Mureș" were the ones being punished instead of those responsible for it, and that the authorities were openly supporting manifestations of anti-minority hatred. Finally, it presented a table showing that in Transylvanian counties, even in those with a Hungarian majority, the proportion of Hungarians among state and local employees was far below that of Romanians.[60]

In my place, a delegation of experts led by Szokai travelled to Bucharest and agreed that the Helsinki Final Act, the documents adopted at the CSCE conferences and the recommendations of the Council of Europe would form the basis of our relations as good neighbors. With State Secretary Meleșcanu,[61] a protocol was prepared showing the issues on which the two countries agreed and disagreed, respectively. I also sent a letter with Szokai to my Romanian colleague, in which—taking note of my partner's position that progress could only be made in small steps—I indicated the issues on which we should reach agreement in order to improve Hungarian-Romanian relations, which I considered a personal matter. I also raised the issue of the intolerable conditions at border crossings (six to eight hour waiting time) and the need to open new border crossings.[62] Năstase's response, made public on July 11, rejected my proposals and stated that the conclusion of a basic treaty between the two countries was a precondition for any further progress.[63]

What was the reason for the Romanian unwillingness and at times hysterical anti-Hungarian attitude? No sober-minded Romanian could believe that Hungary or the Hungarians in Romania were a threat to the territorial integrity of Romania. So, was it the memory of the alleged grievances committed against the Romanians before the First World War? Was it intended as a revenge for the Second Vienna decision? In President Iliescu's view of history, I could recognize the ideas of the Iron Guard, Romania's extremist organization in the 1930s. The image of the Hungarians as the enemy could always be used for domestic purposes. More important for me was the question: What is the antidote to this mentality and attitude? Gestures and friendship did not produce results. Talking tough would not frighten the anti-Hungarians, nor would it change them. Appeal to the West, to Europe? My historian colleague, Béla Borsi-Kálmán who was born in western

---

[60] Romania's Policies and Practices Toward National Minorities. The Record Since Copenhagen (June 1990). The report is among my papers.
[61] Teodor Viorel Meleșcanu (1941–): Romanian politician and diplomat, minister of foreign affairs (1992–1996, 2014, and 2017–2019.
[62] *Népszabadság*, June 29, 1991.
[63] *Külügyminisztériumi tájékoztató, 1991* [Bulletin of the Ministry of Foreign Affairs, 1991] (Budapest: Magyar Köztársaság Külügyminisztériuma, 1991), vol. 2: 39–40. Among my papers.

Romania and who undertook a diplomatic mission in Bucharest at my invitation, was right in his essay sent to me on March 26, 1991:

> Hungarian policy is mistaken when it assumes (hopes) that it can force the Romanian partner to make even the slightest concession by pressure, by constantly informing and influencing the "educated West." On the contrary, Romanian politics needs *Hungarian pressure* to keep its 150-year-old system of arguments fresh and its political instincts in a fighting condition. [...] the traditional Byzantine-style Romanian policy is based on deception, disinformation and—above all—balancing between the strong powers. [...] Though it is no longer effective, the goal of Hungarian policy can only be to prevent or at least delay the end of the Hungarian minority in Transylvania.[64]

Disappointment in Geneva

I summarized my views at the time in an article published in March 1991 in the daily paper *Magyar Nemzet*:

> In the coming years, alongside the success of economic transformation, the issue of national minorities will be a key issue in Europe. It is enough to think that in the member republics of the Soviet Union there are about 75 million people who do not belong to the ethnic group that gave the republic its name, they are national minorities. This justifies the need for Europe to seek a common solution for guaranteeing the rights of these minorities, in harmony with the interests of the majority. This summer, an international conference in Geneva in the framework of the CSCE will examine the possible content of a code on the rights of the national minorities. The Council of Europe has already laid down its own principles. Hungary, with its experience, can play an important role in this work. This is, of course, why it is urgent that a law on national minorities in Hungary be submitted to parliament. One thing is certain: any solution can only be based on guaranteeing the political and cultural autonomy of the individual and the community. The opening up of borders, regional cooperation, multi-country economic ventures—these are not utopias, they are tried and tested models that work well in many areas of the world. If, by adopting and enforcing European

---

[64] Béla Borsi-Kálmán, "Romania's internal situation and the bilateral tasks of Hungarian policy," March 26, 1991. Emphasis in original. Among my papers.

standards, we can pull out the poisonous fangs that the problems of national minorities can represent, the last obstacles to further European integration will be removed. It is unlikely that in this case rivalries between nations will disappear, but they will move from the military and political spheres to the economic, sporting and cultural spheres.[65]

In the summer of 1991, there were still some encouraging signs. In Slovakia, the populist prime minister Vladimír Mečiar was replaced by the leader of the Christian Democratic Movement, Ján Čarnogurský,[66] a brave oppositionist under communism. In him, a lawyer who speaks English well, I recognized a moderate politician, also on the issue of the Hungarian minority. He invited me to climb the 2663-meter high Gerlachovský štít (formerly Franz Joseph Peak, later Stalin Peak) in the Tatra Mountains, the highest peak in Czechoslovakia. On August 15, 1991, I was received at the border by Pavol Demeš,[67] the minister for external affairs in the new Slovak government. In this politician, typical of the new breed (a medical biologist by training, who, like Čarnogurský, spoke excellent English), I encountered a sober, true liberal democrat, a friend, who, like me, has remained a sincere supporter of Hungarian-Slovak friendship. The next day, reaching the summit, we toasted the friendship between Czechs, Slovaks and Hungarians. The descent, which involved the use of chains, was more spectacular than the climb and was well televised on Czech and Slovak television—but it didn't make it onto the Hungarian screens. I would describe Čarnogurský as an enlightened Slovak nationalist who worked consistently since the regime change to create an independent Slovakia and to promote it internationally. From our conversations on the tour, it became clear that we have very different views of our shared history. He proposed a declaration on Slovak-Hungarian reconciliation in a long text condemning the "Hungarian oppression" before 1918 and the Vienna Award of 1938, while devoting only a short paragraph to expressing regret over the total disenfranchisement and attempted expulsion of Hungarians from Czechoslovakia between 1945 and 1948.[68]

From 2663 meters above sea level, the view was unparalleled and the atmosphere in Slovakia did not seem hopelessly polluted. Making the very

---

[65] Géza Jeszenszky, "Magyarország és szomszédai az ezredvégen" [Hungary and its neighbors at the end of the Millenium], *Magyar Nemzet*, March 15, 1991.
[66] Ján Čarnogurský (1944–): Slovak lawyer and politician, prime minister 1991–92.
[67] Pavol Demeš (1956–): Slovak politician and policy analyst, minister for external affairs (1991–92), director of the German Marshall Fund's Bratislava office.
[68] I have dealt with the causes of the disputes between the Hungarians and the Slovaks in a number of writings, including: "A szlovák-magyar viták háttere" [The background of the Slovak-Hungarian disputes], *Magyar Szemle* 16, nos. 11–12 (December 2007): 17–37.

Figure 13. Climbing the highest peak of Czechoslovakia (now Slovakia), Gerlachovský štít (2655 m), with PM Ján Čarnogurský, FM Demeš in the background. August 16, 1991

promising recommendations of the Copenhagen CSCE conference binding offered an opportunity to make minority rights and their correct observance one of the foundations of the "European home." Hungarian diplomacy—together with many non-governmental organizations—worked hard to ensure that the Conference of Experts of the CSCE, convened for July 1, 1991, in Geneva, would adopt binding standards for the protection of the rights of national minorities.[62] It was hoped that the conference would make up for the serious shortcomings of the post-1945 political and legal agreements in this area. The Hungarian prime minister and his foreign minister never failed to emphasize how explosive the issue was but were careful not to make the issue look like some kind of special Hungarian obsession. In April I paid official visits to Oslo and then to Copenhagen; in my lectures there I pointed out that the guarantee of the rights of minorities and therefore of their future was the key to the stability of the new Europe. "Such rights have become almost commonplace in Scandinavia, in Canada, in Spain. In Italy there is a significant German-speaking minority in the south of Tyrol. I believe that the rule should be the same for Hungarians and other minorities as it is already routinely applied in the states I have just mentioned."[69] In another lecture, at the Bologna campus of Johns Hopkins University on May 17, I identified as the key to the security of the "new Europe" honoring the Helsinki principle of the inviolability of European borders, and, as a concomitant, that all nations and national minorities feel safe to preserve their independence, language, culture and religion.[70]

---

[69] *Magyar Külpolitikai Évkönyv, 1991,* 187.
[70] The text of my lecture is among my papers.

The most important points of the proposals put forward by the Hungarian delegation in Geneva were the following: in order to ensure their real equality of rights, national minorities must be granted special rights, recognizing them as a community. The ethnic proportions of the territory they inhabit must not be artificially altered; the designation of administrative units and electoral districts must take into consideration the ethnic setup; in the fields of culture and education the minorities are entitled to have financial support in proportion to their numbers.[71] The United States, traditionally a melting pot of immigrants, was far from being a supporter of the idea of autonomy for national minorities, but it was a staunch opponent of discrimination on the basis of nationality, origin or religion, and in the second half of the 1980s it went from being a supporter of Ceaușescu to a harsh critic of him. I had hoped that Max Kampelman (1920–2013), who led the U.S. delegation to Geneva, would support the implementation of effective minority protection. He did, but only at the level of individual rights and not group rights. He offered American mediation in the Hungarian-Romanian dispute.[72]

Unfortunately, the voice of the nationalists in our neighboring countries grew stronger and stronger during 1991, with a series of false facts and absurd slanders appearing in their media proclaiming that Hungary is continuing to oppress and forcibly assimilate non-Hungarian citizens. The aim was to discredit Hungary's initiatives for the protection of national minorities at the forthcoming international negotiations, especially at the CSCE Conference on Minorities in Geneva in July, and to justify the rejection of Hungarian claims on the basis of the principle of reciprocity, i.e., since Hungary—allegedly—mistreats its minorities, similar treatment is justifiable. It was already apparent that the national differences that had been frozen during the dictatorship had melted away, the wounds had turned gangrenous, and healing them would be a very difficult and lengthy task.

On July 2, Prime Minister Antall voiced a warning at the conference of the Inter-Parliamentary Union in Vienna:

> The polemical question of national minorities has resurfaced in Central and Eastern Europe, just as these countries are consolidating democracy and beginning the transition to a market economy. Respect for minority rights is both a human right and a security issue. The Hungarian Government is determined to ensure that national minorities feel at home in their countries, guaranteeing and respecting their minority rights, and that they have the

---

[71] Draft for the Final Document to be adopted in Geneva, prepared by the Secretariat of the Hungarians Beyond the Border, June 11, 1991. Copy among my papers.
[72] *Magyar Hírlap*, June 15, 1991.

fullest possible opportunity to preserve and develop their ethnic, cultural and religious identity. [...] At the CSCE Conference on National Minorities, which has just opened in Geneva, the Hungarian delegation, together with its *Pentagonale* partners, will put forward proposals for such confidence-building cooperation measures, as well as for dispute settlement procedures and mechanisms to help implement the commitments undertaken.[73]

The escalating crisis in Yugoslavia, the Croatian and Slovenian declarations of independence, and the rebellion of the Serb enclaves among the Croats all created an unfavorable climate for the codification and extension of minority rights. According to several participants, the work of the Hungarian delegation, led by Géza Entz, deserved the praise extended by the Swiss hosts,[74] but—confirming the pessimistic forecasts—the meeting did not agree on binding standards to be observed and held accountable by all member states. Most states did not want to hear about community rights or autonomy. Bulgaria, Yugoslavia and Romania tried to lower the level of rights that was recommended a year earlier, while Britain and the United States were of the opinion that minorities were sufficiently protected if the enjoyment and protection of human rights were adequately guaranteed, and therefore there was no need for further measures. However, there was one significant achievement, thanks to strong US intervention: a declaration was accepted that the issue of national minorities was not a domestic matter but a legitimate subject of international scrutiny. Their representatives must be involved in the decisions that affect them, and they have the right to present their case abroad. The principles of local autonomy and self-government in education were also mentioned in the final document.[75]

At the annual meeting of the Hungarian ambassadors in August, I reported that I considered the conference

> as not having produced the comprehensive decisions and results we would have liked—for example, the promising *Pentagonale* proposals were not adopted—but we did take steps in that direction. [At the same time], it was in Geneva that it became clear to many participants that the way of thinking of some countries still differed from European norms and principles. I heard

---

[73] *Magyar Külpolitikai Évkönyv, 1991*, 254.
[74] Report by Zoltán Pecze (Youth Section of the Hungarian Democratic Forum) quoting Swiss diplomat Paul Widmer, September 21, 1991. Among my papers.
[75] Report by Géza Entz at the 1991 Ambassadors' Conference. Among my papers. Cf. Fedor Mediansky, "National Minorities and Security in Central Europe: The Hungarian Experience," in *Nationalism and Postcommunism*, ed. A Pavkovic, H. Koscharsky and A. Czarnota (Aldershot: Dartmouth Publishing Co., 1995), 117.

from several quarters that Romania's presence in Geneva demonstrated this in many ways, at least to those who were there. [...] Every step taken towards the development of an all-European legal system and the rule of law brings us closer to guaranteeing minority rights, including the situation of Hungarian minorities. However, as the experience of the Geneva Conference showed, the adoption of a single European system of standards, a single document valid for all, is difficult, and it will be a long process.[76]

Results and failures

Due to the democratic transformation of Central Europe and the Antall government's exertions, the political situation and rights of the Hungarian communities outside our borders improved significantly, but no legally binding document guaranteeing their rights at international level was adopted. We could have voiced our disappointment at home and in international forums, but we saw no point in doing so, because it would have had no positive consequences. The only way forward was to continue to argue persistently. The CSCE Human Rights Conference in Moscow in September 1991 provided another opportunity. In my speech there I warned, "Democracy cannot be hostage to ethnic strife. In addition to the more vigorous and *bona fide* implementation of the CSCE commitments on minority rights [...] minorities must also be involved in the process of implementing measures relating to them."[77] I made a similar point in a lecture titled "Europe at a crossroads" at the Institute of International Relations in Paris on September 18. In it I argued for autonomy and collective rights for national minorities as a lesson from the ongoing conflict in Yugoslavia.[78] On October 1, 1991, in a speech at the UN General Assembly, Prime Minister Antall urged the international community to play its part in upholding the rights of national minorities,[79] and on October 28 he did the same at a ministerial meeting of the Atlantic Council in Brussels: "In this region, alongside the cause of human rights, the assertion of minority rights, both in terms of personal and territorial autonomy, is an integral part of security."[80]

Promising initiatives by the Council of Europe raised new hopes. Since Hungary's admission in November 1990, this guardian and promoter of democracy and human rights emerged as the international organization most ready to

---

[76] My opening statement is among my papers.
[77] *Magyar Külpolitikai Évkönyv, 1991,* 294.
[78] *Magyar Külpolitikai Évkönyv, 1991,* 304–7.
[79] *Magyar Külpolitikai Évkönyv, 1991,* 327.
[80] *Magyar Külpolitikai Évkönyv, 1991,* 361.

Chapter 4 – An Attempt at Cooperation

Figure 14. Signing Hungary's accession to the European Convention on Human Rights, with Secretary General of the Council of Europe, Catherine Lalumière, Strasbourg, November 5, 1992

embrace the rights of national minorities and to expand them. The secretary general, Catherine Lalumière, played a significant role in this. It cannot be proven, but I firmly believe that Hungarian diplomacy, and József Antall personally, made a significant contribution to this. The sympathetic and agile secretary general was a person of great influence in many of our formal and informal meetings. She understood the gravity of the issue and that the codification of minority rights, the adoption of binding standards and the monitoring of their observance were the best way to achieve genuine equality of rights and to resolve ethnic and national differences, and that the proper managing of this issue was important for peace and stability in Europe. She strongly supported the adoption of the European Charter for Regional or Minority Languages (in 1992, but its ratification took many years), and its shortcomings were no fault of hers.[81] Although in 1993 the Parliamentary Assembly of the Council passed Recommendation 1201 (which proposed autonomy and special rights), it was not accepted by the majority of ministers. The Framework Convention for the Protection of National Minorities, adopted in 1995, came into

---

[81] "European Charter for Regional or Minority Languages," https://rm.coe.int/16806c7413. The charter does not provide any criterion or definition for an idiom to be considered a minority or a regional language, and the classification stays in the hands of the state in question.

169

effect in 1998, and by 2009 it had been ratified by thirty-nine member states.[82] That, too, fell short of our expectations.

In addition to the international political level, Hungary also tried to promote minority rights at the academic level. In addition to personal contacts, several think tanks and organizations, and also international scholarship programs, such as the USA's Fulbright Grants, enabled many foreign scholars—primarily historians and political scientists—to become familiar with the problems of the Hungarian and other national minorities. Their publications and participation in international conferences helped the struggle for the political and linguistic rights of the Hungarian communities separated from Hungary by borders. Apart from a number of internationally recognized scholars, my personal friends Robert Hammerton-Kelly of Stanford, David F. Marshall from the University of North Dakota, Kathrin Sitzler at the Südost-Institut in Munich, Zsuzsa Csergő (at the time of this writing a professor in political science at Queens University, Kingston, Canada) and others provided important intellectual ammunition to raise the issue in scholarly circles.

Since the Geneva Conference did not make any progress in the field of binding minority rights, and Yugoslavia had been successful in expelling and killing minorities, the nationalists among our neighbors were encouraged to launch a kind of offensive against the Hungarian minorities. On October 25, 1991, on the first anniversary of the adoption of a law declaring Slovak the sole state language, the "cultural" organization Matica Slovenská protested against a provision in that law that allowed the use of a minority language if the proportion of that minority in a municipality reached 20 percent. (State and municipal employees were not, however, obliged to know and apply it.) On that same day *Új Szó*, a Hungarian-language daily newspaper published in Bratislava, printed an opinion on the language law by the eminent Belgian jurist Y. J. D. Peeters of the Center for the Study of Federalism and Ethnic Group Rights. His conclusion was:

> This law contradicts the basic development of minority rights [...], is totally incompatible with the principles laid down in the Council of Europe's recommendations, in particular the proposals of the [forthcoming] Charter for Regional and Minority Languages, or the relevant chapters of the Final Act

---

[82] Council of Europe, "Framework Convention for the Protection of National Minorities and Explanatory Report," Strasbourg, February 1995, https://rm.coe.int/16800c10cf. It came into effect in 1998 and by 2009 it had been ratified by thirty-nine member states. Six months after its exclusion from the Council of Europe, the Russian Federation ceased to be party to the European Convention on Human Rights in 2022 and left the Language Charter.

of the Vienna and Copenhagen Follow-up Meetings of the CSCE. This is by all accounts an example of retrograde legislation.[83]

On October 22, 1991, Slovakia's deputy interior minister Ján Bencúr issued a circular, ordering district offices to remove Hungarian place-names and all non-Slovak signs and public inscriptions. When MPs of the Hungarians protested, Interior Minister Ladislav Pittner replied that "in view of the specific nature of the language law, the general and common definition that what is not prohibited by the law is allowed, cannot apply."[84]

From October 31 to November 2, the European Christian Democratic Union (EUCD) organized a conference on minority issues in Bratislava, with nearly a hundred participants from nineteen European countries. In his introductory speech, Prime Minister Čarnogurský proposed the creation of an international documentation center to collect data on minorities in Central Europe in order to make the minority policies of individual countries comparable. The underlying idea behind the proposal was expressed by a representative of the Matica Slovenská organization (legally not part of the Slovak delegation), who presented a long list of "crimes" committed by Hungarians against Slovaks throughout history. There was a big debate on the themes minority autonomy, self-determination and the "obligatory loyalty" of the minority. The final document was so devoid of content, due to French and Italian opinions that were close to the Romanian and Slovak positions, that the Hungarian participants (László Surján of the Christian Democratic Party and György Csóti of the MDF) did not vote for it, neither did the Romanians, for whom even the modest content was too much. As a consolation, there was the closing speech by Belgian prime minister Wilfred Martens, who said that the view that identifies the state with the nation and the approach that identifies democracy with the will of the majority alone are extremely dangerous.[85]

Two weeks later, the Czechoslovak Committee of the European Cultural Foundation held a conference on the same topic, again in Bratislava. At the opening ceremony on November 13, President Václav Havel condemned the principle of collective guilt and proposed that crimes committed against minorities, especially Hungarians, should be investigated and then reparation would be due![84] Unfortunately, Slovak politics was already on a different track, but that was not noticed in Europe.

---

[83] *Bulletin* of the Secretariat of the Hungarians Beyond the Borders, no. 12, item 4 (1991). Among my papers.
[84] *Bulletin* of the Secretariat of the Hungarians Beyond the Borders, no. 13, item 3. Among my papers.
[85] *Bulletin* of the Secretariat of the Hungarians Beyond the Borders, no. 13, item 2.

After the failure of the Moscow coup, the three Baltic states regained their independence, and Hungary helped them by restoring diplomatic relations. For the agreement's signing ceremony on September 1–2, 1991, we invited Landsbergis, the hero of the drive for independence,[86] and the three foreign ministers to Budapest. The Parliament of the Moldavian Socialist Soviet Republic also declared its independence, and its foreign minister informed me of that in a letter.[87] Romania hoped that Moldova (also known as Bessarabia), with its Romanian majority population, would join it, and thus the Greater Romania of 1920 would be reborn. Sándor Vogel, a Hungarian from Transylvania, a fellow at the Hungarian Institute of Foreign Affairs, noted that for Hungary "a union [between Romania and Moldova] on a federal or confederative basis would be acceptable, which could unravel the centralized Romanian state, based on the idea of a unitary nation-state."[88] Géza Szőcs, then secretary general of the RMDSZ, wrote a confidential letter to Antall and me along the same lines, proposing the recognition of Moldova's independence and outlining the advantages of doing so.[89] I agreed with both. On January 16, 1992, I flew to Chișinău to establish diplomatic relations. Ever since then Hungary has enjoyed excellent relations with the other country with a majority Romanian population, a country where the 300,000-strong Gagauz (Orthodox Turkic) community has territorial autonomy. Unification with Romania depends on the will of the Moldovan population, which includes a significant Russian and Ukrainian minority, too. If it were to happen, Romania would not be able to maintain the fiction of a "unitary nation state," and autonomy for Szeklerland and other regions would be an obvious option.[90] That would obviously be a Hungarian interest, as well, but more importantly, it would be the realization of the principle of self-determination.

The disintegration of Yugoslavia and the collapse of the Soviet Union caused alarm in Bucharest. In an interview I gave to the Hungarian-language newspaper there on September 17, 1991, I pointed out:

---

[86] Vytautas Landsbergis (1932–): Lithuanian politician, head of the Supreme Council renamed Seimas (1990–92, 1996–2000), member of the European Parliament (2004–14).

[87] Foreign Minister Nicolae Țiu to Géza Jeszenszky, August 30, 1991.

[88] Sándor Vogel, "Opinion on the recognition of the independence of Soviet Moldova," October 22, 1991. Among my papers.

[89] Letter from Géza Szőcs to József Antall and Géza Jeszenszky, September 3, 1991. Among my papers.

[90] On that and the perspectives of Hungarian-Romanian relations, Jonathan Eyal, the Romanian-born scientific program director of the British Royal Defense Research Institute, expressed valuable thoughts to our ambassador in London, Tibor Antalpéter, in early 1992.

In the West, as the European Community consolidates, regionalism is gaining ground, and the omnipotence of central bureaucracy is being effectively limited by decentralization, by the decomposition of decision-making processes to the level of direct stakeholders. In Central and Eastern Europe, nations, which had been deprived of their independence are exercising their right to self-determination.[91]

In November 1990, we put forward detailed proposals for resolving the tensions in Romanian-Hungarian relations, which, if adopted, would have led to the conclusion of an inter-state treaty of friendship with Romania. In the wake of this spirit of "détente" the Rompres news agency put questions to me. In my answers, sent on October 10, I welcomed the regionalism that was gaining ground in Western Europe: the decentralization of decision-making, which should be followed in the post-communist world. In the Soviet Union, I said, Hungary respects self-determination processes based on the decisions of statutory bodies, and since we never recognized the Molotov-Ribbentrop Pact, we had restored diplomatic relations with the Baltic States. However, we were not turning our back on the eastern markets, we just could not ship more goods there on credit. I pointed out that there had been some welcome improvements in Romanian-Hungarian relations, such as the initialing of the Education and Culture Agreements, and it would be desirable to accept the proposals we had put forward in November. That would give an impetus to the negotiations on the basic treaty.

The memorable "miners' march"[92] of June 1990 saved the Iliescu/Roman pair from the protesters demanding a real turnaround. At the end of September 1991, economic bankruptcy led to another mining action manipulated by the power elite. Iliescu threw out Roman, who had become a liability, and consolidated his power with the technocrat Stolojan. Commenting on the change, Antall reaffirmed that Hungary was not interested in isolating Romania, but rather in the advance of its democracy, adding that it would be good if the choice of a new head of government were a sign of more pragmatic thinking. A personal meeting would only make sense if it was not for show, he said.[93] Instead of a real détente, after the successful Visegrád

---

[91] My interview in *Romániai Magyar Szó*, September 17, 1991. *Külügyminisztériumi tájékoztató, 1991*, vol. 2: 199–201. Among my papers.

[92] In 1990 and 1991 the Romanian government used the miners, who were dissatisfied with their living conditions, to attack and beat-up pro-democracy demonstrators. The "Mineriads" claimed several deaths and hundreds of wounded. See Dennis Deletant, "The Security Services since 1989: Turning over a New Leaf," in *Romania since 1989: Politics, Economics, and Society*, ed. Henry F. Carey (Oxford: Lexington Books, 2004), 507–10.

[93] *Új Magyarország*, October 3, 1991.

summit in Cracow in October, anti-Hungarian voices in Romania were once again on the rise, ruling out the possibility of cross-border cooperation. Reviving some of the travel restrictions of the Ceauşescu-era, travelers from Hungary were required to present the equivalent of 15 U.S. dollars a day and to indicate their exact destination.[94]

Commenting on the foreign policy debate held in the Hungarian Parliament on October 15, 1991, I stated with regret:

> Our relations with our important neighbor, Romania, did not develop as we had intended. This was no fault of Hungary. We remain ready for a meaningful dialogue. We urge real progress. Confidence-building agreements in the military field are examples of this. Considering the well-known specificities of Hungarian-Romanian relations, we hold it important to avoid campaigns and press polemics that seek to influence public opinion in a tendentious way, and we will act accordingly.[95]

My assessment was borne out by the report of the Romanian Parliamentary Special Committee on the case of "Romanians expelled from the counties of Harghita and Covasna after the revolution," submitted to the Romanian Parliament on October 17. The report, initiated by politicians of the nationalist Romanian National Unity Party, contained numerous nonsensical anti-Hungarian accusations. Two RMDSZ members of the committee, who expressed a dissenting opinion, did not sign it. What did take place during the dramatic events at the end of 1989, in the two Szekler counties, was that Hungarian schools were spontaneously reoccupied by the population and the Romanian officials who had fled on their own were replaced by Hungarians who enjoyed the confidence of the local population. True, there were a few popular outbursts, like the lynching of seven militiamen or members of the dreaded security service, respectively. The parliamentary debate, which lasted for days, was marked by heated, often blindly anti-Hungarian speeches, with some MPs proposing tough measures to "restore order" in Szeklerland.[96]

---

[94] Spokesman János Herman on the new travel restrictions in Romania. *Népszabadság*, October 12, 1991. *Külügyminisztériumi tájékoztató, 1991*, vol. 2: 260.
[95] *Magyar Külpolitikai Évkönyv, 1991*, 338.
[96] Fax report from the Embassy in Bucharest, October 17, 1991. Cf. Csaba Zahorán, "Románüldözés a Székelyföldön? Egy állítólagos etnikai tisztogatás történetei" [Persecution of Romanians in the Sekler counties? Stories of an alleged ethnic cleansing], in *Az új nemzetállamok és az etnikai tisztogatások Kelet-Európában 1989 után* [The new nation-states and ethnic cleansing in Eastern Europe after 1989], ed. József Juhász and Tamás Krausz (Budapest: L'Harmattan, 2009), 268–98.

The RMDSZ, which came in second behind the Salvation Front in the May 1990 elections with 7.2 percent of the national vote, remained a strong element in Romanian politics until the 1996 elections, when Emil Constantinescu[97] won. Both the Hungarian minority and the Hungarian motherland were presented to the Romanian public as permanent enemies. The dashing of their hopes in December 1989 left the Hungarians in Transylvania bitter, but the existence of basic political freedoms also allowed a free flow of internal disputes and conflict between impatient radicals and moderates. The former called for a referendum for October 19, 1991, at the historic site of Agyagfalva (recalling a great public assembly in October 1848), where they planned to proclaim the autonomy of Szeklerland. The Romanian authorities threatened the leadership of the RMDSZ with armed intervention and banned the planned rally. In order to avoid another pogrom like the one in Târgu Mures, only a wreath-laying ceremony was held on October 12 to commemorate the 1848 Szekler Assembly that decided to take up arms against the Habsburg forces and the Romanian rebels.

Major General Lucian Culda, deputy minister of war, speaking at a conference in California, said that Hungarian organizations inside and outside Romania had been trying to destabilize the country for decades, trying to extract illegal privileges for "Romanian citizens of Hungarian origin." They wanted to federalize Romania in order to prepare for the secession of a part of it. The demand for minority rights was segregation (apartheid and a Bantustan in Iliescu's words) reminiscent of the Middle Ages. Parties should not be allowed to be organized on ethnic grounds. There were fourteen national minorities in Romania, but only Hungarians were the problem. The Hungarian government had no right to show an interest in the Hungarian minority of Romania. Hungary was constantly committing aggression against Romania and wanted to Magyarize the Romanians on both sides of the border; cross-border cooperation must be rejected because it would lead to war. Romania had so far tolerated Hungarian aggression only because it was peaceful.[98]

On November 22–23, 1991, a conference on security policy was held at the Center for International Security and Arms Control, at Stanford University, Palo Alto. Among the American participants were the former deputy secretary- and future secretary of defense William Perry, future secretary of state Condoleezza Rice, and Robert Hamerton-Kelly, the organizer of a recent special Romanian-Hungarian meeting. Thanks to my contacts and my visit to the Center in April

---

[97] Emil Constantinescu (1939–): Romanian professor of mineralogy, politician, president of Romania (1996–2000).

[98] Report by László Póti and Sándor Vogel (Hungarian Institute of Foreign Affairs) on the conference. Among my papers.

1990, two Hungarians, László Póti and Sándor Vogel from the Hungarian Institute of Foreign Affairs, were invited to attend. The Americans did not publicly condemn Romania's tone, but in private discussions they did so. However, they considered the Hungarian position on collective rights problematic and proposed a bilateral treaty between the two countries, which would exclude border changes.[99]

Not all Romanians shared the views of Iliescu and his ilk. Dinu Zamfirescu, the foreign policy adviser to King Michael I of Romania, took a diametrically opposed view at a meeting with Géza Entz in Paris, endorsing the Hungarian-Romanian Declaration of June 16, 1989, which both had signed.[100] However, Europe at that time was primarily preoccupied with the ongoing armed conflict in Yugoslavia, and the rhetoric of Slovak and Romanian nationalist politicians was considered negligible in comparison. Hungary, on the other hand, was most sensitive to the fate of its co-nationals in the Serbian Vojvodina and Croatia. But the unfolding crisis in southern Slav lands was indirectly linked to the demise of the Soviet Union and European communism and the end of the bipolar world. And the world was understandably more focused on Moscow than on Belgrade.

---

[99] Ibid. Hamerton-Kelly's report on his earlier trip to Romania was obtained by the Romanian secret service, and Culda admitted that.

[100] Letter of State Secretary Géza Entz, addressed to me, November 4, 1991. Among my papers.

Chapter 5

Accusations and Reality: The New Eastern Policy

The neighboring superpower and its break-up

With the partition of Poland in 1939, Hungary became a neighbor of the Soviet Union, its enemy at the end of June 1941, its satellite by 1948, and its formal ally in 1955, "temporarily" stationing a significant number of Soviet forces on its territory. There can be no doubt that until the dissolution of the Soviet Union in December 1991, the superpower to the east was the most important neighbor of all, one that determined the fate of a small nation.[1]

Those who lived through the Soviet Red Army's presence in Hungary in 1944–45, the communist takeover of 1947–48 as a result of open Soviet intervention, the Soviet Union's two military aggressions in 1956, and the imposition of Kádár's puppet government, knew only too well that regaining freedom was dependent on changes in the Soviet Union, after 1985 dependent on Gorbachev's policies. This situation dictated both caution and courage, taking risks. Caution, lest the intervention of 1956 be repeated, based on the notorious Brezhnev doctrine. In the late 1980s there emerged a new danger: going too far in making internal reforms, taking hasty steps, might contribute to the downfall of the Soviet reformers. But without taking risks, the opportune moment to regain Hungary's independence might be missed—and lost. In other words, the best course appeared to be a gradual easing of dependence, inducing the Soviet Union to withdraw behind its own borders, militarily and politically, without any sense of loss of prestige. It never occurred to the MDF that our relations with the neighboring Soviet superpower and with the

---

[1] On post-1989 Hungarian-Russian relations, see the balanced account by one of the important witnesses and participants using Hungarian and Russian sources: Ernő Keskeny, *A magyar-orosz kapcsolatok 1989–2002* [Hungarian-Russian relations, 1989–2002] (Budapest: Századvég Kiadó, 2012). In this chapter I will supplement that book by my former colleague with my own documents and memories. The diplomatic documents of the Antall government contain a large number of documents on Hungary's relations with the Soviet Union, Ukraine and the Russian Federation in 1990–91. Sáringer, *Iratok az Antall-kormány*, vol. 1: Documents 1–22, 79–188; vol. 2: Documents 1–66, 119–360.

Russian people should in future be anything but friendly.[2] We were also aware that Soviet oil and gas were essential for our energy supply, and maintaining our exports to the Soviet Union was desirable. It was only through ignorance and/or malice suggested by the Socialist opposition, by journalist and writers (e.g., Pál Dunay and Wolfgang Zellner[3]) that the Antall government had deliberately gave up the Soviet market and spoiled relations with its great eastern neighbor because of historical grievances and ideological reservations.[4]

As was shown in Chapter 2, the foreign policy of the Antall government was based on a change of basic orientation; the main goal was to break away from Soviet dependence and to join the Western integration institutions. For that our own will was not sufficient. Even in 1990, we could not withdraw from the Soviet alliance, the Warsaw Pact, "the coalition of the unwilling" by a unilateral act—not with tens of thousands of Soviet troops stationed in the country. The most important first step in foreign policy was to take part in the forthcoming summit meeting of the Political Consultative Council of the Pact, scheduled to take place in Moscow on June 7–8, 1990. Preparing for the meeting, the officials adopted an agenda on the "democratization"' of the alliance, on the "modernization"' and restructuring of cooperation, and thus on its survival.[5] When the Hungarian prime minister and the minister of defense, Lajos Für, arrived in the Soviet capital in the company of the interim head of state, Árpád Göncz, they were received by the Hungarian ambassador in Moscow and the Hungarian diplomats involved in the preparations who relayed the message that not one of our partners—and not even the Western powers—supported the Hungarian position calling for the gradual dissolution of the alliance. Antall, however, could not be swayed, and having effectively refuted the concerns of his entourage, he emerged at the official meeting as "more than the protagonist of the day: as the victor."[6]

As chairman of the first session, Antall simply changed the wording of the previously agreed agenda. Now it read: "An exchange of views on the review and possible radical reform of the nature, functions and activities of the Warsaw Treaty." The silence of shock was broken by Soviet president and general secretary Gorbachev:

---

[2] This was expressed in József Antall's memorable statement in 1989 that if the Hungarian people became free, losing its bondage, it would offer parole and become a good friend to the Russians. See, József Antall, *Modell és valóság* [The model and the reality], ed. Kálmán Soós (Budapest: Athenaeum Nyomda, 1994), vol. 2: 22.
[3] Dunay, "Az átmenet magyar külpolitikája."
[4] In January 1990, the MDF sent a delegation to the Soviet Union, both to express sympathy for the Baltic republics' aspirations for independence and to negotiate in Moscow on the resumption of economic relations. Keskeny, *A magyar-orosz kapcsolatok*, 65.
[5] Für, *A Varsói Szerződés végnapjai*, 132–33.
[6] Für, *A Varsói Szerződés végnapjai*, 131.

"Da, khorosho," (O.K., fine) he said, perhaps not noticing the discrepancy. In his speech that afternoon, the Hungarian prime minister suggested that the military organization should be completely abolished by the end of 1991 and the Warsaw Pact itself merged into a common European security organization.[7] The joint communiqué issued from the meeting also stated that the commissioners of the member states would "begin a review of the nature, functions and activities of the Warsaw Treaty." At the Hungarian-Soviet bilateral meeting, the prime minister left no doubt about Hungary's intentions: our goal was to terminate the alliance through negotiations. Gorbachev rejected this at the time. The next day, at the Soviet Defense Ministry, Minister of Defense Lajos Für announced that Hungary would no longer participate in the Pact's military exercises and would "withdraw its forces from the command of the United Armed Forces."[8]

There can be no doubt that Antall, with great courage and foresight, was the initiator of the process leading to the dismantling of the organization that had institutionalized our dependence. Although some Hungarian authors question or minimize the significance of Antall's actions,[9] senior American contemporaries saw and recognized the leading role of Hungary and of Antall personally in the process leading to the complete dissolution of the Warsaw Pact.[10] Lajos Für's memoirs, far from being uncritical of Antall, and in some places even unfair, provide proof of the Hungarian prime minister's decisive personal contribution to the outcome of the Moscow talks. Although at first the other member states were content to make the Pact more "democratic,"[11] by the end of 1990 the former satellites all rallied behind the Hungarian position. One month after the Visegrád Tripartite Summit, in Budapest on February 25, 1991, the foreign and defense ministers of the Warsaw Pact member states signed the dissolution of the military organization, and on July 1 the heads of state and government signed the dissolution of the Pact itself.

---

[7] Jeszenszky, *József Antall, Prime Minister of Hungary*, 249–56. See also Kodolányi, *Antall Józseffel a világszínpadon*, 252–57.

[8] For the official documents of the meeting, see *Magyar Külpolitikai Évkönyv, 1990*, 207–9, and Sáringer, *Iratok az Antall-kormány*, vol. 1: 112–16 (Doc. 7). The most detailed treatment of the meeting, based on the documentation and personal memories, is Für, *A Varsói Szerződés végnapjai*, 116–56.

[9] Révész, *Antall József távolról*, 125–27; Csaba Békés in several publications, also personally to me.

[10] Gyula Kodolányi, "A mese igaz: Antall József 1990-es külpolitikai kezdeményezései" [The tale is true: The foreign policy initiatives of József Antall], *Magyar Szemle* 10, no. 6 (2001): 20–36 quotes from the works of a member of President Bush's staff: Robert Hutchings, *American Diplomacy and the End of the Cold War, 1989–1992* (Washington D.C.: Woodrow Wilson Center Press, 1997), 143, 238–44. He also quotes a remark by Secretary of State C. Rice to prove the above statement and also that the Americans believed that Antall was the driving force and the brain of the Central European region in foreign policy.

[11] See the letter of September 14, 1990, from Czechoslovak prime minister Čalfa to József Antall. A copy is in my possession.

Figure 15. Dissolving the military part of the Warsaw Pact, together with Minister of Defense Lajos Für, February 25, 1991

The dismantling of the Warsaw Pact did not mean that our country wished to turn its back economically or politically on its largest neighbor, nor that it did not wish to maintain good relations with the Russian people. I had already stressed this emphatically in my discussion with Foreign Minister Shevardnadze at the CSCE meeting in Copenhagen on June 5, 1990, and in an interview with the Soviet newspaper *Izvestia*.

> Historically, there have never been serious differences between the Hungarian people and any of the peoples of the present Soviet Union. [...] Until recently, Hungarian-Soviet relations could be compared to a forced marriage. [...] Stalinism caused no small amount of suffering to Hungary, though of course most of it was inflicted on the Russian people and the other peoples of the Soviet Union. Now we are trying together to get rid of the Stalinist legacy. It is time to move beyond the negative and develop our relations together.[12]

---

[12] The interview was published in the August 7, 1990, issue of *Magyar Hírlap*. See *Külügyminisztériumi tájékoztató, 1990*, 151.

Chapter 5 – Accusations and Reality: The New Eastern Policy

On September 11, Mátyás Szűrös, former speaker of the Hungarian Parliament and before that, ambassador to Moscow, now a Socialist MP, tried to discredit our policy towards the Soviets. He addressed an interpellation to me on the "confusion and misunderstandings in our bilateral relations with the Soviet Union" and asked for a new concept and action program. In reply, I gave a detailed account and explanation on the government's intentions and achievements, and, to my surprise, Szűrös accepted it.[13] At the Hungarian-Soviet meeting held at the time of the signing of the Charter of Paris, we agreed to draw up a new interstate treaty and, after some reluctance on the part of the Soviets, to review their earlier assessment of the events of 1956. Gorbachev rejected the one-sided views on NATO and the Warsaw Pact, and urged the preservation of good relations between the Soviet Union and the countries of Eastern Europe. We agreed with that.[14] While we condemned the Soviet military action in Vilnius in January 1991,[15] on February 25, when the military structure of the USSR was dismantled, I expressed my sincere hope "that the Soviet Union would remain a state which put dialogue before violence, which respected its international obligations, which cooperated in the community of nations and which sought peaceful solutions to its serious problems in accordance with the legitimate aspirations of its peoples. It is this desire that will guide us in our negotiations with the Soviet side on the new treaty that will form the basis of our relations."[16]

In the spring of 1991, Gorbachev's position was shaken, and the voices of hardliner military and political circles against him grew stronger, so my trip to Moscow with József Antall planned for the beginning of the year could not take place. At home, we concluded that it was in our interest (and that of the world) to keep the Soviet president in place and that we should seek to secure recognition of our independence in an inter-state treaty with him, but also to build our relations with the republics that were most important to us, Ukraine, Russia and the Baltic States, which were also in preparation for a possible break-up. There were continuous negotiations about a new inter-state political treaty at the level of experts, but the Soviet condition that neither party would be permitted to join an organization which the other party considered to be directed against it, was rejected. This formula, named after the Soviet deputy foreign minister Kvitsynsky, was accepted by Iliescu's

---

[13] Proceedings of the Hungarian Parliament, September 11, 1990, http://www.parlament.hu/naplo34/039/0390207.html.
[14] Report on the meeting between M. Gorbachev and J. Antall in Paris, November 21, 1990. Among my papers.
[15] On January 14 in the National Assembly Antall and I summoned Soviet ambassador Aboimov.
[16] *Magyar Külpolitikai Évkönyv, 1991,* 158.

Romania, which concluded its own treaty, but we did not accept such a restriction on our sovereignty, bearing in mind our intentions in relation to NATO. I personally communicated this to Kvitsinsky, who visited Budapest in April 1991 in order to persuade us.[17] That is why the Soviet leadership, which did not want to give up its influence completely, was happy to receive not only Gyula Horn, who went to Moscow in April, but also Gyula Thürmer, the general secretary of the unrepentant communist party, who had not even been elected to the National Assembly.

Although Hungarian exports to the Soviet Union had to be halted because of the Soviet insolvency that had become apparent by the summer of 1991 (they were unable to pay for a billion and a half dollars' worth of goods), from then on we sought to maintain economic relations on a commercial basis, with compensation—possibly in the form of barter. On May 22–23, 1991, I finally arrived in Moscow for an official visit. It was the first time I had entered the Empire, which had held us in bondage for forty-five years. As a private individual, a tourist, I had visited other neighboring countries on numerous occasions, but the Soviet Union was only accessible by organized (and strictly controlled) tourist routes, which had no appeal for me. Moscow was still a huge socialist city at the time, and the imperial atmosphere was represented by St Petersburg, which I only got to know years later as a member of the Parliamentary Assembly of the Council of Europe. My first two meetings were not with the Union but with the leadership of the Russian Soviet Socialist Republic. The Chechen-born deputy speaker of the parliament, Ruslan Khasbulatov (1942—2003), smoked a pipe and had the manners of a university lecturer rather than a Soviet apparatchik. With him, and with Kolokolov, Russian deputy foreign minister (the minister, Andrei Kozyrev,[18] was in New York), we discussed primarily the vitality of our economic relations and trade. However, the tense yet hopeful atmosphere was reminiscent of the Hungary of the late 1980s; the birth of a new political system. I was reminded of the title of the great Hungarian author Mór Jókai's novel *Freedom under the Snow*. The voices and questions of the young intellectuals, a large number of whom attended my talk at the Hungarian Scientific, Cultural and Information Center, showed that they were eager for democratic changes, which filled me with optimism that Russia, the "Velikaya Rus", had

---

[17] The negotiations leading to the interstate treaty are described in detail in Keskeny, *A magyar-orosz kapcsolatok*, 71–82.

[18] Andrei Kozyrev (1951–): Russian diplomat, foreign minister under Yeltsin (1990–96), favoring a West-leaning democratic Russia. Constantly criticized "for capitulating to the West," he went into exile in the United States in 2010. Since then, he has been an outspoken critic of Russian policy, particularly the Russian invasion of Ukraine, and of Russian president Vladimir Putin's attitude towards the West. See his memoir: *The Firebird: The Elusive Fate of Russian Democracy* (Pittsburgh: The University of Pittsburgh Press, 2019).

not disappeared, had not been dissolved in the Soviet Union, and we would have genuinely friendly relations with this country.

Alexander Bessmertnykh (1933–) the new Soviet foreign minister, did not behave like a rigid, authoritative communist apparatchik when greeting me. He spoke frankly about the country's serious economic problems, the difficulties of political reorganization, and that they did not want "to push Hungary away by careless steps, nor to draw it closer to themselves against its will." We agreed that in multi-ethnic states, like most of Hungary's neighbors, the key to stability was respect for the will of the various peoples. I indicated that we wanted to develop close relations with our immediate neighbor Ukraine, especially on the minority issue, but we did not intend to act against the central government, so I had come to Moscow before going to Kyiv and Uzhhorod. In addition to international issues, we discussed trade settlements, the pace of the withdrawal of Soviet troops and its financial aspects, memorials, military graves, the easing of border traffic and the Soviet evaluation of 1956 as a "counter-revolution." This meeting was no longer an obligatory salutatory introduction, it was no longer about the relationship between the Empire and a satellite State.

A few days before the agreed deadline, on June 19, the last Soviet soldier left Hungary, and since then we have been celebrating the regaining of our independence every year on June 30 as Freedom Day. At the same time, we made sure that the departure took place in a polite way, with words that would allow for a better future relationship to develop between two countries that had returned to democracy. In Parliament, we said farewell to the army that caused so much pain in 1945 and 1956, with Antall's statesmanlike words: "When great powers withdraw troops from other countries in peacetime, they do not suffer a loss of military prestige, but rather a powerful moral success." Then he repeated his words of nearly two years earlier: "If they take off the handcuffs, we will extend a friendly hand and become reliable good friends of the Soviet Union. We therefore trust that when the Soviet army leaves Hungary, good neighborly and friendly relations will be established between our countries."[19]

President Göncz spoke in a similar vein, thanking Gorbachev in a letter for the withdrawal of troops. In his reply, Gorbachev spoke of future relations based on trust and equality, but urged a settlement of the financial dispute over troop withdrawals.[20] When the six member states of the Warsaw Pact dissolved that imposed alliance by common agreement in Prague on July 1, the Hungarian prime minister

---

[19] *Magyar Külpolitikai Évkönyv, 1991*, 230–31.
[20] Keskeny, *A magyar-orosz kapcsolatok*, 86–87.

called it a moral victory for the Soviet political leadership. "The pseudo-friendship and apparent stability imposed on our region by external forces will disappear," and the road would be opened to join the Europe that was moving towards economic, financial and political union.[21]

Unfortunately, despite our good intentions, in the following weeks, neither the interstate treaty, nor trade relations, nor the financial settlements for troop withdrawals made any progress, due to the Soviet side's unwillingness to compromise. In any case, the Soviet side did not want to accept a "'zero balance" solution, a mutual waiver of financial claims against each other.[22] Antall therefore wrote to U.S. president Bush and German chancellor Kohl[23] asking them "to use their good personal relations with Mr. Gorbachev" to reach a Hungarian-Soviet agreement.[24]

On learning of the attempted coup in Moscow on August 19, 1991, Antall immediately initiated a consultation among the six parties represented in the Hungarian parliament.[25] The Hungarian government, ahead of many Western countries, condemned the coup organizers from the very first moment. The next day, Prime Minister Antall telephoned reformist leader Boris Yeltsin (only President Bush had done so ahead of him), and in a twenty-minute conversation expressed his moral support.[26] This contributed greatly to the extraordinary warm personal relationship between the two. We were reassured by the fact that on the day of the coup, President Bush also telephoned Prime Minister Antall, and I received a call from NATO Secretary General Wörner, both of whom indicated that they would not leave us alone in this dangerous situation.[27] (They did not say, however, that they would protect us from possible Soviet aggression if the coup succeeded.) Antall also contacted the leaders of many other countries around the world—including Polish president Wałęsa, Czechoslovak president Havel and German chancellor Kohl. In Warsaw on August 20, the three Visegrád countries were already coordinating their

---

[21] "Europe's doors are open; its organizations and institutions are open to Central and Eastern European countries committed to democracy and the market economy and ready to work to meet the criteria. All are needed to build a democratic, stable and prosperous Europe." Speech by József Antall at the last meeting of the Political Consultative Body of the Warsaw Pact, Prague, July 1, 1991. My personal copy of the speech.

[22] Dispatch by Sándor Györke, Hungary's ambassador to Moscow, June 13, 1991. The Russian side claimed that the Germans and the Czechoslovaks, on the other hand, were willing to pay, also with a view to future good relations.

[23] Helmut Kohl (1930–2017): chancellor of Germany from 1990 to 1998, before that of West Germany from 1982. A close friend of Prime Minister Antall.

[24] Letter from József Antall to President Bush and Chancellor Kohl, July 26, 1991, both in my possession.

[25] Keskeny, *A magyar-orosz kapcsolatok*, 87–90, summarizes the Hungarian reactions to the coup, I will provide more details below.

[26] The transcript of the conversation is in Sáringer, *Iratok az Antall-kormány*, vol. 2: 207–9 (Doc. 25).

[27] Antall's first day reactions and telephone conversation with President Bush are reported in *Népszabadság*, August 21, 1991. Cf. *Külügyminisztériumi tájékoztató, 1991*, vol. 2: 105–6.

reactions.²⁸ In a statement on August 21, the Hungarian government welcomed "the news of the retreat of the unconstitutional forces" and expressed the hope that this would lead to a more constructive Soviet role in international affairs and "the continuation of the building of new type of relations between Hungary and the Soviet Union, as well as with the individual [member] republics, including economic cooperation."²⁹

Antall sent telegrams of congratulation to Gorbachev and Yeltsin, which Yeltsin thanked in a letter the following day.³⁰ On August 22, Antall wrote to President Bush thanking him for his solidarity in the crisis, expressing his conviction that the Western integration of Central Europe should be accelerated, that since Gorbachev's position was weakened, Yeltsin should be cultivated, and that the independence of the Baltic states and their right to secede from the confederal Soviet Union should be recognized.³¹ French president Mitterrand had earlier contacted Soviet vice president Gennady Yanayev, who was in charge of the coup, but that evening he telephoned Antall to consult him on the situation in Moscow and Yugoslavia. The Hungarian prime minister explained to him that the Soviet Union was moving towards decentralization and that in Yugoslavia a confederation offered some chance of a peaceful solution to the crisis, but that this would require strong pressure on the opposing sides.³²

I held a press conference on the dangers of the coup and spoke of the encouraging attitude of the peoples of the Soviet Union in such difficult hours. I expressed my hope that in the light of what happened, our bilateral relations could develop in a very positive direction, on a new basis.³³ Addressing the heads of the major foreign missions in Budapest on August 23, the Hungarian prime minister stressed that "the events of the past few days have shown that critical situations in our region can still be expected to arise. It has also proved that the Hungarian Government's efforts to dissolve the Warsaw Pact and the Comecon and to withdraw Soviet troops from Hungary as quickly as possible, were the right ones." He proposed international assistance "for the economic recovery of the Soviet Union and confirmed that

---

²⁸ The Hungarian Government was represented by Gyula Kodolányi, state secretary, head of the prime minister's Advisory Council. *Új Magyarország*, August 22, 1991. *Külügyminisztériumi tájékoztató, 1991*, vol. 2: 108.
²⁹ *Magyar Külpolitikai Évkönyv, 1991*, 267.
³⁰ *Külügyminisztériumi tájékoztató, 1991*, vol. 2: 117–19.
³¹ Antall's letter to Bush, August 22, 1991, copy in my possession.
³² Transcript of a telephone conversation between Antall and French president Francois Mitterrand on August 22, 1991. I have a copy.
³³ *Új Magyarország*, August 23, 1991. *Külügyminisztériumi tájékoztató, 1991*, vol. 2: 119–20.

Hungary was ready to participate in this effort."³⁴ At a personal meeting that day, I asked the ambassadors of the European Community in Budapest to speed up the negotiations on our country's associate membership in the Community, and handed over the Prime Minister's letter to that effect. On the same day, Presidents Havel and Wałęsa addressed a similar letter to the EC Member States.³⁵

Antall also sensed—ahead of all his prime ministerial colleagues—that this was the moment for the international acceptance of the Baltic states' demand for independence. He actively contributed to this through his telephone conversations and letters to U.S. president Bush. The Hungarian position was summed up in the government statement of August 24:

> The Government of the Republic of Hungary considers the Molotov-Ribbentrop Pact to be invalid and unlawful. Hungary, like Russia and other states that recognize the independence of the Baltic republics, considers the aspirations of the peoples of Estonia, Latvia and Lithuania to restore their state sovereignty legitimate and supports them. [...] [It] trusts that the Republic of Estonia, the Republic of Latvia and the Republic of Lithuania will receive an internationally valid guarantee that they will soon be able to achieve their declared goal of genuine state sovereignty based on the will of the people.³⁶

On September 2, ahead of the cautious Western countries, Lithuanian president Landsbergis and Lithuanian foreign minister Algirdas Saudargas, Estonian foreign minister Lennart Meri and Latvian foreign minister Janis Jurkans arrived in Budapest at the invitation of the Hungarian government and signed a protocol with them on the resumption of diplomatic relations that had been "dormant" since the Soviet occupation in 1940.

Relations with Ukraine

Ukraine is not a brand-new state. The state built on the River Dnieper is one of the oldest in Europe. Kievan Rus, perhaps founded by Vikings but inhabited mainly by Eastern Slavs, was a large and powerful medieval monarchy; it was destroyed by the Mongol-Tartar invasion in the thirteenth century. The Grand Duchy of Muscovy gradually grew into the Russian Empire; after the Ottoman conquest of

---

³⁴ *Magyar Külpolitikai Évkönyv, 1991*, 268.
³⁵ *Népszabadság*, August 24, 1991. *Külügyminisztériumi tájékoztató, 1991*, vol. 2: 126.
³⁶ *Magyar Külpolitikai Évkönyv, 1991*, 270–71.

Byzantium, the East Roman Empire, Muscovy claimed to be the Third Rome. In the seventeenth century it acquired the territories east of the River Dnieper from the Polish-Lithuanian Kingdom. In the eighteenth, with the partitions of Poland, Russia annexed more territories in its western neighborhood, inhabited by Cossacks and peasants who spoke a Slavic dialect. The Habsburg Empire obtained (and held until 1918) *Galizien* (Galicia), much of today's western Ukraine and southern Poland. The word Ukraine means borderland, and the local language became increasingly distinct from Russian. Despite (or because of) that, in the Russian Empire from the early nineteenth century the Ukrainian language was banned. With Taras Shevchenko and his followers it developed into a literary language in eastern Galicia, in rivalry with Polish, the language of the nobility and the urban middle class.

In the wake of the 1917 Russian Revolution, on November 20, 1917, a Ukrainian National Republic was proclaimed, but, in the ensuing civil war, the Bolsheviks prevailed, and Ukraine became part of the Soviet Union, nominally as a federal unit. As a result of the secret Molotov-Ribbentrop Pact, Poland was destroyed jointly by Germany and the Soviet Union, and eastern Poland was annexed by the Soviet Union and joined to Ukraine. Following the defeat of Nazi Germany, the region beyond the northeastern Carpathian mountain range, until 1919 an integral part of the Kingdom of Hungary, was also annexed by the Soviet Union and added to Ukraine, as Zacarpathia or Transcarpathia, as seen from the east and Subcarpathia, as seen from Budapest. In 1989 a Hungarian population of close to 200,000 lived bordering on Hungary, mainly along the Tisza River. It suffered enormously during the communist period.[37]

---

[37] The most authoritative history of this territory is Paul Robert Magocsi, *With Their Backs to the Mountains: A History of Carpathian Rus'and Carpatho-Rusyns* (Budapest: Central European University Press, 2015), concentrating on its Slavic population. Steven Bela Vardy, "The Hungarians of the Carpatho-Ukraine: From Czechoslovak to Soviet Rule," in *The Hungarians: A Divided Nation*, ed. Stephen Borsody (New Haven, CT: Yale University Center on International and Area Studies, 1988), 209–27, presents the fate of its Hungarian population. *Kárpátalja története: Örökség és kihívások* [History of Subcarpathia: Heritage and challenges], ed. György Csatáry (Beregszász-Ungvár: II. Rákóczi Ferenc Kárpátaljai Magyar Főiskola, 2021) is a massive general history, authored by eighteen local Hungarian historians. The post-1918 history of Subcarpathia is presented in an exemplary joint undertaking by Csilla Fedinec and Vehes Mikola, eds., *Kárpátalja 1919–2009: történelem, politika, kultúra* [Subcarpathia: history, politics, culture] (Budapest: Argumentum, Institute for Ethnic-National Minority Research, MTA, 2010); and László Zubánics, *Tájba írt történelem: Kultúrtörténeti utazás Kárpátalja legmagyarabb városában és vonzáskörzetében* [History written in the landscape: A cultural and historical journey in the most Hungarian city of Transcarpathia and its surrounding area] (Ungvár-Budapest: Intermix Kiadó, 2011); Csilla Fedinec, ed., *Kárpáti Ukrajna: Vereckétől Husztig; Egy konfliktustörténet nemzeti olvasatai* [Carpathian Ukraine: national interpretations of a historical conflict] (Pozsony [Bratislava]: Kalligram Kiadó, 2014). Géza Jeszenszky, *Ukraine and Hungary; The Key to Relations: Sub(Trans)Carpathia* (LAP Lambert Academic Publishing, 2025) is a concise history, in the context of bilateral relations between Hungary and Ukraine.

In the Soviet Union there was a "Ukrainian Soviet Socialist Republic" with a government, a foreign ministry, even its own UN mission. But in reality, Kyiv had no say whatsoever in what happened in Ukraine. When, by the end of the 1980s, the Soviet Union's economy was bankrupt and central power had been weakened because Gorbachev had abandoned political rule based on violence and fear, the population in all member states began to think that independence would make it easier to escape the crisis and that, as an independent state, their standard of living would rise. From 1990, following the independence movement of the Baltic states, the individual Soviet republics, led by Russia and Ukraine themselves, began to exercise their rights, which existed on paper and were enshrined in the Soviet constitution. After the failed coup in Moscow, on August 24, 1991, the Supreme Council of the Ukrainian Soviet Socialist Republic (the Verkhovna Rada) passed a law on the independence of Ukraine. In a nation-wide referendum held on December 1, 1991, on the Act of Declaration of Independence the overwhelming majority, 92 percent of the voters approved the declaration.

Already sensing this trend, the Antall government began to build independent relations with Ukraine. On August 24, 1990, we received Ukrainian foreign minister Anatoly Zlenko in Budapest and agreed to lift the recently imposed suspension of the simplified border crossing.[38] In a telephone interview with the daily *Pesti Hírlap*, my spokesman, János Herman, stressed that we would work with Ukraine to draft a charter on the rights of national minorities and that the transition to a market economy could create new opportunities for our trade with Ukraine, which accounted for a third of the Soviet market.[39] Zlenko saw great potential in the Hungarian relationship, with its precedent-setting support for independence aspirations.[40] In September, President Göncz visited Ukraine, including Uzhhorod/Ungvár and Berehove/Beregszász.[41] Between February 21 and 26, 1991, Géza Entz, head of the Secretariat of the Hungarians Across the Border, held talks in Kyiv, Lviv and Uzhhorod, where he was warmly welcomed, and extensive rights and cultural autonomy to all minorities were promised.[42] On May 30, 1991, Ukrainian President Kravchuk arrived in Budapest and the next day, together with my Ukrainian colleague, I signed the "Declaration on the Principles of Cooperation between the

---

[38] *Külügyminisztériumi tájékoztató, 1990*, 178.
[39] *Külügyminisztériumi tájékoztató, 1990*, 217.
[40] László Póti, *Ukraine's Foreign and Security Policy, 1990–2000* (Budapest: Strategic Defense Research Office, 2001).
[41] Keskeny, *A magyar-orosz kapcsolatok*, 82–85.
[42] Report by Géza Entz, March 5, 1991.

Republic of Hungary and the Ukrainian Soviet Socialist Republic in the Field of Ensuring the Rights of National Minorities."[43]

The Declaration is a unique document in the field of the protection of national minorities, it contains far more and stronger provisions than the Framework Convention for the Protection of National Minorities adopted by the Council of Europe in 1995. It contains very positive principles. It recognizes that the national minorities "constitute an integral part of their society and state;" that they are entitled not only to individual or personal rights but also to community (group) rights ("starting from the fact that the territory of the Parties is inhabited by national minorities who enjoy appropriate rights, at both individual and collective level"). It also addresses the protection of national identity: "The Parties ... take political, legal and administrative steps aimed at creating favorable conditions for the preservation and enhancement of their ethnic, cultural, linguistic and religious identity." The principle of cultural and administrative self-government is also present in the document: the parties "encourage the creation of a status for the national minorities which guarantees their right to participate effectively in public affairs, including in matters relating to the protection and development of their identity, and in the making and implementation of decisions affecting their place of residence." The Declaration prohibits deliberately changing the proportion of the nationalities in a given area: "The Parties shall take no administrative, economic or other steps towards assimilating the minorities or changing the set-up of the population of minority-inhabited regions." Most importantly, "the Parties agree to ensure to the national minorities the necessary conditions for learning, and studying in, their native language at all levels of education." The right is also guaranteed "to use their national first names and surnames" (a change from the Soviet practice). "The preservation and protection of historical monuments and other cultural values" is also guaranteed. Finally, "The Parties confirm their intention to promote the international codification of minority rights at bilateral, regional and universal level. They express their readiness to support efforts along this line in the UNO and the forums of the Conference on Security and Cooperation in Europe." In order to facilitate that commitment, "further states shall be welcome to join the present Declaration," and the parties expressed "their readiness to consult all concerned states on the principles laid down herein." (A few months later, Croatia joined this Declaration, and Slovenia concluded a special treaty with Hungary on the mutual

---

[43] The day before, Soviet ambassador Aboimov, visiting State Secretary Szokai, expressed his reservations about some points of the draft Declaration, but we managed to agree on a wording satisfactory to all three parties. Szokai's notes of May 29 and 30, 1991, are among my papers.

Figure 16. With Ukrainian FM Anatoliy Zlenko in Kyiv, July 9, 1991

protection of national minorities.) In order to implement and monitor the provisions of the Declaration, a separate Protocol provided for setting up a joint committee "composed of representatives of the state institutions of the two Parties and their national minorities."[44]

On August 8–10, 1991, I was invited for an official visit to Ukraine. I had most friendly talks with the Ukrainian government in Kyiv, and then traveled to Lviv (called Lemberg in the Austro-Hungarian Monarchy, and Lwów during its Polish past). I was received with special friendship by the leaders of the opposition movement Rukh, and with touching warmth by the small Hungarian colony there. On August 11, I entered the Carpathian Basin through the Uzsok Pass, the scene of fierce battles in World War I, having a monument to the fallen soldiers of both sides. At the historical border of old Hungary, I was met by a large party composed of members of the Hungarian Cultural Association of Subcarpathia (KMKSZ),

---

[44] For the text of the Declaration and the accompanying Protocol, see *Magyar Külpolitikai Évkönyv, 1991*, 212–22. In English, see "Declaration of the Principles of Cooperation between the Republic of Hungary and the Ukrainian Soviet Socialist Republic in Guaranteeing the Rights of National Minorities," http://www.forost.ungarisches-institut.de/pdf/19910531-1.pdf. For the wider context of the two documents, see Renáta Paládi, "A magyar-ukrán kétoldalú kapcsolatépítés az 1991 májusában aláírt kétoldalú egyezmények tükrében" [The building of Hungarian-Ukrainian contacts in the light of the bilateral agreements signed in May, 1991], *ujkor.hu*, May 31, 2021, https://ujkor.hu/content/magyar-ukran-ketoldalu-kapcsolatepites-az-1991-majusaban-alairtketoldalu-egyezmenyek-tukreben.

Chapter 5 – Accusations and Reality: The New Eastern Policy

Figure 17. Welcome by Hungarians from Visk, Subcarpathia, Ukraine at the Uzsok Pass, August 10, 1991

coming from the municipality of Visk and headed by its president, the unforgettable friend Sándor Fodó. In an impromptu speech, I stressed that in the Great War both sides believed theirs was a good cause for which so many had sacrificed their lives, but in fact they had had no reason to regard each other as enemies. "War memorials are not a tribute to war, but to the man who did his duty and who is an example for the present. [...] Self-sacrifice, heroism are ancient human virtues that we will need now more than ever, when we have a better chance than ever to build a better world." I pointed out that the central and eastern parts of Europe should follow the example of Western Europe, the reconciliation of the Germans and the French, the creation of an atmosphere of tolerance between people of different religions and languages. The civil war in Yugoslavia, which was the opposite of this, was a reminder of where we must not go. "No more mass graves and war memorials in Europe."

Our party then drove to Ungvár/Uzhhorod, the capital city of Subcarpathia, where we were welcomed by the leaders of the regional council. The Soviet flag had just been replaced by the blue and yellow Ukrainian one. In the ensuing discussion, I argued for the need to reopen the recently-suspended Hungarian-Ukrainian local border traffic and to open as many border crossings as possible. I called for the dismantling of barriers to economic and personal relations. In a meeting with the KMKSZ executive committee I advocated the introduction of dual citizenship, as was already practiced in many countries in the West, and that it should be extended

Figure 18. Speaking at the First World War Memorial at Uzsok Pass, August 10, 1991. On my left Sándor Fodó, the leader of the Hungarians of Subcarpathia

to all Hungarians living in the Carpathian Basin.[45] In the evening, a crowd of local Hungarians greeted me when I opened the newly established Hungarian Consulate. They had been waiting for forty-seven years for the official presence of Hungary to return to Ungvár/Uzhhorod. It was a sentimental moment, and I knew how much hardship and suffering that community had endured since the autumn of 1944 and what it meant for them to sing the Hungarian National Anthem again in public under the Hungarian national flag. The next day, at Makkosjánosi, I dedicated a memorial to the Hungarians who died in 1944/45 in the Stalinist camp. I described it as a symbolic grave of the innocent victims and a place of future pilgrimage.[46]

Eight days later, on August 19, a coup by the communist old guard in Moscow frightened the world, only to end with Yeltsin as the leader of Russia. That allowed Ukraine to take its future into its own hands, and the referendum on December 1 legalized that. Russia, Poland and Hungary were the first to recognize the new independent State. Hungary immediately changed the status of its Consulate

---

[45] Reported by the local newspaper *Kárpáti Igaz Szó*, August 14 and 15, 1991. Among my papers.
[46] Ibid., and the journal *Kárpátalja* (August and September 1991).

Chapter 5 – Accusations and Reality: The New Eastern Policy

Figure 19. At the Turul Monument at Tiszaújlak (Vylok), celebrating the Rákóczi uprising, 1703–11

General in Kyiv to an Embassy and designated that building accordingly. Before that, Géza Entz had visited Kyiv and Uzhhorod/Ungvár again on November 5–6, 1991. Not only the Ukrainian government, but also the opposition Rukh, led by Viacheslav Chornovil (1937–1999), usually described as nationalist, had called for better and closer relations with Hungary than any other neighboring country and expressed their readiness to grant territorial autonomy to the Hungarian minority in a federal Ukraine! Dmytro Pavlychko, chairman of the Foreign Affairs Committee of the Supreme Council, announced that deputies had adopted a declaration "guaranteeing the right of minorities to establish administrative self-governing units (so that Hungarians in Transcarpathia can also establish a national self-government) and minorities living in a single block can use their mother tongue as the state language in the territory."[47] So, on the threshold of the independence referendum and independence, Ukraine, the then leadership, had committed itself to an exemplary nationality policy. However, implementation failed to materialize, and twenty-nine years later, it seems as if no one in Ukraine remembered that minority rights were even enshrined in law in 1992.

The new Russia

A real friendship with Russia, which had been an aspiration and a hope, became a reality after the coup failed. A coincidence also contributed to this friendship:

---

[47] Report by Géza Entz, state secretary, November 8, 1991.

Hungary and Its Neighbors, 1988–1994

Figure 20. Wreath-laying at the memorial to the mass deportation of Hungarians of Subcarpathia in 1944/45. Makkosjánosi (Yanoshi), August 11, 1991

the American Aspen Institute held a conference in Budapest, and it was attended by Andrei Kozyrev, the foreign minister of the Russian Socialist Soviet Republic, who had been invited before the coup. He came straight to me from the airport and our long conversation became the basis of a friendship. I can quote his words and answers to questions at the conference from my notes taken at the time. Kozyrev explained the rapid collapse of the coup by the fact that the plotters were unable to immediately arrest the reformists. So they went to the Russian White House and took control of events from there. He was told by the reformists to fly to Budapest, so that if the coup succeeded, they would have a foreign representative to support and defend the democrats from abroad. Fearing that he would be detained at the airport on his departure, he avoided the VIP lounge and was able to leave Moscow unhindered. He observed that revolutions sometimes do not lead to conflict and may give rise to new cooperation. The Russian revolution now entered an economic phase, and this required real cooperation. Sakharov had spoken of the possibility of a new world ideology, of liberal democracy—and now it could be realized. Gorbachev had great merit, and the new leadership did not want to marginalize him, but it was a mistake that in the West they always talked about "helping" him. It was Russian democracy that needed help through, economic transformation and

Chapter 5 – Accusations and Reality: The New Eastern Policy

Figure 21. With Russia's FM Kozyrev in Budapest, August 22, 1991.
In the background is Ivan Aboimov, the ambassador of the Soviet Union to Hungary.

in overcoming bureaucracy. Russians needed to be taught about the market economy. Russia was keen to join the World Bank. But now the West must immediately help it, not with credit but with food! The reforms would not be delayed, everything would be privatized. In the kolkhozes, the privatization of land that had already started would speed up. Russia had so far isolated itself from the world, while in the West, forty years of democracy had created peace between peoples. Peace between the peoples of the Soviet Union was maintained by dictatorship, while at the same time mixing the various ethnic groups. Ethnic boundaries could not be drawn, therefore the current borders of the republics—which were roughly equally offensive to all peoples—had to be accepted. However, there can be talk of changing these borders through negotiations, without the use of force. (Kozyrev often said this publicly, and no one was outraged at the time!) He continued that the point was to have open, permeable borders that may compensate for the unjust borders. On the Russian side, Ukraine's decision to establish independent statehood was taken seriously and accepted. As far as Russians becoming minorities in the independent republics, there was trust in the democratic principles in the successor states, but the international community would be welcome to "intervene" on their behalf. In any case, independent states should be included in the CSCE as its principles also protect minorities. There was an urgent need for both a new economic treaty and a political treaty of alliance between the former member republics. Russia, for its part, was ready for this, the rest was up to the others.[48]

Listening to Kozyrev, a representative of enlightened, democratic Russia, confirmed even more what I had felt in Moscow in May: a real revolution in Russian history was underway; an acceptance of Western and European values. Let it succeed! My next meeting with a Russian confirmed my optimism. At the time of the coup, Soviet ambassador Boris Pankin in Prague took a strong pro-reform stance and became the new Soviet foreign minister. The Moscow Human Rights Conference on September 9–11, 1991, gave me a chance to get to know him. He expressed his appreciation of the Hungarian government's behavior in those critical days. We agreed that now was the time to establish a new kind of genuine friendship between our countries. However, the situation was very serious, as Pankin outlined:

> The economy is in total bankruptcy, and the winter ahead for the Soviet Union could well be a test of democracy. The Soviet Union has taken the decisive step, and now it is up to the Western democracies to seize the great opportunity: they can use economic means to create political stability. It would be desirable for Japan and the Seven [the predecessor of the G-8, the world's most powerful economies] to build more on the economic potential of the Soviet Union and the countries of Eastern Europe. It's a surreal situation: the Central European countries are accumulating goods to sell, and in the Soviet Union there is growing demand for them, but a win-win solution is being blocked by some mysterious force.

For our part, in a difficult economic situation I could only offer to guarantee exports of grain to the Soviet Union and to set up a joint committee to find a solution for further food supplies and their compensation. (The Soviet Union, and later Russia, refused to pay for Hungarian exports with oil shipments and thus settle the accumulated debt.) Our meeting lasted sixty-five minutes, when other foreign ministers had less than half an hour.[49]

The collapse of the Moscow coup removed the obstacle to the conclusion of a fair Soviet-Hungarian treaty that would recognize our sovereignty in all respects. At the same time, as the final text with the Russian Federation was being prepared,

---

[48] Immediately after Kozyrev's departure to attend the Aspen conference I put down the essence of our conversation, to which I later added his intervention at the conference. Prime Minister Antall received the Russian minister; their conversation is in Sáringer, *Iratok az Antall-kormány*, vol. 2: 219–24 (Doc. 28).

[49] Notes of our meeting are among my papers.

we initiated a similar bilateral treaty with Ukraine. In the practical implementation of our "Eastern" policy, the head of the relevant department, István Monori, played a valuable role. An "old hand," he was an expert on the area, and for him, serving the national interest had always trumped loyalty to the Party, not to mention loyalty to Moscow. On December 1, 1991, the referendum in Ukraine gave public endorsement to the country's independence. This was recognized by Hungary on December 3; the Consulate General in Kyiv was upgraded to embassy status and a sign was placed at the entrance to the consulate general's office to reflect the new status. This pioneering step, which was taken ahead of the other countries except Poland, was greeted with enthusiasm in Ukraine. On December 5, I informed the ambassadors of the EC, the United States, Canada, Poland and Czechoslovakia of the reasons for our move. I stressed how important it was that Ukraine should be included in European cooperation (i.e., to follow Hungary's example) and that lately the situation of the over 160,000 Hungarians in Ukraine improved considerably.[50]

By that time, we had three inter-state treaties ready for signature: one with Gorbachev's Soviet Union, another with the Russian Federation under President Yeltsin, and the third with Ukraine. On December 6, 1991, a Hungarian government delegation led by Prime Minister József Antall flew to Moscow. We did not come to the Russian capital to show loyalty but to sign a treaty in the Kremlin with both Gorbachev and Yeltsin as equal sovereign partners. With these treaties, the earlier hypocritical and verbal treaty of friendship, signed under duress, was annulled and replaced by genuine and voluntary cooperation. The two treaties also included condemnation of the Soviet intervention in Hungary in 1956.[51]

After the two ceremonies, in the afternoon, we flew to Kyiv. At the airport, at dusk, we were met by Ukrainian President Kravchuk and a guard of honor to sign the first international treaty of Ukraine, which was restoring its independence after more than three hundred years. The three treaties signed on the same day were the culmination of Hungary's "Eastern policy" and were a curiosity[52] in diplomatic history.[53] The reception of the treaties among the diplomats in Moscow was extremely positive, "a sign of the dynamism of Hungarian diplomacy." In a letter

---

[50] I have a note of my meeting with the diplomats.
[51] At the time of the signing, Gorbachev verbally apologized for the 1956 intervention, and Yeltsin did the same in writing in an appendix to the inter-state treaty. See Keskeny, *A magyar-orosz kapcsolatok*, 91–95.
[52] Sáringer, *Iratok az Antall-kormány*, vol. 2: 255–56 (Doc. 39).
[53] For the communiques on the signing of these contracts, see *Magyar Külpolitikai Évkönyv, 1991*, 388–90. For the report to the Government, see Sáringer, *Iratok az Antall-kormány*, vol. 2: 249–52 (Doc. 38). Endre Marinovich, *1315 nap: Antall József naplója* [1315 days: The diary of József Antall] (Budapest: Éghajlat, 2003), 131–49, gives an authentic account of some of the stages of Antall's Russian policy, recalling details and the authentic atmosphere of these events.

Figure 22. Signing the last international treaty of the Soviet Union with President Mikhail Gorbachev, Moscow, December 6, 1991

dated December 9, Antall informed President Bush of his impressions gained in Moscow and Kyiv that real power had passed into the hands of Yeltsin and Kravchuk respectively, that both of them were expected to pursue a responsible and cooperative policy, and that Ukraine did not wish to become a nuclear power and would radically reduce its armed forces.[54] This was very important and reassuring news at the time.

On December 8, 1991, Russia, Ukraine and Belarus established the Commonwealth of Independent States (CIS). Kozyrev, who had received us in Moscow two days earlier, had already indicated to me as his car was taking us to the Kremlin, that they wanted to create a new framework on the model of the British Commonwealth. On December 21 (coincidentally, Stalin's birthday), the leaders of eight more Soviet republics joined the short-lived CIS.[55] The Hungarian government's declaration on this occasion stated:

---

[54] Letter from József Antall to President George Bush, December 9, 1991. Among my papers.
[55] On that very day, I attended the first meeting of the North Atlantic Cooperation Council (NACC), a group of NATO and former Warsaw Treaty countries, in Brussels. It was there that the Soviet delegate announced the dissolution of the Soviet Union. On instructions from Moscow, he asked for the red flag of the Soviet Union to be removed from the hall immediately! We were standing up on a platform for the group photo with the flags of the participating countries behind us, when a hand reached out from behind the curtain, next to me, and lifted away the Soviet flag with the sickle and hammer.

Mikhail Gorbachev and his policies played a major role in the end of totalitarianism on one-sixth of the world, and the peaceful regime change in the countries of Central and Eastern Europe. [...] The Government of the Republic of Hungary appreciates the political wisdom and dignity with which President Gorbachev voluntarily stepped down from his post after the transformation of the Soviet Union and made way for further necessary democratic changes. [...] We support the aspirations of the Russian Federation to take the place of the Soviet Union in the UN and its Security Council. [...] We applaud the purposeful and responsible policy of the leaders of the successor states in creating the necessary conditions for the peaceful and democratic transformation of the Soviet Union. The decisive role in this process was played by Russian President Boris Yeltsin, who showed personal courage and outstanding statesmanship in averting the August coup.[56]

Diplomatic relations were soon established with all the successor states, and embassies were opened in mineral-rich Kazakhstan, where the Turkic-speaking majority had always showed sympathy towards the Hungarians, and in Moldova, which was important for our relations with the Romanians.

Since December 1991, Hungary's largest neighbor has been Ukraine. While Russia is not an adjacent state, as a great power it remains one of the most important partners in our foreign policy. However, in a figurative sense, as with the Czech Republic, we have continued to regard it as a neighbor. The further development of our bilateral relations is no longer part of this story, and Ambassador Ernő Keskeny gives a detailed and accurate account of the following years in his book.[57] Here I only want to mention a few facts and personal observations in order to provide a better understanding of the much-criticized policy of the Antall government towards the East.

In 1992, we concluded an economic and trade agreement with Russia, and at the end of that year we agreed on the pace and method of repayment of the accumulated Soviet debt. President Yeltsin, in a speech to the Hungarian National Assembly during his official visit on November 11, declared that "the tragedy of 1956 will remain an indelible stain on the Soviet regime forever"[58] and signed seven

---

[56] Declaration of the Government of the Republic of Hungary on its position on the establishment of the Commonwealth of Independent States, December 26, 1991. *Magyar Külpolitikai Évkönyv, 1991*, 402–3.
[57] Keskeny, *A magyar-orosz kapcsolatok*, 98–224.
[58] Minutes of the Hungarian Parliament, November 11, 1992, http://www.parlament.hu/naplo34/244/244/2440083.html. Unfortunately, only those who understood Russian could hear Yeltsin's speech in the Parliament, because the wire that transmitted the interpretation was cut, presumably due to sabotage, leaving the listeners deaf.

Figure 23. President Boris Yeltsin and PM József Antall, Budapest, November 10, 1992

important agreements, including one on cooperation in the protection of the rights of national minorities.[59] (Yeltsin's memorable speech to the Hungarian Parliament was recognized by a special declaration of the Hungarian legislature on December 8, 1992.[60]) During their bilateral talks, Antall reached an agreement on the financial settlement of the withdrawal of the Soviet troops with Yeltsin overruling the resistance of the Minister of Defense Grachev and accepting the "zero-zero" solution.[61] Even in the deteriorating economic and domestic political situation in Russia, the two countries maintained good relations, in which the personal affinity between the leaders[62] played a major role. During Yeltsin's official visit in 1992, after the official meeting, I took and hour-long walk around the Parliament building with Russian foreign minister Andrei Kozyrev, discussing the causes of the fall of communism and the prospects for a definitive end to the East-West conflict. Andrei

---

[59] Declaration on the principles of cooperation between the Republic of Hungary and the Russian Federation in the field of ensuring the rights of national or ethnic, religious and linguistic minorities. *Magyar Külpolitikai Évkönyv, 1992*, 344–48.

[60] *Magyar Külpolitikai Évkönyv, 1992*, 357–58.

[61] The details and the atmosphere of this difficult negotiation are well captured in Marinovich, *1315 nap*, 133–49.

[62] See the half-hour-long telephone conversation between the two leaders on January 21, 1993. Marinovich, *1315 nap*, 148–49. The same is illustrated by a letter from József Antall to President Yeltsin, which I delivered during my official visit on September 20, 1993, and the Russian president's reply a month later. *Magyar Külpolitikai Évkönyv, 1993* [Hungarian Foreign Policy Yearbook, 1993] (Budapest: Magyar Külügyminisztérium, 1993), 282–84.

was an educated, English-speaking, sincerely democratic professional diplomat, well-versed in world affairs. Being an opponent of President Putin's increasingly autocratic policies, in 2010 he went into exile in the United States.

Already during 1992, disappointment replaced earlier hopes in Russia and the so-called "red-brown" forces, who combined nostalgia for the party-state system with extreme nationalism, gained strength. Kozyrev's made a speech in Stockholm in December 1992, in which he wittily set out what the voice of Russian policy again becoming anti-Western would sound like—it was a warning to all. In 1993, a sharp confrontation emerged between President Yeltsin and the majority of the Russian Parliament over the issue of power-sharing. Antall and his government clearly saw in Yeltsin the guarantee for the preservation of Russia's democratic orientation—which was also a strong Hungarian interest. On my official visit to Moscow in September, I was received in a particularly friendly manner, and my ministerial colleague shared many of his concerns and plans with me. Although the nationalist and communist-majority Duma was still reluctant to ratify the 1991 Russian-Hungarian treaty because of the apology for 1956, it did so after the dramatic clash between the Russian Parliament and Yeltsin in September 1993, as Kozyrev had promised a few days earlier. When Kozyrev returned to Budapest in February 1994, his mood was already depressed, his so-called pro-American policies were being widely attacked at home, and he felt that the West was not helping the cause of Russian democracy enough. I believe that defending the cause of Russian democracy was not up to America or NATO, but up to the Russian public. Like Hungarian society, it identified democracy and the West with prosperity, and when the expected prosperity failed to materialize, and many people felt that their financial situation was deteriorating, it looked for new gods.

Despite the excellent relations with Yeltsin's Russia and the Soviet successor states, we stayed sensitive to the manifestations of imperialist nostalgia that had been growing in Russia since late 1992 (at first only among the opposition, especially in Zhirinovsky's party). Antall warned early on, both at home and abroad, of the danger that if "the Russian bear wakes up after a good sleep," it could become a threat again. "Anyone who thinks that the eternal Russia has renounced its political role in the Central European region is a naive man."[63] The first signs of this were seen during the South Slav crisis and then more strongly during the drive of the Central Europeans for NATO membership. However, we did not criticize Russia while I was in office. That is why I reject in the strongest terms Pál Dunay's 2012 statement in the journal *Külügyi Szemle* that "Moscow was shocked by the Antall

---

[63] Debreczeni, *A miniszterelnök*, 217–18 cites this warning.

government's ideological and prejudiced remarks about Russia."[64] It is unlikely that the future researcher of the Russian archives will find documents to support this distorted attitude, finding only evidence to the contrary. The Gorbachev-Antall relationship was cordial, the Yeltsin-Antall relationship was sincere and most friendly, and I would not have any other description for my relations with Foreign Minister Kozyrev. The memoirs of Ambassador György Nanovfszky authentically demonstrate the cordial relations between Hungary, Russia, and the other successor states of the Soviet Union in the mid-1990s,[65] and Ambassador Keskeny provides conclusive proof of this.[66] An important manifestation of this was the visit to Hungary of Alexy II, Patriarch of Moscow and All Russia, in March 1994. As if to give a blessing to Yeltsin's gesture, he said in the Hungarian Parliament: "I, as Patriarch of the Church, who now and forever before God am responsible for my people, hereby ask your forgiveness for our sins of 1956."[67]

What a sad contrast with Putin's Russia and the conduct of the present patriarch, Kirill, who gives a blessing to the war against Ukraine!

---

[64] Dunay's review of Róbert Győri Szabó's synthesis on the history of Hungarian foreign policy, *Külügyi Szemle* 11, no. 4 (2012): 229.
[65] György Nanovfszky, *Nano: Egy soknyelvű diplomata kalandjai öt kontinensen* [Nano: Adventures of a multilingual diplomat on five continents] (Budapest: Alternatív Kiadó, 2014), 67–120.
[66] Keskeny, *A magyar-orosz kapcsolatok*.
[67] Keskeny, *A magyar-orosz kapcsolatok*, 119.

Chapter 6

The Break-up of Yugoslavia[1]

In the first one and a half years of the Antall government, Hungary's foreign policy goals were on the envisaged track. Hungary was the first new democracy to become a member of the Council of Europe, the association of European democracies; Visegrád was a major achievement of our neighborhood policy, averting the real danger of an anti-Hungarian bloc; with our active involvement, the Warsaw Pact was dissolved; the successors of those who crushed our 1956 revolution apologized for their aggression; and our relations with the successor states of the disintegrating Soviet Union, including Ukraine, got off to a promising start. But along our southern border, in Yugoslavia, a serious internal crisis was unfolding, and this presented the Hungarian government with difficult choices.

The issue of the national minorities was at the core of the break-up of Yugoslavia. The Serbs made up only 36 percent of the population, but one third of them lived outside the Serbian Republic, in Croatia their number was about 600,000, in Bosnia-Hercegovina close to 1.5 million. That's one of the major reasons why Serbia did not want to accept the secession of these republics. On the other hand, Serbia had full control over two formerly autonomous provinces, Vojvodina and Kosovo. In the latter, about 90 percent of the inhabitants were ethnic Albanians, while in the former there was a 400,000 strong Hungarian minority, but also 150,000 Croats as well as a sizeable number of Slovaks and Rusyns. In fact, all the southern Slav republics had ethnic enclaves and/or ethnically mixed areas.

We had to strike a delicate balance between our sympathy for those member republics, which wanted to exercise their right to self-determination and had lived with us for many centuries in a state community, and the need to protect the Hungarians in the Vojvodina, who were being held hostage. Our situation was not made any easier by the Western attitude, which insisted on maintaining the status quo and feared a resurgence of territorial disputes in Central Europe, or by the

---

[1] For a more detailed version of this chapter, see Géza Jeszenszky, "Jugoszlávia felbomlása és a magyar külpolitika" [The break-up of Yugoslavia and Hungary's foreign policy], *Külügyi Szemle* 10, no. 4 (2011): 42–79; and a somewhat shorter English version, "Hungary and the Break-Up of Yugoslavia," *Hungarian Review* 2, no. 2 (2011): 42–52, and no. 3 (2011): 65–78.

Serbian propaganda which skillfully built on this, and on the memory of the two world wars. Moreover, in the dispute between the Hungarian Government and the Serbian nationalists in Belgrade, our political opposition and most of the press initially tended to take the side of the Serb Government.

Although the so-called Second Yugoslavia, created by Marshal Tito after the Second World War, was a hardline dictatorship based on a communist one-party system and was held together by force, the federal structure successfully managed the country's multi-ethnic character for decades. The leader of the communist partisan movement during the world war, Josip Tito, wanted to include Albania and Bulgaria in a Balkan federation that he would lead, but Stalin forbade this. This may have been one of the reasons why the Soviet dictator turned against Tito in 1948, trying to remove him from power. The United States and its allies sided with the 'national communist' leader and provided him with substantial political, economic and even military aid. Against the Bulgarian and Albanian leadership loyal to Stalin, Yugoslavia concluded the Balkan Pact with Greece and Turkey in 1953. An idealized image of Tito and his regime as standing up to the Soviet bloc and successfully dealing with national differences, prevailed among the Western governments, press and publications. The outside world, including the "non-aligned" countries of the "third world," embraced Tito's approach, i.e., that the efforts of the member republics and of the national minorities among them to preserve their own separate identity constituted nationalism, a dangerous separatism, against which action was justified. Croatia was viewed with special suspicion, given the memory of the Ustasha puppet state created after the German aggression in 1941.[2]

The 1974 Yugoslav constitution attempted to satisfy the moderate national aims of the six "socialist" republics, and granted autonomous status within Serbia to Vojvodina and Kosovo—to ensure Serb leadership within the Federation, thus to preserve the unity of the country. After the dictatorial head of state's death in 1980, the idea of Yugoslav unity was significantly weakened, with particular national interests coming to the fore—proving that national sentiment is stronger than "internationalist" communism. However, abroad, the seriousness of the internal divisions was still not perceived, and only specialists paid attention to the 1986 Memorandum of the Serbian Academy, which set the goal of uniting all Serbs into a single state. This was not only directed against the autonomy of Vojvodina

---

[2] Tito's ruthless but effective methods and the cult of Tito in the outside world are pointed out in Banac, *The National Question in Yugoslavia*, and Christopher Cviic, *Remaking the Balkans* (London: The Royal Institute of International Affairs, 1991), also Dénes Sokcsevits, *Horvátország a 7. századtól napjainkig* [Croatia from the seventh century to date] (Budapest: Mundus Novus Könyvek, 2011), 660–64.

and Kosovo, but even more so against Croatia and Bosnia and Herzegovina, which were primarily threatened by the "Greater Serbia" plan. The moves of Slobodan Milošević, who took over Serbia in 1987, and the abolition of the autonomy of Vojvodina and Kosovo in 1988 both pointed towards the realization of the Memorandum.

The "Kalashnikov case"

The Antall government was aware of Yugoslavia's internal problems and was sympathetic to the aspirations of the non-Serbs for greater economic and political independence and a genuine federation, but it did not expect the break-up of the federal state. The world could not even imagine it.

Inspired by the fall of the communist dominions in 1989 and the desire for democracy, political parties were allowed to operate in Yugoslavia, too. In the free elections in Slovenia and Croatia in spring 1990 the victory went to the center-right forces, who were dissatisfied with the division of political power and economic resources in Yugoslavia and wanted to assert their own national interest more strongly, and which were politically heterogeneous but united in their national goals, like the MDF in Hungary. In contrast, in its election in December, the majority of votes in Serbia went to the communists, who increasingly identified with Serbian nationalism and, led by Milošević, said no to regime change. Milošević's original goal was a centralized Yugoslav state, led mainly by Serbs, but he had to give that up after the 1990 spring elections.

The Hungarians tended to sympathize more with the Croats than with the Serbs, the beneficiaries of Trianon, despite the memory of the armed conflict in 1848 (which was fomented by the Viennese court) and the political disputes around the 1868 *Nagodba*, the Croatian-Hungarian reconciliation attempt. In addition to the cultural and religious similarities and the memories of the common struggle against the Ottoman Empire, the vision of holidays in the Adriatic made Croatia popular in the eyes of most Hungarians. On the other hand, the Serbs were remembered for the mass murder of Hungarians in 1944, avenging many times the deplorable atrocities committed in 1942 against Serbs.

In Chapter 2 I described my trip to Yugoslavia in July 1990 and the very warm welcome I received in Zagreb. A few weeks later, in September, through Deputy State Secretary Imre Szokai as intermediary, a request was received in Hungary from the government of the Croatian Republic for the purchase of 30,000 (some sources say 40,000) Kalashnikov submachine guns and ammunition for the Zagreb police, which lacked arms for law enforcement. We did not discuss the matter at government level, but József Antall, Minister of Defense Lajos Für and I felt that it was time to restore friendly relations with the Croatian people after the tensions dating back to 1848, and that refusing the request would make this difficult. In addition, the stockpiles of the disbanded Workers' Guards could easily meet the demand. Internal armed conflict in Yugoslavia was unimaginable at the time, and the type and quantity of the weapons request meant that they could not have been used for war purposes. Their significance was more psychological for the new Croatian government with democratic legitimacy, which was engaged in a political dispute with the Belgrade authorities. The Hungarian government had not been informed by Hungarian intelligence that Milošević and the army leadership had already begun arming and training Serbs in Croatia specifically for the purpose of rebelling against the Zagreb government. The Croatian government, however, was probably aware of this, and that is why it had started to set up a Croatian Guard.[3]

Croatian foreign minister Mršić and Defense Minister Špegelj[4] arrived in Budapest on October 5, 1990, to arrange the arms purchase—but no one informed the prime minister or me of their arrival.[5] Subsequently, in accordance with domestic rules, the arms request of the Zagreb-based company Astra (which was conducted through a third-country intermediary) was approved on October 10, 1990, by the interdepartmental committee chaired by the political state secretary of the Ministry of International Economic Relations, László Bogár,[6] in the absence of several other members. It was approved together with several other arms trade contracts. The first batch of ten thousand guns were soon delivered, with proper customs clearance by the Technika Foreign Trade Company, but on October 30 the head of the Intelligence Service of the Yugoslav People's Army contacted Minister of Defense Für with a sharply worded letter from Minister of Defense Kadijević of Belgrade. The letter asked his Hungarian counterpart whether large quantities of arms, ammunition and military equipment had been sold to Zagreb. The Hungarian minister could only say that he was not aware of any such dealings, and that arms

---

[3] Sabrina P. Ramet, T*he Three Yugoslavias: State-Building and Legitimation, 1918–2005* (Bloomington: Indiana University Press, 2005), 374.
[4] Martin Špegelj (1927–2014): Croatian army general and politician, defense minister (1990–91).
[5] I wonder how much was known about those talks by the secret services inherited from the old regime, or whether the whole transaction was handled by the Technika Foreign Trade Company. It would also be useful to know whether Belgrade learned of the sale through its agents in Zagreb or Budapest, or whether the information came from a Hungarian source, probably a ministry.
[6] László Bogár (1951–): Hungarian economist. Having joined the MDF early, was elected to Parliament in 1990, and selected to a post in the government (1990–94). Adviser to Prime Minister Orbán (1998–2002). Later became the supporter and disseminator of extremist conspiracy theories.

sales were not part of his portfolio. The next day, he forwarded the denial of the Hungarian Ministry of International Economic Relations along with a promise to take special care in the future to control the arms trade with Yugoslavia. After a further threatening enquiry from Belgrade, Minister Für asked for the data and documents on which the accusations were based and proposed a ministerial meeting. He never received a reply to the proposal. To avoid further controversy, no further machine gun deliveries were made, with the approval of the prime minister. During his visit to Budapest in December, Yugoslav Prime Minister Marković did not even mention arms sales.[7]

On January 25, 1991, a film on Belgrade television accused Hungary of aiding Croatian separatism with large-scale clandestine arms shipments. It was a manipulated "report," mixing reality with propaganda. In response to a question from the domestic press, I refuted this accusation and sent a note of protest to Belgrade against the false allegations.[8] Hungary's position on Yugoslavia was expressed in the Government's statement of February 2, 1991:

> The Republic of Hungary, based on the generally accepted principles and norms of relations between states, and good neighborliness, strives for mutually beneficial and lasting good relations with the friendly Federal Republic of Yugoslavia. [...] does not wish to interfere in the solution of Yugoslavia's internal problems. It respects the right of the nations and national minorities of Yugoslavia to decide on their internal relations by peaceful agreement, without external interference.[9]

The Hungarian press and the parliamentary opposition at the time seized on the matter, hoping to make political capital out of the criticism of the Hungarian Government in Belgrade and to get at least one or two ministers out of the government. On February 6, 1991, the Government informed the Parliament's Foreign Affairs and Defense Committee of all the details of the case and tightened the

---

[7] Für, *A Varsói Szerződés végnapjai*, 272–82, gives a detailed account of the first phase of the case of the arms sales. Kodolányi, *Antall Józseffel a világszínpadon*, 474–95 published documents on the case, with important details.
[8] *Magyar Külpolitikai Évkönyv, 1991*, 141. See Sáringer, *Iratok az Antall-kormány*, vol. 2: Docs. 162, 744.
[9] *Magyar Külpolitikai Évkönyv, 1991*, 142–43. Sáringer, *Iratok az Antall-kormány*, vol. 2 did not publish it.

regulation of Hungarian arms exports.[10] Antall expressed his regrets to Prime Minister Marković by telephone on February 7, 1991.[11]

This small arms transfer attracted little international attention. Belgrade deliberately exaggerated it in order to discredit Croatia's independence aspirations. Many writings on the South Slav war do not even mention the Hungarian arms sales, or do so only in passing. At the same time, it is clear that the "Kalashnikov scandals" had a very positive impact on the Croats and greatly contributed in Croatian public opinion to the positive perception of our common past. The weapons supplied by Hungary were primarily of psychological significance, but they also proved to be of great political benefit: Croatia perceived that Hungary had stood by its side at a critical time. Hungary gained a good neighbor and a lasting friend in its former sister country. However, independence was still a long way off and involved heavy sacrifices.

Serbian nationalism in communist guise

It is not for me to decide the debate that has been going on for twenty years about who bears the primary responsibility for the war in Yugoslavia. Milošević in his prison in The Hague did not live to see the end of his trial and the verdict, but it is certain that several of his fellow politicians share responsibility with him. The 1974 Yugoslav constitution included the right of the member republics to secede. In the case of Slovenia, where there was virtually no Serb population, Milošević could accept this, but in the case of Croatia only if the eastern half of the country (where half a million Serbs lived, wedged among the Croatian majority—the remnants of the former Habsburg military border zone) were attached to the significantly enlarged Serb member state.[12]

Unbeknownst to the outside world, the leaders of Yugoslavia's member republics had been engaged in intensive negotiations on a new constitutional settlement

---

[10] Joint report of the Foreign Affairs and Defense Committees on arms sales to Yugoslavia. Minutes of the Hungarian Parliament, February 12, 1991. Martin Špegelj in his memoirs (*Sjećanje Vojnika* [Memoirs of a soldier], Zagreb, 2001) gives a detailed list of the countries from which he managed to buy arms and military equipment. Besides Hungary, he mentions Austria, Czechoslovakia, Poland, Romania, Switzerland and Chile. His data (and those from other sources) were accepted by János Jakus, "The Liberation Operations of the Croatian Army in 1995," in *Balkáni füzetek, Különszám 1.* (Pécs: 2009), 37. I can confirm that I was also informed of such deliveries, but with the knowledge of the Hungarian government; we certainly did not sell or deliver weapons to Croatia or any other Balkan state, beyond the 10,000 machine guns mentioned above. If more than that reached Croatia from us, it could only have been done illegally. The international arms embargo imposed upon Yugoslavia in the autumn of 1991 was strictly enforced by Hungary.

[11] *Népszabadság*, February 8, 1991, 3.

[12] Sokcsevits, *Horvátország*, 672; Kocsis, *Egy felrobbant etnikai mozaik*, 37.

for the country since January 1990. Faced with Serbian offers that they found unacceptable, the Croatian and Slovenian leaderships abandoned the idea of maintaining any South Slav unity, however loose, and prepared to declare independence.[13] They began to build their own foreign relations, for the time being by urging countries to set up consulates-general and cultural institutes in Zagreb and Ljubljana, but did not inform the outside world of their plans for secession.[14] However, the Serb army leaders, headed by Minister of Defense Kadijević, were determined to maintain a united Yugoslavia and its so-called socialist system. At that time, Montenegro was still a willing partner of the Serb nationalists. On January 24, 1991, an order of the day was read in every army barracks, starting with approval that a few days earlier in Vilnius, Lithuania, Soviet special forces had killed several peaceful demonstrators who were calling for Lithuanian independence. The Yugoslav defense minister welcomed the fact that a strong crackdown on separatist efforts had finally been undertaken. The order said with confidence, "Socialism in Yugoslavia is not yet defeated, [...] there is a realistic chance that the country can be preserved as a federal socialist community." It went on that the CIA and the anti-socialist elements in the West, were now attacking Yugoslavia from Hungary (the proposal for turning Yugoslavia into a confederation was considered such an attack), but with economic reforms and adequate funding for the Yugoslav People's Army, the "League of Communists—Movement for Yugoslavia" (the proposed new name for the communist party) could save it.[15]

This sounded like a new Communist Manifesto. It can be seen, therefore, that the Yugoslav army, its leadership, in calling for the preservation of the unity of Yugoslavia, became in effect an instrument of Serbian nationalism, but it did so in the name of the communist ideal. Regrettably, two years earlier, the United States and the European Community did not speak out against the abolition of the autonomy of Vojvodina and Kosovo, nor did they object to the fact that the Serb element had thus achieved absolute majority in the federal presidency with four votes (Serbia, the two nominally still autonomous provinces and Montenegro).[16] In the first half of 1991 the West still accepted the fiction of a "Yugoslav nation," even though democratic elections in all the member republics had already confirmed the existence and strength of an independent national consciousness. While the West

---

[13] Ramet, *The Three Yugoslavias*, 374–75.
[14] E.g., on his visit to Budapest on January 22, 1991, Slovenian prime minister Lojze Peterle did not even hint at this. He had probably not yet decided then how to proceed.
[15] The text of the order of the day was published in the newspapers *Borba* and *Vjesnik* on January 31, and the Hungarian press took it over.
[16] Branka Magas in his review of former U.S. ambassador Zimmerman's *Origins of a Catastrophe* (New York: Times Books, 1996), http://www.bosnia.org.uk/about/bi_books/long_reviews.cfm?book=193.

greeted the national movements in the member states with distrust, branding it as nationalism, it refused to see that the real danger for Yugoslavia was the Serbian policy of hegemony, the intention to change the internal borders, and the Serbian military leadership that supported it. Nor were most Western governments and their representatives in Belgrade bothered by the fact that in the escalating crisis, the side that openly called itself communist was pitted against Slovenians and Croats who had democratic legitimacy.

In Budapest, we knew that the deteriorating relations with Belgrade would further aggravate the situation of the Hungarians living in Vojvodina, the former autonomous province which has been incorporated by Serbia. The Belgrade daily *Politika ekspres* reported that "the CIA and the Vatican are working intensively to create a fifth column among Hungarians in Vojvodina."[17] The accusation that the Hungarians of Vojvodina were agents of a hostile foreign country was to recur constantly in the following months and was extremely dangerous. In connection with the arms shipment incident and afterwards, we tried to conciliate the Serbian leadership, primarily in the interests of the Hungarians who were being held hostage in Serbia. The governing coalition in Hungary was happy to recognize the formation of the Democratic Community of Hungarians of Vojvodina (VMDK), an authentic Hungarian political organization, and after a few months the resistance also realized that it could not associate with those who represented Serbian communist nationalism. In June 1991, all the parties represented in the Parliament warmly welcomed the visiting leadership of the VMDK in Budapest.[18]

In the spring, certain Serbian leaders plotted a military takeover with Soviet defense minister Yazov (soon to be one of the organizers of the Moscow coup)[19] and also plotted with Croatian President Tuđman on the partition of Bosnia.[20] Meanwhile, in Croatia's mainly Serb-populated Knin area, a radical Serbian movement, encouraged, armed, and militarily controlled from Belgrade, launched an uprising, and on May 12, 1991, declared its accession to Serbia.

---

[17] Boško Samardžić, "Zavera protiv SFRJ," *Politika ekspres*, February 10, 1991. Quoted in *Magyar Szó* (the Hungarian language daily edited in Subotica/Szabadka) on the same day.

[18] *Magyar Szó*, June 20, 1991.

[19] Dmitry Yazov (1924–2020) was a Marshal of the Soviet Union, minister of defense (1987–1991) before being dismissed for his role in the August Coup of 1991.

[20] Meier, *Yugoslavia*, 157–74. The correspondent of the *Frankfurter Allgemeine Zeitung* reported on the secret negotiations on the basis of interviews, memoirs and on the spot personal experiences. Ante Marković spoke in detail about the negotiations between Milošević and Tuđman and his conflict with the Serbian military leaders in his interview with the Zagreb newspaper *Globus* in October 2003, during Milošević's trial in The Hague. *Magyar Szó*, December 9, 2003, and its sequels in the following days.

At the crossroads: Confederation or separation

In spring 1991 the Western governments barely perceived the gravity of the situation in Yugoslavia. Seeing its growing internal tensions, Hungarian diplomacy repeatedly warned its Western partners of the danger of armed conflict and proposed the convening of a conference on Yugoslavia to avert it. On May 19, 1991, a referendum was held in Croatia on whether the republic should remain an integral part of a Yugoslav federation or whether it should be part of a confederation as a sovereign and independent state, with cultural autonomy for Serbs and other minorities. The latter option was supported by 93 percent of the votes. Nevertheless, U.S. secretary of state James Baker, who arrived in the Yugoslav capital on June 21, declared that Yugoslavia should remain a "unitary" state.[21] On June 25, Croatia and Slovenia declared their independence. Two days later, the "Yugoslav People's Army" went into action in Slovenia, in order to formally regain control of the state border and border crossings. To everyone's surprise, however, the Slovenian Territorial Defense Forces successfully resisted, surrounding several assault units. A "troika" of three EC foreign ministers flew to Belgrade and Zagreb to propose an end to the armed struggle and a three-month suspension of independence by the two republics, during which a new framework for coexistence between the southern Slavs peoples would be worked out. The proposal was accepted by the parties concerned, and an agreement to that effect was signed on July 8 on the island of Brijuni, once Tito's favorite holiday resort.

Back in April, Croatian president Franjo Tuđman visited Hungary. He did not talk about the declaration of independence, which must already have been planned; the talks focused on the situation of Croats in Hungary and Hungarians in Croatia. It was agreed that "Hungary will ensure that Serbs, Croats, and Slovenes living in Hungary will establish their separate associations instead of the previously united South Slavic organization."[22] On the Croatian side, among other things, guaranteed parliamentary representation was promised for the thirty to forty thousand strong Hungarian minority. Soon, Antall created a stir with a statement that Vojvodina had been ceded by the peace treaty to the Kingdom of Serbs, Croats and Slovenes,

---

[21] For revealing observations on Baker's visit, based on contemporary notes, see Kodolányi, *Antall Józseffel a világszínpadon*, 585.

[22] Communiqué on the visit of Croatian head of state Franjo Tudjman to Hungary, April 19, 1991. *Magyar Külpolitikai Évkönyv, 1991*, 195. For more details on the subjects discussed, see Kodolányi, *Antall Józseffel a világszínpadon*, 496, 517–19.

and not to Serbia.[23] The intention was to warn Serbia, where the language of the press was visibly hostile to Hungary and threatening to the Hungarian minority. Some observers, recalling a historical fact, saw in Antall's words a cautious assertion of a Hungarian territorial claim, while others interpreted them as a kind of tutoring of the West, which had little knowledge of history. Indeed, in the preceding decades, historical knowledge in Western Europe had weakened considerably, and the political disadvantages of this became apparent in the Balkan crises, so Europe could have done with some tutoring. However, Antall had a much more obvious reason for this remark: the protection of Hungarian communities outside the borders was a primary concern of the Antall government's attitude during the Southern Slav crisis. It would have been difficult to draw international attention to the worsening situation of the Hungarians in Vojvodina any more effectively.[24] We wanted to prevent the ethnic conflicts from spreading to the Vojvodina, as this would have been fatal for the Hungarians living there. Unfortunately, Antall's statement was not enough to make the world stand up for the rights of Hungarians in Vojvodina to the same extent that it did for Serbs in Croatia and later for Albanians in Kosovo. I regret to say that the struggle of the Hungarian minorities, which is being pursued solely through legal, political means, has never received the attention it deserves. But more radical words, let alone steps, would have been fatal for the Hungarian communities beyond the borders.

Until autumn 1991, when the second strongest army in Europe, led by Serb nationalists, attacked the eastern territory of Croatia, the Hungarian government continued to express the hope, both in public forums and through confidential channels, that greater economic and political autonomy for each of the member republics could bring about a lasting and workable solution within a confederal state. I called attention to the increasingly tense situation in Yugoslavia and the Hungarian position on it in my presentations during my official visits to Norway and Denmark in April, saying that "the Hungarian Government would like to see a peaceful, democratic, prosperous Yugoslavia as its neighbor, in a federal or confederative arrangement, whichever its nations wish to accept."[25]

Hungary's awkward situation was immediately understood and appreciated by my late dear friend, the Croatian-born British journalist and commentator

---

[23] He said that at a press conference following his meeting with President Cossiga of the Italian Republic. *Magyar Szó*, July 6, 1991.

[24] Sympathetic reports about the Hungarians in Vojvodina started to appear in the world press; though there was a deeply unjust comment in the London *Independent*: "Serbian President Slobodan Milošević and his Hungarian counterpart Antall are blowing the horns of nationalism at the top of their lungs," *Magyar Szó*, August 8, 1991.

[25] *Magyar Külpolitikai Évkönyv, 1991*, 187.

on south-eastern Europe, Kristo (Chris) Cviic.²⁶ József Antall deeply felt the responsibility of the Hungarian government as a neighbor of Yugoslavia, which was on the brink of civil war, and as the motherland of the close to 400,000 Hungarians in Yugoslavia. We could not withhold our sympathy from the neighboring Slovene and Croatian peoples, who evoked the principle of self-determination, but we could not allow ourselves to be engaged in an even more strident conflict with Serbia, which was holding the Hungarians of Vojvodina hostage. That is why a balancing act such as this statement, on June 27, 1991, was necessary:

> The Hungarian Government considers it essential that no armed conflict should take place in Yugoslavia. [...] It is in constant contact with the governments of Europe and North America and joins the European Community and Austria in their crisis management initiative. We underline our interest in a peaceful and negotiated solution for the future of Yugoslavia, based on the right of peoples for self-determination and full respect for human and minority rights. [...] We respect any democratic solution found for the future of Yugoslavia.²⁷

At the time, we did indeed consider a Southern Slavic confederation to be a good solution, but we saw that events were moving in a different direction. At our bilateral meeting on June 19, 1991, on the margins of the CSCE Foreign Ministers' meeting, I asked my American colleague, James Baker, whether he saw any similarities between the Slovenian-Croatian declaration of independence and the attitude of the thirteen former British colonies in 1776. Baker looked at me in amazement.

On June 29, 1991, Prime Minister Antall informed Yugoslav prime minister Ante Marković by telephone about the Hungarian government's position.²⁸ The following day Antall turned to the president-in-office of the European Community and also to the presidents of the United States and the Soviet Union:

> The Hungarian Government, like most governments in the international community, believe that the continued existence of the South Slavs in a single entity is definitely desirable. For us, this position is particularly important: half a million Hungarians live in Yugoslavia, most of them in

---

[26] Cviic, *Remaking the Balkans*, 98–99.
[27] *Magyar Külpolitikai Évkönyv, 1991*, 240. The statement was the result the tense cabinet meeting on the same day; its verbatim record is in Sáringer, *Iratok az Antall-kormány*, vol. 2: 756–65 (Doc. 166).
[28] Antall–Marković telephone conversation. *Népszabadság*, July 1, 1991.

the province of Vojvodina, whose autonomous status was suspended last year. In the event of the final break-up of Yugoslavia, a nationalist, communist, post-Tito Greater Serbia may emerge, where, I fear, the rights of Hungarians and other minorities would hardly be respected. I am pleased to note that there is agreement on this issue between the Foreign Ministries of the two countries, as demonstrated by the conversation between Foreign Ministers James Baker and Géza Jeszenszky, and confirmed by the telephone conversation between the Hungarian Foreign Minister and Deputy Secretary of State Eagleburger.[29] I very much appreciate these exchanges. [...] We in Hungary see it as possible and desirable to establish a confederation of sovereign states, the Yugoslav Commonwealth. [...] As I stressed yesterday during the telephone conversation between Marković and myself, our position is that the establishment of a confederation would go hand in hand with the restoration of the autonomous status of Kosovo and Vojvodina. [...] For a successful political dialogue and a lasting solution, all South Slav actors must be encouraged to work for a new constitutional settlement that guarantees sovereignty and internal democracy (including the rights and autonomy of national minorities) for all nations of Yugoslavia. [...] The steps to achieve these goals, I believe, are largely in the hands of the government of the United States.[30]

This Hungarian program, if adopted and implemented, could have avoided wars in Yugoslavia and would have ensured full independence for all the national communities of Yugoslavia, while maintaining the level of integration already achieved in their economic relations. The model was set: the former British Empire which had gradually become a Commonwealth.

Active Hungarian policy in the period of the moratorium

From the moratorium agreed on the island of Brijuni, the European Community and the United States of America expected to preserve Yugoslavia in some form, but the Yugoslav army, which sided openly with Serb nationalism, wanted to create a *fait accompli*, and began armed actions on Croatia's eastern borders, supporting

---

[29] Lawrence Sidney Eagleburger (1930–2011): American diplomat and politician, deputy-, later secretary of state (1989–93).

[30] Letter from Prime Minister József Antall to President George H. W. Bush, June 30, 1991. A copy is among my papers.

the local so-called Chetnik irregulars.³¹ By that time the two republics were determined to secede and used the time to strengthen themselves politically and militarily. In Hungary, a government with a strong knowledge of history knew well the economic consequences of the break-up of a larger entity like the erstwhile Austro-Hungarian Monarchy, but was also aware of the strong appeal of the idea of the nation-state. The Serbian armed action gave the *coup de grace* to the idea of a confederation. However, when the representatives of the Hungarians in Slovenia as well as the Croats and Slovenes in Hungary requested that the government of Hungary recognize the Croatian and Slovenian states, we could only reply with a polite refusal, since we could not risk the safety of the Hungarians in Vojvodina by taking such a step, and we could not go against the still prevailing attitude towards Yugoslavia in the European Community.

While US Secretary of State Baker was still urging the unity of Yugoslavia, his predecessor in that role in the 1970s, Republican Henry Kissinger, arrived in Budapest at the end of June and took a better measure of the situation. He told Antall that the West bore a heavy responsibility for the military action of the Yugoslav army, because it had insisted for too long on Yugoslavia's unity. The prime minister agreed, but saw no chance of ending the military action unless there was strong Western pressure. It would help a lot if Moscow joined in exerting the pressure, Antall said, but given the prevailing perception there, that was unlikely. He added that Croatia and Slovenia should coordinate their actions much better.³² In an interview with the Austrian newspaper *Der Standard*, Antall said that the Yugoslav republics had the right to self-determination and sovereignty and that he supported the autonomy of Vojvodina and Kosovo.³³ President Árpád Göncz was not in line with the government's view, when he said at the end of June, "Hungary is interested in the unity of Yugoslavia, if only because there are a large number of Hungarians living there."³⁴

The military action against Slovenia, and even more so its failure, prompted the international community (especially the Western countries) to reconsider their previous policy. Germany and Austria began to openly declare that the independence of Croatia and Slovenia should be recognized. In mid-July, the EC decided to send observers to the scene of the fighting. However, the Italian and Dutch soldiers clad in white were reluctant to leave Zagreb and were primarily in contact with the

---

³¹ The Chetniks were non-communist Serb partisans fighting against the German occupiers during the Second World War, eventually overshadowed and crushed by Tito's communist partisans.
³² I have a copy of the report on Kissinger's visit, which lasted from June 30 to July 3, 1991.
³³ Reported by *Magyar Nemzet*, July 29, 1991, 3.
³⁴ *Magyar Nemzet*, July 29, 1991, 3.

Yugoslav officers stationed there, most of whom were of Serbian nationality. The Hungarian government received many complaints from the Hungarian population of Eastern Croatia (the historic Slavonia), which was under attack by the Serbian irregulars and the army, that the international observers were biased in favor of the Serbs.[35]

I was in Washington on July 18–19, 1991, on the occasion of an invitation to an American conference. I had a good half-hour conversation with the vice president, Dan Quayle,[36] who was deputizing for the president in his absence. I had met him the previous October during Antall's official visit to the United States, and on this occasion, he was mainly interested in my views on the situation in Yugoslavia. He agreed with me that the starting point of the crisis was the status of the Serb minority in Croatia, which must be settled in a fair and acceptable way for all, but also that the rights of the Albanians in Serbia (Kosovo) and the Hungarians must be guaranteed. The same was the subject of my visit with Defense Secretary Dick Cheney.[37]

On that trip, I also spent an hour and a half with Acting Secretary of State Lawrence Eagleburger, who was very much interested in the situation of countries that escaped from communism. He knew Yugoslavia very well, having been a diplomat in Belgrade at the beginning of his career and then returned there as ambassador between 1977 and 1980. He had a reputation as a pro-Serb, and was often referred to as "Lawrence of Serbia."[38] Now he was pessimistic about the future of Yugoslavia but also fearful of the consequences of its break-up. I did not notice any prejudice in his handling of the South Slav conflict. He understood how difficult the situation was for Hungary, and promised to follow the fate of the Hungarians living there.[39]

It was against this background that a memorable meeting took place in the unique medieval Adriatic port of Dubrovnik, Croatia, on July 26–27, 1991. It was the conference at the prime ministerial level of the regional political and economic cooperation originally of Italy, Austria, Yugoslavia and Hungary, enlarged with

---

[35] This charge was confirmed by the German news correspondent Viktor Meier's experiences on the spot. Meier, *Yugoslavia*, 224.
[36] Dan Quayle (1947–): American politician, Vice President (1989–1993).
[37] Richard (Dick) Cheney (1941–): U.S. politician, Secretary of Defense (1989–1993), Vice President (2001–2009).
[38] A reference to T.E. Lawrence, the legendary British commander of the Arab revolt in the First World War, who wrote his name into Middle East history as Lawrence of Arabia.
[39] I have a copy of the summary of my talks in Washington, prepared by our embassy. I had quite a close relationship with Larry Eagleburger, who sometimes called me from Washington late in the evening (our time) and was a frequent guest at the embassy when I was ambassador in Washington.

Czechoslovakia and then Poland in 1990–91, now called the Hexagonale. In this delicate, even dramatic situation, Antall delivered a speech that was constructive and original, did not antagonize either side in the Yugoslav crisis, and was in line with the goodwill declarations of the international community, while giving voice to the interests of both Hungary and the Hungarian minority in Yugoslavia. He described the venue of the conference as symbolic, saying, "it symbolizes the close links between the Mediterranean region and Central Europe." Taking advantage of the presence of representatives of the international economic and financial institutions—the International Monetary Fund, the World Bank and the European Bank for Reconstruction and Development—the prime minister pointed out that "the economic success of the region is a key factor in its political stabilization." The primary task of the Hexagonale, he said, was also to ensure that the people of the region experience the usefulness of the organization. Antall expressed the hope that the peoples of Yugoslavia would be able to "settle their internal conflicts peacefully and democratically," on condition that "irregular armed forces are not allowed to exist or operate" and that "military forces should not be allowed to play a role that is contrary to a political settlement." With sufficient international support, the federal government led by Prime Minister Marković would be able to do so, provided he could "come into line with the ideas of the member republics of Yugoslavia…" Hungary supported the right of self-determination of nations and the rights of national minorities, and expected the same from the European Community. "When we expressed our position on the idea of a confederation of sovereign republics, it was always in line with international agreements, including the Brijuni Agreement," Antall said. He concluded his speech by saying, "We ask our friends in Yugoslavia never to regard the expression of our concerns as an unwarranted interference, but as a sign of solidarity and a demonstration of willingness to support."[40]

In the same vein of thinking, advocating for a peaceful settlement, the Hungarian prime minister—in my presence—held talks with President Tuđman in a villa by the sea on the evening of July 26. The Croat leader did not mince words and revealed his determination to win independence, by fighting if necessary. In the following weeks, events moved towards armed confrontation, largely through the fault of the Serbian leadership in Belgrade. From this, not the United States, nor the European Community (collectively or separately), nor Hungary could dissuade Milošević, who was harboring plans for a greater Serbian state on the ruins of Yugoslavia and also expressing hopes of restoring the dictatorial regimes he called socialism.[41]

---

[40] *Magyar Külpolitikai Évkönyv, 1991*, 260–64.
[41] József Juhász, László Márkusz, Péter Tálas, and László Valki, *Kinek a békéje? Háború és béke a volt Jugoszláviában* [Whose peace? War and peace in the former Yugoslavia] (Budapest: Zrínyi Kiadó, 2003), 237–48.

France and the United Kingdom had played a decisive role in the creation of Yugoslavia in the First World War. That and Tito's contribution to the defeat of Nazi Germany made it difficult for those two countries to write off Yugoslavia, but at the same time that gave them greater prestige and influence among Serbs than any other countries. This is why the Hungarian prime minister wrote to French President Mitterrand, with whom he had a good personal relationship, on August 1. Reiterating the main points of his Dubrovnik speech, he advised that political control over the Yugoslav army and irregular Serb forces must be restored during the three-month moratorium; to achieve that and to initiate a fruitful dialogue between the republics, strong pressure must be brought to bear on the Serb leaders in Belgrade, and President Mitterrand stood a good chance of doing so. Antall asked the president to intervene at the EC to ensure that international observers extend their operations to Eastern Slavonia, where the population of Hungarian villages was at great risk.[42]

On the same day, a similar letter was sent to President George H. W. Bush. Antall thanked him for his letter of July 19, which expressed the United States' interest in Central and Eastern Europe and concern about the situation in Yugoslavia.[43] The Hungarian prime minister stressed his conviction that the protection of the Serb and Hungarian minorities in Croatia and Serbia would contribute to the resolution of the whole crisis in southern Slavic countries, and that a European guarantee of the rights of national minorities would increase security throughout the continent. The Hungarian references to minority protection were not just a pious wish. As I have already mentioned, in July 1991, the Conference of Experts of the CSCE met in Geneva with a view to drawing up binding international legislation on their rights. In 1990, the international community's position on this was still fragile but promising, and our neighbors had reckoned that an intolerant, repressive policy would not be compatible with the emerging European norms and their aspirations for integration. Two interpretations of the South Slav crisis were possible in this respect. The first was that the emphasis on the right of nations to self-determination and minority rights would lead to crises, conflicts, the disintegration of states and the undermining of European stability. The other, which I believed to be logical but still not valid, was the opposite: ignoring or denying the rights and reasonable demands of national minorities causes serious tensions, possibly wars, and can lead to disintegration, but that can be prevented by guaranteeing and extending those rights, and thus ensuring real and lasting stability. The *bona fide* observance of minority

---

[42] Letter from Prime Minister József Antall to French president François Mitterrand, August 1, 1991. Among my papers.
[43] I do not have President Bush's letter of July 19 in my files, but I knew about it.

Chapter 6 – The Break-up of Yugoslavia

Figure 24. Received by President George H. W. Bush in the White House to discuss the South Slav war, September 1991

rights should be assigned to the mother country of that national minority—with international authorization, as a protective power (*Schutzmacht*). Such a solution has been working really well in South Tyrol.[44]

On August 2, 1991, I too, wrote a letter to the president-in-office of the Committee of Ministers of the European Community, Dutch foreign minister Hans van den Broek. In our previous meetings he had shown a keen interest in the problems of the newly free countries, his helpfulness was sincere, and our personal relationship was most friendly. I summarized the main elements of Antall's letters of the previous day and reported on our talks in Dubrovnik with Croatian president Tuđman, Federal foreign minister Lončar and Slovenian foreign minister Rupel.[45] I also reported on the visit to Budapest a few days earlier by a delegation of mayors and other representatives of the Hungarian minority population in Croatia, who told me how the Serb irregulars were forcing the region's Hungarian and Croatian

---

[44] Italian foreign minister Gianni De Michelis also was of the opinion that the adoption of the South Tyrol model was the solution to the problem of minorities in Yugoslavia. According to him, Serbia and Hungary could act as UN-recognized guardian powers to safeguard the rights of their minorities in their neighboring countries. See *Wiener Zeitung*, August 2, 1991, reprinted in *Magyar Szó*, August 3, 1991.

[45] Dimitrij Rupel (1946–): Slovenian politician who contributed for the independence of the country. Foreign Minister intermittently from 1991 to 2008. Between those years he was mayor of Ljubljana (1995–97), and ambassador to the United States (1997–2000). We have remained personal friends.

population to flee, replacing them with Serb settlers and thus changing the ethnic composition of the area. They called for EC observers to extend their operations to Hungarian villages, to establish a neutral zone on Croatia's eastern border and to get the Belgrade authorities to disarm the Serb guerrillas. The mayors also called for Hungary to recognize Croatia's sovereignty without delay.[41]

On August 19, 1991, the *coup d'état* of the Soviet hardline communists took place—and failed. The Baltic republics, forcibly annexed to the Soviet empire during the Second World War, took advantage of the situation to demand the restoration and recognition of their full independence. In the previous chapter, I described how Hungary had restored diplomatic relations with them. We could not take a similar step in the case of Croatia and Slovenia, partly because of the lack of legal precedents and mainly because of the precarious situation of the Hungarians in Vojvodina. In the wake of the armed clashes, however, we abandoned our earlier position that Yugoslavia could be preserved within a confederal framework. Now it was inevitable to acknowledge the claims for independence. We continued to call for international action to contain the violence[46] and to provide information and analysis to help the leaders of the EC Member States have a clearer picture of the crisis in the Balkan.

In Budapest on August 23, Prime Minister Antall personally briefed the ambassadors of the EC, the G7, the Soviet Union and Austria on the Hungarian government's position and actions on the Moscow coup and the implications for Hungary of the situation in Yugoslavia. He reiterated that Hungary respected the existing borders, i.e., its policy towards Yugoslavia was not based on territorial claims, but also that Hungary considered it essential to guarantee the rights of the Hungarian and other national minorities (including Serbs living in the breakaway republics). He warned that the Yugoslav air force regularly violated Hungarian airspace and that the population of southern Baranya had been chased from their homeland by military means; consequently, Hungary had had to take in large number of refugees. The message, communicated also in writing, concluded:

> All mediation and negotiations failed to bring results, fighting is reaching the border of Hungary, and the non-Serb inhabitants are forced to flee. In view of all that the Government of Hungary repeatedly calls on the members and governments of the European Communities to take an effective and common stand for the resolution of the crisis. That is no longer an internal

---

[46] Statement of the Hungarian Ministry of Foreign Affairs on the situation in Yugoslavia, August 27, 1991. *Magyar Külpolitikai Évkönyv, 1991*, 274–75.

affair; it affects the whole international community. Countries which still have a special prestige in Serbia, like the United Kingdom and France, have a special responsibility to exert pressure [...] All of these worrying developments call for the international community to step up its efforts to resolve the crisis in Yugoslavia. All means at their disposal should be used: the conflict management mechanism of the CSCE, the influence of the EC, of the UN and the Security Council, as well as political pressure.[47]

It was important for Hungary to provide authentic and reliable information to our foreign partners because the Serbian leadership was doing his best to involve Hungary in the conflict—demonstrating that once again it was the Second World War adversaries who wanted to tear Yugoslavia apart.

War along the southern border—towards accepting disintegration

It would have been inappropriate to openly criticize the conduct of our Western partners, but we were aware of the serious consequences of their indecisive and hesitant behavior. Many Western European governments feared that an independent Croatia and Slovenia, together with Austria and Hungary, would once again be part of an economically and politically powerful German sphere of interest. This fear explains, but does not excuse, the position taken by those governments and their diplomats between June and December 1991. This is why Viktor Meier, who was a Balkan correspondent for German newspapers for thirty years, wrote that Western diplomats in Belgrade "bear a heavy responsibility for the disastrous mistakes of Western policy towards Yugoslavia" because they failed to understand that the unity of the country could not be preserved against the determined will of non-Serbs.[48]

In light of the Serb aggression against Croatia and the war crimes committed, it became clear to Hungary that the only way to resolve the crisis was to recognize the independence of the secessionist member states. However, we could not take that step alone, or together with just one or two countries, and not only due to the concern for the Hungarians of Vojvodina. We had, however, begun to build intensive relations with our new future neighbors. I have already mentioned Tuđman's

---

[47] Meeting of PM Antall with the corps diplomatique in Budapest, August 23, 1991. *Magyar Külpolitikai Évkönyv, 1991*, 268–69. Communication of the Government of Hungary for the Foreign Ministers of the European Communities, August 27, 1991. Among my papers.

[48] Meier, *Yugoslavia*, 216–20, quote from 217.

visit in April and meeting his foreign ministers, who were replaced one after the other. They understood that despite extending our sympathy, our options for action were limited. I pointed out that recognition of full independence was a common European cause, and that an independent step by Hungary would be of no use.[49] Antall promised that "Hungary would not be the first to recognize Croatia, but neither will it be the last to do so."[50] Slovenian foreign minister Dimitrij Rupel, who arrived in Budapest on August 26, 1991, was also fully aware of that. In Rupel, Slovenia found a visionary, courageous and capable leader, who played a major role in the acceptance of his country's independence by foreign countries and in establishing its authority. We agreed to set up a working group of experts to strengthen and deepen our relations, to open two new border crossings immediately, in addition to the existing one, and to establish a diplomatic mission in Ljubljana.[51]

The EC foreign ministers met on August 27 to discuss how to enforce the ceasefire, which had been signed several times by the South Slav leaders but then was immediately broken (usually by the Serbs). The ministers were still confident that Yugoslavia could be kept together.[52] Pressed by Hungary, at the meeting of the CSCE Conflict Prevention Centre on September 2 in Vienna, Yugoslavia admitted its violations of Hungarian airspace and promised to do their utmost not to allow that to happen in the future.[53] The EC foreign ministers came up with a new plan, which was adopted by the senior officials of the CSCE on September 3: a new ceasefire on the Croatian fronts, monitored on the spot by foreign observers; a peace conference in The Hague among the six member republics, the Yugoslav federal government and the EC, chaired by Lord Carrington,[54] former secretary general of NATO; and finally, a Court of Arbitration under the leadership of Robert Badinter,[55] former president of the French Constitutional Court. The plan was accepted, and the Yugoslavia Conference began on September 7.

Hungary had already proposed such a conference before the crisis escalated in June, and we had always been of the opinion that the deliberations should include

---

[49] *Népszabadság*, August 29, 1991, 3.
[50] *Új Magyarország*, August 30, 1991; *Külügyminisztériumi tájékoztató, 1991*, vol. 2: 140–41.
[51] *Népszabadság*, August 27, 1991; *Külügyminisztériumi tájékoztató, 1991*, vol. 2: 133.
[52] Meier, *Yugoslavia*, 226–27.
[53] *Népszabadság*, September 3, 1991, 3–5.
[54] Peter Alexander Rupert Carington, 6th Baron Carrington (1919–2018): British Conservative Party politician, Defense Secretary (1970–1974), Foreign Secretary (1979–1982), Secretary General of NATO (1984–1988).
[55] Robert Badinter (1928–2024): French lawyer, politician, Minister of Justice (1981–1986), President of the French Constitutional Council (1995–2011), President of the Arbitration Commission of the Peace Conference on Yugoslavia (1991), President of the Court of Conciliation and Arbitration of the Organization for Security and Cooperation in Europe (OSCE) (1995–2013).

representatives of the minority communities. This was also requested by the VMDK, at our suggestion. Its president, András Ágoston, wrote to Lord Carrington in mid September requesting to be heard, and this took place in early October.[56] They received assurances and the rights of minority groups were included in the settlement that was finally reached.[57] Prime Minister Antall sought to promote both the general settlement and the protection of the Hungarian population of Vojvodina with his visit to Subotica/Szabadka on September 3, 1991, where he met with the federal prime minister, Ante Marković. They agreed on the principles and conditions for a peaceful solution to the crisis: to make another attempt to bring the sovereign South Slav states together in the form of a Commonwealth; to set extensive individual and community rights for all the national minorities; and to place all armed forces under political control. At a press conference, the two prime ministers agreed on the right of nations to self-determination, personal and local autonomy for minorities, and that they "consider all previous conflicts, including arms sales and Yugoslav incursions into Hungarian airspace, to be closed."[58] The Yugoslav prime minister promised that Hungarians and Croats expelled from southern Baranya by the army would be allowed to return to their homes and would receive compensation.[59] The only problem with all this was that by this time Prime Minister Marković had lost all influence and authority. When he resigned at the end of the year, the function itself ceased to exist. Following his meeting with Marković, Antall briefed representatives of the Hungarian community,[60] and then the Croatian and Slovenian deputy prime ministers, inviting them to the Hungarian town on the border, Szeged.[61]

---

[56] On Ágoston's letter, see *Magyar Szó*, September 12, 1991. On the hearing, see "Dr. Ferenc Körmendi presented the VMDK's positions on the situation of Hungarians in Vojvodina to the two vice-presidents of the Yugoslavia Conference in The Hague," *Magyar Szó*, October 2, 1991.

[57] "So, we were the first to reach The Hague, ahead of the Albanians or the representatives of the Serbs from Baranja-Slavonia. [...] At the end of our negotiations, they [the Yugoslavia Conference] expressed their full agreement and support for our requests and demands. This is important, because we also demand that we ourselves could represent our interests, not others," said Dr. Ferenc Körmendi. *Magyar Szó*, October 6, 1991.

[58] *Népszabadság* and *Új Magyarország*, September 4, 1991; *Külügyminisztériumi tájékoztató, 1991*, vol. 2: 148–50.

[59] Communiqué on the working visit of Prime Minister József Antall to Yugoslavia, September 3, 1991. Magyar Külpolitikai Évkönyv, 1991, 277.

[60] After the meeting, András Ágoston, president of the VMDK, told *Pesti Hírlap* in an interview that they had had an encouraging and friendly exchange of views with Prime Minister Antall. "We see him not only as the president of the Hungarian government, but also as a European politician whose prestige is growing due to his creative contribution to the resolution of the Yugoslav crisis." Magyar Szó, September 5, 1991.

[61] *Külügyminisztériumi tájékoztató, 1991*, vol. 2, 150.

In defiance of intensifying international scrutiny and warnings, the Serb-led Yugoslav army launched a new offensive in mid September, a full-scale war, directly south of the Hungarian border. The aim was "merely" to occupy and annex the eastern part of Croatia as far as the town of Virovitica and drive the Hungarians and Croats out of there. At the same time, they launched an attack on the eastern part of Dalmatia and started shelling Dubrovnik, a World Heritage site. This barbaric act shocked world public opinion and turned it against the Serbs. Even their traditional patron, Russia, could not ignore the Serbian war crimes and condemned what had happened. Under these circumstances, the Serbian accusation that Hungary was supplying arms to Croatia could hardly be taken seriously. The accusation was also rejected in the press.[62]

The rapid deterioration of the situation in the southern Slav territories, the bombardment and then occupation of Hungarian villages in Croatia, prompted Antall to telephone German Chancellor Kohl on two occasions. On September 5, he reported on the meeting in Subotica/Szabadka and the fact that the Yugoslav federal government had no influence whatsoever over the armed forces, which were openly cooperating with the Serbian irregulars. He told Kohl that tens of thousands of refugees had arrived in Hungary, 90 percent of them Croats. All parties should be put under constant international pressure, Antall suggested. The Chancellor replied that the pressure was on, and that Yugoslavia had been cut off from all financial and economic aid. If the next round of peace talks fails, the independence of Croatia and Slovenia would have to be recognized. He saw about half of the EC states as currently inclined to do so. He would shortly raise the issue with the reluctant British and President Bush.[63] On September 20, Chancellor Kohl informed the Hungarian prime minister that neither President Bush nor Prime Minister John Major had shown any willingness to take a new initiative to resolve the Balkan crisis, and that the time had come to involve the UN Security Council.[64]

The situation has become an immediate threat to Hungary. We issued a statement that warfare was intensifying near the Hungarian border and that Hungarian airspace was now being violated on a regular basis. We warned that the war could spread to other parts of Yugoslavia and even spill over the borders.[65] Three days later,

---

[62] *Új Magyarország*, September 13, 1991. *Népszabadság* also linked the slander to the intensifying propaganda campaign against the VMDK. Cf. *Magyar Szó*, September 14, 1991.
[63] Transcript of the telephone conversation between Prime Minister Antall and Chancellor Kohl on September 5, 1991. Hungarian copy among my papers.
[64] Transcript of the telephone conversation between Prime Minister Antall and Chancellor Kohl on September 20, 1991. Hungarian copy among my papers.
[65] Statement by the Hungarian Ministry of Foreign Affairs on the violation of Hungarian airspace by Yugoslavia, September 17, 1991. *Magyar Külpolitikai Évkönyv, 1991*, 299–300.

on September 20, we issued a statement calling on the international community to "act in unison and decisively to stop the military action immediately, to prevent it from spreading to other parts of Yugoslavia or outside the country," to protect national minorities in Yugoslavia and to convene the Security Council.[66]

A turn in international reactions?

Knowing that President Bush was not indifferent to his views, Antall initiated a phone conversation with him. He told the president how serious the military situation was, and expressed his opinion that the Serbs could be influenced only by the U.S., Britain, France, and of course Russia, which had finally agreed to stop supplying the Serbs with weapons. Antall asked Bush to tell Gorbachev and Yeltsin that Serbia was in the hands of the very people who attempted the coup in Moscow a few weeks earlier. "If the world is unable to take a common stand in the Yugoslav case, serious destabilization may set in throughout Central Europe." The president sounded understanding and confirmed that he was looking forward to Antall's visit following his address at the UN on October 4. Bush proposed intensive diplomatic action, in concert with the EC, and asked if Lord Carrington's initiatives had indeed failed. Antall mentioned that during his recent visit in Tokyo he had had a long conversation about Yugoslavia with former prime minister Margaret Thatcher, who would be an ideal person on a goodwill mission. The president wondered if Prime Minister Major would be pleased. In any case, he promised to address the issues raised by Antall.[67]

Three days later, Antall had another long telephone conversation, this time with Yugoslav prime minister Marković. The latter said that the latest ceasefire (the Igalo Agreement) brokered by Lord Carrington between Tudjman, Milošević and Kadijević was working (for the time being) and could be lasting if pressure continued to be brought to bear on all parties. Antall noted that although recognition of sovereignty was now on the agenda, this could only be achieved if the whole EC agreed. Marković was ready to accept separation if it was initiated by the Hague Peace Conference. He stated that he supported in principle all forms of local and regional autonomy, including Kosovo and Vojvodina, but that this should also apply to Kosovo Serbs, Serbian Muslims and all three constituent parts of Bosnia and Herzegovina. Antall assured Marković that Hungary would maintain

---

[66] Statement of the Government of the Republic of Hungary on its position on the situation in Yugoslavia. September 20, 1991. *Magyar Külpolitikai Évkönyv, 1991*, 315–16.
[67] Notes of a phone conversation between Prime Minister Antall and President George Bush, September 20, 1991, among my papers.

communications (such as telephone links, gas supplies to Bosnia) with Serbia and all the other republics, and would not restrict border traffic, hoping that these gestures would be appreciated. Hungary continued to welcome the increasing numbers of refugees from Serbia, too, and will also provide schooling for their children.[68]

In my discussions and speeches abroad during my ministerial activities, I have always stressed that in Central and South-Eastern Europe, borders are not drawn along ethno-national lines, the various national groups, especially in border areas, live mixed together, forming a vast ethnic mosaic. Understanding this is essential to understanding the Southern Slavic crisis. As it worsened, I argued with redoubled vigor for the necessary steps to be taken to find a solution, doing so on September 5, 1991, in The Hague at the prestigious Klingendael Institute,[69] on September 10 in Moscow at the CSCE Human Rights Conference,[70] and on September 19 in Paris at the invitation of the IFRI (Institut Français des Relations Internationales). On the Southern Slav crisis, I said that no one should be indifferent to the atrocities committed. In Hungary, the whole transformation was threatened by the war in its neighborhood, and it was keeping away both investors and tourists. The Hungarians in Vojvodina were being held hostage and want to stay out of the war between the southern Slavic peoples. They were protesting against being conscripted into the Serbian army and forced to fight—possibly against Hungarians in Croatia! A few months ago, I argued, a confederation of sovereign republics could have resolved the crisis, but the Serbian guns destroyed that possibility. The first condition for a solution was a ceasefire and the political control of the military. The inviolability of the internal borders of the republics must be accepted by all—which did not preclude their negotiated modification. The political and cultural autonomy of each national minority in each republic must be guaranteed. This would meet the legitimate claims of Serbs in Croatia, but the principle should also apply in Vojvodina, for the Hungarian and other minorities.

In my discussions, I also warned that the ethnic conflict could easily spill over into Bosnia, Kosovo and Vojvodina, where the population was ethnically mixed. The mandate of the international observers should be extended to those areas in order to prevent possible conflicts; if a fire broke out there, it would be difficult to extinguish. Finally, I argued that the negotiations on the future of Yugoslavia should include not only the six republics but also representatives of Kosovo and Vojvodina, which had been deprived of their former autonomy. The Vojvodina is

---

[68] Transcript of the telephone conversation between Prime Minister Antall and Prime Minister Ante Marković on September 20, 1991. Hungarian copy among my papers.

[69] *Magyar Külpolitikai Évkönyv, 1991*, 278–88.

[70] *Magyar Külpolitikai Évkönyv, 1991*, 291–96.

home to a significant number of Croats, Bunevci, Slovaks and Rusyns, in addition to Serbs and Hungarians.[71] I also pointed out in my talks that the Hungarian minorities everywhere were embracing European democratic values, strengthening the fight against retrograde forces in their countries, and that that was particularly important in Serbia.[72]

In Hungarian political life, there was agreement on the course taken by the government. I continuously briefed the experts of the six parliamentary parties, and at my international press conference on September 18, 1991, I was able to confirm that.[73] While the Hungarian government kept providing its international partners with the most up-to-date and accurate information on the southern Slav war, it was an advantage that Germany and Austria gave such a strong support for the independence of Croatia and Slovenia. (Antall was in constant contact with Chancellors Kohl and Vranitzky,[74] while I was with Vice Chancellor and Foreign Minister Mock.) While sympathy grew in Hungarian society for the attacked and clearly weaker Croatian side, there was fear that Hungary might "drift" into war.

Reassuring international action

First the new security forum, the CSCE, and then the European Community proved powerless to prevent or stop the new Balkan war, accompanied by its staggering war crimes. In the diplomatic forums dealing with the South Slav crisis, Antall personally took a most active role, arguing convincingly for decisive action to stop the armed fighting, which was directly threatening Hungary. At the end of September, at the proposal of several countries, the question of Yugoslavia was finally referred to the Security Council. In my statement there, I said:

> Hungary has no intention of siding with either side in the conflict between the southern Slav peoples, but it is obliged to draw the attention of the international community to the deteriorating situation in a country which is our

---

[71] *Magyar Külpolitikai Évkönyv, 1991*, 301–14. For the original English speech, see Jeszenszky, "Hungary and the Break-Up of Yugoslavia" no. 3 (2011): 69–70.
[72] Károly Dudás, a member of the VMDK leadership, told *Vjesnik* that the Hungarians of Vojvodina are unanimous in their support for European integration, the formalization of borders and the single European market. With its current policy, Serbia "has alienated not only the Hungarians, but also all other peoples who do not want to go back to the past. The Hungarians and Serbs can move forward together, but only if the present anachronistic regime of the Serbian Socialist Party is overthrown." *Magyar Szó*, September 5, 1991.
[73] *Külügyminisztériumi tájékoztató, 1991*, vol. 2: 204–6.
[74] Franz Vranitzky (1937–): Austrian politician (Social Democratic Party of Austria, SPÖ), Chancellor of Austria from 1986 to 1997.

neighbor and with which we share a long common border. Our population is already feeling the effects of the hostilities and violence: our borders are being crossed by tens of thousands of refugees, and our airspace was violated on several occasions by foreign aircraft. [...] Hungary believes that the conflict in Yugoslavia is a serious threat not only to the peoples living in that state, but also to the immediate neighborhood, to the distressed democracies of the region, to the whole of Europe and the world [...] We must see it as a threat to international peace and security. [...] Given the gravity of the situation and the urgency of the task, the UN can only discredit itself if it remains marginal or passive, or lacks the necessary determination to make a concerted effort. [...] An internationally acceptable political settlement must reflect the principle of respect for the right of self-determination of the peoples of Yugoslavia and for universal human rights, including the rights of national minorities. It would be a historic mistake to launch the settlement process without allowing not only the nations but also the national minorities living in Yugoslavia, including half a million Hungarians, to express their views and participate in the settlement process. [...] One way to achieve peace could be the presence of foreign observers or, indeed, peacekeeping forces in areas of Yugoslavia not yet affected by internal upheavals. [...] Only the people of Yugoslavia can decide on the future structure of the state. But in our interdependent and cooperative world, we owe it to ourselves to lend a helping hand to these peoples to create the conditions, in accordance with their democratically expressed views, to facilitate the search for a peaceful solution.[75]

It was the first real war in Europe since the Soviet intervention against Hungary in 1956, and the Security Council could not remain silent. However, what Resolution 713 (1991), adopted on September 25, 1991, offered was meager: the reiteration of the pious wish to have a lasting and fair settlement by common consent, and a general and complete embargo on all deliveries of weapons and military equipment to Yugoslavia. The resolution came too late to have any restrictive influence, and in effect it helped the Serbs rather than the Croats, since the former had almost the whole Yugoslav arsenal in their hands. But it was better than nothing. This was reflected in Antall's address to the General Assembly, an eloquent and full exposition of the problem from the viewpoint of Hungary:

---

[75] Géza Jeszenszky, Minister of Foreign Affairs at the UN Security Council meeting, September 25, 1991. *Magyar Külpolitikai Évkönyv, 1991*, 317–20.

World public opinion was under the belief that there was a ceasefire in Yugoslavia, which might be broken by sporadic incidents in towns one has never heard of. Unfortunately, however, a ceaseless and brutal war is going on there. [...] It is essential that in addition to the member republics of Yugoslavia, the representatives of the Albanian and Hungarian ethnic communities and other affected ethnic groups in Yugoslavia be formally involved in the conflict settlement and that their legitimate aspirations be taken into account. We believe that a lasting solution to the Yugoslav crisis can only be found through the simultaneous application of the right of self-determination of nations, universal human rights and the rights of national minorities.[76]

On this basis, the Hungarian prime minister welcomed Security Council Resolution 713.

After his speech, Antall was awarded an honorary doctorate by the University of Connecticut, and then he gave a lecture at a dinner at the prestigious Council on Foreign Relations in New York. The following day, October 3, he spoke at George Washington University in Washington, where he was warmly introduced by Professor Madeleine Albright, later to be secretary of state, who had visited Budapest before the 1990 elections, on behalf the International Democratic Institute. In meetings with lawmakers on Capitol Hill, Antall linked the solution of the South Slavic situation to a proposal for a general role by NATO in crisis management.[77] (Years later, such a role became NATO's practice.) Acting Secretary of State Eagleburger accepted our invitation to dinner that evening at the Hungarian embassy. The main topic of the discussion among the three of us was the Balkan crisis, its consequences and possible solutions. We urged the United States to take a more active role and, if diplomacy were to fail, to support NATO's military engagement to bring peace. I know one person who thought along the same lines: Manfred Wörner, NATO secretary general. In our meeting at the Atlantic Assembly in Madrid on October 21, 1991, he told me privately: "I can only implement a joint decision of the member states. If I were given a mandate, we could stop the killing in a matter of hours. The Yugoslav leadership is aware of what NATO is capable of." At the end of our dinner in Washington, the US secretary of state stood and said, "You convinced me about the best way to resolve this crisis. Tomorrow you will have thirty minutes to convince the president." There may have been more

---

[76] Address by Prime Minister József Antall at the XLVI Session of the UN General Assembly (October 1, 1991). *Magyar Külpolitikai Évkönyv, 1991*, 324–25.
[77] *Külügyminisztériumi tájékoztató, 1991*, vol. 2, 240–41, and my personal memories.

politeness than sincerity in "Larry's" words, but as a former ambassador to Belgrade, he knew that Serbs respected strength.

Our meeting with President Bush the next day lasted forty-five minutes, and the atmosphere could not have been more cordial. However, President Bush did not undertake a course that was unlikely to win the support of both Congress and the public. It took almost four more years for the United States and NATO to commit themselves to military intervention, at the cost of nearly 200,000 deaths in Bosnia. The first armed action in 1995 brought an end to the war, if not in a few hours, then in a few days. In any case, what our messages to America achieved was to strengthen relations between NATO and Central and Eastern Europe and to change U.S. policy towards Yugoslavia.[78]

At this point I recall that at the second summit meeting of the Visegrád Cooperation in October 1991, at a press conference called at the initiative of Polish foreign minister Skubiszewski, we condemned the war crimes committed by the Serbs. On October 8, 1991, at the signing of the Polish-Hungarian treaty in Warsaw, Prime Ministers Mazowiecki and Antall declared:

> The armed activities of the Yugoslav Federal Army on the territory of Croatia were an act of aggression; they were in violation of international law, in particular the Charter of the United Nations. [...] the conflict is not an internal affair, but an armed action against aspirations based on the right of nations to self-determination. The right to self-determination also means the right to statehood, the right to autonomy and the right to guarantee the rights of minorities.

The two prime ministers called for "international peacekeeping forces to be deployed on Croatian territory," and for convening the Security Council as soon as possible.[79]

The September 7 Hague Peace Conference on Yugoslavia, chaired by Lord Carrington, at first aimed to achieve a working and complete ceasefire, but the Serbian attacks only intensified. The intention was clear: to create a *fait accompli* by occupying as much territory as possible and to reach an agreement on that basis. On October 4, Milošević accepted the principle of secession, provided that the Serbs in Croatia were granted far-reaching territorial autonomy. The bombing of Dubrovnik's Old Town may have been the final straw, with the EC responding by threatening Belgrade with sanctions and the suspension of the trade agreement

---

[78] Article about Antall's negotiations in Washington, *Új Magyarország*, October 9, 1991. *Külügyminisztériumi tájékoztató, 1991*, vol. 2: 254.
[79] *Magyar Külpolitikai Évkönyv, 1991*, 331.

with Yugoslavia. On October 8, the three-month moratorium expired, Slovenia and Croatia put their independence decisions into effect, and from then on, the Serbian offensive could only be characterized as aggression. As the fighting intensified, so did Croatian military resistance, while the Serbian side was weakened by mass desertions and growing anti-war protests in Serbia. At the crisis meeting of the high officials of the CSCE held in Prague, István Gyarmati, head of the Hungarian delegation, gave a detailed account of the serious consequences of the fighting in Croatia and proposed that the CSCE ceasefire mission should step up its activities in Baranya and Slavonia and extend them to Vojvodina, also in view of the propaganda campaign being waged by the Serbian mass media against the Hungarians there. He also drew attention to the fact that Hungarians were being drafted into the Yugoslav army in greater numbers than their proportion in the population, and were sent immediately to the front and used as a kind of cannon fodder—one fifth of the fallen soldiers in the Yugoslav People's Army were Hungarians![80] Meanwhile, Yugoslavia requested that the units of its army stranded in Slovenia and their armaments be transported to Serbia by rail via Hungary. Following my proposal, the government rejected the request.

At the parliamentary debate on foreign policy held on October 15, 1991, I summarized our policy in the southern Slav crisis:

> We follow the developments beyond our southern borders with anxiety and alarm, and we do everything in our power to bring that gave crisis to an early and peaceful end, in accordance and cooperation with the other democratic countries. A lasting and just settlement of the conflict requires that the interests of all the concerned sides, of all the nations and national minorities living there, be taken into consideration. Hungary is pursuing a calm and circumspect policy in its approach to Yugoslavia and will lose sight of the interests of the Hungarian minority living there. While we want to keep out of the conflict, we have done and will do our best to protect the security of Hungary and its inhabitants. The Government is conducting regular dialogues with both the leaders and representatives of the individual republics. We are interested in maintaining good-neighborly cooperation with them in the future as well. Meanwhile, Hungary is continuously coordinating its steps with the other European states and with all those countries which are ready to contribute to the settlement of the Yugoslav crisis. This also applies to the recognition of the sovereignty of the independent republics.

---

[80] *Új Magyarország* and *Népszabadság*, October 11, 1991. *Külügyminisztériumi tájékoztató, 1991*, vol. 2: 258.

Thanking the members, including those from the opposition, for their constructive contributions, I assured them that Hungarian foreign policy "will be based on both prudence and courage."[81]

The actions of the Serbian armed forces put an end to Yugoslavia. It is worth noting that the rhetoric of the Belgrade leadership did not challenge the right of the Croats to self-determination but demanded that the Serb community of about half a million living in blocks or scattered in different parts of Croatia, wedged between the Croatian-inhabited areas, be allowed to secede and remain part of Yugoslavia (i.e., a Greater Serbia). To this end, under the protection of the Yugoslav army, several so-called Serb *Krajina*s (autonomous districts) were established, in which the non-Serb population (including Hungarians from Eastern Slavonia and Southern Baranya) were subjected to systematic persecution, killings and expulsions, known as "ethnic cleansing." On October 18, 1991, Lord Carrington and Dutch foreign minister and EC president van den Broek proposed a solution to the problem by recognizing the republics that wanted to secede from Yugoslavia, on condition that the minorities living on their territory were granted far-reaching territorial and/or cultural autonomy, a "special status." That coincided with an idea of Zoran Đinđić,[82] a leader of the Serbian democratic opposition: "The only solution is separation. Where Serbs are in the majority, as in Krajina, they should be allowed to form their own republic. In Slavonia and Banija, on the other hand, broad autonomy should be introduced." In his view, the same should apply to Croats and Hungarians living in Serbia, the Siptars (Albanians) in Kosovo and certain ethnic groups in Bosnia and Herzegovina.[83]

This idea had been proposed months earlier by Italian foreign minister Gianni De Michelis. The problem of the minorities in Yugoslavia, he said, which was the main cause of the ethnic clashes in the country, could be solved in the same way as it had been in the Italian province of South Tyrol, where a foreign state (Austria) was entitled to monitor the protection of the rights of the German-speaking minority. Using a similar principle in Yugoslavia, Serbia could monitor respect for the rights of the Serb minority in Croatia, and as in the case of South Tyrol, Serbia could turn to the UN or the CSCE if the rights of the Serb minority were threatened. In a similar way, Hungary could monitor respect for the rights of the Hungarian minority

---

[81] Minutes of the Hungarian Parliament, October 15, 1991, http://www.parlament.hu/naplo34/136/1360004.html. The speech is also published in *Magyar Külpolitikai Évkönyv, 1991*, 332–47, the place of the quotation is 338–39.

[82] Zoran Đinđić (1952–2003): Serbian politician, an opponent of the policies of Milošević. Following the overthrow of the dictatorship, he was elected prime minister. Assassinated by a political enemy.

[83] Đinđić quoted in the *Wiener Zeitung*, August 2, 1991, reprinted in *Magyar Szó*, August 3, 1991.

in Vojvodina, and Albania could monitor respect for the rights of the Albanians in Kosovo.[84] In addition to the concept of special status, the Carrington-van den Broek plan also stipulated that the borders between republics could be changed by mutual agreement. Originally, of course, the plan applied to all minorities in Yugoslavia, including Kosovo Albanians and Hungarians in Vojvodina, but, sensing protests from Belgrade, the proposal eventually limited the proposed autonomy to the Serbs in Croatia and excluded the possibility of border changes. Hungary welcomed the proposal but pointed out that a real settlement must guarantee the rights of national minorities throughout the whole region.[85] VMDK president András Ágoston, in a letter to Carl Barkman, vice president of the Conference of Yugoslavia, expressed his official position that the proposal put forward by Lord Carrington was acceptable for the Hungarians of Vojvodina.[86]

Five republics, including Montenegro, which until then had unreservedly supported the Serbian position, accepted the offer, but Milošević rejected it.[87] His position in doing so is hard to explain. He could not foresee that subsequent developments would be less favorable to the Serbs, but the current situation was that the Serbs occupied a third of Croatia's territory. Yet the still quiet but sober voices that existed in Serbia at the time were calling for the plan to be adopted. Đinđić expressed his support in a public statement, which was a bold thing to do in the dominant atmosphere.[88] The failure of the Carrington Plan was all the more regrettable as it would have set a precedent for the recognition that the whole of the Balkans, and indeed the whole of Central and South-Eastern Europe could be described as an ethnic mosaic. If the "special status," i.e., autonomy for the national minorities, had become a fundamental principle of the EC and the European Union respectively, a condition for integration and membership, many later tensions and conflicts could have been avoided.

The original Carrington Plan was in line with the Vojvodina Hungarians' concept of autonomy. The leaders of the VMDK came to Budapest to meet with Antall and me on several occasions. They prepared a draft for autonomy, and we disseminated it through our missions abroad. Ágoston, their party leader, and the MP Dr. Ferenc Körmendi were received in several European capitals, and were able to present the worsening situation of the Hungarian community in Vojvodina and their

---

[84] *Magyar Szó*, August 3, 1991.
[85] Géza Jeszenszky to Foreign Minister Hans van den Broek, August 2, 1991. Among my papers.
[86] *Magyar Szó*, October 19, 1991.
[87] Nándor Major, *Elveszejtett ország: Politikai esszék Jugoszlávia széthullásáról* [A country slain: Political essays on the disintegration of Yugoslavia] (Újvidék: Fórum Könyvkiadó, 1993).
[88] *Magyar Szó*, October 18, 1991.

ideas for its long-term survival and for internal peace. While Hungary contributed to the settling of the crisis with a number of analyses and proposals, which eventually were adopted, we were also able to make lasting and reliable friends of our Croatian and Slovenian neighbors, to protect the Hungarians of Vojvodina from even more serious atrocities, and to present their autonomy concept to international forums.

However, the most urgent thing at that moment was to end the fighting and, for Hungary, to avert the terrible political pressure and physical threats to the Hungarians of Vojvodina. The two objectives had to be reconciled. The Serbian armed forces were overwhelmingly superior in numbers and equipment and could only be stopped, it seemed, by an external force, i.e., military intervention within a European, NATO or UN framework, but there was no readiness or political will to do so. Even then, there was a strong fear in Western Europe, which later manifested itself in the Bosnian war, that armed intervention against the Serbs would lead to a protracted conflict with many victims, as had been the case with the partisan war against the Germans in the Second World War, which had been very successful.

As the conflict in Yugoslavia was going from bad to worse, in mid October Hungary put forward new proposals for a solution in a non-paper sent to the governments that were apparently keen to solve the crisis. As expected, the document reached the Serbian government and provoked a strong protest. The Yugoslav deputy foreign minister Milan Vereš called on István Ószi, the Hungarian ambassador in Belgrade, and protested to him "that the Hungarian Foreign Ministry prepared a document on political and ethnic clashes in Yugoslavia. In Yugoslavia's view, the Hungarian document contains unfounded and unwarranted statements. These include the claim that the international community should try to influence the situation by military pressure in addition to diplomatic and economic pressure, and to provide modern weapons for Croatia and Slovenia!" Vereš argued that the document also denied the existence and territorial integrity of Yugoslavia, so Hungary was continuing to interfere in Yugoslav internal affairs. According to his protest, the Hungarian side—despite repeated promises—continued to illegally transfer arms to Yugoslavia even after the relevant Security Council resolution. Vereš demanded that Hungary immediately stop its anti-Yugoslav activities, which were damaging bilateral relations and the interests of the peoples of the two neighboring countries.[89] In our response, we pointed out that the contested proposals were in line with the efforts of the international community to restore peace, and we had explained Hungary's position on the Southern Slav crisis at the recent parliamentary

---

[89] *Magyar Szó*, October 18, 1991.

debate on foreign policy.⁹⁰ The Serbian press, under government control, once again brought up Hungarian revanchism.⁹¹

On October 27, a Yugoslav aircraft dropped a cluster bomb on a house on the outskirts of the border town of Barcs on the Dráva River. It may have been an answer to the non-paper. Fortunately, the action did not result in any loss of life, but it did increase fears among the local population that the war would spread to Hungary. To calm the mood, Antall visited Barcs, and I presented our international efforts to stop the fighting at a town hall meeting in Nagykanizsa. The Barcs bombing was not an isolated, random incident. Since the summer of 1991, Yugoslav military aircraft continued to violate Hungarian airspace—a minimum of eighteen times. This could have happened only with the knowledge of the Serbian government, or, at the very least, the military leadership. The aim was more than just to rattle Hungarian nerves. If Hungary responded to provocations by shooting down a plane, this could have been classified as an act of war, and the claim that the Serbs were waging a defensive war against the same aggressors who had attacked them in the Second World War, would have sounded justified. The Hungarian Ministry of Foreign Affairs sent a note of protest to the CSCE Conflict Prevention Centre, and, probably as a result, airspace violations stopped.

Primarily in order to ease the pressure on the Hungarian population in Vojvodina and to stop the disproportionate military conscription of Hungarians, I invited Serbian foreign minister Vladislav Jovanović⁹² to Budapest to discuss our mutual complaints and the crisis as a whole. A tough nationalist but experienced diplomat, Jovanović recounted the events of the past few months in a completely distorted way, accusing the Hungarian government, as usual, of interfering in Yugoslav internal affairs. In my reply I stressed that "it is not the Hungarian government that claims the right to speak out on issues concerning the Hungarian minority, but they themselves raise them, and we just identify with their complaints. [...] The Democratic Community of Hungarians of Vojvodina is playing politics very wisely in a difficult situation. But we are also sympathizing with the cause of the Serbs in Croatia."⁹³ Jovanović heard my words, understanding that in their increasingly isolated situation the Serbs needed Hungary as a window to the outside world,

---

⁹⁰ The spokesman of the foreign ministry, János Herman, is quoted by *Népszabadság*, October 19, 1991.
⁹¹ "In fact, Hungary, which had lost two world wars, once again declared its revanchist claims. I would, however, point out to Mr. Antall that the Serbian people are strong enough to repel any attack." Budimir Košutić, vice-president of the Serbian government, quoted in *Magyar Szó*, October 24, 1991.
⁹² Vladislav Jovanović (1933–): Serbian diplomat, Minister of Foreign Affairs of the Federal Republic of Yugoslavia (1991–95).
⁹³ *Népszabadság*, October 27, 1991.

especially since their lines of communications with the West had been severed by the war raging in Croatia.

At their meeting in early October, President Bush had asked Antall to put his proposals for resolving the crisis in writing. On October 28, the Hungarian prime minister sent a six-page letter to the American president saying that he was convinced that the underlying cause of the Yugoslav crisis was

> the survival of the communist ideology in the leadership of some republics and the Army, and consequently their conflict with the republics where democratically elected parliaments have rejected the communist traditions. [...] In case the international community is unable to facilitate the democratic solution of the recent crisis it would send a negative message for the nations of Central and Eastern Europe, which liberated themselves and restored democracy, or at least move towards it. At the same time such a failure would give encouragement to the supporters of the old, totalitarian regime, who still exist. It is also obvious that the situation in Yugoslavia has a decisive impact on the outcome of the ongoing transition in the Soviet nuclear superpower.[94] Therefore, Yugoslavia is likely to serve as a precedent, it will show whether international cooperation can or cannot solve such a crisis.

There were also geopolitical implications, Antall continued, observing that the south-eastern flank of NATO was wedged between the Muslim republics of the Soviet Union and the crisis-ridden Middle East. He reiterated that the whole crisis could have been avoided by accepting "the idea of a confederation of sovereign republics. [...] The rights of national minorities could have been guaranteed by ensuring territorial and personal autonomies. In fact, it was the lack of these autonomies which lead to the outbreak of armed conflicts." Now, the "military activities may spread into Macedonia, Bosnia-Herzegovina and also to Kosovo and the Vojvodina."[95]

Among Antall's specific proposals were the exclusion of forcible changes to the borders of the republic, the announcement that those who violate the accepted legal norms of warfare would be held accountable, the need to consider tightening

---

[94] Many, including Antall, believed that if any outside force had any influence on the Serbian leadership, it was the Soviet leadership. I have no information as to what Soviet president Gorbachev, with his diminished weight and influence, had in mind when he invited Milošević and Tuđman to negotiate with him about peace. But neither he, nor Yeltsin, who also met with them, brought peace between the parties.

[95] Prime Minister József Antall to President George Bush, October 28, 1991. My copy of the original English. For more details cf. Jeszenszky, "Hungary and the Break-Up of Yugoslavia," no. 3 (2011): 74–75.

the sanctions, the need to establish an integral link between CSCE crisis management, NATO, the EC and the Western European Union, and, finally, to prepare for the establishment of effective peacekeeping and, if necessary, peace enforcement units. If the Hague Peace Conference were to fail, the sovereignty of the republics wishing to withdraw must be recognized, but Hungary would only take such a step in coordination with the EC and other states. The letter drew the American president's attention to the fact that the unresolved situation of national and ethnic minorities and the deliberate changing of the ethnic composition of the population seriously threatened European stability. On the other hand, guaranteeing the rights of minorities in Yugoslavia would serve as an example for other countries with mixed populations, such as the Soviet republics.[96]

Reading this thoughtful letter thirty-four years later, one is struck by the wisdom of most of the proposals, as they later became cornerstones of any settlement. It is also a testimony to Antall's remarkable foresight about future dangers, including the consequences of not meeting the legitimate demands of the national minorities.

The successful endgame

The conduct of the Serb authorities and their armed forces could no longer be tolerated by the international community. The October 25 meeting of the Yugoslavia Peace Conference and the subsequent meeting of the EC foreign ministers on October 28 could not but condemn Belgrade. Serbia was threatened with sanctions and with the recognition of those Yugoslav republics that requested it and observed human rights, including the rights of the ethnic and national minority groups.[97] Milošević was not yet ready to accept the olive branch, and on November 4 he rejected the ultimatum: "It is not acceptable that national minorities, such as Albanians and Hungarians, should have the same rights in the future community as the Serb people in Croatia, which is not a national minority."[98]

On November 11, the EC put in place sanctions against Yugoslavia (Serbia and Montenegro), an oil embargo and the suspension of all trade agreements with Belgrade. By then, a new actor had also entered the scene: former US secretary of state Cyrus Vance as UN representative. He was tasked with negotiating a permanent ceasefire and deploying peacekeepers, while the EC remained in charge of the political settlement. Vance arrived in Budapest on November 6. After visiting the prime minister, he met with me for about two hours. The problem of minorities

---

[96] Jeszenszky, "Hungary and the Break-Up of Yugoslavia," no. 3 (2011): 74–75.
[97] Declaration on the Situation in Yugoslavia, October 28, 1991. My copy of the original is among my papers.
[98] *Magyar Szó*, November 5, 1991.

was quite new to him, but he seemed to understand it and to accept that attention should be paid to guaranteeing their rights in international fora. His promise that, if necessary, international observers could also come to the Hungarian side of our southern border and that the Hungarian minority in Yugoslavia would not be forgotten was also important.[99] In order to strengthen this finally encouraging trend, I wrote to the dynamic EC president-in-office, Mr. Van den Broek. I drew his attention to the fact that if the settlement plan with Serbia was not accepted and the conflict extended to Bosnia, the Islamic dimension might play a role, but it would also be unfortunate if the crisis were to take on the character of a German-Slavic confrontation, because the "red-brown" forces that are gaining strength in Russia might support Serbian policy in the name of Slavic and Orthodox solidarity.[100]

While most governments were still hesitating, two prominent U.S. senators, Al Gore and Clairborne Pell (both Democrats, the latter's father was U.S. minister to Hungary in 1941), submitted a resolution to Congress for the recognition of Croatia and Slovenia. Their argument was that Serbia had committed aggression in order to change the post-war borders. They also called on Croatia to commit to guaranteeing the rights of its Serb minority and to accept international monitoring to verify this.[101]

The Hungarian political leadership was concerned not only with the security of its own country (then under serious threat from the ongoing war along its southern border) and the future of the Hungarian communities in Yugoslavia but also with the danger that the conflict would spread to Bosnia-Herzegovina. Before that happened, in a letter sent to several highly placed people involved in trying to find a settlement, I wrote the following: "The UN should immediately try to send peace-keeping forces not only to the territory of Croatia but also to those areas of Yugoslavia where there is still a fragile peace: to Bosnia and to the two formerly autonomous provinces, Vojvodina and Kosovo. Without that a wholesale massacre may occur, as reports confirm."[102]

Milošević's tactics of occupying all the territories inhabited by Serbs, expelling non-Serbs from them and replacing them with Serbs, thus creating a *fait accompli*, had not changed. On November 18, the Serbian army occupied Vukovar, which had already been reduced to rubble, and murdered most of its inhabitants,

---

[99] *Magyar Szó*, November 9, 1991.
[100] Minister for Foreign Affairs G. Jeszenszky to H. van den Broek, Foreign Minister of the Netherlands and Chairman of the EC, November 15, 1991. My copy of the original is among my papers.
[101] Memorandum by Gyula Kodolányi, chief foreign policy advisor to Prime Minister József Antall, November 14, 1991.
[102] G. Jeszenszky to Lord Carrington, H. van den Broek and C. Vance, December 8, 1991. My copy of the original is among my papers.

including those in hospital. On November 24, the ancient Hungarian Calvinist village of Szentlászló also fell, but the population was evacuated by Croatian soldiers. The Serbian nationalists thought that with those accomplishments, a ceasefire was now acceptable. It was also easier, for reasons of prestige, to accept the intervention of the UN through Vance than the "diktat" of the EC, which was perceived as German-influenced and biased. On November 23, another ceasefire agreement was brokered by Vance in Geneva, thus fulfilling the precondition for the deployment of UN peacekeepers, which was accepted by the Security Council on November 27. Although the fourteenth cease-fire agreement did not prove to be lasting, the one of January 2, 1992, did bring an end to the war in Croatia. This was due, however, to both the fulfilment of Serbian territorial claims (which turned out to be provisional) and a decision of the EC foreign ministers made on December 16.

On December 3, the Hungarian Ministry of Foreign Affairs published a statement that in recent weeks the political pressure on the Hungarians in the Yugoslav province of Vojvodina had increased beyond all previous levels, the anti-Hungarian campaign in Serbia had intensified, mobilizations continued, and the number of Hungarian conscripts was particularly high. As a result of these incitements and the continuing restrictions on minority rights, the Hungarian and other national minorities were now living in an atmosphere of intimidation, with more and more of them fleeing from their homeland. The leader of the ruling Socialist Party of Serbia in Vojvodina labelled the Democratic Community of Hungarians of Vojvodina, a legitimate Hungarian organization with parliamentary representation, as fascist. In Parliament Serbian MPs called for the VMDK to be banned and for a change in the system of representation in Vojvodina, which would mean a further serious curtailment of the political rights of national minorities. My ministry called this "a major obstacle to the implementation of the intentions of the Hungarian side to improve Hungarian-Serbian relations, which the Hungarian side informed its partner about during the recent visit of the Serbian Foreign Minister to Hungary."[103]

Germany had already been persuading its European partners for weeks to recognize Croatia and Slovenia, and indicated that it was ready to do so, either alone or along with a few other states, expecting Hungary to be among them.[104] On November 29, 1991, the Badinter Commission of the Hague Conference concluded that "Yugoslavia is in a state of disintegration," that the internal borders

---

[103] Statement of the Ministry of Foreign Affairs of the Republic of Hungary on the condition of the national minorities in the Vojvodina of Yugoslavia, December 3, 1991. *Magyar Külpolitikai Évkönyv, 1991*, 384–85.

[104] Alexander Arnot, Germany's ambassador to Hungary, called on me already on November 11, 1991. Sáringer, *Iratok az Antall-kormány*, vol. 2: 776–77 (Doc. 169).

of the republic could only be changed by common consent, and that Croatia's independence could not be recognized until its constitution guaranteed minority rights. On December 4, the Croatian *Sabor* complied with this demand: "The Republic of Croatia shall protect the equal rights of ethnic and national communities (minorities) and stimulate their multifaceted development."[105] As proof of this, on December 15 Croatia signed a convention with Hungary on the mutual guarantee of the rights of national minorities living on each other's territory, taking over the similar convention concluded on May 31, 1991, between Ukraine and Hungary.[106] The time had come for Hungary to act on the recognition of Croatia and Slovenia as independent and sovereign states, and the Foreign Ministry was preparing for that.[107]

The attitude of the United States and the EC towards recognition was thus far much influenced by the state of the Soviet Union. After the restoration of Baltic independence, there was explicit fear of the continuation of independence declarations by other Soviet republics, the creation of new states with nuclear weapons and intercontinental missiles, and the unforeseeable consequences of the break-up of a multinational empire. However, in early December the issue was settled: led by Ukraine, the Soviet member states declared their independence one after the other, and on December 13 the "Commonwealth of Independent States" was established in Minsk. Against this background, the Council of the European Community met on December 16. Antall and I were invited to the informal lunch before the meeting. We knew that it would now be decided whether common recognition of the independence of Croatia and Slovenia would be achieved and whether it would really bring an end to the war in Croatia. We hoped that the terms of recognition would also set an important precedent for the rights of national minorities.

There was no formal seating at the luncheon, and I took advantage of this by taking a seat next to the British foreign secretary, Douglas Hurd. Antall and I ate little so that we could talk more. The subject was almost exclusively Yugoslavia. As we were leaving the lunch, the prime minister told me in the laconic style with which I was familiar: "I think we could contribute to today's decisions."[108] After a long debate, overcoming the objections posed by Vance and Carrington, a unanimous decision was reached: the EC states would be prepared, on the basis of the Badinter Commission's document "Guidelines for the Recognition of New States in the

---

[105] Ferenc Mák, "Horvátország 1991—1999," https://adatbank.ro/inchtm.php?kod=58.
[106] Mák, "Horvátország 1991—1999."
[107] Sáringer, *Iratok az Antall-kormány*, vol. 2: 776–92 (Docs. 170–74).
[108] My personal recollections.

Soviet Union and Eastern Europe," to recognize those republics which so requested and which undertook, on the basis of the UN Charter and the documents of the CSCE, to respect the rule of law, human rights and democratic values, as well as respect for the inviolability of borders and to abide by the rights of national and ethnic minority groups living on their territory, in accordance with the commitments made under the CSCE.[109] On the same day, a document titled "Common Position on the recognition of the Yugoslav Republics" was issued, which set further conditions relating to human and minority rights.[110] The Croatian parliament amended the constitution again almost on the same day, promising broad rights to Serbs and minorities in general.

Although the decision in principle was taken on December 16, and on December 23, Germany, as it had promised, recognized the independence of the two breakaway republics, it still remained to be seen whether the other members of the European Community would find the Badinter criteria satisfactory and whether other major powers would join in. On January 15, 1992, the Community's foreign ministers met again. The decision taken by them was to recognize both republics as independent and sovereign states. Hungary acceded to the recognition on the same day, and the next day announced in a declaration that it would establish diplomatic relations at ambassadorial level with the Republics of Croatia and Slovenia.[111] With that, Hungary gained two new and good neighbors. In a statement to *Népszabadság*, Antall stressed that we were striving to have good relations with the Republic of Serbia as well. "The various South Slav nations and the Hungarians lived side by side for centuries, sometimes as friends, sometimes as adversaries, but it is the duty of our generation to maintain good relations and to create historical reconciliation with all our neighbors. The Hungarian government is ready to do so."[112] The next day, the *New York Times* carried an op-ed written by me: "The Right Choice on Yugoslavia." While welcoming the recognition, I regretted that it had not come earlier, as it could have shortened or even prevented the bloodshed. I urged peacekeepers to be deployed as a preventive measure in the potential conflict zones (thinking particularly about Bosnia-Herzegovina) and stressed that "the world should

---

[109] Sáringer, *Iratok az Antall-kormány*, vol. 2: 786–89 (Doc. 173). Before the decision, on December 11, several member states were still reluctant to endorse recognition, see Sáringer, *Iratok az Antall-kormány*, vol. 2: 783–85 (Doc. 172).
[110] József Juhász, *Volt egyszer egy Jugoszlávia—a délszláv állam története* [Once there was a Yugoslavia. The history of the Southern Slav state] (Budapest: Aula Kiadó, 1999), 245.
[111] *Magyar Külpolitikai Évkönyv, 1992*, 128–29.
[112] *Népszabadság*, January 16, 1992. *Külügyminisztériumi tájékoztató, 1992* [Bulletin of the Ministry of Foreign Affairs, 1992] (Budapest: Magyar Köztársaság Külügyminisztériuma, 1992), vol. 1: 45.

insist on local autonomy for minorities like the Albanians of Kosovo, Hungarians in Vojvodina, Serbs in Croatia and Bosnia, and non-Serbs in Serbia."[113]

In Hungary we knew that the conflict on the territory of Croatia was far from over and that the fate of the Hungarians in the Vojvodina was still uncertain. Prime Minister Antall turned again to President Bush, this time specifically on the issue of the Hungarian minority, befitting someone who carried a brief for all the Hungarians of the world:

> I ask you and your government to use all your influence in order to ensure the personal security and civil and minority rights of the long-suffering Hungarians of the Vojvodina. They wish to remain out of the war, and in order to see that in the international attempts to bring about a settlement of the conflict, those rights should be accorded firm international guarantees. [...] preventing them from falling victim to the possible actions of extremist forces. My government would highly appreciate it if a way could be found for officials of your country to meet the leaders of the Democratic Community of Hungarians in the Vojvodina. [...] I would like to point out that ever since the outbreak of the crisis in Yugoslavia, the government of the Republic of Hungary has striven consistently to promote a democratic resolution of the conflict along our southern border, on the basis of the European-Atlantic system of values and with consideration for the interests of all nations and ethnic minorities in Yugoslavia. I trust that our partners, including Serbia, will appreciate the balanced and moderate policy pursued so far by the Hungarian government towards the Yugoslav republics; this policy is aimed at maintaining constructive relations and cooperation with all South Slav republics, on a basis of common interests with them in the long term.[114]

From a Hungarian point of view, I consider it an extremely important achievement that we managed to avoid the kind of drastic action and "ethnic cleansing" against the Hungarians in Vojvodina that we saw in Bosnia between 1992 and 1995 and in Kosovo in 1999. However, quite a few Hungarians believe that it was a failure that we did not manage to regain from the disintegrating South Slav state at least the northern part of Vojvodina, where in the early 1990s Hungarians still formed

---

[113] Geza Jeszenszky: "The Right Choice on Yugoslavia," *New York Times*, January 16, 1992. "This is the first time that a minister of the Republic of Hungary was published by a prestigious newspaper," *Népszabadság* noted on January 17, 1992.

[114] Prime Minister J. Antall to President G. Bush, January 8, 1992. Copy of the non-official translation is in my possession.

a relative majority. But there was no political or military possibility of doing so. The world, the United States and the European Community were adamantly opposed to any border change for fear that it would trigger an avalanche. Those who used armed force lost all support and goodwill, as we saw in the case of the Serbs. If Hungary had tried to change its borders by force, it would have found itself facing the armies of several countries. It should also be remembered that in 1991 the Yugoslav army was one of the strongest in Europe. Nor would the Hungarian army have been able to protect the Hungarian minority in Vojvodina from "ethnic cleansing," expulsion or massacre. This is why we had been calling for the presence of UN or European Community observers from the very beginning of the crisis. They would have acted as a deterrent, because it is difficult to attack a community when international observers are among them. I am really glad that the serious crisis in the Balkans, the wars, did not require any military action from Hungary.

A debate is still on going as to whether recognition of the breakaway states was "premature." The clear will of the Slovenian and Croatian populations is indisputable, the extent to which the Belgrade leadership and its army deepened the Serb-Croat conflict is undeniable, and the fact that after recognition the guns fell silent in Croatia is also without question. What happened later in Bosnia and years later in Kosovo was not caused by the EC's recognition, but by the further actions of Milošević, Karadžić and other war criminals.[115] Hungary was early to see the inevitability of this step, while our policy during the crisis ensured that Belgrade could not make Hungary a scapegoat for its blunders, and thus create a pretext for anti-Hungarian manifestations and atrocities in Vojvodina. Even though Serbia accused Hungary, along with Germany and Austria, of supporting the disintegration process and even evoked the threat of an armed conflict by regularly and deliberately violating Hungarian airspace during the Croatian war, Antall's South Slav policy effectively protected Hungary from war by means of a calm response. By keeping open an important transit route for Serbia, he successfully averted the deterioration of Hungarian-Serbian relations and ensured that the Hungarians of Vojvodina did not become hostages, victims of the terrible policy euphemistically called "ethnic cleansing." From the outset, Hungary developed excellent political and economic relations with Croatia and Slovenia, and in 1992 it concluded inter-state treaties with both, as well as a treaty with Slovenia on the protection of minorities.

In the southern Slav crisis, Hungarian diplomacy excelled. The prime minister, whose health seemed to have recovered in 1991, played a decisive role in this. His

---

[115] This was supported by sound legal and logical arguments in Richard Caplan, *Europe and the Recognition of New States in Yugoslavia* (Cambridge: Cambridge University Press, 2005).

work was greatly assisted by his chief foreign policy adviser, Gyula Kodolányi. In the Ministry of Foreign Affairs, many of my colleagues worked late into the night in connection with the crisis. Among them I must mention Iván Bába, then deputy state secretary, Ferenc Szőcs, head of the department, his subordinates István Balogh, István Szabó and Imre Varga, as well as Gábor Bagi, consul general in Zagreb, and last but not least Enikő Bollobás, our Washington chargé d'affaires.

The Yugoslav experiment failed. As the last Yugoslav prime minister, Ante Marković, a Bosnian Croat, later said, "At that time, wherever I went, in any city, I was welcomed with warmth and enthusiasm. At every meeting, a great number of people turned up, and all of them assured me of their support. They said that life in Yugoslavia had never been better. Their wages had risen, they travelled, they shopped, they felt free. […] But when they went to the ballot box, everyone voted for his own pack."[116]

And let's add: they shot and killed those of the other pack. One can only hope that the European mentality will sooner or later put an end to the pack mentality in the eastern half of Europe.

---

[116] Interview with Ante Marković in the Zagreb paper *Globus*, translated by *Magyar Szó*, December 9, 2003.

Chapter 7

Successes and Disappointments in 1992

The international acquiescence in the break-up of Yugoslavia did not bring peace to the former communist bloc. Central Europe, as envisaged by the Austrian Erhard Busek,[1] was not born yet. The brutal fighting accompanied by war crimes spread to Bosnia. That was another demonstration that the key to peace and security was and remains the coexistence of communities of different religions, cultures and languages. The starting point for the movements that led to regime change in Europe was the Helsinki Final Act, which virtually codified respect for human and political rights. When democracy and political rights were extended to the eastern half of Europe, Hungarians expected the condition of national minorities to be substantially improved, so that they could exercise their linguistic and cultural rights as self-governing communities, on an equal footing with the majority population in that state. Unfortunately, following the promising recommendations of the CSCE in Copenhagen, the attitude of international institutions with respect to the protection and promotion of such rights slackened and softened increasingly. Hungary's Romanian and Slovak neighbors in particular became more and more unaccommodating in their attitude. In 1992, however, I still hoped that our Western partners would find our arguments convincing enough, and that, with their intercession, the rights of national minorities would be guaranteed through binding conventions. Therefore, Hungary continued to make this issue a priority in its bilateral relations and in multilateral fora. Our approach was well summarized by the Office for Hungarians Beyond the Borders:

> The minority problem is a structural issue which has far-reaching impact on both the internal development of the countries of this region and on inter-state relations. [...] The Hungarian government is convinced that the minority question is not an issue of borders, and cannot be treated as such;

---

[1] Erhard Busek (1941–2022): Austrian politician of the People's Party (ÖVP), vice-chancellor (1991–95). Special coordinator of the Stability Pact for South Eastern Europe (2002–2008). His collection of essays: *Az elképzelt Közép-Európa* [The Central Europe of our imagination] (Budapest: Európai Utas–Századvég Kiadó, 1992).

it is an issue of principle. The creation of ethnically pure states is not possible anywhere in the region by means of border changes, and the attempt to "ethnically cleanse" territories led in the past two years to the most serious crimes against humanity and people committed in Europe since the Second World War. [...] In the last two and a half years, the Hungarian minorities have established their own democratically elected representative and political organizations, and they are continuously formulating their ideas and programs. [...] Depending on the individual situation, various plans for territorial, functional and cultural autonomy have been developed. [...] The realization of the results of the negotiations between the representatives of minorities and their governments would contribute greatly to reducing tensions in this region, to the development of relations based on European values both within and between countries, and thus to the stability and integration of Europe as a whole.[2]

The status of the numerically small national minorities of Hungary was to be regulated by the law under preparation on the basis of collective rights. In addition, we tried to anticipate the hoped-for comprehensive international regulation by bilateral treaties or special agreements. Unfortunately, the fair and far-sighted Hungarian program was not embraced by Western Europe, so the majority of our neighbors had no difficulty in rejecting the aspirations of Hungary and of their own Hungarian minorities.

I attended the Extraordinary Summit of Heads of State and Government of the United Nations Security Council (of which Hungary was a non-permanent member in 1992–93) on January 31, 1992, substituting for the seriously ill Prime Minister Antall. In my speech, I demonstrated the importance of preventive diplomacy and peacekeeping by recalling the events of the Balkan war. Those events demonstrated that "respect for minority rights is not only a legal and humanitarian issue, but also an integral part of international collective security. It is therefore essential that the Security Council takes decisive action to protect these rights." I welcomed the fact that the Security Council had placed under international control the heavy weapons of a UN member state (that is, Yugoslavia) that had committed aggression. Given the significant number of national minorities in all the successor

---

[2] "The issue of Hungarians living beyond the borders in Hungarian government policy," Memorandum of the HTMH, July 30, 1992. Among my papers.

states of Yugoslavia, I said, only territorial and cultural autonomy could secure their future, as Lord Carrington himself suggested.[3]

As I later confirmed in one of my interviews, Hungary of course "fully support[s] the legitimate aspirations of the Serbs in Croatia to preserve their identity. But we find it strange, to say the least, that Serbia does not recognize similar aspirations on its own territory. The selective application of self-determination and the double standard is politically unacceptable: it is not possible to demand the rights of the Serb community in Croatia while denying the rights of the Hungarian, Albanian and other communities in Serbia."[4] Our understanding was in line with the position of the United States and the EC at the time, which, when recognizing the Southern Slavic successor states, called on Serbia to strictly respect the rights of national minorities living on its territory. "A long-term, lasting solution to the conflicts in this region cannot be imagined without full respect for the rights of national minorities and their consistent international monitoring," the Hungarian foreign ministry said in a statement issued upon the recognition of the Southern Slav republics.[5] The two former Yugoslav republics, which, having given guarantees for the rights of their national minorities, were recognized as independent states in January 1992, presented an encouraging picture with respect to such rights.

Croatia and Slovenia

As shown in the previous chapter, Hungary's contribution to the international recognition of those republics was significant. On January 16, 1992, we established diplomatic relations with our two new neighbors. A number of high-level meetings were held with each of them in that year. I paid official visits to Slovenia on May 21 and to Croatia the following day, not to take fresh credit but to lay the foundations for a good, neighborly relationship that would be lasting and exemplary. In Ljubljana, I introduced István Balogh, our first ambassador to Slovenia. The Hungarian newspapers reported in detail on my talks and the results of the meetings.[6] Croatian prime minister Franjo Gregurić (1939–) visited Budapest on August 7, his successor Hrvoje Šarinić (1935–2017) on December 16, and Slovenian speaker France Bučar (1923–2015) on May 7–8. Fulfilling a long-standing local

---

[3] Géza Jeszenszky's intervention at the UN Security Council Summit, *Magyar Külpolitikai Évkönyv, 1992*, 136–42.
[4] Interview by Géza Jeszenszky, *Népszabadság*, January 14, 1992. *Külügyminisztériumi tájékoztató, 1992*, vol. 1: 20.
[5] *Új Magyarország*, March 18, 1992. *Külügyminisztériumi tájékoztató, 1992*, vol. 1: 173.
[6] *Külügyminisztériumi tájékoztató, 1992*, vol. 1: 346–49.

wish,[7] two border crossings with Slovenia, closed since the war, were reopened on August 21, 1992, in the presence of Slovenian president Milan Kučan[8] and Foreign Minister Dimitrij Rupel.

I signed a bilateral convention on "special rights for national minorities" with my colleague Rupel on November 6 in Ljubljana, the Slovenian capital. Our treaty on the protection of the rights of minorities, which is the most far-reaching in the world to date, states that the *de facto* equality of the two minorities and the preservation of their own identity can be achieved through individual and communal special rights. The convention guarantees minorities the possibility of preserving and developing their culture, language, religion and identity. To this end, the two countries will give special attention to the education of the minorities in their mother tongue, from kindergarten to higher education, including instruction in the culture, history and present conditions of the mother nation. To this end, they shall encourage the use of each other's school textbooks. The contracting parties shall ensure the free use and registration of the surnames and given names of members of minorities in private and public life. In the areas inhabited by indigenous nationalities, they shall ensure the equal use of geographical names and public inscriptions of both languages in written and oral communication. The parties shall pay attention to the special interests of the minorities in their regional and economic development plans, promote all forms of cross-border cooperation, and undertake not to establish administrative and territorial organizations of local self-government to the detriment of minorities. To monitor the implementation of the Convention, the parties shall establish an intergovernmental commission on minorities, whose members shall be appointed by the governments on the basis of proposals from the minority organizations.[9]

If we had such an agreement with all our neighbors, and if our partners complied with it in good faith, the continued existence and well-being of the national minority communities, as well as exemplary bilateral relations, would have been ensured with all our neighbors. Slovenian prime minister Drnovšek[10] signed the

---

[7] Before 1992 there was only one border crossing between Slovenia and Hungary, and the inhabitants of the villages were separated by the border. A Cooperation Agreement on restoring trans-border relations was concluded on February 28, 1992, between the Hungarian National Self-Governing Community of the Mura Region and the General Assemblies of Vas and Zala Counties.

[8] Milan Kučan (1941–): Slovenian politician, president of Slovenia (1992–2001).

[9] The text of the Convention is published in *Magyar Külpolitikai Évkönyv, 1992*, 295–301. Cf. Miran Komac and Balázs Vizi, eds., *Bilaterális kisebbségvédelem: A magyar-szlovén kisebbségvédelmi egyezmény háttere és gyakorlata* [The bilateral protection of minorities: The background and practice of the Hungarian-Slovenian Convention on the Protection of Minorities] (Budapest: L' Harmattan Kiadó, 2019).

[10] Janez Drnovšek (1950–2008): Slovene liberal politician, prime minister (1992–2000), president of Slovenia (2002–2007).

inter-state treaty in Budapest on December 1, 1992; it provides a broad framework for our friendly cooperation.

A similarly close relationship was established with Croatia, with a treaty on "friendly relations and cooperation" signed on December 16, 1992, by Hungarian prime minister József Antall and Croatian prime minister Hrvoje Šarinić. It contains a special chapter on the enforcement of minority rights. According to the second paragraph of Article 17 of the treaty,

> the Hungarian nationality living in the Republic of Croatia and the Croatian nationality living in the Republic of Hungary have the right to freely express, preserve and develop their ethnic, cultural, linguistic and religious identity, individually or with other members of their community, without being forced to assimilate against their will. They have the right to use their mother tongue freely in private and in public, to disseminate and exchange information in their mother tongue and to have access to it. They have the right to exercise their human rights and fundamental freedoms fully and effectively without discrimination and in full equality before the law.[11]

Successive Croatian foreign ministers expressed their sincere gratitude for the political support their country received from Hungary. Zdenko Škrabalo, who was a native Hungarian speaker,[12] played an outstanding role. In his later capacity as ambassador to Budapest, he contributed in practical ways to achieving the best possible inter-state relations, sensitive to the problems of Hungarians in Croatia.[13]

I am personally most pleased that Hungary's diplomatic support for their struggle for independence brought reconciliation and friendship with the Croats, overcoming decades of anti-Hungarian sentiment. The political disputes of the eighty years before the First World War faded away, becoming eclipsed by the memory of the personal union that had lasted for eight hundred years until 1918. The kings of Hungary were also kings of Croatia, just as the British monarchs were kings of England and Scotland. In the common struggle against the Ottoman armies the role of the Zrínyi and other aristocratic families resulted in an intertwined history. When Hungarians spend their holidays in Dalmatia, on the Croatian coast,

---

[11] Treaty between the Republic of Hungary and the Republic of Croatia on friendly relations and cooperation. December 16, 1992. http://www.nemzetpolitika.gov.hu/data/files/005.pdf.
[12] Zdenko Škrabalo, (1929–2014): Croatian physician and diplomat, born in Sombor/Zombor, which used to have a large Hungarian population up to the massacres committed by Yugoslav partisans in 1944. Foreign minister (1992–93), ambassador to Hungary (1996–2000).
[13] Letter from Zdenek Skrabalo to Géza Jeszenszky, March 30, 1993. Among my papers.

or walk around Zagreb, they often bump into traces of a common past. It would be desirable for the Slovaks to feel and think in the same way as the Croats, and for the Hungarians to appreciate the contribution of the Slovak people to the achievements of Uhorsko, Hungaria, the historic kingdom.

For many years after international recognition, Croatia faced a very difficult and persistent problem: the Serbian occupation of a good third of the eastern part of the country. This affected the Hungarian minority: both those who remained in the Baranja region after the invasion of the Yugoslav army in 1991, and those who fled to Hungary. Hungary had detailed information on the murders and other atrocities committed in the occupied territories, the systematic intimidation and expulsion of the non-Serb population. Their ancestors had survived the Turkish devastation, yet "now, not a single Hungarian word can be heard among the shattered houses and destroyed churches. [...] The abandoned houses are systematically looted and plundered by armed gangs—in fact, by the representatives of the new regime," I was informed in a report.[14] I received many other credible reports about the reigns of terror, including the elimination of Hungarian language education from the so-called Serbian Republic of Krajina that was proclaimed in the occupied territory.

Finally, on February 21, 1992, on the basis of UN Security Council Resolution 743, 14,000 peacekeepers were deployed to Croatia, in the sectors of Baranja and Eastern Croatia (Slavonia in the history of Hungary), which were declared a UN-protected zone.[15] Unfortunately however, for a long time the peacekeepers, UNPROFOR, stood idly by as atrocities were committed by the Serb irregulars.[16] The situation was improving only very slowly, as I personally experienced in early December 1993, when, with armed protection by UNPROFOR, I visited the ruined, ghost town-like Vukovar in the company of Sándor Jakab, vice president of the Democratic Community of Hungarians in Croatia. We then visited the Hungarian villages of southern Baranya and talked to the Hungarians who had survived the ordeal and remained there. Years later, after the restoration of Croatian sovereignty, some of the displaced Hungarians returned to their homes, but the Hungarian community in Croatia never regained its former strength and strong Hungarian identity.

---

[14] Árpád Pasza and Ferenc Faragó, "The Tragedy of the Hungarians in Croatia." Typescript presented to me in 1992. Among my papers.
[15] József Juhász, László Márkusz, Péter Tálas, and László Valki, *Kinek a békéje? Háború és béke a volt Jugoszláviában* [Whose peace? War and peace in the former Yugoslavia] (Budapest: Zrínyi Kiadó, 2003), 81.
[16] The impotence of the international protection forces was illustrated by President Tudjman's letter to the president of the UN General Assembly on December 9, 1992. Among my papers.

The independence of Hungary's two southern neighbors and the warm relationship with them meant that the Antall government managed to establish excellent relations with four of our seven neighbors. I endeavored to come as close as possible to achieving this with the other three. We were furthest from this goal in the case of the new ("Little") Yugoslavia, which from April was limited to Serbia and Montenegro. Relations with Bosnia-Herzegovina and Macedonia, which had also voted for independence in a referendum, and do not neighbor Hungary, were smooth from the start, and the Bosniaks (Bosnian Muslims) appreciated the diplomatic support we gave them.

Serbia

From February 1991, the Serbian government in Belgrade regarded Hungary as an enemy, calling the Antall government fascist and making absurd accusations. However, for a long time diplomatic relations were maintained for mutual benefit, even at ambassadorial level. In addition to economic relations, which were not negligible, this was necessitated by the existence of the Hungarian community living in Vojvodina and the need to protect them. Hungary rightly feared that the Hungarians of Vojvodina could also fall victim to "ethnic cleansing," as was carried out in Bosnia.

The province of Vojvodina had limited autonomy in the Socialist Republic of Serbia before 1988. The number of ethnic Hungarians in 1960 was 442,000. They had survived the Serbian colonization after 1919, the expulsion and mass murder of Germans and Hungarians in the autumn of 1944, and finally the wars of the 1990s, by which time their number had been reduced to 339,000 according to a 1991 census. By 2002, the number was 290,000, then 251,000 in 2011. Their share of the total population of the province fell from 43 percent in 1910 to 13 percent by 2002.[17] In the war that began in 1991, Hungarians were conscripted and then deliberately put in the line of fire as cannon fodder.[18] Many thousands of young Hungarians fled to Hungary to escape this fate. Those who stayed waited with suitcases packed to see if they would have to leave or be forcibly resettled in Hungary.

---

[17] Károly Kocsis, Zsolt Bottlik, and Patrik Tátrai, *Etnikai térfolyamatok a Kárpát-medence határainkon túli régióiban, 1989–2002* [Ethnic processes in the regions of the Carpathian Basin beyond the borders of Hungary] (Budapest: Magyar Tudományos Akadémia Földrajztudományi Kutatóintézet, 2006); Károly Kocsis and Patrik Tátrai, eds., *A Kárpát-Pannon-térség változó etnikai arculata a 15. század végétől a 21. század elejéig* [The changing ethnic patterns of the carpatho-pannonian area from the late 15th until the early 21st century] (Budapest: MTSA CSFK Földrajztudományi Intézet, 2012), 20, 27.

[18] That was the general opinion of the local Hungarians. Naturally there are no figures to prove that.

The Democratic Community of Hungarians of Vojvodina (VMDK), a party defending the interests of Hungarians, was founded on March 31, 1990, and, defying threats, voiced its serious grievances and, with the support of the Hungarian government, kept foreign countries informed of its situation and demands. After my meeting with US Secretary of State Baker in January 1992, *Magyar Szó* asked me if I had mentioned their critical situation. "Of course, I mention it in every forum. [...] I refer to the positions of the VMDK, to the international activities of András Ágoston. We suggest that the world should listen to what the people concerned, the stakeholders, I would say the sufferers, have to say [...] I would like to stress, among other things, how disciplined and responsible the Hungarians in Yugoslavia are."[19] Since April 1992, when the Serbian army launched a real war against the Bosnian Muslims and Croats who had declared independence in a referendum, the Serb forces had been expelling all non-Serbs from the occupied territories in an organized manner. It was feared that ethnic-based displacement and killings would spread to Vojvodina. From the very beginning of the crisis, I warned the world in every possible forum that an international presence was needed, not only where we had managed to achieve a ceasefire, as in Croatia, but also where there was still a chance of maintaining a fragile peace. I included Bosnia, Kosovo and Vojvodina. I am still convinced today that if the CSCE, the EC and the UN had acted in a timely and decisive manner and sent significant numbers of armed observers and peacekeepers to these areas, it would have been possible to prevent the three years of bloodshed in Bosnia, what happened in Kosovo, and more Hungarians would have remained in Vojvodina, with more rights.

Despite (or perhaps because of) its precarious situation, and indeed in an atmosphere of threat, on April 25, 1992, the party of the Hungarians of Vojvodina, the VMDK, presented its three-level concept of autonomy at its general assembly in Kanizsa: territorial autonomy, local self-government, personal autonomy. (The latter is based on the principle of the individual, i.e., as for religious denominations, regardless of place of residence, the person belongs to the organization of a community.) The document rightly stated that "this could serve as a model for the solution of the minority question not only in the former Yugoslavia, but also throughout in Central and Eastern Europe. The implementation of this concept will enable minorities to decide for themselves (within an appropriate constitutional framework) on issues of importance to their identity."[20] In a statement, the Hungarian Foreign Ministry welcomed it as "a modern, constructive concept based

---

[19] Tibor Purger, interview with Géza Jeszenszky, *Magyar Szó*, January 26, 1992.
[20] *Esély a megmaradásra: A Vajdasági Magyarok Demokratikus Közösségének évkönyve* [A chance for survival: Yearbook of the Democratic Community of Hungarians of Vojvodina], 1992, 5.

on European norms and ideals [...] worthy of the attention and support of the international community [...] a proposal for a peaceful, negotiated solution to the Yugoslav crisis and a stable settlement."[21]

On April 27, 1992, the Federal Republic of Yugoslavia was formed out of Serbia and Montenegro, with the *de facto* leadership of Slobodan Milošević, the president of the Socialist Party of Serbia, which still had a majority in parliament. At the summit of the three Visegrád countries in Prague on May 6, Antall pointed out that three religions and cultures met in Yugoslavia and that if the conflict was not ended by international action, the consequences were unpredictable. That was why he wrote to the three prime ministers of the European Community "troika":

> The European Community must do everything to resolve the crisis as soon as possible. The new Yugoslav state must be compelled to accept UN and CSCE standards and to give guarantees that they will be respected. The latest Security Council resolution on this subject, drafted by the EC, unfortunately falls short of general expectations and does not send a clear signal to the Belgrade leadership that the world body will not tolerate continued violations of these standards. I fear that if the international community does not exert sufficient political pressure on the new Yugoslavia now, it will face an even more serious conflict later.[22]

I had shared the government's dilemmas with all political parties through the Foreign Affairs Committee of the National Assembly. When MPs asked the government to propose concrete solutions, I described the lukewarm reactions from abroad and pointed out that the government had and continued to have many ideas and proposals, but only united, coordinated and tough action could help, while the outside world remained hesitant and indecisive. At the same time, we were also strongly constrained by our responsibility for the fate of the Hungarians in Vojvodina.[23]

On May 30, 1992, UN Security Council Resolution 757 imposed an economic and trade embargo with immediate effect on the Union of Serbia and Montenegro. As a non-permanent member of the Security Council, Hungary was a co-author of the resolution. In this role, we explained in a government statement how the

---

[21] *Magyar Külpolitikai Évkönyv, 1992*, 189–90.
[22] Letter from József Antall to prime ministers Ruud Lubbers of the Netherlands, Cavaco Silva of Portugal and John Major of Great Britain, May 18, 1992. Among my papers.
[23] Minutes of the Foreign Affairs Committee of the National Assembly held on May 27, 1992. Transcript is among my papers. The crucial part in on 65–71.

behavior of "Little Yugoslavia," its continued aggression against internationally-recognized Bosnia and Herzegovina, and its actions in sharp contrast to European standards made this severe measure necessary. The embargo had caused serious losses to the Hungarian economy, amounting to some USD 1.3 billion by the end of 1993. In addition, there were numerous indications and information from sources to show that the oil embargo and other prohibitions were being circumvented or overlooked by several of Serbia's neighbors. While the results of the sanctions were not visible in the short term, they set the Belgrade leadership on a path that led to the abandonment of its aggressive plans.

We could expect more than economic sanctions only from NATO, and primarily from the United States, so at the North Atlantic Cooperation Council meeting in Oslo in June I again called for armed peacekeepers to be sent to Kosovo and Vojvodina.[24] I then wrote to Secretary of State Baker to warn him that if the West failed to protect the Muslims in Bosnia, it could lead to the growth of Islamic fundamentalism in Europe. I also referred to the situation in Vojvodina and Kosovo, which threatened to explode because of displacement of the non-Serbs living there, and I pointed out that, as international action so far has proved insufficient, more robust action was needed against the leadership in Belgrade.[25]

In his speech on July 9, 1992, at a summit of the CSCE countries in Helsinki, Antall concluded that the lesson of the South Slav crisis was that international factors had been lagging behind, and had insisted for too long on the territorial unity of Yugoslavia. The way to resolve the ongoing crisis and prevent similar crises in the future was to recognize the principle of self-determination and to ensure the autonomy of minorities.[26] To date, the world has not learned this lesson. Ten days later, at the summit of the Central European Initiative (the former *Hexagonale*), Prime Minister Antall added that in Bosnia, entire ethnic groups were facing the danger of expulsion, and that that must be prevented, lest similar steps be resorted to elsewhere.[27]

When 3,000 Bosniaks were expelled to Hungary by the Serbs, I reported in detail on that and the problem of South Slav refugees in general, at an international conference on Yugoslavia in Geneva on July 29. I underlined that taking care of the refugees was only treating a symptom, our task was to stop the war, to address the cause.[28] Next day, in Budapest, I had talks with the newly-appointed prime minister

---

[24] Intervention by Géza Jeszenszky, June 5, 1992. *Magyar Külpolitikai Évkönyv, 1992*, 194–96.
[25] Letter from Géza Jeszenszky to Secretary of State James Baker, June 10, 1992. Among my papers.
[26] *Magyar Külpolitikai Évkönyv, 1992*, 231, 233.
[27] *Magyar Külpolitikai Évkönyv, 1992*, 234.
[28] *Magyar Külpolitikai Évkönyv, 1992*, 234–38.

of Yugoslavia, Milan Panić[29] and the old-new foreign minister, Vladislav Jovanović. The latter spoke in a tone that was completely different from that of our previous meetings when he had been aggressive and offensive. Now he declared that the new federal government was a government of peace, that the most important thing in the government's program was a commitment to peace-building and democratization, and that Panić was striving for the cessation of all violent activities. They supported the return of refugees and displaced persons, they said, and were open to securing universally accepted minority rights.[30]

At the initiative of French president Mitterrand, an international conference on Yugoslavia was held in London in August 1992.[31] At that meeting, I presented a detailed proposal for a comprehensive settlement of the Southern Slav crisis, including the accountability of war criminals. As a motto, I quoted Churchill's words condemning the Treaty of Munich: "England has been offered a choice between war and shame. She has chosen shame, and will get war."[32] In my speech I called the conference the last chance to resolve the crisis without external armed intervention. I criticized those who dismissed the aspirations of national minorities as a threat to the integrity of the state and saw their support as interference in internal affairs. Here, too, I argued for minority autonomy as being in the interests of both the majority and the minority while preserving the integrity of the state. Finally, I expressed our desire to be present throughout the settlement negotiations as a country very much affected and to have the minorities concerned participate in the solutions to be worked out.[33] I emphasized our concerns in my speech at the UN General Assembly, where I called attention to the ongoing Serbian colonization in the occupied Croatian territories, and also in the Hungarian-inhabited areas of Vojvodina.[34]

Panić's peacemaking efforts soon ended in failure, as a result of the end-of-year elections, which were boycotted by the opposition, and Milošević retained effective

---

[29] Milan Panić (1929–): Serbian-born American businessman turned politician, prime minister of the Federal Republic of Yugoslavia from 1992 to 1993.

[30] Report on the talks of Yugoslav prime minister Milan Panić and Foreign Minister Vladislav Jovanović in Budapest on July 30, 1992. Among my papers.

[31] The Hungarian Foreign Ministry welcomed the French president's initiative in a statement. *Magyar Külpolitikai Évkönyv, 1992*, 230.

[32] Géza Jeszenszky, "Thesis on the Southern Slav War," August 1992, presented at the Conference. As I discovered later, Churchill did not use these very words in his speech at the House of Commons, but he wrote essentially the same earlier in a private letter to Lord Moyne, September 11, 1938. Martin Gilbert, *Churchill A Life* (New York: Henry Holt & Company, 1991), 595.

[33] *Magyar Külpolitikai Évkönyv, 1992*, 283–87.

[34] G. Jeszenszky's address at the XLVII session of the UN General Assembly in New York, *Magyar Külpolitikai Évkönyv, 1992*, 311–20, esp. 316–17.

power.³⁵ The aggressive tone towards Hungary returned, as did the intolerance towards the Hungarians shown by Serb refugees, coming mainly from Bosnia, who were used for colonizing the Hungarian-inhabited areas. When visiting Budapest in mid October, Serbian transportation minister Katić threatened that Hungary's kin, the Hungarians of Vojvodina, would pay the price of Hungary's policy. He demanded, almost as an ultimatum, that Hungarian oil shipments should be continued, breaching the embargo; he threatened the introduction of visa requirements, high tolls and insurance fees for Hungarian citizens on the Serbian roads, and even the closure of traffic on the Danube. We were obviously not ready to buy the safety of Hungarians in Vojvodina in exchange for continuing the supply of fuel.³⁶ Sándor Hódi, one of the founders of the VMDK, gave a most pessimistic picture of the short-term future of the Hungarians of Vojvodina in an October 13 interview with a Hungarian daily.³⁷

Bosnia and Herzegovina

In this province, Serbs, Croats and Muslims, who speak the same language but use a different alphabet and adhere to different religions, have lived intermingled for centuries. In 1914, Gavrilo Princip, a Serbian student, assassinated the Austro-Hungarian heir to the throne because he hoped to see the whole of Bosnia annexed by Serbia. His now late successor, Milošević, wanted the same thing, and to ensure that his wish coincided with the will of the population, his army and the Bosnian Serb irregulars began to move Muslims and Croats out the way, by any means. Both the restoration of peace in the southern Slav lands, and the security of Hungary were served by an announcement by the Hungarian government on October 30, 1992, that it agreed to allow NATO AWACS reconnaissance aircraft to patrol Hungarian airspace in order to monitor the UN-imposed no-fly zone in Bosnia.³⁸ It had long been clear to us that the fighting in Bosnia and the accompanying crimes would not cease as long as the Serbian side was militarily superior, and as long as foreign powers tolerated that. At a November 25 conference convened by Turkey to assist the Bosnian Muslims I said that in the Balkans it was essential to find a "reassuring, long-term solution to the inter-ethnic relations, which is the center of the conflict,"

---

³⁵ In Panić's government the minister of justice was Tibor Várady, an eminent jurist and member of the Hungarian minority. His type-written recollections are among my papers.
³⁶ My report to Prime Minister Antall on Katić's Budapest talks, October 16, 1991. Among my papers.
³⁷ Interview of Sándor Hódi, *Magyar Nemzet*, October 13, 1991.
³⁸ *Magyar Külpolitikai Évkönyv, 1992*, 290–91.

and that the same criteria should apply to all ethnic communities, i.e., some form of autonomy.[39]

After three years of killing, looting and mass rape (separate camps were set up for that purpose), NATO intervention ended the war. The Dayton Accords established a ceasefire based on the separation of the country's three ethnic groups into so-called "entities," but maintained the fiction of a unitary state. In doing so, it only froze the conflict, but the biggest mistake Dayton made was that it did not apply to Serbia, the root of the problems, and did not even try to defuse the time bomb, Kosovo. When Milošević abolished the autonomy of the Serbian province of Kosovo in 1989, 90 percent of the population was Albanian. Their response was passive resistance for almost ten years. During my visit to Albania in 1992, I informally received a representative of the illegal Kosovo government led by Ibrahim Rugova, and assured him that Hungary would support their demand for autonomy. In 1999, in the wake of an Albanian insurrection, the Serb authorities started to displace and deport nearly a million Albanians from their homes, which led NATO to intervene by air. Finally, fearing a ground invasion, Milošević agreed to the province coming under UN administration. In 2008, Kosovo's parliament declared independence, but to date this has not been recognized by Serbia, Russia, Romania and Slovakia. Since 1999, Hungarian troops have been part of the NATO peacekeeping force, and Hungary has recognized Kosovo's independence and maintains an embassy in the new state.

Macedonia

The leadership, administration, police, economic and political power of the Yugoslav republic, which declared independence on September 8, 1991, was in the hands of Macedonian Slavs, whose language, according to Bulgaria, is simply a Bulgarian dialect. They made up two third of the population and excluded the Albanian minority, that lived a contiguous area on the western periphery, from participating in the government of the county. The Macedonian constitution, like the Slovak and Romanian constitutions, considered the new state as a country of a single nationality, the "Macedonians," i.e., the Slavs. The national demands of the Albanians were not heard by the Slav majority until the Albanians, encouraged by the events in Kosovo, and certainly supported by Albanian fighters there who had kept their weapons, tried to assert their demands by armed force. The government forces failed to control the uprising, and the international community

---

[39] Speech by G. Jeszenszky, November 25, 1992, *Magyar Külpolitikai Évkönyv, 1992*, 307–11.

mediated between the two sides, finally persuading the more sensible Slav politicians to accept most of the Albanian demands, i.e., *de facto* territorial autonomy. Since 2001, one of the Albanian parties has always been in the government, but ethnic peace has remained fragile. Hungary was and has remained interested in the two ethnic groups living together in peace, respecting each other's identity, and setting an example for other countries. But what works well in Switzerland is still far from being the rule in the Balkans.

The results of the break-up of Yugoslavia with each nation living divided among several countries proves that the borders of countries and nations do not coincide in the Balkans, either. The mutual national minorities can no longer be assimilated, expelled or murdered. They want to live in the land of their ancestors, according to their own customs, sending their children to schools teaching their own language, under leaders of their own choosing. The institutional form of this is self-government, autonomy. Sadly, even after the break-up of Yugoslavia, the world has not come to the realization that ethnic minorities, who cling to their national traditions and rightly feel threatened by the ethnic majority, are not satisfied with individual rights, which have no institutional guarantee that they will be respected. It is time to learn from the sad example of the Balkans that, just as discrimination is always based on belonging to a group (of the same ethnic origin or religion), the only remedy is to guarantee group rights.

Austria

As I had expected, Austria was a neighbor with which our good relations have become even more intense and intimate because of common interests, values, and political and personal friendship between the leaders. In return for Vice-Chancellor and Foreign Minister Mock's visit to Budapest in April 1991, I paid my first official visit to Austria on January 27, 1992. I was received by the president of Austria, Kurt Waldheim (1918–2007), Chancellor Franz Vranitzky and Speaker Heinz Fischer.[40] All three praised Hungary's decisive role in the political transition and agreed with me on the need to deepen our relationship on a new basis. On foreign policy issues (the South Slav crisis, Soviet successor states, human rights, EC enlargement, regional cooperation, Danube policy), I fully agreed with Mock on the need for concerted international action.[41] My Austrian partner, by then already a friend,

---

[40] Heinz Fischer (1938–): Austrian social democratic politician, president of the National Council of Austria from 1990 to 2002, president of Austria from 2004 to 2016.

[41] János Sáringer, ed., *Iratok az Antall-kormány külpolitikájához és diplomáciájához*, vols. 3/1–2, *(1992. január–1992. december)* [Papers relating to the foreign policy and diplomacy of the Antall government:

Chapter 7 – Successes and Disappointments in 1992

Figure 25. Austria: the best friend, FM Alois Mock, Vienna, April 14, 1992

understood the problem of Hungarian minorities and consistently supported our legal efforts. On bilateral relations we focused on practical problems, such as the facilitation of Hungary's agricultural exports; increased employment of Hungarians within the agreed framework; Hungary's integration into the Western European energy systems; increasing the number of freight transport permits; a deportation treaty; the opening of more border crossings and speeding up transit; finishing construction of the missing sections of the motorway between the two capitals as soon as possible (overcoming the resistance of the Austrian Greens); and establishing an Austria House in Budapest. For this latter purpose, the Hungarian capital offered a suitable building in the city center. Ambassador Franz Schmid thanked me for my intervention in clearing the bureaucratic obstacles over the transaction.[42]

There is one area where Austria continues to be an important example and reference point for Hungary: South Tyrol. The struggle for the autonomy of the German-Austrian minority in South Tyrol ended with an agreement satisfactory to all the parties concerned: on June 11, 1992, Austria, which had been recognized by the UN as a protective power (*Schutzmacht*) in 1946, accepted in a note that

---

January to December 1992] (Budapest: VERITAS Történetkutató Intézet és Levéltár - Magyar Napló, 2021), vol. 3/2: 249–56 (Doc. 247).

[42] Ambassador Franz Schmied to Géza Jeszenszky, June 2, 1992.

Italy had fulfilled the 137-point package guaranteeing the rights and future of the 300,000 ethnic Germans living in the northern part of the province, which was annexed to Italy in the 1919 peace treaty. On May 30, 1992, at the Congress of the South Tyrolean People's Party, representing the local German-speaking population, it was accepted that Italy had fulfilled the necessary steps required by the German minority for their survival. This put an end to a series of violent acts of local discontent (e.g., blowing up power lines) and ended the long-lasting tension between the two states.[43] The 137 points are an indication of the many issues, both large and small, that need to be resolved before a national minority can feel secure about its future. More importantly, the success of the settlement in South Tyrol proved that with mutual goodwill it was possible to reach a lasting and good solution to disputes over national minorities.

More disputes with Romania

On January 8, 1992, I telephoned Foreign Minister Adrian Năstase to express my concern over a threat against the life of Bishop László Tőkés, the hero of the Timișoara revolt in 1989. According to Năstase, this was either the act of a lunatic or was being perpetrated by circles that wanted to prevent the improvement of Hungarian-Romanian relations. Negotiations on a Romanian-Hungarian treaty began in Budapest at the end of January. Our draft was based on the recommendations of the most recent European cooperation documents and included political, cultural, economic and health issues, with due weight given to the problems of national minorities.[44] I considered how the relationship between the two governments, and even more so between the two peoples, would develop in practice to be more important than the treaty.[45]

The national, local and presidential elections in Romania in 1992 were a success for the extremist, nationalist forces. The most painful manifestation of that was the election of Gheorge Funar, known for his anti-Hungarian rants, as mayor of Cluj-Napoca (Kolozsvár). The thinking on Hungary of the chauvinist organization "Vatra," (the Romanian National Unity Party or, later, the Greater Romania Party) was well reflected in an article published in the February 14, 1992, issue of *Romania Mare* titled "Hungary—an assassin state threatening the tranquility

---

[43] "The legal situation of the German minority in South Tyrol," Summary by the HTMH, undated. Cf. the memo by the Austrian Desk at the Hungarian Ministry of Foreign Affairs, June 24, 1992.
[44] *Népszabadság*, January 29, 1992. *Külügyminisztériumi tájékoztató, 1992*, vol. 1: 65.
[45] The documents published in Sáringer, *Iratok az Antall-kormány*, vol. 3/2: 118–248 (Docs. 218–46) testify to the intensity of this relationship.

of Europe."[46] On February 24, in the run-up to the local elections in Romania, the Romanian ambassador to Hungary, Simion Pop, accompanied by envoy Ioan Donca, called on Ferenc Szőts, the head of the Romanian and Balkan department in the Foreign Ministry. The ambassador read out and handed over a memorandum based on his Foreign Ministry's statement of February 21, and informed us that Romania planned to raise the issue at the next meeting of the CSCE senior officials. The issue in question was that Romania expected an explanation for the words of Minister of Defense Lajos Für on February 21 in the town of Miskolc. The Hungarian minister had said that it was part of the responsibility of the Hungarian state, part of national security, that the Hungarians beyond our borders should not be threatened and that the conditions for their survival should be ensured. According to Romanian perceptions, several of the Hungarian minister's speeches were not in line with international law, the UN Charter, the Helsinki Final Act and the Charter of Paris, because security can only apply to states, not to linguistic minorities. Für's speech was an "outrage," an attack on the rule of law established in Romania, because it guaranteed "the rights of all the citizens of the country, including those belonging to the Hungarian ethnic group," a responsibility that could not be exercised by any other state. The Hungarian minority could not be endangered, the statement said, as it was constantly growing in number. (If the evolution of the number of a given minority is the yardstick, then Romania's policy bears a serious responsibility, given the significant decline in population size of the Hungarian minority in Transylvania over the last twenty years.)

The statement also criticized Géza Entz, state secretary of the prime minister's office, head of the Office for Hungarians Beyond Borders, for "abusing Romanian hospitality," saying he had visited Romania on several occasions and "was engaged in political activities." (In May 1991 he was invited by the RMDSZ and met with several members of the Romanian government and opposition; in September he was a guest of the Roman Catholic Archdiocese of Alba Iulia/Gyulafehérvár.) If Hungarian officials continued this, they would be declared persona non grata, it was said. "Irredentist messages" had appeared in Hungarian media and organizations (specifically in the journal *Erdélyi Magyarság*, on the television program "Panorama," in the film "Returning" by Alajos Paulus, in the World Federation of Hungarians, the Transylvanian Association, the "Holy Crown Association," etc.), which was contrary to the negotiations on the bilateral treaty. The statement also referred to the report of unnamed CSCE experts and rejected the idea that

---

[46] A Hungarian translation was published in the journal *Limes* (edited by Gusztáv Molnár) (March 1992): 24–34.

Hungarian minorities are part of the Hungarian nation. Then, twisting the words of State Secretary Entz in an interview published in *Magyar Hírlap* on February 19, the statement rejected the notion that a Hungarian office could represent ethnic Hungarians living outside its borders.[47] On February 25, foreign affairs spokesman János Herman, citing various statements by Hungarian leaders, denied that Hungary had territorial claims and confirmed that "the Hungarian government consistently acts in the competent international forums to protect the rights of all national minorities, and supports efforts to codify and universally accept minority rights." Contrary to the Romanian accusations, it was precisely the Romanian Parliament that was questioning the current border between Ukraine and Romania.[48]

On March 4, the monitoring of the human rights situation in Romania by the UN Human Rights Committee in Geneva ended, despite the Hungarian representative's argument for its extension. The reason for this was obviously not an improvement in the situation in Romania, but the fact that after the local elections, the outside world had grown tired of the issue and instead of criticizing Romania, was expecting more results from the further "taming" of the forces in power. The following day the next stage in the war of declarations was an interview on Romanian radio with Foreign Minister Năstase's. Referring to this decision, he blamed only the Hungarian side for the unsatisfactory relations between the two countries, for constantly criticizing in international fora the conditions of "persons belonging to the Hungarian minority" living in Romania. The fact that Hungary regularly referred to the wording of the Helsinki Final Act, which prohibits the forcible change of borders and talks about Hungarians from Transylvania, not Romania, led my Romanian colleague to conclude that the intention behind this was a "peaceful" change of borders. He also argued that "Hungarian political science considered and still considers the Vienna Arbitration of 1940 as a 'decision' and not as a dictate."[49] In this context it is worth noting that Romania watched the Visegrád Cooperation jealously. Whether sincerely or just pretending it, they saw in it the nucleus of an anti-Romanian military alliance.[50]

The image of the Romanian political elite in Hungarian society was—and still is—rather one-sided. It is still instructive to read the April 1992 reports of two

---

[47] Report the 4th Regional Department of the Ministry of Foreign Affairs, February 24, 1992, and the attached Romanian Statement. Cf. the cryptic cable from the Embassy in Bucharest on Romania's conditions on the planned bilateral treaty, Sáringer, *Iratok az Antall-kormány*, vol. 3/2: 150–52 (Doc. 228, April 24, 1992).
[48] *Magyar Külpolitikai Évkönyv, 1992*, 146–47.
[49] Press cable from the Hungarian Embassy in Bucharest, March 9, 1992.
[50] Radio interview with Iván Bába, deputy state secretary, March 29, 1992. *Külügyminisztériumi tájékoztató, 1992*, vol. 1: 197–99.

researchers from the Teleki Foundation-affiliated Institute for Foreign Affairs on their discussions in Bucharest. Representatives of the Romanian opposition (National Liberal Party, National Peasant Party, Civic Alliance) were unanimous in blaming the Romanian government for the mishandling of the Hungarian relationship and for Romania's isolation in foreign policy. They regretted their exclusion from Visegrád and the *Hexagonale*. They praised the functioning of the RMDSZ and condemned the behavior of the Romanian extremists. But they, too, considered Lajos Für's words in Miskolc unfortunate, saying that the speech was "a real gift package for the Vatra representatives who stood in the local elections and won the mayor's position in Cluj-Napoca. In Northern Transylvania, the democratic parties lost 15–20 percent of the vote due to the anti-Hungarian propaganda campaign following Für's words." Călin Popescu-Tăriceanu,[51] the representative of the Young Liberals, said that "the acceptance of minority rights can only be achieved by a gradual method, not by violent demands. Romanian public opinion is still shocked by the principle of collective rights, but after delicate preparations it will become acceptable." He also said that victory for the opposition in the Fall elections was possible—and in four years' time, he was proven right. The Hungarian MPs of the Bucharest Parliament also warned that reckless statements would greatly complicate the situation for the Hungarians in Transylvania, and they asked that Hungarian parties in Hungary stop trying to impose the party structure of Hungary on the Hungarians in Transylvania. Finally, they indicated that it would be to their advantage if the Hungarian-Romanian treaty could be concluded as soon as possible—without any concessions in principle.[52]

It was not against my intentions that on April 13, 1992, Géza Szőcs, vice president of the RMDSZ, sent a letter to the two governments negotiating the bilateral treaty to include the Hungarian party in the discussions concerning the fate of the Hungarian minority. I supported this proposal and considered it reasonable, but Năstase rejected it, saying that the situation of the Hungarian national minority in Romania should not be the subject of discussions between the two governments. The analysis of our International Law Department pointed out that the Romanian position was contrary to the various documents and recommendations of the CSCE, which explicitly called for dialogue between the states concerned. The recently signed German-Romanian treaty included the issue of the German minority in Romania, and the refusal to sign in the case of the Hungarians was

---

[51] Călin Popescu-Tăriceanu (1952–): Romanian politician, prime minister (2004–2008), speaker of the Senate (2014–2019).
[52] Report of conversations by Sándor Vogel and János Matus with members of the Parliament of Romania, April 16, 1992. Among my papers.

discrimination, our lawyers argued.[53] State Secretary Meleșcanu's visit to Budapest on May 18–20 promised some progress, but we remembered that in 1989, when holding the same position under Ceaușescu, he had compared the institution of autonomy to the Bantustans in South Africa during the apartheid times. He had also described the funeral of Imre Nagy and his fellow martyrs, at which Romanians and the MDF signed a Declaration on reconciliation, as "chauvinistic, neo-fascist, revisionist."[54] Meleșcanu's manners were definitely better than his boss's. In his discussion with Tamás Katona, the political state secretary, Meleșcanu agreed—in principle—with confidence-building measures, economic, scientific and cultural programs and meetings, improving tourism and transport links, the restoration of the memorial to the martyrs of Arad, and the reopening of the consulate general in Cluj/Kolozsvár, while disagreement over the issue of the national minorities was simply acknowledged.[55]

Soon, another diplomatic clash followed, in line with the Romanian side's stop and go policy. On May 25, 1992, Năstase reiterated in the weekly *Romanul* his spokesman Chebeleu's protests regarding my talk at the Royal Institute of International Affairs in London on May 6. The talks given at Chatham House are public, but what is said is a personal opinion and cannot be quoted (Chatham House rules). In my speech, I gave a factual account of the significant change in the ethnic proportions in Transylvania since 1910, and, in the context of the ethnic clashes in Moldova at that time, spoke about the advantages of the Swiss cantonal system. László Péter, professor at the University of London, wrote to me about the positive reception of my speech.[56] "I cannot understand why it is considered important for Romania to object to what was said [by Minister Jeszenszky] in relation to a third sovereign country," said my spokesman, János Herman. He reaffirmed Hungary's commitment to cooperation with Romania, as it was expressed in my speech at Ártánd in August last year.[57] (The text of my speech was never published in Romania, despite Năstase's repeated promises.) On June 19, at the International Forum on the Future of Europe in the Swiss resort Crans-Montana, Béla Kádár, Hungary's minister for international economic relations, said that Romania's share of Hungarian foreign trade had fallen from 10 percent to 1 percent. In this context,

---

[53] Analysis of Năstase's reply, signed by György Szénási, May 12, 1992.
[54] Note by Géza Entz, political state secretary, April 30, 1992. Among my papers.
[55] Report and memorandum on the negotiations of Political State Secretary Tamás Katona and Romanian state secretary Teodor Meleșcanu, Sáringer, *Iratok az Antall-kormány*, vol. 3/2: 180–86 (Doc. 232, June 3, 1992). Cf. *Új Magyarország*, May 20, 1992.
[56] László Péter to Géza Jeszenszky, May 11, 1992. Among my records.
[57] Ministry of Foreign Affairs spokesman's briefing on the Hungarian perception of Hungarian-Romanian relations, May 26, 1992. Among my papers.

I mentioned that the Romanian government had not agreed to the reopening of the Hungarian consulate general in Cluj, even though it would boost our economic relations. Năstase also attended the conference, at which our private discussion consisted of mutual reproaches. In view of the replacement by Romanians of the ethnic Hungarian prefects in Harghita and Covasna counties (inhabited overwhelmingly by Hungarians), and the multiplication of the police presence in Szeklerland, we did not consider it timely to go forward with a visit to Romania by Hungary's interior minister, Péter Boross, scheduled for the autumn months.[58]

Tensions between the two countries increased further in the wake of the Third World Congress of Hungarians held on August 19–21, 1992, when Hungary traditionally celebrates the founding of the State in A.D. 1000. The event welcomed Hungarians from all over the world to come to see the country after the regime change. The program did not include the conference organized by the "World Transylvanian Federation," founded by István Zolcsák in Brazil, which was to take place simultaneously to discuss "the question of Transylvania." The Romanian press had protested in advance against the statements expected to be made there, and Foreign Minister Năstase wrote to me on August 17 expressing his concerns. In my reply the next day, I explained what it meant to celebrate freely the day of the founding of the Hungarian state and the unity of all Hungarians. I explained also that, in respect of the freedom of assembly and expression, the World Transylvanian Federation had the right to hold an event at which participants could express their views freely. I reassured my colleague that "the Republic of Hungary, building on the increasingly widespread principles of human rights and minority protection, and having a responsibility for the Hungarian communities around the world, has the intention of building good relations with all its neighbors and the democratic countries of the world. I am pleased to read in your letter that Romania intends to address the problem of national minorities in the Romanian Constitution, with full respect to the provisions of the European standards." I informed him that my government's position on the issues of Hungarian minorities and our relations with neighboring countries was set out in the Declaration issued on the same day, and I attached it to my letter.[59] Said Declaration set out the general principles of the Antall government, and, not mentioning Romania, but addressed especially to it, contained principles which have remained valid until today.

---

[58] Letter of State Secretary Entz to Minister of the Interior Boross, July 28, 1992. Among my papers.
[59] Géza Jeszenszky to Foreign Minister Adrian Năstase, August 18, 1992.

> A precondition for the stability and security of Central and Eastern Europe is that the various minorities (national, ethnic, religious and political) should not become victims of the state's power politics. [...] throughout the 20th century [...] the state did not function as an institution for the common good of all citizens, but became the property of the majority nation. [...] Unfortunately, the peoples and states seeking their place after the collapse of the communist system tend to return [...] to the outmoded idea of national exclusivity.[60]

The Congress, which offered many moving and emotional speeches, provided an uplifting and lasting memory for all participants. Bishop László Tőkés distanced himself from the unrealistic dreams of the World Transylvanian Alliance, and Hungary could not be stigmatized by the charge of promoting an irredentism that would destabilize Europe. Ignoring my letter and the proceedings of the Congress, Foreign Minister Năstase gathered the ambassadors of the CSCE member states accredited to Bucharest 8 (except the Hungarian) on August 21 in order to present the events of the World Hungarian Congress in a slanted framework.[61]

János Matus and Sándor Vogel of the Hungarian Institute for Foreign Policy, accompanied by Robert Hamerton-Kelly, a research professor at Stanford University, returned from another trip to Romania in September with some interesting findings. I met with politicians in several towns in Transylvania, and they reported to me that they found the best conditions in Brasov, where the success of the Democratic Convention was largely due to its good relations with the local RMDSZ. They forwarded the request of Hungarian politicians from Transylvania to the Hungarian government to consult with them regularly and not to export party politics from Hungary, rather to follow Austria's attitude towards South Tyrol. The Romanian opposition considered the ruling coalition to be neo-communist, its main base being the army. The nationalist press was funded by the government, they observed, but the Russian secret service also has a hand in it. The Democratic Convention accepted cooperation with the Hungarians, recognized their collective rights, supported the Hungarian school network, and hoped to restore the monarchy by a referendum. The Democratic Convention expected to receive 28–35 percent of the popular vote and be victorious in the elections due at the end of the month.[62] In the parliamentary and presidential elections held on September 27,

---

[60] *Magyar Külpolitikai Évkönyv, 1992*, 272. The Declaration is discussed in detail in Chapter 8, in the section, "The Hungarian aspects of the velvet divorce."
[61] Udvardy Data Bank, August 21, 1992. Among my papers.
[62] Report by János Matus and Sándor Vogel, September 18, 1992. Among my papers.

there were a lot of abuses, irregularities and even fraud, according to convincing arguments from the opposition,[63] and the Convention and Constantinescu lost to Iliescu.

Tamás Sepsey, state secretary, president of the National Office for Compensation and Reparation to the victims of the authoritarian times between 1939 and 1989, made a tour of the major cities of Transylvania from October 8 to 11, 1992, with the cooperation of Hungary's Ministry of Foreign Affairs, the Embassy in Bucharest and the county organizations of the RMDSZ. He informed the large number of affected persons (Northern Transylvania was part of Hungary in 1940–1944) and the Hungarian- and Romanian-language press that Hungary wished to compensate its former citizens (and their descendants) who had suffered harm at the hands of the Hungarian state between 1939 and 1944, regardless of their nationality or religion. This was also appreciated by his official interlocutor Grigore Zanc, prefect of Cluj County.[64] A staff member of the HTMH reported on his visit to Zalău/Zilah, the seat of Sălaj/Szilágy County (with a large Hungarian population), from October 22 to 25, 1992. The impressions he gained were good, and he observed a peaceful atmosphere between the Hungarian and Romanian populations.

In the second half of 1992 there was a proliferation of articles in the Romanian press about alleged Hungarian plans to dismember Romania. They tried to convince Romanian society and Western governments that the official policy of Hungary was to regain Transylvania. An extreme right-wing organ claimed that Hungary wanted to bring the whole Balkans under Hungarian influence, and that the Visegrád Cooperation had been created for that purpose. The implementation of the plan was coordinated by the Secretariat of Hungarians Beyond the Border, headed by a general of the Hungarian intelligence service [sic!] Géza Entz. (Entz came from academic life and was a historian of the arts.) Germany was named as the main supporter of Hungarian nationalists.[65] The article suggested that the visit of Russian president Yeltsin to Budapest and the resulting agreement on the protection of minorities should be answered by reviving the former "Little Entente," the inter-war alliance against Hungary by its neighbors.[66]

---

[63] *HTMH Tájékoztató*, no. 5 (1992): 1–4. The Information Bulletin for the Office of the Hungarians Beyond the Borders (Full name: *HTMH - civil régiók: Tájékoztató a határon túli magyar közösségek civiltársadalmi életének eseményeiről és fejlődési irányzatairól* [HTMH—civil regions: Information bulletin on the events and development trends of the civil society life of Hungarian communities across the border]) was the periodical of the Office.

[64] *HTMH Tájékoztató*, no. 4 (1992):17–19.

[65] The title of the article, published in the weekly *Spionaj-Contraspionaj*, 55–56 (1992), was "The Stake is Transylvania: Growing Hungarian Subversive Activity."

[66] *Dimineaţă*, November 4 and 14, 1992; *Tineretul liber*, November 11, 1992.

Following the September elections, Năstase became the speaker (president) of the National Assembly and Teodor Meleșcanu became foreign minister in the new government formed on November 21. There was a noticeable change in the tone of Romanian politics, as it tried to show a different face to the West after the "marches of the miners."[67] I saw in this a chance for a substantial improvement in our bilateral relations, benefitting the Hungarian community, which I indicated in an article I wrote in December 1992 for *Népszabadság*, the largest-circulation Hungarian daily:

> On the Hungarian side, we are particularly interested in Romania's integrating with the western half of Europe as thoroughly as possible. This would not only be in line with Romania's traditional orientation, but would also mean restoring and strengthening the centuries-old European ties of the Hungarian minority living in Romania. Hungary needs stable and economically prosperous neighbors. We would like Romania to benefit from the Association Agreement with the European Community, to receive "most favored" trade treatment from the United States, to join the political club of European democracies, the Council of Europe, and, as my Central European colleagues and I explained last time in Graz [at the meeting of the CEI, the Central European Initiative], concrete regional cooperation, above all, cooperation in the border regions. All of that could lead to [Romania's] membership in CEI. The memorandum drawn up in May 1992, during Meleșcanu's visit here, summarized in forty-three points the steps that were desirable in bilateral relations and that were agreed at the time to be mutually necessary. These included the promotion of trade in goods, the development of tourism, the opening of new border crossings and the expansion of existing ones, the support for the establishment of joint ventures, the coordination of school textbooks, and the holding of commemorative events to mark each other's national days and historical anniversaries.
>
> Some issues were left open at the time, such as the reopening of the Consulate General in Cluj/Kolozsvár, the establishment of a joint committee on the national minorities, Hungarian access to Romanian documents related to the 1956 Hungarian Revolution, and the restoration of the monument to the martyrs of Arad. This short list shows that Hungary's bilateral relations are far from being focused solely on the situation of the Hungarian minority in Romania. Of course, the greater comfort of minorities would

---

[67] See footnote 92 on page 173 in this volume.

greatly contribute to the positive development of bilateral relations. [Welcoming Meleșcanu's intention to improve our relations, expressed on November 28 on Bucharest radio,] I would like to express my hope that practice and action will make this intention clear. Hungarian public opinion is watching not only to see who will be the prefect in Harghita County, what the national composition of the police will be in Szeklerland, whether justice will be done for Pál Cseresznyés and those convicted for the events of December 1989 and March 1990, and whether Romania will sign the Council of Europe's Language Charter, but also whether it will be difficult or easy to run joint ventures, whether the petrol tax [on tourists buying gasoline in Romania] will be withdrawn, which we have not yet been informed about, whether the new border crossings will be opened, whether Romanian customs will handle passengers as quickly as does Austrian customs, and, in general, how our trade with Romania, which was one of our main trading partners between the two world wars, will develop.

Hungary would of course be happy to anchor our well-established relations in an inter-state treaty. For our part, there is nothing to prevent us from reaffirming, in appropriate legal terms, which are reassuring for both peoples, that we have no territorial disputes with Romania, in line with the Helsinki Final Act, and that we should confirm in specific articles the guarantees for the survival and secure future of the minorities living in each other's countries. If Romania starts on this European path, our relations can become as intense and intimate as the fruitful and friendly relations we have established in recent years with many countries, including many neighboring countries.[68]

My new colleague's response was swift: an invitation to me to make an official visit to Romania, and a willingness to involve the Hungarian minority in Romania in the negotiations on the basic bilateral treaty.

---

[68] Géza Jeszenszky, "Dunának, Oltnak egy a hangja?" *Népszabadság*, December 3, 1992. An English version appeared under the title "Can Danube and Olt Speak with One Voice" in *MFA Current Policy*, no. 28 (1992), it is quoted here with a few editorial corrections.

Ukraine

Interest and emotion have coincided in the unexpectedly close and friendly relationship that evolved between the independent Ukraine and its first international treaty partner, Hungary, in the early 1990s.[69] Consul General András Páldi was appointed ambassador to Ukraine, not as a reward for his flattery towards me, but because of the prestige and popularity that fell into his lap as a result of Hungary's initiatives. Ukraine's first embassy opened in Budapest on March 25, 1992. As a result of our frequent meetings, I formed a close relationship with the foreign minister, Anatolij Zlenko, who, thanks to his intelligence and international experience, quickly shed the Soviet vestiges of his diplomatic past. He understood how important it was for Hungary to have a strong Ukraine that looked to the West. In relation to the territory and population of Ukraine, the Hungarian minority was insignificant, but Zlenko recognized that Hungary's gestures would be best reciprocated if the close to 200,000-strong Hungarian minority living in Transcarpathia, its westernmost district, were given the rights necessary for its survival and the cultivation of its culture.[70] The Minorities Act adopted by the Ukrainian Parliament in the summer of 1992 provided for these rights in a generous way, above the level of the emerging European standards. By that time, the Hungarians in Subcarpathia had already established a political party, KMKSZ, and a Hungarian Studies Institute (within the University of Uzhhorod). They had the right to write personal first and family names and place names in Hungarian, several Hungarian monuments had been restored and new ones inaugurated, and local border traffic had been resumed. More details of the positive phase in our relationship are given in Chapter 9.

Transborder cooperation programs were meant to serve and improve the economic situation throughout in Central Europe. The most important and promising of these, not only for Ukraine, was the Carpathian Euroregion. The conference of the Carpathian-Tisza Foundation and the New York-based Institute of East-West Studies held in Nyíregyháza on May 24–26, 1992, served to prepare the ground for this. The conference was attended by representatives of Subcarpathia, also by representatives of southern Poland, eastern Slovakia and three counties of north-eastern Hungary, but the Romanian government prevented the participation of Maramureș/Máramaros and Satu Mare/Szatmár counties.

Hungary managed to establish excellent relations with Ukraine in all areas, although in the case of a Hungarian autonomous region, demanded by a local

---

[69] A number of documents on bilateral relations in 1992 are available in Sáringer, *Iratok az Antall-kormány*, vol. 3/2: Docs. 334–63, 564–678.

[70] Jeszenszky, *Ukraine and Hungary* 43–46.

referendum, the response of the Kyiv Rada was evasive. This was despite the fact that in 1991, before independence, both the Ukrainian parliament and the then leading opposition party, Rukh, had accepted the principle of self-government for the Hungarians.[71]

Central European solidarity and minority rights[72]

My presentation at the Aspen Institute conference in Bologna, Italy, on February 29, 1992, focused on Central European integration. I argued that the end of the century would see the emergence of radically new forms of economic and political solidarity, that transborder relations between local authorities, cities and regions, and their economic and cultural cooperation could lead to closer cooperation between states. The *Hexagonale*, which had grown out of the Alpine–Adriatic Cooperation, provided a good framework for this.[73] At the summit of the Visegrád Three on May 6, 1992, the Hungarian prime minister said that the integration goals should be achieved as soon as possible, not by rivalry, but by joint, coordinated action. Antall also spoke about the difficulties of the transition, the social tensions and causes of frustration that were common in the three countries. He also stressed the importance of all-European solidarity in their policy towards the successor states of the dissolved Soviet Union, because "it would be naive to believe that centuries of political and foreign policy aspirations would be abandoned overnight. That is why we must unite and pursue a common policy."[74] There was full agreement in the talks on the need to maintain cooperation and to significantly increase mutual trade, and also agreement on the need to coordinate positions on the withdrawal of the Russian troops.[75] In a message to the European Community's governing body, the three leaders expressed their desire for full membership,[76] the three foreign ministers issued a Memorandum of Understanding on cross-border cooperation, on coordination with the Council of Europe on legal issues, and on a proposed program of cooperation with the Benelux countries.[77] In a spirit of growing trust

---

[71] Note by István Íjgyártó, chief adviser of the HTMH, June 22, 1992. This was also the experience of State Secretary Iván Bába at his consultations in Kyiv on June 28–29, 1992. Ibid., 47.
[72] Sáringer, *Iratok az Antall-kormány*, vol. 3/2: Docs. 264–73, 335–64.
[73] *Magyar Külpolitikai Évkönyv, 1992*, 153–62. My paper "Italy and the Central European Integrations" was published in the periodical *Európai Utas*, 1 (1992): 16–20.
[74] *Magyar Külpolitikai Évkönyv, 1992*, 190–95. Cf. Sáringer, *Iratok az Antall-kormány*, vol. 3/2: Doc. 274, 365–68.
[75] I have the record of the informal discussions, too.
[76] *Magyar Külpolitikai Évkönyv, 1992*, 199–200.
[77] *Magyar Külpolitikai Évkönyv, 1992*, 201–5.

and common perceptions among the Three and the EC, the foreign ministers met in Luxembourg on October 5, 1992, and issued a joint Declaration. This was an important milestone in the implementation of the Europe Agreements signed at the end of the precious year, on December 16.[78]

Hungary's commitment to Central European cooperation was not weakened by Slovakia's and Romania's unfriendly—to put it mildly—and anti-minority policies. On July 18, 1992, the heads of government and foreign ministers of the regional cooperation, renamed from *Hexagonale* to the Central European Initiative (CEI), met in Vienna. Here again, Antall stressed the importance of creating economic and financial stability as essential to the functioning of democracy. On the issue of the admission of refugees from the southern Slav crisis, he called attention to the dangers of the world accepting the expulsion of innocent people and entire communities, and the artificial alteration of the ethnic composition of certain areas. The opposite of this, respect for the right of nations to self-determination and the rights of minorities, must, Antall stressed, prevail in the entire Central European region.[79]

On August 18, on the eve of the Third World Congress of Hungarians, the Hungarian government issued the aforementioned Declaration. The document deplored the resurgence of national exclusivity and incitement to hatred against minorities, and it recommended "the constitutional recognition of national and ethnic diversity" and the adoption of various forms of autonomy.[80] At the CEI Foreign Ministers' Conference in Graz on November 21, 1992, I presented the Slovenian-Hungarian and Russian-Hungarian treaties on the protection of minorities, signed a few days earlier, as proof that the collapse of totalitarian regimes did not go hand in hand with the escalation of national-ethnic antagonisms. I supported the admission to the CEI of the new states emerging from the disintegrating Yugoslavia, with the proviso that they must commit themselves to adhering to the accepted European principles and standards on human and minority rights.[81]

In 1993, Hungary took over the presidency of the CEC. The work of the various working groups was not spectacular, but effective. At the end of our presidency, on November 19–20, I welcomed nine of my fellow ministers in Debrecen. The central theme of our discussions continued to be the Southern Slav crisis, the bloody conflict in Bosnia that did not show any sign of ending. We were pleased to see that Belarus, Bulgaria, Romania, Ukraine, Albania, Moldova and even Russia were interested in membership in the CEI. In addition to current political and

---

[78] *Magyar Külpolitikai Évkönyv, 1992*, 321–26.
[79] *Magyar Külpolitikai Évkönyv, 1992*, 263–68.
[80] *Magyar Külpolitikai Évkönyv, 1992*, 272–74.
[81] Speech by Géza Jeszenszky, November 21, 1992. Among my papers.

economic issues of cooperation, we examined the draft European Convention for the Protection of Minorities, prepared by the Minorities Working Group. Welcoming its content, we agreed that once finalized, it would be submitted to the Council of Europe, in the framework of which a comprehensive European agreement was being prepared.[82]

Central European solidarity was one of the guiding principles of Hungarian foreign policy after the regime change. However, the issue of the Hungarian and other national minorities was most difficult to reconcile with that. We have seen how Prime Minister Antall argued on this issue in his international appearances and how he spoke at the Third World Congress of Hungarians. Hungary's principles were clearly set out in the Government Declaration of August 18, 1992.[83] On October 1, at the UN General Assembly, I welcomed the secretary general's report, *Agenda for Peace*, as a means of achieving and maintaining collective security. I pointed out that, as international tensions very often arise from internal conflicts within individual states, their prevention and management was essential. In Hungary's neighborhood, three federal states, claiming self-determination and lacking internal popular support, were disintegrating at a rapid pace. It was wrong to attribute a retrograde character to this, referring to modern integration trends; the key issue was "to accept and support the modern aspirations of peoples for self-determination and the self-organization of national minorities." This also pointed to "the compelling need to address the problem of national minorities in a meaningful way," which would not weaken the stability and internal peace of states, but on the contrary, would strengthen it. This was demonstrated by the settlement of the Alto Adige/South Tyrol issue by the agreement between Italy and Austria. This experience was an opportunity to develop and implement binding international standards and guarantees. I also mentioned the 80,000 people who fled from the former Yugoslavia to our country, whose return should be ensured by UN forces, while at the same time holding accountable those responsible for violations. My conclusion was that the world organization must move beyond the syndrome of doing "too little, too late."[84] On this subject, in an interview with the Hungarian department of the BBC, I mentioned that the treaties on the protection of minorities concluded in 1919 under the auspices of the League of Nations had given national minorities more rights (at least on paper) than they now claimed,

---

[82] *Magyar Külpolitikai Évkönyv*, 1993, 337–46.
[83] *Magyar Külpolitikai Évkönyv*, 1992, 272–74. See above, my letter to my colleague, A. Năstase. For Antall's speech at the Congress, see *Magyar Külpolitikai Évkönyv*, 1992, 276–83.
[84] Speech by Géza Jeszenszky at the XLVII Session of the UN General Assembly, October 1, 1992.

and that between the two world wars it was Czechoslovakia alone that had largely honored those obligations.[85]

Under the auspices of the Lajos Batthyány Foundation, established by József Antall (using the Schuman Prize he had been awarded), and the Komárom-Esztergom County Municipality, an international conference titled "The possibilities of minority self-determination in East-Central Europe on the basis of the Carrington Document" was held in Tatabánya on November 2–3, 1992. Géza Herczegh, a member of the Hungarian Academy of Sciences, vice chairman of the Constitutional Court of Hungary, was presiding. In addition to experts and academics from five Hungarian parliamentary parties, participants included representatives of Hungarian parties and organizations from beyond Hungary's borders, visiting professors András Ludányi and László Kürti from the United States, the ambassadors of Slovenia and Croatia, the minister of nationalities of Vojvodina, the UN Human Rights Centre in Geneva, the Council of Europe, the Badinter Commission of the Yugoslavia Conference and the FUEV.[86] According to the assessment of the HTMH, outstanding presentations were given by Gáspár Bíró, Péter Kovács, László Bodnár, Sándor Hódi, Bela Tonković, István Szépfalusi, János Báthory, Pero Lastic, Rezső Szabó, Jurij Dumnič, Árpád Pasza and András Ludányi, while "the speakers from the UN and the Council of Europe were disappointing, partly with their speeches that contained few new elements and even fewer guarantees, and partly with their absence during the discussion of the Final Declaration."

The Final Declaration described the Carrington Plan IV (of November 1991) as a good starting point, as it "transcends nation-state thinking as a source of conflict" and sees the self-government model as a solution for "the tension-free coexistence of different ethnic groups within a state structure."[87] The first tangible, internationally-approved result was the European Charter for Regional or Minority Languages adopted by the Council of Europe in June 1992, and opened for signature. The signatory countries committed themselves to protect and promote, in the manner and at the level they have indicated, the regional or minority language(s) they have designated as being used on their territory. However, the Charter gives signatories a great deal of freedom in the extent to which they permit the use of these languages; for example, whether minorities can just learn their mother tongue in the schools, or can study predominantly in their own mother tongue. Many European

---

[85] Péter Pallai's conversation with Géza Jeszenszky, October 14, 1992; Radio Observatory, October 15, 1992.
[86] Federalistische Union Europäischer Volksgruppen (Federal Union of European Nationalities), an organization of 84 nationalities from 32 countries, founded in 1949.
[87] *HTMH Tájékoztató*, no. 5 (1992): 6–11.

countries have either not signed, ratified the Charter to date, or do not honor it.[88] Hungary and Austria signed the Charter immediately, while our other neighbors only signed years later, but what counts is how much the country concerned voluntarily implements it. It is telling that Romania committed itself to protecting eighteen languages, which suggests frivolity rather than generosity.

Few states in Western Europe have significant numbers of their citizens living outside their borders, and therefore we had few allies to rely on in our efforts to defend minority rights. Austria was the only country to stand up consistently for these rights, and not only for the sake of the approximately 300,000 German-speakers who had been transferred to Italy in 1919 for strategic considerations in order that the southern side of the Brenner Pass should not be in Austrian hands.[89] During my term of office, Vice-Chancellor and Foreign Minister Mock stood up for those rights in every forum. Romania's opposition was not dampened by the fact that a good 2.5 million people living in Moldova spoke Romanian. Poland, while strongly supporting the culture of Poles living in Lithuania, Belarus and Ukraine, somewhat inexplicably did not support the codification of minority rights in the international arena and remained neutral in the Hungarian-Slovak disputes. The break-up of Yugoslavia created a significant number of national minorities in all its successor states; Slovenia's conduct has always been exemplary, and Croatia, too, has pursued a fair policy on this issue.

The break-up of the Soviet Union, on the other hand, turned nearly 25 million of the 145 million Russians into national minorities, while there are still some 30 million non-Russians living in the present-day Russian Federation.[90] On this basis, it was (also) reasonable to look to Russia as a partner in securing minority rights. As a Foreign Ministry memo noted, "Hungary's efforts on behalf of Hungarians living beyond its borders have until recently been viewed by Moscow with cool indifference, and only occasionally in its policy towards Romania did it mention the situation of Hungarians in Transylvania as a negative example. In recent months, the Russian leadership's view on the issue has changed decisively. As the Counsellor of the Russian Embassy in Budapest recently noted, they are now feeling the weight of this problem on their own skin." Yeltsin's Russia was therefore showing interest in Hungarian minority protection policy.[91] The discussions State Secretary Géza Entz

---

[88] Erzsébet Szalayné Sándor, *A kisebbségvédelem nemzetközi jogi intézményrendszere a 20. században* [The system of international legal institutions for the protection of minorities in the twentieth century] (Budapest: MTA Kisebbségkutató Intézet, 2003).

[89] The formal conclusion of the South Tyrol question was Austria's note to Italy of June 11, 1992, which I have already mentioned.

[90] Jeszenszky, *Post-Communist Europe*, Theme 13, Russians "Near Abroad," 359–68.

[91] Note of Szergely Szűcs, desk officer for Russia, 2134/3 June 24, 1992.

held in Moscow on September 20–24, 1992, were very positive on the growing interest and concern shown by Russia towards the Russian and the Hungarian national minorities.[92] On that basis, the "Declaration on the Principles of Cooperation between the Government of the Republic of Hungary and the Government of the Russian Federation in the Field of Ensuring the Rights of National or Ethnic, Religious and Linguistic Minorities" was signed on November 12, 1992.[93]

While fully in line with Hungary's views on this issue, the Declaration caused real panic in the Romanian press, since a great power appeared to be lining up in favor of national minority rights, which the Hungarians had hitherto been advocating with little success. As an answer, journalists suggested the resurrection of the inter-war Little Entente, coupled with war preparations.[94] Of course, there was also a domestic political calculation in this hysteria: to scare the Romanian population with the "Hungarian threat" and thus divert attention from the serious internal economic and political situation. Unfortunately, the Russian government at the time was primarily concerned with the situation of the fewer than two million Russians left behind in the Baltic countries, essentially as a result of Soviet colonization, while it showed no serious interest in the 11 million Russians in Ukraine or the 6 million in Kazakhstan. Perhaps also because it was not prepared to give its own non-Russian minorities broad linguistic rights and genuine autonomy, fearing their possible secession.

Russia's involvement in the protection of minorities was certainly a promising development and could have made international institutions more receptive to considering the problem. The Council of Europe apparatus, from the secretary general, Catherine Lalumière, to the political director, H.P. Furrer, understood the importance of international regulation and accepted the need for it. The multiparty Hungarian delegation to the Parliamentary Assembly of the Council, led by József Bratinka (1952–2011), an MP of the MDF, and Géza Entz, president of the HTMH, deserves special appreciation. Without Entz, the final document drawn up at the CSCE meeting in Geneva in July 1991 would have been worse; essentially it was he who drafted the government declaration of August 18, 1992, which set out the desirable way of resolving the minority question, and he argued for our minority protection program at numerous international meetings. His visit to Strasbourg of November 17–19, 1992, and his talks with the leaders of the

---

[92] Sáringer, *Iratok az Antall-kormány*, vol. 3/2: 500–505 (Doc. 314).
[93] Keskeny, *A magyar-orosz kapcsolatok*, 101.
[94] E.g., Mihail Fabian's "Budapest–Moszkva tengely?" [A Budapest–Moscow axis?] warned that the Declaration "calls for the dismemberment of Romania." *Dimineața*, November 12, 1992. The press cable from the Embassy in Bucharest is among my papers.

Chapter 7 – Successes and Disappointments in 1992

Council of Europe were enlightening. He presented the situation of the Hungarian minorities created in the millions by the border changes, the frequent intolerant and discriminatory attitude expressed towards them, and everything that made it necessary for an independent Hungarian government office to deal with their problems. He pointed out the difference between the situation of minorities in Western Europe and in Central Europe, and argued in favor of autonomy as the most effective means of establishing security and stability in Europe. He also spoke about the limitations in the rights of the Hungarian communities in Slovakia and Romania, countries which aspire to membership of the Council of Europe. Secretary General Lalumière mentioned that the prevailing perception in most Western countries was that it was unacceptable for an institution to operate in one state to deal with the citizens of another state. In the eyes of many, it "raises fears" that Hungary "deals too much" with Hungarians living beyond its borders, instead of leaving that issue to the Council of Europe. The apparatus of the organization proposed that the Hungarian government and Hungarian minority parties support the admission of Slovakia and Romania into the Council, and said that would help the Hungarian minority ensure their cultural and linguistic rights.[95]

In the early 1990s, the United States paid serious attention to "the new Europe," including to the issue of national minorities. The institutional framework for this was the Project on Ethnic Relations (PER), founded in 1991 by Allen Kassof, former director of the international academic exchange program IREX (International Research and Exchange). PER was established in Princeton, New Jersey, with the support of the Carnegie Corporation of New York and other foundations, in order to address ethnic conflicts in the new European democracies. It organized a number of conferences and meetings in Central and Eastern Europe, and produced studies on the problems and possible solutions.[96] Its co-chair and, after Kassof's retirement, its president, was Livia Plaks (1947–2013), born in Baia Mare/Nagybánya of Hungarian nationality, the niece of Elie Wiesel.[97] She was fluent both in Hungarian and Romanian, understood the plight of the Transylvanian Hungarians, and was a useful go-between between the two nationalities.[98]

---

[95] Report of Géza Entz on his visit to the Council of Europe, November 24, 1992. I would like to thank G. Entz for sharing this document with me.
[96] *Project on Ethnic Relations*, http://www.per-usa.org/. After nearly twenty years of operation, the organization, which had achieved few of its original aims, ceased its activities in 2012. Its archives are available for research at Princeton University.
[97] Elie Wiesel (1928–2016): writer born in Sighet/Máramarossziget in Romanian Transylvania, Holocaust survivor, Nobel Peace Prize laureate.
[98] Zoltán Sipos, "Neptuni találkozók 3: Nagyon ismer minket a PER. De honnan?" [Neptune Meetings 3: PER knows us very well. But from where?], *Átlátszó Erdély*, January 28, 2015, https://atlatszo.ro/velunk-elo-tortenelem/neptun/neptuni-talalkozok-3-nagyon-ismer-minket-a-per-de-honnan/.

PER maintained offices in Bucharest and in several successor states of the Soviet Union; it organized an international conference on ethnic harmony in Budapest on December 11–13, 1992, in collaboration with the László Teleki Foundation. The opening lecture was given by Domokos Kosáry, president of the Hungarian Academy of Sciences, and the closing lecture was given by me. There was a great need for such conferences, for outreach work on this topic, in order to break through the wall of ignorance and malicious misinformation. Since the majority of states wanted to keep minority rights at as low a level as possible, the Hungarian government's minority protection policy received little outside support, and was often—either sincerely or out of self-interest—seen as a destabilizing factor.[99]

The CSCE faced serious challenges after the signing of the Charter of Paris in 1990. First in the disintegrating Yugoslavia, then in the successor states of the Soviet Union. The root cause of the conflicts in the post-Communist countries was intolerance towards national minorities. This was at the heart of my address to the Stockholm meeting of the organization's Ministerial Council on December 14, 1992. I welcomed NATO's offer to contribute to peacekeeping. "There are conflicts in Karabakh, Georgia, Moldova and Tajikistan," I said, emphasizing that these armed clashes between ethnic groups were claiming many lives. The CSCE could mediate, send observers and then strictly impartial peacekeepers, preferably with the participation of Russians and other CIS countries. I warmly appreciated the creation of the institution of the High Commissioner on National Minorities and welcomed its first occupant, Max van den Stoel, who served from 1993 to 2001.[100] I called for the principles and obligations of the CSCE to be made better known and to be enforced, involving not only governments but also NGOs and national minority organizations.[101]

To date, the CSCE recommendations of June 1990 go the furthest in terms of national minority rights, but these are not binding. The same can be said of the UN General Assembly's Declaration on the Rights of Persons Belonging to National or Ethnic, Religious and Linguistic Minorities, adopted on December 18, 1992.[102] The principles laid down in this Declaration are beautiful, implicitly containing the right to autonomy and self-determination, but it is "soft law," it has no coercive force, and its implementation depends on the readiness and goodwill of the individual

---

[99] Memo for a meeting of the Foreign Ministry leadership on the foreign image of Hungary and its neighbors. Among my papers.
[100] Max van den Stoel (1924–2011): Dutch Socialist politician and diplomat.
[101] *Magyar Külpolitikai Évkönyv, 1992*, 360–65.
[102] "Resolution Adopted by the General Assembly, 47/135: Declaration on the Rights of Persons Belonging to National or Ethnic, Religious and Linguistic Minorities," December 12, 1992, http://www.un-documents.net/a47r135.htm.

states.¹⁰³ Nevertheless, the Ministry of Foreign Affairs attached great importance to the fact that the protection of minority rights was enshrined as a basic condition for the democratic functioning of states. In drafting the Declaration, the Republic of Hungary called for a high standard in the definition of these rights, pointing out that this was also a guarantee of security. An essential achievement was the statement that minority rights were not only the rights of individuals but also could be exercised in community with the other members of their group. The Declaration made it the responsibility of states to promote the rights of minorities and to cooperate internationally in this area.

We expressed our hope that this Declaration would be the starting point for a binding codification of minority rights.¹⁰⁴ However, the so-called international community, seeing the opposition by many states, became less and less inclined to adopt binding standards, especially since it had no means of enforcing them. Many states, because of their own minorities, were explicitly opposed to strengthening minority rights. Since 1992, particularly in response to István Csurka's infamous, intolerant pamphlet of August that year,¹⁰⁵ governments have either avoided taking a position in disputes between Hungary and its neighbors on the Hungarian minority issue, or have considered Hungarian concerns to be unjustified or exaggerated.¹⁰⁶ Entering 1993, Hungary nevertheless had high hopes that the new CSCE institution for the protection of minorities, the High Commissioner on National Minorities, and the Council of Europe would be able to enforce their own standards. The test came with the break-up of Czechoslovakia, as both successor states had to apply for admission to both of the institutions promoting the rights of national minorities.

---

[103] This handicap is pointed out by several authors, including Balázs Majtényi, "Az ENSZ és a kisebbségek védelme" [The UN and the Protection of Minorities], *Kisebbségkutatás* 12, no. 1 (2003).

[104] Statement of the Government of the Republic of Hungary on the Rights of Minorities adopted by the UN General Assembly, December 19, 1992. *Magyar Külpolitikai Évkönyv, 1992*, 373–74.

[105] See chapter 2, footnote 45 in this volume.

[106] This is confirmed by a report compiled by the Ministry of Foreign Affairs at the request of the prime minister and submitted on October 9, 1992, entitled "Magyarország és a kelet-közép-európai térség megítélése" [Hungary and the perception of the Central and Eastern European region]. Among my papers.

Chapter 8

Czechs and Slovaks: The "Velvet Divorce"

At the beginning of 1991, the Soviet Union still seemed to be in crisis, but was still holding firm: in January in Vilnius, the capital of the Lithuanian Socialist Soviet Republic, a peaceful demonstration for independence was broken up by Soviet special forces, claiming fourteen lives. In Yugoslavia Milošević was still holding on to power, and in Bratislava there were leaflets calling for military action against "the enemies of the Slovaks: the Hungarians, the Czechs and the Jews, as well as the renegade Slovaks."[1] One wing of the VPN party (Public Against Violence) led by Slovak prime minister Mečiar, barely concealed its efforts to create an independent Slovak State.[2] According to some reports that came to my attention, they were backed by the Soviet secret service, with the aim of driving a pro-Moscow "independent" Slovakia as a wedge, to split the pro-Western Visegrád group. This plan even included making Hungary (or just the Hungarians in Slovakia) believe that the Hungarian-inhabited parts of Czechoslovakia could return to the motherland (thus also scaring the Slovaks). Hungary's ambassador in Prague, György Varga (1954–), warned in a letter: "All political forces at home must know that whatever siren voices one hear from Slovak politicians (whether communists, members of the Slovak National Party or the present-day political leaders) who, naively or under foreign payroll, are calling for the creation of an independent Slovak state, and promise to improve the conditions of the Hungarian minority, must be aware that not a word of this will become reality."[3] The ambassador proved to be a better oracle than many Hungarian politicians in Hungary or Slovakia.

---

[1] The leaflet of the "Slovak Republican Army" was published in *HTMT Tájékoztató*, no. 5 (1991): Item 1 (March).

[2] An early and comprehensive analysis of the story of the break-up of Czechoslovakia is Judit Hamberger, *Csehszlovákia szétválása: Egy föderációs kísérlet kudarca* [The separation of Czechoslovakia: The failure of an attempt for a federation] (Budapest: Teleki László Alapítvány, 1997). Cf. Bohumil Doležal, "A csehszlovák államszövetség felbomlása mint közép-európai stabilitási tényező" [The break-up of the Czechoslovak state union as a factor of stability in Central Europe], *Európai Szemmel*, nos. 2–3 (1999): 51–59. An excellent study, using newly released archival material is Miklós Mitrovits, "Csehszlovákia felbomlása és a magyar politika (1989–1993)" [The break-up of Czechoslovakia and the policy of Hungary, 1989–1993], *Múltunk*, no. 1 (2013): 148–76.

[3] Letter from Ambassador György Varga to Foreign Minister Jeszenszky, March 13, 1991.

In the Czech Republic—as my visit in August 1990 proved—there was little trace of Beneš's blindly anti-Hungarian and pro-Russian attitude. The crushing of the Prague Spring, the signs of solidarity from Hungary, especially in 1989, leading to the "velvet revolution" in November, had cured society of both. From the 1960s onwards, Slovak nationalism was directed more towards the Czechs than the Hungarians; after the political change President Havel and his circle attempted to curb the anti-Hungarian tendencies that were emerging in Slovakia. In the Visegrád Cooperation, the Czechs were active, the Slovaks simply took note of the new friendship. At the tripartite summit in May 1992, the Hungarian prime minister and the president of Czechoslovakia got on very well, and discussed how the likely disintegration of Czechoslovakia would affect the Hungarian community in Slovakia.[4]

Following the May 1991 elections, two forces competed for power in Slovakia, Ján Čarnogurský's Christian Democrats and Vladimír Mečiar's nationalists. Both wanted separation. Of the three parties of the Hungarian community of 567,000 people (in the 1991 census), the Independent Hungarian Initiative was in favor of Czechoslovak unity, and looked to the Czechs to protect the Hungarian minority from Slovak nationalists. At the beginning of September, the Co-existence Party (Együttélés), led by Miklós Duray, asked Czech prime minister Pithart and Deputy Federal Prime Minister Pavel Rychetský about this. According to a report by our consul general in Bratislava, they could not guarantee an improvement in the legal status and living conditions of Hungarians, even if the federation were to survive. Mečiar, on the other hand, promised to meet "special nationality needs" in education and other areas if he came to power, which Duray said was almost certain, and the Slovak prime minister also showed a willingness to build contacts with the MDF. Even Čarnogurský showed some sympathy for the Hungarians' demand for territorial and/or cultural autonomy, but, claiming that it would raise the possibility of border changes, he nevertheless described it as dangerous and unsupportable.[5] I very much regret that this lawyer-politician, who courageously stood up to the dictatorship, has moved farther and farther away from recognizing the grievances of the Hungarian minority, and lately continues to say that "the Hungarians are behaving as if we have stolen something from them." On what basis can he speak in such a way of the Hungarian-Slovak border, drawn in 1920 in gross violation of the ethnic principle?[6]

---

[4] My personal recollection.
[5] Consul General Jenő Boros to Géza Jeszenszky, September 9, 1991.
[6] On the drawing of the border between Czechoslovakia and Hungary, see Géza Jeszenszky, "The British Role in Assigning Csallóköz (Zitny Ostrov, Grosse Schütt) to Czechoslovakia," in *British-Hungarian Relations*

At the end of September 1991, according to our consul general in Bratislava, "the supporters of the federation had already given up the struggle to prevent the declaration of independence, and on the Czech side some people seem to be advocating it. It is increasingly urgent to prepare for such an eventuality on the Hungarian side as well."[7] It seems that the Hungarians in Slovakia, and in their wake the Hungarian representation in Bratislava, had hopes that an independent Slovakia would pursue a more fair policy towards the Hungarian minority. For me it is now clear that this was a deliberate deception on the part of the Slovaks, hoping that the Hungarians in Slovakia would refrain from taking up the idea of self-determination themselves. It was a telling sign of such Slovak thinking that, although the text of the Czechoslovak-Hungarian basic treaty was essentially ready by October 1991, to be signed at the Visegrád summit in Cracow, at the last minute it was postponed, due to Slovak objections to the points on minority protection it contained. However, we were not prepared to conclude a treaty without such articles or with their deletion.[8]

Slovak-Hungarian conflict over the Danube barrage project

The existence of Hungarians in Czechoslovakia was not the only cause of tension with our northern neighbor. In Hungary, many people remember that a catalyst of the regime change was the mass movement in 1988 against building the Gabčíkovo/Bős–Nagymaros Waterworks, which was based on ecological arguments. As a result, the Németh government halted the construction at Nagymaros in May 1989 and began negotiations with its Czechoslovak partner on the future of the joint project. On August 31, 1989, Czechoslovak prime minister Adamec informed Hungary in a letter that if the Hungarian side did not continue with the construction work, the Gabčíkovo/Bős power plant would be commissioned by diverting the Danube into a canal under construction on Czechoslovak territory—a plan known as Variant C. On October 31, the Hungarian Parliament voted that Hungary would definitively abandon the construction of the dam and power plant at Nagymaros and would make the continuation of construction of the Danube dam at Gabčíkovo/Bős subject to a new inter-state agreement.

Since 1848, ed. László Péter and Martyn Rady (London: Hungarian Cultural Centre and School of Slavonic and East European Studies University College, 2004), 123–38.
[7] Consul General Jenő Boros to Géza Jeszenszky, September 20, 1991. A similar conclusion was reached by the HTMH, *HTMH Tájékoztató*, no. 10 (1991): item 3, 5–11.
[8] The somewhat later Slovak draft (March 20, 1992) included a clause on the mutual renunciation of territorial claims, with only a vague reference to the relevant documents of the CSCE on the rights of minorities. I saw no point in signing such a treaty.

After the "Velvet Revolution" in Czechoslovakia, the new government stopped the construction, and on May 21, 1990, it backed out of the project, leaving it to the Slovak government to settle the dispute.[9] Regardless of party affiliation and convinced of the serious danger of environmental damage, a strong majority of the members of the Hungarian National Assembly, formed after the April 1990 elections, staunchly opposed the whole scheme. Irreversible damage to the environment, poisoning the drinking water of millions of people, destruction of flora and fauna, Stalinist mega-investment—this was the prevailing public opinion regarding the project. The majority identified the planned dams with the communist system and believed that this was what the Czechs and Slovaks thought as well, so they would agree that the project was dangerous and should be abandoned. The Hungarian Parliament also accepted without hesitation that we should pay the Austrian contractor of the Nagymaros power station 2,881 billion schillings in compensation for cancelling the construction.

On the Hungarian side, the government tried to keep the debate within a framework of scientific and environmental protection, free of any political character, and it sought agreement on this basis, with international involvement if necessary. Soon, however, both the Czech and Slovak governments treated the power plant plan as a kind of prestige investment and insisted on the implementation of the 1977 interstate agreement, i.e., construction of both stages of the project. After unsuccessful negotiations, on April 23, 1991, Resolution 26/1991 of the Hungarian National Assembly authorized the Hungarian government to negotiate the joint termination of the 1977 interstate treaty and to prepare a new interstate treaty, in which the primary aspect would be the joint protection of environmental-ecological values.

The Czechoslovak government, however, considered that the arguments raised by the Hungarian side were unfounded, that there was no threat of an "ecological disaster," that there was no danger of earthquakes, and that issues of flood protection and navigation would require completion of the whole project. It was prepared to seek the opinion of foreign experts but refused to stop construction on Czechoslovak territory until the studies were completed. In Prague, and even more so in Bratislava, it was felt that the Hungarian side would not listen to Czech and Slovak arguments for domestic political reasons, because of the rigid opposition

---

[9] Sáringer, *Iratok az Antall-kormány*, vol. 3/2 (1992) contains a number of documents pertaining to the debate, 49–117 (Docs. 201–217).
A good, neutral summary of the case is provided in the Wikipedia entry "Gabčíkovo–Nagymaros Dams," https://en.wikipedia.org/wiki/Gab%C4%8D%C3%ADkovo%E2%80%93Nagymaros_Dams;
Cf. Owen McIntyre, "Gabčíkovo-Nagymaros Project: A Test Case for International Water Law?," in *Transboundary Water Management: Principles and Practice*, ed. Anton Earle, Anders Jagerskog and Joakim Öjendal (Stockholm International Water Institute, 2010).

of the majority of MPs. In an unprecedented move, Josef Vavroušek, a respected environmentalist and Czechoslovakia's Minister for Environment, with a laudable opposition record, asked to make his views known in the Hungarian Parliament in the hope of persuading the members. Speaker György Szabad, appreciating the willingness to reach an agreement, allowed him to speak, which was indeed unprecedented. However, the serious arguments put forward did not convince the Hungarian MPs. Clearly there was a cross-party coalition on the "damned dam" issue, determined to prevent at least the Nagymaros plant, so there was no room for compromise or even arguments.

On December 12, 1991, the Czechoslovak government decided to put Variant C into operation the following autumn, i.e., to divert the Danube on Czechoslovak territory into the canal leading to the power plant at Gabčíkovo/Bős. The majority of the MPs believed that Variant C was physically impossible, just a "paper tiger" that the Slovaks were using as blackmail to get the Hungarians to go ahead with the construction of Nagymaros. I am not a technical expert, but I, too, feared that the huge drinking water reservoir, suspected to lie deep below the surface, might be contaminated. However, on the basis of reliable expert opinions I considered the diversion, planned by Slovakia, to be feasible. This would, however, put the key to the whole power plant, the control of the flow of water, into Slovak hands. This was worse than the original plan itself. György Sámsondi Kiss, the extremely well-intentioned Hungarian government commissioner, was eager for a compromise, but the Environment Committee of the Hungarian Parliament overruled him.[10] József Antall was aware that a compromise solution would have provoked fierce opposition in the Hungarian Parliament and would probably have led to the government's defeat. The prime minister's attitude was determined by this.

For my part, I stressed in every forum that the issue of the barrage debate was not a political one, but was primarily a technical and environmental problem that should not be turned into a Hungarian-Slovakian dispute. I also cautioned that the Trianon Peace Treaty designated the middle of the Danube's main drift line (the shipping lane) as the border between Hungary and Czechoslovakia, and the diversion would change that. Would Czechoslovakia be prepared to cede the part of the land south of the canal, the new shipping route, to Hungary? It turned out that the two communist governments understood each other well in this respect and had

---

[10] E-mail from Sámsondi Kiss to me, June 24, 2015. Among my papers. For more details, see György Sámsondi Kiss, *A Duna mégis összeköt—Egy kormánybiztos vallomásai* [The Danube still binds us: Confessions of a government commissioner] (Budapest: Kairosz, 2019).

already agreed in 1958 that "the border line shall not be affected by changes in the course of the border river."[11]

The construction work continued east of Bratislava. The Slovak government commissioner, Julius Binder, who spoke Slovak and Hungarian equally well, made confident statements about its progress, and even teased the Hungarian side that it would sooner or later build the dam and power plant at Nagymaros, too. Almost no one listened to the warning sent to the prime minister's Advisory Council on February 12, 1992, by a sober Hungarian expert, Péter Szabó, a district leader of the MDF. Based on his experience gained visiting the proposed site of the diversion, he concluded that the "paper tiger" was in fact a well-organized effort to divert the Danube and that nothing could stop "the worst," i.e., version C, from being realized. It was a great mistake, he wrote, "not to have tried to weigh the other side's point of view, in the conceited belief of our truth. [...] we did not put forward any proposal smacking of a compromise. In addition, we failed to win over foreign countries, major Western European lobbies and governments are clearly on the Slovak side, at best neutral." This expert also severely criticized the irresponsible advisers of Minister Mádl, who was responsible for the project in the government.[12]

On April 4, 1992, the Hungarian Parliament authorized (practically obliged) the government to unilaterally terminate the 1977 interstate treaty, and it was duly done on May 7.[13] Antall's correspondence with Czechoslovak prime minister Václav Klaus failed to produce any results,[14] so Hungary finally proposed that the two countries take the matter to the International Court of Justice in The Hague.[15] József Antall criticized the planned unilateral Slovak move in a tough speech at the opening ceremony of the Rhine–Main–Danube canal in Nuremberg on September 25, 1992, as "ecologically dangerous, economically unviable, a plan that violates political borders [...] inherited from the communist governments and imposed on us for our lack of sovereignty."[16] Although the EC repeatedly warned both parties to refrain from "unilateral action" (i.e., diversion) and from any violence, Slovakia nevertheless started to block and divert the Danube on October 23, 1991, and successfully completed the job by October 25.

---

[11] Treaty between the Czechoslovak Republic and the Hungarian People's Republic on State Borders, October 18, 1958, Article 3 (1).
[12] Memorandum from Péter Szabó to Gyula Kodolányi, State Secretary, February 12, 1992. Among my papers.
[13] *Magyar Külpolitikai Évkönyv, 1992*, 172–74.
[14] Letter from József Antall to Václav Klaus, May 19, 1992, reply from Klaus, August 6, 1992. Among my papers.
[15] Letter of József Antall to Václav Klaus and Vladimir Mečiar, August 28, 1992. Among my papers. (Strangely, Sáringer, *Iratok az Antall-kormány*, vol. 3 does not contain this important document.)
[16] *Magyar Külpolitikai Évkönyv, 1992*, 268–71, quotation 270.

The Hungarian government's statement condemned the action in the strongest terms, stating that the diversion

> violates the sovereignty and territorial integrity of the Hungarian state, which is protected by the fundamental norms of international law; it is contrary to the principle of the inviolability of state borders; [...] The diversion is also contrary to the 1976 agreement between the two states on the management of water in the border areas, which makes any intervention subject to the agreement of both parties. It is incompatible with the rules and principles of international law on the use of international resources.[17]

The Hungarian government turned to the International Court of Justice in The Hague and to the EU Commission. On October 27, 1992, at a conciliatory meeting organized by the EU, the two parties signed the so-called London Protocol: they agreed to jointly submit the dispute between the two countries to the International Court of Justice in The Hague and to introduce a temporary water-sharing regime until the court's ruling, whereby Slovakia would release at least 95 percent of the Danube water into its original riverbed.[18] However, this has never happened, despite the European Communities' expectations.[19] Finally, the joint submission of the dispute by Hungary and Slovakia to The Hague reduced tensions between the two neighbors. Antall facilitated this with letters to Delors, president of the EC Commission, and Chancellor Kohl and Prime Minister Mečiar.[20]

The debate about what should have been done has been going on ever since. Stop the diversion with a peaceful human blockade? Béla Lipták, who travelled from the United States to the site for that purpose, was joined there by a dozen or so protesters. Or prevent the Danube from being blocked by force, by bombing? Since the diversion was on Czechoslovak territory, that would have been considered military aggression. We knew that in Europe it was not only morally unacceptable to launch an armed action, but that the initiator would pay a very heavy price. The Serbs had done so, the result being hundreds of thousands of dead and a small Serbia with nearly a million Serbs outside its borders. For the government to risk armed conflict would have been political suicide, and such a move would

---

[17] Statement of the Government of the Republic of Hungary on its position on the Bős-Nagymaros barrage system, October 23, 1992. *Magyar Külpolitikai Évkönyv, 1992*, 326–30.

[18] Protocol of the negotiations on the Bős-Nagymaros barrage system in London, October 27, 1992. *Magyar Külpolitikai Évkönyv, 1992*, 330–31.

[19] Letter from F.H.J.J. Andriessen, vice-president of the EC Commission to Foreign Minister Jeszenszky, November 18, 1992. Among my papers.

[20] I have a copy of Antall's letters of February 5, 1993.

have been condemned in the strongest terms by the EC, NATO and the UN. It would also have taken our integration ambitions off the agenda for a long time. The Czechoslovak government made it clear that, despite the ongoing divorce, the entire army was ready to defend the territorial integrity of Slovakia. Several of our neighbors would have sided with Czechoslovakia, and its army alone was much stronger militarily than the Hungarian army.[21] Slovakia was also prepared to use its army against ethnic minorities loyal to another state in the event of internal ethnic unrest.[22] At any rate, the Hungarian electorate did not incline towards military action. Should we have tried international action to prevent Czechoslovakia from taking unilateral action? We tried to do so, and there were some warnings from the European Community to both capitals, but the Czech and Slovak governments refused to allow the planned trilateral committee of experts to draw up its recommendation for a resolution of the inter-state dispute while suspending the river diversion. The Slovaks sensed that the European Community was the paper tiger on the Danube dam issue.

In my opinion, the only better solution would have been a timely compromise, a version D, accepting the operation of the Gabčíkovo plant, controlling the flow of water into the canal from Dunakiliti, on Hungarian territory. Slovakia was ready to accept that. Just think: without the costly and ultimately fruitless Hague litigation, the power plant in Slovakia would be operating, the energy produced would be shared, and the key to water sharing would be in Hungarian hands! But opposition to the waterworks was a symbol of the change of regime in Hungary; rejection of any compromise and confidence in the support of the international environmental lobby were both strong. The majority of the Parliament (not the government!) was intransigent, so the responsibility lies with the obstinate members. We know the rest: the Hague lawsuit ended in an apparently indecisive but certainly unfavorable outcome for us, the power plant at Gabčíkovo is in operation, producing electricity, half of which should belong to Hungary. Sadly, neither a financial nor a technical agreement has been reached in the intervening thirty-three years.

Although Hungary showed restraint throughout the conflict, and even the diversion of the Danube did not provoke widespread anti-Slovak sentiment, in Slovakia the "success" fueled anti-Hungarian nationalism and strengthened Mečiar and his nationalist tendencies.

---

[21] Under the 1989 Comprehensive Force Reduction (CFE) agreement, Slovakia was allowed to have 478 tanks, 683 armored personnel carriers, 115 combat aircraft and 25 combat helicopters after the split, and in 1993 it "inherited" a considerable proportion of arms from Czechoslovakia, with more than 35,000 personnel.

[22] I received an intelligence report about that.

Hungarian aspects of the "velvet divorce"

In the June 1992 elections in the Czech Republic, Václav Klaus's Civic Democratic Party (ODS), which could be called a moderately nationalist party, won most of the votes, while in Slovakia the Mečiar-led Movement for Democratic Slovakia (HZDS) did so. In the course of a few months of negotiations, they came to a smooth agreement on the separation of the two nations. That agreement would surely have been rejected in a referendum (a 1991 poll showed that only 9 percent of Czechs and 15 percent of Slovaks supported the idea of a separate state), nevertheless on January 1, 1993, the separation, usually called the "velvet divorce" did take place. Slovakia became Hungary's neighbor, with which we share our longest border.

Even after the break-up of Yugoslavia and the Soviet Union, the Czechoslovakia split took the world by surprise—although, given a modest knowledge of twentieth century European history, this could not have been unexpected. When self-conscious independent nations emerged from the ruins of federations artificially put together after the Second World War, the only question was whether Slovaks could be satisfied with a hyphenated Czecho-Slovakia or a longer name: the Czech and Slovak Federal Republic. It was not necessary to recall the Slovak State created by Hitler and led by the pro-Nazi puppet Tiso (1939–1945), to know that "at the foot of the Tatra Mountains," there lived a nation whose people were not Czechs. After the change of regime, the federation of the two, in principle equal parties, was welcomed by the majority of the two peoples. The Slovak political elite, however, increasingly saw the Czechs as foreign rulers, who, in 1919, had simply replaced the Hungarians. Václav Klaus, the winner of the 1992 elections, liked to say privately that the Czech Republic, once having gotten rid of the Slovak millstone, would be one of Europe's most successful states.

Why was the West so afraid of the disappearance of its 1918 creation, of the separation of the two kindred nations? It was not unrealistic to assume that, in contrast to the decidedly Western orientation of the Czech Republic, Slovakia would turn towards Russia and the other two members of the former Little Entente, the Serbian strongman and his business partner Iliescu. The suspicion that there was a secret American-Russian deal behind the split was a fantasy.[23] The bloody break-up of Yugoslavia may have indeed been seen as a warning, but the relationship between the Czechs and Slovaks was quite different from the deep religious and historical differences that existed between the southern Slav peoples. There was already a counter-example in the unexpectedly smooth break-up of the Soviet

---

[23] Hamberger, *Csehszlovákia szétválása*, 177–82.

Union. In any case, the Western newspapers tried to "dissuade" the Slovaks from secession by "discovering" the Hungarians in Slovakia. Not since Trianon had so many newspaper articles about them, often illustrated with maps, appeared as in 1992, openly alarming the Slovaks about what would happen if the Hungarians followed their example and "self-determined" their secession from the country? In this situation, Hungary, surrounded by suspicion, could only say that it respected the right of all peoples to self-determination. We knew that not only President Havel, but perhaps the Czech people themselves, were a guarantee that anti-Hungarian Slovak nationalism would be kept in check, and that check was now going to disappear. At the same time, we could only look with understanding at the independence aspirations of the Slovaks, who lived within Hungary for a thousand years, who were similar to the Hungarians in taste, tradition and religion, and who were linked to us by a thousand family ties. I expressed this dual sentiment by participating in the aforementioned "summit" in August 1991 on the highest point in the old Hungary and the defunct Czechoslovakia, the Gerlachovský štít at 2665 meters.

Ahead of the elections, perhaps in the hope of improving his center-right government's chances, or as a kind of political testament, Pavol Demeš, Slovakia's minister for international relations, visited Budapest on April 22. His talks focused on the minority problem. I drew his attention to the Western Europe's experience that a minority with rights and a secure future strengthens the state and does not see its future only in secession. Thinking of the 60,000 strong Slovak community in Vojvodina, he agreed to jointly support the endangered national minorities of Serbia. We agreed that Eastern Slovakia would also participate in the Hungarian-initiated Carpathian-Tisza Working Community. I proposed the (re)opening of several Hungarian-Slovak border crossings. Demeš accepted that the two peoples' views of history should be brought closer together and did not dispute that the Hungarians in Slovakia deserved moral, legal and financial compensation for the persecutions of 1945–48. Although he resented the fact that senior Hungarian civil servants were visiting the Hungarian-inhabited areas of Slovakia without a formal request from the Slovak authorities, he ultimately accepted that there was nothing objectionable about that. We also agreed that we should mutually support the culture and education of our minorities in each other's country. My partner proudly mentioned that in Slovakia, the Ukrainian, or Ruthenian, nationality was "enjoying a renaissance." He said that even given the problems, the situation of Hungarians in Slovakia was better than was the average in Europe. This was, of course, self-deception. In a similar vein, Demeš also had discussions with Géza Entz, who recommended for his attention and accession the Hungarian-Ukrainian minority declaration, which Croatia has since joined. He also suggested that Slovaks and

Hungarians in Slovakia should learn each other's languages. János Wolfart, president of the Office for National and Ethnic Minorities, informed our guest about the work being done for the Slovaks of Hungary.[24]

If Pavol Demeš's understanding and good intentions had not been a rarity in Slovak political life, if a more tolerant policy towards the Hungarian minority had not been defeated in the Czechoslovak elections in June 1992, both the political image of Slovakia and Hungarian-Slovak relations would have been different in the following years. Unfortunately, however, in June, Mečiar's nationalist and populist rhetoric defeated the more enlightened tendencies, and the two victors in the two parts of the country agreed in short order to implement the separation without consulting the citizens. Hungary had no option but to accept this and offer both states close, friendly relations.

There are people in Hungary who ask why Hungary did not make territorial claims against Slovakia separating. According to the 1975 Helsinki Final Act, European borders can be changed by peaceful mutual agreement. (At that time there was the West's hope for the unification of the two Germanies.) Why did the Hungarians in Slovakia and their parties not raise the issue that the outside world feared so much: their secession from Slovakia? The most likely reason was the knowledge that since Trianon, or the first Vienna Award in 1938, ethnic proportions had changed radically. In most towns in southern Slovakia, which used to be inhabited mainly by Hungarians, the post-war expulsion of Hungarians and the population exchange with Hungary, followed by large-scale industrialization and housing development, resulted in many settlements in which Slovaks became the majority. In the event of a referendum, these towns would hardly have voted for Hungary. The Hungarian politicians in Slovakia were aware of this, and it was not cowardice but realism which guided them; their goal was Hungarian autonomy within Slovakia. The attitude of the Hungarian government was determined to a decisive extent by the will and behavior of the Hungarians in Slovakia. The Co-existence Party (*Együttélés*) and the Hungarian Christian Democratic Movement declared that the Hungarian community in Slovakia did not wish to secede from Slovakia but demanded territorial autonomy.[25] In the second half of 1992, Miklós Duray, the president of Co-Existence, told me privately that the situation of the Hungarians in Slovakia might temporarily deteriorate with the loss of the moderating influence of the more enlightened Czechs, but in the future, in a much smaller country,

---

[24] Report to the government on the visit of Pavol Demeš to Hungary, April 30, 1992. Sáringer, *Iratok az Antall-kormány*, vol. 3/2: 755–60 (Doc. 172).

[25] The situation of Hungarians in Czechoslovakia after the elections. Memorandum of the 3rd regional department of the Ministry, June 23, 1992. Among my papers.

having a greater weight in terms of their proportion, the Hungarians would be able to defend their interests more successfully and could win territorial autonomy. He proved to be mistaken.

The Hungarian offer

The precedent, the ideal example, was arrived at in the summer of 1992. On June 11, 1992, Austria accepted that the 137-point package guaranteeing the rights and future of the 300,000 German-speaking inhabitants of the northern part South Tyrol, annexed by Italy in 1919, had been fulfilled. It would have made sense for Slovakia, which was embarking on the road to statehood, to adopt this model, all the more so as the historical background and ethnic composition of South Tyrol and South Slovakia have similarities.

The Government Declaration issued on August 18, 1992, on the eve of the Third World Congress of Hungarians, was a summary of the principles which Hungary held then and has held ever since on the relationship between national minorities and the majority nation. Its wording has remained valid as the foundation for internal stability in states with substantial national minorities, and for tension-free inter-state relations. If a Slovakia that wanted to live in harmony and friendship with its Hungarian neighbor, based on European values and examples, had adopted this program, its historic achievement would have gone beyond the exemplary settlement of relations between two post-communist countries. It is worth quoting in detail from this sensible Hungarian offer:

> A precondition for the stability and security of Central and Eastern Europe is that the various minorities (national, ethnic, religious and political) should not become victims of the state's power politics. In our region, during the 20th century [...] the state did not function as an institution for the common good of all citizens, but became the property of the majority nation. In this context, minorities were viewed with suspicion, their loyalty as citizens was questioned, and efforts to preserve their language and culture were often declared an attack on the order and unity of the state. Unfortunately, the peoples and states that have sought their place after the collapse of the communist regime tend to revert to this double-standard nationalism, to the outmoded idea of national exclusivity. This is one of the greatest obstacles to the democratic transformation of our region. [...] In the wake of the crimes committed in the South Slav lands joint action is needed in order to put an end not only to all bloodshed, but also to incitement to hatred against

minorities, to the efforts of presenting them as enemies of the state, and to endeavor to change the ethnic composition of a territory by artificial means, by expulsions and resettlements.

In the opinion of the Antall government the integration of Western Europe showed that the idea of the nation-state had outlived its time, the "ethnically pure state" is anachronistic, as the nineteenth century Hungarian political scientist József Eötvös noted: "The world is moving towards the general application of the federal principle." The Declaration of August 18 went on:

> The way to the construction of a peaceful new order of states and nations can only come through the constitutional recognition of national and ethnic diversity within states. The necessary compromises should be reached on the basis of a democratic dialogue between the states and the national and ethnic minorities living in their territories. [...] The Hungarian communities living in the Carpathian Basin participate in the legislative and local government bodies of their countries by the will of their voters. Their aspirations do not call into question the given state framework; within it they wish to create the constitutional and legal forms necessary for their self-organization, the exercise of their rights and the guarantee of their cultural autonomy. The various concepts of autonomy are part of this process. Considering the specific situations of minorities, this could be a system of personal autonomy in the case of dispersed minorities, self-government in the case of local minorities, and territorial autonomy in the case when they are the majority in a compact territory. The visions of the national minorities for their own future fit into the current European tendencies, and offer a good basis for cooperation between Hungary and the neighboring states in the field of minority policy [...] thus bringing us closer to the lasting stability and integration of the whole of Europe.[26]

While these principles are followed in many European countries, in Central and Eastern Europe they still seem utopian, but it is precisely their lack of application that is at the root of both the lethargy among the minorities caused by the loss of hope, and the conflicts that are flaring up.

---

[26] Declaration of the Government of the Republic of Hungary on the Hungarian Minorities, August 18, 1992. *Magyar Külpolitikai Évkönyv, 1992*, 272–74.

Figure 26. Ministerial meeting of the North Atlantic Cooperation Council: with Slovak FM Milan Kňažko, December 18, 1992

The Hungarians in Slovakia assumed that if the Slovaks, who were really afraid of the secession of their Hungarian population, calmed down, they would be able to approach with greater generosity the Hungarian demands for internal self-determination, territorial autonomy and bilingualism in southern Slovakia, seeing that their fears were groundless. And in Hungary, many of us hoped that by becoming independent and freeing themselves of a kind of minority complex, Slovaks—like Croats—would actually identify with our common past, and that national minorities living on each other's territory, witnesses to a common past, would indeed form a link, a bridge between the two countries. The Hungarian government knew that the chances of this optimistic scenario in a Mečiar-led government were not very high, but it was worth making an attempt, a gesture. It was in this spirit that I travelled to Bratislava on September 2, 1992, at the invitation of Demeš's successor, Foreign Minister Milan Kňažko.[27]

My talk at the Club of Diplomats in Bratislava was titled "The Road to Slovak-Hungarian Reconciliation," and I started with my personal recollections:

---

[27] Milan Kňažko (1945–): Slovak actor and politician. A leading personality in the Velvet Revolution, he was minister of Foreign Affairs (1992–1993) and Minister for Culture (1998–2002).

Chapter 8 – Czechs and Slovaks: The "Velvet Divorce"

Growing up in the decades of communism, I deeply believed that common suffering would bring solidarity and friendship among the oppressed peoples. In 1956, at the time of our national struggle for freedom, we did not experience any signs of this, either on the Slovak or on the Czech side, but we Hungarians proclaimed and were very serious about reconciliation between the peoples of the Danube region who became free. Although in 1968 Hungarian soldiers were ordered by Moscow to take part in the suppression of the attempt to give socialism a human face, those who remember those tragic days bear witness to the huge scale of sympathy and support for that attempt that Hungarians on both sides of the Danube.

On the issue that concerned Slovaks at the time most, I said: "One of the principles of the reborn Hungarian democracy is that the right of nations to self-determination cannot be applied selectively. [...] Hungary accepts that Slovakia wants to be present in Europe as an independent international entity in the future." The main message of my speech, however, was about the future:

> Reconciliation between nations, especially neighboring nations, is the order of the day at the end of the twentieth century. The peoples of Central and Eastern Europe must turn their old disputes into history, a chapter in the school textbooks, embraced by the teachers, the students and all the citizens, just as the nations of the West have done. [...] It is our common goal and in our common interest that the national communities living in our countries could preserve their identity, possess the necessary constitutional and legal guarantees for this, and be able to foster without hindrance maintain their relations with their mother country, with the nation of which they are an integral part. To this end, they must be able to take an active part in reaching and implementing the decisions that secure their survival. One evidence of the strength of these communities is their own self-organization, and, of course, their ability to take part in the democratic processes through their legitimately elected representatives. One of the conditions for avoiding ethnic conflicts and integrating the minorities within the country is that there be constant communication between the governments and the representatives of the national minorities. These are not radically new ideas. A Briton, Seton-Watson, alias Scotus Viator, perhaps the greatest foreign friend of the Slovak people, and a man whose work I studied myself for several years, included in the Memorandum he sent to President Masaryk in 1928, among other things, a call for bilingual place names, street names

and official announcements, widespread official use of the Hungarian language in districts with a Hungarian majority, the organization of administrative units on ethnic lines, and the full development and maintenance of a Hungarian-language school system, including the establishment of a Hungarian-language university.[28]

My presentation to the Slovak minister, to ambassadors and journalists did not bring forth any tangible response from the Slovak politicians and society to which it was addressed. Nor did the memorandum prepared by the Hungarian Christian Democratic Movement in Slovakia, which realistically presented the situation of Hungarians in Slovakia, have any significant impact. "After the changes of 1989," it said, "our rights have not been extended, but on the contrary, we have to face more and more often the attempts to curtail them." It listed the problems in fourteen points and proposed remedies. The remedy for the decline in numbers and proportions was decentralization and administrative units that reflected ethnic composition. It called for educational and cultural self-government, partial bilingualism and a law on minorities.[29]

The Slovak response

When Slovakia was about to become independent, was it unforgivable naivety to have expected an honest, reasonable policy towards its Hungarian minority, in line with European standards and Western European practice? The omens, the behavior of Mečiar, the Slovak National Party and the organization Matica Slovenská were indeed not encouraging.[30] On September 1, 1992, the National Council of Slovakia ratified the constitution with the wording "We, the Slovak nation," completely ignoring the opinions and proposals of the opposition (not only of Hungarians). The document did not even mention the national minorities, which made up a good 15 percent of the country's population. Apart from empty phrases, it did not provide any concrete guarantees for the linguistic, educational and cultural rights

---

[28] "The Road to Slovak Hungarian Reconciliation." My presentation in Bratislava at the Club of Diplomats on September 2, 1992. *Magyar Külpolitikai Évkönyv, 1992*, 291–301.
[29] Memorandum of the Hungarian Christian Democratic Movement, October 1992. Among my papers.
[30] A typical example is the Slovak leaflet in Hungarian, which was dropped into the mailboxes of Hungarians by Slovak nationalists. It called the Hungarians murderous, yellow Asians who had subjugated the good Slovaks. It insulted these "renegade" Slovaks: Lajos Kossuth, the leader of the 1848–49 War of Independence, Imre Madách, a great figure of nineteenth-century Hungarian literature, and Sándor Petőfi, Hungary's best-known poet and leader of the March 15, 1848, revolution—and Jeszenszky, i.e., myself. The pamphlet was also sent to Speaker György Szabad, who sent me a copy on November 23, 1992.

of minorities; rather, it was promised that they would be regulated by separate laws. (The language law of 1995 and its subsequent amendments justified the Hungarian fears.) The constitution also stated that the exercise of minority rights must not lead to discrimination against other residents of the state. If it were not tragic, it could be called comical that a constitution "protects" the majority that holds state power against the minority.

I have pointed out in several of my writings in the Hungarian media that Hungarian minorities were demanding the same rights (free use of language, an independent education system, territorial autonomy) as Slovaks and Romanians had demanded in Hungary in the nineteenth century.[31] In short, the basic law of our northern neighbor did not promise anything good for the Hungarian minority, and thus it foreshadowed a difficult neighborly relationship. Unfortunately, Slovak society had been brainwashed about Hungarians for a long time. To the old tale of "a thousand years of oppression" was added the completely fabricated claim that since 1920 Hungary had forcibly assimilated the half million members of the Slovak minority left in the truncated country. The reality is that within the borders of Trianon, 141,000 people claimed to be Slovaks in the 1920 census, but ten years later this figure fell to 105,000. The involuntary population transfer from Hungary to Slovakia in 1947 resulted in 73,000 people moving to Slovakia, so it is no wonder that in 1949 there were only 26,000 Slovaks left in Hungary.[32]

Hungary invited both the Czech and Slovak prime ministers to Hungary on the eve of the already announced separation. On September 9, Mečiar had his first one-to-one meeting with József Antall. The Slovak leader thanked Hungary for its attitude towards the divorce and hinted that Slovakia would not build a new Entente, instead it would be keen on the Visegrád Cooperation. Instead of NATO, he envisaged a "Swiss-Austrian-Slovak [neutral] zone." He reiterated that the minority issue was "an internal matter," said that "the necessary rights are guaranteed," and that the situation of the Hungarian minority in Slovakia was far better than in Hungary's other neighbors. Antall made it clear that he was as committed to Hungarian interests as his partner was to Slovak interests, saying, "We want Slovakia to be our neighbor and our friend." The focus of our bilateral relations should be on the economy, "because the exchange of goods is currently unacceptably low between two

---

[31] It is telling that Hugh Agnew, a professor at George Washington University, juxtaposed the 1868 Hungarian Nationality Act and the Slovakian State Language Act on an Internet mailing list in late 1992. He concluded that the latter fell far behind the much-criticized Hungarian legislation of a good hundred years earlier. I have Agnew's letter among my papers.

[32] The origin of the claim about close to half a million Slovaks in post-1920 Hungary, still frequently mentioned in Slovakia, is a false statement by Eduard Beneš's at the Paris Peace Conference in 1919.

neighboring countries." Our disputes, Antall continued, should be settled through bilateral negotiations, if necessary, with the involvement of "an international third party," including an international court—a hint at the dispute about the Danube barrage system. The issue of minorities must be "Europeanized," Antall said in response to Mečiar's rejection of "Duray's ideas of self-determination," and he suggested setting up a joint study group that could "forward its comments to various European forums." Mečiar accepted that—but it was never realized.[33]

Mečiar pocketed the Hungarian gestures and then diverted the Danube at Dunacsúny, a village transferred from Hungary to Czechoslovakia in the 1947 peace treaty. Mečiar returned from a London meeting of the European Community and the Visegrád Three enraged by the mild censure he had received from the EC and the compromise imposed on him on water sharing (which was never respected by Slovakia). He held a press conference in Prague on October 30, 1992, together with Prime Minister Václav Klaus, during which he attacked Hungary in extreme terms. According to him, in Hungarian official circles it was said increasingly often that the Trianon Treaty must be reassessed, and at the same time anti-Semitism, national hatred and fascist ideas [sic!] were being elevated to the level of official policy in Hungary. The foreign press should be more concerned with this than with the problem of the waterworks. He believed that the Danube was not governed by political decisions but by the laws of nature and denied that it had been diverted, rather, it was simply a matter of "redirecting shipping." He said that Hungary's internal political situation was in crisis, that the country was on the verge of collapse, and that this was worrying not only to him but also to Serbia, Romania and Ukraine. He left no doubt that he was thinking of an anti-Hungarian alliance, of the resurrection of the Little Entente, if Budapest continued to make trouble.[34]

With the earlier anti-Czech Slovak nationalism no longer making sense, Mečiar also sought to strengthen his domestic base by exhibiting a strident anti-Hungarian attitude, by frightening his people. "Hungary's state borders with all its neighbors are being questioned, and the only reason for tensions in Central Europe is the ambition to change state borders according to linguistic borders. [...] We are not becoming independent from the Czech Republic in order to lose our independence to Budapest," he told the Slovak press. In stark contrast to reality, he claimed that 5 percent of the Danube water was sufficient for the canal for the Gabčíkovo waterworks, the rest was flowing down the original course.[35] It was not we Hungarians

---

[33] Report to the Government on the visit of Slovakia's prime minister Vladimír Mečiar to Hungary, September 10, 1992. Sáringer, *Iratok az Antall-kormány*, vol. 3/1: 855–65 (Doc. 192).
[34] Personal communication from Prague. Among my papers.
[35] MTI News Summary, November 4, 1992.

but European countries and institutions that should have responded with appropriate condemnation to these unfounded accusations and to the tone of voice that was so contrary to good neighborliness.

But Mečiar could also show a different face. He began courting the leading force in the Hungarian government, the MDF. On November 28, 1992, the MDF delegation that was travelling to the congress of the Hungarian Christian Democratic Movement in Slovakia was virtually kidnapped when he arranged for several hours of talks between the Hungarians and the leadership of his party, the Movement for Democratic Slovakia. He expressed his surprise that the Hungarian Parliament had been able to tie the prime minister's hands regarding the waterworks. He said that the change of regime had not invalidated the international treaty on the barrage system and offered that if Hungary agreed to accept the Gabčíkovo power plant, Slovakia would not insist on building the plant at Nagymaros and paying the 20 billion forints due in compensation. He, Speaker Kovač and Foreign Minister Kňažko, all call for closer economic ties between the two countries. In her response, MDF vice president Gabriella Farkas explained and defended the decision of the Hungarian Parliament. In her report she concluded that the Gabčíkovo/Bős power plant had become a symbol of Slovak achievement, a matter of national pride in the eyes of the Slovaks.[36]

An attempt to enlist foreign mediation

After his visit to Budapest, Mečiar returned to his aggressive statements accusing Hungary of intending to change the borders, of using military threats and even of fascism. Noting this, and that after the diversion of the Danube he did not keep his commitment to the EC on the issue of water sharing, we had to examine whether there were any possibilities to change Slovak policy. Only one instrument offered hope: international pressure. The recognition of the new state and its admission to various international organizations offered a chance. It was clear, however, that if Hungary alone did not recognize Slovakia, we would be isolated, and we would have no means of protecting the Hungarians in Slovakia. The attention of the international community therefore had to be drawn, above all, to the shortcomings of democracy in Slovakia, to the authoritarian features of Mečiar's government, and to his behavior that was leading to conflicts, both at home and with foreign countries. It was expedient to refer to his unacceptably intolerant attitude towards the

---

[36] Károly Herényi's report on the MDF-DSZM meeting in Bratislava on November 28, 1992. Among my papers.

Hungarian minority only afterward because we knew from experience that foreign countries tended to see complaints about Hungarian minorities as a destabilizing factor, an attempt to question the borders.

Our first aim was, that when Czechoslovakia would break up, recognition of the two successor states and their subsequent membership in the UN, CSCE, Council of Europe and Central European Initiative should not be automatic. To this end, we engaged in quiet but intensive diplomatic work, and I wrote to several of my colleagues to explain our position. Having summarized our gestures to Slovakia and the conflict over the Danube, I pointed out the following:

> The 600,000 strong Hungarian community in Slovakia is not only the subject of aggressive rhetoric, its linguistic and educational rights are restricted, the newly adopted constitution does not even mention them, let alone gives any guarantee for their rights. [...] We have no intention of not recognizing Slovakia, because isolating it would be contrary to our fundamental interests, would hinder our bilateral relations, and would cut us off from Poland. However, I believe that this is the last time to put pressure on the current Slovak government to amend their constitution (which has many other flaws, as Mr. Čarnogursky's party noted) and to guarantee the rights of the minorities in a law. Last December, the EC successfully applied this approach to Croatia, and Croatia passed an enlightened law on its minorities, in order to gain international recognition. In my opinion, here is the time to strictly apply the requirements and expectations of the EC and the CSCE. All the new states, including the Baltic ones, which have suffered so much, face serious international scrutiny of their minority policies, and I do not see why Slovakia should be exempt from this. [...] I am afraid that without the necessary guarantees and proper legislation, there will be internal tensions in Slovakia (not only around the Hungarian minority), which could spill over into our relations with our new northern neighbor. However, I hope that with the right steps it will be possible to avoid a new zone of tension in the middle of Europe. If Hungary's fears can be allayed, we will be very happy to support Slovakia's recognition and involvement in all international forums.[37]

On my instructions, our diplomatic representatives in the CSCE countries collected the various states' reactions regarding the recognition of Slovakia. According

---

[37] Letter of Géza Jeszenszky to Polish Foreign Minister Skubiszewski, November 9, 1992. Sáringer, *Iratok az Antall-kormány*, vol. 3/1: 872–74 (Doc. 195). Similar letters were sent to the British, French, Dutch, Spanish and U.S. foreign ministers.

Chapter 8 – Czechs and Slovaks: The "Velvet Divorce"

to Germany, recognition was conditional on minority rights being guaranteed in accordance with European standards, but asked Hungary for patience and exerting a "moderating influence" on the Hungarians in Slovakia. (The message was that they should not even think of demanding secession). Foreign Minister Klaus Kinkel[38] told me that he repeatedly called Mečiar's attention to the importance of the rights of the national minorities. Along with others, he feared (not without reason) that Slovakia might turn away from Europe and pursue a foreign policy orientation "towards Russia, Ukraine and Romania." For similar reasons, Portugal was in favor of automatic recognition. The British promised that, in recognizing Slovakia, "special attention will be paid to the way in which it safeguards the rights of minorities living on its territory," but also advised separating the question of admission to international organizations from our bilateral problems. The French foreign ministry's deputy director said that the EC states had not yet decided whether to apply the doctrine of recognition announced on December 16, 1991, (by the Badinter Commission) but were inclined to do so and expected Slovakia to show flexibility on the issue of both the Danube and the Hungarian minority. The Danish and Dutch position insisted on the recognition criteria. Norway promised to monitor the situation of the Hungarian ethnic group. Austrian foreign minister Mock described the Slovak constitution as "contradictory" and said that the Council of Europe should examine Slovakia's minority policy. Poland reportedly did not want to intervene in Slovak-Hungarian disputes, but opined that the multilateral organizations could influence the behavior of their members. That was an argument in favor of Slovakia's unconditional membership.[39] Unfortunately, as I expected, that did not turn out to be the case.

By early December, at the level of political directors in the EC countries, the view inclined towards Slovakia being recognized unconditionally.[40] The same view was taken with regard to its accession to the CSCE, with the addition that the two successor states should be treated equally and that "if the international community integrates Slovakia into the various international organizations as soon as possible, it will be easier to hold it accountable for its obligations." However, Ambassador István Horváth reported from Bonn that the Hungarian position

---

[38] Klaus Kinkel (1936–2019): German civil servant, later diplomat, minister of foreign affairs (1992–1998) for the liberal Free Democratic Party. In our relationship he was an excellent partner.

[39] Summary report by Ferenc Bősenbacher of the Diplomatic Information Department, November 17, 1992, Sáringer, *Iratok az Antall-kormány*, vol. 3/1: 875–77 (Doc. 196). Cf. the memo of the 3rd Department on the same question, November 27, 1992, Sáringer, *Iratok az Antall-kormány*, vol. 3/1: 882–85 (Doc. 198).

[40] Report of Councilor András Simonyi from Brussels (November 30, 1992) and Ambassador György Granasztói on his visit to Günther Burghardt (director of the EC Commission's Secretariat General), December 7, 1992. Among my papers.

questioning Slovakia's CSCE membership was received with "incomprehension and surprise."[41] I read both nouns with shock, because if people in Bonn had heard anything about Slovak behavior in recent months, they should have been surprised had the Hungarian attitude been any different.

The international reaction was certainly instructive, and it confirmed the negative impression I gained during the Southern Slav crisis. Namely, that the policy of appeasement, which had led to such disastrous results with Hitler, could be banefully haunting, even in the case of a small but aggressive country—even if that country did not cross a certain line, i.e., it did not launch a war or kill its own citizens *en masse*. Violations of freedom of the press, intimidation of the opposition or of minorities, kidnappings, political assassinations may provoke verbal condemnation and criticism, but they seldom lead to harmful sanctions. The European Community, which was the primary institution expected to exert pressure, and which also had the means to do so, was not even willing to consider delaying the recognition of a new country that seriously restricted the language and other rights of the Hungarians in Slovakia. Some individuals and newspapers described merely raising our reservations and misgivings in this regard as "brutal." They paid scant attention to the joint statement issued by the four Hungarian parties in Slovakia on December 5, which condemned the fact that the dissolution of Czechoslovakia was not decided by referendum and stated that "the constitution of an independent Slovakia violates the right of private property, the rights of local self-government, the rights of national minorities and does not take into account the principles agreed in the Helsinki process." The statement also criticized the new Slovakia's refusal to call new parliamentary elections.[42]

The previous paragraphs show that Hungary's Foreign Ministry did not even suggest that Hungary might not recognize Slovakia, it just asked what our partners' position was on recognition. In several capitals, our diplomats' questions led them to conclude that Hungary was trying to block Slovakia's recognition and admission to international organizations, even though we were only trying to create some foreign pressure on Slovakia to change its policy on the Hungarian minority. To make the Hungarian position clear, József Antall wrote a letter to Chancellor Kohl confirming that:

---

[41] Minute by Zoltán Taubner and László Szücs, December 3, 1992. Ambassador Horváth was a long-time confidant of Gyula Horn, more loyal to the former foreign minister than to the Antall government. We soon drew the necessary conclusions and replaced him.

[42] *HTMH Tájékoztató*, no. 5 (1992): Annex 8.

Hungary does not wish to isolate Slovakia in any respect, but on the contrary, it seeks friendly and good neighborly relations with it. [...] Hungarian-Slovak relations are burdened by two serious problems inherited from the past. [...] There are negative tendencies in Slovakia with regard to the treatment of national minorities, and there are several indications that, despite our gestures and offers, the Slovak leadership does not want to pursue a policy of tolerance and cooperation towards the Hungarian minority. The provisions on minority rights in the new Slovak Constitution do not provide adequate protection. Recently, the removal of bilingual place-name signs has begun, the use of Hungarian place-names in Hungarian-language news media in Slovakia has been banned and the registration of Hungarian first names is being refused. All this is coupled with a hostile atmosphere that is deeply disturbing for the Hungarian minority. In order to reverse these negative tendencies, we consider it desirable that the two states should make a binding declaration of support for the general principles and the signed documents of the CSCE (Helsinki Final Act, Charter of Paris, Copenhagen Recommendations) before its accession to the CSCE.

On the Danube, the letter called on the Slovaks to comply with the London Agreement of October 28 on water sharing and to accept the referral to the International Court of Justice in The Hague.[43]

It is most likely due to this letter and subsequent steps taken by Germany that the twelve member states of the European Community agreed to make recognition of the two successor states conditional on the Community resolution of December 16, 1991, and to ask for written commitment to guarantee the rights of minorities.[44] I do not know whether such a commitment was eventually made, but if Slovakia did make such a promise, it is clear that it did not keep it. What we achieved, however, is that we managed to draw the attention of Europe and America to the serious shortcomings of Slovak democracy. The result was that the Council of Europe decided that the two new states must submit a new application for admission to the guardian of constitutional democracy, subjecting themselves to the scrutiny that it entails. On December 15, at the meeting of the CSCE Foreign Ministers in Stockholm, I made a special statement welcoming the Czech Republic and Slovakia, which had long struggled for self-determination and now became independent members of the CSCE, and which had close historical ties with Hungary. I expressed my hope

---

[43] Letter from József Antall to Chancellor Helmuth Kohl, December 8, 1992.
[44] Note from András Simonyi to Ambassador Granasztói, December 16, 1992.

that "the part of the Hungarian nation which was annexed to Czechoslovakia in the peace treaties of 1920 and 1947 will also enjoy a suitable form of self-government in accordance with the wishes of their legally elected representatives." I expressed my expectation that the two new Member States would respect the principles and recommendations for the protection of minorities contained in the Helsinki Final Act and in the CCE documents, as well as the agreements to settle the dispute over the Danube waterworks.[45]

Although Poland's position in the Hungarian-Slovak disputes often appeared to be neutral, it was not. While not deviating from the EC line, Minister Skubiszewski cautiously criticized Czechoslovakia's behavior on several occasions. He also expressed his criticisms privately to me: "We made our views known in Prague and in Bratislava. Among other things, I discussed this privately with Slovak Foreign Minister Kňažko. We are trying to exert influence. I am ready to help. We criticized the removal of bilingual place-name signs. We supported the role of the EC as a mediator and the idea of referring the issue of the dam on the Danube to the International Court of Justice in The Hague. We pointed out that the policy of *fait accompli* should not be used in the Danube case."[46]

In order to ensure good relations in the future, we were ahead of other countries in recognizing the two independent states in a diplomatic note handed over at the Ministry of Foreign Affairs in Prague on December 27, and we upgraded our Consulate General in Bratislava to embassy level. In doing so, we reiterated our commitment to good neighborly relations, refuting the accusations of Slovak nationalist propaganda, easing pressure on the Hungarian community in Slovakia and preventing the success of efforts to revive the anti-Hungarian alliance of Slovakia, Romania and Serbia.[47]

On December 31, 1992 at one minute before midnight, the Czechoslovak flag was taken down in Bratislava Castle and at the main square, and the flag of independent Slovakia was raised. Before that, Mečiar held an international press conference during which he again attacked Hungary in a harsh manner. He declared that Hungarian politicians were unable to bear the losses of Trianon and therefore

---

[45] Remarks by Géza Jeszenszky on December 14, 1992, at the Ministerial Council of the CSCE in Stockholm, *Magyar Külpolitikai Évkönyv, 1992*, 360–65, Statement by Hungary's foreign minister on the accession of the Czech and the Slovak Republic, December 15, 1992. *Magyar Külpolitikai Évkönyv, 1992*, 365–67.

[46] Minister Skubiszewski on the visit of former foreign minister and opposition politician Gyula Horn to Warsaw on December 9–11, 1992. Letter of Ambassador Engelmayer to Géza Jeszenszky, December 16, 1992. Among my papers.

[47] *Magyar Külpolitikai Évkönyv, 1992*, 374. Cf. Miklós Mitrovits, "Csehszlovákia felbomlása és a magyar politika (1989–1993)" [The break-up of Czechoslovakia and the policy of Hungarian politics (1989–1993)], *Múltunk* 58, no. 1 (2013): 175–76, https://epa.oszk.hu/00900/00995/00033/pdf/EPA00995_multunk_13_1_148-176.pdf.

were seeking a revision of the peace treaty—not only in the case of Slovakia but also threatening Ukraine, Romania and Serbia. Again, he argued that "the significant Slovak national minority living [in Hungary] was systematically exterminated, so that today there are only a few brave Slovaks left," while the situation of Hungarians in Slovakia was well above the European average.[48]

Foreign Minister Kňažko, however, in a press conference the next day, took a very different tone: "We are not planning a conflict with Hungary, but multifaceted and advantageous cooperation."[49] A few days later, Mečiar again made the false accusation that some groups in Hungary, including "government representatives," were questioning the Trianon borders. He interpreted Hungary's purchase of military equipment from Russia (MIG 29 fighter aircraft, using Russia's large debt to Hungary) as a threat of war against Slovakia. Interestingly, Co-existence Party leader Miklós Duray saw Slovakia's independence as a "huge chance" for reconciliation among the Central Europeans, while Béla Bugár, president of the Hungarian Christian Democratic Movement, was more realistic: "Slovakia's national minorities are at the mercy of the government and its party."[50]

In some respects, the break-up of Czechoslovakia was a positive development for Hungary, as it was the third neighboring state that surpassed us in terms of territory, population, and economic and military strength, to fall apart, while Slovakia lagged behind us in all these indicators. However, the Slovaks, according to the noted writer Vladimír Mináč, felt a "mythological hatred" towards the Hungarians and compensated for their sense of inferiority with arrogance and a "feigned sense of superiority."[51] The victims of this have been the Hungarians of Slovakia, to this very day. However, this sentiment and thinking is not permanent, and it has been showing a downward trend, although with setbacks. It is largely influenced by the tone and policies of the leaders of the day, which can vary even in the case of a single person. We can see this in the case of the current prime minister, Robert Fico, who once showed strong hostility towards the Hungarians on both sides of the Danube, and today is the best friend of Hungarian prime minister Orbán. I consider it an important achievement that, with the right combination of firmness and patience, we voiced our legitimate objections to Slovak policy, without burning any bridges, and thus we laid the foundations of the friendly, good neighborly relations that we have consistently advocated.

---

[48] *Magyar Nemzet*, January 2, 1993, 3.
[49] *Magyar Hírlap*, January 2, 1993, 1–2.
[50] MTI News Summary, January 5, 1993.
[51] Judit Hamberger, "A szlovákok magyarkomplexusáról" [On the Slovaks' "complex" vis-a-vis the Hungarians], *Magyar Narancs*, November 13, 1997.

Chapter 9

The Hungarian-Ukrainian Treaty and "Nation Policy"

"The 'nation policy' approach is a view of a country's problems from the perspective of the nation as a whole; commitment to one's own nation can be in harmony with respect for other nations."

József Antall[1]

After its absence for more than forty years, József Antall returned the term "nation policy" (*nemzetpolitika*)—the consistent assertion of national interests in the relations with Hungary's neighbors—to the political vocabulary. On the one hand, nation policy is foreign policy, the inclusion of the Hungarian minorities in the objectives of Hungarian foreign policy. But it is also domestic policy, with support from the motherland for Hungarians living outside our borders. It was the government's intention that nation policy would permeate the entire work of the government, and the Office of Hungarians Beyond Borders was set up to coordinate this policy. At the suggestion of Gyula Kodolányi and with the full support of the prime minister, Duna Television was established in 1992 to preserve the spiritual unity of the Hungarian nation and to strengthen its culture.[2] In consultation with Hungarian politicians in neighboring countries, Antall, speaking on minority issues in various forums, supported Hungarian parties across the border to the greatest extent possible, given the political realities, while respecting the political autonomy

---

[1] József Antall, foreword to *Magyarság és Európa: Nemzetpolitikai Szemle; Esélyek és remények a Kárpát-medencében* [Hungarians and Europe: Review of nation policy; Odds and hopes in the Carpathian Basin] (Budapest: Euro-Hungária Alapítvány, 1992).

[2] Duna Television, a special satellite channel named after the river that connects the countries and peoples of Central Europe, went on the air in December 1992 as the first Hungarian TV station to broadcast over satellite. Its mission was to provide news and cultural programs for all the Hungarian speakers of the Carpathian Basin, so as to help maintain their national/ethnic identity. See Gyula Kodolányi, "A Duna Televízió megteremtése" [The creation of Danube Television], in *Szóló hangra: Esszék, beszélgetések* [Essays, conversations] (Budapest: Nap Kiadó, 2012), 104–14.

of those parties. He expected to receive proposals and initiatives from them, rather than imposing on them his own ideas.

At that time, there was no significant difference between the Hungarian parties of the Carpathian Basin and the Budapest government's nation policy goals. They agreed that only the possession of both individual and communal minority rights would ensure the future of Hungarians living as minorities, and that autonomy was the optimal framework for this. "The current avowal of minority rights is nothing else than the modern formulation and assertion of a century-old notion, territorial autonomy," Antall explained in a conversation about South Tyrol with Péter Sárközy, a professor at the University of Rome.[3] In our bilateral neighborhood relations, as we have seen, territorial autonomy has been a crucial thesis,[4] and the fate of the Hungarians living in Subcarpathia, was a crucial element in our relations with Ukraine.[5]

Has Hungary given up Subcarpathia?[6]

Before 1918, the northeastern border region of historical Hungary was not a distinct geographical or political entity, but it was still the subject of special attention due to its history, geographical characteristics, and ethnic and social relations. In the twentieth century, the political status of this territory changed several times.[7] From 1944 until 1989, while annexed by the Soviet Union, its Hungarian minority was cut off from their fellow nationals, and, living under a total dictatorship, they were to suffer the same fate as the other small Finno-Ugric peoples of the Soviet

---

[3] "A közép-európai együttműködés és hazánk" [Central European cooperation and our country], *Európai Utas*, no. 2 (1993). Published in Antall, *Modell és valóság*, vol. 2: 541–55. Sentence quoted: 548.

[4] For strong theoretical, historical and practical arguments in favor of autonomy for the minorities, see Gáspár Bíró, Judit Hamberger, Gusztáv Molnár, Imre Szilágyi, and István Tóth, *Autonómia és integráció* [Autonomy and integration] (Budapest: Magyar Szemle Könyvek, 1993). Similar conclusions and concrete proposals for solutions are provided by László Kiss J., ed., *Európai határok—európai stabilitás* [European borders—stability in Europe] (Budapest: BIGIS, 1994).

[5] Jeszenszky, *Ukraine and Hungary* presents this story against the wider historical background. A short version is Géza Jeszenszky, "Ukraine and Hungary: The Key to Relations is Sub-(Trans)Carpathia," *Hungarian Cultural Studies: Journal of the American Hungarian Educators Association* 17 (2024): 91–107.

[6] For the radical objections to the treaty, see László Dányi, *Miért mondott le az Antall-kormány és az Országgyűlés a történelmi Kárpátaljáról?* [Why did the Antall government and the parliament give up historic Subcarpathia?] (Budapest: Magyarok Világszövetsége, 2017). For the answer, see Géza Jeszenszky, "Az 1991-es magyar-ukrán alapszerződés jelentősége" [The significance of the 1991 Hungarian-Ukrainian basic treaty], in *"Kijevi csirke": (Geo)politika a mai Ukrajnában* ["Chicken Kiev": Geopolitics in today's Ukraine], ed. Csilla Fedinec (Budapest: MTA Társadalomtudományi Kutatóközpont–Kalligram, 2019), 45–62.

[7] Until 1919 it was part of the Kingdom of Hungary. In the Trianon treaty it was assigned to Czechoslovakia. In March 1939, it was re-annexed by Hungary, only to come under Soviet control in October 1944. Since 1991 it is the westernmost district of Ukraine.

Union: assimilation, and disappearance. The political changes that began in 1988 affected the population of Sub-(Trans)carpathia in many ways.[8]

After the disappearance of the communist regimes, it was entirely justified that the—hypocritical and verbal—treaties of friendship and cooperation that the Soviet Union imposed on its satellites should be invalidated. At the same time, also gaining ground in Western Europe was the idea of filling the power and military vacuum created in the center of Europe by the dissolution of the Warsaw Pact with a new system of inter-state treaties. First, after the 1990 reunification, Germany concluded treaties, initially with Poland and Czechoslovakia, in order to make up for a missing peace treaty, and then with other states, including Hungary. The Antall government was also ready to codify in treaties the new Hungarian democracy's transformed system of relations with both the former Warsaw Pact states that had become free and the Western European democracies. Although we were sympathetic to Gorbachev and the Russian reformers, we were unable to conclude a new treaty with the Soviet Union until August 1991, because we were unwilling to accept the so-called "Kvitsinsky formula," which would have severely restricted our sovereignty by denying eventual membership in NATO.[9]

The post-unification treaties that Germany concluded with Poland and Czechoslovakia included a clause that the parties "have no territorial claims against each other and shall not raise such claims in the future." The same approach and the same wording were used by Poland in its interstate treaties with Ukraine, Russia and, finally, Lithuania, which were concluded and ratified between 1991 and 1994. Poland's recognition of the loss of territories that had belonged to it for centuries caused no domestic political tension.

The 1977 constitution of the Soviet Union included Article 72, which granted the right of the constituent republics to secede from the Soviet Union, already promised in previous constitutions. Taking advantage of Gorbachev's policy of "glasnost" (openness), the individual Soviet republics, led by Russia itself and closely followed by Ukraine, began to take independent political action. Sensing

---

[8] For the historical background, see chapter 5, note 37 in this volume. The recent history of Subcarpathia is presented in an exemplary joint venture: Csilla Fedinec, Mikola Vehes, István Chernichko, Roman Oficinsky, Yuri Osztapec, László Szarka, and Marian Tokar, eds., *Kárpátalja 1919–2009: történelem, politika, kultúra* [Transcarpathia 1919–2009: history, politics, culture] (Budapest: Argumentum, MTA Etnikai-nemzeti Kisebbségkutató Intézete, 2010). Cf. Béla Gabóda, "A kárpátaljai magyarság politikai szervezettsége és törekvései" [The political organization and aims of the Hungarians of Subcarpathia], *Valóság* 46, no. 11 (2003). For the post-1990 history of the country, see Csilla Fedinec and Viktória Szereda, eds., *Ukrajna színeváltozása 1991–2008. Politikai, gazdasági, kulturális és nemzetiségi attitüdök* [Ukraine in change: Political, economic, cultural, and national attitudes] (Pozsony: Kalligram, 2009).

[9] For more on the negotiations leading to the interstate treaty, see Keskeny, *A magyar-orosz kapcsolatok*, 71–82.

this trend, the Antall government began to build special relations with Ukraine. Thus, on May 31, 1991, during the official visit of Ukrainian president Kravchuk to Budapest, the "Declaration on the Principles of Cooperation between the Republic of Hungary and the Ukrainian Soviet Socialist Republic in the Field of Ensuring the Rights of National Minorities" and an additional Protocol to this Declaration were signed.

After the unsuccessful *coup d'état* in Moscow in August 1991, the new Soviet leadership did not oppose the independence aspirations of its member states and took note of the will of the people. In Ukraine, a referendum on December 1 approved the declaration of independence, which had already been proclaimed on August 24. Hungary immediately recognized the new state, and the Consulate General in Kyiv was raised to the embassy level. By this time, our "basic" treaty with Ukraine was ready for signature, and on December 6, 1991, József Antall, returning from Moscow with two similar treaties, signed it with President Leonid Kravchuk in Kyiv. It was the first international treaty of independent Ukraine. The aim of the Hungarian-Ukrainian treaty was to establish the best possible relations with our new and largest neighbor, and thus to exclude the possibility of some kind of anti-Hungarian collaboration between neighboring countries and parallel intolerant policies towards the Hungarian minorities. The treaty was also very important from a national point of view: we wanted to improve radically the conditions of the Subcarpathian Hungarians, who had been intimidated and politically disenfranchised under Soviet rule.

That document is still valid today. What is in it regarding "good neighborliness and cooperation?" First and foremost, it sets out a commitment to mutual cooperation in foreign and security policy, economic and energy policy, environmental protection, scientific research, border control and the protection of national minorities. Article 2(2) states: "The Parties respect each other's territorial integrity and declare that they do not and shall not have territorial claims on each other." Hungary did not invent this formula; the Ukrainians adopted it from the German and Polish treaties. But while in this clause Hungary did not renounce any territory, Article 17 of the treaty promised a lot.

> The Contracting Parties, in full conformity with the Charter of Paris for a New Europe and other relevant documents of the Conference on Security and Cooperation in Europe, express their conviction that friendly relations between their peoples and peace, justice, stability and democracy require that the ethnic, cultural, linguistic and religious identities of national minorities be mutually protected and that all conditions be created to ensure this. The

Parties shall take unilateral and joint steps to promote the implementation of the obligations in accordance with the "Declaration on the Principles of Cooperation between the Republic of Hungary and the Ukrainian SSR in the Field of Ensuring the Rights of National Minorities" signed on May 31, 1991, and the "Protocol" annexed thereto. The Parties shall act individually and jointly in their international relations to implement international documents concerning national minorities.[10]

When my experienced colleagues (diplomats and international lawyers) agreed with their Ukrainian colleagues on the text of the treaty, neither they nor I expected it to become a source of controversy. The newborn Ukraine, which did not yet have internationally valid and guaranteed borders, insisted that the German formula, which excluded territorial claims, be included in its inter-state treaties. It would have been an unforgivable mistake if Hungary had missed the opportunity to build a relationship of trust with its largest neighbor, then a nuclear power of 55 million people, ahead of any other country. The signing of the interstate treaty, including the territorial clause, was also essential for the practical implementation of the Declaration on the protection of minorities signed by Ukraine and Hungary in the spring of 1991. By speculating on border changes, Hungry would have jeopardized its western orientation and its integration ambitions—to the delight of some of our neighbors. Moreover, the formula does not exclude the possibility of changing the border peacefully, by referendum or by common agreement. Following the signing of the treaty, the political position of the Hungarians living in Subcarpathia improved spectacularly, and the construction of several new border crossings began.

Between signature and ratification

On April 4, 1992, I shook hands with my colleague, Ukrainian Foreign Minister Anatoliy Zlenko in the middle of the bridge over the Tisza River at Záhony. Then we negotiated, first in Berehove/Beregszász and then in Nyíregyháza. Among the international issues discussed, the most important were the conflicts between and inside the successor states of the Soviet Union, their ending and the elimination of potential new ones. Ukraine was understandably concerned about the conflict in its eastern neighbor, Moldova, between the Romanian and the Russian speakers. We also discussed the ongoing armed conflict in the erstwhile Yugoslavia. On both issues, we agreed on condemning external influences and the need to find peaceful

---

[10] For the text of the treaty, see *Magyar Törvénytár* [Hungarian Law Gazette], Act XLV of 1995.

solutions that respect the rights of the various ethnic groups. We stood for the territorial integrity and independence of the Republic of Moldova.

When the referendum of December 1, 1991, endorsed the independence of Ukraine, on the same day, in a separate ballot, 78 percent of the inhabitants of the Subcarpathian region supported its "special self-governing status." While in the district of Berehove/Beregszász 81.4 percent voted for the establishment of an autonomous Hungarian district. However, the latter two manifestations of popular will were never materialized. I had to raise this with my Ukrainian counterpart. Zlenko asked for patience, citing the 12 million Russians living in the eastern part of Ukraine and the Crimea, where an autonomous Hungarian territory would be a dangerous precedent, a precursor to possible secession; but he had no objection to the idea itself.[11] As I told the (bi-weekly) newspaper *Kárpátalja*, President Kravchuk promised that the administrative changes the people had voted for would eventually be implemented. "That would," I stressed, "prove the thesis in a spectacular way that the minority can really be a link between the two countries and can benefit from that."[12]

We continued our talks in Nyíregyháza, this time focusing on economic issues. The only way to travel between Ukraine and Hungary was over the overloaded and narrow Záhony bridge. Indeed, all the traffic from the post-Soviet region to Hungary used that bridge, so new facilities for our bilateral trade were needed. It turned out that, despite the promises made the previous August, not a single new border crossing had been opened! The former Soviet, now Ukrainian, customs and border guards cited as the explanation for that the lack of roads, water, telephone, and buildings. Nevertheless, we saw a chance for the Hungarian population of Subcarpathia to be the best facilitator and guarantee of our exemplary relations by building as many bridges and by opening as many new border crossings as possible. At the same time as this was under discussion by the ministers, Pál Virágh, the government's representative to Eastern Hungary, discussed it with Mykhaylo Krayilo, the Presidential Envoy of the Subcarpathian *Oblast* (District).[13] Simultaneously, State Secretary Entz and István Íjgyártó, his adviser, met with the leaders of the KMKSZ, who also urged the opening of new border crossings, even before properly equipped buildings for customs and border guards were created.[14]

---

[11] *Új Magyarország* and *Magyar Hírlap*, April 6, 1991. *Külügyminisztériumi tájékoztató, 1992*, vol. 1: 210–13.
[12] *Kárpátalja*, April 21, 1992.
[13] Joint statement on the working meeting of the two foreign ministers, and their declaration on ensuring the protection of national minorities, April 4, 1992. *Magyar Külpolitikai Évkönyv, 1992*, 174–77.
[14] *Népszabadság*, April 6, 1992, 3.

The next step was the official visit to Hungary by Ukrainian prime minister Vitold Fokin on May 21–22, 1992. Preparing for that, presidential envoy for Subcarpathia Mykhaylo Krayilo held talks in Budapest on April 24. After having met him, I summed up our talks thus: "There are no problems in our relations, there are just a lot of tasks to be solved."[15] As a result of Fokin's visit, an agreement was signed on the establishment of an Intergovernmental Committee for Trade and Technical-Scientific Cooperation, the settlement of debts inherited from the Soviet Union, and cooperation between the two national banks and the two ministries of finance, so that henceforth trade would be settled in convertible currency. The prime ministers agreed on the early opening of new border crossings, the return of historical relics, continuation of construction of the hospital in Berehove/Beregszász, further improvements in the conditions of the national minorities and other matters.[16] Antall also urged implementation of the autonomy promised for the Hungarian minority.[17]

Deeds followed the fine words. Ukraine started to implement the principles of the May 1991 Declaration into its laws and the Constitution under preparation. The Kyiv Parliament enacted the Law on National Minorities on June 25, 1992, and on December 7, 1992, the Presidential Envoy of the Subcarpathian *Oblast* issued a decree on enforcing it locally. Among other things, it stipulated that "where the majority of the population is a national minority, officials of state and social bodies, institutions and organizations are obliged to speak both the state language and the language of the national minority at the level necessary for their official duties." Under the decree, the Hungarian national colors were to be displayed alongside the Ukrainian in all official institutions in the Hungarian-inhabited municipalities and in the city of Berehove.[18]

Hungary tried to help Subcarpathia in many ways, foremost regarding the Hungarians, who then still made up a good 12 percent of the population. Public and private foundations, Hungarian individuals at home and abroad provided significant assistance to churches, schools, cultural, health and social institutions, also to businesses. On October 10–11, 1992, at the invitation of the Subcarpathian Foundation, I visited Solotvyno/Aknaszlatina to donate computers to the Ukrainian, Hungarian and Romanian schools in that city. I was saddened to see the ruins of the railway bridge to Sighet/Máramarossziget on the other side of the

---

[15] *Népszabadság*, April 25, 1992. *Külügyminisztériumi tájékoztató, 1992*, vol. 1: 256.
[16] Joint statement on the talks between the prime ministers, May 22, 1992. *Magyar Külpolitikai Évkönyv, 1992*, 207–9.
[17] *Külügyminisztériumi tájékoztató, 1992*, vol. 1: 352–55.
[18] For the text of the decree, see: *Pro Minoritate*, nos. 1–2 (1993): 43.

Tisza, which had been blown up during the war. Six years later, when I rode the rapids of the Ukrainian-Romanian border section of the Tisza River in an inflatable kayak (with special permission from the two governments!), I saw in the water the ruins of several other, smaller bridges that connected the two banks until the end of the Second World War.

On December 18, Mihály Tóth, government representative of the Berehove district, and Árpád Dalmay, the Berehovo district chairman of KMKSZ, arrived in Budapest. They told State Secretary Iván Bába that the demand for autonomy was meeting stiff resistance from the Ukrainian side, and they believed that self-government of the Hungarian region could be established gradually, without using the sensitive term "autonomy." They complained that the representatives of the former communist nomenklatura were more permissive on the issue of autonomy than the opposition led by Chornovil.[19]

On February 14, 1993, the official founding of the Carpathian Euroregion took place in Debrecen. I invited Catherine Lalumière, secretary general of the Council of Europe, Ukrainian foreign minister Zlenko, Polish foreign minister Skubiszewski and John Edwin Mroz, president of the New York-based East-West Institute. Slovakia was represented only at low level, with no authorization to sign the adopted Declaration, the Cooperation Agreement and the Statute.[20] Romania, as a centralized state, did not allow any of its counties to accept our invitation. A week later, at an international press conference, President Iliescu protested the fact that Hungary, far from the Carpathians, had initiated a cooperation named after that mountain range, saying that that "reflects the territorial revisionist claims of certain circles. Unfortunately, Madame Catherine Lalumière, the secretary general of the Council of Europe, allowed herself to be drawn into this game." The comments of most of the Romanian press were even harsher than the president's, and the Romanian Foreign Ministry's weekly press briefing described the initiative as "suspicious."[21] The Euroregion's secretariat was set up in Sanok, Poland. The first programs were aimed at improving infrastructure in border areas (roads, telecommunications—there were no mobile phones yet), opening new border crossings, and also environmental cooperation. In 1997, Romania joined the Euroregion—already

---

[19] Iván Bába's note on the meeting with Mihály Tóth, the district president's representative, December 20, 1992. Among my papers.

[20] Summary report on the founding of the Carpathian Euroregion cross-border cooperation, April 23, 1993, Third Territorial Department of the Foreign Ministry, 1049-6. Among my papers.

[21] The reception of the Carpathian Euroregion in Romania. Press Department of the Foreign Ministry, S/117/29-2/1993. Among my papers.

under the Constantinescu presidency and a democratic government that included the RMDSZ. Romania's participation has since expanded considerably.

In the first half of 1993, Ukrainian-Hungarian relations continued to develop dynamically. On February 26–27, President Kravchuk and Foreign Minister Zlenko paid an official visit to Budapest. New agreements were prepared and signed on mutual transport of goods, closer inter-bank relations, cooperation on border water and flood protection, military-industrial and agricultural relations, simplified border crossings for residents of border counties, additional border crossing points, and the conclusion of an accord on deportation. With Zlenko I discussed the situation in the post-Soviet space and the Balkans and agreed to support the inclusion of three more Ukrainian counties in the Carpathian Euroregion, and to increase the railway and road capacity of the Záhony-Csap border crossing. We agreed that our common understanding on the minority issue is of European importance and is also suitable for addressing Ukraine's internal problems. We talked about solutions such as the legally established use of the "local language" in non-Ukrainian-majority areas, autonomous districts, Ukraine's Western orientation via Hungary towards Austria and Italy. On April 19, 1993, Béla Kádár, minister of international economic relations, attended the inaugural meeting of the Hungarian-Ukrainian Intergovernmental Committee for Trade, Economics and Science and signed the Protocol on the Transport of Goods for 1993.

I venture to say that if Ukraine had continued along the domestic and foreign policy lines of Kravchuk and Zlenko in the years to follow, its history, especially our bilateral relations, would have been different. My view is supported by President Kravchuk's proposal, made public in April 1993, for the creation of an East-Central European security zone. His motive was the Russian suggestion that Russia should be given a mandate by the UN to guarantee security in the territories of the former Soviet Union. Ukraine feared that once in power the aggressive "red-brown" Russian forces, already strong at the time, would threaten the independence of Ukraine and other former Soviet republics. Ukraine's aim was not a new military bloc or organization, and it did not seek to isolate Russia, but rather to create a bridge to the West, with its members mutually renouncing territorial claims and guaranteeing the rights of national minorities. The concept envisaged membership for Slovenia, Croatia, Hungary, the Czech Republic, Slovakia, Poland, Ukraine, the Baltic states, and possibly Belarus. (Romania, which had open territorial claims against Ukraine, was not included.)[22] The proposal was taken off the agenda by the

---

[22] Dispatch from the Embassy of Hungary on Ukraine and on Hungarian-Ukrainian relations, April 15, 1993. János Sáringer, ed., *Iratok az Antall-kormány külpolitikájához és diplomáciájához*, vol. 4, *(1993. január–1993. december)* [Papers relating to the foreign policy and diplomacy of the Antall government:

next Ukrainian presidents, who were drawn to Russia, and also by the subsequent enlargement of NATO.

Disregarding the referendum of December 1, 1991, which voted for declaring the territory of Subcarpathia a special economic zone, the Ukrainian Parliament rejected the government's proposal, citing its potential to set a precedent. Obviously, they were referring to Crimea and other territories with a large Russian-speaking population. Although the leader of Rukh, V. Chornovil, had previously put forward federalist ideas,[23] his party and the majority of the Kyiv Rada eventually sided with the French centralization model. By spring 1993, the government and the Parliament had said neither yes nor no to the creation of a Hungarian autonomous region, but a joint statement issued by the Hungarian prime minister and the Ukrainian president at their meeting in Uzhhorod/Ungvár on April 30, 1993, still held out the prospect of such a move. At the same time, the improvement in the political conditions of the Hungarians in Subcarpathia was accompanied by a deterioration in the overall economic situation in Ukraine, and that left its mark on the mood of the whole population of the country. However, in the spring of 1993, when the Ukrainian-Hungarian treaty was submitted to the Hungarian Parliament for ratification, the general outlook for Ukraine was not bad, and there was no sign of the impatient Ukrainian nationalism that reared its head in the 2000s.

The hot debate over ratification

The ratification of international treaties is usually a routine matter, and the Hungarian Parliament usually adopted the government's proposal without any debate. That is what was envisaged with the treaty with Ukraine. But on June 3, 1992, after the Foreign Affairs Committee, along with several other international treaties, adopted it without objection and was about to forward it to the plenary session for a vote, the committee chairman, Gyula Horn, unexpectedly raised an objection. He warned that when negotiations for a Hungarian-Romanian treaty entered a serious stage, the Romanians might demand a territorial clause similar to the present one. "Would it not have been a better wording," he asked slyly, "that the contracting parties act in accordance with the Helsinki Final Act?" He suggested that the Foreign Ministry renegotiate that paragraph of the treaty. The committee agreed and did not recommend that the treaty be presented before Parliament in its present form.

January to December 1993] (Budapest: VERITAS Történetkutató Intézet és Levéltár - Magyar Napló, 2021), 841–45 (Doc. 155).

[23] Note by István Íjgyártó, Chief Adviser at the HTMH, June 22, 1992. Among my papers.

Chapter 9 – The Hungarian-Ukrainian Treaty and "Nation Policy"

The committee members representing the governing coalition, including Vice Chairman György Csóti, did not see the trap. Horn, a seasoned diplomat, knew full well that Ukraine would not agree to any changes on the border clause. If the Hungarian side raised this issue, Ukraine would join the countries crying wolf over alleged Hungarian attempts to change the borders. If, on the other hand, the current wording remains, the domestic nationalists could be incited against the government. In view of this we put the issue of the treaty aside, but my colleagues confirmed that the treaty was not drawn up as a "rush job" and that the Ukrainian side insisted on the inclusion of the border clause, and that they had stated categorically that they had agreed to guarantee the rights of the Hungarian minority on this condition.[24]

My colleagues also noted that, apart from the clause, the treaty signed with Ukraine was, on a number of points, such as national minorities and security policy, better and stronger than the Hungarian-Russian treaty, and that it guaranteed rights "from which the Hungarians of Transylvania, Slovakia and Vojvodina are still a long way off."[25] Romania's demand for a similar territorial clause could be averted by pointing to the commitments towards the national minorities made by Ukraine and by referring to Romania's thinly veiled ambitions towards Moldova. However, if ratification was not achieved, these gains would be lost, the former Little Entente would be restored in practice, and Hungary's reputation in the eyes of the outside world would be seriously damaged.[26]

Having considered all this, the Ministry of Foreign Affairs submitted the unchanged treaty to the Foreign Affairs Committee of Parliament, which adopted it on January 27, 1993, with one vote against and one abstention. However, the genie had already escaped the bottle, and the right wing of the MDF, led by István Csurka and Gyula Zacsek, began to agitate against the border clause and demanded that ratification be postponed. Ukrainian nationalists found it convenient to attack the "Hungarophile" leaders of Subcarpathia (Krayilo and his two deputies, Serhiy Ustich and Bertalan Molnár), and spoke of the "duplicity" of Hungarian policy. Mihály Tóth, the presidential envoy in Berehove, in consultation with Tibor Szabó, a departmental head at the HTMH, noted that "the delay in ratification is

---

[24] Memo of the 3rd Territorial Department (Ferenc Kontra and István Monori), June 9, 1992. Among my papers.
[25] Memo by Dr. György Szénási of the International Law Department, June 8, 1992. Among my papers.
[26] Analysis of the 3rd Regional Department, February 18, 1993, prepared by Ernő Keskeny, deputy head of department, with the agreement of Iván Bába, deputy state secretary. Among my papers.

increasingly strengthening those who want to portray the aspirations of Hungary and the Hungarian community in Subcarpathia in a negative light."[27]

Seeing that a number of members in the governing coalition were plotting against ratification, Prime Minister Antall proposed a meeting with Ukrainian president Kravchuk. In order to prepare the ground for the meeting, scheduled in Uzhhorod for April 30, 1993, the prime minister sent Kravchuk a letter with a polite request to make progress on the issue of Subcarpathia becoming a special economic zone, and on territorial self-government for the Hungarians.[28] In the discussions, Antall pointed to the likely favorable international reception by ensuring cultural autonomy and local self-government for the Hungarian minority, as well as granting Subcarpathia special economic zone status, which would be a sign of Ukraine's enlightened thinking and conduct. Kravchuk took the point, and his reaction was positive, but without a definite commitment.[29] Given his restricted legal position and the mood of the Ukrainian legislature, we could not expect more.

In the parallel discussion I had with my colleague Zlenko, I regretted the inadequate economic and political assistance the Western democracies were giving to Ukraine, and to the new democracies in general. I offered support for an international conference to examine how to help consolidate its economic and security situation. Following our talks, the joint declaration issued was about broadening cooperation and supporting each other's foreign policy aspirations (including President Kravchuk's security policy proposal). "They stressed *that the development of local democratic self-government* in their countries *is guaranteed by law*. The Hungarian side welcomed with satisfaction the significant steps taken in Ukraine to implement the nationality law guaranteeing all the freedoms to the Subcarpathian Hungarians, and their right to national-cultural autonomy."[30] Following the Ungvár meeting, such a meaningful and intimate relationship with our neighbor was threatened by the voices in Hungary which opposed ratification of the bilateral treaty.

Prior to the ratification debate, our ambassador to the Council of Europe in Strasbourg, János Perényi, who descended from a distinguished Hungarian family in Subcarpathia, addressed a letter to the MPs of MDF:

---

[27] Consultation with presidential envoy Mihály Tóth from Beregszász, April 13, 1993, no. 0019/93. Among my papers.
[28] Sáringer, *Iratok az Antall-kormány*, vol. 4: 846–48 (Doc. 156).
[29] Report to the government on the working meeting of Prime Minister Antall and President Kravchuk in Uzhhorod on April 30, 1993, and their joint communication. Sáringer, *Iratok az Antall-kormány*, vol. 4: 849–59 (Doc. 157).
[30] *Magyar Külpolitikai Évkönyv, 1993*, 202–4. Emphasis added.

Based on my diplomatic experience, it is clear to me that if the disputed passage is strongly condemned by a few members in Parliament, then, even if the Treaty is ratified, the Romanian, Serbian and Slovak propaganda machines will be able to launch an anti-Hungarian campaign. This would make the thesis that Hungarian foreign policy is nothing more than a covert revisionist policy, would sound tangible to the West. We cannot afford this in the current situation. Ratification, on the other hand, would increase the Hungarian Government's room for maneuver and its credibility and opportunities to support the autonomy aspirations of the Hungarian minorities. However, ratifying the Treaty cannot be interpreted as a sign that we have given up on the people of Subcarpathia forever. What matters to me is the opinion of the Subcarpathian Hungarians themselves on the issue, which, as far as I know, is far from negative on ratification.[31]

Less explicitly, Sándor Fodó, president of the MKKSZ, also supported the parliamentary ratification of the treaty, calling it in the interest of further good Hungarian-Ukrainian relations and the interests of the Hungarians of Subcarpathia.[32] In contrast, the executive committee of the World Federation of Hungarians called the border guarantee in the treaty "unjustified and unnecessary."[33] In order to counteract the growing sentiment among MPs of the governing coalition, I personally wrote a four-page paper titled "The importance of the Ukrainian-Hungarian treaty," summarizing the strong arguments in favor of ratification and pointing out how the counter-campaign jeopardized the effectiveness of our efforts on behalf of the Hungarian communities beyond the border. I stressed that we were not giving up anything with the treaty, as our present borders were established by the 1947 peace treaty. On May 3, I discussed the treaty with the members in a closed meeting lasting several hours. My most important argument addressed the question, "With this treaty, did Hungary go beyond the Helsinki Final Act, which prohibits the forcible change of borders and was signed by 35 countries in 1975, and which states, *inter alia*, that [the participating States] consider that their borders may be changed by peaceful means and by agreement in accordance with international law?"

No, because the treaty merely reaffirms the position repeatedly expressed by the Government, the Hungarian Democratic Forum and all parliamentary parties that Hungary has no territorial claims on any of its neighbors. Since

---

[31] János Perényi to the MDF parliamentary group, Strasbourg, April 26, 1993. Among my papers.
[32] Letter of Sándor Fodó to József Antall, April 7, 1993. Among my papers.
[33] Declaration of the Executive Committee of the Federation, April 18, 1993.

all our neighbors have unambiguously indicated that they have no intention of giving up any part of their territory in favor of Hungary, including the areas along our borders, with a large Hungarian population, a peaceful, mutually agreed border change is not realistically conceivable today. Under these circumstances, a "territorial claim" is tantamount to a threat of force, which has been prohibited by international law since the Briand-Kellog Pact of 1928, which is still in force today. It is not possible to renounce a right that does not exist; what has been done is not a renunciation, but a confirmation of an international legal obligation that exists independently of the treaty in question. But this is not a renunciation of the possibility of any legal act permitted by international law.[34]

The overwhelming majority of the coalition government's MPs, convinced by my arguments, understood the importance of the treaty and the arguments against it.

On May 4, 1993, I presented the parliamentary resolution proposing the ratification of the treaty the National Assembly for general debate. First, I said that Ukraine's borders were not decided by the post-war peace treaties, therefore it was understandable that Ukraine insisted on the renunciation of territorial claims by all its neighbors. By quoting the law on national minorities adopted by Ukraine the previous year, I asked:

> Do you know of any other country in Central and Eastern Europe where such a law, such a decree is in force—except this one? This law is being put into practice, and the joint communiqué adopted at the recent high-level meeting also points to further elements in the implementation of minority self-government. At this high-level meeting, the President of Ukraine reaffirmed his personal commitment to both the full guarantee of national minority rights and cultural autonomy, the special economic status of Subcarpathia and the introduction of local self-government. I would like to ask you whether you know of any other head of state in a country with a large Hungarian minority who made a similar statement? It can be said that the Ukrainian-Hungarian treaty and the Ukrainian practice that has evolved since its signing have served and continue to serve the interests of the Hungarian minority living in Subcarpathia.

---

[34] The text of the questions and answers document is among my papers.

After summarizing all the political and economic benefits of the treaty, I turned to the critics:

> When we confirm in this treaty that we have no territorial claims against Ukraine, we are not only acting in accordance with the norms of democratic states and the Helsinki Final Act, but we also take into account the special aspects of Ukrainian-Hungarian relations. The rejection of the territorial claim [...] proves, against the accusations so often levelled against us, through no fault of our own, that we can conclude meaningful treaties with all our neighbors who are prepared to guarantee the rights of minorities living on their territory, promote their survival in their homeland and the preservation of their culture, in accordance with the legitimately expressed demands of the minority concerned. On this basis, I can state with a clear conscience that this treaty is not only in line with the interests of the Hungarian population living in Subcarpathia, and their will expressed through their leaders, but also strengthens the negotiating positions of those Hungarian minorities living elsewhere, whose situation—in terms of their rights and aspirations—is not yet sufficiently reassuring. The Ukrainian Parliament ratified the treaty before you on July 1, 1992. The nearly one and a half years that have passed since it was signed show that Ukraine intends to comply with its obligations under the treaty to a large extent. This was confirmed by the atmosphere at the meeting in Ungvár on April 30, and the joint declaration adopted there. On the basis of the above, I ask the House to ratify the Hungarian-Ukrainian treaty.[35]

The proposal was supported by István Hegedűs, rapporteur of the Foreign Affairs Committee, István Szent-Iványi, on behalf of the Alliance of Free Democrats (pointing out how forward-looking it was in terms of minority rights), Gyula Horn on his own behalf, Csaba Tabajdi on behalf of the Hungarian Socialist Party, and Zsolt Németh on behalf of Fidesz.

Naivety, irresponsibility, ignorance and blindness led some Hungarian politicians to travel to Subcarpathia to stir up sentiment against the treaty. It was not difficult to suggest that, as the consequence of the renunciation of territorial claims, the possibility and chance for a future border adjustment in favor of Hungary was lost. Gyula Zacsek, an MP of MDF, had a few, mainly elderly Hungarians, signed

---

[35] Géza Jeszenszky's presentation, Minutes of the Hungarian Parliament, May 4, 1993, http://www.parlament.hu/naplo34/292/2920092.html.

the following letter: "We, the undersigned Hungarians of Subcarpathia, citizens of Ukraine, declare that we were not aware of the exact content of the basic Ukrainian-Hungarian treaty, that no one consulted us about it, that no one asked our opinion, and that therefore we could not authorize anyone to ask the Hungarian Parliament to ratify this treaty on our behalf."[36] Zacsek also found Ivan Turjanica (presumably a close relative of the person of the same name who orchestrated "popular demand" in November 1944 for the annexation of Subcarpathia by the Soviet Union), the "president" of the highly suspect "Association of the Rusyns of Subcarpathia,"[37] which most probably had a Russian secret service background. This Turjanica protested against the treaty, calling it "a decision on the fate of a people, concluded by Stalinist methods behind their backs," and demanded that the Hungarian Parliament not ratify the treaty.

Several participants in the debate used strongly emotional words that were very badly received abroad. The Slovak pro-government *Národná Obroda* reported the debate under the headline "Strange Voices in the Hungarian Parliament—Dreaming of a Greater Hungary." It quoted MDF MP Izabella B. Király, who said that "it is necessary to unite the Carpathian Basin into a single country by peaceful means," and approved the interventions of MPs Ágnes Maczó, Árpád Miklós and Géza Iván, who spoke in the same vein.[38]

I still believe that there is one quote that best expresses the essence of the debate. It is contained in a speech by Iván Vitányi, whose ancestors were active in Subcarpathia's past and who was a politician in the opposition MSZP:

> The Ukrainian Treaty is not perfect, but it is a step in that direction. It creates the opportunity for Hungarians in Subcarpathia, in Carpatho-Ukraine, to live more freely than before and to establish a free nationality. Therefore, in my opinion, it is a historical necessity for the Parliament to vote in favor of this law. It is not my bread and butter to praise the Government. I say it not because I want to praise the Government, but I say it because I feel that this is a turning point in history, if we miss that, we will bring very serious trouble on our nation.[39]

---

[36] Letter of the members of the KMKSZ pensioners' committee in Beregszász, May 7–9, 1993. Among my papers.

[37] In Soviet times, just as in the independent Ukraine, the Rusyns were not recognized as a distinct people, neither was their language.

[38] *Národná Obroda* (Bratislava), May 10, 1993.

[39] Speech by Iván Vitányi, Minutes of the Hungarian Parliament, May 10, 1991. http://www.parlament.hu/naplo34/294/2940096.html.

Chapter 9 – The Hungarian-Ukrainian Treaty and "Nation Policy"

The debate continued at the plenary session of the National Assembly on May 11. There were statements from those opposing ratification, which some of our neighbors could only welcome as proof of the irreparable irredentism of the Hungarians. In my closing remarks, I said that I understood the passions in the debate and that the many ill-considered statements reflected a sincere sentiment:

> This Parliament, this government, and I myself have never denied that we still feel pain for the decision that for a third of the Hungarian nation Hungary has become a foreign country, that for decades we were separated from them by iron curtains, that for seventy-five years they suffered so much humiliation and injustice, that even today many of them live in fear and have doubts about their future. These terrible memories and more recent experiences explain many of the historical speeches made here—many of which we can agree with—but it is regrettable that some people thought they were in an academic discussion forum and forgot the weight and consequences of their every sentence and reference. When the government concluded and now recommends for ratification the treaty that puts Hungarian-Ukrainian relations and the life of the Subcarpathian Hungarians on a firm foundation, we remember the message, "Forget not the field where they perish'd,"[40] repeated by our own poets, Petőfi and Illyés. No, we do not forget the places of our history, but we think first and foremost of the present and future of our nation, its security, its vital neighborly relations, and not least of all of those Hungarians who carry their daily life outside Hungary. [...]
>
> This treaty represented a breakthrough not only in our neighborhood relations, not only did we make one of the most important successor states of the disintegrating Soviet Union our trusted friend, but we also laid down principles of great importance in the field of minority protection. These principles have not only enabled and continue to enable the Hungarian population of Subcarpathia to improve their conditions, but they also set a real precedent for our other neighbors. Therefore, this treaty is probably the most important of all the interstate treaties concluded by the Antall government so far. [...] Why is it opposed by a few, perhaps a few dozen, members of Parliament and quite a few of our decent compatriots? I understand them, what I respect is not simply their right to dissent, but the voice of conscience and their sense of responsibility for the fate of Hungarians living beyond the borders.

---

[40] Thomas Moore, "Forget not the field where they perish'd, / The truest, the last of the brave, / All gone—and the bright hope we cherish'd / Gone with them, and quench'd in their grave!"

But once again I try to reassure them: it was not us who signed the Trianon treaty, the historic Greater Hungary is not put in the grave now, our greatest national tragedy after Mohács is the consequence of our old misfortune and misjudgments. We are now trying to mitigate the tragic consequences with this treaty. Far from abdicating our responsibility for the Hungarians living in Subcarpathia, we are trying to help them first and foremost with this treaty. In this way, we have dismantled the Iron Curtain in the east, brought them back from isolation, made their difficult lives easier, and brought them into everyday contact with the motherland. [...]

This treaty was conceived in the Central European idea proclaimed by the greatest Hungarians, it is in line with our dreams of a Europe without borders, it is an important milestone on the road to its realization. I ask all Members of this House to reconsider how they vote. Are you voting to protect and even enhance Hungary's international prestige, are you voting to extend the rights of Hungarian communities living beyond Hungary's borders, or are you voting to actually try to forge some kind of hostile ring around Hungary? In the past this Parliament had more than one more difficult decision to make. In 1867, the Hungarians had to choose between [the two great patriots] Lajos Kossuth and Ferenc Deák. In 1921 and 1947, it had to ratify the peace treaty. But now we do not have to choose between two honorable concepts—Kossuth's and Deák's—or between two bad—whether signing the peace treaties or not. We now have to choose only between irrational fears and tangible benefits.[41]

After my replies to further questions, Prime Minister Antall also spoke. He stated, "I assume full responsibility for all the consequences of this treaty, and I signed this treaty in order to secure Hungary's place in the international sphere, and in the interests of Hungarians living beyond the border." After referring to the background and importance of the treaty, the prime minister said that "the Ukrainian-Hungarian basic treaty [and its territorial clause] should not set a precedent in this respect with any neighboring country. It does not oblige us to apply the same formula with other countries." He also responded to those who considered the treaty unpatriotic and even treasonous, saying, "I do not wish to answer whether we were unpatriotic, or you are unpatriotic. Unfortunately, in this House, in its long history, there have been quite a few accusations of being unpatriotic, against people who

---

[41] Concluding speech by Foreign Minister Géza Jeszenszky, Minutes of the Hungarian Parliament, May 11, 1993, http://www.parlament.hu/naplo34/295/2950146.html.

have subsequently become remembered in a very different way." The prime minister concluded with an irrefutable argument:

> All we can aim for is to ensure that the minorities continued to exist. And we must help them, by protecting minority rights, to remain in their birthplace, where there are so many relics of Hungarian history, where so many events are connected with Hungarian history. They should be able to remain in their homeland, and stand their ground as a historical Hungarian minority.[42]

This was József Antall's last speech in Parliament, and to this extent it can be considered his last will and testament. It is symbolic that it was about one of the territories detached from the body of 15 million Hungarians.

On the basis of roll-call votes, Parliament adopted the resolution ratifying the Hungarian-Ukrainian treaty by 223 votes to 39, with 17 abstentions. I was satisfied that the yes vote of the governing coalition secured the required number of votes, but I was also pleased that the opposition SZDSZ, MSZP and Fidesz also supported the treaty. At the same time, however, I was and still am extremely sorry that, against all rational arguments, the votes against were cast by members of the governing coalition, alongside the opposition fraction led by József Torgyán. In an interview with Magyar Rádió, Prime Minister Antall pointed out that "those who, motivated by political intentions and ambitions, argued for rejection on the grounds of the interests of Hungarians, voted against the treaty in the knowledge that the majority, feeling the weight of the decision, would accept it." He also explained the difference between Ukraine, which has no border treaties, and our other neighbors, whose borders are guaranteed by two peace treaties and other international agreements.[43]

Following the successful ratification, Prime Minister Antall informed the Ukrainian president in a letter about the result. The debate, he wrote, showed that even those who were not satisfied with the wording of the treaty were in favor of close and friendly relations with Ukraine. He reiterated the importance of a special economic zone, which would greatly facilitate the economic and commercial ties between our two countries, and that local self-government, which was overwhelmingly supported by the voters in the December 1991 referendum, should be confirmed in a law. The approval of the territorial clause was proof that behind

---

[42] Béla Pálmány, ed., *Antall József országgyűlési beszédei* [József Antall's speeches in Parliament] (Budapest: Athenaeum Nyomda, 1994), 339.
[43] MTI domestic news summary, May 17, 1993. Among my papers.

Hungary's advocacy for territorial self-government there was no hidden claim for border change.[44]

It did not bode well for the future of Ukraine that by a narrow margin of twenty-five votes Parliament voted down the government's bill for Subcarpathia to become a special economic zone.[45] What was behind the vote was the ongoing debate about federalization, demanded by the Donetsk region and Crimea, but in which many saw the schemes of Russia to destabilize Ukraine. As a guarantee against that, the answer was to seek membership in NATO.[46]

The afterlife of the treaty

Our relationship of trust with Ukraine was jeopardized by some irresponsible Hungarian politicians at a time when Serbia, waging a bloody war in Bosnia, was threatening Hungary with terrorist actions, and NATO could give only verbal support. The admission of Slovakia and Romania to the Council of Europe was also on the agenda—the question was whether those two countries would be compelled to change their policies that were disadvantageous to the Hungarian minorities. Two years earlier, in 1991, the world knew very little about ethnic tensions in Europe and the legitimate grievances of the Hungarian minorities; the question now was whether they would see that guaranteeing rights and autonomy offered a solution that would avoid or resolve conflicts, or whether they would see Hungarian support for minority claims as a source of tension. The treaty guaranteeing the rights of the Hungarian community in Ukraine through the exemplary good relations between the two countries, coupled with the Carpathian Euroregion, which built links between peripheral border areas, offered an encouraging alternative and model for the serious conflicts in the Balkans and the post-Soviet space. The Romanian and Slovak extremists, however, who projected Hungarian intentions to resurrect a Greater Hungary, found unexpected allies in the Hungarian Parliament.

Some critics of the Antall government pointed to the fact that it had not concluded a similar treaty with Slovakia and Romania. The accusation was that Hungary refused to include in those treaties the so-called border clause, so as to keep the issue of the borders in abeyance.[47] The real reason was that these two neighbors refused

---

[44] Sáringer, *Iratok az Antall-kormány*, vol. 4: 860–62 (Doc. 158).
[45] Sáringer, *Iratok az Antall-kormány*, vol. 4: 893 (Doc. 163).
[46] Sáringer, *Iratok az Antall-kormány*, vol. 4: 866–88 (Docs. 160, 161, and 162).
[47] The latter thesis is argued in several publications by Dávid Meiszter and Pál Dunay, most emphatically in "Sikerek és kudarcok között: magyar külpolitika 1990–1994" [Between successes and failures: Hungarian foreign policy 1990–1994], *Társadalmi Szemle* 49, nos. 8–9 (1994): 35–52; and "Külpolitika: Amiről

to meet the demands of their Hungarian citizens, based on international standards. The main basis for the critics' bad faith assumptions was the debate on the ratification of the Hungarian-Ukrainian treaty, i.e., the rhetoric of the opponents.

I continued to pay particular attention to our relations with Ukraine during the last year of my mandate. On January 31, 1994, I met my colleague Zlenko again in Uzhhorod/Ungvár, on the occasion of the presentation to the victims of the Subcarpathian floods of a 40-million-forint donation from the government and the Maltese Relief Service. In Berehove/Beregszász, at the district administration office, I informed the interested parties that the Ukrainian government agreed with the establishment of a Hungarian language teachers' training college in Berehove, and I received a promise to establish an independent Hungarian school supervision system in the county. Unfortunately, I could not give any encouraging news about territorial autonomy, as the Ukrainian government failed to fulfill both the will of the people and its own promise, citing unrest among the Russian population of Crimea.[48] No one mentioned the Subcarpathian dimension of the dispute. The president of the KMKSZ district organization thanked me for my visit in a warm letter, without any reference to the ratification debate and its bearing on the Hungarians of Subcarpathia.[49]

After the changes in the governments of both countries in 1994, the replacement of the Kravchuk-Zlenko team, the intensity of cooperation between the two countries decreased, and this affected the situation of the Hungarian community in Subcarpathia. While Hungarian-language education strengthened, thanks to financial support from Hungary, and the Ferenc Rákóczi II Subcarpathian Hungarian Teachers' Training College was established, respect for minority rights weakened, the Hungarian-majority administrative unit was not established, and the Hungarian party split into two. In the new century, Ukrainian nationalism grew to the detriment of the non-Ukrainian nationalities, there was the illusion that Ukrainian national identity could be spread through the school system. Anti-Hungarian incidents were increasingly frequent, which was not a consequence of the treaty, in fact it was contrary to it, rather it was a violation of its letter and spirit. Examples were: the repeated desecration of the Verecke monument to the arrival of the Hungarian tribes in the Carpathian Basin at the end of the ninth century, the removal of Hungarian symbols and relics, and, above all, the Education Law

---

kell és amiről nem (lenne) szabad vitatkozni" [Foreign policy: What should and should not be discussed], *Társadalmi Szemle* 50, no. 1 (1995): 62–67.

[48] *Beregi Hírlap*, February 3, 1994.

[49] Árpád Dalmay to Géza Jeszenszky, February 7, 1994. Years later Dalmay "discovered" how mistaken were the policies of the Antall government.

of 2017, which was to restrict Hungarian-language education considerably.⁵⁰ The Education Law was a serious breach of the 1991 bilateral treaty, and it led to various forms of protest by the Hungarian government.

In the wake of Russia's "special military operation," i.e., its aggression against Ukraine in 2022, members of the Hungarian minority became the indirect victims of the invasion. A substantial number of them, especially men of military age, fled to Hungary. There have been a few cases of hostile acts—arson, bombing of the premises of the Hungarian party—possibly linked to Russian agents. The impression in Kyiv (and in many European capitals) is that the present government of Hungary is inclined to take the side of Russia. According to critics of the Hungarian government, the alleged anti-Hungarian sentiment in Ukraine is simply a tool for turning the public in Hungary against Ukraine—and not without success. However, the prospect of Ukraine eventually becoming a member of the European Union should remove the root of the recent tensions between the two countries, since the EU does not tolerate discrimination based on language or nationality. An amendment to the controversial Education Law was passed by the Ukrainian Parliament on December 8, 2023, and it was immediately signed by President Zelensky. The amendment states, "In educational institutions, the language of the educational process is the state language. In classes (groups) in which the language of instruction for national minorities is one of the official languages of the European Union, the right to use the language of the national minority in question is guaranteed in the educational process." In addition, the right of private universities "to choose a language of teaching" is also acknowledged, provided that it is an official language of the European Union.⁵¹ The amendment should have resolved the long-standing dispute over education in the mother tongue for the Hungarian community of Ukraine, but, inexplicably, in the spring of 2025 the Orbán government started a campaign against eventual Ukrainian membership in the EU. However, the prime minister's opponents support Ukraine both in the war and in the prospect of EU membership.⁵²

The 1991 bilateral treaty laid the foundations for exemplary and intimate relations between Hungary and Ukraine. At the time of this writing, it is still to be hoped that the war will end with Ukraine remaining a sovereign independent state, which would end the present unfriendly atmosphere between the two governments,

---

[50] Géza Jeszenszky, "Ukraine's Blunder—a Nationalist Education Law Leads to International Uproar," *Hungarian Review*, 9, no. 1 (January 2018): 30–38.
[51] "Zelensky Signs Amendments to Law on National Minorities," *Ukrainska Pravda*, December 8, 2023. Online: https://www.pravda.com.ua/eng/news/2023/12/8/7432299/.
[52] Jeszenszky, *Ukraine and Hungary* provides details on this sad turn in Hungarian-Ukrainian relations, including the most recent developments on pages 65–70.

and would open the way for a return to the principles and stipulations of the 1990 Declaration and the 1991 Treaty. The current transformation of Ukraine's administrative system—under wartime conditions—promises to be based on the principle of decentralization. That would be in line with the will of the people expressed in the 1990 December referendum and the promises of the Hungarian-Ukrainian treaty. This would vindicate those who voted for the bilateral treaty in May 1993.

Policy towards the neighbors caught in the crossfire

At the beginning of 1993, seeing the hopes and illusions about the regime change dashed, the HTMH prepared an overview of the situation of Hungarian national minorities. Its main findings were as follows: The changes in world politics were taking place under the principles of democracy, human rights and self-determination, and this brought to the surface the issue of national minorities, which had been frozen for a long time. The problem in Central and Eastern Europe was not the coexistence of various ethnic groups, but the traditionally negative policy of the state towards the national minorities. They were overtly or covertly regarded as second-class citizens, victims of political and economic discrimination, and were prevented from creating and maintaining the conditions necessary to preserve their identity. Anti-minority propaganda and actions were tolerated and sometimes even encouraged. The Hungarian minorities, aware of their modest weight and limited choices, had no separatist aspirations, but instead of being assimilated, they wished to integrate as a community in the states to which history assigned them. They saw internal self-determination, autonomy and co-nation status as suitable means to this end. They rejected the anachronistic concept of the homogeneous nation state as the opposite of the desired stability, as it would create serious internal tensions. International organizations and the powers pursuing responsible policies could exert a beneficial influence on the resolution of these problems by developing mechanisms for the protection of minorities. Neither spontaneous nor organized migration (exodus) into Hungary was seen as a solution. The Hungarian motherland urged economic, cultural and transport cooperation with the neighboring countries, especially in the border areas; that was a common interest. With regard to non-Hungarian minorities in Hungary, the State supported their demands and rejected reciprocity, if only because of the different historical background and the considerable difference in size of the mutual minorities.[53]

---

[53] Theses for dealing with the Hungarian minorities beyond the borders and for international policy pertaining to them. HTMH 00186/93/SZT, January 1993. Among my papers.

In January 1993, Prime Minister Antall also spoke on foreign policy issues on the occasion of the New Year. As much as Hungary was striving to improve relations with our neighbors, he said, this was unthinkable if the rights of the Hungarians living there were not recognized in the way they wanted. "Our basic principle is that we always try to support the political aspirations of the Hungarian minorities living in the country they live in, because they know what their interests are, and our task is to move forward, supporting their political aspirations, in agreement with their representative bodies."[54] In an interview with the Austrian daily newspaper *Kronenzeitung*, in the context of expressing my hope that "the *'Sturm und Drang'* era" of the young Slovakia would soon be over, I said: "The fact that self-government can be achieved in practice through negotiations is demonstrated by the example of South Tyrol. The Hungarian minority wants nothing more than to continue living as Hungarians." I also pointed out that the Hungarian press does not insult Hungary's neighbors, contrary to what one can so often see in the Slovak press. I expected a weakening of national intolerance in Slovakia and in our other neighbors to result from new school textbooks and from the increase in the standard of living. *Kronenzeitung* columnist Kurt Steinitz commented: "Foreign Minister Jeszenszky tries to hold the line of prudence and realism in stormy seas."[55]

Soon after that interview, I wrote in more detail about our neighborhood policy in *Magyar Nemzet*. I stressed that Hungary must not allow the dispute over the hydroelectric plant to overshadow the common economic and political interests of Hungary and Slovakia. Though some were saying that the "damned dam" compelled Hungary to re-evaluate its relations with Bucharest, I thought Romania was beginning to see that a pro-minority policy was a requirement of its Western orientation. Instead of words and symptomatic treatment, we needed action, stronger economic relations, more and faster border crossings. We did not have a border dispute with any of our neighbors, but some Romanian circles were deliberately misleading public opinion on this issue. The better we succeed in restoring the once-united Central European economic area, fragmented after the First World War, the easier it would be to improve political and human relations. It was not Hungary that created conflicts over minorities, I emphasized, but those who used to be oppressed and now wanted to live in greater freedom and without fear for their future. That was why they demand autonomy.[56]

---

[54] József Antall on the radio program "Világóra," January 3, 1993.
[55] *Kronenzeitung*, January 9, 1993. Telefax message from our embassy in Vienna, January 11, 1993.
[56] "A kormány stratégiai célja a legjobb kapcsolat kialakítása a szomszédos országokkal" [The government's strategic goal is to develop the best possible relations with neighboring countries], interview with Géza Jeszenszky by József Martin, *Magyar Nemzet*, February 6, 1993.

Chapter 9 – The Hungarian-Ukrainian Treaty and "Nation Policy"

The Antall government's policy towards Hungary's neighbors was always consistent and, in the spirit of the government program announced in 1990, it strove for sincere and friendly relations with them but was determined not to give up support for the legitimate self-governing claims of the Hungarian minorities. Since by early 1993 there were hardly any permanent foreign correspondents in Budapest or in the neighboring capitals, and even short visits by foreign journalists were rare, the sources of information about Hungary and its neighbors were the news agencies, more often diplomats in Hungary, and especially Hungarian politicians and journalists. Ignoring or misinterpreting the facts, in 1993 several foreign press organs published articles accusing Hungary of irredentism and border revisionism. According to a newspaper review compiled by the Ministry of Foreign Affairs, several newspapers characterized Hungarian minorities as dissatisfied with their situation and therefore they were "radicalized," and the Hungarian government's support for their efforts was a "time bomb." While in 1993 *Le Monde* (January 14), *Helsingen Sanomat* (January 4), the *Guardian* (January 8), the *Daily Telegraph* (February 10) and Barcelona's *El Periodico* (March 4) all reported at least on the responsibility of Slovak and Romanian nationalism for the bilateral tensions, but several others, e.g., the Greek *Kathimerini*, spoke only of Hungarian irredentism and of Hungary's and Albania's alleged territorial claims against Serbia. It was common to mention on the same page Csurka's use of the phrase "Hungarian living space" and Antall's "15 million Hungarians," omitting the cardinal phrase used by Antall in that context, "in spirit, in feeling." In the Serbian press, Elvira Fekete regularly accused Hungary of territorial demands, of wanting to re-create a Greater Hungary, and *Politika* called for the creation of a new Entente against "Hungary, which relies on a strong and active American lobby" and is arrogant and aggressive towards all its neighbors (April 29, 1993). The Czech *Rudé Právo* was content to warn, "What if the Hungarians in Slovakia start demanding to join the mother nation?" (This article, published on January 27, 1993, was intended as much for Bratislava as for Budapest.) István Csurka's pamphlet published on August 20, 1992[57] had a worldwide echo and contained the lion's share of writings and attitudes critical of Hungary. Even after the expulsion of Csurka and his followers from MDF, it was often reported abroad that his influence remained strong in the MDF and with Antall personally. A Hungarian author close to the leftist opposition predicted that in the 1994 election campaign Antall would demand the annexation of Vojvodina to Hungary. This is why the American *Christian Science Monitor*

---

[57] Csurka was one the eight vice-presidents of the MDF, his pamphlet criticized the policy of the government from a radical right angle. See chapter 2, note 45 in this volume.

(February 9, 1993, editorial) could write that "the West should pay attention to the rights of minorities in neighboring states and perhaps attach conditions to support, but at the same time warn Budapest: we keep our eyes on you." Unfortunately, it was only on the airwaves of Voice of America's Hungarian broadcast that the renowned Hungarian-born historian John Lukacs's sober words were heard on January 14, 1993: "History does not repeat itself. There is no new Little Entente. There is no question of Hungary being attacked. The problem is the question of the Hungarian minorities. Especially in Slovakia [...] our Slovak friends are unfortunately drunk with nationalism. Hungary is homogeneous and does not threaten anyone. I do not see any threat of war."[58]

On March 22, 1993, János Herman, my spokesman and head of the Press Department, presented a paper to the leadership of the Foreign Ministry on how to better inform foreign countries about minority problems and Hungarian concepts.[59] We decided to present the Hungarian Minority Act, which was expected to be adopted by the Parliament in the near future, in statements in the major languages and at our diplomatic missions. The László Teleki Foundation would prepare analytical studies and publications and organize conferences on the condition and aims of the Hungarian national minorities and the minority policies of the Hungarian and other governments. We felt we should help the organizations of Hungarians living beyond the borders to regularly inform "the major foreign press, institutions, international organizations and influential personalities" about their life and problems.

In 1993, Hungary took over the presidency of the Central European Initiative. At the March meeting of foreign ministers in Budapest, in the context of the continuing war in the Balkans, I noted that "the spectacular collapse of dictatorial regimes could have been followed by a revival of the cooperation between our countries that had existed for centuries. [...] One of the fundamental factors determining the future of the CEI is the extent to which we can apply the principles and practices generally accepted in the enlightened countries." To promote this, I proposed a CEI conference on national minorities and the creation of a working group to prepare it.[60] The importance of this topic was explained by Prime Minister Antall at the

---

[58] The source of the reports and quotations is a paper compiled by the press department of the Foreign Ministry, "The foreign press on the efforts for border revision attributed to Hungary," January 1–May 17, 1993. Press Department, S/108/11-1/93. Among my papers.

[59] Communication strategy for the presentation of the Hungarian minority policy concept abroad. March 18, 1993. Among my papers.

[60] Géza Jeszenszky's opening speech at the meeting of the CEI foreign ministers, March 22, 1993, *Magyar Külpolitikai Évkönyv, 1993*, 173–77. The rather large domestic and international repercussions of the meeting were reflected in the report of the Press Department of April 2, 1993: S/117/36-4/93. Among my papers.

Inter-Parliamentary Union seminar in Budapest on May 19, 1993, in the context of human rights enforcement, pointing out that guaranteeing individual rights "is not the same as ensuring the rights of minorities." Only respect for all those rights gives peace a chance to be maintained, and their violation threatens international law, security and world stability.[61]

I explained this in more detail in my speech to a number of diplomats and politicians at the Egmont Palace in Brussels on the same day. During my entire tenure as foreign minister, I had never before given to a foreign audience such a full exposition of the problem of national minorities and my proposed solutions:

> Most of the world's states are multi-ethnic, but the problem is not ethnic diversity, rather it is the failure of a state to ensure the equality of national minorities, the preservation of their national identity and their autonomy, if they so wish. This is not bound to lead to secession, but the refusal to do so leads to conflicts when governments, identifying the state with only the dominant national community, suppress the self-asserting aspirations of minorities. [...] I see no greater danger for the new Europe or for the former communist-dominated countries themselves, than a combination of the philosophy and strategy of communist dictatorship with intolerant nationalism. That amounts in fact to a contemporary version of national socialism. What the minorities of Central and Eastern Europe are seeking is neither separatism nor a change of borders, but the right to preserve their language and culture, to have their children educated in the language of their forefathers, and to have local officials—from mayors to police officers—chosen from their own community, who speak and think like everyone else in their town or village.[62]

After establishing this basic principle, I presented the situation and demands of Hungarians living in the seven states neighboring Hungary. I described the attitude of Ukraine, Croatia and Slovenia towards their Hungarian minorities and the joint Hungarian-Russian declaration on national minorities as promising, but said the issue could only be put to rest by "adopting a pan-European law." I urged the adoption of an additional protocol to the Council of Europe's Convention on Human

---

[61] Speech by József Antall at the seminar of the Interparliamentary Union, May 19, 1993, *Magyar Külpolitikai Évkönyv, 1993*, 207–14, quotations 209 and 214.

[62] Address by Géza Jeszenszky at the Royal Belgian Institute of International Relations, May 19, 1993. Hungarian translation in *Magyar Külpolitikai Évkönyv, 1993*, 214–21.

Rights at the forthcoming Vienna Summit.[63] I still had hope that my presentation, which was very well received on the spot, would not be just a cry in the wilderness.

I do not claim that the propaganda of the domestic opposition caused the outside world to refrain from active support for the rights of the Hungarian minorities, but it was undeniably damaging to accuse the government of irredentist ambitions from within Hungary. The latter was exemplified by a full-page article in *Magyar Nemzet* by Miklós Szabó, a Free Democrat member of Parliament, a historian who had been an outspoken critic of the communist regime before 1989. According to his article, the Antall government had no independent concept for the treatment of Hungarians living in neighboring countries, but adopted the approach of the interwar years, and "openly or covertly thought only in terms of territorial change."[64] Szabó's theses were a complete misunderstanding, and even more a misinterpretation, of the thinking of Antall and his government.

Three months after Szabó's article appeared, I was able to refute the accusations of our opposition in the only pro-government newspaper, *Új Magyarország*. In an interview, I pointed out:

> It is not Hungary, but some of its neighbors who keep the issue of borders on the agenda by attributing to Hungary, in the eyes of their own public opinion and international public opinion, an alleged ambition to rectify its borders. [...] If, however, the rights, equality and thus the state-building character of the Hungarians beyond the borders are recognized and guaranteed by our neighbors, then—in an effort to strengthen mutual trust—we can seek a formulation that confirms the validity of the territorial provisions of the peace treaty and the points of the Helsinki Final Act. But the two cannot be separated.

I confirmed that we consider the European integration of both Slovakia and Romania desirable, "if only because we do not wish to keep the millions of Hungarians living beyond the border outside the institutions in which we are or will be participating." However, I wrote, we expected the needs of their Hungarian population to be met. Not with neighboring nations, but "only with certain policies do we have serious reservations."[65]

In June 1993 I was again able to argue for the rights of national minorities in a "live" forum at the UN World Conference on Human Rights in Vienna. There, I called the crimes committed during the Southern Slav war an outrageous violation

---

[63] *Magyar Külpolitikai Évkönyv, 1993*, 214–21.
[64] Miklós Szabó in *Magyar Nemzet*, May 20, 1993.
[65] Géza Jeszenszky in *Új Magyarország*, August 4, 1993.

of human rights, urged that international observers be sent to protect the Hungarian community in Vojvodina, which was living in a climate of intimidation, and called for dialogue and cooperation between governments and minorities, as exemplified by South Tyrol, Schleswig, Finland. Minorities who are satisfied with their situation are loyal to their state, as Arnold Toynbee, one of the great thinkers of the twentieth century, argued in 1915: "Savages wipe out minorities; civilized men take out testimonials from them."[66] I deliberately stated as fact what we actually only hoped and wished for: "The close connection between the violation of human and minority rights and the flood of refugees, and the threat which this problem poses to international peace and security [...] has been wisely recognized by the international community. It is our common responsibility to put this recognition into practice."[67]

We were not so naïve as to think that if the situation of national minorities in Hungary were resolved in an exemplary manner—in law and in practice—our neighbors will follow our example. Act LXXVIII of 1993 on the Rights of National and Ethnic Minorities, passed by Parliament on July 7, 1993, with a 96 percent majority, followed from the principles and program of the Antall government. Its starting point was that minorities in Hungary were state-building factors. Unprecedented and forward-looking in international practice, the Act focused on self-government, cultural autonomy, the recognition of minority rights as group rights and the guarantee of freedom to declare one's choice of identity. The minority self-government structure, the cultural and educational self-administration that was being introduced created the opportunity for minorities to establish and maintain their own institutions.[68] The Act was not a substitute for minority activism, but it was a way of compensating for the disadvantages of being a minority. Despite its shortcomings, which became apparent over time, it has been helping minorities for more than thirty years to preserve their mother tongue, develop their culture and strengthen their self-identity, and has proved to be a good tool for ensuring the survival of minorities as a community. We have presented this exemplary law in speeches, informative publications and in our negotiations abroad. It has been welcomed in words almost everywhere, and has been called exemplary, but based on their own internal situation many countries were not in a hurry to adopt a similar law.[69]

---

[66] Toynbee, *Nationality and the War*, 20.
[67] Géza Jeszenszky's speech at the UN World Conference on Human Rights, Vienna, June 15, 1993. *Magyar Külpolitikai Évkönyv, 1993*, 241–48.
[68] *Magyar Közlöny*, no. 100 (1993): 5273–86. The government issued a statement on the occasion of the passing of the Act: *Magyar Külpolitikai Évkönyv, 1993*, 257–58.
[69] Compilation of the Ministry of Foreign Affairs for the government on the perception of Hungary and its neighborhood, November 12, 1993. Among my papers.

The Hungarian-Ukrainian treaty debate in the Hungarian Parliament awoke concerns about Hungary's alleged territorial claims, and that the emphasis on the rights of minorities was a threat to European peace. In Berlin on November 2–3, 1993, in addition to giving two lectures, in a meeting I reiterated that we did not have a border dispute with any of our neighbors, and those who spread this accusation only wanted to divert attention from the existing disregard for the legitimate demands of the Hungarian minorities. I also spoke about growing disillusionment in our region, because people were expecting more tangible support during the difficult process of economic transformation. I warned that the message was spreading that the West had always let Central Europe down.[70]

In September 1993 I proposed the establishment of an inter-ministerial committee of senior officials from the Ministries of Foreign Affairs, Interior, Education, Agriculture, International Economic Relations, Welfare, and Finance to counter misinformation about Hungary. That same month, the expert advisors of the CSCE High Commissioner on Minorities visited Budapest and Bratislava. The following month I personally informed the high commissioner himself, Max van der Stoel, about the situation of the Hungarian minorities and asked for his assistance in redressing Hungarian grievances in Slovakia and Romania. On November 8 he sent a letter to Jozef Moravčík, Slovakia's foreign minister,[71] very tactfully welcoming the promise that the rights of the Hungarian minority would not be curtailed in the course of the reform of the administrative organization of Slovakia. He gave cautious advice in support of Hungarian-language education and inter-ethnic dialogue.[72] The Slovak response spoke about the planned introduction of bilingual place-name signs and the promise of setting up a government office for minorities, also authorizing the use of personal names in the Hungarian style and spelling, thus giving the impression that the Slovak government was pursuing a generous minority policy and was only waiting for the Hungarian government to solemnly declare the inviolability of the Slovak-Hungarian border. This exchange of letters was sent to all Member States via the CSCE Secretariat.[73] In my letter to the High Commissioner, I informed him on the causes of the Hungarian-Slovak disputes and raised the issue of border crossings, where the Slovak side was delaying the opening of new ones.[74] The response was inconclusive and therefore disappointing:

---

[70] *Új Magyarország*, November 4, 1993.
[71] Jozef Moravčík (1945–): Slovak lawyer and former politician. Foreign minister (1993–94), prime minister (1994).
[72] Max van der Stoel to Foreign Minister Moravčík, November 8, 1993. Among my papers.
[73] CSCE Communication no. 38, Prague, November 25, 1993. Among my papers.
[74] Géza Jeszenszky to Max van der Stoel, November 29, 1993. Among my papers.

the former Dutch Foreign Minister showed concern not for the conditions of the Hungarian minority in Slovakia but for the situation of the (quite small) Slovak minority in Hungary. Regarding the Beneš decrees and the border crossings, he promised to follow up with his experts.[75]

Hungary's CEI presidency concluded with a meeting of foreign ministers in Debrecen on November 19–20. The substantive discussions between the ten member states resulted in a very substantial final declaration. We noted with regret that the situation in Bosnia and Herzegovina had deteriorated further and that there was no progress in the implementation of UN plans in the occupied territories of Croatia. We reaffirmed our commitment to strengthening Central European cooperation for the purpose of European integration, and we identified the economic, scientific and cultural measures needed to achieve this. We welcomed the willingness of our neighbors to the south and east to join our organization. We urged the Working Group on National Minorities to formalize a document on the protection of minority rights as soon as possible, in order to strike the necessary balance between the rights of the state and those of minorities, in close cooperation with the Council of Europe.[76] The Hungarian radical rightist periodical *Magyar Forum* described the meeting as a failure, quite unjustifiably, writing: "Hungarian diplomacy was left alone with its blind hopes, obsessions and obsessive optimism," and adding that even the Hungarian opposition admitted that freedom and democracy would not solve the problem of national minorities.[77]

By the end of 1993, with the admission to the CSCE and the Council of Europe of Czechoslovakia's two successor states, Slovakia and Romania, all with so many shortcomings in the field of minority rights, the problems of the new Central European democracies, and particularly the issue of national minorities, were pushed into the background.

---

[75] Max van der Stoel to Géza Jeszenszky, January 10, 1994. A few years later, Moldovan representatives showed me a letter from the High Commissioner warning Moldova against granting autonomy to their Gagauz minority, mentioning that this would strengthen the demand for autonomy by the Hungarians in Transylvania. Unfortunately, his successors also argued that the purpose of the HCNM was not to help minorities but to avert conflicts over the issue of the national minorities.

[76] *Magyar Külpolitikai Évkönyv, 1993*, 337–42.

[77] Imre Krajczár in *Magyar Forum*, November 25, 1993.

Chapter 10

Slovakia and Romania Join the Council of Europe

Hungary did not wish for the break-up of Czechoslovakia, if only because President Václav Havel and the democratically-minded Czechs were trying to curb the mildly anti-Czech and strongly anti-Hungarian Slovak nationalism. The split created a Czech Republic similar in area and population to Hungary, and a Slovakia roughly half the size of Hungary. It may have raised faint hopes in Hungary that it might result in some Hungarian-inhabited territory being returned to it, but in reality, it offered a much greater opportunity: the creation of an independent Slovakia in close friendship with the Republic of Hungary, which is the central area of the former common homeland, Hungaria, Uhorsko, which Slovaks named Maďarsko after 1919. This is what I personally wanted to see, but it was shipwrecked on the rock of Slovak nationalism and was left off the agenda indefinitely, because of Mečiar and the Danube barrage system. I hope that is not permanent, however, since Hungary and Slovakia have so much in common: history, religion, family relationships, and cuisine.

A new state unfriendly towards its minorities

According to the 1991 census data, the number of Hungarians in Slovakia was 567,296, while the number of native Hungarian speakers was 682,621 (11.5 percent of the country's population), a difference that could only be explained by voluntary and involuntary assimilation. In southern Slovakia, in a contiguous area, the proportion of Hungarians was 61.7 percent, as opposed to 86.5 percent in 1938. The explanation is the post-1945 expulsions and the subsequent involuntary population exchange, and assimilation.[1] The constitution begins "We, the Slovak Nation," declaring the country to be comprised of the Slovaks' state, effectively

---

[1] Hungarians in Slovakia, compiled by the Office of Hungarians Beyond the Border, January 1993. Cf. Károly Kocsis and Eszter Hodosi-Kocsis, *Ethnic Geography of the Hungarian Minorities in the Carpathian Basin* (Budapest: Hungarian Academy of Sciences, 1998), 64 and 68–76. Also, Kocsis and Tátrai, *A Kárpát-Pannon-térség*, 18–19.

downgrading the Hungarian minority to second-class citizenship.² In the budget, per capita cultural funding for Slovak projects in 1992 was three times higher than for Hungarian ones. With effect from November 18, 1992, Slovak television broadcasts in Hungarian were forbidden to use the Hungarian names of settlements in Hungarian-language programs, with the threat of immediate dismissal for those who violated the provision. It was a grave injustice that the Czechoslovak reparation law only applied to violations of property rights following the communist takeover in February 1948, and thus did not affect the earlier deprivation of rights affecting Hungarians.³

Although the Hungarians in Slovakia in 1992 feared a nationalist and anti-Hungarian Slovakia, they also saw a chance to improve their situation considerably, to gain territorial autonomy and co-nation status, as they still made up almost 12 percent of the total population.⁴ Miklós Duray, president of the Coexistence (*Együttélés*) movement, saw in the new state a "tremendous chance" for reconciliation of the peoples of Central Europe. Béla Bugár, leader of the Hungarian Christian Democratic Movement, was more realistic: he thought national minorities would be at the mercy of the government. László A. Nagy (Hungarian Civic Party) expected "sobriety and sobering up" on the part of those "who have been taken over by the stupor of national independence." The head of the Hungarian mission in Bratislava had the fewest illusions. Jenő Boros, formerly the consul general and now the new embassy's chargé d'affairs, noted that independent Slovakia, at the moment of its birth, carried a permanent image of Hungary as its enemy.⁵

Boros's view was born out as Prime Minister Valdimir Mečiar continued his sharp anti-Hungarian tirades, even making the absurd accusation that Hungary wanted to change the Trianon borders with Slovakia by using armed force. Jozef Prokeš, the chairman of the Slovak National Party, compared Hungarian policy towards Slovakia to Hitler's propaganda against Czechoslovakia and Poland in 1938–39.⁶ Speaking to the AFP news agency, Duray described the Slovak constitution as "a democratic framework for the oppression of minorities." Richard Ingham of AFP wrote that according to a poll, 50 percent of Slovaks consider the

---

² The wording recalls the fiction of the much-maligned "political nation" of the Hungarian Nationality Act of 1868. The official interpretation of the term is that it covers all the citizens of the country. Interview with Foreign Minister Milan Kňažko, *Heti Magyarország*, February 12, 1993.
³ Hungarians in Slovakia, compiled by the HTMH, January 1993.
⁴ This was the conclusion of the booklet "From Minority Status to Partnership," published in early 1993 (also in English) by the Co-Existence Political Movement led by Miklós Duray, which supported the arguments with graphs and tables.
⁵ Responses to a questionnaire in the daily newspaper *Új Szó*, MTI News Summary, January 5, 1993, 1–2.
⁶ MTI News Summary, January 5, 1993, 2.

"relocation," i.e., expulsion, of Hungarians to be the solution to the minority question.[7] A compilation of laws and practices that violated the linguistic and cultural rights of Hungarians in Slovakia was prepared by the Hungarian Human Rights Foundation (HHRF), headed by László Hámos. It showed undeniable evidence of discrimination against Hungarians.[8]

Despite all this, we had to strive for good neighborly relations, because a Hungarian-Slovak "cold war" could only have worsened the situation of Hungarians in Slovakia, and the outside world would have been unlikely to side with Hungary. In contrast to the widespread anti-Hungarian atmosphere in Slovakia, there was no noticeable antipathy towards the Slovaks in Hungary. In addition to acknowledging the crimes committed against each other, the distinguished Slavic philologist István Käfer, based on the many positive aspects of a thousand years of coexistence, called for Hungarian support for the newborn Slovakia and for the rejection of anti-Hungarian sentiment among the Slovaks.[9] Prime Minister Antall, in a letter to his Slovak counterpart expressed his conviction that "the Prime Minister clearly sees the compelling interests in establishing trust and cooperation between our peoples, inevitably linked by historical and geographical circumstances, and in our rapid and fuller integration into the European integration process."[10] A "Hungarian-Slovak TV Bridge" was held on February 12, 1993, with the intention of starting a productive dialogue; in it, journalists and the two foreign ministers discussed bilateral relations in a live broadcast. It is possible that this program also contributed to Foreign Minister Milan Kňažko's replacement.

Already at the moment of the separation and the formation of the new state, it was clear that Mečiar was striving for the opposite of a reasonable minority policy in line with Western European practice. His aim was the creation of a centralized, homogenous nation-state, and the abolition of existing—modest—minority rights. The Council of Europe, to which the two new states had to apply for membership, represented a chance to thwart this. The common threat from Slovak nationalism united the Hungarian parties in Slovakia, which had been at odds with each other on several issues. In their memorandum, addressed to the COE, they explained that the Slovak constitution considered Slovaks, who made up 85 percent of the population, to be the 'state nation', their language to be the state language; it did not

---

[7] MTI News Summary, January 5, 1993, Appendix.
[8] "Minority Rights in Slovakia: Litmus Test for Democracy," January 18, 1993. Among my papers.
[9] István Käfer, "A megalázott völgy esélye" [A chance for the humiliated valley], *Vigília*, no. 5 (1993): 338–43. It was a rejection of the author's hopes that the essay was published in *Slovenske Pohľady*, no. 9 (1993), in a translation not approved by the author, omitting several sensitive passages showing examples of Slovak bias.
[10] József Antall to Vladimir Mečiar, February 5, 1993. Among my papers.

guarantee equal rights for minorities, or the free use of their language; it protected the state nation against them, and allocated far less money to their culture and education than their population-based share. The most recent violations cited were the mass removal of Hungarian place-name signs and the frequent refusal to register Hungarian first names (instead the Slovak version). The Hungarian parties' memo considered it essential to amend the Constitution, to repeal the discriminatory provisions adopted between 1945 and 1948 and to mitigate their consequences through compensation (together with the amendment of the compensation law), and also to sign and ratify the COE's Charter of Local Self-Government and its Language Charter.[11]

The planned administrative division of the country threatened to abolish Hungarian-majority districts, thus, splitting up contiguous Hungarian-inhabited areas, merging them into Slovak-majority districts.[12] A delegation of the Coexistence and the Hungarian Christian Democratic Movement visited Budapest on March 29, 1993, and met with Hungarian leaders. They asked the Hungarian government to use the COE admission process to bring about an amendment to the Slovak constitution and the abolition of measures adversely affecting Hungarians. The Hungarian leaders in Slovakia were pleased to note that "the Hungarian government's position is fully in line with the needs of the Hungarian people" of Slovakia, and expressed their hope that it would be possible to establish a partnership on an equal footing with the Slovaks.[13] A few days later, a delegation from the Slovak National Council (Parliament) arrived in Budapest, led by Speaker Ivan Gašparovič (1941–). At our meeting they complained about the decreasing number of Slovaks in Hungary, but I received no substantive response to my words about the problems of the past and present.[14] The real answer was a report by Tibor Szabó, head of the Slovak department at the HTMH, on the manifestations of growing anti-Hungarian sentiment in Slovakia.[15]

---

[11] Memorandum on the admission of the Slovak Republic to the COE by Co-Existence, the Hungarian Christian Democratic Movement, the Hungarian People's Party and the Hungarian Civic Party, February 4, 1993.
[12] The counter-proposal of Coexistence was published in the paper *Szabad Újság*, March 20, 1993.
[13] Note of the HTMH on the visit of the Hungarian party coalition of Slovakia to Budapest on March 29, 1993. Among my papers.
[14] Based on my notes from our meeting of April 7, 1993.
[15] Report on the Hungarian aspects of the internal political situation in Slovakia, April 13, 1993. HTMH/0026/93. Among my papers.

Democracy in Slovakia—a cursory examination

After Hungary's accession in November 1990, I noticed a disappointing tendency in the COE: lowering the standards for admission of new members and insisting less and less on the basic democratic requirement that the rights of national minorities be fully respected. The Hungarian communities in Slovakia (and Romania) expected Hungary, as a member of the Council, to support their efforts to secure and, if necessary, enforce their rights in the course of the admission process. Hungary's aim was not, of course, to veto the admission of our northern neighbor (which was not practically possible, and could only be delayed), but with the help of the COE to change the unacceptable Slovak practices. Slovakia (and the Czech Republic) expected to become members of the COE automatically on January 1, 1993, the date of separation, but the Council of Ministers did not accept this, and on January 13, 1993, asked the Parliamentary Assembly of the Council of Europe (PACE) to give its opinion on the two applications for admission.

On February 1, the Assembly adopted its now famous Recommendation 1201, which was extremely forward-looking: "The Assembly recommends that the Committee of Ministers adopt an Additional Protocol to the Convention on Human Rights on the Rights of National Minorities." The draft containing twenty articles included legal and administrative measures and actions to ensure that national and ethnic communities in each country enjoyed the rights essential for their survival and well-being. The most important was Article 11: "In the regions where they are in a majority the persons belonging to a national minority shall have the right to have at their disposal appropriate local or autonomous authorities or to have a special status, matching the specific historical and territorial situation and in accordance with the domestic legislation of the state." However, the Recommendation did not become a Resolution, due to stiff opposition by several States.[16]

On March 8, 1993, the international Helsinki Watch organization wrote a letter to Prime Minister Mečiar describing the situation of the Hungarian minority as worrying, and on March 9, High Commissioner on National Minorities Max van der Stoel proposed the establishment of an independent commission to examine minority rights in Slovakia. On March 10–12, the three-member PACE committee, chaired by Finnish Social Democrat MP Tarja Halonen (who was president of

---

[16] "Recommendation 1201 (1993) of Council of Europe Sunday, 31 January 1993," https://www.sznt.org/en/documents/international-documents/892-recommendation-1201-1993-of-council-of-europe-sunday-31-january-1993. Years later I published an article commenting on the subject: "Elfeledhető-e az 1201-es?" [Is it possible to forget Recommendation 1201?], *Magyar Hírlap*, May 11, 1995, 6.

Finland from 2000 to 2012), visited Slovakia and submitted its report on June 11, 1993. Sir Basil Hall, member of the European Commission of Human Rights, visited Slovakia on March 18–19, 1993. In his report, based on his meetings with the Slovak minister of the interior and the minister of culture, he said he was impressed by the commitment of the authorities to support minority culture and arts. While he acknowledged that there were complaints about the use of place names and first names, it was explained to him that allowing place names other than the official ones would create serious problems in mapmaking, also for motorists and the postal service. He concluded that Slovak laws and their implementation were "fully in line" with the human rights standards of the Council. Louis-Edmon Pettiti, a judge of the Court of Human Rights, was unable to visit Slovakia, but in his own report he concluded that human rights promises and implementation are not yet in line, including on the use of first names, and that it would be desirable to introduce the teaching of the Hungarian language in Slovak-language schools if there were an interest.[17]

The new Slovak foreign minister, Jozef Moravčik, who replaced Milan Kňažko (who must have been found to be not nationalistic enough and too independent-minded), wrote a letter to PACE Committee Chair Halonen on April 27, 1993. In it, he—misleadingly—said that a change in the use of place names had not been ruled out.[18] During an official visit to Vienna, Mečiar announced that the ban on the registration of Hungarian names would "soon" be lifted and bilingual place-name signs would be reinstated.[19] Speaking to the COE ministers on May 6, 1993, Moravčik acknowledged the problems of minorities as a legacy of the past and expressed his readiness to implement four recommendations of the Committee of Ministers: the authorization of the use of Hungarian first names, bilingualism of place names, the annulment of the Beneš decrees and the equitable modification of the administrative system.[20] At the meeting of the COE foreign ministers on May 13, I warned my colleagues that Slovakia had not yet taken any steps to fulfil the conditions prescribed by the Council and its own commitments.

On May 19, 1993, the four Hungarian parties of Slovakia issued a Declaration. In it, they supported the admission of the Slovak Republic to the COE, but on condition that the government sign the Language Charter, remove from the agenda

---

[17] Report on human rights in Slovakia. Document of the Parliamentary Assembly, April 28, 1993. Among my papers.
[18] Marc Langendoen, "The Admission of the Slovak Republic to the Council of Europe" (MA thesis at Leiden University, Manuscript, 1999), 71.
[19] Fax message of Péter Keresztesi from the Hungarian Embassy in Vienna, May 4, 1993. Among my papers.
[20] Langendoen, "The Admission of the Slovak Republic," 74–75.

the draft law on the administrative structure which was contrary to the interests of minorities and revise it with the involvement of minorities, submit to the National Council by September 30, 1993, a draft constitutional law on the rights of minorities to self-government on the basis of the 1201 recommendation, and start constructive dialogue with the legitimate representatives of the Hungarians of Slovakia on the issues set out in their Memorandum of February 4, 1993.[21] This was submitted as a proposal to the Slovak Parliament, which did not put it on the agenda, and then, after it was submitted in a new form, blocked the vote on it on May 21 by a filibuster.[22] Subsequently, on May 25, 1993, two Hungarian parties, Coexistence and the Christian Democrats, in agreement with the Hungarian Civic Party and the Hungarian People's Party, sent a letter to the COE. They pointed out discrimination against minority communities and asked that Slovakia's accession be conditional on the following conditions being met: the amendment of the Slovak Constitution on the basis of Recommendation 1201; changes to the regulation of language use; the signing of the Language and Self-Government Charter; the repeal of discriminatory provisions adopted between 1945 and 1948; the taking into account of the interests and proposals of minorities in the restructuring of the administrative structure; and, finally, the opening of negotiations with the legitimate representatives of minorities on the constitutional settlement of their situation under the supervision of the COE.[23]

If the new Slovakia really had wanted to ensure the equality and legitimate aspirations of all its citizens, it would have accepted these proposals. In that case, Hungary would of course have warmly supported its admission to the Council, and relations between the two countries would have been harmonious ever since. The fact that this did not happen is primarily the responsibility of the Slovak political parties of the time, but the COE shares the responsibility.

It was against this background that Minister Moravčik arrived in Budapest on May 27, 1993, for an unofficial visit. The next day, our talks covered all areas of our relations: water sharing in connection with the power plant on the Danube; the opening of old-new border crossings; the location of the Hungarian Cultural Centre in Bratislava; the Deportation Agreement; compensation for Hungarians expelled from Slovakia after 1945; the reopening of the Adriatic oil pipeline; the

---

[21] Declaration of the Hungarian participants of the Round Table of the President of the Slovak Republic, May 19, 1993.
[22] Langendoen, "The Admission of the Slovak Republic," 66.
[23] Position of the Hungarian Parties Represented in the Slovak Republic's Parliament on the Question of Slovakia's Admission into the Council of Europe. Bratislava, May 25, 1993. Signatories: Árpád Duka-Zólyomi, Pál Csáky, Miklós Duray, Béla Bugár, László A. Nagy and Gyula Popély.

absence of Slovakia from the Carpathian Euroregion; and, in particular, the situation and wishes of the Hungarians in Slovakia. Moravčik made a point of saying that he could negotiate in English, but I got the impression—on other occasions too—that he did not really understand other people's English, but could only—sort of—express what he had to say in English. In any case, he did not want to understand my arguments in favor of the needs of Hungarians in Slovakia, nor did he want to understand my toast at the dinner on the evening of the 27th, when I offered him a choice: either our neighbor, who lived with us on good terms for a thousand years, complies with the May 25 memorandum of the Slovakian Hungarians, following the Western European models, as a result of which we would then have a close friendship between the two independent nations, or they refuse to reach an agreement with their own fellow Hungarians, and thus the tension between us would be perpetuated, to the detriment of all. I did not get a substantive answer from my colleague; I had the feeling that he did not dare to deviate from his boss's line.[24] In his lecture at the László Teleki Foundation's Institute for Foreign Affairs and Central Europe, Moravčik spoke of many—unfounded—grievances about the conditions of the Slovaks in Hungary in the past, while offering no apologies for the measures taken against Hungarians in Slovakia between 1945 and 1948.[25]

The mechanism of abandoning principles

On June 2, the COE's Political Affairs Committee recommended Slovakia's admission.[26] The Halonen-led panel of three rapporteurs from the Commission, who had visited Slovakia, published its report on June 11. They met only with Slovak leaders, and no Hungarian politicians; instead of the latter they met with Hungarian and Gypsy (Roma) cultural experts at Nitra/Nyitra. The document was based on the premise that there had been no human rights problem in Czechoslovakia, and they were only looking at whether anything had changed with Slovakia's independence. They admitted that they had had very little time, that they had heard "a lot of accusations and rumors" from the Slovak and Hungarian sides about different intentions, that there was a lack of mutual trust, and that this should be helped by dialogue. It was noted that the promised language law on the use of the Hungarian language had not yet been completed, that some localities lacked Hungarian street names, that some "difficult to pronounce" Hungarian first names were not among

---

[24] My handwritten notes of the negotiations of May 28, 1993.
[25] The distributed text of Moravčik's presentation, among my papers, and my personal recollections.
[26] Interestingly, the bulky 4th volume of Sáringer, *Iratok az Antall-kormány külpolitikájához* does not publish any document on Hungary's conduct in the process of Slovakia's admission to the COE.

the authorized names, and that the planned administrative division may be unfavorable for the Hungarians. However, they were reassured by Slovak promises to sign the Language Charter (which was not signed until 2001, eight years later!), to accept the principles of Recommendation 1201 (which was never done) and to respect the interests of minorities in the administrative division (the opposite is still the case today). The report also welcomed the fact that Slovakia would accept the recommendations of the High Commissioner on Minorities, including the establishment of a committee of experts to study the situation of minorities in the two countries. Hungary was ready for this, but it was never established.[27] This statement was clearly untrue and does not reflect well on the politicians who produced the report, especially the one who later became president of Finland.

In a note dated June 16, 1993, György Misur, head of the Central European Regional Policy Department (a Hungarian diplomat of Slovak origin from Békéscsaba), expressed strong (justified) criticism of the Slovak political elite in power, and optimistically believed that the COE, democratic Europe, had noticed this. He proposed a firm stand on the demands of the Hungarian minority in their Memorandum and believed that the Council of Europe would be ready and able to force the Slovak government and legislature to meet the demands of the minorities before accession.[28] This might have been the case if the PACE and the representatives of the governments had stood their ground. On June 15, 1993, the Slovak government agreed that both first and surnames could be registered according to the style and spelling of the parents of the minority individual, and submitted this to the National Assembly by special procedure,[29] but it did not go further.

The events of the next few days are worth recounting in detail, because they reflect the resolute actions for minority protection of the Hungarian side, the insincere maneuvers of the Slovak side, the softness of the COE and its member states and of the so-called "international community" in general, and the refusal to take tough but justified action that promises results.

On June 17, 1993, János Perényi, Hungary's ambassador in Strasbourg accredited to the Council of Europe, announced in the Committee of Ministers (which is actually a meeting of ambassadors) that until Slovakia changed the laws and bills that the legal representatives of the Hungarian minority objected to, Hungary would not support its admission. This caused great alarm not only in Slovakia, but

---

[27] Report on the Application by the Slovak Republic for Membership in the COE, document 6864 of the Parliamentary Assembly, June 11, 1993. https://pace.coe.int/en/files/7217.
[28] Slovakia's membership of the Council of Europe. Note by György Misur, June 16, 1993.
[29] Letter from Eva Mitrová, Slovakia's ambassador to the Council of Europe, to Hans-Peter Furrer, political director of the COE, June 18, 1993.

also in the Czech Republic and among most of the EU member states. The next day, the Slovak ambassador in Strasbourg, Eva Mitrová, in the letter to Political Director Furrer already quoted, asserted the Slovak readiness to change some of the contested laws and plans in the near future. On June 18, I sent a non-paper (an informal document seeking the reaction of the other party(ies)) to the foreign ministries of all COE member states:

> The Hungarian government still hopes that Slovakia will become a member of the Council of Europe as soon as possible. [...] Though Hungary is interested in the possible widest cooperation and in transforming the "Visegrád Three" into "Visegrád Four," we cannot accept the restriction of the rights of the Hungarian minority, [...] the nationalism of the current Slovak policy, the increased reduction in the rights of the Hungarian minority and the sometimes hostile tone towards Hungary. [...] On that basis the Hungarian government agrees with the clearly expressed position of the legitimate representatives of Hungarians in Slovakia, according to which the Slovak Parliament and government are expected to make further steps to win Hungary's support of Slovakia's joining the Council of Europe.
>
> As a consequence of this, the Hungarian government cannot accept the June 12 recommendation of the Political Affairs Committee of the Parliamentary Assembly of the Council of Europe on Slovakia.
>
> We are of the opinion that the promises of the Slovak government are not in harmony with its deeds, therefore we do not consider the conditions included in the rapporteur's report secured without legal and parliamentary guarantees. The requirement of these guarantees is in line with the system of norms of the accession to the Council of Europe, and meets the practice applied during the earlier accession processes, so also in the case of Hungary's accession to the Council of Europe.
>
> The Hungarian citizens and parties in Slovakia expect the following steps from the Slovak Parliament and government to strengthen their confidence and to ensure guarantees:
>
> – Before the accession, the Slovak Parliament should accept the laws on the use of names and the denomination of settlements, also included in the rapporteur's report as a precondition of the accession.
>
> – In the field of the transformation of the public administration, the Slovak government should grant authentic guarantees that the transformation would not bring the Hungarian ethnic minority into disadvantageous position. The restructuring should take place in accordance with the ethnic

aspects and the Recommendation 1201 of the Parliamentary Assembly of the Council of Europe. It would be useful if the Slovak party included the experts of the Council of Europe into the administration reform.

The Slovak government should make the necessary steps to ensure the financial and institutional basis for the long-term training programs for Hungarian teachers. The right for education in the Hungarian language is in line with the Recommendation 1201 (1993) of the Parliamentary Assembly of the Council of Europe and with the European Charter for Regional or Minority Languages. Slovakia should join this convention.

It is desirable and essential that the Slovak government should renounce in a political declaration the 1945–48 laws (Beneš decrees), discriminating on the basis of ethnic status.

In an attached two-page annex in English, I summarized the discriminatory measures taken in 1945–48, their consequences to date, the recent measures taken against the Hungarian minority and how this was holding back a full democratic transition.[30] On June 19,1993, the Slovak Foreign Ministry sent a *note verbale* objecting to Ambassador Perényi's remarks on June 17. On June 22, Foreign Minister Moravčik, summoning our Bratislava representative, indirectly withdrew the objection. The minister said that "the problems raised by the Hungarian Ambassador" were being resolved, but that a Hungarian veto would seriously set back the "normalization" of relations between the two countries. However, on June 21 a memo by our Foreign Ministry's Slovak desk officer reported that Slovakia was in fact blocking the Hungarian minority's demands in all the areas under discussion (territorial reorganization, education in the mother tongue, the number of Hungarian teachers and students, and the registration of Hungarian names).[31]

On June 23, 1993, Prime Minister Mečiar initiated a meeting with the heads of mission of the COE countries in Bratislava. He claimed that the Hungarian government's members, who were themselves historians (i.e., the prime minister, the foreign minister and the defense minister) did not know enough about history. The demands of the Hungarian minority in Slovakia were not in line with European practice [sic!] and no one could force Slovakia to take ethnicity into account in its administrative reform. Any reference to the Beneš decrees would

---

[30] Reflections on Slovakia's Membership in the Council of Europe. June 18, 1993. I personally oversaw the composition of the document.
[31] Judit Láng's comments, June 21, 1993. Among my papers.

mean "the rehabilitation of fascism and fascists," "fascists and former nobles would be returned to office" and would also put the Czech Republic in a seriously difficult position.

Then, instead of condemning Mečiar's nonsense and virtually rejecting the conditions for EC membership that had just been adopted in Copenhagen, the Danish ambassador in Prague, speaking on behalf of the European Community, read out the EC's position: they supported Slovakia's accession and were *putting pressure on Hungary to adopt a similar position*.[32] I found the report I received on this shocking. Even back in 1991, it was a major disappointment that so many European democracies were rejecting the inclusion of collective minority rights in a binding convention, but there was some explanation as to why. Even today, however, I see no serious reason why the COE and its Member States did not apply their own standards to a new state that was seeking and in need of European recognition but had a proven record of violating the declared principles of minority protection.

On the facts, the memo submitted by Ambassador Mitrová to the COE Secretariat on June 23, 1993, was a sham. In it, she promised to negotiate an amendment to the law regulating the use of "names of foreign origin" by July. She announced that there would be bilingual place and street names in the language of the minorities "in literal translation of Slovak names," that the administrative division of the administration will return to the traditional county system "on the basis of geographical and economic conditions" but taking into account the rights of national minorities, and finally that a faculty of national cultures would be established at the Pedagogical College in Nitra, starting in the fall term. The issue of the Beneš decrees was mentioned in the memorandum, as they had no bearing on the relationship between the Slovak government and national minorities. The covering letter stressed that "the fact that both the Slovak Republic and the Czech Republic" complied with the Statute of the Council of Europe when they were admitted in 1991 should not be ignored, and that therefore only changes that had occurred since January 1993 should be considered in the readmission process. These changes were all positive and in line with Recommendation 1201 of the PACE. With regard to the Beneš decrees, the letter claimed that only the property of Czechs and Slovaks who collaborated with the Nazi regime was confiscated, while Hungarians and Germans who participated in the anti-fascist movement were not affected by the decrees, so there was no question of collective guilt on ethnic grounds. That was a blatant lie. The crowning item among these false statements was the assertion

---

[32] Report to Prime Minister Antall for his meeting with EC ambassadors from Slovak desk officer, Judit Láng, June 25, 1993. My italics. Among my papers.

that Slovakia was sincerely striving to protect national minorities on the basis of the COE recommendations, and that Slovaks and Hungarians were living in peace and friendship on the country's territory.[33]

On the same day, the Foreign Affairs Committee of the Hungarian Parliament held a closed session to discuss possible Hungarian steps regarding Slovakia's accession to the EU. According to the chairman, László Kovács, a solution was needed that would do the least harm to Hungarian-Slovak relations while not doing significant damage Hungary's international prestige and bringing practical results for the Hungarian minority. Unfortunately, he did not say what this solution would consist of. Government and opposition speakers agreed that since all COE member states were in favor of admission, there was no point in blocking it, because the best we could do was to postpone it until the next meeting of the ministers. State Secretary János Martonyi, representing the government, suggested to the Hungarian PACE representatives that they should submit amendments and additional proposals, and if these were rejected, they should indicate their position by abstaining or voting "no." That would make it easier for the Hungarian ambassador in the Committee of Ministers to abstain and would make an interpretative statement. The Committee agreed to the proposed procedure.

On June 24, 1993, we replied to the Slovak note of June 17 in a verbal note. We stated:

> [Hungary] cannot remain indifferent to the fact that the legal representatives of the indigenous and numerous Hungarian population and Hungarian settlements in Slovakia have complained in recent months in a series of memoranda to Slovak and international forums that their rights in the new Slovak state had been weakened and had become uncertain compared to the period of the existence of the Czechoslovak state, that official preparations had been made for the reorganization of their historically established administrative system and educational institutions. [...] It is legitimate demand to expect the Slovak parliament to adopt the laws on the use of names and place names, as formulated in the relevant report of the COE rapporteurs, before accession to the Council.

---

[33] Aide-memoire of the Ministry of Foreign Affairs of the Slovak Republic concerning the membership of the Slovak Republic in the Council of Europe. Bratislava, June 23, 1993. Cf. *Slovakia—the Road to the Council of Europe: Selections from Documents concerning the Acceptance of the Slovak Republic into the Council of Europe* (Bratislava: Ministry of Foreign Affairs of the Slovak Republic, 1994), 28–30. Among my papers.

We stressed that the planned administrative reorganization should not adversely affect the Hungarian minority and said that we would like Slovakia to accede to the COE Language Charter and "to distance itself in a political declaration from laws discriminating on the basis of nationality, the so-called Beneš decrees." We also accepted the Slovak proposal made two days earlier "to start negotiations without delay on relations between Hungary and Slovakia," including representatives of the COE and the national minorities.[34]

On the same day, the EC Troika (then Denmark, the United Kingdom and Belgium) ambassadors in Budapest and the EC mission called on State Secretary Martonyi to present the EC's common position. According to their statement, Slovakia's accession to the COE as soon as possible was desirable, as this would improve the situation of the Hungarian minority in Slovakia. Slovakia had already taken steps to correct the criticized legal situation, therefore "the EC strongly urges the Hungarian government to change its position and accept Slovakia's accession." State Secretary Martonyi said in his reply that Hungary was interested in Slovakia's European integration, but the haste with which the COE member states were handling the matter was incomprehensible. Everyone recognized that basic standards must be met for accession, but it was clear that "the Slovak government does not comply with the recommendations of the COE rapporteurs' report, and does not intend to do so." Proof of that was Slovakia's foreign minister Moravčik's statement in relation to the administrative reform, that minorities should not be allowed to make up more than 50 percent of the population in any administrative unit. Martonyi proposed that Slovakia should be given time to fulfil its promises, "or if it does not do so, the member states will see the value of verbal promises." Lowering admission requirements was dangerous, he said, and "if Slovakia were admitted to the COE despite not meeting the requirements, the responsibility would fall on the COE and the countries that sponsor the admission."[35]

The question rightly arises: why did the European Community and the COE Member States close their eyes to Slovakia's anti-minority behavior? My tentative explanation is as follows. Foreigners visiting Bratislava have an unexpectedly positive impression of a city steeped in history and culture. A country having such a capital cannot be much different. The Slovak interlocutors proved to be very willing and promised everything. It was easy to presume that the Hungarian government and the Hungarian politicians in Slovakia were exaggerating the grievances.

---

[34] Verbal note from the Hungarian Ministry of Foreign Affairs to the Slovak Ministry of Foreign Affairs, June 24, 1993. Among my papers.
[35] Minutes of the meeting between State Secretary Martonyi and the EC Troika, June 24, 1993. Among my papers.

The collective rights of minorities were not recognized, and indeed were explicitly rejected by the Western governments. They feared that Mečiar was ready to push the new country into the arms of the Russians if the West was too harsh. In addition, in the Western democracies the particular sympathy for the Czechs went back as far as the First World War, and especially to the remorse over the Munich Treaty of 1938. Following the separation, why should the international treatment of the Czech Republic and Slovakia and their admission to the various organizations differ? The Czech Republic's admission to the COE was a foregone conclusion, and this also helped Slovakia. The Czech government supported Slovakia in every forum and firmly rejected the idea of rescinding the Beneš decrees. No one said it, but it was also part of the decision that after the Second World War Czechoslovakia was considered a victor and Hungary was remembered as an ally of Nazi Germany. Only one event could have made Western Europe think twice: some spectacular action by the Hungarians in Slovakia. Mass demonstrations and demands that went as far as demanding self-determination and possibly secession. It seems that neither the Hungarian politicians in Slovakia nor their voters were prepared to do this. And the West always tries to appease the harder-liners.

The reports we received from the capitals of the COE countries showed that no member state—except us—supported the postponement of Slovakia's accession, and everyone cautioned Hungary against isolation on this issue. Denmark (as President-in-Office), Austria, which saw great potential in the new country, and naive Finland were the most vigorous opponents of postponement, while only Poland, the United Kingdom, Sweden and the Netherlands showed some understanding for the Hungarian position and considered it necessary to have adequate Slovak guarantees. The COE apparatus, and Secretary General Lalumière herself, understood the Hungarian concerns and proposed the creation of a monitoring mechanism as a compromise solution.[36]

On June 23, the National Council of Slovakia agreed to follow in its policy towards minorities the recommendation of PACE 1201.[37] (It also calls for autonomy and special status, among others, in areas predominantly inhabited by minorities.) On the same day, the Slovak government promised to comply with the Halonen report in legislation in the near future. Two days later, however, the Slovak National Council, sensing the expected favorable decision of the COE, postponed even the decision on bilingual place and street names and did not react to the other Hungarian demands. As the author of a dissertation at Leiden University on the

---

[36] Background paper for the prime minister on Slovakia's admission to the Council of Europe, June 25, 1993. Among my papers.
[37] Langendoen, "The Admission of the Slovak Republic," 72.

subject, Marco Langendoen, rightly observed, "When the COE had to decide on Slovakia's application for membership, none of the four conditions was accepted by the Slovak legislature."[38]

Making another attempt, I phoned Swedish foreign minister Margaretha af Ugglas, a conservative (Moderate) party member of the Swedish Parliament, with whom I had a very good collegial relationship. I asked her to propose, on the basis of our arguments, to postpone Slovakia's admission until the legislative amendments requested by the COE and largely promised by Slovakia had been passed. With kind words of understanding, she tried to persuade me that greater pressure could be brought to bear on Slovakia to take the necessary legislative steps and to hold Slovakia to account once it became a member of the organization. I did not approach Polish foreign affairs minister Krzysztof Skubiszewski, because I knew that, despite our personal friendship and all his sympathy for the Hungarians, he would not take our side against the Slovaks, especially against the Council of Europe and EC Member States.

On June 26, 1993, at a Slovak initiative, I held talks with Foreign Minister Moravčik at the Hotel Silvanus in Visegrád. I expressed my regret that relations between our countries were not developing as I had indicated in my speech in Bratislava/Pozsony the previous September, and in our discussions with my Slovak counterparts. I listed the issues that the Hungarian parties in Slovakia objected to, highlighting that the administrative reform was openly aimed at preventing the Hungarian minority in Slovakia from forming a majority in any single entity. Hungary did not want to prevent Slovakia's accession to the COE, but to give it time to change the wrong tendencies. If this happened, Hungary would be Slovakia's strongest supporter on all issues and in all forums.

Moravčik denied that the Hungarian minority was seriously dissatisfied and that its situation was worse than it had been in Czechoslovakia. He did not rule out that the situation of the Hungarian minority would be further improved in the future, but said that this could not be done under pressure, as it would only provoke a backlash. The principles of administrative reform were economic, geographical and historical, and ethnic considerations were firmly rejected. The Hungarian government should urge the Hungarian parties in Slovakia to show moderation. On the whole he gave no positive response to our suggestions.[39] Apparently, Moravčik had no mandate to do so, the minister was merely a less than eloquent spokesman for Mečiar and his party. On returning from his visit to Romania, Prime

---

[38] Langendoen, "The Admission of the Slovak Republic," 77.
[39] Note of the meeting between Géza Jeszenszky and the Slovak Foreign Minister. June 28, 1993.

Minister Mečiar contrasted the declining number and assimilation of Slovaks in Hungary with the condition of minorities in Slovakia, which was "above European standards." He was satisfied that Hungary could at most delay, but not prevent, Slovakia's accession to the COE.[40]

In the afternoon of June 28, Slovak president Michal Kováč called Prime Minister Antall in the absence of President Göncz. He informed him that his government was ready to guarantee minority rights in appropriate laws, but said that the current Hungarian position did not provide the right climate for the adoption of such laws by Parliament. He asked Hungary to consider supporting Slovakia's accession to the EU in order to suppress the manifestations of intolerant nationalism[41] in both countries. Antall reiterated that we supported Slovakia's accession, but that we considered it necessary that "minority rights are legally settled in a way that meets European standards" before that could happen, and there was currently no guarantee of this.[42] On the eve of the decision, therefore, referring to representatives of the Hungarian minority in Slovakia, we were right to say in a statement by the foreign ministry that "the government of Slovakia has stepped back from its previous promises in the area of guaranteeing human rights, especially the rights of the Hungarian national minority, and lacks the political will or the political strength to enforce those rights consistently."[43]

A premature decision

Our international efforts were not entirely in vain. On June 28, Halonen presented a proposal to the Parliamentary Assembly to monitor the commitments of the new Member States every six months.[44] Naturally, ex post facto accountability is much less effective than imposing requirements before admission, but it eased the consciences of those who supported immediate admission. Most of them probably believed it would be effective. In the Assembly debate on June 29, József Bratinka, the MDF leader of the Hungarian delegation, found Slovakia's promises insufficient and proposed several amendments. He proposed the annulment of the Beneš decrees, which was accepted by the Assembly, and that Slovakia should

---

[40] *Magyar Nemzet*, June 28, 1993, 1–2.
[41] All this happened shortly after the heated debates in Hungary surrounding the ratification of the Hungarian-Ukrainian treaty and the formation of an independent political group by István Csurka and his followers.
[42] Summary of a telephone conversation between Prime Minister Antall and President Kováč, June 29, 1993.
[43] Announcement by the Ministry of Foreign Affairs, June 29, 1993. *Magyar Külpolitikai Évkönyv, 1993*, 249–50.
[44] Motion for an order on the honoring of commitments entered into by new member states, presented by Mrs. Halonen and others. COE document 6882, June 28, 1993.

remove from its laws group discrimination based on collective guilt. The Assembly also adopted the proposal that Slovakia could be held accountable for all points of Recommendation 1201. David Atkinson (UK, Conservative, later my personal good contact, 1940–2012), chair of the Committee of Non-Member States, criticized Halonen's monitoring proposal for abandoning the idea that membership should be based on strict conditions to be met before admission. On the Slovak side, MP Fogas confirmed that they would abide by Recommendation 1201 on minorities. Walter Schwimmer (Austrian People's Party) said that the Hungarian minority would benefit from the fact that the Strasbourg Court of Human Rights would now be open to them. In the vote, the majority—reassured by the Halonen proposal to monitor commitments—voted in favor of Slovakia's inclusion, but far from unanimously, as had been the case with the Czech Republic a few hours earlier.

The following day, June 30, the Committee of Ministers (i.e., the ambassadors of the Member States) voted on the admission. The previous day I had sent a last appeal to my ministerial colleagues, with a detailed explanation why Slovakia's admission should be postponed until they fulfilled their own pledges.[45] For the Czech Republic, the decision was unanimously "yes." In the case of Slovakia—taking into account the vote of the PACE the previous day—I sent instructions to our ambassador, János Perényi, to end his speech explaining our abstention with the following sentences:

> The Government of Hungary regrets that Slovakia has not yet fulfilled its promise to the Council of Europe. However, the amendments made by the Parliamentary Assembly in the Recommendation will allow for continuous monitoring of the developments in Slovakia and may promote better democracy and minority rights in Slovakia. The Council of Europe and its Member States have made it clear in the debate so far that they will require Slovakia to comply with the conditions set out in the Council's recommendations and the rapporteurs' reports after its accession. In our view, the chances of achieving the objectives of the Council of Europe as set out in the PACE would have been better served if Slovakia's accession had been delayed until the steps that were generally considered necessary had been taken by Slovakia. Thus, the Council of Europe has taken the responsibility for the decision. Hungary places the future of the Hungarian minority in Slovakia under the protection of the Council of Europe. The Hungarian Government considers it its duty to continue to monitor the legislative process in Slovakia

---

[45] Géza Jeszenszky to the foreign ministers of the Council of Europe, June 29, 1993. Among my papers.

and, if necessary, to draw the attention of the Council of Europe member states to this. It will endeavor to ensure that the human rights mechanisms of the Council of Europe are effectively implemented. For the above reasons, Hungary will abstain in the vote.[46]

The other ambassadors voted in favor, making Slovakia a member of the Council of Europe. I issued the following statement on the same day.

> The Hungarian government did not and still does not aim to isolate Slovakia and prevent its integration into Europe [...] The Hungarian parties in Slovakia have made public their concerns and expectations in several documents since February 1993. In their common view, the situation of Hungarians in Slovakia is complicated by a number of problems, the solution of which is inevitable. [...] The Hungarian government's position was, and remains, that the new member states of the Council of Europe should give guarantees on minority rights issues, preferably before full membership is achieved. Unfortunately, this did not happen in the case of Slovakia. Since we only received promises, we were compelled to express our reservations emphatically. In recent months, Hungarian diplomacy repeatedly drew the attention of Slovak partners and other European partners to the need to resolve these problems. [...]
>
> The Hungarian government does not consider the steps made by the Slovak government and legislature to comply with the recommendations of the Council of Europe on minority issues to be sufficient and convincing. [...] However, it considers the acceptance of the requirements set out by the PACE for the admission of Slovakia as a clear achievement. Therefore, the Hungarian delegation did not veto Slovakia's accession. However, it is crucial that the amendments adopted by the PACE yesterday significantly strengthened the requirements included in the recommendation for Slovakia's membership. [...] In our view, the chances of achieving the objectives also expressed by the PACE would have been better served if Slovakia's accession had taken place only after the steps that were generally considered necessary for Slovakia had been taken. The Council of Europe has taken on a greater responsibility than before. The Hungarian Government feels entitled, and continues to feel obliged, on the basis of the debate and the decision, to

---

[46] Instruction from minister Jeszenszky to Ambassador Perényi, June 30, 1991. Among my papers.

monitor the legislative process in Slovakia and to draw the attention of the member states to this wherever it is necessary.[47]

With the statement above, we made it clear that Slovakia's minority policy did not comply with the principles of the Council of Europe. It was not possible to veto the admission because if we had voted 'no,' the ministers of the Member States would have had to meet within a few days, and we alone would not have been able to prevent Slovakia's membership. However, we would have provoked a reaction of defiance in the Slovak legislature and in the majority population that would have made meeting the demands of the minority hopeless well into the future. Last but not least, in Western Europe and America the repercussions of our move would have been very bad and would have hindered our European and NATO integration efforts. Slovak-Romanian cooperation against the interests of Hungarian minorities would have been further strengthened.

Despite what happened, Hungary continued its efforts to make the contacts of the Hungarians of Slovakia with the motherland easier, therefore in August we agreed with Slovakia to open three old-new border crossings.[48]

There was a suggestion abroad, and at home, too, that our "tough" behavior was motivated by a domestic political consideration, to "appease" the nationalist right after the Ukrainian treaty dispute. This is a completely unfounded assumption; our position was based on the principles to which this work bears witness. As a kind of aftermath, on July 12, 1993, Prime Minister Antall congratulated Czech prime minister Václav Klaus, on his country's accession to the Council of Europe. In the letter, Antall indicated that he was counting on the Czech Republic to use the Council of Europe's monitoring mechanism to ensure that Slovakia "following the confidence it received in advance, would, shape its legal order in accordance with international standards and guarantee the rights of minorities." He also called it "indispensable for Slovakia to abolish discriminatory laws based on nationality."[49] Knowing Klaus's personality and outlook, the reply letter came as no surprise. He wrote that his country's position was that "the protection of minorities in Slovakia meets the general standard of protection under the international instruments in force." (Based on the Copenhagen recommendations of the CSCE and Resolution 1201 of the Council of Europe, this claim was completely unfounded.) As regards

---

[47] Announcement of the Ministry of Foreign Affairs on the relations between Hungary and Slovakia, June 30, 1993. *Magyar Külpolitikai Évkönyv, 1993*, 253–56.

[48] Protocol on negotiations on the opening of new border crossings on the Hungarian-Slovak state border, August 12, 1993. Among my papers.

[49] Letter from J. Antall to V. Klaus, July 12, 1993. Among my papers.

the Beneš decrees, he considered that it would be unhelpful to adopt a political or legal position on them, writing, "Let history itself be the judge of the actual role of these laws."[50] Also, speaking as a historian, I do not believe that judgement regarding inhumane laws should be left merely to history. They should be invalidated and condemned first and foremost by the states that once enacted them. Germany, Hungary and even Romania, among others, have done so, but the Czech Republic and Slovakia are still in arrears to this day.

Langendoen rightly stated in his dissertation that "Slovakia signed a number of international documents, including some that other countries had not yet accepted, but in practice it did not take measures to improve the situation of minorities."[51] Yet the result was that, together with the Hungarian parties in Slovakia, the several blatantly intolerant measures were repealed, including the provision banning the use of the Hungarian form of women's names, the halting of the attack on the Hungarian school system, progress in the use of Hungarian place names, and the biannual monitoring mechanism which limited the Slovak majority's anti-minority intentions. Even in the face of Slovakia's worrying behavior, the Council of Europe member states did not agree to postpone admission, and they deluded themselves that membership would make it easier to persuade the Slovak government to be more tolerant towards its minorities. A similar position was taken by the COE a few months later on Romania's application for membership, although to facilitate it Romania did make some minor gestures towards both Hungary and its own Hungarian minority. This made possible the first official visit by a Hungarian leader after the regime change.

A new tone in Romania?

Due to the replacement of Romanian foreign minister Năstase with the smiling Teodor Meleșcanu, who used a much friendlier tone than his predecessor, and even more so due to Romania's admission into the Council of Europe being on the agenda, in the summer of 1993 there was a noticeable decrease in anti-Hungarian outbursts in Romania. RMDSZ, the Hungarian Party of Romania, felt that my accepting the invitation to pay an official visit to Romania in September 1993, was justified. Since the Târgu Mureș pogrom of March 1990, and knowing Năstase's arguments, I had no illusions. I knew that the Romanian majority would disregard the fact that at the Romanian rally in Gyulafehérvár/Alba Iulia on December 1,

---

[50] Letter from V. Klaus to J. Antall, July 15, 1993. Among my papers.
[51] Langendoen, "The Admission of the Slovak Republic," 72.

1918, demanding the "unification" of Transylvania with the Romanian Kingdom, autonomy had been promised to the Hungarians. The cultural autonomy of the Saxons and Szeklers, as provided for in the Treaty for the Protection of Minorities, signed by Romania in 1919, was never even mentioned. The majority of Romanian society saw Hungary as an enemy who, with the support of external powers, wanted to regain Transylvania. The Hungarians of Transylvania were seen as Hungary's allies in this, who, therefore, must be kept firmly in check, at a distance from power even at local level, and made to feel at every turn that Romania belongs only to the Romanians. Since this mentality was far from European principles and practice, and Romania also wanted to be included in the organizations of European integration, I had thought that the improvement of the situation of Hungarians in Transylvania could be brought about primarily by the position and pressure of these organizations. In turn, with better inter-state relations, we could reduce the anti-Hungarian sentiment of Romanian public opinion, we could promote the assertion of the political strength of the Hungarians of Romanian, the acceptance of their demands, and possibly the formation of a Romanian government with a different composition.

On February 26, 1993, the leadership of the Hungarian Democratic Alliance of Romania met with the leaders of Hungary in Budapest and a communiqué was issued on our discussions. These included the establishment of permanent and institutionalized contacts and the support of the RMDSZ in its efforts to strengthen the social, economic and cultural position of the Hungarians in Romania, to achieve their internal self-determination and autonomy. We agreed on the desirability of adopting a law regulating the situation of national minorities in both countries, of concluding a bilateral agreement on the protection of minorities, and of concluding the inter-state basic treaty as soon as possible. The Antall government's fundamental position, which also applied to other Hungarian communities across the border, was expressed in Point 7 of the Announcement. "The Prime Minister of Hungary and the leaders of the Hungarian Democratic Alliance of Romania agree that the issue of the Hungarian minority beyond the border should not be used for party political and electoral purposes. To this end, they consider it necessary to put the politics of the Hungarian minority beyond the border on a unified basis, with multi-party consensus."[52]

On March 20, 1993, in response to an invitation by the city of Gyula and the Association of Romanians in Hungary, I participated together with my Romanian

---

[52] Announcement by the Hungarian Government and the Hungarian Democratic Alliance of Romania, February 26, 1993. Among my papers.

colleague in the unveiling of the statue of Liviu Rebreanu, a renowned Romanian writer, who, as a young lieutenant served in Gyula for years before the First World War. At my suggestion, the representative of the Romanians in Hungary, György Petrusán, and representatives of the RMDSZ also attended the meeting. In my speech I presented a tentative program for improving Hungarian-Romanian relations:

> In the midst of freedom, these two peoples must put into practice the ideals that our writers and poets have professed. [...] Our goal is to have throughout Europe, and especially in Central and Eastern Europe, contented minorities living in ethnically non-homogeneous countries. A contented minority is a resource for the country in which it lives and promotes friendship and cooperation with its brothers and sisters living beyond its borders, with the country we call, in a very nice word, motherland. [...] our great writers, poets, artists, who served the friendship of our two peoples in significant numbers, offer a good example.

I then recalled the events and atmosphere of Christmas 1989.

> We must not allow narrow-minded politicians or publicists to erase from our memories these historic days when Romanians and Hungarians did not care who spoke what language: they fought together, and celebrated together the dawn of the hoped-for freedom. Together, we made declarations and shook hands in the belief that a better world must be born when dictatorships are gone. It is very important that the joined hands of that time do not let go of each other and do not let the prejudices of false prophets or simply of people long excluded from European ideas prevent this spirit of Timisoara/Temesvár from spreading and taking hold on a broad scale.

For me, the life of Rebreanu carried the message that "very many people were able to unite the cultures of the two peoples and wanted to serve the culture and friendship of the two peoples."[53]

It was agreed to open two new border crossings in the coming months at Méhkerék and Battonya. The Romanian response to the reopening of the consulates general was that "the issue can be dealt with in principle." However, Meleșcanu

---

[53] Speech by Géza Jeszenszky at the unveiling of the statue of Liviu Rebreanu in Gyula, March 20, 1993. Among my papers.

stressed that the Hungarian-Romanian basic treaty should include the fact that Hungary has no territorial claims.[54] He confirmed this when he participated in the NATO seminar in Budapest on June 5, 1993, saying that he considered it important to conclude the basic treaty with Hungary, and that Hungary should support Romania's accession to the Council of Europe. I replied, "I would hurry to Bucharest if I saw any hope of progress on the points of the 41 Hungarian proposals on the table." Hungary was ready to support Romania's admission to the COE "if the situation of minorities is settled in a reassuring way."[55]

Romania on the threshold of the Council of Europe

Romania's application for membership of the Council of Europe submitted in 1990 reached the stage in the spring of 1993 where the competent committees were able to take a position. Following the example of the Hungarian parties of Slovakia, the RMDSZ also formulated those changes Hungarians in Transylvania considered necessary for Romania to meet the requirements of COE membership. The list was—with good reason—quite long: The constitution defined the country as a unitary nation-state whose only official language is Romanian. Despite the arguments of the RMDSZ, the Hungarian party, that has not changed. This discriminates against some 3 million national minority citizens. In 1993, as a result of heightened Romanian nationalism, minorities were excluded from control in all areas of public life—public administration, the judiciary, and the state-controlled economy. Local administration was dependent on the political will of the central government due to lack of financial resources. In the judiciary, those who did not (sufficiently) speak the official language could only present their case with the help of an interpreter—at their own expense. The use of Romanian was compulsory at meetings of local bodies, even if all members belong to a minority. Submissions to the authorities could be made in the minority's mother tongue, but only if accompanied by a certified translation into Romanian. There was no law on the restitution of nationalized land and property. The independence of public service media was not guaranteed by law, and the Audio-Visual Council was controlled by the political majority.

The RMDSZ then addressed the steps needed to be taken. The status of national minorities and their linguistic, cultural and religious rights should be guaranteed by law, in accordance with COE Recommendation 1993/1201 and the CSCE Copenhagen recommendations. The European Charter of Human Rights, the

---

[54] "Hungarian-Romanian negotiations," *Népszabadság*, March 22, 1993. For a detailed account of the meeting, see Sáringer, *Iratok az Antall-kormány*, vol. 4: 605–11 (Doc. 111).
[55] *Magyar Hírlap*, June 8, 1993.

European Charter of Local Self-Government and the European Charter for Regional or Minority Languages should be signed and ratified. An education law should guarantee an independent network of schools with instruction in the mother tongue of the minorities, and administered by them. The (Hungarian language) Bolyai University, closed in 1959, should be restored. Until the necessary changes were made in Romania's legal order, Romania was not suitable for membership, the document stated. It was signed by President Béla Markó and Executive President Csaba Takács.[56]

I hoped that a translation or summary of this Memorandum had been prepared in Romanian, English and French, and had been sent to the various COE committees. Unfortunately, the committees had already dealt with the issue earlier, in April and May, and on July 1 the Political Affairs Committee voted 14:12 in favor of Romania's inclusion, with a decision expected at the September PACE meeting. As most of the previous objections to Romania concerned the laws and their application, the position of the Legal Affairs Committee was very important. The appointed rapporteur was Gunnar Jansson, a representative of the Swedish-speaking Åland Islands, which belongs to Finland. (I was a member of this committee between 1994 and 1998, and I came to know Jansson as an upright, honest, well-intentioned Scandinavian politician. He simply could not imagine how amoral people could be elected to national parliaments in democratic elections.) His report, dated August 17, 1993, suggested that it was unlikely that he had become familiar with the points raised by the RMDSZ. It accepted that the elections of September 1992, with all the doubts about their fairness, were democratic. The role of the secret service (SRI) "gives cause for some concern and caution," it read; the legal control of SRI was adequate, but the crucial issue was its practical implementation. Jansson quoted a Helsinki Watch report that detainees in police stations suffered systematic and brutal ill-treatment in order to extract confessions. "Romania has undoubtedly done a lot for minorities," the report said, adding that "not all the demands of the 1.6 million-strong Hungarian minority are justified." Referring to an article in the July 21 issue of the *International Herald Tribune*, the report saw an improvement in the situation of the Hungarian and German minorities, as negotiations with the U.S. Project on Ethnic Relations in July "resulted in the admission of 300 more Hungarian students to the Babes-Bolyai University in Cluj, increasing the teaching of history and geography classes in minority languages in primary schools, and installing multilingual street name signs in areas where the

---

[56] Memorandum of the Hungarian Democratic Alliance of Romania on the admission of Romania to the Council of Europe, August 5, 1993. Among my papers.

minority population is 30 percent or more." Much remained to be done in the area of fundamental rights and freedoms; legislation, while seemingly adequate, was not so in executing the laws.

The question arises, Jansson noted in his report, whether there was any guarantee that Romania would honor its commitments after accession, especially given how many of the people in high positions had held similar positions under the Ceaușescu regime. He concluded, however, that Romania was on the road to democracy and that membership in the COE could further encourage positive developments; therefore, he recommended its admission to the organization. "However," he noted, "it is understandable if some members of the Parliamentary Assembly will abstain or vote against Romania's membership, as happened in the Political Affairs Committee." Jansson was reassured that Romania itself was aware of the need for change and that the ongoing monitoring already agreed for Slovakia would allow the COE committees to monitor developments. During the Legal Committee's visit to Romania in April, a number of questions were put to the Romanian authorities, to which satisfactory answers were given, including regarding the case of the Hungarian and Roma defendants convicted for the events in Târgu Mureș in March 1990, and the case of Hungarians convicted for the December 1989 popular demonstrations in Zetelaka and Oroszhegy (the lynching of Securitate officers). György Frunda, a member of the PACE visiting delegation in Romania, representing the RMDSZ, rebutted the official Romanian reply on several points.[57] Both Jansson and F. König, the COE rapporteurs, suggested that it would have been a good idea to grant presidential pardons to those (exclusively Hungarians) who had been convicted in a legally dubious manner after the 1989/90 turnaround. President Iliescu promised to do so, and Foreign Minister Meleșcanu confirmed in writing that "the President of the country will examine the possibility of taking action before the end of the year. The action will be a positive signal in the resolution of this issue."[58] I raised the matter in my subsequent negotiations, and the leaders of the RMDSZ were adamant in their calls for the release of those sentenced to a long prison term without a fair trial. Finally, on March 25, 1994, Iliescu granted a partial pardon and reduced the length of the sentence for the Hungarians and the Roma, while the Communist leaders still in prison were all released.[59]

---

[57] Draft Opinion on the application for membership to the COE submitted by Romania. Rapporteur G. Jansson, Finland, Liberal, August 17, 1993. Detailed critical comments by István Gyarmati, of the Department for Security and European Cooperation, from August 25, 1993, are among my papers.

[58] On the basis of my instructions, the Romanian ambassador in Budapest, Ioan Donca, was reminded of the promises about the pardon in a letter by Deputy State Secretary Iván Bába, in early January 1994.

[59] Udvardy Data Bank, https://udvardy.adatbank.ro/?action=helymutato&helymutato=Zetelaka%20 (RO)&kezd=31. "A total of thirteen persons of Hungarian nationality were unjustly convicted in

The Jansson report, which saw encouraging developments in the situation of the Hungarian minority, also referred to the so-called "secret Neptun negotiations." The PER (Project on Ethnic Relations), described in Chapter 7, first brought together representatives of the Romanian government and the RMDSZ in Switzerland in January 1992. The *Washington Post* reported on April 3, 1993, that the Romanian government was for the first time showing willingness to take concrete steps to ease tensions with its Hungarian minority. Among the concessions promised were the return of the Bolyai Grammar School in Târgu Mures/Marosvásárhely to the Hungarian community, a university quota for minorities, the submission of a law on the rights of national minorities, the publication of place and street names in Hungarian in Hungarian-inhabited areas, and the creation of a Council for the National Minorities.[60] A crucial meeting took place on July 15–17 at the Black Sea resort of Neptun. On behalf of the RMDSZ, Senator György Frunda and MPs László Borbély and György Tokay met with Viorel Hrebenciuc, head of the National Minority Council, and agreed on concessions published in the *New York Times* on July 20. PER director Kassof and its co-director, Livia Plaks, attended the meeting as observers. On July 21, PER opened an office in Târgu Mures/Marosvásárhely with the aim of building trust between the two communities. (I met with PER leaders on several occasions, and my impression was that their intentions were sincere, but they gave credence to the Romanian assumption that the real goal of both the Hungarians in Transylvania and the Budapest government was to change the borders.)

László Tőkés, at the time honorary president of the RMDSZ, sharply attacked what he said were secret and unauthorized negotiations, and in a press conference on July 29, 1993, he called the outcome of the meeting a shambles.[61] Two days later, Béla Markó, president of the RMDSZ, responded that there could be no speaking of secret negotiations, as the participants had made statements to the press afterwards and had informed the executive board. But he added: "The promises made in Neptunfürdő have, however, already been on the agenda of the Minority Council, which has so far also turned out to be a showcase institution, and even in the reports

---

connection with the events of 1989 in Romania. Four defendants in Oroszhegy (Dealu) in Székelyland were sentenced to 66 years imprisonment, three defendants in Zetelaka (Zetea) to 58 years and six defendants in Kézdivásárhely (Târgu Secuiesc) to 21 years. Of the 145 years of cumulative prison sentences in the three trials, 34 years and 7 months were served, and three of the thirteen defendants died, two of them by suicide." Hungarian Human Rights Foundation, New York, March 3, 2003. http://www.hhrf.org/kezdivasarhely/.

[60] David Ottaway, "Romania Makes Overtures to Ethnic Hungarian Minority: American-Brokered Deal Grants Special Rights, Sets Up Committee," *Washington Post*, April 3, 1993.
[61] Udvardy Data Bank, July 29, 1993, https://udvardy.adatbank.ro/index.php?action=helymutato&helymutato=Neptunfurd%C3%B5.

of the COE." In his opinion, "these issues should not be resolved in such deliberations. There is the right political framework. The RMDSZ has clearly stated its goals at its Congress in Brasov in January and will not be satisfied with half-solutions, even if we know that it is a long process."[62]

The Hungarian government was not aware of these talks, but later it became obvious that the Romanian government did not really want to make any concessions, and only wanted to maintain the appearance of being ready for a dialogue with "moderate" minority politicians. I did not join those who criticized the negotiations because I trusted the RMDSZ, respected its autonomy, and also trusted the good intentions of the PER. I thought that only by negotiating (bargaining, if you like) with the Romanian majority was there any chance of improving the situation of the Hungarians in Transylvania. Doing the latter was the primary purpose of my visit to Romania in September.

My official visit to Romania

According to the program agreed in advance, following my talks in Bucharest, I was to visit the predominantly Hungarian *Székelyföld* region,[63] then Timișoara, the scene of the great turn of 1989, before returning to Bucharest to sum up the results of the visit. Before my departure for Romania, I gave a long interview to the Romanian news agency Rompres, which was published on September 14. I started from the premise that "Romania was one of Hungary's most important economic partners between the two world wars, our trade between us declined during the communist period and continued to decline as a result of the transition to a market economy," and said that this urgently needed to change. "Romania is home to the second largest Hungarian community after Hungary, but the two peoples do not know each other well enough." After presenting the achievements of regime change in Hungary, I reaffirmed that it was our goal

> to build good neighborly, preferably friendly, relations with all our neighbors, based on common destiny and interests, on a new basis, [...] our immediate objective is to stabilize the whole Central and Eastern European region as soon as possible, both politically and economically. It is in our interest that Romania followed the same path and became, together with us, a prosperous

---

[62] *Romániai Magyar Szó*, July 31, 1993.
[63] Székelyföld is a historical region, comprising the counties of Harghita, Covasna and Mures, predominantly inhabited by Hungarians. It had nominal autonomy in the 1950s, which the post-1990 Romanian governments refuse to restore. See Bottoni, *Sztálin a székelyeknél*. Cf. Chapter 3, footnote 72 in this volume.

country ready for membership in the European organizations and institutions, including the Council of Europe and then the European Community.⁶⁴

In our bilateral relations, I continued, we should be aware that, despite the tensions, there were many encouraging elements, such as the Open Sky Agreement in the military field,⁶⁵ cooperation in the field of internal affairs against international crime, and the existence of around a thousand joint ventures registered in Romania, "cultural institutes have been opened, the joint committee of historians is functioning again, the Hungarian-Romanian Friendship Society is very active in Pécs, and I also follow with confidence the activities of the Interethnic Society based in Cluj and the Dialogue Group in Bucharest." Following this *captatio benevolentiae*, trying to create a favorable atmosphere for the reception of my words, I pointed out the serious problems that needed to be addressed:

> There is no border dispute between Hungary and Romania, the peace treaties of 1920 and 1947 were guaranteed by the great powers, and Hungary does not question their validity. Consistent adherence to the Helsinki principles and the Charter of Paris precludes any citizen of Romania from mistrusting Hungary. However, I am bound to recall that at the time of the signing of the peace treaties, the Hungarian minority living in Romania undoubtedly had many more schools, cultural institutions, rights and properties than today. Although the institutions of Hungarian culture and the Hungarian churches suffered a great deal of damage in the 1920s, in 1947 the Bolyai University was still in operation in Cluj, there was an extensive network of Hungarian schools and bilingualism was widely practiced. The nationalizations after 1948, the show trials and then the measures taken against the Hungarian population during the Ceaușescu period caused very serious wounds to the Hungarian population in Romania.
>
> In my view, the Hungarian Democratic Alliance of Romania is pursuing a sensible and responsible policy, its aim is to harmoniously settle the relationship between the majority and the minority, and above all to ensure that the Hungarian population of Transylvania, which has lived there for more than a thousand years, feels that its basic living conditions and cultural needs have been met, and that it can look forward to a secure future. I do not

---

⁶⁴ Géza Jeszenszky, statement to the Rompres news agency, September 14, 1993. Among my papers.
⁶⁵ The Treaty on Open Skies, negotiated between the members of NATO and the defunct Warsaw Pact, established a program of unarmed aerial surveillance flights over the entire territory of its participants. The agreement was signed in Helsinki, Finland, on March 24, 1992, but in 2021 Russia withdrew from the treaty.

understand why the RMDSZ memorandum on Romania's accession to the Council of Europe, issued at the end of August, has provoked such strong criticism. I do not consider it my duty to comment on the proposals that fall within the competence of the Romanian Parliament, but I agree with those Romanian opinions that propose studying the wishes of the Hungarian community, in line with the aspiration of all democracies in the world to investigate citizens' complaints and, as far as possible, to meet their needs. I have said many times that my emphasis in Romanian-Hungarian relations is not exclusively on the satisfactory settlement of the situation of the Hungarian minority in Romania, but on a broad community of interests between the two countries, however, I feel it is impossible to try to improve and tighten relations over the heads of the Hungarian and Romanian minorities living in the two countries, without consulting them. It is almost a cliché, but it cannot be stressed enough that the development of the situation of national minorities living in individual countries influences internal and international security and stability, and that those nationalities can play a useful, mediating role in economic, political and cultural relations between states. [...] I consider the most important thing to do is to strengthen our economic relations and cooperation. [...] A primary and extremely urgent task is to change the impossible situation that has developed at the border crossings between the two countries. While at most border crossing points in Hungary, passengers spend minutes, crossing the border at our eastern border takes several hours for passenger traffic and several days for freight traffic. This situation is not good for Romania's international relations. In addition to the increase of the number of the functioning border stations, the opening of new border crossings, or more precisely the reopening of the once operational crossing points closed during the communist era, is an urgent priority. This is a prerequisite for the complementary economies of the two countries to revive old ties and for Romania and Hungary, both of which are striving for European integration, to pave the way for the free movement of goods, money, labor and services between them. The existing significant economic turnover and mutual tourism, based on a wide range of kinship and friendship ties, require and justify the opening of consular representations, or more precisely the reopening of consulates-general closed by the dictatorship and promised to be reopened after the December 1989 turnaround. In addition to the reciprocal traffic, the unfortunately increasing number of infringements and accidents also make it necessary to avoid citizens having to go to distant capitals to deal with these matters.

It is often said that there is a need to strengthen trust between the two countries, the two peoples. I feel that Hungary and the Hungarian people, through their selfless help at Christmas 1989 and afterwards, have shown that they deeply felt the suffering of the Romanian and Hungarian populations of Romania and have striven to establish a genuine and lasting friendship between the two peoples under the two national flags, with the hated communist coat-of-arms torn from them. Despite the disappointments that we have suffered since then, we affirm and maintain this goal. It is perhaps little known that large quantities of humanitarian aid (food, medicine, clothing) are constantly arriving in Romania from Western Europe, and that Hungary waives tolls and other charges for such goods. Although it is hardly possible to compare the situation and needs of the Romanians in Hungary, who make up about one hundredth of the Hungarian population in Romania, with those of Hungarians in Transylvania, I am pleased to see that Romanians in Hungary are satisfied with their situation and appreciate the minority law passed by the Hungarian Parliament this year, which, in addition to the already substantial cultural support, gives them far-reaching self-government and self-administration opportunities.

With the above I tried to show that there were encouraging trends in relations between our countries, but there was still a lot to be done. I elaborated:

We need to ensure the convertibility of the two countries' currencies and to conclude agreements on tourism, railways and aviation. We need to make the documents of the history of the two peoples accessible for research, and we need to appreciate and restore the tangible monuments and memorials of our history, which are closely linked, and to inaugurate new statues and memorials where appropriate and possible. In parallel with all this, it is appropriate to conclude a new treaty between the two states, in which we must provide a remedy for perceived or real fears and grievances. With political will and goodwill, this can be done, but it really requires that we know each other, because this is a prerequisite for understanding and trust. I am travelling to Romania with the same goodwill and sense of friendship that I felt when, as a private citizen, I visited Romania's beautiful landscapes and cities on countless occasions, that I represented as a historian at the International Congress of Historians in Bucharest in 1980, and that I used to teach my university students about the difficult but beautiful history of the Romanian people, a history full of suffering. I very much hope that my visit will lead to better relations between us and I am sure that many people at home and abroad sincerely wish that.[66]

Although my statement did not impress the blinkered anti-Hungarian Romanian nationalists, its echo was decidedly positive. Only the mayor of Cluj-Napoca/Kolozsvár, the notorious Gheorge Funar, president of the Romanian National Unity Party, demanded that the foreign minister withdraw my invitation.

By previous agreement, my Romanian colleague Melescanu gave an interview to *Népszabadság*, the Hungarian newspaper with the largest circulation. He put the emphasis on the conclusion of the bilateral "basic" treaty, including the territorial clause, but also called the signing of conventions on mutual protection of investments and the avoidance of double taxation an important goal. He recalled:

> In most of the treaties concluded so far, including the recently ratified Hungarian-Ukrainian treaty, there is a territorial clause. The problem for us is whether we will give up the idea of having such a clause in the treaty. The answer is no. Because it is now a standard practice between the countries in this region, and I think that if we were to waive it—as opposed to the Ukrainian treaty, for example—it would be a signal that would be very badly received by Romanian society. As far as the specific wording is concerned, we have no prejudices or obsessions, but the basic idea would be that the two sides have no territorial claims on each other.

"Do you seriously believe that any significant political force in Hungary would make territorial claims against any of its neighbors?" asked the Hungarian newspaper.

> No, I don't believe in such a possibility, and I think that's an opinion shared by quite a few people. [...] It's about fixing a legal rule, even if we are convinced that this is the case, all the more so because there have been statements contrary to this. The clause also has a psychological value at the level of Romanian society, because if there were a very clear legal clause, it would not be possible to interpret a whole series of actions initiated by, say, the Hungarian authorities as a veiled manifestation of territorial claims.[67]

---

[66] Géza Jeszenszky's statement to the Rompres news agency, September 14, 1993. Among my papers.
[67] *Népszabadság*, September 14, 1993.

There were certainly well-meaning people in both countries who expected a border guarantee in a basic treaty to silence extremism and radically improve relations. In 1996, the Socialist-Free Democratic government finally gave that guarantee. Has that improved relations between the two countries? Experience shows that for a long time, not substantially—and what improvement there was not due to the treaty but to the policy of the RMDSZ, and its participation in the government after 1996.

On September 15, 1993, I arrived in Bucharest with my wife, some colleagues and journalists in a modest Soviet-made military aircraft (Antonov-26). There I was greeted by a host of Romanian journalists, along with Meleșcanu and Ambassador Ernő Rudas. First, I met Foreign Minister Meleșcanu, who handed over Romanian Foreign Ministry documents relating to the 1956 revolution and the deportation of Imre Nagy and his colleagues to Romania. Our discussions continued the next day, lasting a total of seven hours. I explained in detail what we considered necessary for a real improvement in relations between the two countries. I listed in detail the international documents relating to the protection of minorities (including the COE 1201 recommendation, which also envisages autonomy), which we would like to see adopted by the Romanian legislature and implemented. We agreed to organize future symposia on the status of minorities. Radically speeding up the border crossing, which then took several hours, was not only in the interest of the Hungarian minority, I explained, but was also essential for strengthening our economic and cultural relations. My colleague agreed that queues at the borders should be eliminated, agreed that two new border crossing points should be opened immediately and that more should be opened later.[68] Textbooks would be reviewed with the help of experts and diplomas would be mutually recognized. On the issue of the Consulate General in Cluj-Napoca/Kolozsvár, I pointed out that its reopening was not simply in the interest of the Hungarian minority, it was primarily in the interest of visiting Hungarian citizens, just as the Romanian Consulate General in Debrecen would be primarily in the interest of Romanian citizens. My partner was surprised by my announcement that we intended to open further Hungarian consulates in addition to Cluj-Napoca/Kolozsvár, since the Romanian capital is located at "one end" of the country, and consular matters usually do not arise there. As regarded the basic treaty, I reiterated our willingness in principle and our expectations as to its content. I did not make any specific pledge to support Romania's accession to the European Council, but, referring to the legitimate expectations of the RMDSZ

---

[68] Dr. György Ruzsa, the mayor of Méhkerék, a village in Hungary inhabited partly by Romanians, wrote me a letter on November 2 thanking me for my support in establishing a kindergarten for the Romanian children.

memorandum, I said that it was in our common interest that Romania, which professes European values, should also become a member of the European institutions. At the end of our talks, we signed the agreement prepared on the elimination of double taxation and mutual investment protection.

On the first day, I was received by Prime Minister Nicolae Văcăroiu. According to his assessment, there were no outstanding problems on the issue of bilingual signs and the situation of Hungarian-language education in Romania was satisfactory. On the morning of the 16th, I met with the leaders of the opposition, Emil Constantinescu of the Democratic Convention and Corneliu Coposu, president of the National Christian Democratic Peasant Party, followed by a meeting with representatives of former prime minister Petre Roman's party, the Democratic Party. I visited Ovidiu Gherman, the president of the Senate, and in the early afternoon I had a relaxed and informative meeting with the leaders and representatives of the RMDSZ at the association's headquarters. This was followed by my presentation at the Foreign Policy Society on "Romania and Hungary in post-communist Europe." In it I pointed out that in the post-Cold War world, rivalry based on the exploitation of power differences was an anachronism, and then I cited the examples of Hungarian and Romanian historical and cultural personalities who had stood up for cooperation between the two nations. I refuted the favorite subject of Romanian nationalists that communism was brought to Romania by Hungarians and Jews. "Everyone suffered under communism, but minorities always suffered more. The tragedies of many peoples of the former Soviet Union are proof of this, and the Hungarians in Romania have also experienced it bitterly. If statistics were compiled on the ethnic composition of the concentration camps in the Danube Delta, or on those imprisoned for political reasons, my thesis could be proven exactly." The fall of the dictatorship offered a good opportunity for cooperation between the two peoples, and it would be good to "bring back and resurrect the intertwining of the two national flags with their torn-apart coats of arms."

I then summarized the achievements of Hungary's domestic and foreign policy:

> Despite the remaining problems, especially concerning the situation of the Hungarian minority, we have high hopes that relations with Slovakia, Romania and, after the international settlement of the crisis, with Serbia, too, will be fully normalized. [...] The priorities of Hungarian foreign policy include supporting the legitimate aspirations of the Hungarian minority living across the border and the legitimate organizations of the indigenous Hungarian minority living in their place of residence, which operate in accordance with democratic principles and the principles of European

integration, in a manner that respects international standards, and making their situation and legitimate goals known to a broad international audience. [...] On July 7, 1993, the Hungarian Parliament adopted the Minorities Act, which sets an example in regulating the rights of all persons and communities in Hungary who claim to belong to an ethnic or religious minority.

I went on to present the recent advances in relations between the two countries, the arguments in favor of the reopening of the Consulates General and the obstacles to be overcome, such as the anomalies in border traffic and tourism:

Hungary, for its part, has long been calling for the establishment of standards and rules in Europe, especially in the former communist countries, which—similar to the 1919 agreements on the protection of minorities—lay down the rights of minorities, the preconditions for the use of their language and the preservation of their culture. Since one of the basic requirements of democracy is that decisions about citizens should not be taken without consulting them, I believe that it is entirely justified to involve the legally elected representatives of individual minorities, including the ethnic Hungarians in Romania, in the preparation of plans and ideas concerning them. That should apply also the planned bilateral treaty between our two countries. Since 1990, Romania and Hungary have shared the same basic goals: to create democracy and a well-functioning market economy, to join the European integration process and, through all this, to ensure the best possible well-being of citizens. Hungary has an interest in seeing Romania move as much as possible along this path with its western neighbor. The Hungarian nationality of Romania enriches Romania with its accumulated knowledge and traditions and can greatly contribute to the above goals. The aspirations of the Hungarians in Romania do not pose any threat to the majority nation, the accusation of separatism is unrealistic, given the geographical location of the Hungarian population, and is completely frivolous in the light of European realities.

After listing the positive examples in Western Europe concerning minorities, I reminded the audience:

European and transatlantic integration forums (COE, European Community, NATO) consider the way in which the aspiring states implement internal democracy, local democracy, minority rights and overcome tensions between themselves as a precondition and touchstone of enlargement. They do not want to include quarrelsome countries in their own circle, but since the Balkan crisis they have paid even more attention to the causes of conflicts and who was responsible for them. One of the secrets of the success of Western democracies has been their ability to embrace and integrate the aspirations of different social groups and communities and not to hinder those aspirations that can be fulfilled. In the relations between states, too, a policy of genuine compromise has prevailed, rather than a policy of force and overstretched national interest. By following the lessons and example of Western Europe, Romania and Hungary can successfully solve their internal and external problems. It is the task and responsibility of the present generation of politicians to recognize and realize this.[69]

That evening, I paid a protocol visit to President Iliescu, scheduled for one hour. The head of state began the conversation with a monologue that lasted almost an hour and consisted of a rather odd, completely distorted presentation of Hungarian-Romanian relations in the past. For example, he outlined the centuries of Ottoman Turkish rule over the two Romanian principalities, Wallachia and Moldova, governed and exploited by the Greek Phanariot princes. This had reduced the Romanians to total misery, but he described it as better than the Hungarian or Habsburg supremacy had been in Transylvania! He likened the government of Hungary's patronage of the Hungarian minorities to Hitler's pre-war policy of using German minorities for subversion, and called the Hungarian minority of Romania Hungary's "fifth column." At this point, I could have stood up and left my host, who was being unprecedentedly rude and so out of touch with reality. However, I thought it was an opportunity to set out facts that Iliescu had never faced. I did what the Hungarian opposition, especially Gyula Horn, often accused me of doing, giving historical lectures instead of negotiating. I literally lectured the Romanian president, who coupled his ignorance of the history of Romanian-Hungarian relations with bad faith. On the issue of language use, for example, I referred to instances of multilingual signs I had seen from North America to Israel. After my responses, Iliescu's tone became friendlier, and the visit stretched on for two hours. After our meeting, Iliescu told MTI that he was in favor of direct dialogue and was therefore happy with our frank exchange of views, adding that he was ready to meet the Hungarian head of state or prime minister at any time, as long as the two countries did not interfere in each other's internal affairs on the treatment

---

[69] Géza Jeszenszky's lecture is published (with omissions) in *Magyar Külpolitikai Évkönyv, 1993*, 285–92.

of the minorities.⁷⁰ (Years later, on an occasion of Iliescu visiting Washington and meeting with me, he recalled our most friendly conversation!)

On the evening after this meeting there was a reception given at the Hungarian Embassy. It was attended by the leader of the opposition, Constantinescu, a civilian geologist and university professor, who had done much better than Iliescu in the 1992 presidential elections in Transylvanian. At his initiative, we had a confidential meeting in a separate room where he told me that Iliescu was a member of the reorganized Securitate, with strong anti-Yeltsin Russian connections. If Hungary were to block Romania's membership in the COE, or even veto it, it would radically reduce support for the Democratic Convention, and Hungarian-Romanian coexistence in Transylvania would take a tragic turn. In order to divert attention from the threatening economic conditions and the real causes of Romania's international isolation, the Romanian secret service was preparing for a bloody ethnic conflict similar to the one in Târgu Mureș/Marosvásárhely in 1990'. He was aware of the problems of the Hungarians in Transylvania and would like to develop a coordinated strategy with the RMDSZ to solve them, but its memorandum to the COE had also put him in a difficult position, triggering a condemnatory campaign by the authorities.

I explained to Constantinescu that the memorandum pointed at real shortcomings, that the remedies proposed were in line with the principles of the COE, and that several European countries, from the Netherlands to Scandinavia, had strong reservations about Romania's democracy. According to Constantinescu, Hungary's position was crucial; if we supported Romania's accession to the COE, we would pull the rug out from under the feet of the Romanian President and his think-tank. Once in Europe, the current Romanian leadership would be exposed; their face as neo-communist functionaries, would emerge from behind the European mask.⁷¹ I judged Constantinescu's words to be sincere, not a manifestation of two-faced Romanian politics. His presidency in 1996–2000 and the invitation to the RMDSZ to participate in the government, confirmed that he was indeed being sincere with me, as did also our private meetings after his term ended.

On September 17, I set off on a tour of the Székely counties. Everywhere I went, I not only met local Hungarian and Romanian leaders but also had the opportunity to talk to the Hungarian population, who welcomed me with touching enthusiasm. In Târgu Mureș/Marosvásárhely, the traditional center of the region, I laid a wreath

---

⁷⁰ Report on Foreign Minister Géza Jeszenszky's official visit to Romania, September 20, 1993. Sáringer, *Iratok az Antall-kormány*, vol. 4: 655–58 (Doc. 115).

⁷¹ The Hungarian embassy in Bucharest's record of the conversation between the Hungarian foreign minister and the president of the Democratic Convention in Romania on September 16, 1993.

Figure 27. In Transylvania: visiting András Sütő, the renowned author at Marosvásárhely/Târgu Mureș, September 17, 1993

at the monument to the Szekler martyrs of the 1848–49 War of Independence and the heroes of December 1989, and presented a collection of books at the Bolyai Farkas Lyceum. At the *Vártemplom* (Castle Church) I was warmly welcomed by Pastor Dénes Fülöp, who had been imprisoned during the Communist years, and his congregation. We sang the Hungarian National Anthem, which my official escort, State Secretary Marcel Dinu, protested indignantly, but he was calmed by the pastor who showed him that the Anthem is in the Calvinist hymnal, the last item of the psalms and hymns. (I learned later that there was a special directive from the government to all officials not to show the Hungarian national colors or allow the singing of the Anthem during my visit.) In the afternoon, my wife and I visited András Sütő, a highly respected author who lost an eye when attacked by a Romanian mob in March 1990.

In Erdőszentgyörgy the following day, I visited the grave of Claudia Rhédey, the great-grandmother of the British monarch, to lay a wreath, then went on to Szováta, Korond, Farkaslaka and Székelyudvarhely—all locations well known to most Hungarians. The very fact that the Hungarian foreign minister travelled in a car with a Hungarian flag and stopped at each place to greet the local population, which welcomed him tumultuously, was something that had not happened in Transylvania since the province was annexed by Romania. In Parajd, I showed the

Chapter 10 – Slovakia and Romania Join the Council of Europe

Figure 28. Visiting the house of my first visit to Transylvania in 1969 (Parajd/Praid), with the leaders of RMDSZ, Béla Markó and László Borbély

RMDSZ leaders the farmhouse where I had stayed on my first trip to Transylvania in 1969—unfortunately, Farmer Ambrus was no longer alive.

The set itinerary was increasingly "delayed," which my official Romanian escorts did not mind, as they expected that my meeting with the people waiting for me at the Udvarhely town hall would therefore be cancelled. I avoided this trap by making an impromptu speech at the packed town hall instead of attending the lunch waiting for us at the Küküllő Hotel. In it, I spoke about my vision of a Europe without borders, the significance of membership in the Council of Europe and what it implied, the future of nations and national minorities. Perhaps the most timely element was a response to Iliescu's oft-mentioned claim (in the press and to me) that the duty of a national minority is loyalty to the state. An approximate paraphrase would be: "Every citizen is loyal to the authorities if the authorities are also loyal to him. [...] A good country can count on the support of its citizens. So, the loyalty of the Romanian Hungarians should not be questioned or required, but earned." I also referred to an issue which is still prevalent in the countries around Hungary, particularly in Romania:

> Here I see the flag of Romania side by side with the flag of Hungary. The red-white-green is not simply the flag of the State of Hungary, it is the flag

of all Hungarians. And when the borders looked different, those who said that the Romanian students in Transylvania could, of course, use their own national colors, were right, and they did show it. There were Hungarians who did not like that, but the time has passed for people not to respect each other's national colors.

I also talked about the most topical issue:

> In front of the Council of Europe headquarters in Strasbourg there is the European flag and there are also the flags of the Member States. I very much hope that the Romanian national flag will soon be hoisted on a mast there. How could we, Hungarians be against this, because if Romania were not allowed to join the various European organizations, it would mean that the Hungarians in Romania would not be allowed to join them either. This would be against Hungarian national interests. It is not we, the Hungarian government, but the member states of the Council of Europe, that in order to become a member of the Council, one must meet the expectations and rules that are common in this organization, in this political club. The leaders of Romania have indicated that they respect these rules, and I think that the sooner this is achieved, the better. Then it will not be Hungary, but all the Member States of the Council of Europe who will, by a public declaration, admit Romania to the Council of Europe. The decision, this public declaration, is not up to Hungary and not up to the RMDSZ. Everyone should be aware of this...[72]

My second day's program ended in Fehéregyháza (Albești) with a wreath-laying at the Petőfi monument, where the great Hungarian poet fell in the battle against the invading Russians on July 31, 1849. At Sighișoara/Segesvár, Hungarian schoolchildren welcomed me with the ancient Székely hymn "Jesus, bless the people of Transylvania." There was one dissonant element in my tour of Székelyföld: the prefects of Mures/Maros and Harghita/Hargita counties instructed the (Hungarian) mayors of the settlements to address the Hungarian foreign minister in the official language of the state, with the assistance of an interpreter. In some places they did so with embarrassed reluctance, but in most places, they ignored the arbitrary order. To the best of my knowledge, they were not reprimanded.

---

[72] My taped speech was published in *Magyar Külpolitikai Évkönyv, 1993*, 293–99.

In the evening of September 18, I flew to Timișoara/Temesvár, where the next morning, a Sunday, I laid a wreath at the monument of the 1989 Revolution. I was greeted there by Romanians protesting against the Bucharest government. Then I attended the Reformed (Calvinist) service, where Bishop László Tőkés said in his sermon that many people remained silent because they felt it was safer. However, whoever remains silent is not a patriot, "Love for the homeland urges us never to be silent. [...] Sacrificing the collective rights of the Hungarian minority and risking its very survival is a political gamble." At the Orthodox Archdiocese headquarters, Archbishop Nicolae Corneanu hosted the Hungarian foreign minister and the leaders of the denominations, Roman Catholic bishop Sebastian Kräuter, Reformed bishop László Tőkés, Chief Rabbi Ernő Neumann, and representatives of the Greek Catholic and Baptist Churches. The discussion was frank and intimate.

From Timișoara, we flew back to Bucharest, where I had a joint press conference with Foreign Minister Meleșcanu to assess the visit. I voiced that the Hungarian government insisted on the re-opening of the Consulate General in Cluj/Kolozsvár. Education in the mother tongue must be guaranteed. With regard to the basic treaty, I stressed that the border issue between the two countries had been settled by the peace treaties in force, that Hungary had no territorial claims against Romania, and that minority rights must be guaranteed. Meleșcanu announced that two joint committee meetings would be held on the minority issue in order to explore the problems.

My visit attracted more attention in the Romanian press than in the Hungarian. "Bucharest and Budapest choose clear skies" (*Tineretul liber*), "Reflecting on Franco-German history, two diplomats have made the news" (*Adevarul*), "We will follow the path of Franco-German reconciliation" (*Romania libera*). These were headlines of the first reports. Commentaries ranged from "successful" to "insignificant agreements." Those Romanians who expected a turnaround and Hungarian promises on the COE accession or the basic treaty were disappointed: "Everywhere, Jeszenszky was dignified and reserved, but did not make any clear commitments."[73]

The hopes in Hungary that Romania would radically change its attitude towards the demands of the Hungarian minority were not fulfilled. Béla Markó, president of the RMDSZ, was under no illusion that their demands would be at least partially met any time soon, but he appreciated that I had drawn attention to the problems of the Hungarian minority and that the wider Romanian public had been able to see Hungary's perception without having it be distorted. I feel

---

[73] Embassy Press Telegram, Bucharest, September 17, 1993; Ministry of Foreign Affairs, summary by the Press Department, S/Nk/2-09.28. Among my papers.

that the Transylvanian-born correspondent Mihály András Beke best summed up the benefits of my trip: "The outstretched hand towards the Romanians, the embracing arm towards the Hungarians of Transylvania reflected firm intentions."[74] Indeed, the last time a leading Hungarian politician had visited Székelyland was in 1958, but communist prime minister János Kádár's declaration of loyalty to the Romanian leadership had only provoked exasperation. In addition to the results already mentioned, the good news was that the issue of bilingual inscriptions was soon brought before the Romanian government, and that on September 22 Foreign Minister Meleșcanu received Béla Markó, president of the RMDSZ, and Executive President Csaba Takács and gave his positive assessment of his talks with Foreign Minister Jeszenszky. They exchanged views on the RMDSZ's ideas on education, the Minorities Act, and organizing a Romanian-Hungarian dialogue series.[75]

Membership—with conditions

Even before my visit to Romania, I wrote to several of my foreign minister colleagues informing them of the changes that the elected representatives of the Hungarian community in Romania expected from the Romanian government as a precondition for membership in the Council of Europe. I found that, based on rapporteur Jansson's report, the member states were reassured by the promises of the new Romanian government headed by Nicolae Văcăroiu (1943–), whose tone was different from that of its predecessor. They were satisfied that the monitoring, introduced at Slovakia's accession to the COE, could be applied to further accessions. In line with the Hungarian government's intentions, the Hungarian Parliament's Foreign Affairs Committee on September 24, 1993, recommended Hungary's support for Romania's full membership in the COE on condition that it fulfill the necessary conditions by providing accountable guarantees.

The Parliamentary Assembly of the COE discussed Romania's application for membership on September 28. Only one Dutch and one Austrian MP opposed the admission. The PACE recommended that Romania be invited to the COE, subject to a continuous six-monthly monitoring of the commitments made by Romania. At the same time, it called on Romania to sign the European charters on the self-government of local authorities and the use of languages by minorities, also to guarantee freedom of the press and to adopt a new law on minorities and education, to return nationalized church property, to take action against anti-Semitism, nationalism,

---

[74] *Heti Magyarország*, September 24, 1993.
[75] "RMDSZ leaders at the foreign minister," *Romániai Magyar Szó*, September 25, 1993.

national and religious discrimination, to improve prison conditions, and to review the release of political and ethnic prisoners.[76] The RMDSZ was pleased to note that the nine-point conditionality largely corresponded to the terms of the RMDSZ's memorandum to the COE. Speaking to the BBC's Romanian program, Senator György Frunda said it was the first time that the COE had imposed so many conditions on a prospective new member state.

At its meeting on October 4, the COE Committee of Ministers (the Strasbourg ambassadors), admitted Romania as a member, with Hungary abstaining. The conditions proposed by the PACE could not be included in the Resolution because France rejected the proposal of Denmark, the Netherlands, Switzerland and Belgium for that, but the conditions remained in force. Looking back from the present, it can be said that the August Memorandum of the RMDSZ contributed to the imposition of strict conditions for admission. Twenty years later, in 2013, the then leadership of the Hungarian party rightly claimed that this was "the document that put Romania in order."[77]

On October 7, Foreign Minister Meleșcanu, in an interview with the daily *Romániai Magyar Szó*, assessed the recent visit to Romania by the Hungarian foreign minister: it could be considered a historic event if both sides took advantage of the opportunities created by the visit through concrete actions and measures. The Hungarian side seemed to be ready to enshrine the inviolability of borders in the basic treaty, with a reference to the Helsinki Final Act. On the issue of minorities, the Romanian side was willing to accept wording that committed it to respect international standards. At Romania's admission to the Council of Europe, nine recommendations were voted. Those recommendations were not binding, Meleșcanu said, but they must be implemented. He said no constitutional amendment was needed, but that some laws should be changed.[78]

President Iliescu must have been annoyed by the Council of Europe's recommendations, because *Dimineata*, a newspaper close to him, wrote that since Romania's neighbor was "a hot-tempered and vindictive Hungary," the question arose whether Romania should get closer to NATO or Russia. The answer was revealing: "Why should we fear a Russian alliance? Only the blind cannot see the advantage in this situation, when Hungary has not modified its irredentist demands, and the West openly encourages it." In the October 9–10, 1993, issue of this newspaper,

---

[76] Opinion 176 (1993) of the Parliamentary Assembly of the Council of Europe on Romania's application for membership of the COE. https://pace.coe.int/en/files/13915/html.

[77] *Erdélyi Riport*, August 28, 2013. http://erdelyiriport.ro/politika/a-dokumentum-amely-rancba-szedte-romaniat

[78] *Romániai Magyar Szó*, October 7, 1993.

the president said that in his meeting with Géza Jeszenszky, he explained that the Hungarian policy of attachment to the Hungarian minority outside the border is similar to Hitler's practice of playing the role of the subversive fifth column with the German minority. Iliescu's words caused consternation in Budapest, said foreign affairs spokesman János Herman at the beginning of his October 12, 1993, press briefing. He recalled that the meeting of the two foreign ministers had been described by both countries as positive, and that the Hungarian government had not put obstacles in the way of Romania's membership of the Council of Europe. The spokesman said that at the meeting with the president Mr. Jeszenszky had rejected this blatant accusation, but did not make the remarks public in the interest of better relations.[79]

The Summit of the Council of Europe

On October 8–9, 1993, a summit of heads of state and government of the COE took place in Vienna. In a letter to the meeting, the Central European Initiative (CEI) proposed enlarging the COE, and the early adoption of a convention to ensure the protection of the national minorities.[80] It is instructive to note how the European leaders present at the meeting spoke—some honestly, some misleadingly. Due to his ongoing medical treatment in Cologne, Prime Minister Antall had requested that I represent Hungary, therefore, on the basis of my own notes, I can recall what was said. The host, President Thomas Klestil, pointed out that while the Congress of Vienna in 1815 was trying to restore the old order, we were now creating a new order in Europe. Secretary General Catherine Lalumière spoke about the transformation of the Council of Europe through the enlargements, and said that the importance of minority rights was a consequence. According to President Václav Havel, the nation state favored by eighteenth century philosopher Johann Gottfried Herder must be surpassed, and minorities must be allowed to prosper, overcoming national parochialism; but this did not mean enacting the right to self-determination by calling into question the existing borders, because that is what leads to wars, as 1938 showed. Chancellor Helmut Kohl spoke of the happiness he felt about an enlarged free Europe, and called for the adoption of an additional protocol guaranteeing the protection of minorities. This was supported by Lord Chancellor Lord Mackay, representing the United Kingdom. The prime minister of Denmark, Poul Nyrup Rasmussen, warned against watering down the

---

[79] *Magyar Nemzet*, October 13, 1993.
[80] The English text is in my possession, but it is undated.

COE standards and proposed mutual protection of minorities on a bilateral basis, following the example of the German-Danish relationship. Slovenian prime minister Janet Drnovšek called the protection of minority rights the key to the loyalty of the minorities. Dutch prime minister Ruud Lubbers called for the adoption of legally binding minority protection standards. Iliescu, for his part, claimed that his country's tolerant and minority-friendly attitude was demonstrated by the fact that the representatives of fourteen minorities had guaranteed seats in parliament and were loyal to the majority. That international law overrides national law was another guarantee, he said. Norwegian prime minister Gro Harlem Brundtland characterized the new generation of the new Europe as being based on tolerance. Sweden's prime minister, Karl Bildt, said that it was necessary not to allow human rights to be diluted and that the fulfilment of commitments had to be monitored. Austrian chancellor Franz Vranitzky also stressed the importance of legal guarantees and said that "ethnic cleansing" should not be rewarded by changing borders. On the French side, Foreign Minister Alain Juppé warned against national passions, stressed the need for the permanent nature of borders, talked about the danger of minority ghettos, stressed the importance of preventive diplomacy, and said he expected a political document (i.e., non-binding legal standards) from the summit. I have no better word for Slovak prime minister Mečiar's speech than that it was eye-opening: "Minorities are the apple of our eye, they enrich our country," he claimed, but they cannot have more rights than the majority, collective rights do not exist, only individual rights. The guarantee of borders is the key to peace. There must be Europe-wide regulation, not separate treatment of East-Central Europe, he said, knowing that Western Europe does not have the large historical minorities that we see here. What he meant was that if some regulation is inevitable, Western Europe would help to dilute it.[81]

In my own speech, I expressed my delight that today we live in "a different Europe and [have] a different Council of Europe" than when Hungary joined it three years ago. Referring to the two newly admitted states, I explained:

> Recently my country expressed certain reservations concerning the latest admissions. My government is satisfied that the Parliamentary Assembly and the Committee of Ministers, by making some recommendations and provisions, has assumed a most welcome responsibility over the fulfilment of the pledges made by the countries concerned. I am confident that the governments of these countries will be able to pass the necessary legislation and

---

[81] The above summaries are based on my notes.

will not be prevented by extremist forces, like the "red-brown" ones recently seen in Moscow, from honoring the recommendations of the Council of Europe. [...]

In Central and Eastern Europe, the countries must embark upon the same road that the founders of the Council of Europe took some forty years ago. Inter-state confidence must grow, and sources of tension or bias must be removed. One of the best ways to do so is encouraging and facilitating regional and trans-frontier cooperation. This was started four years ago by Italy, Austria, Hungary and Yugoslavia, and it has developed into the Central European Initiative. This association has been also following with utmost interest and sympathy the activities of the Council of Europe aimed at the protection of national minorities, including the elaboration of a legally binding document. Upon the decision of the Prime Ministers, the CEI member countries embarked on working out an instrument for the protection of national minorities as a CEI contribution to the Council of Europe's efforts in this field.

There, before the highest forum of the Council of Europe, I repeated my *ceterum censeo*, my constant message and warning:

1) In Central and Eastern Europe, the ethnic composition of existing states and the history of the present borders is fundamentally different from that of Western Europe. Despite the brutal ethnic cleansing carried out by Hitler and Stalin, and more recently by others, the eastern half of Europe has remained and must remain a colorful ethnic mosaic, since one of our most fundamental human rights is to live one's life in his or her native land.
2) The ethnic and national tensions in Central and Eastern Europe are not as serious as the media often portray them. The former Yugoslavia is the exception, not the rule.
3) Tensions are caused not by the existence of minorities, or by their claims, but by their disadvantageous position. If they were guaranteed their basic desire to preserve their identity, ethnic tensions would be reduced or even eliminated.
4) Many people dispute the existence of collective rights. But almost no one denies that xenophobia, racial and ethnic discrimination exist. The latter is always the result of being a member of a group or community. If rights can be denied on a collective basis, it is logical that legal guarantees should be available to an entire community.

5) Recently, some governments have begun to argue that members of national minorities should be obliged to show loyalty to the state. Since loyalty is nothing more than obedience to the law, loyalty presents no problem where the state is neutral on nationality issues—as President Havel proposed yesterday—where the state respects the rights of minorities to manage their own cultural affairs, to use place names that their ancestors have kept for centuries, and so on. Citizens, whether they belong to the majority or the minority, will only be loyal to a government that is loyal to them in return.[82]

As is customary at major international meetings, the declaration adopted by the summit was drafted in advance by the officials of the member states, and the speeches delivered did not change it. The text stated that the protection of national minorities was a vital element of the stability and security of the continent. Appendix II expressed the COE's determination to translate the recommendations adopted in Copenhagen into legal obligations "to the fullest extent possible." (The latter phrase weakened rather than strengthened the intention.) It stressed the importance of bilateral treaties for the protection of national minorities and instructed the Committee of Ministers to prepare a draft framework treaty for the protection of minorities by June 1994, and to begin work on a protocol to the Convention on Human Rights on the cultural rights of persons belonging to minorities.[83] As usual, this was more than nothing, but it did not offer much hope that my arguments would not remain mere words. Still, at the Committee of Ministers meeting in Strasbourg on November 4, 1993, I tried to strike while the COE's iron was still warm—if no longer hot. Referring to the Vienna summit resolution calling for a campaign against xenophobia, I pointed out that "xenophobia can also take various forms of expression of hostility towards a country's national minorities." At the same time, "national minorities can be transformed from sources of discontent into useful and contented communities of citizens" if their defense "is given its rightful place in the country's legislature."[84]

---

[82] Speech by Géza Jeszenszky at the Summit of Heads of State and Government of the European Council, October 8, 1993, *Magyar Külpolitikai Évkönyv, 1993*, 309–13.

[83] Declaration of the Council of Europe's First Summit (Vienna, October 9, 1993), https://www.cvce.eu/obj/declaration_of_the_council_of_europe_s_first_summit_vienna_9_october_1993-en-d7c530b5-a7c9-43f9-95af-c28b3c8b50d3.html.

[84] Contribution by Géza Jeszenszky at the 93rd meeting of the COE Committee of Ministers. *Magyar Külpolitikai Évkönyv, 1993*, 314–15.

With little hope of success, I warned my foreign minister colleagues at our meeting in Rome at the end of that year that resolving the situation of national minorities was a key requirement for European stability.[85]

Semi-Private visit to Háromszék

In addition to the many kind letters and messages I received from ordinary Székely people, there was a memorable aftermath to my official visit to Romania. The September trip had not even been planned yet when I received a letter in June 1993 from Botond Turóczy, a retired engineer from Târgu Secuiesc/Kézdivásárhely, in the southeastern corner of Transylvania, the old center of the district of Háromszék. It informed me that his town was erecting a statue to Mózes Turóczy, a coppersmith, an 1848 freedom fighter and a fellow cannon founder of Áron Gábor, who cast sixty-four copper cannons in Kézdivásárhely for the Hungarian army. I was asked to dedicate the bust, because the founder of the Turóczy family, which spread over the whole of the Háromszék district, was István Jeszenszky, a goldsmith and relative of my ancestors, who had moved from Turóc County to Kézdivásárhely in 1647. As proof of the connection, they sent me the family coat of arms of the Turóczy family—which was indeed identical to that of the Jeszenszky family of Nagyjeszen! This request could only be accepted. András Vetró, a renowned Transylvanian sculptor, completed his work by the end of October, and the unveiling was scheduled for November 6, 1993. Meleşcanu was abroad, so he sent State Secretary Marcel Dinu to represent the administration on my whirlwind visit, termed as private.

When my military plane landed at Târgu Mureş airport on a Saturday morning, Ambassador Rudas informed me that the promised helicopter was not available due to overcast skies, so I would not be able to make the statue's unveiling scheduled for noon. With a strong push, he managed to get state cars sent from somewhere to transport our small delegation to the Székely town, a good 200 km away. The ceremony was rescheduled for the afternoon, the audience went home, but faithfully returned in time. In Romanian and Hungarian, Mayor Csaba Szőts greeted the thousands of people who had gathered in the small town despite the drizzling rain, including the girls dressed in beautiful Székely costumes. After the Romanian national anthem, the brass band of Réty played the *Szózat*, the unofficial second national anthem of Hungary.

---

[85] Contribution by Géza Jeszenszky at the meeting of the Council of Foreign Ministers of the CSCE Member States in Rome, November 30, 1993. *Magyar Külpolitikai Évkönyv, 1993,* 347–52.

Chapter 10 – Slovakia and Romania Join the Council of Europe

Figure 29. In Transylvania: dedicating the bust of Mózes Turóczy, who cast the copper guns in the War of Independence, 1849, Kézdivásárhely/Târgu Secuiesc, November 6, 1993

After unveiling the statue of my freedom fighting distant relative and laying the numerous wreaths accompanied by the orchestra playing the famous popular song "Gábor Áron rézágyúja" (The copper canon of Áron Gábor), I began my speech by saying that the Hungarian War of Independence of 1848–49 was also a struggle for the best European ideals and world freedom. My presence, welcomed by the Romanian government, refuted those who would see the Hungarian citizens of Romania and the majority of the Hungarian nation living across the border as some kind of threat:

> Three days ago, I myself stood in Strasbourg when the Romanian flag was raised in front of the building of the Council of Europe. The Government of Romania has made a promise, a commitment, to enact the laws that already exist and are in force in other countries of Europe, which come with membership of the Council of Europe. Hungary has made no attempt to prevent or even to put a brake on Romania's accession and, in the spirit of anticipated confidence, congratulates Romania on having chosen the European path.[86]

---

[86] *Heti Magyarország*, November 12, 1993, and my private notes, among my papers.

I thanked the people of the city for their loyalty to their nation and its history and told them that I had visited Kézdivásárhely before, but that today's celebration was only made possible by the change of regime. Then Béla Markó, a native of the town and president of the RMDSZ, recalled the fervor of Turóczy and of the whole of Transylvania in those valiant times:

> Bowing my head to the memory of Mózes Turóczy, I would now like to refer to a different kind of courage, the courage of reason. In 1848, it was not enough to promise a cannon, but it was also necessary to make one. Now it is not enough to say that there will be a Hungarian school, culture, and self-government, but we must also do something about it. If we do not do everything ourselves, there is nothing and no one to look forward to.[87]

After a brief historical presentation by the renowned Transylvanian historian Ákos Egyed, State Secretary Dinu greeted me on behalf of his minister. "Those who claim that nothing has changed in Romania since '89 are contradicting themselves, and nothing proves it better than the presence of the Hungarian foreign minister." The "statue-installing gathering" ended with the singing of the Hungarian and Székely anthems throughout the city. State Secretary Dinu did not protest this time.

Unfortunately, recounting all the things I saw and heard, all the people I talked to in the next twenty-four hours in Csíkszereda, Sepsiszentgyörgy and Ilyefalva (Miercurea Ciuc, Sfântu Gheorghe and Ilieni in Romanian) would require too many pages. Clearly there was a thaw in Romanian-Hungarian relations, and the response from the Romanian press, consisting of fair reports and commentary, far exceeded the response in September and could be taken as an encouraging sign. Unfortunately, however, a senator from the Romanian government party, Ion Solcanu, objected at Monday's meeting in Parliament to the display of "the flag of a foreign state" during the Hungarian foreign minister's private visit to Târgu Secuiesc. Béla Markó responded by saying that his fellow senator had questioned a customary and internationally established right, and recommended that Solcanu travel abroad more often in order to become better informed. In addition, he added, it had not been strictly a private visit, as the Romanian government was represented at the ceremony by State Secretary for Foreign Affairs Dinu. In any case, the right to use their own national symbols was one of the demands of Romanians living beyond the borders. RMDSZ member György Frunda said that Romania should stop saying one thing in the Council of Europe and doing something very different

---

[87] *Heti Magyarország*, November 12, 1993, and my private notes, among my papers.

at home. Solcanu remarked that Béla Markó did not represent the Hungarian state and therefore had no right to respond. His Romanian colleagues applauded.

My second trip to Romania in two months was also covered in detail by the press in Hungary, sensing that I may have broken the ice in Hungarian-Romanian relations. I was very sorry that Reformed bishop László Tőkés, with whom I had been in constant and intensive contact since 1990, and who had often visited our apartment in Budapest, had criticized both those trips in the autumn of 1993. On the TV program *Nap-kelte* on December 6 he said he thought that it would give the false impression, both in Romania and abroad, that relations between the two countries and the situation of Hungarians in Transylvania were improving, which was not the case.

On the basis of my detailed report above, I claim that the bishop was wrong. In the previous three years, a Hungarian minister could not have toured Székelyland, genuinely strengthening hope and activity among the Hungarians there, and publicly expressing the Hungarian wishes, with arguments broadcast by the Romanian-language media. Even if the reason for the changing behavior in Romania was the intention to "soften" the Council of Europe—and I think it was more than that—important progress was made, the atmosphere became calmer, and we broke through some minor walls. "All or nothing" is not a good policy. The emotional side of the visit was also important, as was testified by Mihály András Beke, son of the renowned Székely writer György Beke, who gave an authentic account of the visit:

> What is missing from the media reports is that Jeszenszky once again emphasized the principle of dual loyalty, that Hungarian minorities have the right to be loyal to their nation in addition to the constantly demanded obligation of citizenship and loyalty. Missing from the reports are the tearful crowds in Kézdivásárhely, the people waving by the roadside, and the profound emotion of the RMDSZ leader [Csaba Takács], which stifles all cynical voices. Missing is everything that may not be big politics, but for which the Hungarian foreign minister visited the land of the Székely. A visit to relatives, but not only to his own personal relatives.[88]

---

[88] *Heti Magyarország*, November 12, 1993, and my private notes, among my papers.

Chapter 11

Instead of Stabilization, Conflicts Are Put in the Freezer

The death of the hero of the transition

On December 12, 1993, after a three-and-a-half-year-long battle with non-Hodgkin lymphoma, József Antall, the architect of Hungary's regime change, died. I do not need to speak of his achievements here, I have done so elsewhere, as have others.[1] On December 11, 1993, the Executive Committee of his party, the MDF, sent a moving message to its leader in his last hours: "Mr. President, your historic activity as prime minister, your work ethic and your political good sense are an example for us all."[2] As described in Chapter 1, Antall was a versatile statesman, with a special flair for foreign policy. He knew when to take risks, when to rush ahead and when caution was warranted. Referring to the example of Yugoslavia, he always argued for the need for a preventive rather than a defensive foreign policy, not just following the beaten track, and was always thinking in strategic terms. His decisive role in shaping Hungarian foreign policy is also evident in the contents of this book; and his surviving contemporary adversaries, too, speak very highly of him.

During the fight against the disease that was destroying him physically, the prime minister's attention never wavered. The final summary of his foreign policy goals was in a letter he sent to the participants of the 1993 Ambassadors' Conference. On Central Europe and our neighborhood relations, his message was:

> We have to maintain a strong relationship between the Visegrád countries. Slovenia and, after peace is achieved, Croatia might join the group. Close political partnership with Poland is a fundamental Hungarian interest. While cultivating our relationship with the Czech Republic, we must take

---

[1] Jeszenszky, "József Antall and the World"; Kodolányi, *Antall Józseffel a világszínpadon*; Otto Hieronymi, *Prime Minister József Antall and the Regime Change in Hungary, 1989–1993* (Budapest: Magyar Napló Kiadó, 2024). These are many favorable mentions of Antall by his foreign colleagues, but as yet I have not seen any serious assessment of Antall by non-Hungarian writers.

[2] The document has not been published; I have it among my papers.

into account the heritage of almost seven decades of Czech-Slovak coexistence, their common benefits, and their common political philosophical heritage, going back to Tomáš Masaryk and Edvard Beneš. That is why we must always be free of illusions, not overestimating the differences between them.

This letter reaffirmed the need for agreement between the parties, the government and the opposition on the fundamental national strategic issues he had aspired toward from the outset. He said it was intolerable for either political side to weaken Hungary's positions on the country's most sensitive issues by making statements that serve selfish party goals. This warning—like Antall's entire political life's work—is still valid and worth heeding today.[3]

Even during his treatment in a Cologne hospital, he made a contribution to world politics. In a letter to U.S. president Clinton, he referred to the domestic political crisis in Russia the previous month, when President Yeltsin used armed force against the retrograde majority of the Parliament, and to the still-volatile situation in the Balkans, and he called for accelerating the integration of Hungary and the whole of Central Europe into NATO—they should not remain in a no-man's-land.[4] The outgoing president, George H. W. Bush, thanked Antall with moving words: "He was a true friend to me and to the American people. We have stood together in many difficult historical situations: at the beginning of Hungary's transformation, during the Gulf War, the collapse of the Soviet Union and now the crisis in the former Yugoslavia and the famine in Somalia. Throughout these events, your firm stance and your honest and wise counsel have been indispensable to me and to the whole world."[5]

These good wishes, received in the hospital's sterile tent, came from a U.S. president who had played a key role in regime changes in Central Europe, and they represented the highest recognition of a lifetime's work. "This is just a simple note from someone who admires you, respects you and is pleased to have had the opportunity to work with you in a mutually satisfying way."[6] I don't think there will ever be a Hungarian head of government who will receive a similar letter from the leader of the world's most powerful nation.

---

[3] Message of József Antall to the participants of the Ambassadors' Conference, July 19, 1993.
[4] József Antall to William J. Clinton, October 4 and October 19, 1993. Cf. Ronald D. Asmus, *Opening NATO's Door: How the Alliance Remade Itself for a New Era* (New York: Columbia University Press, 2002). Foreign Minister János Martonyi wrote on his death: "On the Passing Away of Ron Asmus," *kormány.hu*, May 2, 2011, https://2010–2014.kormany.hu/en/ministry-of-foreign-affairs/news/on-the-passing-away-of-ron-asmus.
[5] Marinovich, *1315 nap*, 206. I do not have the original English text.
[6] Marinovich, *1315 nap*, 198–99.

The esteem in which Antall was held by leading foreign politicians is clear from the condolences, letters and obituaries that followed on his death and from the large number of dignitaries who attended his funeral.[7] The Hungarian public has been traditionally ill-informed about foreign policy and not particularly interested in it, but for the better-informed Antall's views on international issues were convincing and reassuring.[8] I remained foreign minister in the succeeding Boross government; as Antall willed, the government's foreign policy, including its neighborhood policy, remained unchanged.[9] However, there were attempts to change it.

On November 25, 1993, when so many of us were still confident that the prime minister's treatment in Cologne would be successful, three prominent Hungarian leaders of the Hungarian minorities, Miklós Duray, László Tőkés and András Ágoston, all familiar names from the precious pages, wrote a letter to the prime minister. It stated: "We need a universal Hungarian policy. [By this] we mean that the Hungarian government policy in Hungary and the political ideas of the Hungarians in the successor states should be harmonized and become complementary, and that the politicians in charge do not take any steps that could diminish the common chances of the Hungarian people." There was nothing new in this demand; that was the view and practice of the government. They were right, the goal of the government was "the fullest possible autonomy," i.e., territorial self-government for the beyond-the-border Hungarian communities. The letter's three authors, however, called for "a comprehensive concept" and coordinated action. They felt that for the sake of good economic relations with the neighboring states, the "Hungarian government circles" were marginalizing the Hungarians beyond the border as well as their "most authentic" leaders, with whom they (allegedly the government) "neither consult nor coordinate their strategic nor tactical moves. [...] There is no blueprint as to what and which Hungarian support is useful, and which is harmful for the socially organized Hungarians outside Hungary." This was a totally unfounded and insulting accusation, and even more so the conclusion of the letter: "Seeing how the question of the Hungarians beyond the border is slipping out of the government's hands, our fears are growing. [...] We see the greatest danger in the fact that to this day we have not been informed what concrete

---

[7] *A politikus Antall József*, 465–530; Jeszenszky, "József Antall and the World," 40–48.
[8] Professor Rudolf Tőkés proved right in a note sent to me on the death of Antall: "History will be more generous to him than have been his contemporaries."
[9] *A Boross-kormány programja, 1994. január* [The Program of the Boross government, January 1994], Chapter 4, 44–50. (Typescript, among my papers.) For the relevance of Antall's foreign policy for the future, see László Csaba, Géza Jeszenszky and János Martonyi, *Helyünk a világban—A magyar külpolitika útja a 21. században* [Our place in the world: The path for Hungarian foreign policy in the 21st century] (Budapest: Éghajlat Kiadó, 2009).

intentions and possibilities the Hungarian government have, nor do we see the will behind any of these ideas."[10]

This letter could only be interpreted as meaning that, after the debate over the Ukrainian treaty and Csurka's radical faction founding of a new party, the impatient, radical-leaning leaders of the understandably dissatisfied Hungarian minorities believed that the government, including the pro-Western Atlanticists Jeszenszky, Entz and Martonyi, were willing to give up the claim for autonomy for the Hungarian minority communities in the interests of early Euro-Atlantic integration and the requirement of "good neighborly relations," in the hope of economic benefits. The letter also implied that in political contacts and financial support, we preferred the "moderate" leaders (presumably the signatories of the letter were thinking of Béla Markó, Pál Csáky, Béla Bugár and Sándor Hódi), who understood the need to cooperate with the majority nations to achieve the aims of the Hungarian minorities.

It was not simply a misunderstanding on their part to ignore the government's consistent stand for autonomy, but rather it reflected the thinking that a strong, radical voice was more effective than quiet diplomacy, than patient dialogue with the leaders of neighboring nations, than a policy of trying to win over Western democracies. For me, it was a long-standing principle to be "*suaviter in modo, fortiter in re*," i.e., restrained in tone but forceful in the matters themselves. If they did not understand or agree with the government line, that was no excuse for their letter, since all three of them met the prime minister regularly, most recently in mid-September, and me even more often, and if I was not available, they left messages for me with my wife.

In the months and years that followed, I came to see that the letter was connected with intrigues within the MDF, and the desire of those preparing for the post-Antall era to turn the government's policy in a more "national" direction, using some of the well-known and respected leaders of the Hungarian minorities. A typical example of this was a suggestion made in the MDF's internal forums and then at its congress in February 1994 by György Csóti, vice-chairman of the Foreign Affairs Committee of the National Assembly, that good neighborly relations should be subordinated to support for Hungarians living beyond the border. Upon learning about the letter, I thought that it was just a sign of the authors' radical temperaments, but in view of later developments it was an attempt to replace me as foreign minister after Antall's death.

---

[10] Miklós Duray, László Tőkés and András Ágoston to Prime Minister József Antall, November 25, 1993. The letter is among my papers.

On December 20, 1993, András Ágoston, the leader of the Vojvodina Hungarians, sent me a letter, expressing his concerns about the Pact on Stability in Europe under preparation.[11] In my reply I tried to allay his fears:

> On the basis of our conversation on December 8 and our contacts so far, I was surprised to hear the fear that the present government of the Republic of Hungary might 'give in' and 'give up' the protection and support of the Hungarian minorities living in the Carpathian Basin. I believe that you and other minority leaders are experiencing day by day that the government has made the representation of the interests of Hungarians living abroad in all international forums one of the priority areas of foreign policy. There is no reason to doubt that our foreign policy stance in this respect will remain unchanged, and I can assure you that we will endeavor to fulfil our responsibility towards the Hungarian nation as a whole with the same consistency as before.

I went on to inform Ágoston about our role in the preparation for the Pact on Stability in Europe, our achievements, and that "in my opinion the most important feature of the envisaged Pact is that it is practically the first and only international codification attempt since the 1919 peace treaties to attempt to settle the rights of national minorities."[12]

In early April, I learned about a more serious matter than the three beyond-the-border leaders' letter: an unexpected intrigue and a crisis of confidence. On his Transylvanian tour in March, at the writer András Sütő's home and in wider circles as well, my deputy, Political State Secretary András Kelemen, spread the word that in the past year and a half there had been a break in the Hungarian government's "nation policy," in the attitude towards the Hungarian minorities, because József Antall had become ill and could no longer influence his government's activities in that area. He, however, enjoying the confidence of the new prime minister, Péter Boross, had taken minority policy issues into his own hands.[13] This was the second seriously disloyal move by Kelemen, my ambitious political deputy, who had replaced Tamás Katona. Kelemen often showed embarrassment while talking to me, and this was not his first act of disloyalty. I think I am right to assume that the prime minister was counting on Kelemen as his foreign minister in case the election

---

[11] On the planned European conference and pact, see the sub-heading in the present chapter.
[12] Géza Jeszenszky to András Ágoston, January 11, 1994. Among my papers.
[13] Messages from Ambassador Ernő Rudas, Executive President Csaba Takács and MP László Borbély to Ferenc Oberfrank, chief of my Cabinet. Personal verbal communication.

results kept him in his position. This was indicated by the fact that before the meeting between Prime Minister Boross and the beyond-the-border leaders on February 10, 1994, State Secretary Kelemen held a podium discussion with the prime minister and the three minority politicians in Székesfehérvár, which was reported in long interviews in the pro-government newspaper.[14] What most bothered me was not the intrigue against my person but the uncertainty implanted into those politicians and their electorate about the intentions of the Hungarian government, and involving them in the internal tensions of the MDF after the loss of its leader.

A cancelled visit

The debates surrounding the Hungarian-Ukrainian treaty had been slow to subside, and on May 31, 1993, the MDF members who had opposed the treaty formed the Hungarian Justice and Life Party (MIÉP) under the leadership of István Csurka. In the debate on the Ukrainian treaty Antall explained the reasons for the inclusion of a border clause, and why this would not be necessary in the case of other countries. Our Slovak and Romanian neighbors, however, lulled themselves into believing that only such a clause could protect them from the Hungarian schemes to change the borders. In Hungary, on the other hand, naïve nationalists believed Csurka and his supporters' position that with such a clause, Hungary was abandoning the Hungarian minorities, while without it there was a chance of changing the borders. My personal opinion was that it was precisely the strong minority protection points in the Ukrainian treaty that should serve as a precedent, and we should insist on similar guarantees in any Slovak or Romanian treaty. If such guarantees were given, we would be ready to consistently reaffirm the fact that Hungary respects the peace treaty signed in 1947.

As expected, Slovakia did not keep the promises and commitments it made when it joined the Council of Europe. On July 14, 1993, just two weeks after the COE expressed its confidence that Slovakia would keep its promises about changing the antiminority laws, the Slovak Ministry of Transport and Telecommunications ordered the removal of Hungarian-language place-name signs in the predominantly Hungarian southern region. On January 17, 1994, the report of the visiting experts of the COE accepted the plan for the new territorial-administrative division of the country, which failed to consider the national-ethnic composition of the population, carving up the southern Hungarian rim. The Coexistence (*Együttélés*) movement sent its protest to Secretary General Lalumière, citing the principle of

---

[14] *Új Magyarország*, February 10, 1994.

subsidiarity, Recommendation 1201 of 1993 and the Charter of Self-Government of the COE. All those justified the creation of an independent Hungarian administrative unit.[15]

While Mečiar's tales of Hungary's warlike intentions were not taken too seriously in the West, Moravčik's propaganda, cleverly emphasizing multiculturalism and the rejection of collective minority rights, could find more sympathetic ears. He argued in his exposition of Slovakia's foreign policy:

> It is important for the stability of Central Europe that the issue of minority rights does not remain a permanent problem. Indeed, a stabilizing solution must be found as soon as possible in order to avoid a situation in which the fulfilment of one demand becomes an incentive for further demands. It is also important to bear in mind—especially for those of us who live in an ethnically mixed area—that minority rights should not create artificial boundaries between the different ethnicities. I am thinking of the so-called collective rights of national minorities. It is the principle of a multi-ethnic society, and not the principle of creating ethnically compact units, who can be useful for a unifying Europe.[16]

I would have been happy to respond to his words by publicly demonstrating the many injustices and insults that had been inflicted on the Hungarian community in Slovakia lately. At the end of January 1994 in a letter to Moravčik I presented irrefutable facts showing that Slovakia did not comply with the commitments made at the time of its accession to the Council of Europe.[17] It is possible that my two trips to Romania, their reception by the Hungarian minority on the one hand, and the Romanian public on the other, played a role in the Slovak government's eventual withdrawal of the invitation to me to pay an official visit to Slovakia, because it would have given credible insight, without the intervention of distorting prisms, into Hungarian policy and thinking towards Slovakia. The Slovak nationalist leadership feared that the presence of a Hungarian leader in the Hungarian regions of Slovakia would strengthen the psychological status of the Hungarian minority, as had happened in Transylvania. Even today, I see that nationalist Slovaks have a particular dislike for those Hungarians, who, on their part, have friendly feelings towards the Slovaks.

---

[15] Letter of Miklós Duray to Catherine Lalumiere, February 8, 1994. Among my papers.
[16] Prime Minister Moravčik on the fulfilment of the foreign policy tasks of the Slovak Republic, February 2, 1994. Among my papers.
[17] Géza Jeszenszky to Jozef Moravčik, January 25, 1994. Among my papers.

Two trips to Serbia

The UN sanctions against the Union of Serbia and Montenegro ("Little Yugoslavia") had an increasing impact. The standard of living continued to decline, and the Hungarians of Vojvodina were no longer concerned with political attacks but with food and heating. Their dependence on aid from Hungary increased.[18] The government forces on the Bosnian battlefields halted the Serbian advance and a stalemate set in. The exclusion of Belgrade from international air traffic made Budapest Serbia's airport, and Serbian citizens aiming to leave for abroad rode busses to the Hungarian capital. However, getting a visa to the West was a rare privilege.

Telecommunication lines and natural gas transport lines to Bosnia via Hungary were not subject to sanctions, and we could have cut these last links if we had wanted to, but that would not have had any positive effect. What we expected, happened: the Belgrade government turned to us to ease its isolation. Upon my advice, the government agreed that I try to make use of that opportunity. Taking advantage of an invitation to the twentieth anniversary of the Hungarian Theater in Novi Sad/Újvidék, I flew on a military plane to Belgrade on January 27, 1994, for a whirlwind visit. A crowd of journalists, larger than in Bucharest, was waiting for me. My main aim and expectation from this trip were that the pressure on Hungarians in Vojvodina would abate (if possible, through the deployment of international observers) and that the hitherto sharply anti-Hungarian Serbian press would change its tone. We were not prepared to deviate one iota from the policy of the international community, but we wanted to show the Serbian leadership that there was a way out of the hole into which they had led their country.

For the opposition at home and abroad, Deputy State Secretary Iván Bába shed light on the background to my visit in a long statement to a Hungarian news agency:

> It is in Hungary's elementary interest to do everything in its power to bring the whole Southern Slav crisis to an end as soon as possible, to stop the bloodshed, the suffering of the civilian population and the restrictions that are causing serious economic disadvantages for our country. Since the beginning of the crisis, it has been clear that a settlement requires the political will of all those involved, and the international community can help to achieve this through the instruments of reward and punishment. A major success of Hungarian foreign policy since 1990 has been the settlement of

---

[18] Letter of András Ágoston to György Szabad, speaker of the National Assembly, October 4, 1993. Among my papers.

Croatian-Hungarian relations, which have been fraught with tensions for some 150 years, and the establishment of friendship that has restored the spirit of centuries-old coexistence. As early as July 1990, Géza Jeszenszky paid an official visit to Belgrade. The 10,000 machine guns delivered to the Zagreb police were a regular commercial transaction, and when Belgrade objected to the deliveries, the Hungarian side stopped them. The Hungarian side did not contribute in the slightest to the Serb-Croat conflict, which started almost a year later, and Croatia armed itself from other sources, with the help of other countries. The sanctions against Serbia and Montenegro were imposed by the Security Council with the aim of persuading Belgrade to change its policy in Bosnia. When the Security Council decided last April to significantly tighten sanctions, Hungary's action in the Security Council played a significant role in ensuring that no measures were taken that would have completely halted human contacts. [...] Hungary is known to have suffered extremely heavy losses under the sanctions regime, with a loss of USD 1.3 billion so far. Of course, we are aware of how badly the people of Serbia and Montenegro are affected by inflation, energy and goods shortages, including those who cannot in any way be held responsible for the policy in question, among others, the minorities. In this context, the Hungarian foreign minister stressed in an interview published in the Belgrade daily last November that Hungary would be among the first to support the lifting of sanctions, but added that he saw a chance for this only if the expectations of the international community were met.

As Foreign Minister Jovanovic indicated in a statement to a correspondent of the Hungarian News Agency, the settlement of bilateral relations is important for both peoples and countries. We welcome the fact that Jovanovic distanced himself from the anti-Hungarian statements of extremist forces in Serbia and the threats to Hungarians in Vojvodina, stating that the VMDK is a legitimate and constitutional organization and a legitimate negotiating partner for the Yugoslav leadership. It is particularly reassuring for the Hungarian public that Foreign Minister Jovanovic reaffirmed that there would be no provocations against the Hungarians in Vojvodina. However, I should note that it is hardly true (and it would be contrary to our interests) to claim that the 35–40 thousand Hungarians who have fled Vojvodina in the last two years, 12–15 percent of the Hungarian community, left their homeland and property behind as a result of some kind of Hungarian propaganda. The Serbian claim that the "positive change" in Hungarian policy is in contradiction with the behavior of official Hungarian representatives in international forums is not substantiated. At the UN General Assembly, Hungary voted in favor of a resolution reaffirming the principles laid down by the 1992 London Conference and the Security Council resolutions and calling on the parties for an immediate ceasefire. It reaffirms the unacceptability of the consequences of ethnic cleansing, calls on the Bosnian Serbs to lift the siege of Sarajevo and other cities, and recommends that the Security Council consider lifting the arms embargo on Bosnia, allowing it to exercise the right of self-defense. The resolution was voted by more than a hundred member states, including the United States, and some twenty CSCE member states, including Hungary.

In addition to supporting the above principles, our positive vote was also motivated by the resolution's concern about the continuing grievance of the national minorities in the Federal Republic of Yugoslavia, including the Hungarians in Vojvodina. Could Hungary have voted for this resolution otherwise than in the affirmative? When Géza Jeszenszky received an invitation from the Hungarian-language theater in Novi Sad to participate in a performance to be held on January 27, 1994, the 20th anniversary of its foundation, he felt that it was appropriate to combine the invitation with accepting the earlier invitation of Yugoslav foreign minister Jovanovic to pay an official visit to Belgrade. The Hungarian government is trying to seize every opportunity to ease the difficult situation of the people living on both sides of the Serbian-Hungarian border, to improve Hungarian-Serbian relations, to settle disputes, and to contribute to ensuring the rights of the Hungarian community struggling for survival in Vojvodina and to better understanding and implementation of its aspirations for self-government by the Serbian side.[19]

A part of the Hungarian and foreign press commented on my visit to Belgrade in a slanted way, and in response we issued a ministerial statement saying:

> Foreign Minister Jeszenszky travelled to Belgrade as a member of the CSCE "troika" and in agreement with other members of this group. He raised the possibility of sending CSCE monitors to the ethnically mixed regions of Serbia. He reiterated that the lifting of sanctions depended on Belgrade changing its policy. Hungary sensed some positive changes in the attitude towards the Hungarian community. By easing ethnic tensions in northern

---

[19] Statement by Deputy State Secretary Iván Bába to MTI news agency, January 31, 1994. Among my papers.

Serbia, by reducing the pressure on ethnic minorities in this region, and by easing fears that the conflict could spread to this area, the risk of the Balkan crisis deepening would also be reduced. In this way, Hungarian diplomatic action could reduce the risk of the further escalation of hostilities, help prevent a flood of refugees, and prevent the need for further humanitarian aid operations. This is in the interest of all democratic states. [...] Hungary is actively contributing to the management of the conflict in the Balkans and to international efforts to reach an agreement between the warring parties, to restore peace in the region and thereby consolidate stability in the heart of Europe.[20]

During my visit to Washington on March 1–2, 1994, the Southern Slav crisis was again the main topic of my discussions and presentations at the State Department. I confirmed that the purpose of my trip to Belgrade was to ease tensions between the two countries (primarily in defense of the Hungarians of Vojvodina), not to reduce Serbia's international isolation.

An important element of our policy was my tour in Vojvodina on March 12–13 to celebrate the 1848 revolution. While there, I said that the lesson of the 1848–49 War of Independence was that the interests of the peoples of the Carpathian Basin were common ones and peaceful coexistence was an imperative. The claim for autonomy by the Serbian minority in 1848 was rightful, just as was autonomy for the Hungarian minority today. Breaking the atmosphere of fear, I paid tribute to the statue of Lajos Kossuth in Magyarittebé, a small village in Vojvodina. At that time, tensions among the leaders who had founded the VMDK were already running high. There were political disagreements over whether territorial autonomy was a reality but even sharper differences over the distribution of the 80 million Hungarian forints in humanitarian aid from Hungary. Starting from the conviction that pluralism among minority Hungarians could be ensured not by separate and quarreling parties but by pluralism within a single Hungarian party, by joint decisions based on a free exchange of opinions, I tried to mediate between the leaders. I held these leaders in equal esteem at the time, especially András Ágoston and Sándor Hódi.

Unfortunately, my efforts were without success. Shortly after my departure, the break-up of the VMDK was formalized. Ágoston's account of the split differed

---

[20] Statement of the Ministry for Foreign Affairs on the relations between Hungary and Serbia, February 15, 1994. *Magyar Külpolitikai Évkönyv, 1994* [Hungarian Foreign Policy Yearbook, 1994] (Budapest: Magyar Külügyminisztérium, 1994), 134–37.

from my personal experiences.[21] I refute and reject in the strongest possible terms the allegation by Ágoston that the modest financial support to the VMDK by the Hungarian government of the time was conditional, was connected to certain persons, and that we did not support the autonomy program, or only did so hesitantly. Chapter 6 of this book and the substantial practical help given to the VMDK's concept of autonomy, should prove the opposite. Autonomy was already included in the MDF's 1989 program:

Figure 30. Visiting war-torn Sarajevo, March 17, 1994

The MDF attaches great importance to the establishment of a system of local and community autonomy in the legal settlement of the minority question. [...] It is desirable to realize territorial autonomy as the autonomy of traditional, historical territorial units or as the autonomy of the residential areas of minorities living in a larger block. Autonomous territories should be endowed with all rights that do not endanger the sovereignty of the state concerned [...] In the case of small, dispersed minorities, cultural autonomy can provide minorities with the possibility of preserving their identity and self-organization.[22]

On March 16 I discussed the situation in the Balkans with my Croatian colleague, Mate Granić,[23] in Zagreb. I welcomed the Croatian-Bosnian accord and signed an agreement on cultural, educational and scientific cooperation between our

---

[21] András Ágoston on the causes of the crisis. *VMDP Hírlevél*, 2/47 (June 22, 2004). One of the founders of the VMDK told me that in the account Ágoston was " blatantly dishonest and shameful. The facts are exactly the reverse of what he wrote."

[22] A Magyar Demokrata Fórum programja [Program of the Hungarian Democratic Forum], October 1989, 144–45.

[23] Mate Granić (1947–): Croatian politician, minister of foreign affairs (1993–2000).

Chapter 11 – Instead of Stabilization, Conflicts Are Put in the Freezer

Figure 31. Meeting Bosnia's FM Irjan Ljubijankić in Sarajevo, March 17, 1994

countries. I participated in the celebrations of the Hungarians remembering March 1848. The next day, with the assistance of international peacekeepers, I flew in their military aircraft to Sarajevo, which was still under Serbian siege. In an armored vehicle, wearing a bulletproof vest and helmet, I was taken to the dilapidated government building for talks with Foreign Minister Irfan Ljubijankić—who a year later was killed in action. We talked about the Hungarian efforts to bring about peace. I handed over our humanitarian aid shipment to the recently formed Hungarian Association in Sarajevo. Serbs had hit the Bosnian capital with bombs and sniper attacks for two years, and not a single house was left intact. The shocking sight reminded me of Budapest after the siege of 1945. I thought that if peace talks were to continue in this city, everyone would see that the killing had to be stop immediately. Unfortunately, the calm proved to be only momentary, and the European Community, as an integrating and conflict-resolving force, failed that test.[24] The siege continued for another year and a half, until NATO intervention, prompted by the United States, put an end to it.

During their severe ordeal, the impact of our friendship with the Bosnian (mainly Muslim) leadership, and, personally, with former foreign minister Haris

---

[24] My thoughts at that time are authentically expressed in János Kőbányai, *Balkáni krónika: Szarajevói jelentés* [Balkan chronicle: Report from Sarajevo] (Budapest: Múlt és Jövő Kiadó, 1998, 2nd ed. 2013), 172–74.

Silajdžić, left its mark on our inter-state relations until recently, when the Hungarian government established a close relationship with the leader of the Serbian entity Republika Srpska, Milorad Dodik, who is bent on secession.

Election campaign linked to neighborhood policy

The goals of Hungarian foreign policy formulated in 1990 were not disputed by the opposition, but the consensus that was truly desirable in this area—and which usually is a characteristic of Western democracies—did not work in practice. Even today, I can only say that I did my best to enlist the opposition parties' support for the foreign policy of the government. During the Southern Slav crisis of 1991–92, the government's policy proved to be so correct and effective that the opposition's initial loud criticism died down. The aims of our European integration and NATO policies could not be questioned either, and their results could not be denied. So there remained only the neighborhood policy and the related "nation policy," the support for the Hungarian minorities. It was not the government's fault that from the second half of 1993—obviously with a view to the elections—a strong attack was launched on this front against the Antall-Jeszenszky line. Not only from the left but—even more sharply—from the right, from Csurka's MIÉP and its hidden supporters.

Gusztáv Molnár, a political scientist with a courageous opposition background in Transylvania, rightly wrote, "The future of our region is at stake. Now that Csurka & Co. are attacking from the right and the MSZP from the left, trying to change Hungarian foreign policy, we need to go back to the beginning, so as to better understand where they want to divert us from." He recalled the Declaration of the MDF and the Romanian emigration to the West of June 16, 1989, and the agenda of the Antall government that "the cause of the nation, of the Hungarian nation as a whole, can only be served with the necessary strength and effectiveness if the country becomes an integral part of the Western world again." However, Molnár went on, "there are those who claim to be committed supporters of the Hungarian national cause, but in fact, like their predecessors in the 1940s, they are servants of foreign interests." He compared Romanian and Hungarian nationalists who flirt with irredentism to Russian right-wing populist politician Vladimir Zhirinovsky.

> The Hungarian sham-nationalists [...] wildly scorn the alleged communists and the Jews, and the result is increasing public sympathy for the opposition, and above all for the MSZP. They harangue against the Hungarian foreign minister and occasionally the late prime minister for having "ceded"

Subcarpathia to Ukraine, and tomorrow they will erupt in frenetic cheers when a KGB creature will tell us not become NATO's shoe-shine boy, because, if we behave, he will give us back Transylvania.[25]

Prophetic words, especially in light of some of the manifestations of our times!

My predecessor as foreign minister, Gyula Horn, now president of the Socialist Party, became active in opposition to the foreign policy of the government in early 1993. On foreign trips and in interviews at home, he proposed the creation of a Slovak-Austrian-Slovenian-Hungarian regional group as opposed to the Visegrád cooperation. In his view, Visegrád was created by the leaders alone and had no prospects, whereas his proposal was based on economic and geographical factors and common problems.[26] Csaba Tabajdi, a socialist member of the Teleki Foundation's board of trustees, embedded his professional objections in accusations of "a vague illusionism, a kind of stealthy, sometimes even openly proclaimed desire for revenge [on Trianon]."[27] László Kovács, chairman of the foreign affairs committee, also criticized the strict Hungarian attitude towards Slovakia's accession to the COE,[28] but the full frontal attack came from the offended former state secretary, Ferenc Somogyi. He denounced our foreign policy in words such as, "destabilizing," "over-ideologized," "came to a dead-end and lost its momentum," "the issue of Hungarians living beyond the border has become its almost exclusive element." According to him, we were trying to discredit our neighbors in the eyes of the outside world, and we incurred the disapproval of our Western partners, but we did not want to notice it. His only specific accusation was that we tried to isolate Slovakia in the Council of Europe's admission process.[29]

I still consider our actions in trying to tie the membership of our new neighbor to the redress of the legitimate grievances of the Hungarian community there to have been fully justified, and the situation has not significantly changed since then, for which the 1993 decision of the Council of Europe allowing untimely admission was largely responsible. In another article, Somogyi strongly criticized the fact that

---

[25] Gusztáv Molnár, "Geopolitika és nemzetpolitika" [Geopolitics and nation policy], *Új Magyarország*, January 5, 1994. Republished in Molnár, *Alternatívák könyve*, 389–95.
[26] He came up with his proposal while visiting the Austrian socialist chancellor Vranitzky in Vienna. *Népszabadság*, January 30, 1993.
[27] Csaba Tabajdi, "A nemzeti stratégiai alapkérdésekben egyeztessen a kormány az ellenzékkel" [The government should consult with the opposition on key national strategic issues], *Magyar Nemzet*, April 28, 1993.
[28] László Kovács, "A kormányzat nem hallgatott a követségi jelzésekre" [The government did not listen to the signals from the embassies], *Magyar Hírlap*, July 26, 1993.
[29] Ferenc Somogyi, "A párt küldte őket a posztra: Kimondhatjuk immár: a király meztelen!" [The party sent them to their posts: We can now say: the king is naked!], *Népszabadság*, August 12, 1993, 12.

"in the last three years, more than half of the civil servants of the Foreign Ministry have been replaced, and the actual role of professionally qualified, experienced staff has been reduced even more."[30] In terms of the ratio, the figure was excessive, and the replacements resulted in better quality work. I take responsibility for my HR policy, the changes in personnel, and I maintain that our diplomats, old and new, sent to the neighboring countries, were conscientious and did a good job. The debate was not closed by the reply of my state secretary, János Martonyi, nor by the rejoinder of his predecessor.[31]

Unfortunately, to this day, the stable and professional company of civil servants, loyal to the government of the day, which I sought to create in line with Antall's intentions, has not been established. Indeed, today I am reminded of the mood of the 1960s. László Kovács, the chairman of the foreign affairs committee of the National Assembly, made unfounded accusations, which, through frequent repetition, became accepted in the coming years:

> We have never questioned the principles of the government's foreign policy; what we have criticized is the historical nostalgia, the sense of a Hungarian mission, ideological sympathy and antipathy. [...] the government deliberately destroyed relations with the dying Soviet Union and its successor states, and its vehement attacks made it impossible to maintain economic relations. [...] Hungary must not be seen as a troublemaking, unpeaceful, devious country.[32]

I believe that this book convincingly refutes these accusations, but they continued to appear in the press. "There can be no European integration without genuine good neighborliness," appeared in another article, which called Slovakia and Romania's membership in the COE, despite Hungary's objections, a diplomatic defeat. The article criticized György Csóti, the MDF vice-chairman of the foreign affairs committee, who in a press statement did not rule out that border changes

---

[30] Somogyi, "A Párt küldte őket a posztra," *Népszabadság*, August 12, 1993.
[31] János Martonyi, "A kampány alatt a munka zavartalanul folyik" [During the campaign, work is going on smoothly], *Népszabadság*, August 4, 1993, 12; Ferenc Somogyi, "Jól, vagy csak zavartalanul?" [Going well or just smoothly?] *Népszabadság*, August 4, 1993.
[32] László Kovács on the foreign policy views of the MSZP, *Magyar Hírlap*, September 10, 1993. In *Pesti Hírlap* (December 30, 1993), he called it an achievement that "our relations with Slovakia and Romania have not deteriorated further," and said that it was to the credit of the Foreign Affairs Committee chaired by him that in the process of the admission of Slovakia to the COE "recommendations were made so that Slovakia could be held accountable." In the weekly newspaper *Respublika* 3 (1994), already after the elections, Kovács reiterated that the previous government had a "sense of mission" and constantly referred to the historical past.

in the Carpathian Basin could still be on the agenda.[33] The same author described Antall's foreign policy as flawed and ineffective, not a policy of successes but of failures, mainly because of his "eastern" and neighborhood policy.[34] I never boasted that our foreign policy was a success story, but it was hardly a failure.

In the final stages of the 1994 election campaign, Tabajdi criticized me using more specific arguments. In his opinion, the government should not be solely blamed for the regrettably escalating internal disputes of Hungarians living beyond the border, however, "it did not act as a conciliator, but by its ideological and party positions, its financial support, and its client policy of extending its clientele policy to Hungarians living beyond the border, it did not calm but rather fueled the disagreements and disputes that were bound to arise." This book proves the opposite: on the one hand, we always respected to the maximum the independent opinions of the Hungarians living beyond the borders, and on the other hand, we always encouraged them to stay united and to preserve their unity. The accusation that we considered the cause of the Hungarians beyond the border more important than dealing with domestic economic and social issues does not stand either. Tabajdi's view that the economic and entrepreneurial activities of Hungarians living beyond the border, the strengthening of their civil society, and the development of border regions should be supported, were all in line with the government's policy.

I don't think it was the government's fault that, as Tabajdi wrote, "Hungary's quite legitimate and internationally justified efforts were met with more suspicion and mistrust than warranted [?], not only in Central, but also in Western Europe." Didn't the opposition have a role in this? While most of our critics have accused the government of excessive attention to the minority issue, Tabajdi alleged that we failed to study the issue in a scientific way, that we had no ready proposals for the international community, we presented what was a general Central and Eastern European problem as an exclusively Hungarian issue. But Tabajdi's warning that it would be a great mistake, even a sin, if the next government "would want to place the issue of Hungarians beyond the borders lower down on the list of tasks" was not meant to be addressed to the Boross government, but to the likely successor, the Socialists.[35]

The wording of Somogyi's criticism was sharper, "Hungary's foreign policy needs a conceptual and practical change of course," but his censure was weaker on substantive issues. In his view, Euro-Atlantic integration must become the number

---

[33] *Népszabadság*, December 17, 1993, 20.
[34] *Népszabadság*, March 18, 1994, 21.
[35] Csaba Tabajdi, "Fordulat kell a magyar kisebbségi politikában" [A turnaround is needed in Hungarian minority policy], *Népszabadság*, April 11, 1994. Reprinted in Tabajdi, *Az önazonosság labirintusa*, 361–65.

one goal, and gestures must be made to our neighbors, who, if they reject our initiatives, would be compelled to take a defensive position. According to Somogyi, "The only way to directly help solve the problem in practice is to improve bilateral relations as a whole. The final solution is the social and economic advancement of the countries concerned and, ultimately, their integration into Europe."[36]

If the Antall government was under the illusion that foreign and international pressure would promote settlement of the situation of the Hungarian minorities, the Socialist-Free Democrat opposition, which was counting on coming to power, was under the illusion that gestures and border guarantees to the neighbors and their majority nations would bring about the desired change, i.e., a generous minority policy and autonomy. Finally, Somogyi's advice on Hungarian organizations beyond the border was justified but illusory: "Official Hungarian foreign policy should not distinguish between them on the basis of political-ideological considerations, and it is generally desirable that the Hungarian government of the day should keep only its eye on these movements and organizations, not its hand."[37] Meaning it should not try to control them or dictate to them. The foreign policy front man of the Free Democrats, István Szent-Iványi, was even more radical: "In few areas has the government been as successful as in discrediting noble goals and ideals." Considering solidarity with Hungarians beyond the border a European value, he called efforts to defend their rights a failure, but admitted that the policies of the government were not solely to blame. He expected improvements from better inter-state political and economic relations, and urged the more effective functioning of the HTMH: "Its activities are less characterized by administrative discipline than by enthusiasm."[38] At the same time, in an interview with, Szent-Iványi said that "Hungarian foreign policy must be set on a new course," but his proposals were largely open-ended, listing what the steps taken and intentions were of the Antall government. He said—realistically, and in full agreement with my understanding and policy—that improving neighborhood relations was a difficult and long task. "I am not naive, because I'm not saying, like Gyula Horn, that we should sign the treaty immediately and everything will be solved." Szent-Iványi stated, in full agreement with my understanding and our policy, that "the treaty can only be signed if it contains possibilities for substantial progress on minority rights."[39]

---

[36] *Népszabadság*, April 16, 1994.
[37] *Népszabadság*, April 16, 1994.
[38] István Szent-Iványi, "Kisebbségi politika: Erkölcsi és alkotmányos felelősség" [Minority policy: A moral and constitutional responsibility], *Népszabadság*, April 18, 1994.
[39] Interview with István Szent-Iványi, *Pesti Hírlap*, April 20, 1994, 11.

From the newspaper articles comparing the foreign policy agendas of the parliamentary parties, I concluded that there were no real arguments or substantive proposals behind the verbal criticism. Not even the MIÉP called for a border revision, only József Torgyán's Smallholder faction[40] hinted at it. The MSZP program was dominated by criticism of the MDF-led government. Clumsiness, constant reference to historical grievances and historical merits, a sense of mission, long lectures—these were the recurrent accusations. Zsolt Németh and Csaba Lőrincz from the opposition criticized the Socialists' foreign and security policy concept. In addition to the uncertainty about NATO membership, the "post-communist Socialist Party" would be satisfied if the neighboring countries guaranteed the rights of Hungarian national minorities only in accordance with currently accepted international standards—which is in line with the declared Slovak and Romanian positions, but falls short of the demands of interested Hungarian organizations.[41] In the same issue of *Népszabadság* as Németh and Lőrincz's opinions appeared, László Kovács rejected their criticism and denied that the MSZP would put good neighborly relations before minority protection.

In the debate on foreign policy in the daily paper *Magyar Nemzet*, the SZDSZ, like me, called the improvement of neighborly relations interrelated with ensuring the rights of Hungarians living beyond the border, and equally important but for the time being with small steps. On behalf of Fidesz, József Szájer called for the continuation of the previous foreign policy and described the Antall government's minority policy as basically correct "but lacking empathy towards the [majority] nations of the neighboring countries." Concerning the basic treaties, he considered it important to lay down guarantees for the protection of minorities, and "they should be based on existing economic, cultural and ecclesiastical agreements."[42] Since its formation, the opposition Fidesz paid special attention to the neighborhood policy, including the rights of the Hungarian minorities. Its concept did not differ on substantive issues from that of the MDF, as the sum of the statements and writings of its leaders in the press and in international forums attested.[43]

Looking back in 2025 to the debate more than thirty years ago, while I still think that it was unfairly critical of the government's foreign policy and it magnified insignificant differences among the parliamentary parties, it was lively, and

---

[40] József Torgyán (1932–2017): Hungarian lawyer and politician, president of the Independent Smallholders' Party (1991–2002), Deputy Prime Minister and Minister of Agriculture and Rural Development (1998–2001) in the government of Viktor Orbán.

[41] Zsolt Németh and Csaba Lőrincz, "Az MSZP utódpárti külpolitikája" [The foreign policy of the post-communist MSZP], *Népszabadság*, April 8, 1994.

[42] *Magyar Nemzet*, April 23, 1994, 13.

[43] Lőrincz et al., *Nemzetpolitika*.

thanks to the diverse press, it involved the public. Sadly, today there is hardly any serious discussion, hardly any discussion on foreign policy in the media, and even less in the Parliament; the present government pays no attention to those who question its stance on the European Union, Russia, Ukraine and China.

The 1993/94 electoral campaign spread to Slovakia, where Mečiar's government fell on March 11, and a government was formed by Jozef Moravčik, the self-styled "liberal" foreign minister. However, he made his planned meeting with Prime Minister Boross in Bratislava conditional on Hungary confirming in a joint statement afterwards the guarantee of the border between the two countries. This was precisely the pitfall of the long-drawn-out bilateral agreement: the Hungarian government tied such a reconfirmation (which was unnecessary under the peace treaty in force) to the guaranteeing of the rights of the Hungarian minority, enshrined in law; non-binding verbal flourishes and promises at a possible later meeting between the two prime ministers could not replace guarantees enacted in law. Therefore, the idea of an official meeting between the two prime ministers was dropped.

The opposition, however, tried to capitalize on the cancelled meeting, allegedly through the fault of the Hungarian government. On April 18, 1994, Gyula Horn travelled to Bratislava and met Moravčik, no doubt promising a much more flexible attitude on behalf of his party. On the SZDSZ side, a few days later, prime minister-designate Gábor Kuncze and his foreign affairs spokesman Szent-Iványi went to Bratislava to attend the inaugural congress of the Slovak Liberal Democratic Union (Moravčik's party). In view of all this, I was right to claim on April 21 at an event organized by the social-democratic-oriented Friedrich Ebert Foundation that some opposition politicians were underbidding the government, promising or implying that they would be more accommodating on the rights of Hungarian minorities if they were successful in the elections. László Kovács and Szent-Iványi rejected my assumption.[44] Horn's response was to charge "inept foreign policy, conscious misrepresentation," and he also made the totally unfounded accusation in *Népszabadság* that I had proposed sending Hungarian irregular volunteers to Romania with Antall at Christmas 1989.[45] (For the real story see Chapter 1.)

The SZDSZ was much more ideological in its thinking than the MDF. Its radical representative, Miklós Szabó, who knew me well through our common profession as historians, but who, due to party differences, completely misjudged me, expressed his criticism in a long article. He rejected my view of the Hungarian

---

[44] *Magyar Hírlap*, April 23, 1994, 3.
[45] *Népszabadság*, April 23, 1994, 3.

Holocaust as an enormous loss for the whole nation requiring common mourning,[46] and accused me and my party of being a "generation of politicians offended by Trianon," who "believe that under the Carpathians one is allowed to cry only over Trianon. All other weeping is impermissible, because it weakens the effect of this only permissible weeping."[47] This assumption was truly improper and biased against Antall and his government. Ferenc A. Szabó contributed to this debate—already after the elections—in an impartial and balanced article, pointing out that real reconciliation with the neighbors was unthinkable without satisfying the claims for autonomy, and therefore the reconciliation offer of the Socialists and Free Democrats was frivolous and self-indulgent.[48]

Finally, on the evening of May 1, 1994, a few days before the elections in Hungary, an informal Hungarian-Slovak prime ministerial meeting took place between Péter Boross and Jozef Moravčik at a dinner in Komárom. They visited both the Hungarian and Slovakian sides of the city. Accordingly, the Slovak government was not so sure that the new government would be formed by the Hungarian opposition. Even if, understandably, no agreements were reached at that time, positions were converging on the deportation agreement, border crossings, a committee of experts on minorities, cultural cooperation, and cooperation on plant protection and veterinary matters.[49]

At the end of the parliamentary term, on May 4, I and my senior colleagues held a press conference to take stock of our four years of activity. I believed that we had achieved most of the government's foreign policy agenda: we had restored our sovereignty, we had maintained peace in the midst of the break-up of the neighboring countries, we were respected in the world, our relations with all our neighbors were good, and with the majority of them were friendly and intimate. Although the situation of the Hungarian minorities was not what they and the Hungarian government would have liked, by now the whole world was aware of their problems, and appreciated that they were committed to democratic and European values and were fighting for their goals by peaceful, political means. State Secretary János Martonyi highlighted our successful European policy; Iván Bába stressed our successful regional and eastern policy, and our excellent relations with both Russia

---

[46] My words were greeted with loud disapproval by a group at the 1994 International Holocaust Conference in Budapest. I expounded my feelings in detail in several essays and talks, see "A zsidóság tragédiája mint magyar tragédia" [The Holocaust as a Hungarian tragedy], *Hitel*, 20 (April 2007), 21–31; "A vészkorszak mint kettős tragédia" [The Holocaust as a double Tragedy], *Élet és Irodalom*, October 5, 2012.

[47] *Magyar Hírlap*, April 26, 1994, 7.

[48] Ferenc A. Szabó, "Kiegyezés vagy önfeladás?" [Reconciliation or self-surrender?], *Új Magyarország*, May 31, 1994.

[49] Note by Iván Bába, May 9, 1994, 001549/5/1994. Among my papers.

and Ukraine. Deputy State Secretary János Herman highlighted the Ministry's open information policy as the best tool for image building.[50]

At the elections the center-right government was defeated, but the fundamentals of foreign policy had not changed, just as I expected. The new government also decided to seek NATO membership and was committed to a Western orientation. It granted the border guarantees requested by the Slovak and Romanian governments in bilateral treaties in 1995 and 1996 respectively, but, unlike its predecessor, accepted that the demands of the Hungarian minority living there were at best partially met. Only the election of Constantinescu as head of state in Romania and the formation of Mikuláš Dzurinda's government[51] in Slovakia brought some positive changes. Over the past thirty years, open intolerance and hate-speech against the Hungarian minorities receded but did not disappear, and their demands for territorial self-government was nowhere met.

The Balladur Plan—the last attempt to mitigate minority problems

In 1994 it was already clear that Hungary's Romanian and Slovak neighbors would not in the foreseeable future, of their own free will, treat their Hungarian minorities in the way that those Hungarians, their mother country, and Western principles required. However, I still hope that the Western democracies, international pressure, and also common sense eventually will bring about a positive turnaround. French Prime Minister Éduard Balladur[52] put forth an initiative that seemed to offer a good chance for that. He made his proposal in the spring of 1993, in the wake of the disintegration of three European federations that were not created by the free will of the constituent peoples, and the ethnic conflicts that accompanied it. The experienced French politician proposed that the member states of the CSCE should, in order to prevent future conflicts, confirm existing borders and also the rights of their national minorities by means of a convention, possibly with minor border adjustments. (This essentially coincided with Antall's view on the importance of preventive diplomacy.) As a precondition for EC membership, the Central and Eastern European countries should agree on a bilateral framework for dealing with minority problems. In June 1993 the Council of the European Community raised the initiative to Community level, but the possibility of border changes and

---

[50] Based on my own notes and the MTI summary of May 4, 1994. Among my papers.
[51] Mikuláš Dzurinda (1955–): Slovak center-right politician, prime minister of Slovakia from 1998 to 2006.
[52] Édouard Balladur (1929–): French politician, prime minister from 1993 to 1995.

the mention of collective rights were dropped from the draft, citing opposition from the Eastern European states.[53]

On September 7, 1993, I discussed the Balladur Plan with senior colleagues. Our conclusion was that it was justified to welcome it and to participate actively in it. We would seek to involve the legitimate representatives of the national minorities concerned in the bilateral negotiations, while the mother country also would have the right to speak out in their interest. Our only fear was that our suspicious Romanian and Slovak neighbors would reject the very idea.[54] In the second half of September, Prime Minister Antall met in Budapest with the leaders of the Hungarian parties beyond the border—Béla Markó, Miklós Duray, Paul Csáky, András Ágoston and Sándor Milován—to discuss the plan. They saw a better chance than ever to address their problems in an agreement with international legal obligations. They saw a case for involving their parties in the negotiations preparing the pact.[55] The Hungarian government was in full agreement with this, and I officially presented the proposal in Brussels.

The EC presidency entrusted Prosper Thuysbaert, a retired Belgian ambassador, with the diplomatic negotiations in preparation for the convention. He held consultations in Budapest on October 22, and I had a long discussion with him. We explained that Hungary welcomed the proposal and expected the convention to resolve, or at least to alleviate, minority problems and to reduce the separating effect of the borders. During the talks the ambassador did not show any reservation or disagreement with our position, therefore I was struck when our contacts informed me that Thuysbaert had prepared a report sharply criticizing the Hungarian position. Completely, perhaps willfully misunderstanding us, he claimed that Hungary rejected the recognition [sic!] of its borders and demanded autonomy for all national minorities. He shared his views with the ambassadors of the EC states in Budapest, which provoked criticism from several of them. The ambassador of the Netherlands, Hans Sondaal, informed his ministry that Thuysbaert had misinterpreted the Hungarian position, thinking that the collective or group right of minorities was tantamount to "ethnic-based regionalization," and that was a dangerous idea.[56]

---

[53] Miklós Boros, "Kisebbségvédelem és határok: a Balladur-terv" [Minority protection and borders: the Balladur Plan], in Kiss J., *Európai határok*, 51–54; Pál Dunay and Wolfgang Zellner, "The Pact on Stability in Europe—A Diplomatic Episode or a Lasting Success?," in *OSCE-Yearbook 1995/1996* (Baden-Baden 1997), 299–312.
[54] Memo from Gyula Kodolányi to József Antall, September 9, 1993. Among my papers.
[55] *Heti Magyarország*, September 24, 1993.
[56] Conversation with Dr. H. Sondaal, Dutch ambassador in Budapest, minute by Dr. István Csejtei, November 8, 1993. Among my papers.

The French, just like Romania (and even Hungary before 1918), traditionally stood by the concept of a unitary nation-state. Balladur, who held Antall in high esteem, accepted that in ethnically-mixed Central Europe that was not feasible.[57] Mayor of Paris Jacques Chirac, the center-right RPR party leader, spoke at UNESCO on October 14, 1993, of the need for "a degree of administrative autonomy" for the national minorities.[58] The original version of the Pact on Stability in Europe (PSE), as it was officially known, mentioned the possibility of minor border revisions, that was received with horror in western Europe, so the idea was soon dropped. Hungary, wisely, did not jump on the idea. Prime Minister Klaus of the Czech Republic warned that some countries could make demands for border changes, creating tensions rather than stabilization. Poland showed disinterest in the whole plan, saying that no Balladur Plan could resolve the Polish-Lithuanian differences because the key lay with the Lithuanians. If Hungary could reaffirm the validity of its borders with its neighbors, Poland would be better able to support Hungary on minority issues. Romania just hoped that the very idea would fade away. Thuysbaert did not recommend involving mediators in the bilateral talks, let alone the participation of representatives of the national minorities. The open and the confidential diplomatic reports Hungary received showed that the countries of the eastern half of Europe welcomed the idea of reaffirming existing borders, but were reluctant to link that to the treatment of the minorities. Most of them claimed that they had no problems with their minorities and therefore did not wish to discuss such issues under the auspices of the EU, still less to accept international legal obligations. Russia, on the other hand, supported the plan to provide protection for the national minorities, preferring to base it on the CSCE and its institutions. It saw a case for extending it to Central Asia and the countries of the Caucasus region—obviously thinking of the Russian minorities. Germany welcomed France's commitment to such a role in the interests of European security, and recommended that the countries of Central and Eastern Europe should conclude treaties with each other, along the lines of the treaties Germany had with its eastern neighbors, renouncing any territorial claims while safeguarding the rights of the national minorities. The Bavarian government, on the other hand, warned that bilateral agreements on the protection of minorities had not worked after the First World War.[59]

---

[57] Antall's letters of October 4 and 19, 1993, and the reply of his French counterpart on December 9, 1993. Minute by State Secretary Kodolányi, December 9, 1993. Among my papers.

[58] Note by Ádám Balázs (8th Regional Department of the Ministry), November 3, 1993. Among my papers.

[59] The above reactions were compiled by the Department of Diplomatic Information of the Foreign Ministry. The report is among my papers.

The original aim of the Convention was to improve the situation of national minorities in countries liberated from communist rule, and thus increase stability in the eastern half of Europe. This would have been a good preventive measure, reducing tensions both within and between states. The newspaper *Új Magyarország* rightly warned, however, that many countries would seek to throw out the part of the PSE relating to the minorities, and "that is unacceptable for Hungary, as there is no point in having a new Trianon treaty wrapped in tissue paper."[60] In *Magyar Nemzet*, Tibor Pethő called the initiative a substitute action, but said it could bring results "if we can prove with our internal relations that our country is the most balanced country in our region and an important factor of European stability."[61]

In the early 1990s, the Council of Europe took the lead in the fight for minority rights. After the adoption of the Language Charter in June 1992, the drafting of an additional protocol to the European Convention on Human Rights establishing the rights of national minorities was on the agenda. As I have shown in the previous chapter, the Parliamentary Assembly adopted Recommendation 1201 in 1993, but the Committee of Ministers did not adopt it, and it did not become a resolution. The Vienna Summit of Heads of State and Government of the Council of Europe on Minority Rights on October 8–9, 1993, agreed to draft a weaker framework convention instead of Recommendation 1201, and this foreshadowed the possibility that the Stability Pact would not fulfil its original purpose. My last attempt to convince our Western partners was put forth primarily in my speech to the CSCE Foreign Ministers' meeting in Rome. After outlining the achievements, shortcomings and new tasks of the organization, I spoke about the Stability Pact, which was intended to prevent conflicts:

> With this initiative, the European Union has undertaken to tackle an issue to which my government has attached the utmost importance since the very first moment it took office. It is doing so not only because Hungary is in the unique position of almost a third of the nation living in the neighboring countries, but also because we recognize that resolving the situation of minorities is a prerequisite for stability in Europe. This is particularly true at a time when we are witnessing the rise of intolerant nationalism in the formerly communist-ruled parts of the continent, and not only there. Neither majorities nor minorities are 'inoculated' against this disease. However, it is the national minorities who are more in need of protection because, as

---

[60] *Új Magyarország*, October 8, 1993.
[61] *Magyar Nemzet*, November 5, 1993.

their name suggests, they are in a numerical minority in states where not all civil servants and citizens are impartial in terms of nationality and religious beliefs. The solution to the minority issue has nothing to do with changing borders. On the contrary, while European borders have already been fixed in several binding international treaties, the same has not been done for minority rights, unlike the binding international rules of 1919. Since the Second World War, there have been only very weak documents on minority rights—and most of them have not been respected. Hungary is not thinking of solving the situation of national minorities by changing borders. What is needed is autonomous self-governments that guarantee both the territorial integrity of the state and the preservation of the identity of the minorities. This task is closely related to, but not identical with, the question of democracy and the guarantee of individual human rights, and therefore requires special regulation.[62]

At the end of 1993, the NATO program Partnership for Peace was announced during the visit of US Secretary of State Christopher to Budapest, and then NATO membership came within reach at the January 1994 summit of President Clinton and the Visegrád countries, which pushed the PSE somewhat into the background. However, NATO, too, required the guarantee of minority rights from its prospective new members. It was generally felt that Hungary's attitude was crucial to the success of the Stability Pact: signing bilateral treaties that included minority rights, would give meaning to the initiative. However, the countries with Hungarian minorities could easily explain the ineffectiveness of any bilateral negotiation by citing the excessive demands of Hungary. This could be answered by the involvement of mediators in the negotiations. As far as we were concerned, the Stability Pact only made sense if it could go beyond the non-existent problem of borders and promote the solution of the minority problem, which was a real problem and which undermined stability.

We continued to insist that representatives of national minorities should have their voices heard in the preparation of decisions affecting them. The draft did not foresee the participation of the Union of Serbia and Montenegro before the ending of the conflict in the Balkans, but we considered it necessary that all the Balkan countries should become parties to the Convention in due course. The dilution of Balladur's plan did not make most of our neighbors' enthusiastic supporters of the

---

[62] *Magyar Külpolitikai Évkönyv, 1993*, 349–50. (The Hungarian version of the speech in English is quoted from my own documents, it differs in style in places from the text published in the Yearbook.)

Chapter 11 – Instead of Stabilization, Conflicts Are Put in the Freezer

Figure 32. Discussing NATO membership with Secretary of State Christopher, Budapest, October 21, 1993

PSE, but they were wary of blocking the implementation of the version promoted by the EU. It was therefore already clear in the spring of 1994 that the PSE would fall far short of its original purpose and our own expectations, but it would have been a mistake to withdraw from the process and not participate in the preparatory conference in May. At one of the cabinet meetings, Prime Minister Boross suggested boycotting the conference—who knows on whose advice, but most probably in connection with the letter from the three beyond-the-border leaders sent to Antall on November 25, 1993. Earlier, in a radio interview, and without any consultation with me, Boross had put forward the idea of banning NATO AWACS aircraft, which monitored the airspace of the Balkans from our airbase at Taszár. The cabinet managed to talk him out of it, but the alarm it caused could not be repaired in NATO circles. Both of these ideas were in stark contrast to Antall's foreign policy.

In addition to the foreign policy arguments in favor of NATO participation in Paris, I also warned the new prime minister that our opposition in the election campaign was just waiting to say that after the government had spoiled our relations with our neighbors, it was now spoiling our relations with the West. The majority of my fellow ministers, in light of my arguments, stood by me and were prepared to go as far as resigning with me, and so this unexpected and unnecessary internal crisis passed. At a meeting between Prime Minister Boross and all Hungarian leaders beyond the border on February 10, it was agreed that despite anachronistic nation-state aspirations by Hungary's neighbors, impatience and moving away from democratic politics, Hungarians beyond the border have maintained their political sanity and commitment to parliamentary democracy. They continue to strive for their recognition as a national community, for territorial and community self-government rights based on the principle of subsidiarity, and for the establishment of partnerships with the numerically majority nations of each country. It was also stated that the principles of the Stability Pact were suitable "for resolving the situation of numerical minority communities and ethnic groups, [but that such a pact] can only fulfil its mission of stabilizing Central and Eastern Europe if an agreement was reached between the governments of each country and the legitimate representatives of the national communities concerned on the status of the community concerned."[63]

The government was facing the parliamentary elections with the unity of the MDF and the government in foreign policy preserved. If the result was not unexpected, the proportions were. The MDF's share of the vote in the first round on May 8 was down to half of what it had received in 1990 (12%), which was not as bad as was considered then and seen later, given all the difficulties and disappointments of the transition. The potential coalition partners (including Fidesz) did much worse, barely reaching the election threshold of 5 percent. I travelled to the opening conference of the Stability Pact in Paris on May 26 already as a minister in a defeated government.

During the final consultations it became clear that the majority of the participating states did not support the Hungarian proposal to include the representatives of the minorities in the conference and in the bilateral or multilateral negotiations planned afterwards. The Research Directorate of the European Parliament argued very unconvincingly that the RMDSZ did not want its community to be represented by the Hungarian government and that the presence of minorities would disturb the atmosphere in the sensitive inter-state negotiations.[64] That statement was a deliberate lie, or at least a deliberate misunderstanding. The RMDSZ, in a public statement sent to the conference secretariat, explicitly requested its participation in the conference and its involvement in the subsequent negotiations. It supported the principle of the inviolability of borders, with the addition that personal, local and territorial autonomy and special status should be guaranteed

---

[63] Government Spokesman's Office, February 10 and 11, 1994. Among my papers.
[64] Background Note on the Pact on Stability in Europe, November 24, 1994. SDI/CH/iv. Among my papers.

at the national and international level.[65] As their request to be heard was turned down, party president Markó wrote me a letter asking that "I ask the Minister of Foreign Affairs to represent our position at the opening conference of the Pact on Stability in Europe."[66]

On the eve of the conference, I summarized for the Hungarian press the causes of the national-ethnic conflicts that hinder stability and how to resolve them. I expressed my conviction that "every democratically elected Hungarian government will support the legitimate aspirations of Hungarians living in the neighboring states, as expressed by their political parties, organizations and elected representatives." When bilateral negotiations stall, multilateral diplomacy can help, and since 1990 various international institutions produced numerous recommendations, proposals and even agreements:

> In my view, governments should not be afraid to enshrine the rights of national minorities in a protocol to the Council of Europe's Convention on Human Rights. Unfortunately, this proposal was shelved at the Council of Europe summit in October 1993. The Pact on Stability in Europe, which is currently in preparation, aims to improve the situation of national minorities in the former communist countries and thus increase stability in the eastern half of Europe. It would be a good preventive measure, and its strict application and observance would prevent tensions and possible crises from developing. It is the only way to ensure that democracy in the former communist countries is on a firm footing.[67]

In my speech in Paris, I summarized the positive results of the regime change in Europe, explaining how the problem of national minorities arose:

> One indispensable requirement for stability and good-neighborly relations in the case of many Central and Eastern European countries is to reach a settlement of the situation of the national minorities based on applying the principles of democracy, participation in public affairs by those who

---

[65] Position of the Democratic Alliance of Hungarians in Romania on its Participation in the Conference on Stability in Europe, May 20, 1994. Among my papers.
[66] Béla Markó to Géza Jeszenszky, Bucharest, May 24, 1994. Among my papers.
[67] *Magyar Nemzet*, May 25, 1994. My article conformed with the article "Autonomy without democracy" by Zoltán Balassa, a resident of Kosice/Kassa in Slovakia, *Új Magyarország*, May 31, 1994. Cf. Géza Jeszenszky, "Variations on Autonomy," in *The Balkans and the Balkans*, vol. 3, ed. Ferenc Glatz (Budapest: Europa Institut, 2009), 171–74.

are governed, and of subsidiarity and decentralization. In the view of the present Hungarian government, and of all the political forces represented in the new Hungarian Parliament due to convene in the near future, no agreement affecting the position of the minorities can conceivably be reached without consulting them and without their participation. [...] The national minorities did so much for the collapse of the communist dictatorships and expected so much from democracy.

Since the document to be adopted did not accept Hungary's proposal to allow the minorities to be involved in the forthcoming negotiations, an interpretative statement was distributed to as a supplement to my speech. It reflected a six-party consensus:

> The initiative of the European Union is designed to initiate a process in which talks will take place between two neighboring countries, with the presence of the Union and its contribution as a mediator, and as a result of these, good-neighborly agreements will be reached in the knowledge and with the cognizance of the minorities' interests and opinion. An important and integral factor in these negotiations will be for a continual dialogue to commence between the minority and government concerned in the presence of an EU mediator, with the purpose of settling the questions in dispute, and for it to continue in order that the agreements devised may be satisfactory to both sides.
>
> The Hungarian government cannot formally represent the citizens of other countries who belong to a Hungarian national minority, but it considers it an essential requirement that the representatives of the minorities concerned should be able to present their opinions during the process and state their views on the agreements that are reached. This is in accordance with the interests of the minorities, of the governments concerned and of all participants in the conference alike, since only an agreement that is also accepted by the minorities can establish permanent stability.[68]

Thus, Hungary felt compelled to take it upon itself to represent the interests of the Hungarian national minorities in the whole PSE process.

The final document of the Paris conference identified good neighborly relations based on international conventions and standards as the key to European stability,

---

[68] *Magyar Külpolitikai Évkönyv,* 1994, 167–70.

and saw conventions based on the principles and obligations of the CSCE, the UN and the Council of Europe as a means to achieve this through bilateral and multilateral negotiations and regional roundtables. The text said that the EU and the High Commissioner on Minorities would be ready to contribute to the negotiations as facilitators, and the Stability Pact should be concluded, preferably at the final conference to be held within a year, and its implementation would be monitored by the CSCE. The domestic and international press response was cautiously optimistic, but Mihály Fülöp, the director of the Institute on Foreign Policy, noted in the daily paper *Magyar Nemzet* that with the EU's involvement, the original Balladur Plan lost its original aim, the protection of minority rights, and also the economic incentives that would have stimulated exemplary minority policy. However, Fülöp was wrong to say that the EU's willingness to "play a mediating role in bilateral negotiations between the countries of this region" was also left out.[69] (Subsequently, Romania refused to accept any mediation.)

Figure 33. Addressing the Paris Conference of the Pact on Stability in Europe, May 26, 1994

The ideas I expressed in Paris were in line with my conduct as foreign minister and were also present in my speech to the CSCE Standing Committee in Vienna on June 8, 1994. In the latter, I called the full realization of the rights of minorities a condition of democracy, "the international community should recognize and accept its responsibility not only for maintaining the territorial integrity of its member states but also for the treatment of national minorities living on their territory."[70]

---

[69] *Magyar Nemzet*, October 20, 1994, 11.
[70] *Magyar Külpolitikai Évkönyv, 1994*, 179–80.

Many people abroad expected that the election defeat of the MDF-led coalition would end the disputes between Hungary and its neighbors, that the MSZP-SZDSZ coalition would pay much less attention to the Hungarian minorities, and that this would remove the obstacle to good neighborliness. Outgoing prime minister Péter Boross expressed his hopes and fears in a letter to Bishop László Tőkés in June 1994:

> I am aware of the possibilities and limitations of the Pact on Stability in Europe (formerly the Balladur Plan). This is why our interpretative statement, issued in the interests of Hungarians beyond the borders, in fact in the interests of the Hungarian nation as a whole, is so important. In every forum and in the face of all opposition, we must strive for the acceptance of the minorities as political subjects. [...] I very much hope that the new government will not forget its obligations towards the Hungarians beyond the borders, will use every possible means—including international forums—to act in their interests, and will always consult the legitimate leaders of the organizations of Hungarians beyond the borders in advance about the political steps it will take in this subject. I also hope that the new government will endeavor to make our policy towards the Hungarians beyond the borders based on the consensus of the parliamentary parties. I will be able to draw the attention of my successor as prime minister to this commitment.[71]

The final act of my tenure as foreign minister was during President Clinton's visit to Warsaw and the related meeting between Secretary of State Warren Christopher and his Central European counterparts on June 7. I thought it appropriate to invite my designated successor, László Kovács, and his political state secretary, István Szent-Iványi, to join our delegation. We travelled to Warsaw in our special military aircraft, so we could return the same night, and the next day I was able to fly to the United States, where I was teaching a summer course at my old university in Santa Barbara. In Warsaw, I was invited by my foreign colleagues to give a kind of farewell address. I spoke about the importance of bilateral and multilateral cooperation and mutual trust between the countries of Central and Eastern Europe, and about NATO membership as a guarantee of our security. On my return from the States, I found a letter from my American colleague Secretary of State Warren Christopher thanking me for our cooperation and for my work for stability in Central Europe, with photos of our meeting in October 1993.[72]

---

[71] Reply of Prime Minister Péter Boross to Bishop László Tőkés's letter of April 11, 1994, June 7, 1994. *Magyar Külpolitikai Évkönyv, 1994,* 171–73.
[72] Secretary of State Warren Christopher to Géza Jeszenszky, June 10, 1994. Among my papers.

My 1500 days—the balance and the lessons learned

Everybody likes to look back on important and productive periods in their lives, and this is certainly the case for those actively involved in the 1989/90 *annus mirabilis*, the fall of the communist dominoes. I was in charge of the Ministry of Foreign Affairs of the Republic of Hungary for 1500 days, and, as a historian, I was fully aware of the responsibility for giving a new frame to Hungary's relations with the outside world. The months leading up to the regime change were indeed valiant times, full of hope and good intentions. For the first time in the 450 years since the Turkish occupation of Buda Castle, Hungary became fully independent, in control of its own destiny. The freely and democratically elected government and parliament felt that it had been given a historic task. Aware of this, the great majority of us worked with all our heart and soul to change the fate of the country and the Hungarian nation for the better. It was painful, but understandable that after four years, the decision of the people, disappointed in their unrealistic expectations, the governing coalition was defeated in a fair competition. The same happened to all the first non-communist governments in Central Europe. I am convinced that my colleagues in the Foreign Ministry did a good job in advancing our foreign policy goals. We charted a course for our successors, for future governments, and even if the words, the people and the circumstances changed, the direction remained steady for two decades. It was not through our will or our talent that we were not able to heal the trauma of Trianon, but the patient remains alive and the efforts to heal must continue.

Although most of the foreign policy goals we set ourselves in 1990 were on track to be achieved, there were also serious disappointments. Those that came from my domestic political adversaries, was the corollary of democracy. Those that came from within our own ranks, from my party, from my colleagues, I attribute to human frailties. I have shown how our neighborhood policy came under fire in the final six months of my term. However, I believe that, in addition to the successful change of orientation and the friendly, even trusting, relations with the leading powers of the West, we also achieved a great deal in the field of neighborhood relations. Despite the rapid dissolution of the Warsaw Pact at our instigation, our relations with the new Russia remained good, even intimate, with the conclusion of its first international treaty with us. And in November 1992 President Yeltsin, on behalf of his people, apologized for the aggression of 1956. We created the Visegrád Cooperation, which, despite repeated predictions of its demise, stood the test of time—until recently, but in time it is bound to revive. We played a key role in the Central European Initiative. During the break-up of three neighboring states, we did not allow ourselves to be drawn into the bloody Balkan conflicts, and we did not give in to any advice encouraging adventurism. Between the two world wars, we were sworn enemies with three of our four neighbors, and our relations with Austria only became good in the years before the Anschluss. In 1990 the number of our neighbors grew to seven; under the Antall government we managed to establish a distinctly friendly relationship with four of them: Austria, Ukraine, Croatia and Slovenia. Slovakia was a difficult partner but was linked to us in the Visegrád association. By the end of my term, relations with Romania and even Serbia had improved substantially from their 1991 low. I am very pleased that we managed to restore our historic friendship with the Croats. Our close friendship with the Poles grew even stronger.

We consistently pursued a policy of outstretched hands with everyone, but we were not prepared to forget that there were those who refused to meet the legitimate demands of their sizeable Hungarian minority. Nor were we prepared to sacrifice those minorities on the altar of Euro-Atlantic integration—as some of our opposition claimed, while others imagined that this was exactly the government's intention. We did try to improve bilateral relations with the neighbors by small steps. The most important element of this was the promotion of cross-border multilateral cooperation, in the knowledge that the direct beneficiaries of this measure would be the inhabitants of the border districts, where the vast majority consisted of Hungarians. As a first step, I initiated the reopening of border crossings on the Slovak, Ukrainian, Romanian and Yugoslavian borders, which had been closed during the communist era. Even if this process was slower than desired due to the procrastination of some of our neighbors and the limited financial resources, in four years the previously impassable border was reopened at four points on the Ukrainian border and at two (instead of the previous single one) on the Slovenian border, and five border crossings were reopened with the other three countries. As a result, the isolation and dead-end nature of many settlements was eliminated, local border traffic was boosted, living standards on both sides of the border improved somewhat and normal human and economic relations began to return.[73]

The complaint (by some: or accusation) that we were not able to modify our borders, at least by regaining the Hungarian-majority areas along the borders, is heard occasionally; that cannot be taken seriously by a sober, informed person.

---

[73] For a collection of case studies on the economic and foreign policy relevance of cross border cooperation and regional policy, see László Zsinka, ed., *Modernizáció és regionalitás: A külpolitika térbeli összefüggései* [Modernization and regionalism: Spatial contexts of foreign policy] (Budapest: Közszolgálati Tanulmányi Központ, 1996). Cf. György Éger, *Regionalizmus, határok és kisebbségek Kelet-Közép-Európában* [Regionalism, borders and minorities in East-Central Europe] (Budapest: Osiris Kiadó, 2000).

Only superficial or deliberately misleading thinking asserts that the break-up of three neighboring countries could have been, and should have been, used to increase Hungary's territory. The internal administrative borders of the states that broke up changed only from administrative to international borders. The world, the foreign powers, however, were so afraid that the slightest change in the European state borders would set off a chain reaction leading to wars, that they were most adamantly opposed to even the most sensible, obvious change, i.e., the exchange of territory. This did not happen between Kosovo and Serbia. The Russian Federation, which remained a nuclear superpower even after the collapse of the Soviet Union, did not claim territory from its neighbors Ukraine and Kazakhstan, inhabited by millions of Russians—at least not before 2014. If Hungary had asked any of its neighbors to accept holding a referendum on the status of certain territories predominantly inhabited by Hungarians, all its neighbors and all the foreign countries would have rejected the idea with indignation. Our EU and NATO membership would have been off the agenda for a long time. But our borders would not have changed, because the answer to the Hungarian slogan, common between the two world wars, "no, no, never" shall we accept the loss of territories is still valid today: "We will not give back a single furrow." However, in view of the ethnic changes (practically colonization) that took place in the course of a hundred years, the towns beyond the border having lost their Hungarian majority, and such a referendum would not have produced a result favoring Hungary. Therefore, the Antall government's policy was supporting the linguistic and cultural rights of the Hungarian communities outside the borders, and their demand for self-government, and it tried to obtain broad international support for this.[74] I admit that we have not been able to achieve the aim of significantly improving the condition of these Hungarian communities, and to guarantee their future to the degree we and those minorities had hoped for. However, this was no fault of the first freely elected government. A "softer," more conciliatory policy would not have produced a different result—twelve years of socialist-led governments are proof of this. Neither has tougher, louder, more radical action, as shown in the last fifteen years by Orbán's government, led to different results.

The most effective way to achieve the protection of national minorities is autonomy, whether territorial or cultural. The oft-mentioned solution, integration, is bound to end in assimilation, the disappearance of the minority community. Why was the autonomy of South Tyrol, such an obvious and well-functioning model

---

[74] A fair summary of the steps Hungary took to protect Hungarian minorities is Mediansky, "National Minorities and Security."

for Central Europe, not accepted by Hungary's neighbors? The reason is that the model was not the federal system, but the strongly centralized nation-state, with the national group that forms the majority (the titular nation) controlling the state. The communist model created a highly centralized country, nationalism forbidden, but under the guise of internationalism Stalin followed the aims of the expansionist Czars, suppressing the non-Russian peoples.[75] All the other communist dictators gradually adopted the Stalinist model of oppression of their national minorities; the best example was Romania. Following the collapse of communism, intolerant nationalism revived, in some countries with vehemence. Tolerance, fairness and compromise in settling disputes, the concomitants of democracy, did not take roots automatically.[76]

I already knew that my advocacy of self-government and collective rights for the national minorities fell on almost deaf ears, when, as a swansong, I summarized what I thought all European democrats should stand up for. This was at the "Europe and Us" conference in Prague on May 13, 1994. I quote from it extensively here, because I think it is a valid explanation of how the issue of the national minorities of Europe should be approached and handled:

> There should be no mistake, it is not patriotism, dedication to a nation's traditions and legitimate interests, that is to blame for the current national tensions. Nor is it the demands of the national minorities that are causing the trouble. Whatever tension may emerge is caused by the inadequate application of democracy, by unwillingness on the part of some governments to meet the aspirations of their national or ethnic minority groups, which have so far been unable to assume responsibility for running their own affairs, and so to ensure their future for generations to come. [...] the problem is caused less by the multi-national nature of the population than by the policy dating back to the 19th century, whereby governments started to identify themselves and the state increasingly with just one ethnic group—the dominant majority of the population. [...] there are many promising and well-functioning present-day models as well. Belgium, Switzerland, Spain and the South Tyrol in Italy, where the various national communities have their own autonomy, are all worth serious study, with a view to adapting these solutions to the eastern half of our continent. The introduction of democracy on every level

---

[75] Robert Conquest, *The Nation Killers: The Soviet Deportation of Nationalities* (New York: Macmillan, 1970); Rogers Brubaker, "Nationhood and the National Question in the Soviet Union and Post-Soviet Eurasia: An Institutionalist Account," *Theory and Society* 23 (February 1994): 47–78.

[76] See my interview with the Polish daily *Gazeta Wyborcza*, May 5, 1994.

and into local self-government is in line with the principle of subsidiarity, which maintains that decisions should be made at the lowest possible level. This should apply not only to the decision-making process in the European Union, but to the minority national communities in Central and Eastern Europe as well. [...] It is not the need for self-determination, self-administration, but the lack of them, that makes the question of national minorities in Central and Eastern Europe a source of tension. [...] What the minority communities of Central and Eastern Europe are seeking is neither separation nor a change in borders, only the right to preserve their language and culture, to have their children educated in the language of their forefathers, and have local officials chosen from their own community who understand their way of life. This is what autonomy and collective rights are about.

The current attitude towards national minorities in many post-communist countries is characterized by intolerance (especially identifiable in some press organs) and by a barely concealed intention of making them disappear from the map by either forcefully assimilating them or forcing them to emigrate. In practice they come close to being second-class citizens, and this is shown even by the constitution in some states, by not recognizing them as 'constituent elements of the state.' (Hungary today follows a different pattern, in its constitution, legislation and day-to-day practice.) [...] Under the policies currently pursued, harassment of the minorities is indeed a source of tension both in domestic and external affairs, especially when the minority concerned belongs to a nation with a state of its own just beyond the frontier, as the case is with the minority Russians, Hungarians, Serbs and Armenians, to take only a few examples.

Bearing all these facts in mind the idea of the exclusive nation-state is not in line with modern democracy. The only way to create homogeneous nation-states would be through exchanges of population on a vast scale, involving tens of millions of people, at enormous financial cost and causing untold human sufferings. A variant of this is the practice of 'ethnic cleansing' whose hideousness can be observed in Bosnia and the occupied parts of Croatia. It follows that the only real solution for the 30–40 million people who form national minorities in the states of Central and Eastern Europe is to introduce genuine self-government, in which every national group could participate in accordance with its proportion. Where the minorities are more dispersed, they could still enjoy the institutions of cultural autonomy following the pattern of the various denominations: the Catholic, Calvinist, Lutheran and Jewish churches enjoy autonomy in every European country. The minorities need guarantees of a decent life and a safe future. This can be achieved through specific constitutional and legal rights, and international guarantees. Until the constitutional guarantees of minority rights remain unformulated in states with a substantial Hungarian minority, any Hungarian government is bound to support the aspirations of the Hungarians in the states neighboring us, as expressed by the elected representatives of their political parties and other organizations. Since there are also Germans, Slovaks, Slovenes, Romanians, Croats and Serbs living in Hungary, it is only natural that those minorities must be involved in the negotiations Hungary is conducting with the neighboring states over bilateral treaties. There are indeed some promising developments in this issue. In 1991, Hungary signed a treaty with Ukraine that specified the rights of the mutual national minorities. Since Ukraine is a new state, not the successor of the Soviet Union, Hungary was willing to reconfirm the present border, and the treaty has been ratified by both parliaments. Hungary and Ukraine now have an operative committee on national minorities to work out the details needed. Croatia acceded to the declaration on the principles of the treatment of the minorities drawn up by Hungary and Ukraine. There is also a joint Hungarian-Russian declaration on the rights of the national minorities, which supports the idea that there should be international codification of these rights. Hungary and Slovenia have signed a special treaty on the mutual protection of the Slovenian and Hungarian communities living in each other's country. Hungary repeatedly proposed negotiating such treaties to all the neighbors.

Since solutions and agreements on a bilateral level appear to be difficult to reach, a multilateral, international approach could be helpful. An all-European code of conduct safeguarding the rights of minorities would be the best thing. Much work has already been done here. The CSCE conference on the human dimension, held in Copenhagen in 1990, has already broken much ground, and elements of it can be found in the Paris Charter of November 1990. The Council of Europe and its experts have also made serious studies and came up with some excellent ideas. A Charter of Regional and Minority Languages has been drawn up and several countries, Hungary included, have already signed it. I hope our neighbors will soon do it, without exception. Governments should not be reluctant to work for the codification of the rights of the national minorities in the form of an additional protocol to the Convention of Human Rights adopted by the Council of Europe. This was unfortunately set aside at the Vienna Summit of the Council in October 1993.

The proposed Pact on European Stability envisages improving the situation of the national minorities in the formerly communist countries and this would indeed enhance stability in the eastern half of Europe. It would be a good preventive measure, and its strict application and observance would pre-empt tensions and crises likely to emerge. This is the only way to make the former communist countries safe for democracy.[77]

Autonomy is the exercise of democracy at the local level, in municipalities, cities and larger territorial units. In the United States, where I represented Hungary for four years, all fifty states have a degree of autonomy, as do cities and counties within each state. The native Indians have autonomous reservations. All the churches, the various denominations have autonomy—within the framework of the law. There are many different kinds of communities in the world, all based on solidarity with each other, but perhaps the most important community is the nation, based on a common language, culture and history. The national minorities are parts of a nation, but they live detached from the main body it by an international border. They are also communities, not just "persons belonging to a national minority." Among Hungary's neighbors, Austria, Croatia and Slovenia, and more recently Serbia, too, recognize the Hungarians living there as a community. All national minorities form a community, and demand—by peaceful, political means—the legal, economic and political conditions that are indispensable for their survival. The usual argument of those opposing autonomy is to favor integration, "deepening coexistence," and this is—in good faith—an argument widely shared in Western Europe and North America. The proponents fail to see that the result of "deepening coexistence" is assimilation, the disappearance of the community in question. This is precisely the unacknowledged aim in many countries, because then the minority problem will be "solved" once and for all. I do not want to stigmatize this as inhumane, but the end result of assimilation is the disappearance of the minority.

I confess that in my ministerial career, as a rational intellectual, I overestimated the role of facts and arguments, of rationality in the discussions and negotiations. In the first year, I believed that in the new world order after 1990, the lofty principles of the UN Charter, the 1975 Helsinki Final Act, and the 1990 Charter of Paris would prevail, that Western democracies would understand that securing

---

[77] "Nations and Minorities in Europe," *The Hungarian Observer*, 7, Central Europe for Stability. Special Issue (May 1994): 1–6.

the rights of national minorities was indeed a precondition for stability and they would be willing to exert pressure to this end. This illusion was largely shared by my Hungarian contemporaries, the generation of the regime change. It was also shared by Hungarian politicians beyond the borders. Béla Markó once complained about the lack of or weakness of "Mister International Pressure."[78] Hungary's bilateral agreements on the protection of minorities (with Ukraine, Slovenia, Croatia and Russia) went beyond the so-called international standards, the international obligations and recommendations in force, but Western Europe did not want to notice those agreements, lest they become a precedent.

What do I see as the reason why the hoped-for European support for minority rights has not materialized? A fundamental difficulty was that most countries in the world were opposed to the collective rights of national and ethnic minorities, because they themselves had significant minorities to whom they did not want to give the rights that the Hungarian minorities demanded. Typical examples: Turkey, Spain, Greece, and almost all Asian and African countries. Most states fear the threat to their stability and *status quo* from the demands of minorities. Behind the fear lay a misinterpretation of events and history. Since one of the triggers (or just a pretext) for modern wars has been territorial disputes and the minority grievances associated with them, Western Europe linked the mere mention of the minority issue to the danger of war. This was confirmed by the totally unexpected crisis in Yugoslavia. There was a strong fear that every minority problem was a potential Cyprus, Karabakh or Bosnia. Western governments, fearing a repeat of the Balkan horrors, sought to cool and freeze potential conflicts, not resolve them.

Unfortunately, at times opinions coming from Hungary (not also my own) also fed these concerns. The most distressing example of this was when, in 1993–94, certain press organs, not sympathetic to the government of the day, published articles announcing that the government would be ready to start armed conflict with one or more of its neighbors, ostensibly to protect the beleaguered Hungarian minorities, but in reality to postpone the elections and keep the "arrogant, insensitive, nationalist" government in office. Such irresponsible voices severely damaged Hungary's international image and limited the room the country had for maneuvering in foreign policy.

The Hungarian position on minority rights was wholeheartedly supported only by Austria, personally by Vice-Chancellor and Foreign Minister Mock, who would have liked to see the successful South-Tyrolean model applied in the eastern half of Europe. Although the United States emphasized individual human rights, it was

---

[78] *Népszabadság*, August 1, 2015, 5.

sensitive to all violations of minorities and was not opposed to the assertion of self-government. America was largely permissive in the use of languages: Spanish gradually became a *de facto* second language, and the use of non-English inscriptions, flags and other national symbols was common in various ethnic quarters and churches. A respected American journalist who knew our region well said something to me that was not atypical, to wit: the United States would not expose itself on behalf of the autonomy of Hungarian minorities, but would welcome it if it came about.

The Antall government's support for the passage of laws claimed by the Hungarian minorities were made more difficult by the fact that the most prestigious and influential organs of the world press did not sympathize with the Hungarian coalition government from the outset, which was perceived as right-wing, nationalist and sometimes even antisemitic. We did our best to counter unfounded accusations, and we were also on good terms with the left-of-center European governments, but there was little recognition of this in the press. The main subject of concern and criticism was the neighborhood policy, including the so-called excessive support for Hungarian minorities, which was seen as a threat to stability. The aforementioned statements made by István Csurka and a few other politicians were not only inaccurately quoted and/or exaggerated by the international media, but the actual influence of the Hungarian radical right was also greatly overestimated. Anyone skeptical about this claim will find it well supported by a very thorough analysis of the German press by Zsolt K. Lengyel.[79] The hypercritical stance of the foreign media was greatly aided by the left-wing opposition to the Hungarian government at home, and by its very powerful media outlets at the time.

The Socialist-Free Democrat government formed in 1994 had to cool the concerns they themselves had contributed to when in opposition by criticizing the "excessive" support for Hungarian minorities. Many foreign politicians and observers accepted that Hungary and the Hungarian minority communities were destabilizing factors. During the election campaign, the leader of the Socialist Party, Gyula Horn, proclaimed "if I win, I will bring peace." My answer was that there was no need for peace, because fortunately Hungary was not at war. The Antall government concluded nineteen interstate treaties, three of them with neighboring countries (Ukraine, Slovenia and Croatia), but Slovakia and Romania refused to accept the specific points on minority protection contained in those treaties, and therefore the "basic treaty" was not concluded with those two states. Those treaties

---

[79] Zsolt K. Lengyel, *Tükrözés és torzulás: Magyarország és a magyar kisebbségek képe a német politikai irodalomban 1993–1994* [Mirroring and distortion: Hungary and the image of Hungarian minorities in German political literature 1993–1994] (Budapest: Méry Ratio–Pro Minoritate Alapítvány, 2014).

were finally concluded by the Horn government, but the articles on minority protection fell short of the demands of the Hungarian communities concerned, and the agreements we really signed against their will.[80]

I see another reason for Western Europe's reluctance, for stalling the process of strengthening the protection of minority rights: the new, non-European, mainly Muslim immigrants, lately referred to as migrants. The governments did not distinguish between the autochthonous, historic minorities, who had never crossed the borders (the borders crossed over them), and the new minorities. They refused to think about granting collective rights to millions of migrants, who were causing serious social and public security problems. That is why the Committee of Ministers of the Council of Europe rejected the idea of creating an additional protocol on the protection of minorities to the 1950 European Convention on Human Rights, and rejected the implementation of Recommendation 1201 of the Parliamentary Assembly in 1993. The Framework Convention on Minority Rights, which was adopted in their place in 1994 (and, due to the delays in ratification, came into force only at the end of that decade), contained only modest provisions.

Most Western democracies fail to recognize the fact that in most multi-ethnic countries, and in Central and Eastern Europe in particular, ethnicity, religion and language are the fundamental sources of loyalty, the basis of belonging to a nation. The Western ideal of an integrated multi-ethnic society, where the majority nation recognizes minorities and ensures them special rights, has not found many adherents in the east of Europe. In the eastern half of Europe, the state has traditionally not been neutral in matters of language and culture, and has often been the instrument of ill-treatment of the national minorities, in the vain hope that ethnically diverse populations can be "homogenized" and assimilated, so that countries that proclaim themselves nation states will in time become true nation states. However, these countries are not "melting pots," and should not try to work toward such an end.

The link between minorities and international security is now recognized by many experts.[81] Almost ninety years ago, János Esterházy, leader of the United Hungarian Party in Slovakia and later martyr of communist repression, pointed this out: "A just nationality policy is a much greater security coefficient than many written laws ... it is more secure than any Maginot Line, because nothing strengthens a state more when not only the majority but also the minority citizens feel

---

[80] As an opposition MP, I regularly called attention to those deficiencies in my speeches in parliament and in the press between 1994 and 1998. For more on this, see chapter 12 in this volume.

[81] Rudolf Joó, "Nemzetiségi konfliktusok és nemzetközi biztonság Közép-Kelet-Európában" [Ethnic conflicts and international security in Central and Eastern Europe], *Külpolitika* 2 (1996): 11–27.

fully at home in it."[82] Showing his pessimism about the immediate prospects, State Secretary Géza Entz pointed out in an interview summing up our policy: "The concern of the motherland and the Hungarian government for the Hungarian people in neighboring countries has a stabilizing effect in our region. Because if we don't do this, if we don't take on this responsibility, the deterioration of their situation would risk giving voice to extremism, and this would have a destabilizing effect."[83]

Oszkár Jászi, wrote a fundamental book on the problem of national minorities well over a hundred years ago, and in his essay, "The Irresistibility of the National Idea" (1925), published forty years after his death in 1995, he wrote that the policy towards the national minorities after the First World War brought him to the conclusion that only the fullest possible national-minority self-administration and self-government would be able to resolve the ethnic conflicts in Central Europe. He considered the creation of nationally neutral states to be an indispensable condition for that.[84] In Western Europe, the *de facto* equality of citizens of different nationalities has been largely achieved, while this is not the case in the former Eastern bloc. However, it is impossible to imagine lasting good relations between Hungary and its neighbors without satisfied Hungarian minorities having constitutional rights. Hungary, for its part, has done much to improve the political and cultural situation of its national minorities: Germans, Romanians, Croats, Slovenes, Serbs and Ukrainians (Ruthenians). The treatment of minorities is not the only element of neighborhood relations, but it is misleading and hypocritical to talk about good neighborliness, friendship, and "strategic partnership" if there is a painful point in the bilateral relationship, if the national minority communities that could be truly linking countries are dissatisfied with their situation and do not see their rights and future secured. This does not mean that the Hungarian government of the day should give some sort of blank cheque or veto to Hungarian communities across the border. There are unpeaceful, insatiable minority groups and politicians in the world, but the Hungarian minorities of the Carpathian Basin do not fall into this category. The Hungarian communities of Slovakia, Ukraine, Romania, Yugoslavia, Croatia and Slovenia, their elected leaders and members of parliament, only make demands and formulate demands that are in line with international recommendations and conventions, not least the practice of many Western European countries. This is the strength of Hungarian minority protection policy, and it is

---

[82] Imre Molnár, *The life and martyrdom of János Esterházy* (Budapest: Méry Ratio, 2011).
[83] Géza Entz, "Látványos áttörésre nem lehet számítani" [A spectacular breakthrough is not to be expected], *Magyar Nemzet*, February 12, 1994.
[84] Oscar Jászi, *Homage to Danubia*, ed. György Litván (Boston, London: Rowman and Littlefield, Inc., 1995), 23–29.

therefore justified to adhere to the principles and practical foundations on which the Hungarian minority communities base their political programs. It is neither theoretically nor practically true that the interests of the national minority and the interests of the majority nation are irreconcilable, a "zero-sum game." It is unfortunate that in some of Hungary's neighbors, not enough have understood to date that meeting the moderate demands of national minorities is a prerequisite for real democracy. There can be no internal stability if a significant proportion of citizens, the members of the national minorities, are unhappy and dissatisfied; and if they are not listened to at home, they will necessarily seek support from outside, from the mother country and from the international community.

After so many disappointments, after so many failed reconciliation initiatives, after the bilateral treaties, it is time to say and make clear to the world: good relations between Hungary and its neighbors do not depend on inter-state relations but on relations between the majority nations and the Hungarian communities, which make up a significant minority. The desired harmony can only be ensured by a good-faith agreement between the Hungarian minorities and the majority nations, by reconciliation. By now, public opinion in our neighboring nations has been driven to the point that the idea that autonomy is unacceptable and will lead to the disintegration of the country has become an obsession. Yet numerous examples, most recently Kosovo, prove that the opposite is true. In Kosovo, the at first peaceful protests and later bloody conflict began when the autonomy of the province was abolished in 1988. Serbia's intolerant policy led to Kosovo's secession from Yugoslavia.

In the early 1990s, there were recurring demands from our neighbors to reassure them that they were no longer threatened by Hungarian "revisionism," to add a new pledge to the internationally guaranteed peace treaty, that we not claim any part of their territory and not do so in the future. Because—so they said—if they were not so afraid of the Hungarian government's hidden agenda, they would be ready to grant more rights to the Hungarian minorities. The demands were met in the "territorial clause" of the treaty with Ukraine, in the statement that the contracting parties did not and would not have any territorial claims against each other. However, it is now clear that even with a territorial clause, intolerance towards the Hungarian minorities did not disappear. Unfortunately, there are signs of fatigue among the ranks of the Hungarian minorities beyond the border, manifested in low voter turnout and accelerating assimilation and emigration. The target of the latter is no longer Hungary but Western Europe, which offers much more in financial terms. Today, these processes threaten the future of the Hungarian communities living outside our borders just as seriously as the intolerant, discriminatory policies aimed against them.

Could the Antall government have pursued other, more effective policies? I believe that the answer from any objective observer and analyst can only be no. We were not driven by party or individual interests. I always sought to ensure that foreign policy was based on a six-party consensus of the whole Parliament, including the opposition. It was in the area of neighborhood policy that the most serious disagreement between the government and its opposition could be seen. On the basis of my first year as minister, I could see that merely with gestures, visible goodwill, the legitimate demands of the Hungarian minorities would not be met, the intolerant policy towards them would not cease. Counting on international factors, we tried to bring about an improvement by the codification of both individual and community minority rights, unfortunately with little success. However, there is no other way even today. We have to convince the foreign powers, including all our neighbors, by persistent arguments that the issue of harmonious coexistence of national minorities, communities of different languages, religions and consciousness is a global problem, a precondition for internal and international stability. The overwhelming majority of the world's countries are multi-ethnic and multi-religious, and the resulting conflicts prove that oppression and intolerance sooner or later lead to explosions.

In addition to my readings, my personal experience has led me to the conviction, which has not changed but has only grown stronger over the past thirty-five years, that the attempt to create homogeneous nation states has failed, but that the alternative is not supranationalism, but integration of the states, eliminating their borders, a Europe of cultural nations, of regions, and the extension of this model to the other continents.[85] A fine task for future generations if we do not want our world, all that human civilization has created over thousands of years, to be destroyed in wars and anarchy.

The key was—and remains—in the hands of the Western democratic powers. Even if a policy of insistence on the rights of national minorities has not yet prevailed in the European governments, experts and high-minded politicians, who know the issue well, have already made it clear what can ensure peace and stability in a Europe of multi-ethnic states. A comprehensive proposal was drawn up at a conference organized by the Friedrich Naumann Foundation. Held in Berlin on September 14–16, 2000, it brought together representatives of thirty-eight national

---

[85] Géza Jeszenszky, "More Bosnias? National and Ethnic Tensions in the Post-Communist World," *East European Quarterly* 31, no. 3 (1997): 283–99.

and ethno-cultural minorities and indigenous peoples.[86] According to a resolution adopted by the Parliamentary Assembly of the Council of Europe in 2003:

> Most present-day conflicts no longer occur between states but within states and are rooted in tensions between states and minority groups which demand the right to preserve their identities. These tensions are partly due to the territorial changes and the emergence of new states which followed the two world wars and the collapse of the old communist system, and also reflect the inevitable development of the concept of the nation-state, which, hitherto, viewed national sovereignty and cultural homogeneity as essential. Autonomy as applied in states governed by the rule of law can be a source of inspiration in seeking ways to resolve internal political conflicts. Autonomy allows a group which is a minority within a state to exercise its rights, while providing certain guarantees of the state's unity, sovereignty and territorial integrity. In order to provide the right conditions for the permanence of autonomy, the report recommends compliance with a number of basic principles, including the creation of a legal framework for autonomous status, a clear division of powers and the establishment of democratically elected legislative and executive bodies in autonomous regions.[87]

Resolution 1985 (2014) went further, stating that since "manifestations of extreme nationalism, racism, xenophobia and intolerance have not disappeared; on the contrary, they appear to be on the rise [...] The Assembly invites its members to follow more closely the issue of national minorities, to play an active facilitating and problem-solving role and to draw up proposals for direct political representation of national minorities."[88]

The so-called Kalmár report, adopted in 2014, recommended important further steps:

> The protection of minorities should remain a priority on the political agenda in order to address minorities' needs and protect their rights and human

---

[86] "A kisebbségek jogai: Nyilatkozat az etnokulturális és nemzeti kisebbségekre, valamint őshonos lakosságokra vonatkozó liberális demokrata elvekről" [The rights of minorities. Declaration on liberal democratic principles concerning ethno-cultural and national minorities and indigenous populations], *Magyar Kisebbség* 3 (2000): 120–34.

[87] Council of Europe, Resolution 1334 (2003). The positive experience of autonomous regions as a source of inspiration for conflict resolution in Europe. https://pace.coe.int/en/files/17120/html

[88] Council of Europe, Resolution 1985 (2014). The situation and rights of national minorities in Europe, https://pace.coe.int/en/files/20772/html.

dignity. An efficient protection of the rights of national minorities contributes to preventing conflicts, to achieving the vision of Europe as a home for all, and to creating a peaceful and prosperous environment. The Assembly therefore asks the Committee of Ministers to: [...] draw up training programs and organize seminars for history teachers and media representatives, especially for those working in ethnically mixed regions, in order to educate young people in the spirit of tolerance and co-operation throughout Europe.[89]

One of the sad features of today's Europe is that these recommendations and resolutions have remained dead letters, without triggering any meaningful action or action. In Central and Eastern Europe today there are still millions of national minorities whose fate is unacceptable, and this is a constant threat to the stability of the whole continent.

One may ask whether it was not naïve of me to have tried to persuade our partners, the European democracies, in my negotiations and in speeches at important international forums, to adopt conventions and laws and measures to safeguard the rights of the national minorities, using logical arguments, referring to the basic conditions of lasting peace and stability. But given Hungary's size, the size of its population, its economic or military strength, the support of only a few far-sighted foreign politicians—what other means did I and my government have? Today, unfortunately, a deadly illusion has reared its head once again, the illusion that, having been disappointed in the West, we should turn to the East, where we can gain economic and political support against our neighbors and our hard-won Western allies. A part of Hungarian society once believed that with the help of an aggressive great power it would be possible to regain the territories lost in the Trianon peace. The outcome was not as predictable then as it would be today. An attempt to have recourse to such a policy would be bound to end in a failure, and a vast tragedy.

What is the solution, is there a chance for reconciliation in the Carpathian Basin? The principles, patterns and framework for a solution are there. Decentralization, local democracy, self-government and autonomy are now common practice in the western part of Europe. The policy towards national minorities in the eastern half of Europe must break with a bad tradition that has been in place for more than a century: to deny or at least to restrict the rights of the national minorities. Until this is

---

[89] Council of Europe, Recommendation 2040 (2014). The situation and rights of national minorities in Europe, https://pace.coe.int/en/files/20773/html. Cf. Péter Varga, "A Kalmár-jelentés: Újra napirenden a kisebbségi jogok" [The Kalmár-report: Minority rights are again on the agenda], *Kisebbségkutatás* 2 (2014).

done, there will be constant tension between the majority nation and the minority national communities on the one hand, and the minorities' mother country on the other. It is in the interest of the countries of Europe, and a special responsibility of the great powers that drew up the 1920 Hungarian peace treaty, that the greatest victims of Trianon, the Hungarian minorities, should finally be able to breathe again and feel at home in their homeland, the land of their ancestors.

Central and Eastern Europe have certainly fallen behind the international legal order based on respect for common values, but the goal, that the peoples of Central Europe should live in friendship and alliance with each other, which Lajos Kossuth dreamed of as a "smiling future," shall never be given up.

Chapter 12

The Outstretched Hand and the Embracing Arm

On November 6, 1993, in Kézdivásárhely/Târgu Secuesc, I dedicated the bust of Mózes Turóczy, the companion of Áron Gábor, the celebrated cannon-maker in the Hungarian War of Independence in 1948–49. Mihály András Beke, reporting on the event, summed up my sentiments about and politics towards Transylvania: "The outstretched hand towards the Romanians, the embracing arm towards the Hungarians of Transylvania."[1] I believe that the simultaneous application of these two approaches is what the Hungarian motherland can do to heal the hundred-year-old wound of the Trianon trauma, the unjust peace. The Antall government's neighborhood policy was based on these principles.[2] Even after 1994, Hungarian politicians in successive governments have continued this policy—to varying degrees—trying to improve the situation of the Hungarian minorities. It is debatable whether the bilateral treaties concluded with Slovakia in 1995 and Romania in 1996 had any positive effect. Although those the treaties did include the then-existing international standards for the protection of minorities, both neighbors tried to evade the conventions and recommendations contained in them. The governments led by Viktor Orbán have demonstrated their commitment to the cause of Hungarian national minorities by various means—financial aid, investments, preferential treatment, preferential naturalization, support for the Hungarian media in the neighboring countries. Behind this, Hungarian domestic political goals (increasing the votes for Fidesz) were also evident, but this was only natural.

---

[1] *Heti Magyarország*, September 24, 1993.
[2] For reviews of the first Hungarian edition of this book (Jeszenszky, *Kísérlet a trianoni trauma orvoslására: Magyarország szomszédsági politikája a rendszerváltozás éveiben* [An attempt to heal the Trianon trauma: Hungary's neighborhood policy in the years of regime change], 1st ed. [Budapest: Osiris, 2016]), see Géza Entz, "Jeszenszky Géza Trianon meghaladásának kísérletéről: Átfogó mű az Antall-kormány szomszédság-politikájáról" [Géza Jeszenszky on the attempt to overcome Trianon: A comprehensive work on the Antall government's neighborhood policy], *Magyar Szemle* 25, nos. 7–8 (2016): 48–58; Béla S. Király, "Az Antall-kormány Teleki-térképe" [The Antall government's Teleki map], *Magyar Idők*, June 19, 2016, and Béla S. Király, "Trianon jegyében" [With respect to Trianon], *Háromszék*, June 11, 2016; Csaba Gy. Kiss, "A külügyminiszter visszanéz" [The Hungarian foreign minister looks back], *Bécsi Napló*, January 12, 2017.

Changes under the Horn Government

In the conclusion of the first edition of this book, I wrote that, although the situation and opportunities of Hungarian minorities had improved as a result of the regime changes, political parties and press outlets representing their interests had been established, international conventions and recommendations had been concluded to serve their present and future, yet despite the hopes and efforts of the Antall government, the best means of remedying the Trianon trauma, namely establishing the territorial or local autonomy of Hungarian minorities, had nowhere been realized. This situation has not changed to this day in 2025. The problem of national minorities has been relegated to the background at international level, and the European Union has not been willing to take up the issue, which is still a national (state) responsibility.

The situation of Hungarian minorities after the regime change, their goals, strategies, and the functioning of the individual governments have been discussed in a considerable number of high-quality books.[3] While the legal self-government of the towns has been established in all our neighbors, the extent of their actual powers and financial capacities varies from country to country. Collective or group rights, or personal autonomy (which is common for religious denominations) would mitigate the consequences of having become a diaspora, but that has not been recognized in the Central European countries except in Hungary, and, to a limited extent, in Vojvodina, a province of Serbia.[4] Autonomy is the guarantee for the lasting survival of the national minorities; autonomy and democracy are interlinked. However, international law and European institutions, foreign politicians and political scientists do not yet accept that. (It is not an exclusively Hungarian notion.). For many there is the fear (real or just feigned) that the concept of group rights, or collective minority rights, may lead to separatism, to serious internal and external conflict. Governments and political scientists abroad assume that it is sufficient to guarantee individual (minority) rights. (The minority protection system

---

[3] Bárdi, *Tény és való*; Nándor Bárdi and György Éger, eds., *Magyarok Romániában 1990–2015: Tanulmányok az erdélyi magyarságról* [The Hungarians in Romania, 1990–2015] (Budapest: Károli Gáspár Református Egyetem–L'Harmattan Kiadó, 2017); Nándor Bárdi, Csilla Fedinec, and László Szarka, eds., *Minority Hungarian communities in the twentieth century*, trans. Brian McLean (Boulder, CO, Highland Lakes, NJ, New York: Social Science Monographs; Atlantic Research and Publications; Distributed by Columbia University Press, 2011).

[4] On August 31, 2009, the Serbian House of Representatives adopted the Law on National Councils for the National Minorities. It regulates the conditions for the establishment of national councils and the election of their members, the way they are financed, and their place in the political system of the country. https://hu.wikipedia.org/wiki/Magyar_Nemzeti_Tan%C3%A1cs_(Vajdas%C3%A1g).

under the League of Nations was based on collective rights.) Alas, there is also no distinction made between indigenous (autochthonous) minorities, which are historical (national) minorities created by border changes, and new minorities, which are mainly the result of immigration, mainly of peoples of non-European origin. In the latter case, their integration is encouraged, rightly, but in the case of historic national minorities, integration is the path to assimilation and the gradual elimination of the minority. However, the common, implied view that territorial autonomy can only be ethnic-based is wrong, it is always based on territory, with its diverse population.[5]

Looking back, the situation of the Hungarian minorities in the mid-1990s was certainly worse than it is today. Proof of that is offered in an article I wrote in the summer of 1995 in the weekly *Magyar Narancs* in response to Mátyás Eörsi, then chairman of the Foreign Affairs Committee of the National Assembly:

> He [Eörsi] claims that "in Brussels, Paris and Madrid, the problem of Hungary evokes just as much pain as the Basque, Northern Irish or Rwandan conflicts in Budapest." It would be painful if in the Western European capitals every word that tries to draw attention to the deteriorating situation of the Hungarian minorities fell on deaf ears, but in that case, we should redouble our efforts and instead of debating each other in public, we should discuss common strategy and tactics in a closed session of the Foreign Affairs Committee. However, Mátyás Eörsi is entirely wrong when he equates the Basque problem, which has been fairly settled with the federative Spanish constitution and autonomy, with the behavior of Slovakia and Romania, who are, instead of introducing regional self-government, centralizing, and do not want to hear about the very moderate Hungarian demands. British policy, which is based on strong local self-government in Northern Ireland, and today maintains an equal distance between the Catholic minority and the Protestant majority, seeks a solution that satisfies both parties, while the Slovak and Romanian governments see autonomy as blasphemy and seek to radically curb the Hungarian education system and the use of the

---

[5] Zsuzsa Csergő, a distinguished American scholar on post-Cold War nationalism and minority issues, wrote in a private letter to me regarding the demand for autonomy that "Hungarians should be able to live in Transylvania as if they lived in Hungary and the Romanians did not live with them." I consider such a wish to be understandable, though not, of course, in the sense that they should ignore the state in which they live. Autonomy is more a way of avoiding tensions and conflicts than a cause of them. See Zsuzsa Csergő, "Kin-State Politics in Central and Eastern Europe: The Case of Hungary," Wilson Center Meeting Report 315, 2005, https://www.wilsoncenter.org/publication/315-kin-state-politics-central-and-eastern-europe-the-case-hungary.

Hungarian language. Can the good situation in Spain and the improving situation in Northern Ireland be compared with the increasingly rigid Slovak and Romanian attitude, which rejects any reasonable European solution?

Eörsi's argued that however justified our criticism of some of our neighbors may be, we should not speak out publicly on neighborhood issues, as doing so would be in vain. We should do so only at the buffet table ("That is where the real politics takes place!"), and let others hear and talk of the complaints of the Hungarian minorities. His argument may sound convincing, but I disagreed:

I don't share the view that the real arena of parliamentarianism is the buffet. I do not see the most prestigious members of the Parliamentary Assembly of the Council of Europe, such as Lord Finsberg or Tarja Halonen, Jaques Baule or Rudolf Bindig sitting in the buffet, but I know them as the most knowledgeable speakers in the chamber. I am also witness to the fact that although it is possible to persuade our friends to speak out on some good issue that concern us, but they expect us not to be complacent and not to try to induce others to get the hot chestnut out of the fire (to quote the favorite phrase of Comrade Stalin), but to take a stand ourselves. It may sometimes be tiresome to hear a Greek, a Turk, a Cypriot or a British speaker, who is not strictly on the subject, but is it not the duty of Hungarian MPs to draw attention to the growing anti-Hungarian mood in our neighborhood, to the hate campaign that is targeting and victimizing nearly two million Hungarians in Romania and 600,000 Hungarians in Slovakia, when, in the Year of Tolerance the debate is about the great danger that national and sectarian intolerance, xenophobia poses to Europe? [...]

[On June 28, 1995, at the Parliamentary Assembly of the Council of Europe] Zsolt Németh (Fidesz-MPP) said that the principle of self-government is an essential element of the Hungarian Minorities Act, and that it provides cultural autonomy for the minorities, including the Roma population, which is often mentioned in the debate. The Hungarian Parliament has created a special fund for the youth campaign against xenophobia. He spoke the urgent need for legislative or law-amending activity in national parliaments, and drew attention to the fact that a language law is being drafted in Slovakia which seeks the language of the majority to "protect" against the language of the minority. [In my own intervention, I reminded the Assembly that] there are at least thirty, if not forty million citizens in Central and Eastern Europe whose mother tongue and national identity are different from those of the majority. I regret to say that a significant number of them are often disadvantaged because of their ethnic origin and are victims of discrimination, intolerance and sometimes even a real hate campaign. [I drew the attention of the Assembly to the fact that] in Romania, Slovakia and Serbia, which are neighbors of Hungary, despite the recommendations and mechanisms of the Council of Europe and the OSCE, the fate of the significant number of Hungarians is deteriorating rather than improving. They are law-abiding citizens who have never resorted to violence and try to preserve their rights, or are seeking to restore them through legal means, through their elected representatives. Because of discrimination and the mood of the press, for many, especially young people, emigration is the way of escape. [I pointed out that the language law being drafted in Slovakia] makes a mockery of the commitments made by Slovakia when it was admitted to the Council of Europe. In Romania, Hungarian inscriptions are being forcibly removed from towns and villages where the traditions of Hungarian culture go back to centuries. Recently in Cluj-Napoca/Kolozsvár, an enlightened Romanian was fined for putting the name of his foundation, which worked for inter-ethnic reconciliation, on his sign in three languages, Romanian, Hungarian and German. Such behavior is contrary to the standards, conventions and recommendations of the Council of Europe. We know where such tendencies lead, and we must act against them.[6]

Nándor Bárdi, in a book using many sources, analyzed Act LXII, which provides preferential treatment for the Hungarian minorities, and its reception. He reviewed the changing interpretations of "nation policy," and summarized the policy of the Budapest governments between 1918 and 1989. He, too, rightly criticized "the international community"—primarily the Western European governments—for their position on and policies towards the national minorities. He also spoke critically of some of the steps taken by successive Hungarian governments—in my opinion the criticism was not always well founded. However, his answer to the question of why Hungary must address the problems of Hungarians living beyond its borders was to the point. Comparing the policies of the Antall, Horn, and Orbán governments, Bárdi identified common and contrasting features. He is mistaken to think that in the Antall government there was rivalry between the Ministry of Foreign Affairs and the HTMH on the one hand, and the Ministry of Education on the

---

[6] Géza Jeszenszky, "Eörsi törököt fogott, avagy mi történt Strassburgban" [Eörsi's blunder in Strasbourg], *Magyar Narancs*, August 24, 1995, 14.

other. (Whether there were internal disputes and rivalries later, I do not know). Whether it is justified to speak of "often well-intentioned, ambitious initiatives by the Antall government, which did not take sufficient account of international realities," is for the reader of the previous chapters to judge. It is also up to the reader to decide if Bárdi was right to assert that "in the execution of foreign policy, Euro-Atlantic integration and policy towards the Hungarian minorities were the priority, and thus at the beginning neighborhood relations were a series of unresolved conflicts."

Bárdi rightly concluded:

> The Horn government did not consider it its historical and national mission to deal with the affairs of Hungarians beyond its borders, [...] this government was characterized by a striving for concreteness and pragmatism in Hungarian policy. [...] Because of the competition for integration and the strained neighborly relations, it was considered a basic principle that *raising issues related to Hungarians beyond the borders should not endanger—even ostensibly—the stability of this region*. Thus, the issue became a foreign policy issue, subordinated to (integration) priorities within it. It was under these circumstances that with Slovakia and Romania the basic treaties were concluded. ... [As a result,] the electoral results and the emergence of Euro-Atlantic integration as a top priority in the neighboring countries led to a significant change in their policy towards the Hungarian minority: the discriminatory political approach of the past was replaced by an integrative policy. This does not mean that the longer-term homogenization of the nation-state was automatically abandoned. Rather, the policies of the Czechoslovak bourgeois democracy and Titoist Yugoslavia, integrating the elite, came to the fore in Slovakia, Romania, Ukraine and Serbia. The other part of the process was the behavior of the political elites of the Hungarian minority: *the entry of the Hungarian minority parties into coalition governments or the external support of the governing party*. The result was a reduction in anti-Hungarian attitudes and allowing a wider the use of the Hungarian language, as well as allowing a small share of development funds for Hungarian regions.[7]

On the changes that took place in the first fifteen years, Bárdi rightly observes of the Hungarian parties:

---

[7] Bárdi, *Tény és való*, 22–29. Emphasis in original.

Instead of developing into a people's party, they are operating as ethnoregional electoral parties, with a diminishing ability to mobilize. The decision-making power of local government leaders in Hungarian-majority regions and municipalities increased. Minority elites increasingly see the minority issue as something that can be dealt with through legal and political deals and decrees, and social self-organization was devalued or became of interest only from the point of view of party politics. At the same time, there was a growing sense of political apathy and abandonment in local Hungarian communities. In the same way, the proportion of Hungarians who do not vote or vote for other parties was steadily rising. The new type of minority politician no longer stood for the protection of cultural interests, but legitimacy was ensured by how much development and funding sources could be obtained for the [Hungarian] electorate.[8]

Bárdi's two books were a kind of continuation of the story of the policies of the Antall and Boross governments. What follows is a summary of my personal involvement after 1994 in the efforts to heal the trauma caused by Trianon. Between 1994 and 1998, I worked as an opposition member of Parliament. Many of my speeches dealt with the neighboring countries and the Hungarian minority living there. My writings on this subject were also published.[9] At the Budapest University of Economics and Business Administration (today Corvinus University of Budapest) I continued my lectures and seminars on modern international and Hungarian history, also on Central Europe and its national problems.

In the spring of 1996—for reasons not explained here—the MDF split, and half of the MDF's thirty-two members of Parliament—mainly the former senior officials of Antall's government who swore by his policies—formed an independent political organization, the Hungarian Democratic People's Party (MDNP). Its foreign policy program, drafted by me, stated that its founders "have for decades demonstrated their commitment to the fate of Hungarian communities outside our borders through their actions." It continued:

---

[8] Nándor Bárdi, "Magyarország és a kisebbségi magyar közösségek 1989 után" [Hungary and the Hungarian minority communities after 1989], *METSZETEK—Társadalomtudományi folyóirat* 2, nos. 2–3 (2013): 56–69.

[9] Just the two most important ones: Géza Jeszenszky, "More Bosnias? National and Ethnic Tensions in the Post-Communist World," *East European Quarterly* 31, no. 3 (1997): 283–99; and Géza Jeszenszky, "Magyarország kétoldalú szerződései a szomszédos országokkal és a kisebbségi kérdés" [Hungary's bilateral treaties with the neighboring countries and the issue of national minorities], in *Ars boni et aequi: Tanulmányok az ezredvég nemzetközi rendszeréről Bokorné Szegő Hanna 75. születésnapjára* (Budapest: BKÁE Nemzetközi Kapcsolatok Tanszék, 2000), 450–69.

We see the future of them in extending the borders of the European Union, in the gradual softening of the artificial borders that ignore historical, economic and geographical factors, in regionalism and subsidiarity, keeping decisions at the lowest possible level. It is regrettable to note that in many neighboring countries there has been growing intolerance and trampling of rights against the Hungarian population, and that the Horn government's policy of "reconciliation" announced in 1994 has proved fruitless. [...] Therefore, in the spirit of preventive diplomacy, we intend to launch a broad international awareness-raising movement to ensure that these trends, which threaten European stability, are not allowed to continue unabated. At the same time, we must make it clear that "national radicalism," lacking strength and supporters, cannot achieve any real results in foreign policy in the interests of Hungarians beyond the border, while it only reinforces fallacious and unfounded prejudices against the Hungarians. The People's Party does not seek to serve the interests of Hungarians living as minorities with words, but with deeds, by weighing up the opportunities and risks. It wants them to find solutions to their problems not in emigration, but in remaining in their homeland.[10]

On my initiative, the MDNP launched a minority protection offensive, addressed to the OSCE High Commissioner on Minorities, the member states of the Council of Europe and the European Parliament.

The Hungarian-Slovak treaty

The Horn government, formed after the 1994 elections, wanted to demonstrate that, unlike its predecessor, it could establish good relations with Slovakia. Even during the election campaign, party chairman Horn promised, "If I win, I will bring peace." Although there was no sign of war, the new government, which placed great emphasis on its international reception, wanted to take advantage of the fact that the Moravčík government was facing elections and was also seeking international support, therefore was itself interested in a spectacular improvement in its relations with Hungary. The Horn government was willing to include the border guarantee in the treaty without any significant strengthening of minority rights. On the eve of the signing of the Pact on Stability in Europe in Paris, at the strong urging of the EU and the United States, the Hungarian and Slovak prime ministers agreed on the

---

[10] The foreign policy program of the Hungarian Democratic People's Party. In Hungarian. Among my papers.

Chapter 12 – The Outstretched Hand and the Embracing Arm

text of the treaty, and it was signed in Paris on March 19, 1995.[11] The agreement was based on the mutual acceptance of international documents on minority rights. As these contained few concrete conditions beyond the declaration of fine principles, both countries considered the agreement a victory. The most sensitive point was Recommendation 1201 of the Parliamentary Assembly of the Council of Europe, adopted in 1993, which recommended the establishment of autonomous local government in areas predominantly inhabited by a given national minority. Although the Recommendation was included among the documents referred to in the treaty as a means of guaranteeing minority rights, at the signing ceremony, to the surprise of the representatives of the Hungarian government, the Slovak foreign minister attached an interpretative note to the treaty with a paper clip. The note stated that the reference did not imply the adoption of any form of autonomy by Slovakia, and they did not recognize collective minority rights. (Prime Minister Horn rightly declared that this action did not have relevance to the treaty, and the note might as well have been a recipe for *strapachka*, the popular Slovak sheep's curd dumplings.)

I saw the shortcomings of the treaty as the following: it did not include the free use of national symbols (Hungarian national colors and the coat of arms), the right to practice religion in the mother tongue, guarantees of training for Hungarian clergy and of higher education in the Hungarian language, and the development of the Hungarian-inhabited areas in proportion to their population. Also missing from the agreement was the financial support for minority institutions and trans-border cooperation. More than a shortcoming, it was a serious error to accept a clause stating that the precondition for any commitment was that it did not conflict with the provisions of the "internal legal order" in Slovakia.[12] At that time, it was already clear that the Mečiar government was about to curtail the existing rights of the Hungarian minority by means of a discriminatory language law, an administrative reform. That led to a sensible reaction: the formation of the Hungarian Coalition in Slovakia, the integration of the three Hungarian parties. The undeniable decline in the minority rights and the desirable solution was published in 1997.[13]

---

[11] Treaty between the Republic of Hungary and the Slovak Republic on good neighborly relations and friendly cooperation. *Magyar Külpolitikai Évkönyv, 1995* [Hungarian Foreign Policy Yearbook, 1995] (Budapest: Magyar Külügyminisztérium, 1995), 195–206.

[12] Géza Jeszenszky: "Félresiklott magyar-szlovák megegyezés?" [A Hungarian-Slovak agreement that went astray?], *Magyarország*, April 14, 1995. Jeszenszky, "Tető falak nélkül? A magyar-szlovák szerződés veszélyei és esélyei" [The dangers and opportunities of the Hungarian-Slovak treaty], *Magyar Nemzet*, June 10, 1995, 4.

[13] Hungarian Coalition in Slovakia, *The Hungarians in Slovakia* (Bratislava: Information Centre of the Hungarian Coalition in Slovakia, 1997).

The Hungarian-Romanian treaty

In 1995, despite international pressure, no similar treaty was signed with Romania. The obstacle was the Hungarian expectations regarding minority rights, above all the need to incorporate Council of Europe Recommendation 1201 of 1993 into the treaty, as it was in the case of the Slovakian one. Sensing deteriorating electoral prospects, President Iliescu and his government, knowing the predictably favorable international reception, and in the hope that this would have a significant domestic political impact, abandoned their earlier objections and in August 1996 agreed to include Recommendation 1201 (1993) in the treaty. However, it had a footnote stating that "the contracting parties agreed that Recommendation 1201 did not imply collective rights and did not oblige the Parties to grant a special status of ethnic autonomy." The Hungarian opposition parties immediately objected to the footnote narrowing the recommendation. They voiced concerns that there would be disappointment among Hungarians in Romania, as many of their basic demands, such as Bolyai University and expropriated properties, were not mentioned in the treaty, while autonomy and collective rights were now dropped with Hungary's approval.

It was a serious disappointment for the RMDSZ that its long-standing fundamental demands were now ignored by the Hungarian government, too. In its resolution of August 16, 1996, the political party of the Hungarians of Romania declared its commitment to the reconciliation and Euro-Atlantic integration of the two peoples, welcomed the provisions of the treaty on education in the mother tongue and bilingualism, but deplored the lack of agreement on the fate of confiscated church and community property, and that there were no guarantees for the implementation of the treaty. It stated that "the many forms of collective rights are indispensable for the future of the Hungarians in Romania," and that therefore a basic treaty was needed "to regulate the minority issue in a way that is reassuring for all parties concerned."[14] The historical Hungarian churches in Romania spoke in similar terms. The Hungarian media were also full of discussions of the treaty.[15]

The Hungarian Parliament discussed the treaty on September 3, 1996, in an extraordinary session that ran into the night, and the opposition parties rejected it

---

[14] The position of the Steering Committee of the Hungarian Democratic Alliance of Romania on the Romanian-Hungarian basic treaty, which is about to be finalized. Târgu Mures/Marosvásárhely, August 16, 1996.

[15] In the spirit of the party-neutral administration, the Ministry of Foreign Affairs sent the opposition a preview of Radio and Television Program No. 47, where I discussed the treaty with State Secretary István Szent-Iványi and international lawyer László Valki, August 28, 1996.

in strong terms. Speaking on behalf of the Hungarian Democratic People's Party, I did not question "that the representatives of the governing coalition sincerely wish to improve Hungarian-Romanian relations and to fulfil the legitimate wishes of the Hungarians in Transylvania," but I said I believed that "they themselves do not believe that this treaty will have the desired result." The political good will of the partner, which was present in the case of the Ukrainian, Slovenian and Croatian treaties concluded by the previous government, was clearly lacking in the case of Romania. After a detailed list of the treaty's shortcomings, I turned to its much vaunted positive reception abroad: "I sincerely thank Washington, London, Bonn and Brussels for being so happy about the good news, the imminent conclusion of the Hungarian-Romanian treaty, but I fear that our friends are very wrong if they think that this treaty really solves the problem." Western governments needed to know what was happening to Hungarians in Transylvania, and we urged them "to take deadly seriously the principles they laid down in Copenhagen, Geneva, New York on minority rights. If these Western friends of ours see these principles and Western practices reflected in our neighborhood treaties and put into practice in Slovakia and Romania, then they will have a reason to offer congratulations. But until they do, they should feel free to put pressure on all those who need it."[16]

Objections were swept aside, and the treaty was signed in Timișoara on September 16, 1996.[17] Iliescu expected the foreign policy success to turn around at least some of the city and its surrounding area, which were traditionally opposed to him. The signing ceremony and the banquet that followed were accompanied by the voices of the crowds protesting against him and his regime. The demonstrators emphasized that they were not protesting against Hungarian-Romanian reconciliation but against the Romanian government. This voice was heard by the Romanian electorate, which had voted in in two rounds in November to defeat the regime that had been in place since December 1989, and against its leader, Ion Iliescu. He certainly bears the main responsibility for the failure to maintain the spirit of Romanian-Hungarian reconciliation and friendship after the unforgettable Christmas of 1989. There was an apt cartoon in the September 14 issue of *Magyar*

---

[16] Minutes of the Hungarian Parliament, session of September 3, 1996, 23420–24. Cf. Géza Jeszenszky, "Hungary's Bilateral Treaties with the Neighbours," *Ethnos-Nation* (Köln), nos. 1–2 (1996 [1997]): 123–28; and Jeszenszky, "Viták a magyar-román szerződés körül" [Disputes over the Hungarian-Romanian treaty], in *Magyarország Politikai Évkönyve 1997* [Hungarian Political Yearbook 1997], ed. Sándor Kurtán, Péter Sándor and László Vass (Budapest: Demokrácia Kutatások Magyar Központja Alapítvány, 1997), 220–27.

[17] "Szerződés a Magyar Köztársaság és Románia között a megértésről, az együttműködésről és a jószomszédságról" [Treaty between the Republic of Hungary and Romania on understanding, cooperation and good neighborliness], *Magyar Kisebbség* 2, no. 6 (4) (1996): 59–69.

Nemzet, in which the two prime ministers, Iliescu showing his feigned good-natured smile, sign the treaty over the head of Béla Markó, the leader of RMDSZ, who is lying under the table.

Emil Constantinescu, who won the election and became the president of Romania, was a true democrat. I can testify to that based on our exchanges both before and after his presidential term. It was thanks to this decision of the Romanian electorate, and not to the treaty, that the Hungarians in Romania were not abandoned under the table but shared in the responsibility of government and tried for four years to improve their economic and political situation together with the Romanian majority. This broke a taboo: in Romania, which was declared a unified nation state, Hungarian ministers worked—to the public's satisfaction—to lift the country from its poor condition, and even if they only achieved a portion of their goals, that was not insignificant. Sadly, the joint committees set up by the Slovak and the Romanian treaty to monitor their implementation did not produce much as a result.[18]

The scene in Western Europe on the subject of regional self-government was more hopeful. On September 11, 1997, the people of Scotland voted in a referendum to accept the British Labour government's offer that Scotland, which had been an independent kingdom until the seventeenth century, could elect its own Parliament, so that it would be governed from Edinburgh rather than London. A week later, a similar decision was taken by the people of Wales, whose Parliament sits in Cardiff. So, the United Kingdom, together with its two provinces, the land of Burns and the Bards, known to and sympathetic to Hungarians mainly through our poets, joined an expanding circle of European countries. Those are countries where, alongside the central Parliament and government, provincial parliaments with considerable powers ensure a tangible local exercise of democracy, where the specific interests of larger historical and geographical regions are represented by politicians and authorities close to the citizens, and where their affairs are managed locally. In 1998, the British Parliament passed legislation specifying the powers of each province. The previous Conservative government opposed such "devolution," fearing that it would start the disintegration of the United Kingdom, but Labour politicians, analysts and the majority of the interested public argued the opposite. I recall once having read in the *Economist* that provincial autonomy is not a threat

---

[18] Róbert Győri Szabó, "A parlamenti pártok és alapszerződések (1994-1997)" [The parliamentary parties and the basic treaties], *Magyar Kisebbség* 6, no. 4 (2000): 168–87. Cf. Bárdi, "Magyarország és a kisebbségi magyar közösségek," 57; Miklós Bakk on the "basic treaties" in *Magyar Kisebbség* 2, no. 3 (1996): 103–10; and the studies by Árpád Sidó, János Fiala, Dávid Vincze and Balázs Jarábik in *Regio* 14, no. 1 (2013).

to the UK, but a guarantee for keeping it together. Lord Robertson, the former Secretary General of NATO, once told me the same thing about devolution.

The benefits of internal self-determination are demonstrated by European examples. Since the Second World War, most countries in Western Europe have embarked on decentralization, on the vertical sharing of power, accepting the EU principle of subsidiarity. The political and economic benefits of this process have been undeniably significant: regional tensions (often based on ethnic and historical grounds) have been reduced; many previously underdeveloped regions are prospering. The Flemish regions of Belgium are one of the most visible, if little known, examples. Since 1945, Germany's *Länder* (federal states) have extensive rights, autonomous parliaments and governments, and that contributed to the economic and political success of the Federal Republic. During Franco's dictatorship, Catalans and Basques in Spain were not even allowed to use their own language and were sworn enemies of the government, even resorting to terrorism in protest; the democratic transformation of that country largely eliminated old antagonisms and resulted in an unprecedented boom in the previously neglected and underdeveloped provinces. Nevertheless, Spain, has remained one state, the majority of Catalonia's population does not support the independence of the province. In the 1980s, France, which had been a bastion of centralization for two centuries, also decentralized its administration, and this is working increasingly well. It can be said that the western half of Europe is now characterized by different levels of self-government, and it is therefore right to speak of a Europe of regions and autonomies.[19]

From the law on benefits to simplified naturalization

In February 1996 I was invited by the University of Michigan, Ann Arbor, to give a seminar on "Post-Communist Europe and the Ethnic Problem." In 1998 I held a seminar course at Pázmány Péter Catholic University on "The Hungarian Minorities in International Politics." After the 1998 elections, Prime Minister Viktor Orbán asked me to represent Hungary in the United States as ambassador. During the subsequent four years I gave many talks, lectures, and speeches at conferences to demonstrate that discrimination against national minorities is a global problem, not just a Hungarian preoccupation. Bloody proof of that was the genocide in Kosovo, which NATO finally halted with armed intervention. Hungary, as

---

[19] See my essay: "A régiók és autonómiák Európája felé: Skócia és Wales a belső önrendelkezés útján" [Towards a Europe of regions and autonomies: Scotland and Wales on the road to internal self-determination], *Bécsi Napló* 18 (1997): ix–x; also in the Transylvanian periodical *Sóvidék* 2, no. 1 (May 2010): 62–66.

a new NATO member state, took an active role in that. The process of the break-up of Yugoslavia, which dragged on for ten years, enabled me to draw the attention of American decision-makers and the media to Vojvodina, a province of Serbia, and to the Hungarian minority living there. I gave the keynote address at a conference on "ethnic cleansing" held on November 16–18, 2000 at Duquesne University, Pittsburgh. It was organized by Hungarian-American historian Béla Várdy. Later, my address appeared in an enlarged version in a book.[20]

One of the strongest Hungarian-American organizations is the Hungarian Communion of Friends (Magyar Baráti Közösség). At its summer camp at Lake Hope (Ohio) on August 14, 2001, I presented another summary of my understanding of the minority problem. I started with this premise:

> In the Balkans and elsewhere, national (historical) minorities can no longer be assimilated, expelled or murdered. They want to live in the land of their ancestors, according to their own customs, sending their children to schools teaching in their own language, under leaders of their own choosing. The institutional form of this is local democracy, self-government, or, in Greek, autonomy. Unfortunately, the world has not yet come to the realization that ethnic groups who cling to their national traditions and rightly feel that they are threatened, are not satisfied with individual personal rights. They need institutional guarantees for respecting their rights. It is time to learn from the sad example of the Balkans that, just as discrimination is always based on belonging to a group (of the same origin or religion), the only antidote to this is to guarantee group rights.

The Hungarian communities detached from Hungary in 1920 have lost a great deal in terms of numbers, institutions, real estate, economic strength and organization over eight decades. The aim of autonomy is to stop the decline, to stop the deterioration, to promote the survival and prosperity of the Hungarians in their homeland, in other words, to preserve peace and tranquility. That serves the interests of both the majority and the minority. We Hungarians can cite examples of autonomies that are functioning well: South Tyrol, Catalonia, and most recently Scotland and Wales. There are also lesser-known examples involving smaller groups, such as the autonomy of about sixty thousand of Germans in Belgium. Even the case of Canada shows

---

[20] Géza Jeszenszky, "From 'Eastern Switzerland' to Ethnic Cleansing: Is the Dream Still Relevant?," in *Ethnic Cleansing in Twentieth Century Europe*, ed. Steven Béla Várdy and T. Hunt Tooley (New York: Columbia University Press, 2003), 11–30.

that the separation of the English and French ethnic groups, the latter's provincial autonomy, proved the best way of keeping the country together. An even more obvious example is the cantonal system in Switzerland; it ensured the peaceful coexistence of German, French, Italian and Romansh-speaking people living in the Confederation Helvetica.

The Hungarian ethnic groups outside Hungary need rights, acceptable economic conditions and, above all, to feel at home, to be free from discrimination, in order survive. It may not sound good to Hungary's neighbors and many outside observers, but they want the village, the town, the county, the region where they live to be a kind of small Hungary. They understand that the sovereignty of the Hungarian state cannot return, but they do not accept that in the territory they inhabit they could live as mere aliens, outcasts. They have no objection to other people living together with them, but they should not find that they can use their mother tongue only in private life, and even on the street only with caution. Fundamentally, it is the mentality of the majority nation that should change, it must accept that Hungarians will not disappear from the lands where they lived for more than a thousand years. The desired change in mentality would be greatly facilitated by a change in the international community's position. Since 1990, many promises and many drafts have been made, which have included the autonomy of national minorities, but in the end, seeing the resistance of governments and the majority nations, the international community always backed down.

Today European integration is no longer a utopia, it is a well-functioning reality. One day it will achieve what existed in Central Europe before 1919: eleven nations without borders, common economic space, currency, foreign policy and army, many regional parliaments. For the ethnic mosaics, a centralized state declaring itself to be a nation-state is not acceptable; their goal is a Europe where borders are open, where there is free movement of people, goods and capital, but where nations remain, even if they are divided into eight countries. For us Hungarians, the only solution is a virtual Homeland, above the borders.[21]

During my term as ambassador, I met over breakfast with the ambassadors of the other three Visegrád countries on a monthly basis. Jerzy Koźmiński and his successor, Przemysław Grudziński of Poland, Slovak ambassador Martin Bútora and his

---

[21] Géza Jeszenszky, "A nemzeti autonómia, a balkáni válságok le nem vont tanulsága" [National autonomy, the unlearned lesson of the Balkan crises], *Itt-Ott Kalendárium* 34, no. 2 (2001): 14–16.

Czech colleague Alexandr Vondra, were excellent partners and friends, and we participated in many activities and programs together, demonstrating the close cooperation between our countries.

From the mid-1990s to the mid-2000s, I was associated with the Princeton-based Project on Ethnic Relations, an organization supported by a number of well-known foundations, including the Soros Foundation. Its president, Allen H. Kassof, was particularly active in Romanian-Hungarian relations, and he organized highly controversial meetings with Transylvanian Hungarians, with the help of Livia Plaks.[22] The organization was supported by successive Romanian governments and thus was inclined toward the Romanian position, but in our conversations, I tried to make it be more open to Hungarian arguments.

Financial support arriving from Hungary gradually increased as the country's economic situation improved, but this did not change the political situation of the Hungarian minorities.[23] Seeing that and in order to ensure their survival, Act LXII of 2001 "On Hungarians Living in Neighboring States" was passed by the Hungarian Parliament. It provided for various benefits for Hungarians living beyond the border and having a "Hungarian identity card," which entitling them to the benefits. The genesis of the law and the controversy surrounding it abroad were

---

[22] The Transylvanian portal *Átlátszó* published a series of articles on the activities of the organization, which operated between 1992 and 2012. "Based on the available documents, there is no reason to believe that György Tokay, László Borbély and György Frunda did not try to represent the interests of the Hungarian community in Transylvania. Nor is it entirely correct the often-heard claim that the Hungarian participants negotiated and agreed with the representatives of the Bucharest authorities without a mandate, behind the backs of the RMDSZ leadership and in secret. From unpublished documents in the possession of *Átlátszó*, and a series of background interviews, the most plausible interpretation seems to be that Hungarian politicians in Transylvania were not prepared to successfully represent the interests of the community in these high-level meetings. They were unable to assess their own room for maneuver, failed to see the foreign policy context and made several mistakes that ultimately weakened their negotiating positions." I believe this is a correct interpretation. Zoltán Sipos, "Neptuni találkozók 1: Több száz oldalnyi belső levelezést találtunk," [Neptune Meetings 1: Hundreds of pages of internal correspondence found], *Átlátszó Erdély*, January 26, 2015, https://atlatszo.ro/velunk-elo-tortenelem/neptun/neptuni-talalkozok-1-tobb-szaz-oldalnyi-belso-levelezest-talaltunk/; Zoltán Sipos, "Neptuni találkozók 3: Nagyon ismer minket a PER. De honnan?" [Neptune Meetings 3: PER knows us very well. But from where?], *Átlátszó Erdély*, January 28, 2015, https://atlatszo.ro/velunk-elo-tortenelem/neptun/neptuni-talalkozok-3-nagyon-ismer-minket-a-per-de-honnan/. On the American mediation revived in 2014, see "Kassof: az én ötletem volt a brassópojánai román-magyar találkozók megszervezése," *Transindex.ro*, December 2, 2014, https://web.archive.org/web/20240303212042/https://itthon.transindex.ro/?cikk=24811.

[23] Nándor Bárdi and Tibor Misovicz, "A kisebbségi magyar közösségek támogatásának politikája" [The policy of support for the Hungarian minority communities], in *Határon túli magyarság a 21. században: Konferencia-sorozat a Sándor-palotában* [Hungarians beyond the border: a series of conferences in the Sándor Palace], ed. Botond Bitskey (Budapest, Köztársasági Elnöki Hivatal, 2010), 119-32.

detailed in a book edited by Zoltán Kántor,[24] which resulted in a volume of studies in English with major foreign contributors, published by Hokkaido University.[25]

The law was fiercely opposed—on flimsy legal grounds—by Slovakia and Romania, countries hoping for the gradual disappearance of their Hungarian minorities. Within two years they managed to induce the European Union and even the Council of Europe to raise legal objections to the law, leading to the new Hungarian government of Péter Medgyessy[26] readily amending it, reducing its effectiveness. In my article for *Heti Válasz*, I called attention to the opinion of the liberal Slovak newspaper *SME*: "If anyone is bothered by the term [used by the previous prime minister, Viktor Orbán] 'the unification of all Hungarians without border change,' that person is obviously unaware that it is precisely this process that can guarantee the stability of our region."[27] On the morning of June 24, 2003, the Parliamentary Assembly of the Council of Europe—in the presence of one sixth of the members—voted in favor of the Jürgens report criticizing the Hungarian law. But that very afternoon it also adopted a most forward-looking report, which called for territorial autonomy for the national minorities. It was drafted by a Swiss socialist member, Andreas Gross, who had a political outlook different from Jürgens. The recommendation stated that local autonomy should be reached through negotiations, it should be included in the constitutions and be given sufficient funding to operate. My own conclusion was: "The European institutions should urge our neighbors, who are railing against the status law, to break with an eighty-five-year-old bad tradition. Until this happens, there will be constant tension between the majority nations and the minority national communities on the one hand, and their mother country on the other."[28]

After returning from Washington, I resumed teaching at my old university, now called Corvinus University of Budapest, instructing the increasing number of foreign students about the history of Central Europe, the regime change, the transformation that followed, and the national-ethnic conflicts in our region. For the

---

[24] Zoltán Kántor, ed., *A státustörvény—Dokumentumok, tanulmányok, publicisztika* [The status law. Documents, studies, newspaper articles] (Budapest: Teleki László Alapítvány, 2002). Reviewed by Sára Görömbei, *Külügyi Szemle* 2 (2003): 248–54. Cf. Miklós Bakk and Barna Bodó, *Státusdiskurzus* [Talk on the status] (Temesvár: Szórvány Alapítvány, 2003).

[25] Also, Zoltán Kántor, Balázs Majtényi, Osamu Ieda, Balázs Vizi, and Iván Halász, eds., *The Hungarian Status Law: Nation Building and/or Minority Protection* (Sapporo: Slavic Research Centre, Hokkaido University. 2004).

[26] Péter Medgyessy (1942–): Hungarian (formerly communist) politician, minister in the last communist governments, between 2002 and 2004 prime minister of the Socialist–Free Democrat government.

[27] Géza Jeszenszky, "Kinek a kudarca a státustörvény?" [Whose failure is the 'Status Law'?], *Heti Válasz*, July 11, 2003, 60–61.

[28] Jeszenszky, "Kinek a kudarca a státustörvény?"

latter topic I compiled a reference book consisting of lecture outlines and excerpts from articles and other studies.²⁹ Between 2003 and 2008 I gave lectures and courses on the modern history of Central Europe, including on the question of national minorities, at the following universities abroad: Babes-Bolyai University, Cluj-Napoca/Kolozsvár; College of Europe, Warsaw-Natolin; Mississippi State University; and Pacific Lutheran University in Tacoma, Washington. My views, writings and words on the problem of the national minorities are well summarized in a long private letter I sent to President Ferenc Mádl, in preparation for his visit to Transylvania in March 2003:

> I believe that the Antall government's fundamental principle was correct: we should help our compatriots who have ended up outside our borders in every way we can, where justified and possible, but we must respect their sovereign conduct. We also believed that "unity is strength" and that there was no need for multiple Hungarian parties in Slovakia, as we saw the effectiveness of unity in the case of the Swedish community in Finland and the Südtiroler Volkspartei. In 1990 we were unable to induce the Hungarian parties in Slovakia to unite, but Mečiar did us this favor, which proved useful and resulted in strong Hungarian representation in the National Council. I personally tried to preserve Hungarian unity in Vojvodina, but internal conflicts (mainly rivalry over limited funds) tore the VMDK apart.³⁰

I referred to the fact that after the death of Ferenc Csubela, the Hungarian Association of Vojvodina (led by József Kasza, following the fall of Milosević) achieved serious results thanks to its common-sense policies: in 2002 a National Council, elected by ethnic Hungarians, was established. I continued my letter by saying that the RMDSZ was a strong party in many respects similar to the MDF, and with MDF's help, it was accepted into the international organization of the conservative and Christian democratic parties. Although it did not achieve everything that was expected of it after 1996 when it entered the government, it got Romanian society accustomed to the idea that Hungarians have a say in Romanian affairs; it even became apparent that RMDSZ politicians are better and more honest than most of their Romanian colleagues. The example of the Catalans shows that minorities can achieve results if they regularly hold the balance between the

---

²⁹ Géza Jeszenszky, *The New (Post-Communist) Europe and its Ethnic Problems* (Budapest: Kairosz Publishers, 2005); expanded edition, Jeszenszky, *Post-Communist Europe and Its National/Ethnic Problems* (Budapest: Kairosz, 2009).
³⁰ Letter of Géza Jeszenszky to Ferenc Mádl, March 14, 2003. Copy among my papers.

Chapter 12 – The Outstretched Hand and the Embracing Arm

Figure 34. Speaking in Transylvania at the cemetery of fallen Hungarian soldiers in the Úz valley in the Carpathians, in today's Romania, August 26, 1996

rival parties and are an indispensable element in successive governments. (This is generally the case with the Swedish People's Party in Finland and the Südtiroler Volkspartei in the Italian Tyrol.) This explains the RMDSZ's decision in 2000 to support the post-communist government from outside. (My old confrontative partner, Adrian Năstase, now prime minister, proudly told me during his visit to Washington, that the RMDSZ had achieved more under his government than when it was formally part of the previous government.)

In the letter to President Mádl, I expressed my view that in In Romania there was still a climate of authoritarianism, therefore a party that is part of the government holds a different position in the eyes of the local authorities than does a party in the opposition. This is why it is important for the RMDSZ to once again be part of the governing coalition. With Hungarian unity and high voter turnout, the Hungarian party could tip the balance! Most Hungarian politicians in Transylvania want to make the Székely Land a kind of internal motherland for the dispersed Hungarian population of Transylvania, so that they would prefer to move there rather than to Hungary. To achieve this, the two Székely counties (three, including Mureș/Maros County) would have to be joined within one development region. For the time being, the Romanian authorities do not want to hear about Székely Land as a territorial unit or a development region and, unfortunately, the idea is not supported by the Council of Europe or the European Union, even though the aim is not to create an "ethnic-based territorial autonomy." The Hungarians of Transylvania should push for territorial autonomy, not ethnic autonomy, but rather a German-style "*Land*" province in the Székely region, which would be able to shape its own economic policy (also to the benefit of the Romanians who live there), have its own internal administration (even its own police force), and have an educational system that is not controlled from Bucharest.[31]

The United States had been monitoring Hungarian-Romanian relations since the 1980s, and in the 1990s it had a consulate general in Cluj-Napoca/Kolozsvár, primarily to monitor the situation of the Hungarian minority.[32] I contributed to the adoption of a resolution by the US House of Representatives on May 23, 2005, introduced by Representatives Lantos and Tancredo, that urged the Romanian government to return church property confiscated by communist regimes.[33]

As a reaction to the flawed and unfortunate referendum on the preferential naturalization of Hungarians born outside Hungary, held on December 5, 2004, the 2010 amendment to the law on Hungarian citizenship introduced simplified naturalization, making it possible for persons not living in Hungary but proving their Hungarian origin to acquire Hungarian citizenship. Although this strengthened the Hungarian identity and cultural preservation of Hungarians living in neighboring countries, it failed to secure the rights necessary for their future and survival. Contrary to its intention, it actually made it easier for them to leave their homeland and take up employment in any country of the European Union and even settle there. It is interesting to note that this amendment did not provoke such a strong reaction either at home or abroad as did the Benefit Law passed ten years earlier, even though its effects and consequences are much more serious.

In December 2004, the Forum of the Hungarian Representatives of the Carpathian Basin (KMKF) was established as a consultative body to assist the work of the Hungarian National Assembly. It is comprised of representatives of the parliamentary parties of Hungary and of the Hungarian parties operating in neighboring countries, as well as Hungarian members of the European Parliament. The body, which meets at least once a year, deals primarily with issues of national strategy.[34]

---

[31] Letter of Géza Jeszenszky to Ferenc Mádl, March 14, 2003. Copy among my papers.

[32] Levente Salat, "A Rapprochement without Reconciliation: Romanian-Hungarian Relations in the Post-Communist Era," in *Hungary and Romania Beyond National Narratives: Comparison and Entanglements*, ed. Anders E. B. Blomqvist, Constantin Iordachi, and Balázs Trencsényi (Bern: Peter Lang, 2013), 655–90.

[33] H. Res. 191 on May 23, 2005, urging the "Government of Romania to recognize its responsibilities to provide equitable, prompt and fair restitution to all religious communities for property confiscated by the former Communist government."

[34] Bálint Ódor and Ádám Szesztay, eds., *Nemzetpolitikai konszenzus dokumentumokban: A KMKF nemzeti együttműködési stratégiája és szakpolitikai koncepciói, 2004–2009* [The strategy of national cooperation

"Requiem for a former province"

Rezső Peéry, a Hungarian writer born in 1910 in Pozsony (today's Bratislava, the capital of Slovakia), where many kings of Hungary were coronated, wrote a slender book first published in Munich in 1975. It presented the last 150 years of the ethnically diverse province that once was called Upper Hungary, *Hungaria Superiora, Horno Uhorsko, Felvidék* (Uplands), and where Hungarian, Slovak and German (Zipser) people used to live more or less in harmony for centuries.[35] It is about how national intolerance destroyed peaceful coexistence, reduced the Hungarian population of present-day Slovakia from 30 to a mere 10 (today 8) percent, and how it continues to poison relations between these two Central European nations that share a common destiny. The cancer of the relationship is the territorial question, for which the greed of Eduard Beneš (then the right hand of Professor Masaryk, the would-be head of state of Czechoslovakia) at the 1919 peace conference is to blame.[36]

Because of Prime Minister Mečiar's anti-democratic policies, impatient nationalism and pro-Russian foreign policy, Slovakia was left out of NATO enlargement in 1999. Mikuláš Dzurinda's government made up for this by bringing his country into the European Union alongside the Atlantic Alliance. Together with Hungarian Prime Minister Orbán, and in the presence of then-EU enlargement commissioner Günter Verheugen, on October 11, 2001, the two inaugurated the Danube bridge linking Esztergom to Štúrovo/Párkány, rebuilt with EU financial support. However, in 2006, the Slovak elections were won by the Smer party led by Robert Fico,[37] a self-styled social democrat who formed a coalition government with the notorious nationalist Jan Slota's party. This marked a return to a policy of discrimination against the Hungarian minority and a hostile tone towards the Hungarian government. In response to the reaction of the Slovak prime minister to

---

and political concepts of the Forum of the Hungarian MPs of the Carpathian Region] (Budapest: KMKF Titkárság, 2009).

[35] Rezső Peéry, *Requiem egy országrészért* [Requiem for a former province] (Munich: Aurora, 1976); republished with an insightful foreword by András Görömbei (Pozsony: Pannónia Könyvkiadó, 1993).

[36] I have dealt with this in a number of my writings. I will highlight three of them: "Trianon az európai tragédia" [Trianon, the European tragedy], *Magyar Szemle* 14, nos. 5–6 (2005): 7–24; "Trianon: Az önrendelkezési elv megcsúfolása" [Trianon, the mockery of the principle of self-determination], *Rubicon* 6 (2005): 4–5; "A Csallóköz elvesztése: Esettanulmány Trianon történetéhez" [The loss of Csallóköz: A case study in the history of Trianon], *Rubicon* 6 (2005): 6–7; "The British Role in Assigning Csallóköz (Zitny Ostrov, Grosse Schütt) to Czechoslovakia," in *British-Hungarian Relations Since 1848*, ed. László Péter and Martyn Rady (London: Hungarian Cultural Centre and School of Slavonic and East European Studies University College, 2004), 123–38.

[37] Robert Fico (1964–): Slovak politician, prime minister from 2006 to 2010, from 2012 to 2018, and since 2024.

the call of the Hungarian party for Slovak-Hungarian reconciliation,[38] I wrote the following in the December 2007 issue of *Magyar Szemle*:

> How can it be called "brazen impudence" when the Hungarian Coalition in Slovakia proposes a declaration of reconciliation to the legislatures of the two countries? Prime Minister Fico's comment added fuel to the fire by the resolution of the Slovak National Council (National Assembly) confirming the Beneš decrees, and as expected, it triggered protests from all Hungarian political factions. In order to make things worse the Slovak Education Minister wanted to ban the Hungarian (often original) version of place names from Hungarian school textbooks—clearly also to brainwash Hungarian consciousness from the minds of students. And just when this Slovak behavior reached the threshold of the EU and America's attention, a declaration was made by Prime Minister Fico in memory of the Csernova [Černová] massacre that took place a hundred years earlier, "Bearing in mind the mostly negative experiences of more than 1100 years of neighborly relations, and taking into account the recent actions of our southern neighbor, which are once again unilateral, unfounded and increasingly aggressive in their demands, we cannot remain indifferent." Therefore Fico called on the Hungarians to repent for their sins, express regret, and pay compensation. What should the many Hungarians and Slovaks who want to see friendship rather than a cold war between the two neighboring nations do now?[39]

The law restricting the use of the Hungarian language, which was adopted in Slovakia in 1995 over the protests of Hungarian MPs, was further tightened in 2009.[40] The news portal *Felvidék Ma* asked me, "The Slovak ambassador in [Budapest] said that the EU had not raised any objections to the language law, which came into force on September 1. Is this true?" I responded:

---

[38] "Fico szerint pimaszság bocsánatkérést követelni a szlovákoktól" [According to Fico it is impudent to demand an apology from the Slovaks], *Paraméter*, September 10, 2007, https://parameter.sk/14997/fico-szerint-pimaszsag-bocsanatkerest-kovetelni-a-szlovakoktol/.

[39] Géza Jeszenszky, "A szlovák-magyar viták háttere" [The background of the Slovak-Hungarian disputes], *Magyar Szemle* 16, nos. 11–12 (December 2007): 17–37; . Cf. Jeszenszky, "Falak helyett: A magyar-szlovák viták gyökere és az ellenszer" [The Root of the Hungarian-Slovak Disputes and the Antidote] *Magyar Nemzet*, November 22, 2008, 28; Reprinted in *Itt-Ott Kalendárium* (2009): 150–56.

[40] For a thorough, objective critique of the law, see Anna Porter, "Second-rate citizens," *Macleans.ca*, October 26, 2009, https://macleans.ca/news/world/second-rate-citizens/.

The Slovak language law does not violate any EU regulations, because there are no regulations on this issue. It does, however, violate the Framework Convention on Minorities adopted by the Council of Europe and signed by Slovakia, as well as the Language Charter, and, last but not least, the 1995 Slovak-Hungarian Treaty. Even more so the spirit of these agreements. It significantly restricts and curtails existing, hard-won language rights. There is no need for a language law, there is no language law in Hungary. No one is stipulating that only the Hungarian language should be used in certain situations or in general.[41]

Tensions between the two neighboring states were further heightened when Hungary's president, László Sólyom, was refused entry to Slovakia when he was on his way to Komarno/Komárom to inaugurate the statue of St Stephen on August 20, 2009. This was in violation of the Schengen agreement on the free movement of persons. My answer to a question from György Batta, a Hungarian author in Slovakia, was:

> This was a blatant case that a self-respecting government cannot remain silent about. I think that for too long in recent years the Hungarian government has followed the principle that if we give in, if we make gestures, if we swallow a lot, then Slovak nationalism will run away, will blow itself out, and relations will improve. As far as I can see, this passive or insufficiently assertive Hungarian foreign policy has not lived up to expectations, and has even emboldened Slovakia. Of course, the EU has also taken note of and swallowed many things that it does not swallow in other countries (such as Haider's policy in Austria) or in the case of injustices elsewhere. When Fico included a nationalist party of an extremist nature in his government, it was first criticized by European social democrats and Fico's party membership was suspended. A year later, however, they forgot about it and lifted the suspension. No wonder that Fico and his associates were even more emboldened after that.[42]

On July 22, 2009, the Slovak language law was condemned by the European Security Organization, the OSCE. On January 4, 2010, the High Commissioner on National Minorities, Knut Vollebaek[43] (former Foreign Minister of Norway and

---

[41] *Felvidék.ma*, September 3, 2009.
[42] *Felvidék.ma*, September 3, 2009.
[43] Knut Vollebaek (1946–): Norwegian politician, minister of foreign affairs (1997–2000), ambassador to the United States (2001–2007), OSCE high commissioner on minorities (2007–2013).

Figure 35. Celebrating March 15, 1848, in Bratislava/Pozsony, 2008

later Ambassador to Washington, with whom I have remained on friendly terms), called on the Slovak government in a very diplomatic way to "balance the strengthening of the Slovak state language with the protection of minority rights," especially in view of the extremely high fines for violating the law. In a face-to-face meeting on February 10, 2010, I told the high commissioner that our relations with Slovakia had been excellent under former Slovak prime minister Dzurinda, but they had deteriorated significantly under Fico and his coalition partner, the extreme nationalist Slota. "Why do we need a language law?" I asked. It does not apply to English or Czech, only to Hungarian, to Slovak citizens of Hungarian nationality. It only serves the purpose of forced assimilation, to banish the Hungarian language from the administration and official communication to the kitchen, or perhaps only to the bedroom. No other country has such laws, and in the United States even ATMs offer the choice to use English or Spanish, which in Florida is on a par with English. Slovakia does not punish obscene language, but it does punish Hungarian. The immediate aim is to eliminate Hungarian from public life in the south of Slovakia, which, until 1945, was inhabited almost solely by Hungarians, and replace it with the language of the Slovaks who were moved there.

During those difficult times, I deliberately visited Slovakia often. As one of the founders and board members of the Rákóczi Association, established in 1988 to support Hungarians there, I often visited Hungarian schools there to hand out enrollment grants. On March 1, 2010, in the ceremonial hall of the Selye János Gymnasium, as a guest of the Lélekharang Civic Association in Komárom,

Chapter 12 – The Outstretched Hand and the Embracing Arm

Figure 36. Speaking at the birthplace of the poet Kölcsey, Sződemeter, August 8, 2010

I presented a book I had written together with László Csaba and János Martonyi.[44] A year later, at the invitation of the Hungarian Cultural Institute in Bratislava, I spoke to politician and journalist Pál Csáky at a sold-out event with the framework of a two-hour forum. Among other things, we discussed why it would have been irresponsible and counterproductive for the Antall government to make territorial claims against Slovakia. The *Felvidék.ma* portal asked why the European fair nationality policy had not been implemented in Slovakia, and I replied that I believe that the (unacknowledged) aim of Slovak policy was and has remained to turn the Hungarians in Slovakia into an insignificant, small ethnic group, and thus to make the possibility of changing the borders completely unrealistic.[45] I have often spoken or written about the failure to rehabilitate János Esterházy, the martyr-politician.[46] I said at Kráľovský Chlmec/Királyhelmec on April 26, 2016, that "I am

---

[44] Csaba, Jeszenszky, and Martonyi, *Helyünk a világban*.
[45] *Felvidék.ma*, May 5, 2011.
[46] János Esterházy (1901–1957): Hungarian politician in Czechoslovakia, leader of the United Hungarian Party in the late 1930s. Following the First Vienna Award he became the leader of the Hungarians in the newly independents Slovakia, and voted against the deportation of its Jewish citizens. In 1945 he was arrested and deported to the Soviet Union, only to be returned to Czechoslovakia to be tried and sentenced to death. The verdict was commuted to life imprisonment, and he died in captivity. See Géza Jeszenszky, "Egy ítélet, mely a bírákat minősíti: Még egyszer Esterházy Jánosról" [A judgment that tells for the judges: Once more on János Esterházy], *Magyar Szemle* 16, nos. 5–6 (June 2007): 191–98.

convinced that the main reason for the bias and malice is that Esterházy, and with him the entire Hungarian community in Slovakia, continues to be the necessary scapegoat for Slovak nationalists."

In the 2010s and 2020s

I started writing this book in the early 2000s, while teaching at a university. It is both a memoir and an analysis. As a private person, I travelled extensively to Hungary's neighbors, paddled on the whitewater section of the Upper Tisza in Ukraine, and on the river Arieș/Aranyos in Transylvania, led ski tours in the Harghita Mountains, visited Vojvodina and Croatia several times. In 2011, I was appointed Hungary's ambassador to the Kingdom of Norway and to Iceland. My decision was influenced by the fact that in Washington I had become good friends with Norwegian ambassador Vollebaek, who, like me, had previously been his country's foreign minister and who became the OSCE High Commissioner on Minorities in 2007. Although his office was in The Hague, he returned to Norway frequently to visit his family, and I had the opportunity to meet him again in person. His tenure ended in 2013, after which our relationship deepened. His naïve good faith, born of his Christian Democratic outlook, saw the solution to the conflicts arising from the situation of national minorities in their integration. To this end, he believed that

Figure 37. At the peak of the Hargita Mountains in Transylvania, February 2020

it was desirable to replace mother-tongue schools at secondary level with a school teaching in the majority language. I got the impression that this was the view of his mixed international staff. However, he welcomed and supported my proposal for an international conference in Oslo on the "Protection of the Indigenous, Historical Minorities." I put together the theme and proposed the participants, but after my resignation as ambassador in the autumn of 2014, the topic was taken off the agenda. During my term in Oslo, the Hungarian embassy became the meeting place for the growing Hungarian colony in Norway, and also the scene of a moving ceremony for the handing over of passports granting citizenship to Hungarian residents coming from Transylvania.

Figure 38. Talk at Subotica/Szabadka in Serbia, 2006

In response to Roger Scruton's essay "Indispensable Nations," published in the August 2013 issue of *Magyar Szemle*, I wrote about the importance of the survival of national minorities and their secure future:

> It is high time to realize that in most multiethnic countries, and in Central and Eastern Europe particularly, ethnicity, religion and language are the source of primary loyalty, and they are the basis of belonging to a nation. The fashionable western ideal, an integrated multiethnic society where the majority national group does not aim at undermining the position and reducing the size of the national minorities, has no appeal here, at least not to the majority national groups. In the eastern half of Europe, the State has traditionally not been neutral in matters concerning language and culture, it rather served as a tool for the harassment of the national minorities, in the futile hope that the ethnically heterogeneous population can be "homogenized," assimilated, and thus the nominal nation states can become real nation states. These countries are not melting pots; the present national

minorities emerged not by people crossing borders but by borders crossing people. Attempts to turn this region into a melting pot can transform it into a powder keg, as older and most recent history amply testifies. [...] The EU is right to stand up for the rights of the Roma, but it would be far easier to eradicate discrimination and intolerance against national minorities than to lift millions of Roma out of poverty and illiteracy. Then we face the familiar problem of lack of means for enforcing the existing—admittedly rather mild—conventions and recommendations. If the EU politely passes the issue to the OSCE or the Council of Europe, the situation will be the same as we know from the failure of these two institutions to enforce their conventions and recommendations.[47]

Between 2002 and 2023 I published about fifty essays and articles on national minorities in book chapters and in many Hungarian journals and newspapers, including *Magyar Szemle, Hungarian Review, Heti Válasz, Magyar Nemzet, Bécsi Napló, Magyar Hang* and other publications. Even before the current war, I was particularly concerned with the deteriorating Ukrainian-Hungarian relationship, which is in sharp contrast to the spirit of the 1991 bilateral treaty and the practices of the 1990s. In 2008 a decree was issued that threatened the survival of Hungarian schools in Subcarpathia (Transcarpathian Ukraine). I protested in a letter sent to the then foreign minister, Volodymyr Ohryzko, whose guest I had been not long before:

> Last year, on December 27, I had the honor to celebrate the 90th anniversary of the creation of the independent diplomatic service of Ukraine together with you in Kyiv. I was pleased to see that the present leaders of Ukraine continue to appreciate the role Hungary played in 1991 in the international recognition of the independence of your State. [...] Decree No. 461, issued by the minister of education on May 26, 2008, is tantamount to replacing the language of instruction in the schools of the national minorities with Ukrainian. [...] The measure planned has caused deep concern among Ukrainian citizens of Hungarian nationality, and had very negative publicity in Hungary, too. It is very likely that similar objections will be heard from the Romanians, and also from the Russian Federation.[48]

---

[47] Géza Jeszenszky, "The Need for Satisfied National Minorities," *Hungarian Review* 4, no. 5 (August 2013): 32–35.
[48] Géza Jeszenszky, Open Letter to H.E. Volodymyr Ohryzko, the Foreign Minister of Ukraine, June 27, 2008. Among my papers.

The reply sought to reassure me that better teaching of the Ukrainian language would not be at the expense of education in Hungarian. Then the measure was dropped. In 2016, the conversion of Hungarian schools into mixed-language schools, i.e., Ukrainianization, and the Ukrainian-only university entrance exams were back on the agenda. At an international conference on Ukraine held in Budapest in November 2016, I warned with cautious optimism that "such a change would be a serious violation of the treaty and of the intimate relationship between the two countries."[49] When the Ukrainian parliament passed the education law on September 5, 2017, I criticized it in several forums.[50]

The echoes of the 100th anniversary of the Trianon Peace Treaty in 2020 resonated beyond our borders. In addition to numerous commemorative events, a large number of publications were produced, including some of considerable academic value. Expressing grief is understandable today, but anger is meaningless. Most of the research and analyses have focused on the circumstances of the drawing of the new borders and have added useful new details and insights to the existing picture. Few have looked into the deeper causes, those that preceded the world war, or whether it was possible to avoid or prevent the tragic outcome before the collapse of October–November 1918. It would also have been worthwhile to give more attention to the question of how the trauma of Trianon could be mitigated today, and what the way out is, what could be done to ensure that the primary victims of Trianon, the Hungarians on the other side of the new borders, could live and prosper, preserving their identity and number, enjoying the rights necessary for that. Most importantly, examining what the mother country could do to achieve that.

Research carried out at Kodolányi János University in Székesfehérvár between 2012 and 2015 sought to answer the question of whether Hungarians have come to terms with the major traumas they suffered in the past. According to the survey, the Trianon Peace Treaty is Hungary's greatest historical tragedy. Primarily it meant the break-up of the historic country, the loss of so many of the scenes of Hungary's thousand-year history. As the great Hungarian poet Petőfi echoed Thomas Moore: "Forget not the field where they perish'd,/ The truest, the last of the brave." It is primarily up to us Hungarians to ensure that the memories and tangible objects

---

[49] I summarized our deteriorating relations with Ukraine in the essay "Az 1991-es magyar-ukrán alapszerződés jelentősége" [The significance of the 1991 Hungarian-Ukrainian basic treaty], in *"Kijevi csirke": (Geo)politika a mai Ukrajnában* ["Chicken Kiev": Geopolitics in Today's Ukraine], ed. Csilla Fedinec (Budapest: MTA Társadalomtudományi Kutatóközpont–Kalligram, 2019), 45–62.

[50] Jeszenszky, "Ukraine's Blunder"; Jeszenszky, "Ukraine's Conflict with Two of Its Neighbours," *Hungarian Review* 9, no. 5 (September 2018): 42–49. Also in Hungarian in *Heti Válasz*, February 22, 2018, 27; and *Magyar Szemle* 27, nos. 11–12 (Nov.–Dec. 2018): 96–108.

of our past do not fall from our consciousness. It is a fundamental requirement of Hungary that the Hungarian national minorities, which have been annexed to our neighboring countries and have been reduced from 3.5 million to today's 2 million, should not disappear. Their many grievances are wounds torn open, and untreated they will never heal. Caring for the fate of the Hungarian communities that have become a national minority in their homeland is a constitutional responsibility and duty of Hungary, but it is also a moral and legal duty of its neighbors. Many Hungarians believe that it is also a moral obligation and political responsibility of the European Union.[51]

In my own reflections, I have shown the path from the early twentieth century to the treaty, how the erroneous steps and decisions of Hungarian politics played a major role in the tragedy, and that instead of looking for real and fake scapegoats, we should look at the lessons to be learned.[52] I would like to see the teaching of history in Hungary reflect what I said in response to a question in *Történelemtanítás*, a journal about the teaching of history, asking what future generations of Hungarians should know about Trianon.[53] I would certainly emphasize that the non-Hungarian minorities could have been placated through the implementation of Oszkár Jászi's program ("the people need good schools, good administration, and good justice—in their own language"). It should also be made clear that at the turn of 1918 into 1919, the exhausted, hungry, ragged Hungarian soldiers returning home from the front were unwilling to continue fighting, while their neighbors were fired up by the possibility of fulfilling their national dreams. French policy hoped to prevent Germany from regaining strength and waging a war of revenge by creating larger and stronger allies located behind its rival, which is why Czechoslovakia, Romania, and the new south Slavic state were given territories with significant Hungarian populations.

---

[51] József Nagy, a MEP in the European Parliament (European People's Party) on behalf of the Slovak-Hungarian Most-Híd Party from 2015–2019, presented a comprehensive report on "minimum standards for minorities in the EU." On November 13, 2018, the Parliament adopted the report in a resolution—481 voted in favor, 112 against, with 73 abstentions.

[52] On that subject I published two essays in the journal *Magyar Szemle* 29, nos. 5–6 (May–June 2020): 11–25; and 29, nos. 7–8 (July–August 2020): 34–48. Cf. Géza Jeszenszky, "Overcoming the Baneful Legacy of Trianon," *Hungarian Review* 11, no. 4 (July 2020): 105–16n. My major piece on the issue: "Elkerülhető volt-e a Magyar Királyság végzete?" [Was the fate of the Kingdom of Hungary avoidable?], in *Trianon 100: Emlékező Magyarország* [Trianon 100: Hungary Remembers], vol. 1, ed. János Gyurgyák (Budapest: Osiris Kiadó, 2020), 484–92.

[53] "Mit tanítsunk Trianonról?—nemcsak az iskolában" [What should we teach about Trianon?—not only in the schools], *Történelemtanítás Online* 11, no. 4 (2020). https://www.folyoirat.tortenelemtanitas.hu/2020/11/tortenes zek-trianonrol-11-03-02/.

In their international forums, primarily in the Council of Europe, Hungarian representatives have constantly kept the issue of national minorities on the agenda. Ferenc Kalmár (a member of Parliament from 2010–14, since then ministerial commissioner for the Development of Hungary's Neighborhood Policy, and co-chair of the joint committees set up to examine bilateral treaties with neighboring states) together with Katalin Szili (since 2015 the prime minister's commissioner and from 2023 onwards, the prime minister's chief advisor) have summarized the proposals and resolutions on minority protection adopted in international fora since 2000.[54] Szili has also detailed these in a book.[55] Kalmár pointed out that Hungary—unlike most of its neighbors—recognizes its own national minorities as state-building factors.[56]

On January 14, 2021, the European Commission rejected the seventy-four-page-long, well-drafted citizens' initiative on minority protection, known as the Minority SafePack (MSP). It was backed by well over a million signatures by EU citizens from eleven countries. Its legal basis, content and reception have been thoroughly elucidated by Balázs Tárnok.[57] It is clear that the EU apparatus is not aware of the serious and legitimate complaints of the national minorities of Central Europe. They are not aware of the difference between social integration and forced assimilation and do not realize how large the gap is between the way the issue is handled in Western and Northern Europe and the everyday practice in Central and Eastern Europe. In my opinion, this is not something worth lamenting, or perhaps reacting to angrily, but rather we must continue to explore every opportunity to improve the situation of the national minorities. Věra Jourová, until 2024 one of the eight Commission vice-presidents, was in charge of values and transparency in the EU government, and she explained in twenty-two pages how EU legislation and its various actions supported the aims of the initiative, the rights of "persons belonging to national minorities," and Europe's cultural diversity. The reply offers an opportunity to take the Commission at its word, to point out the inadequacy of the measures cited (measures that Jourova viewed as positive), and to point out which points of the MSP can be implemented—with some good will—without

---

[54] Ferenc Kalmár and Katalin Szili, *Proposed Basic Principles for the Protection of National Minorities in the EU*, 2nd ed. (Bethlen Gábor Alapkezelő Zrt. [n.d.]).

[55] Katalin Szili, *Ten out of Thirty: Aspirations for Autonomy, Neighbourhood Policy and the European Minority Protection, 2010–2020* (Budapest: Bethlen Gábor Fund, 2022).

[56] Balázs Borsi, "Kalmár Ferenc: 'Magyarország elismeri államalkotó tényezőként a nemzeti kisebbségeit, Románia nem'" [Ferenc Kalmár: Hungary recognizes its national minorities as state-forming factors, Romania does not], *Maszol.ro*, October 12, 2022, https://maszol.ro/belfold/Kalmar-Ferenc-Magyarorszag-elismeri-allamalkoto-tenyezokent-a-nemzeti-kisebbsegeit-Romania-nem.

[57] Balázs Tárnok, *Mire elég egymillió aláírás? Az európai polgári kezdeményezés mint a nemzeti kisebbségek jog- és érdekérvényesítési eszköze* [What is a million signatures enough for? The European Citizens' Initiative as a tool for the rights and interests of national minorities] (Budapest: Ludovika Egyetemi Kiadó, 2023).

specific legislation. The reply lists the amounts allocated to the Roma, migrants and gender minorities. The counter-argument is obvious: how many more people are affected by intolerance, discrimination and violations against national minorities compared to the number of people in the groups mentioned. Prejudice and discrimination against the Roma or sexual minorities can be combated primarily through education, while the situation of national minorities can be improved primarily through legal measures and laws.

It is encouraging that the European Parliament supported the MSP proposals on December 18, 2020, after a thorough debate. Supporting MEPs can continue to argue in favor of it in their own countries. Every day we see and experience how intolerance towards national, linguistic and religious minorities leads to tensions and even wars, not only in Asia and Africa, but also in Europe, a continent so proud of its civilization. Yugoslavia fell apart not only due to the desire of its constituent republics for independence; the Croatian-Serbian war was directly caused by the Serb minority in Croatia, which wanted to belong to Serbia despite separated from it by non-Serb territories. The consequences and the memory of the "ethnic cleansing" against Muslims in Bosnia and Albanians in Kosovo (before it was helped to secede from Serbia), still cause serious tensions, and sometimes lead to armed clashes. The perceived and real grievances of some ten million Ukrainian citizens, most of whom spoke Russian, provided Russia with a pretext—not a reason, but an excuse—to commit its aggression. At the root of the Azeri-Armenian conflict was Nagorno Karabakh, which, until very recently, was an Armenian island surrounded by Azerbaijan. By today, that two-thousand-year-old Christian territory has been conquered by Islam, chasing away the Armenians. By recognizing and enforcing the collective rights of national minorities, the EU could prevent the emergence of many tensions and armed conflicts, above all in Central and Eastern Europe. These facts can be used to persuade governments. The Hungarian government is entitled to propose measures to the EU for the protection of national minorities. However, to have them adopted, it would have to convince the opposing member states (and not just several of Hungary's neighbors!) to endorse them. For that, Hungary needs friends and allies, systematic and consistent diplomacy, so that at least some of the MSP proposals become binding EU norms.[58]

The situation today and the perspectives

Throughout this book, the experience is manifest that the outside world, and more specifically democratic countries, our allies, who stress the importance they attach to

---

[58] My detailed analysis of the MSP appeared in *Országút* 2, no. 20 (October 8, 2021): 9–11.

respect for human rights, are showing a decreasing rather than a growing sensitivity to the cause of national minorities. This is particularly striking in comparison to recent concerns, first for the Roma, and more recently for LGBTQ persons and groups, which have been referred to as a community. The eradication of all discrimination is desirable, but the support for the latter is seen by many as exaggerated, even unjustified, and perhaps a passing fad. Unlike LGBTQ individuals, the national minorities are real communities with tangible and legitimate grievances, affecting millions.

Among the reasons for the passivity toward and even refusal to acknowledge the problem of the national minorities I highlight the following factors. In English and Western speech in general, the term "nation" is synonymous with the state. The state is seen as a melting pot, and ethnic or linguistic minorities should identify with the state (country) in which they live. As Boutros Boutros-Ghali, the former UN secretary-general, explained in a meeting with me in September 1992, if all claims for autonomy were allowed to materialize, this would result in the break-up of existing states and would increase the number of states in the world to some five hundred, not to mention triggering the wars that would ensue. As I see it, the status quo is sacred—until someone or something overturns it. Then the new status quo will be sacred. As an example, as long as Kosovo was part of Serbia, the "international community" condemned the discrimination and murder of Albanians but did not support the idea of separation. When Slobodan Milošević's policy appeared to be genocidal, then came the international intervention, and the process ended in the recognition of Kosovo as an independent state. (Unlike Hungary, several countries, including Russia, Serbia and Slovakia, have not yet recognized it.) From then on, the Serbian minority has been expected to reconcile itself to its new status as a national minority, of course with all the rights that are due. Kosovo, however, is in no hurry to respect the right of its Serb minority to organize themselves as a community. (The situation is familiar for Hungarians: before 1914, the territorial integrity of the Austro-Hungarian Monarchy was not even questioned by its critics abroad. The war overturned this, creating a "new Europe," and from then on no one was to tamper with the new borders.)

The mentality of fear of the slightest conflict, coupled with a policy of appeasement in the face of aggression, reminiscent of the 1930s, still haunts us today. The more vociferous party is always feared and appeased, and the more sober (usually Hungarian) party is expected to be patient and to make concessions. Foreign observers are also characterized by a kind of sterile legalistic approach, which sees national minorities first and foremost as citizens with loyalty due to the state they live in. Finally, there is the "realpolitik" consideration: in the case of Hungarian minorities, Hungary stands alone against all its neighbors, therefore it is not advisable to support the one against the many. The only way to break out of this situation is for Hungary to have considerable weight and prestige, not to be accountable on any issue, and, most importantly, not to be suspected of questioning the borders, harboring territorial claims. However, with a strong economy and stable domestic conditions, it is not hopeless to argue the case for the Hungarian and other national minorities.

If we take stock of the past thirty-three years of Hungary's neighborhood policy and its support for the Hungarian minorities, the result is both encouraging and disheartening.[59] For seventy years, from 1919, when historic Hungary was divided into five parts, our neighborhood relations were characterized by armed conflict, revenge, mutual territorial claims, distrust of, and open discrimination against the Hungarian minorities. There was pressure for assimilation, forced displacement was called population exchange, and, under the communist dictatorship, the minorities were under dual repression—both as citizens of the country (along with all their compatriots) and as national minorities. With the change of regime, the bad memories were not forgotten, but the Hungarian minorities could breathe a sigh of relief and start to feel at home in the land where they had been born. This relief was due to the common sense of the governments, the foreign powers' expectations for respect for all the political freedoms, the sensible politics of the Hungarian minority parties, and the financial and political support of the motherland. At the same time, demographic trends (declining fertility, improving living standards, free movement and emigration across borders, and natural assimilation) have reduced the number of Hungarians living in the Carpathian Basin from 13,000,810 to approximately 11,425,000 in thirty years.[60] As a result of artificial resettlement and industrialization, the proportion of Hungarians in cities that once had a large Hungarian majority (Kolozsvár/Cluj-Napoca, Nagyvárad/Oradea, Szatmárnémeti/Satu Mare, Arad, Rozsnyó/Roznava, Kassa/Košice) or a relative Hungarian majority (such as Pozsony/Bratislava or Újvidék/Novi Sad) has been radically reduced to a maximum of one third. Their share in the total population is also slowly but steadily declining. Since 2016, the year of the first edition of this book, emigration of the

---

[59] Myra Waterbury, "National Minorities in an Era of Externalization: Kin-State Citizenship, European Integration, and Ethnic Hungarian Minority Politics," *Problems of Post-Communism* 64, no. 5 (2017): 228–41.

[60] Anita Élő, "Már 11,5 millió magyar sincs a Kárpát-medencében—lesújtó friss adatok" [There are no longer 11.5 million Hungarians in the Carpathian Basin—devastating recent data], *Válasz Online*, March 6, 2023, https://www.valaszonline.hu/2023/03/06/magyarorszag-karpat-medence-magyarsag-demografia-nepszamlalas-elemzes/. This is somewhat compensated for by the fact that the number of Hungarians who have moved to the West is likely be in the hundreds of thousands, but the disappearance of their descendants and the loss of their Hungarian identity is inevitable—unless changing circumstances cause a significant number of them to return home.

Hungarian minorities from their homeland has continued, albeit at a slowing pace, and as a result of EU membership (2004) and preferential naturalization providing Hungarian citizenship (2010), they are now increasingly moving from Hungary to Western Europe, where incomes are higher. Among the Hungarians living in the diaspora (less than 15 percent of the population in a given region), the process of assimilation into the majority nation seems unstoppable, mainly through mixed marriages and the children born of those marriages. This would only change somewhat if the diaspora Hungarians moved to cities with (still) significant Hungarian populations or to Hungary.

My distinguished colleague, Pál Pritz, has stated resignedly, "The events of the past thirty years in world politics and within the EU have made the national component virulent again, and the reality of the neighboring countries' allowing the Hungarian minority in a co-nation position has been postponed to the unforeseeable future." This timeframe can/should be shortened, however, by giving up the demand for territorial autonomy and by a wise neighborhood policy. "In the meantime," Pritz continued, "the mills of industrial and urban development are grinding the Hungarian nationality smaller and smaller."[61]

Has autonomy, co-nation status—the need for which this book has so fervently argued—been postponed to an indefinite future? As a legally realized institution, perhaps so. But in everyday practice, it has been achieved to some extent. Towns and villages have self-governments—with varying authority and power—in which Hungarians are roughly proportionally represented. In those settlements where the proportion of Hungarians exceeds 20 percent (in some countries 15 percent), the Hungarian place name is displayed (sometimes being regularly painted over), there are Hungarian street names, company signs, and in some large grocery stores the Hungarian language is (also) used, so there is bilingualism in practice, even if not in enough places. With conscious, organized local campaigns, this situation can be improved—but if the Hungarians' mood is passive, it can be made worse.

The situation and rights of Hungarian minorities abroad are regulated by the laws of their own countries. These cannot be directly influenced by the mother country, the Hungarian state, but better inter-state relations could provide a more favorable climate for the Hungarian communities to have their demands fulfilled through political means and parliamentary channels. The most obvious means of achieving this is a high turnout in both national and local elections. In this respect, the Hungarian minorities beyond the borders fall far short of their potential, and

---

[61] Pál Pritz, "Trianon—a közel messziről" [Trianon—from near and far], *Történelemtanítás Online* 11, nos. 3–4 (2020). https://www.folyoirat.tortenelemtanitas.hu/2020/11/torteneszek-trianonrol-11-03-02/.

in general they also lag behind the participation of the members of the majority nation. If the opposite were the practice, the Hungarian minorities would have greater influence in the legislature, and in a favorable case the Hungarian minority could even tip the scale in the formation of governments. Of course, this would require a strong Hungarian party in each country, supported by the whole Hungarian community. Pluralism within these parties could be ensured by creating platforms, without forgetting the basic common goal.

Hungary and the Hungarian government's relations with its neighbors are radically different today from the 1990s. The closest relations are with Serbia, with which it had the worst relations between 1991 and '93, through no fault of our own. However, the Hungarian community in Vojvodina, which is numerically in sharp decline, does not benefit much from this. The good relations with Austria are overshadowed by the fact that the Orbán government is backing the Freedom Party, which has a bad image in Western Europe. Relations with Croatia and Slovenia are good, but they were better, and could be better. The Hungarian minorities in those two countries have become little more than an ethnographic curiosity. The Hungarian population of Romania, partly thanks to the money flowing to them from Hungary, feels a great deal of gratitude towards Hungarian prime minister Orbán personally, and is more concerned with politics going on in Budapest than in Bucharest. The original aim of the summer university in Transylvania (now in Tusnádfürdő/Baile Tusnad) was to build trust and understanding between Hungarians and Romanians by inviting Romanian politicians. Once even President Traian Băsescu attended it. Today, relations with Bucharest are cool, and the Hungarian government does not seem eager to improve this, even though Romania is playing an increasingly important role in the alliance system (EU and NATO) of which both are members. At the moment, the party of the Hungarians (RMDSZ) is a member of the governing coalition and has good local government positions in the Hungarian-inhabited regions, but it has to fight hard to maintain the representation of Transylvanian Hungarians in the Bucharest Parliament. The Hungarian electorate does not seem to care much about this. In the case of Slovakia, achieving Hungarian representation in Parliament seems hopeless at the moment, and Budapest politics is partly to blame for this. In recent years, anti-Hungarian nationalism in Slovak society and politics has declined (though it did not disappear and there are even signs of it increasing), thanks in large part to the previous head of state, Zuzana Čaputová, and the previous governments. I consider it a mistake to bank on Robert Fico, the present prime minister, who was at the forefront of anti-Hungarian sentiment around 2010, and who had the Parliament vote a separate law to stave off the results of the Hungarian naturalization law of 2010, which allows dual citizenship. Bilateral relations with Ukraine have deteriorated since 2010, mainly due to growing Ukrainian nationalism and the adoption of the school law, which threatened Hungarian-language education, but was withdrawn in December 2023. The relationship has been further aggravated by the Hungarian government's increasingly hostile policy towards Ukraine in its defensive war against Russia. Ukrainian membership in the EU, no matter how far away, would be a great benefit for the Hungarian minority in Subcarpathia, and, of course, for bilateral relations in general.

On the face of it, today's Hungarian foreign policy priority is not given to improving relations with our neighbors and Euro-Atlantic allies. The close cooperation of the Visegrád countries has been a victim of the war in Ukraine. Hungary's isolation is exacerbated by its cordial relations with Russia and China. Right now, the question cannot be answered whether or not the Orbán government's apparently warm ties to President Donald Trump and his administration can counterbalance the ever-louder criticism received from the rest of the EU on account of the alleged large-scale corruption, violation of the state of law, curtailment of the independence of the judiciary, and control of the public media by the government. Emphasis on sovereignty and patriotism and intimate party ties with and open support for the right radical movements in Europe do not help the cause of the Hungarian national minorities in Hungary's neighbors.

For years, there was a strong view in the European Union that the future does not lie in centralized and bureaucratic governance that disdains national specificities, but in local democracy at all levels. Subsidiarity is the principle that all decisions should be taken at the lowest possible level, as close as possible to the citizen, and it has become widespread in the West. Its concomitant is that taxes should be used for the benefit of the citizen, based on their decisions, so that villages, towns and provinces can manage their own affairs to their public's satisfaction through their elected representatives and authorities. That is the model to emulate throughout Central Europe!

Hungary cannot change by political means the demographic trends that are unfavorable to the Hungarian minorities, but the emigration of those minorities can be slowed down and even stopped to a great extent by strengthening local democracy (self-government), extending language rights (official bilingualism in areas with a significant Hungarian population), improving local economic opportunities and reducing anti-Hungarian sentiment. It would help a lot if Hungary were in a better position in terms of economic power and international prestige. If that were the case, the emigration destination of the Hungarian minorities would be, to a decisive extent, the mother country. Politically, economically and militarily, the European Union and NATO have brought the Hungarians, who were

Figure 39. Decorated with the Commander's Cross of the Order of Merit by President Duda of Poland, Budapest, March 20, 2016

divided by the Trianon Treaty, into one camp, into both one federal system and the Schengen system, which has removed borders; all that makes it possible to reconnect the personal, economic, trade and transport links that were severed by history.

A few practical steps could also greatly improve both the situation and well-being of the Hungarian minorities and their attachment to Hungarian culture. It is a clear Hungarian interest to give priority support to the development of border areas, which often have a nationally mixed population. The importance of investment in job creation is obvious. A prerequisite for this is also the significant improvement of infrastructure (roads, railways), which has deteriorated as a result of the closed borders set up by the Trianon peace and negligence during the communist era. There have been numerous concepts and impact studies for the restoration of bridges destroyed during the wars and of closed railways and roads, for which substantial EU funding is available, but only a fraction of the plans has been implemented so far. The closure of trans-border railways towards Slovakia is contrary to Hungarian national interest. The restoration of the Drégelypalánk–Sahy/Ipolyság line would improve the economic and social orientation of the whole of Central Slovakia towards Hungary. It is essential to increase and promote, rather than reduce, rail and bus services across the borders, adapting timetables to local needs. Non-Hungarians moving to Hungary because of lower real estate prices demand better transport links. Bilingualism in these regions could be established and strengthened by the mutual teaching of the languages. One day bilingualism should become legal and official. Hungarian newspapers and books should be distributed to shops and department stores on the other side of the Hungarian border and in the Székely region (Szeklerland). Hungarian identity, commitment to Hungarian causes can be preserved within the Carpathian Basin, but it can also be maintained outside it, among people living in other European countries and in America: the Internet, low telephone rates, inexpensive trains and flights all facilitate and simplify personal contacts.

In conclusion, if the basis and possibility of border change is not available, is there any other way to ensure and guarantee the rights and future of the Hungarian minorities? Only European integration offers a chance. The European Union and its Schengen Agreement practically abolish borders. If all Hungary's neighbors are part of this, the Carpathian Basin and its surroundings will form a single economic space, with the unhindered movement of people and goods, and sooner or later, with a common currency. The EU cannot order everyone to treat Hungarian minorities fairly, but it is moving in the direction of prescribing such policies. Border areas, big cities, economic zones separated by the Trianon border are integrated, transport links can be revived. The guardian of constitutionality, the Council of Europe, has adopted conventions and resolutions that should greatly promote the rights of the Hungarian-speaking minority—if the signatory states, including all Hungary's neighbors, would respect them. If Hungary can find friends who will stand by it, it could reach the point where all the human rights and minority rights documents were actually respected. It is desirable that this should also be a condition of EU financial support. Only the help of foreign powers offers a chance to heal the wound caused by Trianon. The scar will remain, but if Hungarians living across the border can use their language and national symbols and have a say in the decisions that govern their lives without restrictions, then the future of the Hungarian word and Hungarian culture in the former historic country will be assured. It is Hungary's essential goal that the European Union becomes an active supporter of the rights of historical national minorities and will contribute to the Hungarian nation's ability to preserve its sense of unity without changing its borders. This is what all the Hungarian communities and all Hungarian political forces must work for in the future. This is the only way to heal the Trianon trauma.

Bibliography

Official documents and other sources

Antall, József. *Modell és valóság* [The model and the reality]. Edited by Kálmán Soós. Budapest: Athenaeum Nyomda, 1994.
Jeszenszky, Géza, ed. *József Antall, Prime Minister of Hungary: Selected Speeches and Interviews (1989–1993)*. Budapest: József Antall Foundation, 2008.
Külügyminisztériumi tájékoztató, 1990 [Bulletin of the Ministry of Foreign Affairs, 1990]. Budapest: Magyar Köztársaság Külügyminisztériuma, 1990.
Külügyminisztériumi tájékoztató, 1991 [Bulletin of the Ministry of Foreign Affairs, 1991]. 2 volumes. Budapest: Magyar Köztársaság Külügyminisztériuma, 1991.
Külügyminisztériumi tájékoztató, 1992 [Bulletin of the Ministry of Foreign Affairs, 1992]. 2 volumes. Budapest: Magyar Köztársaság Külügyminisztériuma, 1992.
Magyar Külpolitikai Évkönyv, 1990 [Hungarian Foreign Policy Yearbook, 1990]. Budapest: Magyar Köztársaság Külügyminisztériuma, 1990.
Magyar Külpolitikai Évkönyv, 1991 [Hungarian Foreign Policy Yearbook, 1991]. Budapest: Magyar Köztársaság Külügyminisztériuma, 1991.
Magyar Külpolitikai Évkönyv, 1992 [Hungarian Foreign Policy Yearbook, 1992]. Budapest: Magyar Köztársaság Külügyminisztériuma, 1992.
Magyar Külpolitikai Évkönyv, 1993 [Hungarian Foreign Policy Yearbook, 1993]. Budapest: Magyar Köztársaság Külügyminisztériuma, 1993.
Magyar Külpolitikai Évkönyv, 1994 [Hungarian Foreign Policy Yearbook, 1994]. Budapest: Magyar Köztársaság Külügyminisztériuma, 1994.
Magyar Külpolitikai Évkönyv, 1995 [Hungarian Foreign Policy Yearbook, 1995]. Budapest: Magyar Köztársaság Külügyminisztériuma, 1995.
Pálmány, Béla, ed. *Antall József országgyűlési beszédei* [József Antall's speeches in Parliament]. Budapest: Athenaeum Nyomda, 1994.
Sáringer, János, ed. *Iratok az Antall-kormány külpolitikájához és diplomáciájához*. Volume 1, *(1990. május–december 1990)* [Papers relating to the foreign policy and diplomacy of the Antall government: May to December 1990]. Budapest: VERITAS Történetkutató Intézet és Levéltár - Magyar Napló, 2015.

———, ed. *Iratok az Antall-kormány külpolitikájához és diplomáciájához*. Volume 2, *(1991. január–1991. december)* [Papers relating to the foreign policy and diplomacy of the Antall government: January to December 1991]. Budapest: VERITAS Történetkutató Intézet és Levéltár - Magyar Napló, 2018.

———, ed. *Iratok az Antall-kormány külpolitikájához és diplomáciájához*. Volume 3/1–2, *(1992. január–1992. december)* [Papers relating to the foreign policy and diplomacy of the Antall government: January to December 1992]. Budapest: VERITAS Történetkutató Intézet és Levéltár - Magyar Napló, 2021.

———, ed. *Iratok az Antall-kormány külpolitikájához és diplomáciájához*. Volume 4, *(1993. január–1993. december)* [Papers relating to the foreign policy and diplomacy of the Antall government: January to December 1993]. Budapest: VERITAS Történetkutató Intézet és Levéltár - Magyar Napló, 2021.

Books and articles

A politikus Antall József—az európai úton: Tanulmányok, esszék, emlékezések a kortársaktól [József Antall, the politician: Studies, essays and recollections by the contemporaries]. Edited by Géza Jeszenszky, Károly Kapronczay, and Szilárd Biernaczky. Budapest: Mundus Magyar Egyetemi Kiadó, 2006.

Ablonczy, Balázs. *Trianon-legendák* [Legends about Trianon]. Budapest: Jaffa Kiadó, 2010 (2nd edition 2015).

Arday, Lajos. *Nemzetállamok és kisebbségek: Történelem és identitás Közép-Európában* [Nation-states and minorities: History and identity in Central Europe]. Budapest: L'Harmattan, 2016.

Bába, Iván. *Irányváltás a magyar külpolitikában, 1990–1994* [Change of direction in Hungarian foreign policy]. Budapest: Windsor Klub Füzetek 2, 1994.

Banac, Ivo. *The National Question in Yugoslavia: Origins, History, Politics*. Ithaca, NY: Cornell University Press, 1984.

Bárdi, Nándor. "Magyarország és a kisebbségi magyar közösségek 1989 után" [Hungary and the Hungarian minority communities after 1989]. *METSZETEK—Társadalomtudományi folyóirat* 2, nos. 2–3 (2013): 40–79. https://ojs.lib.unideb.hu/metszetek/article/view/12347

———. *Tény és való: A budapesti kormányzatok magyarságpolitikája és a határon túli magyarok társadalomtörténete; Problémakatalógus* [Fact and reality: The "nation policy" of the Budapest governments and the social history of the Hungarians beyond the border]. Pozsony: Kalligram, 2004.

———. *Útkeresés és integráció* [Search for a path and integration]. Budapest: Teleki László Alapítvány, 2000.

Bárdi, Nándor, and György Éger, eds. *Magyarok Romániában 1990–2015: Tanulmányok az erdélyi magyarságról* [Hungarians in Romania, 1990–2015: Studies on the Hungarians of Transylvania]. Budapest: Károli Gáspár Református Egyetem–L'Harmattan Kiadó, 2017.

Bárdi, Nándor, and Tibor Misovicz. "A kisebbségi magyar közösségek támogatásának politikája" [The policy of support for the Hungarian minority communities]. In *Határon túli magyarság a 21. században: Konferencia-sorozat a Sándor-palotában* [Hungarians beyond the border: a series of conferences in the Sándor Palace], edited by Botond Bitskey, 119-32. Budapest, Köztársasági Elnöki Hivatal, 2010.

Bárdi, Nándor, and Zoltán Kántor. "Az RMDSZ a romániai kormányban, 1996–2000" [The RMDSZ in the government of Romania, 1996–2000]. *Régió* 11, no. 4 (2000): 150–86.

Bárdi, Nándor, Csilla Fedinec, and László Szarka, eds. *Minority Hungarian Communities in the Twentieth Century*. Translated by Brian McLean. Boulder, CO; Highland Lakes, NJ: Social Science Monographs; Atlantic Research and Publications; Distributed by Columbia University Press, 2011.

Benedek, Márton. "Conditionality and Kinship: Hungarian Neighbourhood Policy towards Romania and Slovakia, 1990–2004." D. Phil. Thesis, Oxford University, 2009.

Bessenyey Williams, Margit. "European Integration and Minority Rights: The Case of Hungary and Its Neighbors." In *Norms and Nannies: The Impact of International Organizations on the Central and East European States*, edited by Ronald H. Linden, 227–59. Oxford: Rowman & Littlefield Publishers, 2002.

———. *Foreign Policy and Transitions to Democracy: the Case of Hungary*. Bloomington, IN: Indiana University, 1997.

Bibó, István. *Democracy, Revolution, Self-Determination: Selected Writings*. Edited by Károly Nagy. Boulder, CO: Atlantic Research and Publications, 1991.

———. "The Miseries of East European Small States." In *The Art of Peacemaking*, edited by Iván Zoltán Dénes, 130–80. New Haven, CT: Yale University Press, 2015.

Borsody, Stephen, ed. *The Hungarians: A Divided Nation*. New Haven, CT: Yale University Center on International and Area Studies, 1988.

Bottoni, Stefano. *Sztálin a székelyeknél: A Magyar Autonóm Tartomány története, 1952–1960* [Stalin at the Székelys: The history of the autonomous Hungarian province]. Csíkszereda: Pro-Print, 2008.

Braun, Robert. *The Dismemberment of Hungary and the Nationalities*. Budapest: Hornyánszky, s.d. [1919].

Brubaker, Rogers. *Nationalism Reframed: Nationhood and the national question in the New Europe*. Cambridge: Cambridge University Press, 1996.

Cadzow, John F., Andrew Ludanyi, and Louis J. Elteto, eds. *Transylvania: The Roots of Ethnic Conflict*. Kent, OH: Kent State University Press, 1983.

Cartledge, Bryan. *The Will to Survive: A History of Hungary*. London: Timewell Press, 2006 (2nd ed. London: Hurst & Company, 2011).

———. *Trianon egy angol szemével* [The Treaty of Trianon as seen by an Englishman]. Budapest: Officina Kiadó, 2009.

Case, Holly. *The Transylvanian Question and the European Idea during World War II*. Stanford: Stanford University Press, 2009.

Chmel, Rudolf. *Jelen és történelem—Az etnokráciától a demokráciáig és vissza* [The present and history—from ethnocracy to democracy and back]. Budapest: Kalligram, 2014.

———. *Nagykövet voltam Magyarországon* [Ambassador in Hungary]. Pozsony: Kalligram, 1997.

Csaba, László, Géza Jeszenszky, and János Martonyi. *Helyünk a világban—A magyar külpolitika útja a 21. században* [Our place in the world: The path for Hungarian foreign policy in the twenty-first century]. Budapest: Éghajlat Kiadó, 2009.

Csergő, Zsuzsa. "Beyond Ethnic Division: Majority-Minority Debate about the Post-communist State in Romania and Slovakia." *East European Politics and Societies* 16, no. 1 (2002): 1–29.

Csergő, Zsuzsa and James Goldgeier. "Nationalist Strategies and European Integration." In *The Hungarian Status Law: Nation Building and/or Minority Protection*, edited by Zoltán Kántor, Balázs Majtényi, Osamu Ieda, Balázs Vizi, and Iván Halász, 270–302. Sapporo: Slavic Research Center, Hokkaido University, 2004.

Csergő, Zsuzsa, Ognen Vangelov, and Balázs Vizi. "Minority Inclusion in Central and Eastern Europe: Changes and Continuities in the European Framework." *Intersections: East European Journal of Society and Politics* 3, no. 4 (2017): 5–16.

Cviic, Christopher. *An Awful Warning: The War in ex-Yugoslavia*. CPS Policy Studies, No. 139. London: Centre for Policy Studies, 1994.

———. *Remaking the Balkans*. London: The Royal Institute of International Affairs, 1991.

Deak, Francis. *Hungary at the Paris Peace Conference: The Diplomatic History of the Treaty of Trianon*. New York: Columbia University Press, 1942.

Debreczeni, József. *A miniszterelnök: Antall József és a rendszerváltozás* [József Antall and the regime change]. Budapest: Osiris, 1998.

Deets, Stephen. "Reconsidering East European Minority Policy: Liberal Theory and European Norms." *East European Politics and Societies* 16, no. 1 (2002): 30–53.
Dunay, Pál. "Az átmenet magyar külpolitikája" [The foreign policy of the transition in Hungary]. *Mozgó Világ* 30, no. 2 (2004): 51–65.
Dunay, Pál, and Wolfgang Zellner. *Ungarns Außenpolitik 1990–1997: Zwischen Westintegration, Nachbarschafts- und Minderheitenpolitik*. Baden-Baden: Nomos Verlagsgesellschaft, 1998.
Duray, Miklós. *Kutyaszorító* [Dog collar]. New York: Püski, 1983.
———. *Kutyaszorító II* [Dog collar II]. New York: Püski, 1989.
Edwards, Lee, ed. *The Collapse of Communism*. Stanford: Hoover Institution Press, 1999.
Fedinec, Csilla, ed. *Kárpáti Ukrajna: Vereckétől Husztig; Egy konfliktustörténet nemzeti olvasatai* [Carpathian Ukraine: national interpretations of a historical conflict]. Pozsony [Bratislava]: Kalligram Kiadó, 2014.
———, ed. *"Kijevi csirke": (Geo)politika a mai Ukrajnában* ["Chicken Kiev": Geopolitics in today's Ukraine]. Budapest: MTA Társadalomtudományi Kutatóközpont és Kalligram, 2019.
———, "Ukrajna helye Európában és a magyar-ukrán kapcsolatok két évtizede" [The place of Ukraine and the two decades of Hungarian-Ukrainian relations]. *Külügyi Szemle* 11, no. 4 (2012): 99–123.
Fedinec, Csilla, and Vehes Mikola, eds. *Kárpátalja 1919–2009: Történelem, politika, kultúra* [Subcarpathia: history, politics, culture]. Budapest: Argumentum, Institute for Ethnic-National Minority Research, MTA, 2010.
Fedinec, Csilla, and Norbert Tóth. *Romantikus jog—fapados gyakorlat: A magyar-ukrán szerződéses viszony* [Romance in law—prosaic practice: Hungarian-Ukrainian treaty relations]. Budapest: TK Kisebbségkutató Intézet–L'Harmattan Kiadó, 2022.
Földes, György. *Magyarország, Románia és a nemzeti kérdés 1956–1989* [Hungary, Romania and the national question]. Budapest: Napvilág Kiadó, 2007.
Fowler, Brigid. "Fuzzing Citizenship, Nationalising Political Space: A Framework for Interpreting the Hungarian 'Status Law' as a New Form of Kin-State Policy in Central and Eastern Europe." In *The Hungarian Status Law: Nation Building and/or Minority Protection*, edited by Zoltán Kántor, Balázs Majtényi, Osamu Ieda, Balázs Vizi, and Iván Halász, 177–238. Sapporo: Slavic Research Center, Hokkaido University, 2004.

Frank, Tibor, ed. *Discussing Hitler: Advisers of U.S. Diplomacy in Central Europe, 1934–1941*. Introduction by Tibor Frank. Budapest and New York: Central European University Press, 2003.

Fülöp, Mihály. *The Unfinished Peace: The Council of Foreign Ministers and the Hungarian Peace Treaty of 1947*. Boulder, CO: Social Science Monographs; Wayne, NJ: Center for Hungarian Studies and Publications, 2011. Second, revised and enlarged edition, Budapest: Ludovica University Press, 2025.

Für, Lajos. *A Varsói Szerződés végnapjai—magyar szemmel* [The final days of the Warsaw Pact—from a Hungarian perspective]. Budapest: Kairosz Könyvkiadó, 2003.

Gál, Kinga. "A kisebbségek nemzetközi védelme: az 1990-es évek jogi és politikai kerete" [The international protection of the minorities: its legal and political framework]. *Pro Minoritate* 1 (2001): 131–49.

Garton Ash, Timothy. *The Magic Lantern: The Revolution of 1989 Witnessed in Warsaw, Budapest, Berlin, and Prague*. London: Random House, 1990.

Gecse, Géza. *Állam és nemzet a rendszerváltás után: A Magyar Rádióban elhangzott riportok és a Tolcsvay klubban tartott Határok nélkül vitaestek szerkesztett változata* [State and nation after the regime change: The edited version of the reports on Hungarian Radio in the debates 'Without borders' in the Tolcsvay Club]. Budapest: Kairosz Könyvkiadó, 2002.

Gerencsér, Balázs, and Albin Juhász. "A kisebbségvédelem megvalósulása a nemzetközi szervezetekben (ENSZ, ET, EBESZ, KEK)" [The implementation of minority protection in the international organizations (UN, COE, OSCE, CEI)]. *Magyar Kisebbség* 7, no. 1 (2001): 287–312.

Gilberg, Trond. *Nationalism and Communism in Romania: The Rise and Fall of Ceausescu's Personal Dictatorship*. Boulder, CO: Westview Press, 1990.

Gow, James. *Triumph of the Lack of Will: International Diplomacy and the Yugoslav War*. London: C. Hurst & Co., 1997.

Győri Szabó, Róbert. "A parlamenti pártok és alapszerződések (1994-1997)" [The parliamentary parties and the basic treaties]. *Magyar Kisebbség* 6, no. 4 (2000): 168-87.

———. *Kisebbség, autonómia, regionalizmus* [Minority, autonomy, regionalism]. Budapest: Osiris Kiadó, 2006.

———. *Kisebbség-politikai rendszerváltás Magyarországon: a Nemzeti és Etnikai Kisebbségi Kollégium és Titkárság történetének tükrében (1989–1990)* [Regime change in Hungary in minority policy: The history of the College and Secretariat on Ethnic Minorities]. Budapest: Osiris, 1998.

Gyurácz, Ferenc. *Egy "populista" följegyzései: Politikai esszék, tanulmányok, cikkek, 1981–1993* [Notes by a "populist": Political essays, studies, articles]. Szombathely: Életünk, 1993.

Hamberger, Judit. *Csehszlovákia szétválása: Egy föderációs kísérlet kudarca* [The separation of Czechoslovakia: The failure of an attempt for a federation]. Budapest: Teleki László Alapítvány, 1997.

–––. "Közép-Európa politikai dimenziójának megvalósítási kísérlete: a visegrádi együttműködés" [An attempt at realizing the political dimension of Central Europe]. *Külügyi Szemle* 9, no. 2 (2010): 35–51.

Hévizi, Józsa. *Autonómia-típusok Magyarországon és Európában* [Types of autonomy in Hungary and in Europe]. Budapest: Püski, 2001.

Hieronymi, Otto. *Prime Minister József Antall and the Regime Change in Hungary, 1989–1993*. Budapest: Magyar Napló Kiadó, 2024.

Hinsley, F. H. *Power and the Pursuit of Peace: Theory and Practice in the Relations between States*. Cambridge: Cambridge University Press, 1962.

Horn, Gyula. *Cölöpök* [Piles]. Budapest: Zenit Könyvek, 1991.

Horváth, István. *Az elszalasztott lehetőség: A magyar-német kapcsolatok 1980–1991* [The missed opportunity: Hungarian-German relations, 1980–1991]. Budapest: Corvina, 2009.

Hupchik, Dennis P., and William R. Weisberger, eds. *Hungary's Historical Legacies*. Boulder, CO: East European Monographs, 2000.

Hutchings, Robert L. *American Diplomacy and the End of the Cold War*. Washington D.C.: Woodrow Wilson Center Press, 1997.

Illyés, Elemér. *National Minorities in Romania: Change in Transylvania*. Boulder, CO: East European Monographs, 1983.

Janics, Kálmán. *Czechoslovak Policy and the Hungarian Minority, 1945–1948*. New York: Social Science Monographs, 1982.

Jászi, Oscar. *The Dissolution of the Habsburg Monarchy*. Chicago: University of Chicago Press, 1929.

Jeszenszky, Géza. "A dunai államszövetség eszméje Nagy-Britanniában és az Egyesült Államokban az I. világháború alatt" [The idea of a Danubian Confederation in Great Britain and the United States]. *Századok* 122, no. 4 (1988): 648–63.

–––. "A magyar külpolitika fő irányai a század utolsó évtizedében" [Key fields in Hungarian foreign policy in the last decade of the century]. In *Magyarország helye a XX. századi Európában* [The place of Hungary in twentieth century Europe], ed. Pritz Pál et al., 169–84. Budapest: Magyar Történelmi Társulat, 2002.

―――. "A 'visegrádi gondolat' és az euro-atlanti integráció" [The "Visegrád idea" and Euro-Atlantic integration]. *Magyar Szemle* 7, nos. 7–8 (1998): 124–34.

―――. "Antall, a külpolitikus." In *Antall József: Modell és valóság*. Vol. 3, 1106–58. Budapest: Antall József Tudásközpont, 2015.

―――. "Az 1991-es magyar-ukrán alapszerződés jelentősége" [The significance of the 1991 Hungarian-Ukrainian Basic Treaty]. In *"Kijevi csirke": (Geo)politika a mai Ukrajnában* ["Chicken Kiev": Geopolitics in today's Ukraine], edited by Csilla Fedinec, 45–62. Budapest: MTA Társadalomtudományi Kutatóközpont - Kalligram, 2019.

―――. "Az Antall-kormány szomszédsági- és nemzetpolitikája" [The policy of the Antall government toward the neighbors and their Hungarians]. *Korunk* III 30, no. 12 (2019): 95–106.

―――. *Az elveszett presztízs: Magyarország megítélésének megváltozása Nagy-Britanniában (1894–1918)*. [Lost prestige: The changing image of Hungary in Great Britain, 1894–1918]. Budapest: Magvető, 1986; 2nd ed., Budapest: Magyar Szemle Kiadó, 1994; 3rd enl. ed., Budapest: Fekete Sas Kiadó, 2020.

―――. "Hungary and the Break-Up of Yugoslavia" [Part 1]. *Hungarian Review* 2, no. 2 (2011): 42–52; [Part 2] no. 3 (2011): 65–78.

―――. "Hungary in the Second World War: Tragic Blunders or Destiny." In *July 1944: Deportation of the Jews of Budapest Foiled*. Edited by Géza Jeszenszky, 65–101. Reno, NV: Helena History Press, 2017 [2018].

―――. "Hungary's Foreign Policy Dilemmas." *Hungarian Quarterly* 34 (Summer 1993): 3–13.

―――. "Hungary's Foreign Policy Dilemmas after Regaining Sovereignty." *Society and Economy* 29, no. 1 (2007): 43–64.

―――. "József Antall and the World." In *József Antall: Prime Minister of Hungary; Selected Speeches and Interviews* (1989–1993). Edited by Géza Jeszenszky. Budapest: József Antall Foundation, 2008.

―――. "Jugoszlávia felbomlása és a magyar külpolitika" [The break-up of Yugoslavia and Hungary's foreign policy]. *Külügyi Szemle* 10, no. 4 (2011): 42–79.

―――. *Kísérlet a trianoni trauma orvoslására: Magyarország szomszédsági politikája a rendszerváltozás éveiben* [An attempt to heal the Trianon trauma: Hungary's neighborhood policy in the years of regime change]. 2nd ed. Budapest: Osiris, 2023.

―――. "Közép-Európa veszte: Az I. világháború" [The catastrophe of Central Europe: The First World War]. *Magyar Szemle* 13, no. 10 (2014): 36–52.

———. *Lost Prestige: Hungary's Changing Image in Britain 1894–1918*. Reno, NV: Helena History Press, 2020.

———. "Magyarország és a kommunista dominók eldőlése" [Hungary and the fall of the communist dominoes]. *Hitel* 22, no. 10 (2009): 70–79.

———. "Magyarország kétoldalú szerződései a szomszédos országokkal és a kisebbségi kérdés" [Hungary's bilateral treaties with the neighboring countries and the issue of national minorities]. In *Ars boni et aequi: Tanulmányok az ezredvég nemzetközi rendszeréről Bokorné Szegő Hanna 75. születésnapjára*, 450–69. Budapest: BKÁE Nemzetközi Kapcsolatok Tanszék, 2000.

———. "More Bosnias? National and Ethnic Tensions in the Post-Communist World." *East European Quarterly* 31, no. 3 (1997): 283–99.

———. "Peace and Security in Central Europe: Its British programme during World War I." In *Etudes historiques hongroises 1985*, 457–82. Budapest: Akadémiai Kiadó, 1985.

———. *Post-Communist Europe and Its National/Ethnic Problems*. Budapest: Kairosz, 2009.

———. "Questions about the 25 Years of the Visegrad Group." In *Russia and Central Europe in the New Geopolitical Realities*, 38–47. XI International Scientific Conference, Moscow, December 1–2, 2016.

———. "Tanulmányok a szuverén Magyarország külpolitikájáról" [Studies on the foreign policy of Hungary after the restoration of sovereignty]. *Külügyi Szemle* 4, nos. 1–2 (2005): 274–90.

———. "The British Role in Assigning Csallóköz (Zitny Ostrov, Grosse Schütt) to Czechoslovakia." In *British-Hungarian Relations Since 1848*, edited by László Péter and Martyn Rady, 123–38. London: Hungarian Cultural Centre and School of Slavonic and East European Studies University College, 2004.

———. "The Genesis of a Lasting Quarrel in Central Europe." *The Hungarian Quarterly* 44 (Winter 2003): 113–18.

———. "The Origin and Enactment of the 'Visegrad Idea.'" In *The Visegrad Group—a Central European Constellation*, 60–62. Bratislava: International Visegrad Fund, 2006.

———. "Transylvania: Its Past and Present." In *Transylvania Today: Diversity at Risk*, edited by Csaba K. Zoltani, 23–47. Budapest: Osiris, 2013.

———. "Ukraine and Hungary: The Key to Relations is Sub-(Trans)Carpathia." *Hungarian Cultural Studies, Journal of the American Hungarian Educators Association* 17 (2024): 91–107.

———. *Ukraine and Hungary; The Key to Relations: Sub(Trans)Carpathia*. LAP Lambert Academic Publishing, 2025.

———. "Ukraine's Blunder—a Nationalist Education Law Leads to International Uproar." *Hungarian Review*, 9, no. 1 (January 2018): 30–38.

———. "Válasz egy doktrinernek" [Reply to a doctrinarian]. *Külügyi Szemle* 4, nos. 3–4 (2005): 290–93.

———. "Visegrád: Past and Future." *Hungarian Review* 2, no. 4 (2011): 20–23.

Joó, Rudolf, ed. *Report on the Situation of the Hungarian Minority in Rumania: Prepared for the Hungarian Democratic Forum*. Budapest, 1988. [New ed.]

Joó, Rudolf, and Andrew Ludanyi, eds. *The Hungarian Minority's Situation in Ceausescu's Romania*. New York: Columbia University Press, 1994.

Juhász, József. *Volt egyszer egy Jugoszlávia—a délszláv állam története* [Once there was a Yugoslavia. The history of the Southern Slav state]. Budapest: Aula Kiadó, 1999.

Juhász, József, László Márkusz, Péter Tálas, and László Valki. *Kinek a békéje? Háború és béke a volt Jugoszláviában* [Whose peace? War and peace in the former Yugoslavia]. Budapest: Zrínyi Kiadó, 2003.

Kállay, Nicholas [Miklós]. *Hungarian Premier: A Personal Account of a Nation's Struggle in the Second World War*. Westport, CT: Greenwood Press, 1954.

Kalmár, Ferenc, and Katalin Szili. *A nemzeti kisebbségvédelem javasolt alapelvei az EU-ban / Proposed Basic Principles for the Protection of National Minorities in the EU*. Budapest: Bethlen Gábor Alapkezelő, 2020.

Kántor, Zoltán, ed. *A státustörvény—dokumentumok, tanulmányok, publicisztika* [The Status Law: Documents, studies, essays]. Budapest: Teleki László Alapítvány, 2002.

———. "Hungary's Kin-State Politics, 2010–2014." *Minority Studies*, no. 17 (2014): 23–32.

Kántor, Zoltán, Balázs Majtényi, Osamu Ieda, Balázs Vizi, and Iván Halász, eds. *The Hungarian Status Law: Nation Building and/or Minority Protection*. Sapporo: Slavic Research Centre, Hokkaido University, 2004.

Kárpátalja története: Örökség és kihívások [History of Subcarpathia. Heritage and challenges]. Edited by György Csatáry. Beregszász–Ungvár: II. Rákóczi Ferenc Kárpátaljai Magyar Főiskola, 2021.

Kárpáti, Ferenc. "A román forradalom és Magyarország 1989" [The revolution in Romania and Hungary's reactions, 1989]. *História* 22, no. 4 (2000): 26–29.

———. *Puskalövés nélkül...* [Without a shot...]. Budapest: Duna International, 2011.

Keskeny, Ernő. *A magyar-orosz kapcsolatok 1989–2002* [Hungarian-Russian relations, 1989–2002]. Budapest: Századvég Kiadó, 2012.

Király, Béla K., and Veszprémy, László, eds. *Trianon and East Central Europe: Antecedents and Repercussions*. Boulder, CO, Highland Lakes, NJ: Atlantic Research, 1995.

Király, Béla K., and András Bozóki, eds. *Lawful revolution in Hungary, 1989–94*. Boulder, CO: Atlantic Research, 1995.

Király, Béla K., Peter Pastor, and Ivan Sanders, eds. *Essays on World War I: Total War and Peacemaking, A Case Study of Trianon*. New York and Boulder, CO: Atlantic Research, 1982.

Kis, János. "Nation-Building and Beyond." In *Can Liberal Pluralism Be Exported?*, edited by Will Kymlicka and Magda Opalski, 220–42. Oxford: The University Press, 2002.

Kiss J., László, ed. *Európai határok—európai stabilitás* [European borders—stability in Europe]. Budapest: BIGIS, 1994.

———, ed. *Nemzeti identitás és külpolitika Közép- és Kelet-Európában* [National identity and foreign policy in Central and Eastern Europe]. Budapest: Teleki László Alapítvány, 2003.

Kocsis, Károly. *Egy felrobbant etnikai mozaik esete* [The case of an exploded ethnic mosaic]. Budapest: Teleki László Alapítvány, 1993.

Kocsis, Károly, and Eszter Hodosi-Kocsis. *Ethnic Geography of the Hungarian Minorities in the Carpathian Basin*. Budapest: Hungarian Academy of Sciences, 1998.

Kocsis, Károly, and Patrik Tátrai, eds. *A Kárpát-Pannon-térség változó etnikai arculata a 15. század végétől a 21. század elejéig* [The changing ethnic patterns of the carpatho-pannonian area from the late fifteenth until the early twenty-first century]. Budapest: MTSA CSFK Földrajztudományi Intézet, 2012.

Kocsis, Károly, Zsolt Bottlik, and Patrik Tátrai. *Etnikai térfolyamatok a Kárpát-medence határainkon túli régióiban, 1989–2002* [Ethnic processes in the regions of the Carpathian Basin beyond the borders of Hungary]. Budapest: Magyar Tudományos Akadémia Földrajztudományi Kutatóintézet, 2006. https://hungarian-geography.hu/konyvtar/kiadv/etnika/indexCD.html.

Kocsis, Károly, Patrik Tátrai, Norbert Agárdi, Dániel Balizs, and Anikó Kovács. *A Kárpát–Pannon-térség változó etnikai arculata a 15. század végétől a 21. század elejéig: Térképmagyarázó/Changing Ethnic Patterns of the Carpatho–Pannonian Area from the Late 15th until the Early 21st Century: Accompanying Text*. 3rd, revised and enlargened edition. Budapest: MTA CSFK Földrajztudományi Intézet, 2015.

Kodolányi, Gyula. *Antall Józseffel a világszínpadon* [With József Antall on the world stage]. Budapest: Batthyány Lajos Alapítvány, 2023.

---. "A mese igaz: Antall József 1990-es külpolitikai kezdeményezései" [The tale is true: The foreign policy initiatives of József Antall]. *Magyar Szemle* 10, no. 6 (2001): 20–36.

Kollai, István. *Meghasadt múlt: Fejezetek a szlovákok és a magyarok történelméből* [Shattered past: Chapters from the history of the Slovaks and the Hungarians]. Budapest: Terra recognita alapítvány, 2008.

Kollai, István, and Bence Bánki. "Populism in the Making: The Case of Slovakia." In *Economic Policies of Populist Leaders: A Central and Eastern European Perspective*, edited by István Benczes, 125–47. London: Routledge, 2024.

Köpeczi, Béla, ed. *History of Transylvania*. 3 vols. Boulder, CO, Highland Lakes, NJ, New York: Social Science Monographs; Atlantic Research and Publications, 2001–2002.

Kymlicka, Will. "National Minorities in Postcommunist Europe: The Role of International Norms and European Integration." In *Ethnic Politics after Communism*, edited by Zoltan Barany and Robert G. Moser, 191–217. Ithaca-London: Cornell University Press, 2004.

Langendoen, Marco. "The Admission of the Slovak Republic to the Council of Europe." MA thesis at Leiden University, Manuscript, 1999.

Lengyel, László. "Külpolitika vagy nemzetpolitika" [Foreign policy or "nation policy"]. In *Kormány a mérlegen, 1990–1994* [Government—the balance sheet], edited by Csaba Gombár, Elemér Hankiss, László Lengyel, and Tibor Várnai, 346–68. Budapest: Korridor Politikai Kutatások Központja, 1994.

---. "Rendszerváltás: fordulópont és gyorsítás, 1990–1994" [Regime change: Turnaround and speed up]. In *Illeszkedés vagy kiválás* [Integration or separation], 143–72. Budapest: Osiris Kiadó, 2006.

Lőrincz, Csaba, Zsolt Németh, Viktor Orbán, and Zoltán Rockenbauer. *Nemzetpolitika '88–'98* [Nation policy '88–'98. Studies, essays, speeches, interviews]. Budapest: Pro Minoritate Alapítvány, 1998.

Macartney, C. A. *Hungary and Her Successors: The Treaty of Trianon and its Consequences 1919–1937*. Oxford: Oxford University Press, 1937 [1965].

---. *Hungary*. With a Foreword by H.A.L. Fisher. London: Ernest Benn Ltd. 1934.

---. *The Habsburg Empire, 1790–1918*. London: Weidenfeld & Nicolson, 1968.

Magocsi, Paul Robert. *With Their Backs to the Mountains: A History of Carpathian Rus' and Carpatho-Rusyns*. Budapest: Central European University Press, 2015.

Mák, Ferenc. "Az új nemzeti politika és a Határon Túli Magyarok Hivatala (1989–1999)" [The new national policy and the Office for Hungarians Beyond the Border]. *Magyar Kisebbség* 6, no. 3 (2000): 237–93.

Marinovich, Endre. *1315 nap: Antall József naplója* [1315 days: The diary of József Antall]. Budapest: Éghajlat, 2003.

Martonyi, János. *Európa, nemzet, jogállam* [Europe, nation, Rechtstaat]. Budapest: Magyar Szemle–Európai Utas, 1998.

May, Arthur. *The Passing of the Hapsburg Monarchy, 1914–1918*, volume 2. Philadelphia, PA: University of Pennsylvania Press, 1966.

Mediansky, Fedor. "National Minorities and Security in Central Europe: The Hungarian Experience." In *Nationalism and Postcommunism*, ed. A Pavkovic, H. Koscharsky, and A. Czarnota, 101–20. Aldershot, England: Dartmouth Publishing Co., 1995.

Meier, Viktor. *Yugoslavia: A History of Its Demise*. Translated by Sabrina Ramet. London and New York: Routledge, 1999.

Meiszter, Dávid. *Biztonságpolitikánk a gyakorlatban* [Hungary's security policy in practice]. Budapest: Politikai Tanulmányok Intézete, 1993.

Molnár, Gusztáv. *Alternatívák könyve*. Vol. 3, *Összmagyar alternatíva* [Book of alternatives, vol. 3, All-Hungarian alternative]. Kolozsvár: Pro Philosophia Kiadó, 2014.

Montgomery, John Flournoy. *Hungary: The Unwilling Satellite*. New York: Devin-Adair Co., 1947.

Nagorski, Andrew. *The Birth of Freedom*. New York: Simon & Schuster, 1993.

Nanovfszky, György. *Nano: Egy soknyelvű diplomata kalandjai öt kontinensen* [Nano: Adventures of a multilingual diplomat on five continents]. Recorded by Nemere István. Budapest: Alternatív Kiadó, 2014.

Nyitrai, Árpád-Attila. "A román-magyar kapcsolatok és a román-magyar alapszerződés megkötése (1990–1996)" [Romanian-Hungarian relations and the conclusion of the Romanian-Hungarian basic treaty]. Dissertation at the Babes-Bolyai University, 2008.

Ódor, Bálint, and Ádám Szesztay, eds. *Nemzetpolitikai konszenzus dokumentumokban: A KMKF nemzeti együttműködési stratégiája és szakpolitikai koncepciói, 2004–2009* [The strategy of national cooperation and political concepts of the Forum of the Hungarian MPs of the Carpathian Region]. Budapest: KMKF Titkárság, 2009.

Oplatka, András. *Egy döntés története* [History of a decision]. Budapest: Helikon, 2008.

Oplatka, Andreas. *Der Eiserne Vorhang Reisst*. Zürich: *Neue Zürcher Zeitung*, 1990.

———. *Der erste Riss in der Mauer: September 1989—Ungarn öffnet die Grenze*. Zürich: Zsolnay-Verlag, 2009.

Páldi, András. *Egyre távolabb Moszkvától* [Farther and farther away from Moscow]. Budapest: Belvárosi Könyvkiadó, 1996.

Péter, László, ed. *Historians and the History of Transylvania*. Boulder, CO: East European Monographs, 1992.

Pilon, Juliana. *The Bloody Flag: Post-Communist Nationalism in Eastern Europe; Spotlight on Romania*. New Brunswick, NJ: Transaction Publishers. 1992 (Routledge, 2021).

Poulton, Hugh. *The Balkans: Minorities and States in Conflict*. London: Minority Rights Publications, 1993.

Pritz, Pál. *Iratok a magyar külügyi szolgálat történetéhez 1918–1945* [Papers relating to the history of Hungary's foreign service]. Budapest: Akadémiai Kiadó. 1994.

———. *Magyar diplomácia a két háború között (Tanulmányok)* [Hungary's diplomacy between the two wars. Studies]. Budapest: Magyar Történelmi Társulat, 1995.

Pritz, Pál, Balázs Sipos, and Miklós Zeidler, eds. *Magyarország helye a 20. századi Európában* [Hungary's place in twentieth-century Europe]. Budapest: Magyar Történelmi Társulat, 2002.

Ramet, Sabrina P. *The Three Yugoslavias: State-Building and Legitimation, 1918–2005*. Bloomington: Indiana University Press, 2005.

Ránki, György, ed. *Hitler 68 tárgyalása keleteurópai államférfiakkal 1939–1944* [Hitler's sixty-eight negotiations with East European statesmen, 1939–1944]. Budapest: Magvető, 1983.

Reisch, Alfréd A. "Hungarian Foreign Ministry Completes Reorganization." *RFE/RL Research Report* 1, no. 13 (March 27, 1992).

Révész, Sándor. *Antall József távolról* [József Antall from a distance]. Budapest: Sík, 1995.

Rhodes, Matthew. "National Identity and Minority Rights in the Constitutions of the Czech Republic and Slovakia." *East European Quarterly* 29, no. 3 (1995): 347–69.

Romsics, Ignác. *From Dictatorship to Democracy: The Birth of the Third Hungarian Republic 1988–2001*. Boulder, CO: Columbia University Press, 2007.

———. *The Dismantling of Historic Hungary: The Peace Treaty of Trianon, 1920*. Translated by Mario D. Fenyo. Boulder, CO: Columbia University Press, 2002.

———. *Volt egyszer egy rendszerváltás* [Once there was a change of regime]. Budapest: Rubicon Könyvek, 2003.

Royer, Laura. "The Implications of the Hungarian Nation Policy in Central Europe since 1989: Between Tension and Integration." https://www.academia.edu/66850462/The_Implications_of_the_Hungarian_Nation_Policy_in_Central_Europe_Since_1989_Between_Tension_and_Integration?auto=download&email_work_card=download-paper.

Salat, Levente. "A Rapprochement without Reconciliation: Romanian-Hungarian Relations in the Post-Communist Era." In *Hungary and Romania beyond National Narratives: Comparisons and Entanglements*, ed. Anders Blomqvist, Constantin Iordachi, and Balázs Trencsényi, 655–90. Oxford: Peter Lang AG, 2013.

Sárközy, Péter. "A Közép-Európai Kezdeményezés és Magyarország: Beszélgetés Antall József miniszterelnökkel" [The Central European Initiative and Hungary: A conversation with József Antall]. *Európai Utas* 4, no. 2 (1993): 2–10.

Seton-Watson, Hugh. *Nations and States: An Enquiry into the Origins of Nations and the Politics of Nationalism*. London: Methuen, 1977.

Seton-Watson, Hugh, and Christopher Seton-Watson. *The Making of a New Europe: R.W. Seton-Watson and the Last Years of Austria-Hungary*. London: Methuen, 1981.

Seton-Watson, R. W. [Scotus Viator]. *Racial Problems in Hungary*. London: Methuen, 1908.

Sokcsevits, Dénes. *Horvátország a 7. századtól napjainkig* [Croatia from the seventh century to date]. Budapest: Mundus Novus Könyvek, 2011.

Sugar, Peter F., ed. *A History of Hungary*. Bloomington: Indiana University Press, 1990.

Szabad, György. "Román forradalom és Magyarország, 1989" [The Romanian revolution and Hungary]. *História* 22, no. 8. (2000): 26–27.

Szabó, Tamás. "Magyar-román államközi viszony és az RMDSZ kapcsolatrendszere a rendszerváltástól a könnyített honosítási eljárás bevezetéséig" [Hungarian-Romanian inter-state relations and the contact system of the RMDSZ from the regime change to the introduction of simplified naturalization]. PhD dissertation, Budapest: Budapesti Corvinus Egyetem, 2019.

Szarka, László. *Duna-táji dilemmák: Nemzeti kisebbségek—kisebbségi politika a 20. századi Kelet-Közép-Európában* [Danubian dilemmas: national minorities and minority policy in East-Central Europe in the twentieth century]. Budapest: Ister Kiadó, 1998.

Szarka, László, and István Tóth. *A magyarországi szlovákok* [The Slovaks of Hungary]. Budapest: Magyar Nemzeti Levéltár, 2023.

Szilágyi, Imre. "Magyarország és a délszláv térség 1990 után" [Hungary and the South Slav territory after 1990]. *Külügyi Szemle*, 3, nos. 1–2. (2004): 4–27.

Szili, Katalin. *Ten out of Thirty: Aspirations for Autonomy, Neighbourhood Policy and the European Minority Protection, 2010–2020.* Budapest: Bethlen Gábor Fund, 2022.

Szűts, Pál. *Bukaresti napló* [Bucharest diary]. Budapest: Osiris, 1998.

Tabajdi, Csaba. "A kedvezménytörvény 1989-ben kezdődött a kisebbségi rendszerváltozás folyamatában" [The Status Law goes back to 1989]. *Magyar Kisebbség* 1 (2001): 87–102.

———. "A nemzetközi kisebbségvédelem időszerű kérdései" [Current questions in the international protection of minorities]. *Magyar Kisebbség* 1, no. 1 (1995): 49–53.

———. *Az önazonosság labirintusa* [The labyrinth of self-identity]. Budapest: CP Stúdió Bt., 1998.

Takács, Ferenc. "Románia Erdély-politikája 1989 után" [Romania's policy towards Transylvania after 1989]. *Magyar Kisebbség* 4, nos. 3–4. (1998): 312–30. https://epa.oszk.hu/02100/02169/00010/m980323.htm

Tar, Pál. *In Memoriam Antall József: Tanú és szereplő* [In memoriam Jósef Antall: Witness and actor]. Budapest: Kairosz, 2003.

Tárnok, Balázs. *Mire elég egymillió aláírás? Az európai polgári kezdeményezés mint a nemzeti kisebbségek jog- és érdekérvényesítési eszköze* [What can one million signatures achieve? The European Citizens' Initiative as a means of asserting the rights and interests of national minorities]. Budapest: Ludovika Egyetemi Kiadó, 2023.

Temperley, H. W. V., ed. *A History of the Peace Conference of Paris.* Published under the auspices of the Institute of International Affairs. 6 vols. London: H. Frowde, and Hodder & Stoughton, 1920–1924.

Tismăneanu, Vladimir, and Sorin Antohi, eds. *Between Past and Future: The Revolutions of 1989 and Their Aftermath.* New York: Central European University Press, 2000.

Tőkés, Rudolf L. "From Visegrád to Cracow: Security and Cooperation in Central Europe." *Problems of Communism* 40, nos. 5–6. (1991): 100–114. https://babel.hathitrust.org/cgi/pt?id=uc1.31210008684167&seq=8

Toynbee, Arnold J. *Nationality and the War.* London and Toronto: J.M. Dent, 1915.

Udvardy, Frigyes. *A romániai magyar kisebbség történeti kronológiája 1990–2009* [Historical chronology of the Hungarian minority in Transylvania]. *Erdélyi Magyar Adatbank.* https://udvardy.adatbank.ro/.

Ujvári, Gábor, ed. *Történelmi traumáink: Közös sebek és a gyógyításukra tett kísérletek a Kárpát-medencében* [Our historical traumas: Common wounds and attempts at their healing in the Carpathian Basin]. Székesfehérvár: Kodolányi János Főiskola, 2014.

Vizi, Balázs. "A kisebbségek politikai képviseletének keretei nemzetközi színtéren" [The frameworks of the political representation of the minorities on the international scene]. In *Etnikai pártok Kelet-Közép-Európában, 1989–2014* [Ethnic political parties in East-Central Europe], edited by Csilla Fedinec, László Szarka, and Balázs Vizi, 15-19. Budapest, Gondolat Kiadó, 2018.

———, ed. *Magyarország és szomszédai: A kisebbségvédelem kérdései a kétoldalú szerződésekben* [Hungary and the neighbors: Minority protection in the bilateral treaties]. Budapest: Társadalomtudományi Kutatóközpont Kisebbségkutató Intézet - L'Harmattan, 2021.

Vizi, Balázs, Balázs Dobos, and Natalija Shikova, eds. *Non-Territorial Autonomy as an Instrument for Effective Participation of Minorities*. Budapest, Skopje: Centre for Social Sciences (CSS), University American College Skopje, 2021.

Waterbury, Myra. "National Minorities in an Era of Externalization: Kin-State Citizenship, European Integration, and Ethnic Hungarian Minority Politics." *Problems of Post-Communism* 64, no. 5 (2017): 228–41.

Zahorán, Csaba. "Románüldözés a Székelyföldön? Egy állítólagos etnikai tisztogatás történetei" [Persecution of the Romanians in the Székely land? Stories of an alleged ethnic cleansing]. In *Az új nemzetállamok és az etnikai tisztogatások Kelet-Európában 1989 után* [The new nation-states and the ethnic cleansings in Eastern Europe], ed. József Juhász and Tamás Krausz, 268–98. Budapest: L'Harmattan–ELTE BTK Kelet-Európa Története Tanszék, 2009.

Zeidler, Miklós, ed. *Trianon*. Budapest: Osiris, 2003.

Zoltani, Csaba K, ed. *Transylvania Today: Diversity at Risk*. Budapest: Osiris,

Appendix

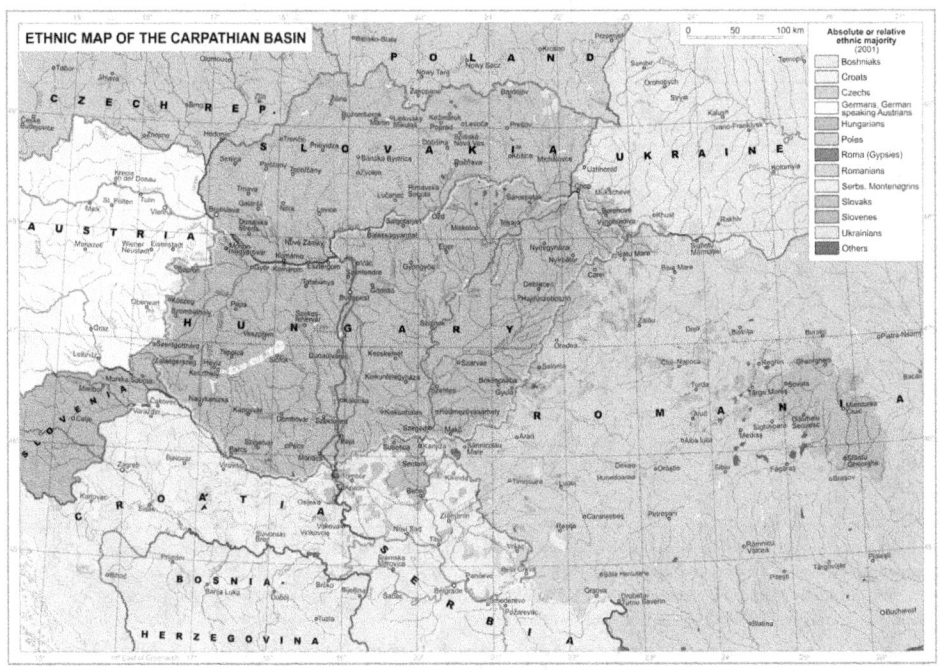

Map A1. Ethnic map of the Carpathian Basin, 2001
(Author: Károly Kocsis; Cartography: Zsolt Bottlik and Zoltán Keresztesi © Hungarian Academy of Sciences, Geographical Research Institute, Budapest, 2009)

Table 1. Ethnic structure of the population of the Kingdom of Hungary (1495–1910)[a] and the Carpathian Basin (1930–2001)[b] in thousands (and percentages).

	1495[c]	1787[d]	1840[e]	1880[f]	1910[g]	1930[h]	1941[i]	1960[j]	1990[k]	2001[l]
Total population	3,100	9,362	12,877	15,642	20,886	22,723	24,305	26,335	30,200	29,456
Hungarians	2,050[m] (66.1%)	3,250 (34.7%)	4,822 (37.4%)	6,445 (41.2%)	10,051 (48.2%)	10,526 (46.3%)	11,953 (49.2%)	12,508 (47.5%)	12,843 (42.5%)	11,822 (40.1%)
Romanians	180 (5.8%)	1,581 (16.9%)	2,206 (17.1%)	2,404 (15.4%)	2,949 (14.1%)	3,283 (14.4%)	3,434 (14.1%)	4,133 (15.7%)	5,764 (19.1%)	5,464 (15.5%)
Slovaks	170 (5.5%)	1,432 (15.3%)	1,687 (13.1%)	1,865 (11.9%)	1,968 (9.4%)	2,508 (11.0%)	2,582 (10.6%)	3,709 (14.1%)	4,624 (15.3%)	4,717 (16.0%)
Croats[n]	340 (11.0%)	1,003 (10.7%)	1,313 (10.2%)	1,460 (9.3%)	1,928 (9.2%)	1,932 (8.5%)	2,043 (8.4%)	2,488 (9.4%)	2,686 (8.9%)	2,833 (9.6%)
Serbs	100 (3.2%)	620 (6.6%)	828 (6.4%)	892 (5.7%)	1,106 (5.3%)	1,096 (4.8%)	1,071 (4.4%)	1,487 (5.6%)	1,560 (5.2%)	1,497 (5.1%)
Ukrainians[o]	30 (1.0%)	278 (3.0%)	443 (3.4%)	356 (2.3%)	473 (2.3%)	595 (2.6%)	641 (2.6%)	784 (3.0%)	1,084 (3.6%)	1,119 (3.8%)
Roma	-	-	-	-	121 (0.6%)	178 (0.8%)	172 (0.7%)	107 (0.4%)	465 (1.5%)	576 (2.0%)
Germans	200 (6.5%)	928 (9.9%)	1,270 (9.9%)	1,954 (12.5%)	2,037 (9.8%)	1,885 (8.2%)	1,854 (7.6%)	682 (2.6%)	393 (1.3%)	367 (1.2%)
Slovenes	10 (0.3%)	37 (0.4%)	41 (0.3%)	62 (0.4%)	93 (0.4%)	120 (0.5%)	103 (0.4%)	115 (0.4%)	95 (0.3%)	82 (0.3%)
Unknown/Unspecified[p]	-	-	-	-	-	-	-	-	73 (0.2%)	722 (2.5%)

Source: based on Károly Kocsis, Patrik Tátrai, Norbert Agárdi, Dániel Balizs, and Anikó Kovács, *A Kárpát–Pannontérség változó etnikai arculata a 15. század végétől a 21. század elejéig: Térképmagyarázó/Changing Ethnic Patterns of the Carpatho–Pannonian Area from the Late 15th until the Early 21st Century: Accompanying Text*, 3rd, rev. and enl. ed. (Budapest: MTA CSFK Földrajztudományi Intézet, 2015), 34.

[a] Kingdom of Hungary (1495–1910) includes the territories of the provinces Transylvania, Slavonia, and (between 1787–1910) Croatia / [b] Carpathian Basin (1930–2001) includes the territories of present-day Hungary, Transylvania, Slovakia, Pannonian Croatia, Vojvodina, Transcarpathia, Burgenland, and the Transmura region / [c] Calculations by Károly Kocsis partly based on the following publications: András Kubinyi, "A Magyar Királyság népessége a 15. század végén," *Történelmi Szemle* 38, nos. 2–3 (1996): 135–161; István Szabó, *A magyarság életrajza* (Budapest, Magyar Történelmi Társulat, 1941) / [d] Calculations by Károly Kocsis partly based on the following publications: J. H. Benigni von Mildenberg, *Handbuch der Statistik und Geographie des Grossfürstentums Siebenbürgen* (Hermannstadt, 1837); Dezső Dányi and Zoltán Dávid, ed., *Az első magyarországi népszámlálás (1784–1787)* (Budapest: KSH, 1960); Dezső Dányi et al, *Pótlás az első magyarországi népszámlálás-hoz 1786–87* (Budapest: KSH, 1975); J. A. Demian, *Darstellung der Oesterreichischen Monarchie nach der neuesten statistischen Beziehungen*, vol. 4, *(Statistische Beschreibung der Militär-Gränze)* (Vienna, 1806); Joseph Leonhard, *Lehrbuch zur Beförderung der Kenntnis von Siebenbürgen* (Hermannstadt, 1818); Lajos Nagy, *Notitiae politico-geographico-statisticae Hungariae, partiumque eidem adnexarum* I–II. (Buda: Landerer, 1828); Gusztáv Thirring, *Magyarország népessége II. József korában* (Budapest: MTA, 1938) / [e] Based on Elek Fényes, *Magyarország statistikája* (Pest: Trattner–Károlyi, 1842) / [f] Based on mother tongue data of the Hungarian censuses / [g] Based on mother tongue data of the Hungarian censuses / [h] Based on ethnic and mother tongue data of the Austrian (1934), Czechoslovak (1930), Hungarian (1930), Romanian (1930), Yugoslav (1931) censuses / [i] Based on ethnic, mother tongue, and colloquial language data of the German (1939), Slovak (1940), Hungarian (1941) and Romanian (1941) censuses; and authors' estimates (on Croatian and Serb territories) based on the Yugoslav (1931) census / [j] Based on ethnic, mother tongue and colloquial language data of the Austrian (1961), Czechoslovak (1961), Hungarian (1960), Romanian (1956), Soviet (1959), Yugoslav (1961) censuses / [k] Based on ethnic, mother tongue and colloquial language data of the Austrian (1991), Czechoslovak (1991), Hungarian (1990), Romanian (1992), Soviet (1989), Yugoslav (1991) censuses / [l] Based on ethnic and colloquial language data of the Austrian (2001), Croatian (2001), Hungarian (1990), Romanian (1992), Serbian (2002), Slovak (2001), Slovenian (2002), Ukrainian (2001) censuses / [m] Including Jász and Cuman people / [n] 1495: Slavonians; 1787–2001: including Bunjevci, Šokci, and Krašovani / [o] 1495–1930: Rusyns / [p] Including persons who did not declare ethnic affiliation and persons with regional identity.

Appendix

Table A2. Ethnic structure of the population of the countries and regions of the Carpathian Basin (in thousands, 1990–2011)

		Total population	Hungarians	Romanians	Slovaks	Croats[1]	Serbs	Ukrainians[2]	Roma	Germans	Slovenes	Czechs	Yugoslavs	Unknown/Unspecified[3]
Hungary	1990	10,375	10,142	11	10	14	3	–	143	31	2	–	–	–
	2001	10,198	9,416	8	18	16	4	6	190	62	3	–	–	571
	2011	9,938	8,314	26	30	24	7	9	309	132	2	–	–	1,456
Transylvania (Romania)	1992	7,723	1,604	5,684	19	4	27	50	203	109	–	5	–	–
	2002	7,222	1,416	5,394	17	4	21	49	244	49	–	3	–	1
	2011	6,789	1,217	4,795	14	5	16	42	271	33	–	2	–	378
Slovakia	1991	5,274	567	–	4,519	–	–	30	79	5	–	59	–	9
	2001	5,379	521	–	4,615	1	–	35	90	5	–	47	–	55
	2011	5,397	458	–	4,353	1	1	41	106	5	–	34	–	382
Pannonian Croatia (Croatia)	1991	3,207	20	1	5	2,549	385	5	6	2	12	12	73	41
	2001	3,010	15	–	4	2,712	150	4	8	2	7	10	–	12
	2011	2,873	13	–	4	2,623	131	3	15	2	5	9	–	124
Voivodina (Serbia)	1991	2,014	339	39	64	98	1,144	22	24	4	3	2	174	21
	2002	2,032	290	30	57	76	1,322	20	29	3	2	2	50	79
	2011	1,932	251	25	50	64	1,290	18	42	3	2	–	12	124
Transcarpathia (Ukraine)	1989	1,246	156	29	7	–	7	977	12	3	–	–	–	–
	2001	1,255	152	32	6	–	6	1010	14	4	–	–	–	–
	2012	1,252	:	:	:	:	:	:	:	:	:	:	:	:
Burgenland (Austria)	1991	271	7	–	–	19	–	–	–	239	–	–	–	–
	2001	278	7	–	–	20	1	–	–	242	–	–	–	–
	2012	286	:	:	:	:	:	:	:	:	:	:	:	:
Transmura Region (Slovenia)	1991	90	8	–	–	2	–	–	1	–	78	–	–	2
	2002	82	5	–	–	1	–	–	1	–	70	–	–	4
	2012	80	:	:	:	:	:	:	:	:	:	:	:	:
CARPATHIAN BASIN	1990	30,200	12,843	5,764	4,624	2,686	1,560	1,084	465	393	95	78	247	73
	2001	29,456	11,822	5,464	4,717	2,833	1,497	1,119	576	367	82	62	50	722
	2011	28,234	:	:	:	:	:	:	:	:	:	:	:	:
CARPATHIAN BASIN (in %)	1990	100.0%	42.5%	19.1%	15.3%	8.9%	5.2%	3.6%	1.5%	1.3%	0.3%	0.3%	0.8%	0.2%
	2001	100.0%	40.1%	18.5%	16.0%	9.6%	5.1%	3.8%	2.0%	1.2%	0.3%	0.2%	0.2%	2.5%
	2011	100.0%												

Based on ethnic data of the given censuses. *Source*: Kocsis et al., *A Kárpát–Pannon-térség*, 35.

[1] Including Bunjevci, Šokci and Krašovani.
[2] Including Rusyns.
[3] Including persons who did not declare ethnic affiliation and persons with regional identity.

Hungary and Its Neighbors, 1988–1994

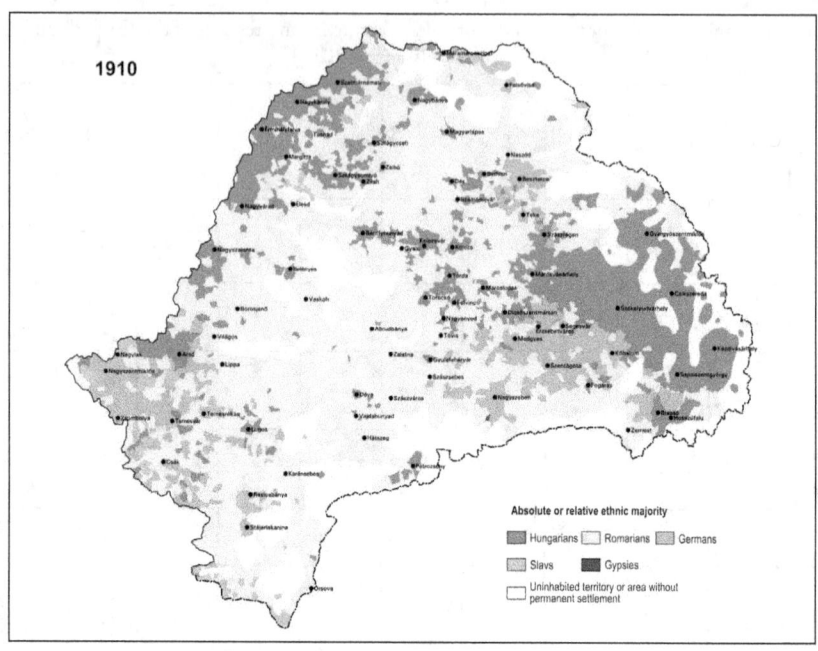

Map A2. Ethnic map of the present territory of Transylvania in 1910
(Author: Károly Kocsis; Cartography: Zoltán Farkas and Zoltán Keresztesi © Hungarian Academy of Sciences, Geographical Research Institute, Budapest, 1997)

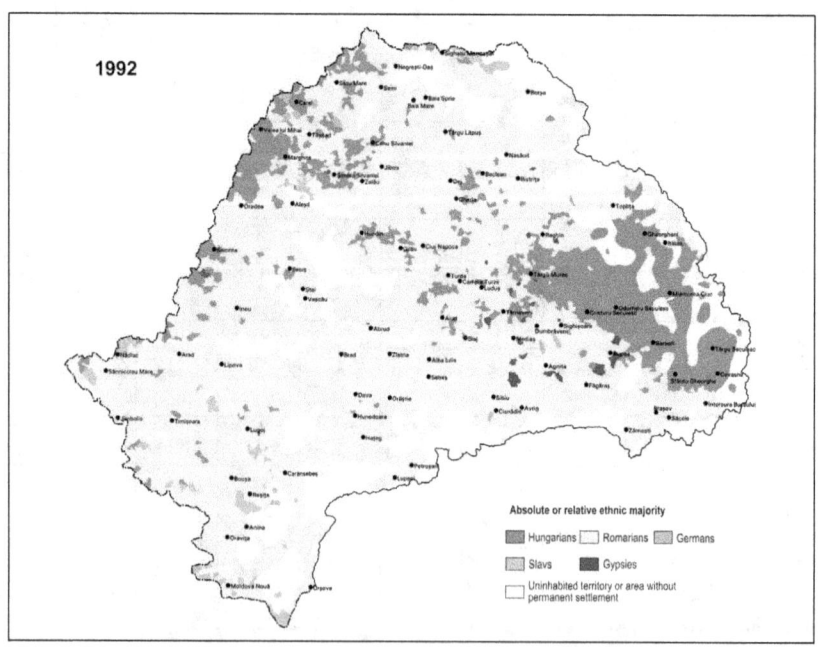

Map A3. Ethnic map of the present territory of Transylvania in 1992
(Author: Károly Kocsis; Cartography: Zoltán Farkas and Zoltán Keresztesi © Hungarian Academy of Sciences, Geographical Research Institute, Budapest, 1997)

Appendix

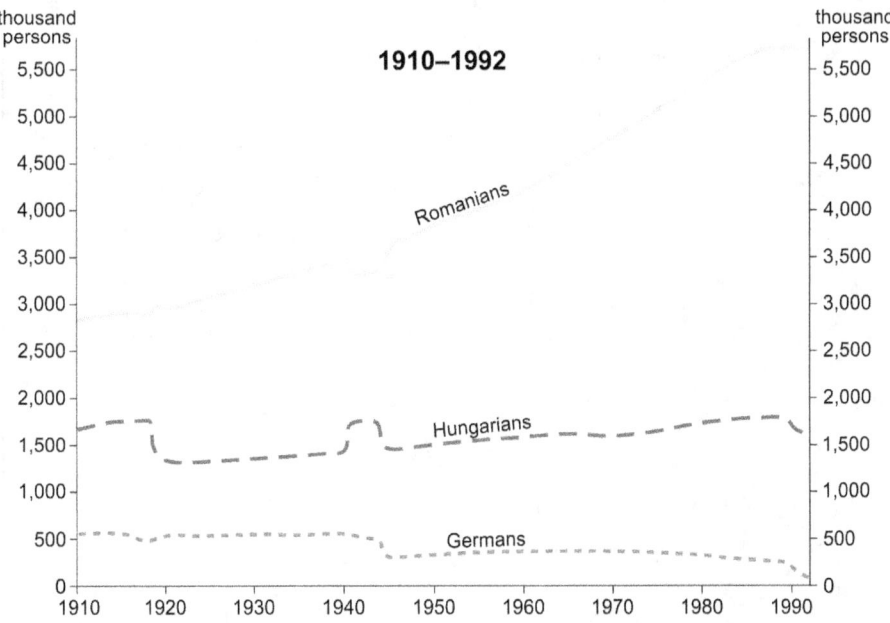

Figure A1. Change in the number of Romanians, Hungarians and Germans on the present territory of Transylvania (historical Transylvania, Maramureş, Crişana, Rumanian Banat), 1910–1992

(Author: Károly Kocsis © Hungarian Academy of Sciences, Geographical Research Institute, Budapest, 1997)

Hungary and Its Neighbors, 1988–1994

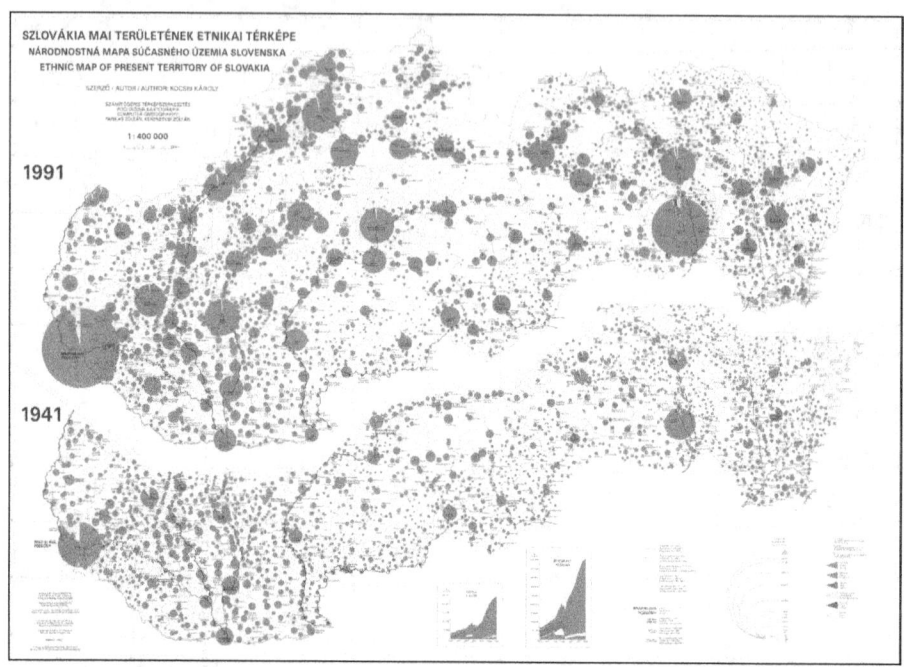

Map A4. Ethnic map of the settlements of the present territory of Slovakia in 1941 and 1991
(Author: Károly Kocsis; Cartography: Zoltán Farkas and Zoltán Keresztesi © Hungarian Academy of Sciences, Geographical Research Institute, Budapest, 1997)

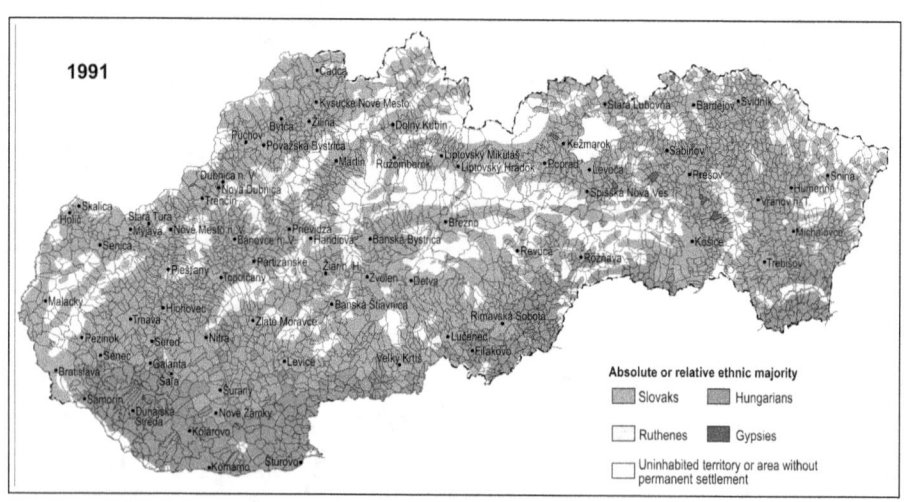

Map A5. Ethnic map of Slovakia, 1991
(Author: Károly Kocsis; Cartography: Zoltán Farkas and Zoltán Keresztesi © Hungarian Academy of Sciences, Geographical Research Institute, Budapest, 2000)

Appendix

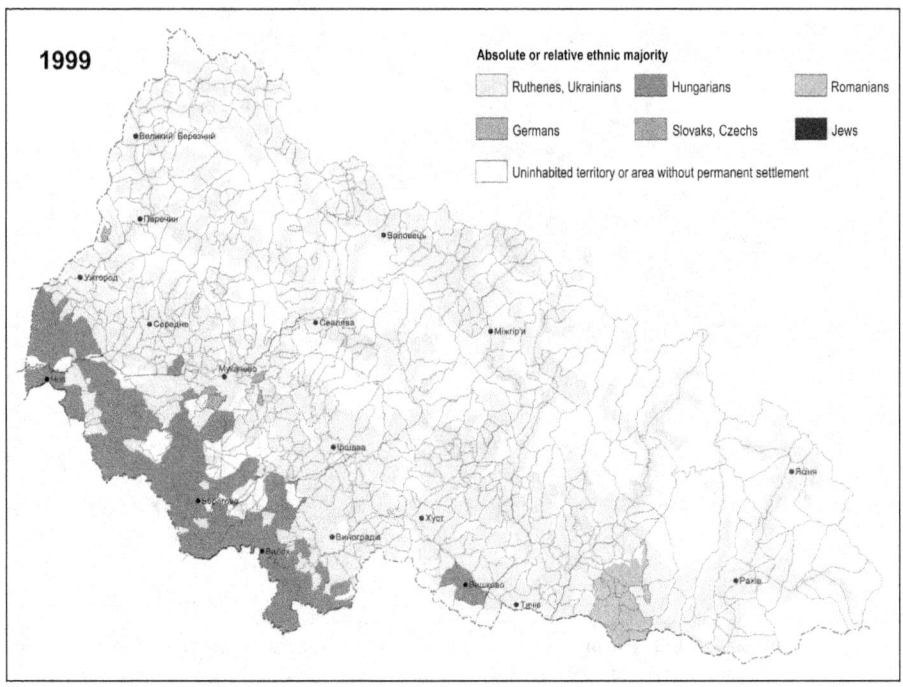

Map A6. Ethnic map of Sub(Trans)-Carpathia, Ukraine, 1999
(Author: Károly Kocsis; Cartography: Zoltán Farkas and Zoltán Keresztesi © Hungarian Academy of Sciences, Geographical Research Institute, Budapest, 2001)

Hungary and Its Neighbors, 1988–1994

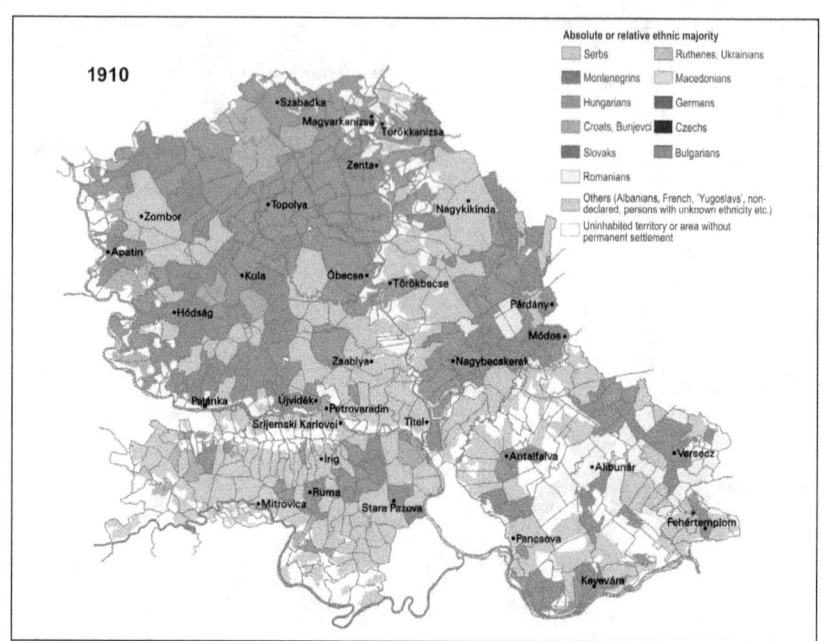

Map A7. Ethnic map of the present territory of Vojvodina, Yugoslavia, in 1910
(Author: Károly Kocsis and Saša Kicošev; Cartography: Zoltán Farkas and Zoltán Keresztesi ©
Hungarian Academy of Sciences, Geographical Research Institute, Budapest, 2004)

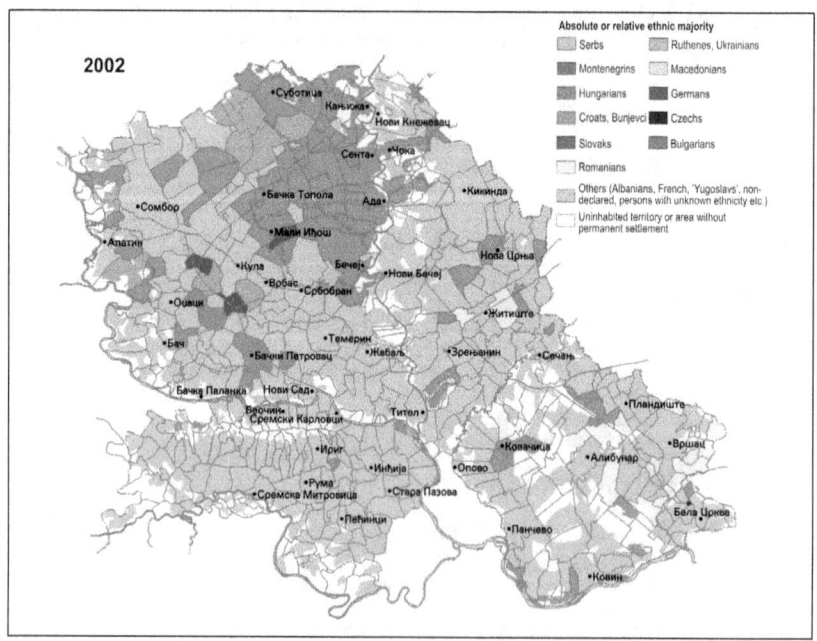

Map A8. Ethnic map of the present territory of Vojvodina, Serbia, in 2002
(Author: Károly Kocsis and Saša Kicošev; Cartography: Zoltán Farkas and Zoltán Keresztesi ©
Hungarian Academy of Sciences, Geographical Research Institute, Budapest, 2004)

Index

Page numbers in italics refer to figures and tables.

A. Nagy, László, 340, 345
Aboimov, Ivan Pavlovich, 181n, 189n, *195*
Adamec, Ladislav, 283
Áder, János, 63
Ady, Endre, 137
Agnew, Hugh, 297n
Ágoston, András, 96, 223, 233, 252, 393, 394n, 395, 398n, 401–2, 413
Albright, Madeleine, 93, 229
Alexy II, 202
Alföldy, Tádé, 159
Andersson, Sten, 32
Andriessen, Frans, 287n
Annus, József, 37
Antall, József, 20, *30*, 53, 76–77, *139*, *140*, *141*, *198*, *200*, 325, 391–92; as seen/described by others, 48, 52, 75, 94, 122, 134, 144, 179, 212, 223n, 251, 331, 334, 391, 392–93, 407, 410–11; as leader of the MDF, 20, 31, 32–33, 36, 39, 44, 46–47, 48, 49–50, 78; as prime minister, 59, 76–77, 142; Antall government, 3–4, 66, 69, 80, 83, 89, 168, 203, 205, 331, 360, 393, 404, 409, 423–25, 431–32, 435, 439, 443–44, 463; neighborhood policy of, 32–34, 48, 64–69, 98, 109, 113, 136, 173, 188, 206–7, 211–13, 222, 225, 227–28, 235, 241, 243, 249, 251, 286, 297–98, 302–3, 307, 310, 318, 323, 324–25, 341, 355, 391–92, 396, 424, 439; and Hungarian minorities in neighboring countries, 20, 69, 70–72, 75–76, 124, 168, 212–13, 218, 223, 228–29, 233, 242, 249, 251, 293, 298, 303, 307–8, 313, 318, 325, 330, 331, 360, 393–94, 408, 409, 413, 439; and national minority rights, 72, 75, 76, 106, 114, 124–25, 166, 168–69, 218, 220, 230, 237, 249, 265–66, 272, 293, 325, 332–33, 335, 355, 358; and Central European cooperation, 20, 39, 84, 116, 132–33, 135, 136, 140, 142, 147, 148, 150, 151, 155, 217, 271–73; and European integration, 20, 185, 271, 293, 355, 358; and Western relations, 20, 44, 54, 57, 90, 98, 105, 124, 128, 153, 178, 184, 212, 215, 216, 218, 224, 225, 227, 229–30, 287; and Soviet/post-Soviet relations, 83, 92, 147, 151, 172, 177n, 178, 181, 183, 194–86, 188, 197–98, 199–202, 220, 271, 309–10, 323, 392; and international crisis resolution, 215, 217, 218, 224, 225, 227–30, 236–37, 253, 254, 412; and the Warsaw Pact, 138, 140, 144, 178–79;
Antall, József, Sr., 20
Antalpéter, Tibor, 172n
Apostol, Gheorghe, 33

Apponyi, Albert, 12
Ara-Kovács, Attila, 37
Atkinson, David, 356

Bába, Iván, 130, 146, 157n, 158, 244, 262n, 271n, 314, 317n, 364n, 398, 400n, 411
Badinter, Robert, 222; Badinter Commission, 239, 240, 241, 274, 301
Bagi, Gábor, 244
Bajcsy-Zsilinszky, Endre, 31, 121, 137
Baker, James, 92, 147, 148, 211, 213, 214, 215, 252, 254
Balassa, Zoltán, 419n
Balázs, Ádám, 414n
Bălcescu, Nicolae, 110
Balladur, Édouard, 412, 413, 414, 421, 422
Balogh, István, 244, 247
Barcza, György, 78n
Bárdi, Nándor, 28, 443–45
Barki, Eva Maria, 161
Barkman, Carl, 233
Bartók, Béla, 21
Báthory, János, 274
Batta, György, 461
Beke, György, 389
Beke, Mihály András, 380, 389, 439
Bencúr, Ján, 171
Benczédi, Pál, 32
Benda, Kálmán, 37
Benedek, Dezső, 56
Beneš, Edvard, 11, 137, 282, 297n, 392, 459; Beneš decrees, 102, 337, 344, 349, 350, 352, 353, 355, 359, 460
Berindei, Mihnea, 37
Bertalan, Imre, 56
Bessmertnykh, Alexander, 183
Bethlen, Gábor, 99
Bibó, István, 15, 72, 75, 137, 144

Bielecki, Jan Krzysztof, 133, 140, *141*
Bildt, Karl, 383
Biller, Stephen, 127n
Binder, Július, 286
Bíró, Gáspár, 274
Bíró, Zoltán, 48
Bismarck, Otto von, 136
Bodnár, László, 274
Bodor, Katalin, 32
Bodor, Pál, 37
Bogár, László, 206
Bojtár, Endre, 37
Bollobás, Enikő, 45, 244
Borbándi, Gyula, 18n, 24
Borbély, László, 365, 395n, 454n
Boros, Jenő, 102n, 105, 106–7, 282n, 283n, 340
Boross, Péter, 265, 395–96, 410, 411, 417, 422; Boross government, 393, 407, 455
Borsi-Kálmán, Béla, 83, 163
Borsody, István, 24
Bősenbacher, Ferenc, 301n
Botez, Mihai, 56
Boutros-Ghali, Boutros, 471
Bratinka, József, 276, 355
Broek, Hans van den, 147, 219, 232, 233, 238
Brucan, Silviu, 33
Brundtland, Gro Harlem, 383
Bučar, France, 247
Bugár, Béla, 305, 340, 345n, 398
Burghard, Günther, 301n
Busek, Erhard, 245
Bush, George H. W., 1, 35n, 54, 124, 147, 179n, 184–85, 186, 198, 214n, 218, *219*, 224, 225, 230, 236, 242, 392
Bútora, Martin, 453

Čalfa, Marián, 140, 179n
Călinescu, Matei, 56
Čarnogurský, Ján, 102, 105, 164, *165*, 171, 282, 300
Carrington, Peter, Lord, 222–23, 225, 230, 232, 233, 238n, 240, 247, 274
Ceauşescu, Nicolae, 17n, 19n, 30, 31, 33, 46–47, 51, 108, 114, 118, 166, 264; regime/era of, 19, 34, 35, 39, 45, 54n, 116, 120, 124, 161, 174, 364, 367
Celac, Sergiu, 92
Chászár, Ede, 81
Chebeleu, Traian, 111, 264
Cheney, Dick, 216
Chirac, Jacques, 54, 414
Chmel, Rudolf, 106–7
Chornovil, Viacheslav, 193, 314, 316
Christopher, Warren, 416, *417*, 422
Churchill, Winston, 24n, 255
Clesse, Armand, 144
Clinton, Bill (William Jefferson Blythe), 392, 416, 422
Combes, Ariadna, 37
Constantinescu, Emil, 175, 267, 315, 372, 375, 412, 450
Coposu, Corneliu, 372
Corneanu, Nicolae, 379
Cossiga, Francesco, 212n
Cs. Szabó, László, 24
Csaba, László, 81, 463
Csáky, Pál, 345n, 394, 413, 463
Csejtei, István, 413n
Csengey, Dénes, 115
Cseresznyés, Pál, 269
Csergő, Zsuzsa, 170, 441n
Csőgör, Lajos, 37
Csoóri, Sándor, 37, 39, 82
Csóti, György, 171, 317, 394, 406

Csubela, Ferenc, 456
Csurka, István, 78n, 279, 317, 331, 355n, 394, 396, 404, 431
Culda, Lucian, 175, 176n
Cviic, Christopher, 213
Czettler, Antal, 81
Czigány, Lóránt, 24, 80

Dalmay, Árpád, 314, 327n
De Gasperi, Alcide, 126
De Michelis, Gianni, 54, 93, 219n, 232
Deák, Ernő, 24, 74
Deák, Ferenc, 324
Deák, István, 24
Del Medico, Imre, 81
Delors, Jacques, 287
Demeš, Pavol, 164, *165*, 290–91, 294
Dienstbier, Jiří, 102, 103, 139, 140, *141*, 147
Dinu, Marcel, 37, 386, 388
Diószegi, István, 81
Diószegi, László, 82
Dobrovsky, Luboš, 103
Dodd, Christopher, 27n, 160
Domokos, Géza, 53n
Donca, Ioan, 261, 364n
Drnovšek, Janez, 284, 383
Dubček, Alexander, 100, 138
Dudás, Károly, 227n
Duka-Zólyomi, Árpád, 345n
Dumas, Roland, 92
Dumnič, Jurij, 274
Dunay, Pál, 178, 201
Dunn, Newton, 127
Duray, Miklós, 25, 27, 28, 282, 291, 298, 305, 340, 345n, 393, 394n, 397n, 413
Dzurinda, Mikuláš, 412, 459, 462

Eagleburger, Lawrence, 54, 57, 214, 216, 229
Egyed, Ákos, 388
Ellemann-Jensen, Uffe, 92
Eminescu, Mihai, 110
Engelmayer, Ákos, 45, *139*, 304n
Entz, Géza, 32, 36, 74, 98, 108n, 114n, 159, 167, 176, 188, 193, 261, 262, 264n, 265n, 267, 275, 276, 277n, 290, 312, 394, 433
Eörsi, Mátyás, 441–42
Eötvös, József, 293
Esterházy, János, 102, 432, 362–64
Eyal, Jonathan, 172n

Farkas, Ádám, 32
Farkas, Gabriella, 299
Farkas, Zoltán, *500, 501, 503, 504, 505, 506*
Fáy, Gedeon, 81
Fejtő, Ferenc, 56
Fekete, Elvira, 331
Fiala, János, 450n
Fico, Robert, 153, 305, 459, 460, 461–62, 474
Finsberg, Lord, 442
Fischer, Heinz, 258
Fodó, Sándor, 191, *192*, 319
Fodor, Gábor, 41
Foias, Ciprian, 56
Fokin, Vitold, 313
Forrai, Kristóf, 82
Forrai, Tibor, 81
Frunda, György, 364, 365, 381, 388, 454n
Fukuyama, Francis, 88
Fülöp, Dénes, 376
Fülöp, Mihály, 421
Funar, Gheorghe, 17n, 260, 370

Für, Lajos, 36, 39, 48–49, 178, 179, *180*, 206–7, 261, 263
Furrer, Hans-Peter, 276, 347n, 348

Gábor, Áron (1814–1849), 386, 387, 439
Gábor, Áron, 113n
Galló, Béla, 3n
Garton Ash, Timothy, 135
Gáspár, Ödön, 80
Gašparovič, Ivan, 342
Gáti, Charles, 93
Genscher, Hans-Dietrich, 148
Geran-Pilon, Juliana, 56
Geremek, Bronisław, 133
Gherman, Oliviu, 372
Giscard d'Estaing, Valéry, 54
Goma, Paul, 37, 56
Göncz, Árpád, 37, 99, 106, 109, 121, 140, *141*, 142, 178, 183, 188, 215, 355
Gonzalez, Felipe, 54
Gorbachev, Mikhail Sergeyevich, 76, 83, 139, 143, 145, 177, 178–79, 181, 183–84, 185, 188, 194, 197, *198*, 199, 202, 225, 236n, 309
Gore, Al (Albert, Arnold), 238
Granasztói, György, 301n, 303n
Granić, Mate, 402
Greguric, Franjo, 247
Gross, Andreas, 455
Grósz, Károly, 31
Gruber, Karl, 126
Grudziński, Przemysław, 453
Gyallay-Pap, Domonkos, 81
Gyarmati, István, 231, 364n
Gyekiczki, András, 37
Győri Szabó, Róbert, 202n
Györke, Sándor, 184n
Gyurácz, Ferenc, 40

Gyurcsány, Ferenc, 135n
Gyurgyák, János, 13n, 37

Hall, Sir Basil, 344
Halonen, Tarja, 343, 344, 346, 353, 355–56, 442
Hamberger, Judit, 308n
Hamerton-Kelly, Robert, 108, 175, 176n, 266
Hámos, László, 24, 27, 37, 56, 341
Hanák, Péter, 23, 81
Hargitai, Zsuzsanna, 131, 132n, 156, 157
Harrach, Vilmos, 81
Harsányi, Endre, 56
Havel, Václav, 27n, 44, 99–100, 107, 135, 136, 138, 140, *141*, 142, 148, 150, 151, 156, 171, 184, 186, 282, 290, 339, 382, 385
Hegedűs, István, 321
Heller, Ágnes, 56
Herczegh, Géza, 34, 274
Herder, Johann Gottfried, 382
Herényi, Károly, 299n
Herman, János, 83, 122, 174n, 188, 235n, 262, 264, 332, 372, 382, 412
Hitler, Adolf, 87, 289, 302, 340, 374, 382, 384
Hódi, Sándor, 265, 274, 394, 401
Hodža, Milan, 137
Horn, Gyula, 46, 48, 49n, 50, 53, 106, 129, 145, 182, 302n, 304n, 316–17, 321, 374, 405, 408, 410, 431–32, 443, 444, 446, 447
Horthy, Miklós, 112
Horváth, István, 128, 129, 157, 301, 302n
Howe, Geoffrey, 32
Hrebenciuc, Viorel, 365
Hunya, Gábor, 37

Hurd, Douglas, 240

Íjgyártó, István, 271n, 312, 316n
Ilia, Mihály, 37
Iliescu, Ion, 47, 52, 53, 108, 117, 121–22, 124n, 127, 160, 162, 173, 175, 176, 181, 267, 289, 314, 364, 374–75, 377, 381–82, 383, 448, 449–50
Illyés, Gyula, 25, 74, 323
Illyés, Mária, 37
Ingham, Richard, 340
Ionesco, Eugène, 37, 56
Ionesco, Marie-France, 37
Iván, Géza, 332

Jakab, Sándor, 250
Jansson, Gunnar, 363–35, 380
Jászi, Oszkár, 9, 73, 137, 156, 433, 468
Jelačić, Josip, 97
Jessenius, Johannes, 99
Jeszenszky, Péter, 21
Jókai, Mór, 182
Jolsvai, Sándor, 158
Jónás, Pál, 56
Joó, Rudolf, 30, 32, *33*, 39, 44, 61n
Josipović, Ivo, 96
Jovanović, Vladislav, 235, 255, 399, 400
Juhász, Gyula, 23
Juppé, Alain, 383
Jurkans, Janis, 186

K. Lengyel, Zsolt, 451
Kádár, Béla, 264, 315
Kádár, János, 18, 19, 110n, 177, 380
Kadijević, Veljko, 206, 209, 225
Käfer, István, 341
Kaifu, Toshiki, 54
Kállay, Kristóf, 81

Kállay, Miklós, 88n
Kalmár, Ferenc, 469
Kampelman, Max, 166
Kántor, Zoltán, 455
Karadžić, Radovan, 243
Károlyi, Mihály, 11, 95
Kárpáti, Ferenc, 40n, 48, 49
Kassof, Allen, 277, 365, 454
Kasza, József, 456
Katić, Dejan, 256
Katona, Tamás, 77, 100, 139, 158, 264, 395
Kelemen, András, 78, 395–96
Kemény, G. Gábor, 23
Kende, Péter, 25, 157
Keresztesi, Péter, 344n
Keresztesi, Zoltán, *497, 500, 501, 503, 504, 505, 506*
Kertész, István, 78n
Keskeny, Ernő, 199, 202, 317n
Khasbulatov, Ruslan, 182
Kinkel, Klaus, 301
Király, B. Izabella, 322
Király, K. Béla, 18n, 24, 56
Király, Károly, 53n
Kircsi, Júlia, 82
Kiss, Gy. Csaba, 45, 81
Kissinger, Henry, 215
Klaus, Václav, 151, 286, 289, 298, 358, 414
Klestil, Thomas, 382
Kňažko, Milan, 106, 294, 299, 304, 305, 341, 344
Kocsis, Károly, *497, 498, 500, 501–6,*
Kodolányi, Gyula, 25, 36, 45, 54, 66, 77, 98n, 147, 185n, 238n, 244, 286n, 307, 413n, 414n, 467
Kohl, Helmut, 54, 184, 224, 227, 287, 302, 303n, 382

Kolokolov, Boris, 182
Komorowski, Bronisław, 132
König, Friedrich, 364
Konrád, György, 135
Kontra, Ferenc, 317n
Körmendi, Ferenc, 223n, 233
Körmendy, István, 130, 158
Korné, Mihai, 37
Kosáry, Domokos, 82, 278
Kossuth, Lajos, 2, 137, 296n, 324, 401, 438
Košutić, Budimir, 235n
Koszorús, Ferenc, 24, 27
Köteles, Pál, 34, 35
Kováč, Michal, 299, 355
Kovács, László, 351, 405, 406, 409, 410, 422
Kovács, Péter, 274
Kövi, Pál, 56
Koźmiński, Jerzy, 453
Kozyrev, Andrei, 182, 194, 195–96, 198, 200–201, 202
Krajczár, Imre, 337n
Kräuter, Sebastian, 379
Kravchuk, Leonid, 188, 197–98, 310, 312, 315, 318, 327
Krayilo, Mykhaylo, 312–33, 317
Kriston, Károly, 147n
Kućan, Milan, 98, 248
Kulin, Ferenc, 37
Kuncze, Gábor, 410
Kundera, Milan, 135
Kürti, László, 274
Kutasi, Márta, 157n
Kvitsinsky, Yury, 153, 182, 309

Ladislaus IV of Hungary, 21
Lalumière, Catherine, 116, 169, 276, 277, 314, 353, 382, 396, 397n

Landsbergis, Vytautas, 172, 186
Láng, Judit, 350n
Langendoen, Marco, 354, 359
Lantos, Tom, 458
Lastic, Pero, 274
Lauer, Edith K., 56
Lauer, John, 56
Lengyel, Zsolt K., 431
Lenin, Vladimir Ilyich, 153
Lieberman, Joseph, 160
Lipták, Béla, 81, 287
Litván, György, 37
Lloyd George, David, 12
Lončar, Budimir, 96, 153, 219
Lőrincz, Csaba, 156, 159, 409
Lovinescu, Monica, 37
Lubbers, Ruud, 253n, 383
Ludányi, András, 274
Lukacs, John, 24, 81, 332
Lukyanov, Fyodor, 143

Mackay, James, 382
Maczó, Ágnes, 322
Madách, Imre, 296n
Mádl, Ferenc, 286, 456, 457, 458n
Magas, Branka, 209n
Maior, Petru, 110
Maizière, Lothar de, 113
Major, John, 224, 225, 253n
Maksić, Milivoje, 99
Mănescu, Corneliu, 33
Manoilu-Manea, Maria, 56
Marković, Ante, 96, 98, 207, 208, 210n, 213, 214, 217, 223, 225, 244
Marshall, David F., 170
Martens, Wilfred, 171
Martin, József, 330n
Márton, Áron, 111

Martonyi, János, 78, 351, 352, 392n, 394, 406, 411, 463
Masaryk, Jan, 10, 102n, 295, 392, 459
Matus, János, 263n, 266
Mazilu, Dumitru, 117n
Mazowiecki, Tadeusz, 132, 230
Meciar, Vladimír, 100, 102, 105, 139, 145, 148, 164, 281, 282, 286n, 287, 288, 289, 291, 294, 296, 297, 298–99, 301, 304–5, 339, 340, 341, 343, 344, 349–50, 353, 354–55, 383, 397, 410, 447, 456, 459
Meier, Viktor, 216n, 221
Meiszter, Dávid, 146n, 156, 159, 326n
Melescanu, Teodor, 162, 264, 268–69, 359, 361, 364, 370, 371, 379, 380, 381, 386
Meri, Lennart, 186
Mesić, Stjepan, 97
Michael I of Romania, 37, 44, 176
Miklós, Árpád, 322
Miklósházy, Attila, 56
Mikloško, František, 99, 103, 105
Mikloško, Jozef, 103
Milošević, Slobodan, 95, 96, 205, 206, 208, 210n, 217, 225, 230, 232n, 233, 236n, 237, 238, 243, 253, 255, 256, 257, 281, 456, 471
Miłosz, Czesław, 135
Milován, Sándor, 413
Mináč, Vladimír, 305
Miskolczy-Simon, János, 22
Misur, György, 347
Mitrová, Eva, 347n, 348, 350
Mitterrand, François, 54, 185, 218, 255
Mock, Alois, 90, *91*, 143, 227 258, *259*, 275, 301, 430
Molnár, Ágoston, 56
Molnár, Bertalan, 317

Molnár, Gusztáv, 37, 81, 156, 404–5
Molotov, Vyacheslav Mikhaylovich, 173, 186, 187
Monori, István, 197, 317n
Moravčik, Jozef, 336, 344, 345–46, 349, 352, 354, 397, 410, 411, 446
Mroz, John Edwin, 153, 314
Mršić, Zdravko, 97, 98n, 206

Nádosy, Péter, 56
Nagy, Imre, 18n, 36, 41n, 110, 264, 371
Nagy, József, 468n
Nagy, Károly, 24, 56
Nagy, László A., 340, 345n
Nagy, László, 33
Nanovszky, György, 202
Năstase, Adrian,
Neagu, Romulus, 108–9, 111, 120, 121–22
Németh, Miklós, 42, 47, 49n, 60, 106, 125, 283
Németh, Zsolt, 42n, 63, 159, 321, 409, 442
Nemoianu, Virgil, 56
Neumann, Ernő, 379
Nitti, Francesco Saverio, 12

Oberfrank, Ferenc, 82, 395n
Ódor, Lászkó, 45
Orbán, Viktor, 69, 87n, 153, 156, 206n, 305, 451, 455, 459, 474; Orbán government, 3, 87, 328, 409n, 425, 439, 443, 474, 475
Őszi, István, 234

Palacký, František, 137
Palade, George Emil, 56
Palánkai, Tibor, 81
Páldi, András, 270

Pallai, Péter, 274n
Panić, Milan, 255, 256n
Pankin, Boris, 196
Papp, József, 157
Pasza, Árpád, 274
Paulus, Alajos, 261
Pavlychko, Dmytro, 193
Pecze, Zoltán, 167n
Peéry, Rezső, 459
Peeters, Yvo J. D., 170
Pell, Claiborne, 238
Perényi, János, 80, 318, 319n, 347, 349, 356, 357n
Perry, William, 108n, 175
Péter, László, 24, 264
Peterle, Lojze, 209n
Pethő, Tibor, 415
Petőfi, Sándor, 296n, 323, 378, 467
Petrusán, György, 361
Pettiti, Louis-Edmond, 344
Piłsudski, Józef, 137
Pithart, Petr, 100, 282
Pittner, Ladislav, 171
Plaks, Lívia, 277, 365, 454
Pop, Simion, 112, 122–23, 158, 261
Popély, Gyula, 345n
Popescu-Tăriceanu, Călin, 263
Póti, László, 175n, 176
Pozsgay, Imre, 31, 56, 74, 106
Princip, Gavrilo, 256
Pritz, Pál, 473
Prlja, Aleksandar, 98
Prokeš, Jozef, 340
Puchly, János, 22
Pugh, Helen, 32

Quayle, Dan, 216

Radičová, Iveta, 106n
Radványi, János, 41, 79
Rákóczi, Ferenc II., 137, *193*, 327, 462
Rákosi, Mátyás, 19, 21
Ránki, György, 26
Rasmussen, Poul Nyrup, 382
Rațiu, Ion, 37
Rebreanu, Liviu, 361
Révész, Sándor, 75
Rhédey, Claudia, 376
Ribbentrop, Joachim von, 173, 186, 187
Rice, Condoleezza, 108n, 175, 179n
Roman, Petre, 53, 108, 128, 144, 160, 161, 173, 372
Róna, Péter, 56
Rudas, Ernő, 117n, 121, 160, 371, 386, 395n
Rugova, Ibrahim, 257
Rupel, Dimitrij, 219, 222, 248
Ruzsa, György, 371n
Rychetský, Pavel, 282

Sakharov, Andrei Dmitrievich, 194
Sámsondi Kiss, György, 285
Sáringer, János, 64n
Šarinić, Hrvoje, 247, 249
Sárközi, Mátyás, 24
Sárközy, Péter, 308
Saudargas, Algirdas, 186
Schmid, Franz, 259
Schmidt, Mária, 87
Schultz, George, 32
Schwimmer, Walter, 356
Scotus Viator. *See* Seton-Watson, Robert William.
Scruton, Roger, 465
Sepsey, Tamás, 267
Seton-Watson, Christopher, 16

Seton-Watson, Hugh, 16
Seton-Watson, Robert William, 16, 295
Shakespeare, William, 69
Shevardnadze, Eduard, 92, 180
Sidó, Árpád, 450n
Siklós, István, 24, 57, 80
Sikorski, Władyslaw, 137
Silajdžić, Haris, 403–4
Sillár (Szíjj), Emőke, 82, 148n
Silva, Cavaco, 253n
Simonyi, András, 301n, 303n
Şincai, Gheorghe, 110
Sitzler, Kathrin, 170
Škrabalo, Zdenko, 249
Skubiszewski, Krzysztof, 132–34, 140, *141*, 230, 300n, 304, 314, 354
Slota, Ján, 459, 462
Solcanu, Ion, 388–89
Sólyom, László, 461
Somogyi, Ferenc, 66, 78, 122, 146, 405, 407–8
Sondaal, Hans, 413
Soros, George, 56; Soros Foundation, 41n, 454
Špegelj, Martin, 206, 208n
Stalin, Josif Vissarionovich, 19n, 87, 164, 198, 204, 384, 426, 442
Steinitz, Kurt, 330
Stephen I of Hungary, 7n
Stoel, Max van der, 278, 336, 337n, 343
Stolojan, Theodor Dumitru, 173
Surján, László, 171
Sütő, András, 376, 395
Szabad, György, 46, 48, 285, 296n, 398n
Szabó, Ferenc A., 411
Szabó, István, 244
Szabó, Miklós, 334, 410
Szabó, Péter, 286

Szabó, Rezső, 274
Szabó, Tibor, 317, 342
Szájer, József, 409
Szalai, Katalin, 82
Szarka, László, 45, 60
Szávai, János, 45
Szegedy-Maszák, Aladár, 78n
Szelényi, Iván, 56
Szénási, György, 264n, 317n
Szent-Iványi, Domokos, 78n
Szent-Iványi, Gábor, 81
Szent-Iványi, István, 68, 321, 408, 410, 422, 448n
Szépfalusi, István, 24, 274
Sziklay, Andor, 81
Szili, Katalin, 469
Szőcs, Ferenc, 244
Szőcs, Géza, 172, 263
Szokai, Imre, 29, 62, 66n, 96, 109, 111, 117n, 120–21, 159, 162, 189n, 205
Szőts, Csaba, 386
Szőts, Ferenc, 261
Szűcs, Jenő, 135
Szücs, László, 302n
Szűcs, Szergej, 275n
Szűrös, Mátyás, 28, 31, 32, 34n, 181
Szűts, Pál, 31n, 108

Takács, Csaba, 363, 380, 389, 395n
Takács, Ferenc, 55
Takács, József, 81
Tamás, Gáspár Miklós, 63, 127n
Tancredo, Thomas, 458
Tar, Pál, 80
Tar, Sándor, 81
Tárnok, Balázs, 469
Taubner, Zoltán, 302n
Teleki, Béla, 56, 113

Teleki, László, 82; László Teleki Foundation, 82, 135, 144, 263, 278, 332, 346, 405
Teleki, Pál (1879–1941), 20, 56
Teleki, Pál, 56
Thatcher, Margaret, 54, 69, 225
Thürmer, Gyula, 182
Thuysbaert, Prosper, 413, 414
Tismăneanu, Vladimir, 56, 124n
Tiso, Jozef, 289
Tito, Josip Broz, 95, 97n, 204, 211, 215n, 218, 444
Țiu, Nicolae, 172n
Tokay, György, 365, 455n
Tőkés, László, 45, 51, 55, 260, 266, 365, 379, 389, 393, 394n, 482
Tőkés, Rudolf, 56, 143–46, 149, 160n, 393n
Tonković, Bela, 274
Torgyán, József, 325, 429
Tóth, Mihály, 314, 317, 318n
Tóth, Sándor, 51
Toynbee, Arnold, 153, 335
Tudman, Franjo, 97, 210, 211, 217, 221, 236n
Tudoran, Dorin, 56
Turjanica, Ivan, 322
Turóczy, Botond, 386
Turóczy, Mózes, 386, *387*, 388, 439

Újpétery, Elemér, 78n
Ustich, Serhiy, 317

Văcăroiu, Nicolae, 372, 380
Vágvölgyi, B. András, 37
Vajay, Szabolcs, 81
Vajda, Tünde, 45
Valki, László, 81, 448n
Vance, Cyrus, 237, 238n, 239, 240

Várdy, Béla, 452
Varga, Bálint, 45
Varga, György, 281
Varga, Imre, 244
Várkonyi, József, 113n
Vásárhelyi, Miklós, 37, 41, 81
Vavroušek, Josef, 285
Végh, Béla, 81
Vereš, Milan, 234
Veress, Bulcsú, 27
Verheugen, Günter, 459
Vetró, András, 386
Vianu, Ion, 37
Világi, Oszkár, 156
Vincze, Dávid, 450n
Virágh, Pál, 312
Vitányi, Iván, 322
Vogel, Sándor, 172, 176, 263n, 266
Vollebæk, Knut, 461, 464
Vondra, Alexandr, 454
Vranitzky, Franz, 90, 227, 258, 383, 405n

Waldheim, Kurt, 258
Wałęsa, Lech, 133, *139*, 140, *141*, 148, 150, 151, 184, 186
Widmer, Paul, 167n
Wiesel, Elie, 277
Wigner, Jenő, 56
Wilson, Thomas Woodrow, 11
Wolfart, János, 72, 291
Wörner, Manfred, 150, 184, 229

Yanayev, Gennady, 185
Yazov, Dmitry, 210
Yeltsin, Boris, 182n, 184, 185, 192, 197–98, 199–202, 225, 236n, 267, 275, 392, 423

Zabolai Csekme, Éva, 32
Zacsek, Gyula, 317, 321–22
Zalatnay, István, 81, 129, 130, 157
Zamfirescu, Dinu, 37, 176
Zanc, Grigore, 267
Zeidler, Miklós, 13n
Zellner, Wolfgang, 178
Zhirinovsky, Vladimir, 201, 404
Zlenko, Anatoliy, 188, *190*, 270, 311–12, 314, 315, 318, 327
Zolcsák, István, 113, 265
Zwack, Péter, 80

www.ingramcontent.com/pod-product-compliance
Lightning Source LLC
Chambersburg PA
CBHW052128070526

44586CB00016B/2133